# The Critical Response
# to D.H. Lawrence

**Recent Titles in**
**Critical Responses in Arts and Letters**

# The Critical Response to D.H. Lawrence

Edited by Jan Pilditch

Critical Responses in Arts and Letters, Number 38

GREENWOOD PRESS
Westport, Connecticut • London

**Library of Congress Cataloging-in-Publication Data**

The critical response to D.H. Lawrence / edited by Jan Pilditch.
     p.   cm.—(Critical responses in arts and letters, ISSN 1057–0993 ; no. 38)
    Includes bibliographical references and index.
    ISBN 0–313–30853–5 (alk. paper)
    1. Lawrence, D.H. (David Herbert), 1885–1930—Criticism and interpretation.   I.
Pilditch, Jan.  II. Series.
    PR6023.A93 Z62327   2001
    823′.912—dc21       2001033622

British Library Cataloguing in Publication Data is available.

Library of Congress Catalog Card Number: 2001033622
ISBN: 0–313–30853–5
ISSN: 1057–0993

First published in 2001

Greenwood Press, 88 Post Road West, Westport, CT 06881
An imprint of Greenwood Publishing Group, Inc.
www.greenwood.com

Printed in the United States of America

# Copyright Acknowledgements

The author and publisher gratefully acknowledge permission for use of the following material:

Abercrombie, Lascelles, review of *Sons and Lovers* in *Manchester Guardian* 2 July 1913, reprinted with permission.

Anonymous article, "Imaginative Fiction", *Nation and Athenaeum*. XXVIII, 21 January 1921

Anonymous, "Review of *The White Peacock* by ", 18 March 1911, reprinted with permission of *The Glasgow Herald*.

Beirne, Raymond M. "Lawrence's Night Letter on Censorship and Obscenity", reprinted with permission from *The Review*, 7, 1974.

Bien, Peter, "The Critical Philosophy of D.H. Lawrence", reprinted with permission from *The Review*, 17:3, Summer 1984.

Bryden, Ronald, "Strindberg in the Midlands", Copyright *The Observer*, reprinted with permission from *The Observer*, 19 March 1967.

Carswell, Catherine. "D.H. Lawrence in His Letters" reprinted from *Nineteenth Century* CXII, November 1932, with permission of the Carswell family.

Cowan, James C. "D.H. Lawrence's 'The Princess' as Ironic Romance", reprinted with permission from *Studies in Short Fiction*, 4, 1967. Copyright 1967 by Newberry College.

Davies, Cecil, "D.H. Lawrence '*The Merry-Go-Round*': A Challenge to the Theatre", reprinted with permission from *The Review*, 16:2, Summer, 1983.

Draper, R. P. "The Defeat of Feminism: D.H. Lawrence's *The Fox* and 'The Woman Who Rode Away'", reprinted with permission from *Studies in Short Fiction*, 3, 1966. Copyright 1966 by Newberry College.

Ellis, David, "D.H. Lawrence and the Female Body", reprinted with permission from *Essays in Criticism: A Quarterly Journal of Literary Criticism*, 46:2, April, 1996, and Oxford University Press.

Engelberg, Edward, "Escape from the Circles of Experience: D.H. Lawrence's *The Rainbow* as a Modern *Bildungsroman*" reprinted by permission of Edward Engelberg and the Modern Language Association of America from *PMLA: Publications of the Modern Language Association of America*, 78, 1963.

Fisher, William J. "Peace and Passivity: The Poetry of D.H. Lawrence", *South Atlantic Quarterly*, 55:3 (July 1956), pp. 337-48. Copyright 1956, Duke University Press. All rights reserved. Reprinted with permission.

Garnett, Edward, "Introduction" to *A Collier's Friday Night* by D.H. Lawrence (first edition), 1934, reprinted with permission from the estate of the late Edward Garnett.

Gurko, Leo, "D.H. Lawrence's Greatest Collection of Short Stories— What Holds It Together", reprinted with permission from *Modern Fiction Studies*, 18, 1972.

Hinz, Evelyn J. "The Beginning and the End: D.H. Lawrence's *Psychoanalysis* and *Fantasia*", reprinted with permission from *Dalhousie Review*, 52, 1972.

Hoffman, Frederick J. "From Surrealism to 'The Apocalypse': A Development in Twentieth Century Irrationalism", reprinted with permission from *English Literary History* XV, June 1948, pp. 147-165. Copyright © 1948 The Johns Hopkins University Press.

Holmes, Colin, "A Study of D.H. Lawrence's Social Origins", reprinted by permission from *Literature and History*, No. 6, 1980.

Humma, John, "The Imagery of *The Plumed Serpent:*The Going-Under of Organicism", reprinted with permission from *The D.H. Lawrence Review*, Fall, 1982.

Huxley, Aldous, "The Censor", *Vanity Fair*, November 1929, reprinted with permission from the Aldous Huxley Literary Estate.

Ingersoll, Earl G., "Gender and Language in *Sons and Lovers*", reprinted with permission from *Midwest Quarterly:: A Journal of Contemporary Thought*, 37:4, Summer, 1996.

Janik, Del Ivan, "D.H. Lawrence's 'Future Religion': The Unity of Last Poems" reprinted with permission from *Texas Studies in Literature and Language* 16:4, 1975, pp. 739-754.   Copyright © 1975 by the University of Texas Press. All rights reserved.

Kalnins, Mara, "'Terra Incognita': Lawrence's Travel Writings", reprinted with permission from *Renaissance and Modern Studies*, 29, 1985, and Mara Kalnins.

Lainoff, Seymour, "*The Rainbow*: The Shaping of Modern Man" reprinted with permission of *Modern Fiction Studies*, 1 May 1955.

Macy, John, "The American Spirit", reprinted with permission from *Nation* CXVII, 10 October 1923.

Moore, Harry T. "Some New Volumes of Lawrence's Letters", reprinted with permission from *The D.H. Lawrence Review*, 4, 1971.

Murry, John Middleton, "Dr Leavis on D.H. Lawrence," *The Times Literary Supplement*, 28 October 1955, reprinted with permission of The Society of Authors as the literary representative of the Estate of John Middleton Murry.

Orwell, George, [pseud. of Eric Blair], "'The Prussian Officer' and Other Stories", reprinted with permission from [London] *Tribune*, 16 November 1945.

Panichas, George A. "D.H. Lawrence's Biblical Play *David*", reprinted with permission from *Modern Drama*, 6:2, September 1963.

Ruderman, Judith, "Rekindling the 'Father-Spark': Lawrence's Ideal of Leadership in *The Lost Girl* and *The Plumed Serpent*, Reprinted with permission from *D.H. Lawrence Review* 13:.3, Fall, 1980, pp. 239-59.

Rudrum, Alan, "Stage Sons, Stage Lovers", reprinted from *Listener and BBC Television Review*, LXXV, 10 February 1966, with permission of BBC.

Sackville West, Edward, " A Modern Isaiah", *New Statesman*, XXVII, 10 July 1926. Reprinted with permission from Lord Sackville.

Sagar, Keith, "Open Shelf and Open Poem: The Stages of D.H. Lawrence's Poetic Quest", reprinted with permission from *The  Review*, 24:1, Spring, 1992.

Schorer, Mark G.   "Technique as Discovery", reprinted with permission from *The Hudson Review*, Vol. I, No. 1, Spring, 1948.   Copyright © 1966 by Mark Schorer.

Schulz, Volker, "D.H. Lawrence's Early Masterpiece of Short Fiction: 'Odour of Chrysanthemums'", reprinted with permission from *Studies in Short Fiction*, 28, 1991. Copyright 1991 by Newberry College.

Spilka, Mark, "Lawrence's Quarrel with Tenderness" reprinted with permission from *Critical Quarterly*, 9, 1968, and Mark Spilka.

Squires, Michael,  "Lawrence's *The White Peacock*: A Mutation of the Pastoral" from *Texas Studies in Literature and Language*, 13, pp.263-283. Copyright © 1972 by the University of Texas Press.  All rights reserved.

Stanford, Raney, "Thomas Hardy and Lawrence's *The White Peacock*", reprinted with permission from *Modern Fiction Studies*,  Spring, 1959.

Stewart, Jack F. "Primitivism in *Women in Love*", reprinted with permission from *The D.H. Lawrence Review*, 13, 1980.

Twitchell, James, "Lawrence's Lamias: Predatory Women in *The Rainbow* and *Women in Love*", *Studies in the Novel*, v. 11, Spring, 1979. Copyright 1979 by North Texas State University.  Reprinted by permission of the publisher.

VanHoosier-Carey, Kimberley, "Struggling with the Master: The Position of Kate and the Reader in Lawrence's 'Quetzalcoatl' and *The Plumed Serpent*", reprinted with permission from *The  Review, 25*, 1993-1994.

Vickery, John B. "Myth and Ritual in the Shorter Fiction of D.H. Lawrence", reprinted with permission from *Modern Fiction Studies*, V, Spring, 1959.

West, Rebecca,  "Notes on Novels", from *New Statesman* XVII, 9 July 1921, reprinted with permission of The Peters Fraser and Dunlop Group Ltd.

Williams-Ellis, A. "Mr D.H. Lawrence's Work". Reproduced from *The Spectator*, 1 October 1921. Reprinted with permission.

Winn, Harbour, "Parallel Inward Journeys: *A Passage to India* and *St. Mawr*", reprinted with permission from *English Language Notes*, 31:2, December 1993.

Excerpts from the work of D.H. Lawrence are reprinted by permission of Laurence Pollinger Limited and the Estate of Frieda Lawrence Ravagli.

FOR

CONRAD, CRISTIAN AND FLETCHER

# Contents

# Preface

The work of D.H. Lawrence has always created controversy among critics. From the early prosecution of *The Rainbow*, to more recent disputes about feminist criticism, D.H. Lawrence is a writer who engenders strong feeling, both for and against his work. His appeal, both artistic and intellectual, knows no boundaries. His work remains in print and it is widely taught, read, anthologised and translated throughout the world. It has engaged some of the best critical and artistic minds of the past ninety years. A volume of this size and type cannot attempt to be inclusive. The critical response to his work in this volume is represented, in the interests of lucidity, by a selection of essays written in English chosen according to critical theme. Included are essays which, it is hoped, will indicate the breadth and range of Lawrence criticism, its concerns, innovations and ongoing interests, and some of the many critics and scholars who have contributed to our understanding of Lawrence and his times. The essays are arranged chronologically and according to the work considered. Further explorations can be made by consulting the Selected Bibliography at the end of the book, as can information regarding the complete publishing record of Lawrence's work which is not given in the Chronology. The essays in this volume represent the diversity of the critical response to Lawrence's life and work over a period of some ninety years. Those wishing to know more are urged to consult the Selected Bibliography at end of the book.

# Acknowledgements

My thanks go to Marshall Walker, who generously advised. I owe a debt of gratitude to the staff of the National Library, London; the Bodleian Library, Oxford; and to the staff at the Library of the University of Waikato, particularly Rae Riach. I thank Sonia Wells, for her encouragement, support and for the preparation of the manuscript. I am grateful for the generosity and support for this project to Charles Rossman and the editorial board of the *Review*, and to Mark Spilka and Richard Garnett for their correspondence. I thank the Research Committee of the University of Waikato for making the project financially possible, and George Butler for his commitment to it. Finally, my very special thanks to the late John Carswell, for sharing some of his early memories of Lawrence, and to Allan Green for showing me his Cornwall.

# Chronology

| | |
|---|---|
| 1911 | *The White Peacock*, [novel] (New York: Duffield & Company). London: Heinemann. |
| 1912 | *The Trespasser*, [novel], London: Duckworth & Co. |
| 1913 | *Love Poems and Others*, [poems], London: Duckworth & Co. *Sons and Lovers*, [novel], London: Duckworth & Co. |
| 1914 | *The Widowing of Mrs Holroyd*, [play], New York: Mitchell, Kennerley. *The Prussian Officer and Other Stories*, [stories], London: Duckworth & Co. |
| 1915 | *The Rainbow*, [novel], London: Methuen & Co. Ltd. |
| 1916 | *Twilight in Italy*, [travel], London: Duckworth & Co. *Amores*, [poems], London: Duckworth & Co., (New York: B.W. Huebsch). |
| 1917 | *Look! We Have Come Through!*, [poems], London: Chatto & Windus. |
| 1918 | *New Poems*, [poems], London: Martin Secker, (New York: B.W. Huebsch). |
| 1919 | *Bay*, [poems], (hand-made paper copies.) |
| 1920 | *Touch and Go*, [play] London: C. W. Daniel, Ltd. *Foreword to Women in Love,* (Privately printed). *Women in Love*, [novel], Privately printed, (London & New York), First trade edition, London: Martin Secker. *The Lost Girl,* [novel], London: Martin Secker. |

1921          *Movements in European History*, [by Lawrence H. Davison],
               London: OUP.
          *Psychoanalysis and the Unconscious,* [essays], New York:
               Thomas Seltzer.
          *Tortoises*, [poems], New York: Thomas Seltzer.
          *Sea and Sardinia*, [travel], New York: Thomas Seltzer.

1922          *Aaron's Rod*, [novel], New York: Thomas Seltzer.
          *Fantasia of the Unconsicous*, [essays], New York: Thomas Seltzer.
          *England my England*, [stories], New York: Thomas Seltzer.

1923          *The Ladybird*, in America—*The Captain's Doll*, [stories],
               London: Martin Secker, (New York: Thomas Seltzer).
          *Studies in Classic American Literature*, [Essays], New York:
               Thomas Seltzer.
          *Kangaroo*, [novel], London: Martin Secker.
          *Birds, Beasts, Flowers*, [poems], New York: Thomas Seltzer,
               (London: Martin Secker).

1924          *The Boy in the Bush*, with M. L. Skinner, [novel], London:
               Martin Secker.

1925          *St Mawr:* together with *The Princess*, [stories], London:
               Martin Secker, (New York: Alfred A. Knopf).
          *Reflections on the Death of a Porcupine*, [essays], Philadelphia:
               The Centaur Press.

1926          *The Plumed Serpent*, [novel], London: Martin Secker.
          *David*, [play], London: Martin Secker.
          *Sun*, [story], London: E. Archer.
          *Glad Ghosts*, [story], London: Ernest Benn Ltd.

1927          *Mornings in Mexico*, [travel], London: Martin Secker.

1928          *Selected Poems*, Augustan Books of English Poetry series, [poems],
               London: Ernest Benn Ltd.
          *Rawdon's Roof,* [story], Woburn Books 7, London: Elkin,
               Mathews & Marot.
          *The Woman Who Rode Away*, [stories], New York:
               Alfred A. Knopf.
          *Lady Chatterley's Lover,* [novel], Privately printed.
          *The Collected Poems of D.H. Lawrence*, [poems], Vols. 1 & II,
               London: Martin Secker.
          *Sun*, [story], unexpurgated edition, Paris: The Black Sun Press.
          *Sex-Locked-Out*, [essay]. Privately printed.

1929        *The Paintings of D.H. Lawrence,* [paintings],with Introduction by
               D.H. Lawrence, London: The Mandrake Press.
            *Pansies*, [poems],  London: Martin Secker.
            *My Skirmish with Jolly Roger*, [essay],  New York: Random House.
            *The Escaped Cock,* [story—later "The Man Who Died"], Paris:
               The Black Sun Press.
            *Pornography and Obscenity*,  [essays],  London: Faber & Faber.


1930        *Nettles*, [poems],  London: Faber & Faber.
            *Assorted Articles,* [articles],  London: Martin Secker.
            *A Propos of Lady Chatterley's Lover*, [essay—an expansion of *My
               Skirmish with Jolly Roger*],  London: Mandrake Press Ltd.
            *The Virgin and the Gipsy,* [story],  Florence: G. Orioli.
            *Love Among the Haystacks*, [stories], with a Reminiscence by
               David Garnett. London: The Nonesuch Press.


1931        *Apocalypse*, [essay], Florence: G. Orioli.
            *The Triumph of the Machine,* [poem],   London: Faber & Faber.


1932        *Lady Chatterly's Lover*, [novel—abridged edition], London:
               Martin Secker,  (New York: Alfred A. Knopf).
            *Etruscan Places*, [travel essays], London: Martin Secker.
            *The Letters of D.H. Lawrence* [letters], ed. and with Intro. by
               Aldous Huxley, London: Heinemann, (New York: The Viking
               Press).
            *Last Poems*, [poems], ed. by Richard Aldington and Giuseppe
               Orioli, with an Introduction,  Florence: G. Orioli.


1933        *The Lovely Lady and Other Stories*, [stories], London:
               Martin Secker.
            *We Need One Another*, [essay], Intro. by Henry Hart, New York:
               Equinox.
            *The Plays of D.H. Lawrence,* [plays], London: Martin Secker.
            *The Tales of D.H. Lawrence,* [stories], London: Martin Secker.


1934        *A Collier's Friday Night*, [play], with Intro. by Edward Garnett,
               London: Martin Secker.
            *A Modern Lover,* [stories],  London: Martin Secker.


1935        *The Spirit of Place*, [prose anthology], ed. with Intro. by
               R. Aldington, London: Heinemann Ltd.


1936        *Foreword to Women in Love,* San Francisco: Gelber Lilienthal, Inc.
            *Phoenix,* [posthumous papers], ed. E. D. McDonald, New York:
               Viking Press.

1940          *Fire and Other Poems,* [poems], Foreword by Robinson Jeffers and Note by Frieda Lawrence. Printed at the Grabhorn Press for the Book Club of California.

1944          *The First Lady Chatterley*, [novel], New York: Dial Press.

1948          *Letters to Bertrand Russell,* [letters], ed. H. T. Moore, New York: Gotham Book Mart.

1949          *A Prelude*, [story], Thames Ditton, Surrey: The Merle Press.

1955          *The Complete Short Stories of D.H. Lawrence*, 3 vols., Melbourne: London: Toronto: Heinemann Ltd.

1956          *Eight Letters to Rachel Annand Taylor*, [letters], Foreword by Majl Ewing, Pasadena, California: Grant Dahlstrom at the Castle Press.

1957          *The Complete Poems,* [poems], London: Heinemann

1958          *Look We Have Come Through*, [poems], with Intro. by Frieda Lawrence, Notes and Foreword by Warren Roberts, Marazion, Cornwall: Out of The Arc Press.

1959          *Lady Chatterley's Lover*, [novel—first authorised unexpurgated American edition], with Intro. by Mark Schorer, New York: Grove Press.

1961          *Lady Chatterley's Lover*, [novel—first authorised unexpurgated British edition], London: Penguin Books.

1962          *The Collected Letters*, [letters], ed. H. T. Moore, New York: Viking Press.
*The Symbolic Meaning: Uncollected Versions of Studies in Classic American Literature*, ed. Armin Arnold, Preface by Harry T. Moore, Philadelphia: Centaur Press Ltd.

1964          *The Complete Poems,* [poems], ed. V. De Sola Pinto and W. Roberts, London: Heinemann.

1965          *The Complete Plays*, [plays], London, Heinemann.

1968          *Phoenix II*, [uncollected, unpublished and other prose works], ed. W. Roberts and H. T. Moore, London: Heinemann.
*Lawrence in Love*, ed. with Intro. and notes, James T. Boulton, [letters], Nottingham: University of Nottingham Press.

1970        *The Quest for Rananim,* ed. with Intro., by George J. Zytaruk,
                [letters], Montreal and London: McGill-Queens University
                Press.
              *Letters from D.H. Lawrence to Martin Secker: 1911-1930,*
                Privately published.

1972        *John Thomas and Lady Jane*, [the second draft of *Lady
              Chatterley's Lover*, novel], London: Heinemann.

1973        *The Escaped Cock*, ed. Gerald Lacey, [with new material, story],
              Los Angeles: Black Sparrow Press.

1979        *The Letters and Works of D.H. Lawrence* (ongoing), Cambridge:
              Cambridge University Press, 1979-

NB. This Chronology is limited to first editions, in book form, of publications by D.H. Lawrence. Reprints, pamphlets of only a few pages, and translations are not listed, nor are works published in periodicals. Readers needing further detail are directed to the book-length bibliographies listed in the Selected Bibliography at the end of this book.

# Introduction

From his arrival on the literary scene Lawrence was recognised as a talent; possibly a genius. Born in 1885, in Eastwood, a Nottinghamshire mining village, David Herbert Lawrence was the son of a miner. His mother was a schoolteacher. He won a scholarship to Nottingham High School, taught elementary school between the ages of seventeen and twenty-one and was a brilliant student. Teaching examinations were passed effortlessly, and after two years at Nottingham University he was teaching secondary school when he came to the attention of Ford Maddox Hueffer [Ford], editor of *The English Review*. Ford prided himself on an ability to recognise new talent. He published four of Lawrence's poems in the November 1909 issue of his periodical and facilitated the publication of Lawrence's first novel, *The White Peacock*, with Heinemann.

Early reviews of Lawrence's work were mixed and cautious. Most agreed with Ford that the author had promise. Many commented upon the lyricism and poetry of Lawrence's prose, but Violet Hunt, perhaps following Ford's notion that England needed a novelist to speak for the working classes, suggests in a review published in *The Daily Chronicle* that *The White Peacock* should be read by all those superior persons engaged in public works in order to discover "something of the mind of the classes" who vote for them. Lawrence, she declares, is "supremely unconscious of class" and his characters "extraordinarily and bewilderingly" cultured. In her view *The White Peacock* was "a political document, developed along the lines of passionate romance." (Hunt: 1911) Hunt's liberal opinion is one that hints, simultaneously, of the origins of the author and the British class system. That Lawrence was a provincial writer, and was of lower middle, or even working class origin, was indisputable, but these facts were allowed to temper views of his genius. His was a natural genius, it was said, but one deprived of the benefits of fine culture and education. Nevertheless, as an unsigned review in *The Morning Post* of February 1911 declared, *The White Peacock* was not only worth reading, "but worth reckoning with, for we are inclined to believe that its author has come to stay." (*Morning Post*: 1911)

Lawrence was viewed, then, as a serious writer, but he made his critics uneasy. During his lifetime this unease centred, most obviously, on reactions to his treatment of sexuality. Heinemann had insisted on editorial changes to *The White*

*Peacock*, to avoid offending Edwardian sensibilities. *The Trespasser*, too, was viewed as a deeply sensual book. An unsigned review of the time praises Lawrence's "unobtrusive art" and "psychological intensity," but complains that "Siegmund, at the age of thirty-eight, is credited with the ecstatic passions of youth" (*Athenaeum*: 1 June 1912). Lawrence's overt descriptions of human sexuality caused discomfort, and to this was added more serious criticism. Galsworthy, in a letter to J.B. Pinker in the autumn of 1915, remarks that: "the sexual instinct is so strong in all of us that any emphasis upon it drags the whole being of the reader away from seeing life steadily, truly, and whole. . . ." This comment, of the type Matthew Arnold might have made, epitomised much of the debate that surrounded Lawrence in his lifetime. On one hand, a popular view of Lawrence saw his works as obscene. These views culminated in the destruction of some one thousand copies of *The Rainbow* in 1915, by order of the court, and precipitated a censorial interest in Lawrence's work that affected his poetry, paintings and, most notoriously, prohibited the publication in Britain of *Lady Chatterley's Lover*. On the other hand, more serious critics of Lawrence found his work antipathetic to civilised life. T.S. Eliot, spokesman for tradition and a disciplined sensibility, in his essay "The Contemporary Novel," finds Lawrence uninterested in civilisation or the civilised man, and Middleton Murry, in the *Athenaeum*, calls Lawrence "the outlaw of modern English literature." Murry, and others like him, chose rather to "stand by the consciousness and the civilisation of which the literature we know is the finest flower." However, if Lawrence was the literary outlaw of English Literature, he was also, Murry finds, "the most interesting figure" in it (Murry: 1921).

By 1916, in the midst of World War I, Lawrence wanted to leave Britain for America. Made miserable by his expulsion from Cornwall, largely brought about because locals suspected his German wife, Frieda, he wanted to exchange the old world for a new one. He had travelled in Europe since 1912, to Germany, Austria and Italy, but the war had confined him to Britain. In 1919, finally free to go, he travelled once more in Europe, before leaving for Taos, New Mexico, in 1922, travelling by way of Ceylon, Australia and New Zealand. Lawrence had been published in the United States from the very beginning, and reviews in America reflected caution similar to that in Britain. Controversy made apologists of many of his American supporters and if Lawrence was never actually banned in America, B.W. Huebsch, *The Rainbow*'s American publisher, did, silently, expurgate the novel. However, it was an American, Alfred Kuttner, who wrote the first of many Freudian interpretations of *Sons and Lovers* . His innovative approach to Lawrence criticism saw Freud's theories as central to a proper understanding of the novel. "Without the Freudian psycho-sexual theories *Sons and Lovers* remains an enigma," Kuttner remarks. "With it we see that artist and scientist supplement each other, that each in his own way attests to the same truth." (Draper:1970, p.79) For his part, Lawrence's imagination was engaged by America. In 1923, and again in 1924, he visited Mexico, but as his oscillations between Mexico and the United States continued, his critics perceived a deepening rejection of Western civilization. L.P. Hartley, writing of *The Plumed Serpent* in *Saturday Review* found Lawrence's imaginative powers as great as ever: "He tears the heart out of Mexico as he tore it out of Australia." (Draper:

1970, p.266) Lawrence's capacity for descriptive prose was never in doubt. Clive James, the Australian critic,writing in 1973, found the situations in *Kangaroo* to be mainly imported, but the settings he remarks: "have no trouble in being the most acutely observed and evocative writing about Australia that there has so far been" (Spender: 1973, p.166). But in 1926, for Hartley, as for Katherine Anne Porter, it was felt that a catastrophe had overtaken D.H. Lawrence (Draper:1970, p.271). Illness, finally, forced the Lawrences to return to Europe.

Lawrence died in Venice in 1930. It was an event that touched many and deeply grieved and saddened his friends. "When I lie awake," wrote Catherine Carswell to Koteliansky, "I cannot bear it that Lawrence is dead" (Carswell: 14 Jan.1931). The two planned a collection of his reviews, which did not eventuate but inevitably, in the decade after Lawrence's death, a quantity of reminiscences by friends and devotees appeared. Each had a story to tell, even those who, like Murry, had quarrelled bitterly with Lawrence. A series of "Reminiscences of D.H. Lawrence" that appeared in the *New Adelphi* were expanded by Carswell as *The Savage Pilgrimage: A Narrative of D.H. Lawrence*, which remains one of the best personal recollections of Lawrence. That work, in part, was intended as a refutation of Middleton Murry's own "Reminiscences of D.H. Lawrence" and his *Son of Woman: The Story of D.H. Lawrence* which appeared in 1931. Murry, employing loosely Freudian concepts, had attributed a perceived failure in Lawrence's life and work to an inability to normalise his feelings for his mother. The resulting conflict between Murry and Carswell led to the withdrawal of Carswell's biography by the publisher. Such conflicts were not uncommon after Lawrence's death. Many reminiscences took the opportunity to assess the writer's own relationship with Lawrence. Ada Lawrence and G. Stuart Gelder's *Young Lorenzo: Early Life of D.H. Lawrence* emphasises the importance of family and education, while Jessie Chambers's *D.H. Lawrence: A Personal Record*, published under the pseudonym "E.T.", returns to herself as Miriam in *Sons and Lovers* and feels that the mother is allowed to prevail. Frieda Lawrence's *Not I, But the Wind* relates her version of Lawrence's life. The early biographies, recollections, and memories are all informative about Lawrence's personal life, his travels, and his friends, but they are individual views of Lawrence. Observations were not always supported by the collections of Lawrence's letters, that began with *The Letters of D.H. Lawrence*, edited by Aldous Huxley, in 1932. Edward Nehls, in his *D.H. Lawrence: A Composite Biography*, which appeared in three volumes in 1957, 1958, and 1959, juxtaposes reminiscences and memoirs with letters written by Lawrence and other documents and materials, in chronological order. The method exposes the problems that a wealth of biographical material can create.

Alongside the memoirs of the 1930s were critics who attempted to judge the work of Lawrence and place it in the canons of literature. Murry's view of Lawrence in *Son of Woman* was endorsed by T.S. Eliot in a review in the *Criterion*. There he characterised his objections to Lawrence's life's work as stemming from a kind of "ignorance" in Lawrence. This "ignorance" led Lawrence to adopt "crazy theory to deal with the facts" as evidenced by his use of Christian terminology to describe his non-Christian philosophy, and a hopeless attempt to discover a mode of spiritual unity between two human beings.

Lawrence's history, and that of his novels, Eliot insisted, was a record of his attempts to maintain his rightness, despite his "mother-complex," possibly nourished "by the consciousness of great powers and humble birth" (Draper:1970, p.360-1). Huxley's "Introduction" to the *Letters* presented a differing view, as did others. David Garnett, reviewing Huxley's collection in *The Saturday Review of Literature*, expected the letters to change attitudes to Lawrence, who is, he says, "one of the easiest of great writers to get hold of by the wrong end." "Aldous Huxley," he remarks, "certainly emphasizes the right end" (Garnett:1932, p.141). Huxley had countered the biographical and psychological explanations of Lawrence's work with an emphasis on Lawrence as artist. Not all, however, were convinced.

By the late thirties the New Criticism was already entering the academies. Mark Spilka, in his Introduction to *D.H. Lawrence* (1963), comments that, with its close attention to textual analysis, as opposed to biographical and ideological approaches, and particularly by the way that it accounts for ideas as a formal element of text, the New Criticism should have benefited Lawrence's reputation. If it did not, Spilka remarks, it was because the "New Critics also favored 'tradition,' conscious and impersonal artistry, and tenable contextual beliefs, and Lawrence fell short (or so it seemed)" (Spilka:1963, p.2). If Lawrence, however, could not join the ranks of writers who responded well to the New Critics, like Yeats, Eliot, and Joyce, he could be incorporated into their midst in terms of a perceived and elitist inability to adjust to society by virtue of his sensitivity as an artist. By the late 1930s Lawrence's political position was again the subject of debate. Peter Preston, in his essay "Lawrence in Britain" points out that the Scottish critic, David Daiches in his *Literature and Society* (1938) discerns a retreat from society in Lawrence's realisation of instinct and emotion at the expense of reason, as it is expressed by modern civilisation, although, as Preston remarks, he stops short of calling Lawrence a Fascist (Takeo Iida:1999, p.7). Nevertheless, Lawrence's reputation did diminish among the younger, and often Marxist, critics. World War II slowed Lawrence criticism further, although Eric Russell Bentley's 1942 essay, "D.H. Lawrence, John Thomas and Dionysos" offered Lawrence's insistence on tenderness to refute the charge of Fascism. Then, in 1948, Mark Schorer's seminal essay "Technique as Discovery", appeared in the *Hudson Review*. His essay considered the ways in which form determines content and theme in *Sons and Lovers*, but so doing usefully demonstrated that good criticism could incorporate conflicting opinions. By the early 1950s, a number of critics were emerging whose influence on Lawrence scholarship would be profound.

F.R. Leavis's *D.H. Lawrence: Novelist* (1955) placed Lawrence in the "Great Tradition". Leavis's *The Great Tradition* (1948) had argued that, in fiction as in poetry, there was a tradition of serious writing. That tradition was moral, intellectual, largely humanist, and included Jane Austen, George Eliot, Henry James, and Joseph Conrad. Leavis's moral criteria were characterised by vitality. He favoured an individual morality, rather than one shaped by external codes and guides. Lawrence could have seemed a natural link to modern literature. In his "Introduction," and elsewhere, Leavis attacked Eliot's position on Lawrence. Eliot himself had modified his earlier views, but not enough. Eliot's view, that

Lawrence's art suffered from the failure of his early environment to provide him with a living and central tradition, remained unchanged. Leavis, for his part, claimed that Eliot had failed to understand English culture. In particular he had failed to understand the strong intellectual and moral seriousness of congregationalists, which seemed so surprising to Violet Hunt. Lawrence's intellectual life, his wide reading, and the vitality and vigour of a provincial aesthetic had all escaped Eliot. Leavis incorporated a number of his critical essays in his book that had been published as part of a series called "The Novel as Dramatic Poem" (*Scrutiny*: 1950-52). These essays read fiction as if it were poetry. The technique enabled Leavis to demonstrate the symbolic patterns of Lawrence's work in relation to the function of his ideas. In Leavis, *The Rainbow* and *Women in Love* appear as Lawrence's finest artistic achievements. For Murry, in his review of Leavis's book, they appear to the exclusion of other aspects of Lawrence's work. Nevertheless, Leavis's readings were persuasive and very influential. He clarified and accounted for the psychological and cultural conflicts in Lawrence's work without reduction, and he revitalised reading by demonstrating Lawrence's richness of character, his life, his wit, and his creative intelligence.

The American critic, Harry T. Moore, also emerged in the early 1950s. Moore had declared, in the 1940s, that Lawrence should be read, but in his *Life and Works of D.H. Lawrence* (1951) he made an early and comprehensive survey of Lawrence's writing. Spilka remarks that Moore brought to the task of biography ". . . an incomparable advantage: he had never met the author" (Spilka: 1963, p.5). Moore, who had no personal stake in Lawrence's reputation, brought sound judgment to his task, and his work functioned as a corrective to earlier views. In his later work *The Intelligent Heart: The Story of D.H. Lawrence* (1954) Lawrence emerges as man of contrast. His origins were working class, but he married Frieda, a German baroness. His English roots were strong, but he travelled relentlessly. He sympathised with conscientious objection during World War I, but his concerns with male leadership and power are central to much of his work. He rejected Christianity, but his religious impulse remained strong. The valuable perspective that Moore provided on Lawrence was reinforced by the Edward Nehls's composite biography when it began to appear in 1957.

Other critics, too, were beginning to make serious book-length studies of Lawrence's work. Mark Spilka's *The Love Ethic* (1955) considered Lawrence a religious artist. Spilka saw Lawrence, not as an incredible mystic, but one for whom "the resurrection or destruction of the human soul, within the living body, was central to his work; and by resurrection Lawrence meant no more . . . than emergence into greater fulness of being" (Spilka:1955, p.112). It is in this sense, Spilka comments, that we should understand the struggle to transcend "blood intimacy" with the "life-force" in *The Rainbow*, or understand the struggle to regain vitality in *Lady Chatterley's Lover*. Graham Hough's *The Dark Sun: A Study of D.H. Lawrence* (1956) also concentrated on the novels. He argued that Lawrence expanded the experience of his readers through the explorations of consciousness in his work. This revival in critical assessment corresponded with Penguin's publication of Lawrence's work in paperback. It was the unexpurgated paper-back edition of *Lady Chatterley's Lover* which instigated the British censorship trial, under the Obscene Publications Act of 1959, (Regina v. Penguin Books, Ltd.). It is some indication of the impact of Leavis and others that, by then, the defence was able to muster some of the finest literary minds in England as witnesses. The trial generated both popular and academic debate, but Penguin won their case and the book was finally published in Britain. The second unexpurgated edition of *Lady Chatterley's Lover* (1961) appeared with an Introduction by Richard Hoggart, which reiterated the argument that Lawrence's purpose was to encourage men and women to think about sexual matters cleanly and honestly. *The Trial of Lady Chatterley: Regina v. Penguin Books Limited*, edited by C.H. Rolph, documented the proceedings.

That Lawrence should have become an icon of British counter-culture during the 1960s and 1970s is perhaps unsurprising, in view of the popular debate surrounding the unexpurgated publication of *Lady Chatterley's Lover*. The reasons for his status, based loosely on an idea that Lawrence was against industrialised civilisation and for the free expression of physical love, were probably more imagined than real. This was, after all, the Lawrence who disapproved of people appearing in their undergarments, and of whom Catherine Carswell observed: "It would indeed be easy to call him prudish" (Carswell: CUP, 1981, p.65). But if there was little in Lawrence's work to support the prevalent view, it is fair to say that Lawrence had never enjoyed such popularity. A successful film of *Sons and Lovers* (Jack Cardiff, 1960) was made. In 1965 and 1967 Granada Television screened a sequence of adaptations of Lawrence short stories (ten in 1965, three in June 1967, and three in October 1967). This was followed by more films: *The Fox* (Mark Rydell, 1967), *Women in Love* (Ken Russell, 1969), *The Virgin and the Gypsy* (Christopher Miles, 1970). Lawrence's fiction responded well to the medium of film, and the success of these works served to familiarize a general public with the scope of Lawrence's work. This period also saw Lawrence acknowledged as a serious British dramatist. In 1967 there was an Edinburgh production of *The Daughter-in-Law*, which was also produced on BBC radio. Peter Gill's productions of *A Collier's Friday Night*, *The Daughter-in-Law*, and *The Widowing of Mrs Holroyd* at The Royal Theatre, London, in 1968, were acclaimed for their naturalistic attention to the details of the set. Other provincial centres followed suit. Then, in 1970, a Lawrence festival in Taos provided a forum for panel discussions for those who had known Lawrence. The festival proved a valuable venue for Lawrence scholars to meet and forge relationships. Lawrence scholarship grew rapidly.

James C. Cowan, in his annotated bibliography of D.H. Lawrence, points to the fact that the "increased interest in in the fifteen-year period from 1960 to 1975 is indicated by the fact that Volume II of his bibiography is of comparable length to Volume I, which included some 2061 annotated entries for the years 1909 to 1960" (Cowan: 1982, p.xxi). The period is also marked by a diversity of form and approach. Even after Nehl's composite biography in three volumes, memoirs and reminiscences continued to flow, from Frieda Lawrence and others. Some approached biography differently. Rose Marie Burwell's "A Catalogue of D.H. Lawrence's Reading from Early Childhood", for instance, demonstrates Lawrence's voracious appetite for knowledge (Burwell: 1970). New psychoanalytic critical techniques continued to engage with the unconsious and psychological subtext of Lawrence's work. Daniel A. Weiss, in his *Oedipus in Nottingham:* (1962), finds that an unresolved Oedipal complex can be discovered almost everywhere in Lawrence's works. Others suggest that Lawrence failed to resolve his relationship with his mother or with Jessie Chambers. J. F. C. Littlewood, in his article "Son and Lover" suggests that Lawrence betrayed the truth of his early relationships with Jessie Chambers and his mother's life by a refusal to emphasise the joy and harmony experienced. The vividness of much of *Sons and Lovers*, comments Littlewood: "is the instrument of the author's will to distort" (Littlewood: 1969). Other critics commented on Lawrence's views of women more generally. Kingsley Widmer's essay, "The Pertinence of Modern Pastoral: The Three Versions of *Lady Chaterley's Lover*" finds the final version of that novel flawed by Lawrence's strident misogyny, discovering: ". . . in the thought-over final version, a more misogynistic down-playing of the man's weakness and a harsh attack on "harpies," on "beaked" females, who are sexually aggressive for their own satisfaction . . ." (Widmer: 1973). Lawrence's own theories of the unconscious were examined, as were his illnesses and sexual practices. Other critics compensated for earlier neglect, by explicating the difficulties of Lawrence's leadership novels: *Kangaroo, Aaron's Rod, The Plumed Serpent*.

Another approach, especially after Leavis, was to consider Lawrence in relation to literary tradition. Lawrence was seen as a continuation of the realistic tradition in English fiction (Moynahan: 1963). or as heir to the English Romantic Poets (Clarke: 1969). Keith Sagar (1966) divides Lawrence's works into four phases placing Lawrence in the tradition of a Tolstoy or a Shakespeare, for whom the action of daily life had its basis in a larger quest (Sagar: 1966). Thus, if the early Lawrence explored that which was dead or declining in society, then movement of Lawrence's work and its exploration of alternatives, is toward the more certain vision of life and death that Sagar finds in the last poems (Sagar: 1992). Some critics discussed Lawrence's relations to other writers such as Hardy, George Eliot, Forster, and the American Whitman, or, like George J. Zytaruk, discussed Lawrence's response to Russian Literature (Zytaruk: 1971) or correspondences with the European artists. Studies were made of Lawrence's individual novels and other genres, and casebooks and study aids proliferated. Lawrence's historical and social backgrounds were discussed; others traced the geography of Lawrence's own travels and its literature. To point to the activity in Lawrence scholarship during this period, however, is not necessarily to subscribe to the view inherent in the title of an omnibus review in the *Times Literary Supplement* : "The Lawrence Industry"(London: 1970). James C. Cowan remarks on the injustice of so characterising the Lawrence criticism of these decades. Rather, he suggests, the items covered by his own bibliography "attest to both the breadth and depth of scholarly interest in Lawrence. Some of them are distinguished" (Cowan:1985, p.xxi).

Lawrence's appeal was not just confined to the literary. He had always been viewed by some as a visionary or prophet, which made some sort of sense of his popular status in the early sixties. As Edward Sackville West remarks in his 1921 review of *Reflections on the Death of a Porcupine* and in *David*, "A Modern Isaiah": "it is no good, as Mr. Lawrence says, arguing about it and intellectualising his imaginative appeal. We must let ourselves understand him, as one understands poetry, and let him 'incite us to an attitude,' . . . *The religious state of mind is disappearing from Western Europe*, as a result [by no means necessary] of the progress of scientific knowledge" (Sackville West:1921). Subsequent critics have explained Lawrence's vision as one that seeks to divest society of its Victorian observances, of responsibility and social duty, and to replace it with a social model based upon a perceived human impulse toward community. This impulse, opposed by its opposite resistant impulse, would see the individual develop toward a paradoxically free acceptance of community, in an act devoid of duty or obligation (Goodheart: 1963). H.M. Daleski identified the opposing terms of Lawrence's dualism as the male and female principles, as developed in his *Study of Thomas Hardy* (Daleski: 1965). Critics examined other aspects of Lawrence's thought. E. W. Tedlock Jr. saw Lawrence's revolt against convention as a rebellion against those institutions that inhibit the discovery of one's true nature and the formation of a real relationship with the natural world (Tedlock: 1963). A similar view had been expressed by Lainoff in his 1955 essay, "*The Rainbow*: The Shaping of Modern Man", in which he observed that: "What characterizes the modern most in *The Rainbow* is vacancy of spirit and barrenness of instinct". Lawrence's urge, however, was always towards reform.

Many critics saw the reforming nature of Lawrence's thought as inseparable from his art. Lawrence's one-time wish to found a colony of like-minded people to be called Rananim, in part as a reaction to the brutalities of the First World War, is well known. Harry T. Moore remarks that: "Rananim was doomed from birth. Katherine Mansfield collected some practical information about islands and began asking Lawrence solemn questions. He knew she was jeering at him, and he fell silent" (Moore:1974, p.213). Later critics, like George A. Panichas, in his *Adventure in Consciousness: The Meaning of Lawrence's Religious Quest* (1964), nevertheless viewed Lawrence's work as a journey of discovery. Del Ivan Janik makes a similar point when he comments that Lawrence's *Last Poems* should be read as if it were a single long poem. It is, he suggests: "a poem that expresses Lawrence's fervent and very personal religious understanding of life as a preparation for death and ultimate rebirth. *Last Poems* asserts the primary importance of each individual's relationship with the world of experience, so that in the context of Lawrence's whole career it strongly qualifies the collectivistic emphasis of *Apocalypse*, Lawrence's other late religious statement" (Janik: 1975). Other critics considered Lawrence from the perspective of Christianity or other religions, but, in a sense, questions about Lawrence's alternative to orthodox religious thought remained.

One method used to discover Lawrence's meaning was through the close study of his use of archetypal myths and symbols. Evelyn J. Hinz's trilogy of articles, published in the *D.H. Lawrence Review* (Summer: 1970, Summer: 1971, Spring: 1972) uncovers Lawrence's archetypal imagination. John B. Vickery's essay, "Myth and Ritual in the Shorter Fiction of D.H. Lawrence" (1959), had earlier worked to indicate the extensive use Lawrence made of material from anthropological and comparitive religious sources and to demonstrate the ways in which this practice could be used to elucidate structure, theme, and motive. Vickery discovered Lawrence's use of this material to be extensive and his book,

*The Literary Impact of the Golden Bough* (1973), includes two chapters on Lawrence. James C. Cowan's *D.H. Lawrence's American Journey: A Study in Literature and Myth* (1970) also considered the fiction of Lawrence's American period, together with his psychological and critical works, in terms of a quest for regenerative myths and symbols.

The most influential new direction for Lawrence scholarship in the 1970s, however, was that of the feminist critics. Feminist criticism of Lawrence was not new. Simone de Beauvoir's *The Second Sex* (Paris: 1949, trans. New York: 1953) presented one of the earliest sustained feminist critiques of Lawrence, suggesting that Lawrence believed passionately in male supremacy, and that his novels merely rediscovered a very bourgeois tradition, that women should be subordinate to men. Nevertheless, it was Kate Millet's *Sexual Politics* (New York: 1970) that began Lawrence feminist criticism, as it emerged during the following decades. *Lady Chatterley's Lover* marked, for Millet, the elevation of male supremacy to the status of mystical religion, and Lawrence's canon was viewed in terms of a progression, not of religious or philosophival thought, but of a fear and hatred of women on the part of Lawrence, and a desire for sexual mastery. Norman Mailer effected some sort of reply in "The Prisoner of Sex" that first appeared in *Harpers Magazine* (March 1971). Lawrence, he suggested, understood women and was not trying to instigate a dictatorial formula for male/female relations, but was also trying to destroy them. The problem, for feminist critics, however, lay not only with Lawrence, but with Leavis, among others, and with a whole set of assumptions that underlay the "great traditon" and the canon as it was taught in academies throughout the world. Feminist critics redefined the terms of Lawrence debate and, like Cornelia Nixon in *Lawrence's Leadership Politics and the Turn Against Women* (1986), investigated Lawrence's imaginative attempts to control female power and sexuality, while allowing for acceptable male bonding. Others saw Lawrence as an essentially patriarchal writer, but one whose responses to women were not without ambivalence. Margaret Storch, in her article "The Lacerated Male: Ambivalent Images of Women in *The White Peacock*", notes that: "The glorification of masculine power and the phallic mystique of many of the middle and later works testify to animosity against female dominance, yet Lawrence continues to create strong and independent females . . . whose strength can barely be crushed" (Storch:1989, p. 117). In common with other feminist critics Storch concludes that Lawrence's contradictory feelings about women are finally feelings about mothers. This was not an uncommon strain of Lawrence criticism, yet feminist views of Lawrence have been seen as, at best, reductionist, and, at worst, destructive. Keith Cushman weighs the case against feminist views when he remarks that: "It's not as if feminist critics . . . don't have a case to make. No one (except Peter Balbert in *D.H. Lawrence and the Phallic Imagination* [1989]) longs for a return to F.R. Leavis's heroic, ceaselessly life-affirming, faultlessly visionary 50s Lawrence. But those who assault Lawrence for his sexual politics tend to overlook how he championed sexual liberation (particularly the liberation of women) and also the fact that his more appalling attitudes are in part culture-bound" (Takeo Iida: 1999, pp.152-153). However, it would be wrong to underestimate the part played by feminist critics in the redefinition of critical boundaries, for Lawrence as for others. As Ellis was able to remark at the beginning of a recent essay: "Although Lawrence's attitude to sexual matters is very important, given the kind of novelist he chose to be, serious discussion of it is still in the early stages" (Ellis:April 1996, p.136).

Lawrence's literary output is complex and is unlikely to be encompassed by a single critical approach. This was made apparent by the controversy surrounding the publication of the Cambridge University Press editions of Lawrence's letters and works. While feminist critics appeared to be marginalising Lawrence, these prestigious editions should have served to centralise and cement Lawrence's literary reputation. Volume I, *The Letters of D.H.L.: September 1901 to 1913*, edited by J.T. Boulton, appeared in 1979. These Lawrence letters were unexpurgated and annotated to impeccable scholarly standards. As the project extended to the works, with Maria Kalnins edition of *Apocalypse* appearing in October 1980, editions became available to scholars and readers that restored Lawrence's punctuation and had the potential to clarify obscurities. Nevertheless, some critics found the volumes too expensive, particularly when Cambridge University Press abandoned its plan for cheap scholarly editions. The very idea of a definitive edition was called into question. Annotations and appendices detracted from the pleasures of Lawrence's writing, it was said, and introductions were editorial rather than critical, limiting the usefulness of these editions to new scholars. Scholars argued, as Peter Preston remarks: "that the notion of a fixed, definitive or authoritative text [was] fallacious, particularly in the case of an author like Lawrence, who constantly revised his work" (Takeo Iida: 1999, p.31). Charles L. Ross and Dennis Jackson edited a collection of essays entitled *Editing Lawrence* (1993) which allowed scholars an opportunity to challenge editorial procedures, but it was not until The Penguin Lawrence editions of 1994, which used the Cambridge text, but with fewer annotations and critical introductions, that controversy lessened and the place of the Cambridge texts was assured.

The place of Lawrence is also assured. The plaque in Westminster Abbey that commemorates his life and work, and the extensive celebrations for his centenary in 1985, attest to his abiding worth. Critics, working in a post-structuralist era are less inclined to view Lawrence as a prophet or guru, but are discovering that, while much has been said, much also remains. Volker Schulz points out that J. H. Harris's work of 1984 was the first book-length study of Lawrence's short fiction and that: "many of the sixty-odd short stories have yet to receive the detailed critical appreciation they deserve"(Schulz:1991, p.363). Recent critical studies are concerned to place Lawrence's philosophy into a relationship with other major trends, and comparitive critical works include those of feminist critics such as Cynthia Lewiecki-Wilson. (Lewiecki-Wilson:1994). Critics, like those featured in Keith Cushman's and Dennis Jackson's *D.H. Lawrence's Literary Inheritors*. (1991) have begun the consideration of Lawrence's influence on others. Changes in Lawrence criticism occur gradually, and when they do occur, they tell us something new of Lawrence. So much was Lawrence's finger on the pulse of humanity that a change in our view of him is a reflection of change in ourselves.

NB. Publication details for all works cited in this Introduction can be found in the Selected Bibliography at the end of this book.

# I

# THE WHITE PEACOCK

**Anonymous, "Review of *The White Peacock* by D.H. Lawrence"**

It is no uncommon occurrence nowadays for a reader to turn from the last page of a novel to the first in irritated query as to the connection between the story he has just perused and the title provided by its author. Take for example such a title as *The White Peacock,* a first novel of undoubted merit by one D.H. Lawrence (6s. London: Heinemann). Such a title is not only strictly unsuggestive to begin with but entirely without reference to the concluded story, or if there be a reference it is so recondite that much thought and time would have to be expended on its discovery. Otherwise the novel is an interesting one, and has a peculiar flavour, not wholly agreeable, of its own. . . .

*The Glasgow Herald*, 18 March 1911
(Review probably by Catherine Carswell)

**Raney Stanford, "Thomas Hardy and Lawrence's *The White Peacock*"**

It has long been a tenet in the criticism of D.H. Lawrence that the two most important influences on the early Lawrence were Thomas Hardy and George Eliot and that the former of these two depictors of provincial England is by far the more important. There are the evidences of various commentators who knew the young Lawrence and his reading habits, there is the early ballad-like dialect poetry of Lawrence, and there is "A Study of Thomas Hardy," the longest study

Lawrence ever did of another's work, even though it contained opinions and feelings about a multitude of things other than the achievement of Thomas Hardy.

Also there is *The White Peacock,* Lawrence's first novel, generally regarded as the most Hardyesque of any of Lawrence's work, and generally dismissed as derivative therefore. This influence, most of Lawrence's critics agree, is in the description of and in some vague feeling for nature and rural setting that both writers share.[1]

Now it is obviously true that both Hardy and Lawrence are among the greatest sensuous apprehenders of what Lawrence and many of his critics call "a sense of place" in English fiction. They both excel—Lawrence from the very start, Hardy as his career developed—in rendering physical men and women in a physical world. Yet there is always a subtle but striking difference in the use of this physical. In Lawrence the physical world serves to illuminate the characters and situations in which they are involved, whereas in Hardy the physical world generally takes on a character of its own that operates over and beyond the human characters. Hardy's famous Egdon Heath, in Lawrence's own words, reminds us "that there exists a great background, vital and vivid, which matters more than the people who move upon it" (*Phoenix*, 419). In the material depicted by Lawrence the scene is part of the narrative, but part of the human narrative; it extends the meaning of the actions of the human characters but does not overawe or override them. In "The Princess," for example, the cruelty and wildness of the nature of the American Southwest serves to illustrate the wildness of nature that will ultimately exact its toll from the heroine; in *Lady Chatterley's Lover* the natural world of the estate of her husband symbolizes the life that life with Clifford Chatterley would deny her. Readers of Lawrence can immediately summon to mind dozens more such profound uses of natural environment to supplement and to reveal human reality in a reciprocal relationship.

The relationship of Hardy and Lawrence revealed in *The White Peacock* is then more profound than the ability to communicate vivid impressions of the physical scene. The real relationship here is Lawrence's development of Hardy's technique of using symbolic scenes as structural devices; and the interest, even the obsession, that both writers display for feminine psychology embodied in uprooted or distressed heroines.

# II

The importance of symbolic scenes for dramatizing Hardy's fictional meanings has been noted by most of his modem critics but has been investigated in detail by few.[2] All those who have noted this technique have either implied or stated outright that the dramatizing of meaning through the symbolic scene helps greatly to explain the significance of Hardy's work, and its ability to live on and be widely read, despite Hardy's complicated mechanical plots, his stereotyped minor characters, and his irritating obsession to intrude everywhere a mechanistic, malevolent fate that blights all human endeavor. Hardy's use of symbolic dramatics, however, is always subordinate to his plot-making, and is often awkward and heavy handed. Such scenes as the oft-cited dominating of Bathsheba Everdene by the glittering sword of the glittering Sergeant Troy in *Far from the Madding Crowd,* or the rarely noticed offer of herself and life that Bathsheba makes to Troy while the latter sickens himself and the readers with self-pity over the coffin of Fanny Robin, emerge from the cluttered plots and break off from the rest, as Virginia Woolf put it. Furthermore, Hardy's insight is often unsure; he often will compose a scene from his will and not from his imagination. The death of Tess in the ancient ruins of Stonehenge and the hanging of the children of Jude and Sue are examples of the scene that is as yet insufficiently imagined, that violates principles of dramatic probability for the sake of the author's point.

A comparison of several symbolic scenes of both Hardy and Lawrence will show how the beginnings of the technique of the former become the full-fledged operational procedure of the latter.[3] Hardy often uses the death of animals to portray the innate cruelties of the world, and one such example of this comes in *Jude the Obscure,* when Sue Bridehead has fled her husband Phillotson to seek refuge with Jude. From his aunt's house at night Jude hears the "shrill squeak" of a rabbit caught in a trap somewhere outside. The aural impression is followed by a paragraph of heavily ironic commentary in which Hardy explains that if the rabbit is unfortunate it will escape and die slowly in the woods, and if it is lucky its trapper will appear in five or six hours and smash its skull. Then Sue appears in a nearby window, condemns the trapping of rabbits in heart-felt tones, and goes on to condemn the "trap" of marriage, in which society cripples the innocent who wander into its snares without knowing what intimate life with another person really is. The application of meaning is arbitrary, and the scene is rather like a fable with a moral tagged on at the end (Modern Library, 258-60).

Now let us consider another use of the physical to reveal the human world, this time in *The White Peacock.* Lettie and Cyril Beardsall, the narrator, with Leslie Tempest, walk out into the fields of the Saxton farm where George Saxton and his father are mowing grain. Along the way, delicate Lettie, even with gloves on, gets a blackberry thorn in her finger and Leslie carefully squeezes it out for her. But in the fields the sun, the smell of the mown hay, George with his tousled hair and bare back showing through torn shirt, all kindle Lettie to move toward him, to touch his arm. Then George matter-of-factly pulls out a pen knife and excavates a thorn deeply buried in his own hand. As Lettie, shocked but fascinated, stands absorbed, a rabbit is kicked out of the underbrush and all the men pursue it avidly until the poor animal is finally caught and killed. Back at the house Lettie announces that "men are all brutes" and George grins. Leslie contributes that "When it comes to killing it goes against the stomach." George answers, "If you can run . . . you should be able to run to death. When your blood's up, you don't hang half way." The argument ends as abruptly as it began, unresolved, neither side quite understanding the other, and neither side wishing to push the conflict to a break. That night, however, under the spell of moonlight, Lettie suddenly opens up, demands to dance in the meadow and does, first with her brother Cyril and then wildly with George. Only under the soft mask of the moon, then, will Lettie allow herself to respond to the physical, to respond to the spontaneous violence of George. She fears the love, that like Marvell's would

Tear our pleasures with rough strife
Through the iron gates of life.

Fearing, she stands fascinated, until night and the traditional sentimental mask of moon emerges, when she comes alive, vivacious and enticing and then flees, leaving baffled George not knowing what to make of it all (London, 1911, 71-86). The meaning of this evocative scene, done by weaving images together, is reiterated in other symbolic scenes throughout the book, until finally frustrated George marries a barroom slut in rage and hostility and drifts off to alcohol and confusion and Lettie marries her selfish intellectual Leslie, who is the first of a long line of life-denying intellectuals like Gerald Crich and Clifford Chatterley, and settles down to that modern domestic unlife that Lawrence depicted so well in all its dreary meaninglessness.

We note here that meaning is conveyed unusually and dramatically, but in a leisurely fashion. Meaning is not arbitrary, as in Hardy, but movement is not smoothly flowing; many digressions interrupt the flow and divert the meaning. Later on in his career, however, Lawrence will present these scenes in a more intensely dramatic fashion.

For the illustration of the mature Lawrence, we shall consider our last and most famous rabbit, the one which Gerald Crich and Gudrun Brangwen lift out of its hatch in *Women in Love*. Gudrun reaches into the container for the animal, which promptly panics and scores her hands and wrists heavily with lashing feet. Responding to its fear with cruelty, she seizes it with determination and holds it outstretched, crying "It's most fearfully strong." Excitedly, Gerald steps in and stuns the creature with the edge of his hand. The unfortunate rabbit is tossed into a pen and he cowers, motionless. The sensuality-intoxicated Gudrun turns to Gerald and cries "Isn't it a sickening fool?" Then she shows him a long red gash down her arm and Lawrence says:

> . . . it was as if he had knowledge of her in the long red rent of her forearm, so silken and soft. He did not want to touch her, deliberately. The long, shallow red rip seemed torn across his own brain, tearing the surface of his ultimate consciousness, letting through the forever unconscious, unthinkable red ether of the beyond, the obscene beyond. (Modern Library, 272-77)

Here we see that the meaning is rendered dramatically by Lawrence, implicit everywhere but explicit nowhere. The world is close to the world of Hardy, where men and women torture one another as well as rabbits, but there is no explanatory passage stating how Gudrun perverted love into a desire to possess and hurt, and how Gerald feels a corresponding desire to *be* hurt by her. Lawrence renders this by imaginatively transferring the gash from Gudrun's arm to Gerald's brain, and the metaphor conveys the meaning with something of the impact of the original event.

Lawrence's method shown here, then, is to take the symbolic scene and base the entire narrative upon it, in contrast to Hardy's technique of using it to supplement the narrative meaning. The mature Lawrence—i-e., the author of *The Rainbow* and *Women in Love*—will then weave such scenes together to make an imagistic "narrative," what Horace Gregory has called a "symphonic pattern," in which meaning is dramatized and then is juxtaposed with scenes before or after, in order to depict the various conflicts of familial love in three generations of Brangwens in *The Rainbow* and to contrast the destructive sado-masochistic love of Gerald and Gudrun with the creative, constructive kind of Birkin and Ursula in *Women in Love.* Both these books depend upon a thread of dramatic images rather than conventional narratives, a fact that probably accounts for the bewilderment of so many critics upon confronting these two novels.[4]

## III

Just as important an impact of Hardy upon Lawrence revealed in *The White Peacock* is the interest in female psychology common to both. Hardy critics as varied as Albert J. Guerard, and Virginia Woolf have noted that Hardy's women dominate his books; outside of Michael Henchard, all the commanding figures are women: Bathsheba Everdene, Eustacia Vye, Tess, Arabella Donn, and Sue Bridehead. Lawrence is a creator of more varied characters but again and again women dominate the interest; also, they tend to be the center of consciousness from which the world is seen. Typical here is *Lady Chatterley's Lover,* where Mellors is real enough, but is made so through the sensibility of Constance Chatterley; she communicates the experience we receive.

However, along with a psychological affinity for experiencing the world through a woman's psyche, there is a definite Hardyean influence—the meaning of the exasperating life of Jude's Sue Bridehead. In Lawrence's study of Hardy the most space devoted to any Hardy novel is spent upon *Jude,* and fourteen of its twenty-one pages are devoted to a provocative detailed analysis of Sue. In a sense, the complex sado-masochistic complex that is Sue fascinated Lawrence the rest of his life, and uprooted, dispossessed women occur again and again throughout his work, beginning with the most interesting character of his first novel, Lettie Beardsall of *The White Peacock.*[5]

Lawrence's discussion of *Jude* is alternately brilliant and muddled. He tends to turn Arabella into something of a heroine because she alone possesses the animal vitality that Lawrence finds so necessary to real life, but this vigor makes him overlook the fact that it is largely a destructive force in her, used to satisfy her own lazy sensual greeds. But he is unerring in his judgment of Sue Bridehead, seeing her as more than just a capricious woman in a sad tale of frustrations. "Sue is the production of the long selection by man of the woman in whom the feminine is subordinated to the male principle" (496). As many others have observed, she is a dark counterpart to the Ibsen-Shavian new woman, for whom happiness was to bloom with access to a ballot box. "One of the supremest products of our civilization is Sue, and a product that well frightens us" (497). Since she is a product of generations of anti-human gentility, of ascetic Christianity ("In her the pale Galilean had indeed triumphed" [501]), intellectual emancipation has meant psychological deracination, and her new-found mental powers lead her not to a new fulfillment, but to a new horror, a new destruction.

> The suppressed, atrophied female in her, like a potent fury, was always there, suggesting to her to make the fatal mistake. She contained always the rarest, most deadly anarchy in her own being. (497)

Torn between her sensual ("pagan") needs and idealistic desires for psychological security, she typically finds relief for her frustration in torturing others, and eventually herself. All investigators of the psyche have observed this sado-masochistic behavioral complex in which the unfortunate victim expresses a failure to have real human and sexual relationships by hurting others or the self. Sadism and masochism, all the psychologists agree, are variants of the same behavioral pattern.[6]

The joining link is the irrational urge to destroy or hurt one's self or others instead of having respect, if not regard, for the feelings of another separate being. Erich Fromm, whose socially oriented theories are perhaps most pertinent here for the study of the world of the novelist, points out that aggressions directed against the self or others are the result of fears or hates created by social pressure isolating the individual from a wholesome, creative, and satisfying life. Driven by feelings of powerlessness and isolation, such a frustrated individual avoids the responsibility of entering a mature relationship with another human being, in which one's own will is simultaneously expressed and subordinated to another in a vital, reciprocating flux; but instead "escapes" into purely selfish attachment, in which the individual either tries wholly to master the other, tries wholly to be absorbed by another, or else alternates between these anxious extremes.[7] As will be remembered by all, this phenomenon of love perverted into a clash of wills manifests itself in Sue through an ever-intensifying series of nightmarish scenes of pain and deprivation. From the simple teasing of slow, idealistic Jude, she proceeds to psychological torture when she prevails upon his kindness to make him participate in her wedding with Phillotson, climaxed with the intense and macabre scene in which she makes Jude stand in for the bridegroom in a mock wedding rehearsal in the actual church in which the wedding is to take place. Later, momentarily breaking through to reality, she flees Phillotson to come to Jude, but much of her life with him consists of torturing and frustrating him with a sense of the wrongness of their acts, making their life together an anxiety-ridden, insecure thing. With the famous murder of the children by the implausible, impossible Little Father Time (who refuses to smile for historical reasons and murders to demonstrate Malthus[8]), she relapses into a masochistic trauma, grovels and crawls before her vision of Christ as the torturer of righteousness, leaves Jude to drink himself into disease and death, and returns to the dull unalive Phillotson as a perverted penance.

As Albert J. Guerard has pointed out, we do not see Sue as a child, so we cannot analyze the factors in her childhood that influence her actions in the novel. But Hardy is not interested in personal psychology *per se*, nor for that matter is Lawrence; both are interested in how their feminine characters reveal the world about us. We first see Sue employed in ecclesiastical designing, but very soon see her personal tastes—two reproductions of a classic Apollo and a Venus. These images of the ascetic-sensual conflict within Sue are more to be relied upon than her conversation, for much of Sue's citing of eighteenth and nineteenth century sceptical writers—Gibbon, Swinburne, and the revisionists of Bible criticism—to justify her predicaments is often rationalization she offers for her behavior after the behavior has already been executed. Primarily Sue suffers from desires that she has been taught are punishable, not capable of being gratified; and from an isolation-derived fear that stems from her desire to be something more than a nineteenth century village matron, when she is not able to visualize what she wants to be. Real sexual desires terrify her, yet she cannot avoid them. One of her efforts to extricate herself from her terrible dilemma is to rationalize sexual feelings in the ethereal Romantic manner; it is significant that at one crisis she quotes movingly from Shelley's "Epipsychidion," finding in his confused Platonism a solution that transcends (that is, ignores) the body. The only thing that we do know about her childhood is her daring games with local boys that earned her the name of tomboy, but when the boys cheered her she fled and would not return. The pattern follows throughout her life, and she fails to achieve stature in the masculine world or fulfillment in the world of women.

This profound portrayal of tortured character is, as Lawrence immediately recognized, not just a preliminary exercise in the type of female psychotic mechanism whose boring perversions make up such a large part of the many paper-backed volumes that fill our drugstores. Sue's charms and desire to love never fail, even in her most terribly wrong acts, so that her final fall is not meaningless but evokes pity throughout the world that reads of her experience, and creates meaning beyond her own value to her self. Sue is the potential Lover-Wife-Mother, and when she falls, the family falls, the community falls, and the significant, valuable world falls.

That Lawrence feels this about Sue, and, through her, women in general, is obvious from his treatment of her in the Hardy study, in his numerous essays on the plight of modern women, and through his creation of numerous women whose complex quest for meaning and fulfillment is the subject of such a large bulk of his fiction. And the first of these "lost girls," as Mark Spilka calls them, is Lettie Beardsall.

The pattern of Lettie's behavior as traced in the scene of the rabbit chasing followed by moonlight dancing is the basic pattern for her relationship with George Saxton. She is both repelled and drawn by the animality of the world expressed in George, and like that of Sue, her conflict of contradicting forces is expressed in morbid tantalizing, a playing with sex, a now-you-see-it-now-you-don't kind of teasing of slow George that attracts and confuses him. The torturing of Jude by Sue in the church wedding is repeated by the torturing of George by Lettie at her engagement party, where she taunts him with the ring given her by Leslie Tempest. She fears not only passion and the will of George but also her own desires that would sweep her away from being the domesticated matron that she has been taught is the proper wife. Eventually she chooses Leslie, the child man, even though he "does not seem real" (199) to her. Their love at best is a pathetic mother-son relationship (263-64) but more often is the modern middle. class slag heap of wasted human talent for life. "Leslie adored her when he had the time and when he had not, forgot her comfortably" (443).

The pattern of behavior of the Lettie-George relationship is the same as the one between Sue and Jude. Both girls, fearing the unknown male will and the unknown passion of sex, try to resolve their dilemma by token, superficial offers of themselves—that is, offers that are not real, are simply tantalizations that unsuccessfully pretend to be sexual relationships, but are not rewarding because nothing is risked or committed. Both girls confuse, hurt, and eventually destroy the men so confused and shammed with, but neither of them intends to; it is their uncontrollable fear of real life and love that drives them to do as they do. Both also use superior intellects to bedazzle the slower men; this cleverness enables them to express their wills against the sexual forces latent within the men. The intellectual triumphs of both girls are in reality defeats, as the subsequent denouements of their affairs show.

As has been pointed out, Sue is not merely a study in private neurosis, and neither is Lettie Beardsall. The meaning of the latter's conflict, however, is more clearly analyzable than that of Sue, for, although Hardy formulated no general theories about the place and purpose of women in his world, Lawrence, as all know, formulated many. Much of this theorizing is contradictory; much is couched in florid metaphor in which Lawrence endeavors to create a feeling where unfortunately no concept seems to exist. But much is vital and coherent and serves as commentary upon the many Lawrencean daughters of Sue Brideshead. Women are different from men, he writes, and it is fatal, he says again and again, for them to imitate masculine behavior and modes of living. When imitation does take place, especially of contemporary commercial middle-class man in his drive for power and status, women cut themselves off from their necessary roots and drift off into sterile, frustrated patterns of life. Women rely upon emotional patterns for order and stability, patterns created by life with men and with their children, as men do not.

This reliance does not mean that men who cut themselves off from a vital physical and emotional life are not crippled thereby, for they are; but it does mean that the crippling is immediately recognizable as destructive in the case of women, because their existence is necessarily closer to the emotional center of life as Lawrence saw it. Men can exist without this emotional fulfillment, Lawrence notes bitterly: alienated, with creative forces often turned to destruction and the will to power, but existing nevertheless. But women in such a state are immediately more poignant, Lawrence seems to recognize. They are not merely individual women who wander through private wastelands of the spirit, but are archetypes of the mother, the creator of the children and the living center of the family. As crippled creatures, they serve Lawrence, and perhaps his readers, even better than men to show the loss of meaning that Lawrence finds as the core of futility of modern life. These young women are not just victims of an alien world; they are fundamental symbols of the alienation itself and so reveal the pathetic society to itself.

These reasons undoubtedly explain why Lawrence returns to such tortured women in book after book. A pathetic procession of such women pass, seeking fulfillment and rarely finding it: Ursula Brangwen in *The Rainbow,* Gudrun Brangwen in *Women in Love,* Alvina Houghton of "The Lost Girl", Kate Leslie of *The Plumed Serpent*—central figures in almost all of the novels except the two political novels, the novels concerned with leadership, *Aaron's Rod* and *Kangaroo.* The theme is perhaps most fully and happily exercised in *Lady Chatterley's Lover,* in which her childhood and her loveless marriage lead Connie Chatterley into the valley of death-in-life, from which she is reclaimed for life by Mellors. It is featured in dozens of short stories, with the sterility of frustrated woman receiving its most terrible image in one of Lawrence's most successful stories, "The Woman Who Rode Away."

Undoubtedly Lawrence would have created such women even if Hardy had not done so in Sue Bridehead. Certainly it is true that Lawrence would have created his technique of narration by image patterns rather than plot-event patterns without Hardy's use of the symbolic scene. But Lawrence would have spent more time than he did seeking objective correlations for his intensely felt but often awkwardly conceptualized visions if he had not had the vivid example of Sue Bridehead ready there for him, to dramatize the horror of the present actuality and the beauty of the possible future in the life of modern men and women.

*Modern Fiction Studies*: *D.H. Lawrence*, V, Spring 1959.

## Notes

[1] W. Y. Tindall, *Forces in Modern British Literature* (New York, 1949). p. 369; Richard Aldington. *Portrait of a Genius But . . .* (London, 1950), p. 97; Anthony West, *D. H. Lawrence* (Denver, 1950). pp. 88-89. It is true that "E. T." (Jessie Chambers) in her memoir of Lawrence speaks only of George Eliot in connection with the composition of *The White Peacock*, but all critics have cited Hardy as the most likely parallel with the work, and rightly so.

[2] Hardy's metaphorical structure is praised by Carl R. Anderson, "Time, Space and Perspective in Thomas Hardy," *Nineteenth Century Fiction*, 9, 3, 194-208. Some of the prominent image motifs of *Jude* are discussed by Norman Holland, Jr., in "Jude: Hardy's Symbolic Indictment of Christianity," *NCF*, 9, 1, 50-60. Perhaps the best overall discussion so far is Walter Allen, *The English Novel* (London, 1954), pp. 241-46.

[3] By "symbolic scene" I mean the scene that creates its meaning primarily by images, and whose meaning tends beyond the immediate confines of the explicit narrative in such a manner indicated in Allen Tate's discussion of Emma Bovary's suicide attempt in his "The Technique of Fiction," in *Forms of Modern Fiction*, ed. William Van O'Connor (Minnesota. 1948). pp. 41-45. See also W. Y. Tindall, *The Literary Symbol* (New York, 1955), pp. 9-11.

[4] The importance of narrative by image cluster rather than by plot event for Lawrence has been briefly indicated by Allen, pp. 347-48.

[5] Graham Hough, *The Dark Sun* (London, 1956), p.24, has noted that "Lettie [owes] something to Hardy's capricious and unsatisfied ladies," and Allen, p. 246, points out Sue's importance for Lawrence.

[6] Theodor Reik, *Masochism in Modern Man* (New York, 1941), pp. 169-71.

[7] Erich Fromm, *Escape from Freedom* (New York, 1941, pp. 141-45. As do the novelists discussed here, Fromm writes of the social neurosis, not the private psychosis, the sexual perversions to which these tendencies at their most powerful lead.

[8] Albert J. Guerard, *Thomas Hardy* (Cambridge, Mass., 1949), p. 69.

## Michael Squires, "Lawrence's *The White Peacock*: A Mutation of the Pastoral"

D.H. Lawrence almost surely had *The White Peacock* in mind when he wrote to Sydney Pawling in 1910, calling one of his novels "a decorated idyll running to seed in realism."[1] Lawrence's remark accurately describes his first novel, *The White Peacock*. Rewritten several times, it was published finally in 1911 when Joyce and Proust were spading the ground for the modern novel and when a temporary equilibrium settled over Georgian England. Yet its roots lie deep in nineteenth-century fiction. Graham Hough points out that in the major sections of the novel "Lawrence approaches most nearly to George Eliot or Hardy—to the traditional novel of English provincial life."[2] Walter Allen has also observed that, when Lawrence began to write *The White Peacock,* "it seems to have been with George Eliot and with *The Mill on the Floss* particularly in mind."[3] Like *Sons and Lovers* (1913) or *The Rainbow* (1915), *The White Peacock* is a transitional novel between the nineteenth and twentieth centuries, between traditional and modern; what makes it distinctive is that it begins as a nineteenth century novel but ends on a dissonant, twentieth-century chord.[4]

The link between *The White Peacock* and the early "pastoral" novels of George Eliot and Hardy is stronger than we might at first imagine.[5] All the novels reveal the same structural pattern, the same kind of human conflict: a young woman living in the country is forced to choose between two dissimilar suitors, one rural and one urban. In each novel the motivation for much of the action lies in the conflict that this double attraction ignites in the lives of its characters. In *The White Peacock* Lettie Beardsall, cultured and lovely, must choose between Leslie Tempest, son of a wealthy industrialist, and George Saxton, a farmer's son. The conflict, which follows the vagaries of courtship and culminates both in Lettie's marriage to Leslie and in George's decline, forms the essence of the plot. In Hardy's pastoral novels, Fancy Day in *Under the Greenwood Tree*, Bathsheba Everdene in *Far from the Madding Crowd,* and Grace Melbury in *The Woodlanders* face exactly the same kind of choice. Hetty Sorrel in George Eliot's *Adam Bede* must choose between Arthur Donnithorne and Adam Bede, and the pattern of *Silas Marner* is only slightly different: Eppie chooses, not between two lovers, but between two "worlds"—one humble, one proud and wealthy. If we look ahead to *The Rainbow,* Ursula Brangwen must choose between the gardener Anthony Schofield and the soldier Anton Skrebensky. And in *Lady Chatterley's Lover*, Connie Chatterley chooses between her husband, Sir Clifford, and his gamekeeper, Mellors. These fictional conflicts between urban and rural connect the novels and represent, moreover, the actual class conflict at the center of much nineteenth-century social history—the conflict between the working class and the.nobility or landed gentry. The fictional pattern has most significance if we see it within this broad context of a historical reality that the novels reflect.

Despite its impressive link with the structural pattern revealed in the pastoral novels of George Eliot and Hardy, one comes to study *The White Peacock* apologetically, for it is frequently dismissed by its critics. Dr. Leavis calls it "painfully callow," an "extremely immature novel";[6] and Keith Sagar recently argues that as a novel in its own right, "*The White Peacock* is hardly worth attention."[7] As a novel, it is easily dismissed because it lacks formal perfection. But to reject it too quickly, we shall see, is to miss much that is worthwhile 'for the novel is still readable and still alive and absorbing as a work of the imagination. It is not a great novel; it survives as a collection of striking parts rather than as an aesthetically coherent whole. But it will seem most successful to us if we follow Lawrence's suggestion and view it not as a realistic or naturalistic novel, but as a mutation of pastoral.

Mark Schorer has already noticed the pastoral element in *The White Peacock*: "The background of . . . *The White Peacock*, is a slow cultural convulsion. . . in which the ancient pastoralism of the yeoman way of life yields to the new mechanization of the industrial way of life, and in which, incidentally, a lovely landscape yields itself to an iron horror. What was lovely and peaceful in that older life and landscape was Lawrence's peculiar treasure; what was ugly and new, his special anathema."[8] George H. Ford has similarly written that in the novel "the action seems less important than the loving evocation of a pastoral setting, —the brooks, hayfields, and wild flowers which the characters observe in their walks."[9]   Yet other critics differ sharply. W. J. Keith most recently has argued that the predominant tone of the novel is one of frustration and disillusion.[10] But this argument denies a large portion of our actual experience of *The White Peacock*, for the naturalistic portions of the novel do not create the dominant impression that the novel makes on the reader's mind. Keith's remarks, like those of Julian Moynahan[11] account for only one aspect of the novel, its realism. The long, lyrical, very frequent passages of farm life and landscape description at the heart of the novel are virtually ignored.

Now the realism of the novel is to be neither disputed nor denied: bees, mice and rabbits are sportingly (though not maliciously) killed;  an injured cat is of necessity drowned; wild dogs kill the squire's sheep;  the characters gradually become disillusioned; and the world *beyond*  idyllic Nethermere is bleak. The bulk of such realism, however, is concentrated in the walking trips outside the valley of Nethermere and in the final chapters and does not provide the novel with its central focus.[12] On the other hand, the novel is not pure idyll, either, but, as suggested, is best discussed as a mutation of the pastoral genre. It is not little "a giddy little pastoral—fit for old Theocritus," as one character says. Instead, it is a modified or modern pastoral novel characterized by its lyrical landscapes, its circumscribed pastoral valley, its pointed contrast between city and country modes of life, its tension between rural and urban values, its full representation of a pastoral picnic, its inverted pastoral conclusion, and its nostalgic backward look to the little world that once functioned for the characters as a Golden Age.

What makes the novel complex for the critic are the many impulses  at work in the novel. These impulses are numerous because the novel  is a mixture of lyrical, elegiac, and harshly realistic elements. In particular, the novel has posed a problem for the critic in that it manifests two strong but opposing tendencies: a tendency toward romanticism and a tendency toward naturalism. Recent critics have concentrated mainly on the naturalistic strain. This essay, however, while fully recognizing the novel's realism, sets out deliberately to discuss the romantic-idyllic-pastoral strain, which seems frankly to make the dominant impression.

## II

What emerges in a study of the novel as a pastoral (or rather modified pastoral) novel is a matrix of four attitudes toward rural life, four different expressions of the pastoral impulse: a tinge of antipastoral reflected in the occasionally harsh passages about rural life; a modified or realistic pastoral, close to Hardy's, that is reflected in the often idyllic portrait of life at Strelley Mill farm; a portrait of the Beardsall family—Mrs. Beardsall, Lettie, and the shadowy narrator, Cyril—who live in a remote rural setting and who enjoy not regular agricultural labor, but the fruits of culture, the beauty of nature, and freedom from any necessary work; and, last, a burlesque of a traditional pastoral picnic, artificial and self-consciously humorous, which depicts cultured urbanities affecting dialect and pretending to be Theocritean rustics. To account for the complexity and the disparate impulses in the novel and to illuminate the varied treatment given to rural life, we should consider separately each of the four expressions of pastoral.

The antipastoral impulse is by far the least fully developed and does not emerge very clearly until the novel has, in Lawrence's words, "run to seed in realism." We have an early glimpse of sordid rural life in the brief picture of the gamekeeper's family living in disorder. Much later, when the family has moved to Selsby, the couple who replaces them— a "mouse-voiced" shrew and her "mouse-voiced man"—are cleverly caricatured by Lawrence. Near the end of the novel, Cyril and Emily return to Nethermere to visit Strelley Mill farm and find the house occupied "by a labourer and his wife, strangers from the north." They possess  none of the Saxtons' charm and are repulsively characterised: "He was tall, very thin, and silent, strangely suggesting kinship with the rats of the place. She was small and very active, like some ragged domestic fowl run wild" (p. 291).[13] The charm of the Saxtons has soured. Yet such a description can occur only in the final chapters, when the pastoral world has dissolved and the novel has become realistic.

The pastoral region of the novel is the small, magnificent, rather isolated valley of Nethermere; and the largest portion of the novel evokes, through description of landscape and character, the pastoral atmosphere that permeates the first of two of the three main sections of the novel. The valley is a pastoral hollow of happiness. Like George Eliot's Raveloe and like Hardy's Mellstock or Little Hintock, it is secluded and enclosed; inside, a multitude of birds and wild flowers live in pristine freshness. As Robin Magowan writes of nineteenth-century pastoral narrative, the pastoral haven becomes a felt experience "through the sensual concreteness with which its details are presented. Presented with sufficient pictorial skill, these details form the image of a world rich and satisfying, the perfect complement in space to the lives of the pastoral characters."[14] So it is with the snug bollow that harbors the two families at the center of the novel: the Saxtons who live at Strelley Mill farm and the Beardsalls who occupy Woodside nearby.

Lawrence sees the Saxtons nostalgically, as living an admirable life; yet he also sees that their life has a realistic side, and thus he does not oversimplify it, creating a modified version of pastoral very much like that found in the pastoral novels of George Eliot and Hardy. Often enough, realistic details qualify or rupture the pastoral atmosphere of cowslips and violets. The squire allows rabbits to invade the Saxtons' pasture lands and to crop their grass. External urban forces, such as industrialism and education, invade the stability of the pastoral valley. Even the hooters from the nearby mines can be heard. And occasionally George himself, the center of narrative interest, is discontented with the sameness of his life. It is George who also provides the focus of the transition from country to town, which is part of the novel's theme of the dissolution of human character when its roots in the ancient rhythms of agriculture are cut by aspiration for the world beyond.

A September harvest spent with George at Strelley Mill farm evokes the nostalgic lyricism that is so notable a strength in the novel. Cyril, the narrator, works through the quiet autumn mornings, sharing his knowledge of books with George; this particular autumn "fruited the first crop of intimacy between us":

> We tramped down to dinner with only the clinging warmth of the sunshine for a coat. In this still, enfolding weather a quiet companionship is very grateful. Autumn creeps through everything. The little damsons in the pudding taste of September, and are fragrant with memory. The voices of those at table are softer and more reminiscent than at haytime.
> Afternoon is all warm and golden. Oat sheaves are lighter; they whisper to each other as they freely embrace. The long, stout stubble tinkles as the foot brushes over it; the scent of the straw is sweet. When the poor, bleached sheaves are lifted out of the hedge, a spray of nodding wild raspberries is disclosed, with belated berries ready to drop; among the damp grass lush blackberries may be discovered. Then one notices that the last bell hangs from the. ragged spire of fox-glove. The talk is of people, an odd book; of one's hopes—and the future. . . . The mist steals over the face of the warm afternoon. The tying-up is all finished, and it only remains to rear up the fallen bundles into shocks. The sun sinks into a golden glow in the west. The gold turns to red, the red darkens, like a fire burning low, the sun disappears behind the bank of milky mist, purple like the pale bloom on blue plums, and we put on our coats and go home. (pp. 66-67)

The concrete, metaphorical language of this striking passage approaches the concentration and evocation of poetry in its marked rhythm and alliteration and consonance. Such poetic prose looks back to Sidney's *Arcadia.* The labor of the farm is apprehended lyrically so that the emphasis falls on the beauty and fulfillment that accompany the harvest work. The passage maintains the easy, wistful rhythm of the September harvest. Its mood is one of bounty and fullness, aroused by the heavy pull of adjectival words and phrases, yet saved from languor by the opposing pull of vivid verbs and striking figurative language. Especially notable is the restrained use of personification to suggest that inanimate nature is as active and involved as the human harvesters. Because personification integrates man and nature by causing nature to assume human qualities, man and nature seem equal. In all, the artistic success of the passage lies in its rich variety, with sentences evoking a response from all five senses.

The climax of the hymn to farm life comes in a well-known chapter, "A Poem of Friendship," famous for its unguarded expression of homosexual love or *Blutbrüderschaft*. When his vacation from college begins, Cyril yearns to help George gather in the hay for the last time before the Saxtons are forced to leave Nethermere. In excitement,

> I rose the first morning very early, before the sun was well up. The clear sound of challenging cocks could be heard along the valley. In the bottoms, over the water and over the lush wet grass, the night mist still stood white and substantial. As I passed along the edge of the meadow the cow-parsnip was as tall as I, frothing up to the top of the hedge, putting the faded hawthorn to a wan blush. Little early birds—I had not heard the lark—fluttered in and out of the foamy meadow-sea, plunging under the surf of flowers washed high in one corner, swinging out again, dashing past the crimson sorrel cresset. (p. 243)

Surrounding him everywhere on his path, the flowers and birds create an aptly lyrical mood. After a brief swim in the pond, Cyril and George

> went together down to the fields, he to mow the island of grass he had left standing the previous evening, I to sharpen the machine knife, to mow out the hedge-bottoms with the scythe, and to rake the swaths from the way of the machine when the umnown grass was reduced to a triangle.  The cool, moist fragrance of the morning, the intentional stillness of everything, of the tall bluish trees, of the wet, frank flowcrs, of the trustful moths folded and unfolded in the fallen swaths, was a perfect medium of sympathy. The horses moved with a still dignity, obeying his commands. When they were harnessed, and the machine oiled still he was loth to mar the perfect morning, but stood looking down the valley.
> "I shan't mow these fields any more," he said, and the fallen, silvered swaths flickered back his regret, and the faint scent of the limes was wistful. . . .
> "But merely to have mown them is worth having lived for," he said,  looking at me.
> . . . . . . . . . . . . . . . . . . . . . . . . . . . . . . . .
> Later, when the morning was hot, and the honeysuckle had ceased to  breathe, and all the other scents were moving in the air about us, when all the field was down, when I had seen the last trembling ecstasy  of the harebells,  trembling to fall; when the thick clump of purple vetch had sunk; when the green swaths were settling, and the silver swaths were glistening and glittering as the sun came along them, in the hot ripe morning we worked together turning the hay, tipping over the yesterday's swaths with our forks, and bringing yesterday's fresh, hidden flowers into the death of sunlight.
> It was then that we talked of the past, and speculated on tthe future.  As the day grew older, and less wistful, we forgot everything, and worked on,  singing, and sometimes I would recite him verses as we went, and sometimes I would tell him about books. Life was full of glamour for us both. (pp. 245-24)

In the first paragraph, work and beauty blend into unison as Cyril and George work in the lushly beautiful fields. The vision of man in harmony with his natural environment has always been a prime attraction of the  pastoral genre; and here, as in all pastoral, we find "a scene and some  means for expressing man's accord with it."[15] Since the human sphere is  in perfect sympathy with the natural world, the morning is perfect. This "perfect morning" then mirrors the idea in a preceding paragraph that "our love was perfect for a moment," so that the human and the natural mirror and interpenetrate each other. The relationship between Cyril and George and the relationship between Cyril and nature are both conceived in lyrical terms. George and nature both elicit a rapturous affection from the narrator (although the relations between the opposite sexes are fraught with the usual romantic conflicts). Thus, to the narrator, Cyril, George is more closely identified with nature than the other characters, not merely because we often see him working on the farm, but because at a deeper level of the narrator's consciousness George is conceived of and then presented to the reader in the same imaginative terms as nature is—with the same images, the same sympathy, the same pure feeling. Because the human and the natural are perceived and described in the same terms, they seem in accord.

Throughout the passage the details are primarily visual. As in the novels of both George Eliot and Hardy, the eye dominates the book, recording the look of landscape and characters and catching the movement of eyes and limbs with as much precision as it catches the fluttering of a cowslip, the shape of a lark's nest, or the scent of honeysuckle. The love of rural life is created, not through summary, but through evocation, through the poetic mastery of the language that creates in the reader the feeling and atmosphere of country life. The poetic quality is evident particularly in the onomatopoetic effects and in the rhytlm. Especially effective in the penultimate paragraph is the way in which the prose rhythms, the accumulation of *when* clauses, and the heavy use of gerunds and participles capture the rolling physical movement of turning the hay, or the way in which the scents of flowers create the feeling of exquisite sensuousness. The artistic achievement of *The White Peacock* lies as much in the sensuous apprehension of the natural world as it does in the creation and interaction of the characters.

### III

Living also in the valley are the Beardsalls, different from the Saxtons because they are financially independent and place a high value on culture. Their dialogue is in its way as stylized as that in *Under the Greenwood Tree*. Since they uphold the urban values of culture, sophistication, and complexity, they are not the "realistic" pastoral figures that we find in George Eliot and Hardy or that we see in the Saxtons; instead, they fall between the Saxtons and the artificial figures of traditional pastoral, who had only leisure and music to occupy their time. The Beardsalls' frequent allusions to literature, painting, music, and foreign languages sometimes suggest the artificiality of traditional pastoral—largely, one suspects, because Lawrence transposed his own family, in fiction, from the mining town of Eastwood into a middle-class country setting. The Beardsalls' basic attitudes often resemble those we encounter in traditional pastoral—particularly the praise of rural life from an urban-committed point of view.

The complexity of *The White Peacock* is increased because it is a double pastoral, a pastoral within a pastoral. That is, we see the valley of Nethermere from the urban point of view of the Beardsalls; and within the valley of Nethermere we see life at Strelley Mill farm from the perspective of life at Woodside. Lettie and Cyril, already within Nethermere, frequently admire the kind of solid rural life that is lived at Strelley Mill farm. With admiration, Lettie says to George when he pauses from mowing the oats on the hillside: "'You are picturesque. . . quite fit for an Idyll'" (p. 54). Then he shows her how to bind the grain. Cyril's attitude is similar. His desire to leave the cultured life (p. 157) is expressive of the pastoral impulse in one who lives already in pastoral Nethermere. Lettie and Cyril want to become like George, but they are already committed to a life that is essentially urban in outlook, and thus cannot transform their desires into action.

The creation of a pastoral world is complicated, then, by characters living in a pastoral world but ultimately adhering to the cultured views of the urban world. The pastoral world is complicated also by the dissatisfaction and unrest that the culture of Lettie and Cyril brings to George, a figure fully immersed in rural life. George says to Lettie, for example, that "'things will never be the same—You have awakened my life—I imagine things that I couldn't have done'" (p. 130). And to Cyril: "'But you see, you and Lettie have made me conscious'" (p. 260). In this respect Cyril and Lettie function, paradoxically, as anti-pastoral figures. Although Cyril and Lettie inhabit a beautiful world ("We had lived between the woods and the water all our lives") and although they are free from responsibility, like traditional pastoral figures, they also create unrest with their cultural values. They inhabit a pastoral world, but their allegiance to its values is only partial. They praise, often ecstatically, the world and life of Nethermere, yet with their sophistication they place this world and its life in the perspective of the urban world. It is such a perspective that classical and Renaissance pastoral had always accomplished.

Pastoral narrative has been called "an art of perspective."[16] In *The White Peacock* perspective is effectively achieved by placing the valley of Nethermere in the larger context of cultured urban life: the sophisticated allusions to literature, art, and music suggest a framework through which to see the simple rural beauty of Nethermere and the simplicity of life at Strelley Mill farm. Because Lawrence lets us see both sets of values, he shows us the strengths of both and so uses, as often in pastoral, one way of life to criticize the other. Only after we have a firm sense of this perspective do we see that the novel is prorural and antiurban, even anti-cultural, in its denouement and conclusion. The characters are led down the road of disillusion toward sophistication. They see then (as we do) the past through the perspective of the present.

In addition to Strelley Mill farm, what the narrator remembers through this lens of the present is the diversion and adventure in the pastoral valley  The young people of Nethermere amuse themselves with frequent walks into the rapturously beautiful countryside around Woodside and Strelley Mill farm, where they go "wandering round the fields finding flowers and birds' nests," sensitive to the beauty around them, laughing and teasing, and discovering afresh the wonder of human and natural life. The writing of such passages is vivid, unusually metaphorical, and characteristically idyllic in quality. The sordidness that the characters occasionally find in or beyond the valley—the life of the gamekeeper's family, for instance—only heightens, by contrast, the beauty that they find. The many superb descriptions of the natural world are the chief means used to create the lyrical atmosphere characteristic of all versions or mutations of pastoral. The lush texture of the landscape is often rapturously evoked, weaving a verbal arabesque; and the evocation of landscape, in its pictorialism and in its suggestion of nature's independent life, helps to place Lawrence alongside Hardy in the first rank of novelists who write of rural life.

A major part of the evocation of landscape consists of detailed descriptions of flowers: primroses, violets, cowslips, forget-me-nots, snowdrops, dog-mercury, wood-anemones, bluebells. In addition to contributing to the lyricism of the novel, flowers gradually assume a symbolic value. They are a concrete and objective manifestation, a symbol, of the quality of life that is lived in the Nethermere valley. The emphasis on flowers, moreover, suggests a yearning for beauty that intensifies the pastoral escape from the ugliness and squalor of the surrounding industrialism. Though occasionally set pieces, the evocations of flowers nurture the pastoral quality that is the source of the novel's charm.[17]

The pastoral world and the garden-world of Eden are, of course, related; the concept of the Garden of Eden is a later Christian version of the pastoral myth of the Golden Age, when innocence, leisure, and contentment blossomed freely.[18] The implication throughout *The White Peacock* is that Nethermere is a kind of Eden out of which the characters are gradually lured. Even in winter, Edenic overtones appear in the landscape description: "On the second Saturday before Christmas the world was transformed; tall, silver and pearl-grey trees rose pale against a dim-blue sky, like trees in some rare, pale Paradise" (p. 102). In other passages the Edenic overtones are more explicit. When the group wanders into a field of yellow cowslips, Lettie draws near to George, surprised:

> "Ah!" she said. "I thought I was all alone in the world—such a splendid  world—it was so nice."
> "Like Eve in a meadow in Eden—and Adam's shadow somewhere on the grass," said I. (p. 228)

The quotation comes from a chapter entitled "The Fascination of the Forbidden Apple" (a reference to the fact that both Lettie and George are fascinated by each other but forbidden to each other by Lettie's engagement to Leslie Tempest). This chapter title echoes an earlier one, "Dangling the Apple"—both alluding clearly to the Christian myth. At another point, George says of Lettie: "'She is offering me the apple like Eve'" (p. 105). Eden was most certainly in Lawrence's mind when he wrote the novel. The specific cause of the Fall remains obscure, but one suspects that it has much to do with Lettie's luring George out of Nethermere because he picks the apple of temptation that she dangles. The allusions to Eden are significant; we understand the characters better if we see that they trespass beyond their Eden and are in effect cast out, in the same way that Adam and Eve were expelled from Paradise. In the final chapters of the novel, perhaps the most significantly repeated word is *exile*. The characters, except for Emily, feel that they have been expelled from their pastoral paradise. The numerous short excursions that they take outside Nethermere—excursions that reveal the ugliness of life beyond—seem to serve as a warning to them. Once the characters have moved too far from Nethermere and stayed too long, they cannot return, as the final chapters prove. The novel, though far more than mere allegory, nonetheless makes vivid use of the myth of the Fall. If the parallels are imperfect, they are yet strong enough to show Lawrence's indebtedness in the novel to the Christian myth of Eden and to the earlier pastoral myth of the Golden Age.

## IV

The final expression of the pastoral impulse in *The White Peacock* is found in the chapter called "Pastorals and Peonies," which closes Part 2 of the novel. This chapter, describing in detail a picnic, is a mock pastoral—a burlesque of the *Idylls* of Theocritus. Leslie Tempest, Lettie's fiancé, asks Mr. Saxton "if a few of his guests might picnic that afternoon in the Strelley hayfields," for the wedding guests at Highclose, the Tempests' home, are "anxious to picnic in so choice a spot" (p. 248). The wedding guests, it turns out, are sophisticated, intelligent, refined urbanites who wish to escape for a few hours into the farm life of Nethermere. Thus we have a simulated, conventional situation like those of traditional pastoral, one of the characters even affecting speech thought to be country dialect, then pretending to be a Theocritean shepherd. The chapter may have been suggested by Theocritus' Idyll VII, "The Harvest Home," in which three urban friends dressed as herdsmen join a harvest feast in the country, then sit on piles of leaves and straw, eat pears and apples and plums, and drink wine. The details of the singing-contest and the allusions to the pastoral figure of Theocritus probably derive from Idyll VI, a country singing-match between Dameotas and Daphnis, and again from Idyll VIII, a second match in which Daphnis and Menalcas contest for a shepherd's pipe; the allusions to Amaryllis and to the ripening apples probably refer to Idyll Ill.

The group wants to help, not to hinder, in the haymaking, so Mr. Saxton gives them light hay-forks and they begin "just tipping at the swaths." They soon tire of the work:

> "Ain't it flippin' 'ot?" drawled Cresswell, who had just taken his M.A. degree in classics: "This bloomin' stuffs dry enough—come an' flop on it."
>
> He gathered a cushion of hay, which Louie Denys carefully appropriated, arranging first her beautiful dress, that fitted close to her shape. . . .
>
> Cresswell twisted his clean-cut mouth in a little smile, saying:
>
> "Lord, a giddy little pastoral—fit for old Theocritus, ain't it, Miss Denys?"
>
> "Why do you talk to me about those classic people—I daren't even say  their names. What would he say about us?"
>
> He laughed, winking his blue eyes:
>
> "He'd make old Daphnis there,"—pointing to Leslie—"sing a match with me, Damoetas—contesting the merits of our various shepherdesses—begin Daphnis, sing up for Amaryllis, I mean Nais, damn 'em, they were for ever getting mixed up with their nymphs."
>
> "I say, Mr. Cresswell, your language! Consider whom you're damning," said Miss Denys, leaning over and tapping his head with her silk glove.
>
> "You say any giddy thing in a pastoral," he replied, taking the edge of her skirt, and lying back on it, looking up at her as she leaned over him.  "Strike up, Daphnis, something about honey or white cheese—or else the  early apples that'll be ripe in a week's time."
>
> "I'm sure the apples you showed me are ever so little and green," interrupted Miss Denys; "they will never be ripe in a week—ugh, sour!"

He smiled up at her in his whimsical way:

"Hear that, Tempest—'Ugh sour!'—not much! Oh, love us, haven't you got a start yet?—isn't there aught to sing about, you blunt-faced kid?"

"I'll hear you first—I'm no judge of honey and cheese."

"An' darn little apples—takes a woman to judge them; don't it, Miss Denys?"

"I don't know," she said, stroking his soft hair from his forehead, with her hand whereon rings were sparkling.

"'My love is not white, my hair is not yellow, like honey dropping through the sunlight—my love is brown, and sweet, and ready for the lips of love.' Go on, Tempest—strike up, old cowherd. Who's that tuning his pipe?—oh, that fellow [George] sharpening his scythe! It's enough to make your back ache to look at him working—go an' stop him, somebody."

"Yes, let us go and fetch him," said Miss D'Arcy. "I'm sure he doesn't know what a happy pastoral state he's in—let us go and fetch him." (pp. 250-251)

Miss D'Arcy approaches George:

"They are spinning idylls up there. I don't care for idylls, do you? Oh, you don't know what a classical pastoral person you are—but there, I don't suppose you suffer from idyllic love—" she laughed, "—one doesn't see the silly little god fluttering about in our hayfields, does one? Do you find much time to sport with Amaryllis in the shade?—I'm sure it's a shame they banished Phyllis from the fields—"

He laughed and went on with his work. She smiled a little, too, thinking she had made a great impression. (p. 252)

Wandering about, the group picks flowers and talks until teatime, when a manservant comes with the tea-basket. Seated on tufts of bay, with "the manservant waiting on all," the pastoral picnickers savor the delights of "fruits, grapes and peaches, and strawberries, in a beautifully carved oak tray," while "the talk bubbled and frothed over all the cups" (pp. 253-254). Soon, they leave Strelley Mill farm.

The scene is entertaining in an artificial way, and our view of the whole is well expressed in George's initial reaction to the picnickers: "George at first swore warmly; then he began to appreciate the affair as a joke" (p. 248). It is true, as Dr. Leavis has said of the novel, that "there is a great deal that is literary and conventional in the style and the treatment."[19] But we will be less critical of the scene if we view it as mock pastoral rather than as a realistic portrayal of urban picnickers or as an attempt to be merely elegant. Like most scenes of traditional pastoral, this one lacks verisimilitude: we do not regard it as believable or convincing in its own right. Thus considered, we can accept the artificiality of the picnic. Like Theocritus, Lawrence presents a kind of jesting masquerade in the pastoral picnic and wishes us to recognize friends of his own circle (the Pagans) behind the clever disguises.

The picnic is an interlude in the evocation of farm life and shows the city-dweller's view of the farm. What makes the pastoral picnic difficult to analyze is the prominence in the scene of divergent views of rural life. Along with the polished Arcadians relishing flowers and munching on fresh fruit from a beautifully carved oak tray, we find George scything the hay, his hand calloused with work. In the garden of voluptuous peonies stands a calf sucking on George's finger; nearby are what Miss D'Arcy calls "smelly" cows, and, as Freddy Cresswell points out, with his "whimsical affectation of vulgarity," "'the stink o' live beef ain't salubrious'" (p. 254). Tle scene is still more complex because the picnickers are both admired and satirized—satirized for their affectation yet admired for their superior culture and refinement. But because there is no suggestion that they think of rural life as superior to urban life, the scene does not represent pure traditional pastoral, but a mock variation of it.

The picnic chapter is like another mock variation of pastoral, *As You Like It*. There is, in fact, a surprising correlation between the three levels of pastoral life in Lawrence's scene and the three levels of pastoral life that Shakespeare dramatizes in *As You Like It*. The counterparts of Shakespeare's Arcadians, Silvius and Phebe, are the group of wedding guests from the city. The exiled followers of the Duke, courtly but less artificial than the refined Arcadians, find counterparts in Cyril and Lettie—characters who are urban in outlook but who have a particular fondness for rural life and who vocally prefer their rural setting. Last, the counterpart of Shakespeare's real peasants William and Audrey is of course George, who is described more realistically in this scene than earlier in the novel. Although the characters stand in a different relation to each other, both Rosalind and Lettie are beloved by characters who represent two opposmg worlds. Lawrence therefore uses the same pastoral situation as did Shakespeare in his pastoral play. But more significant is the fact that both writers express similar attitudes toward their conventional pastoral characters and regard them as lovely and refined, but insubstantial and unreal—as elegant decorations rather than vital men and women. It is possible that the play was, in addition to the pastoral poems of Theocritus, a direct influence on the picnic chapter.[20]

The picnic scene, with its urban elements, prepares us to leave the rural-pastoral world and to move toward the ugly industrial world. With the pastoral picnic, we move in terms of aesthetic distance from the rural world to the urban world; the position of this increased distancing in the final chapter of Part 2 prepares us for change. If this final chapter contrasts real and artificial country experience in the form of the pastoral picnic, Part 3 embodies still another contrast to both these representations of country life.

Part 3 (or more precisely, the last six chapters of the novel) is much more naturalistic than the first two parts. The two contrasting portions of the novel— the first three-quarters and the last quarter—thus pose a problem for reader and critic not only because they are difficult to reconcile to each other, but also because they do not cohere as  an aesthetic whole. The novel modulates into a minor key when the techniques of romanticism give way to those of naturalism and when George's new town environment appears to control him and to be significant in his decline. The last quarter is rushed, and scenes shift rapidly, as though Lawrence were impatient with the denouement, as though the subject matter were unsuited to his genius and failed to call forth his fullest powers. A letter to Blanche Jennings, written by Lawrence in 1909, reveals that he had rewritten the novel: "I have added a third part, have married Lettie and Leslie and George and Meg, and Emily to a stranger and myself to nobody. 0 Lord—what a farce."[21] We should not be surprised that the artistic level of the last quarter (when George has left Nethermere) shows a falling off in quality, so that the freshness and vitality of the novel exist mainly in the first three-quarters.

The opening pages of Part 3 are nostalgic and elegiac in tone. After Lettie marries Leslie and they leave for France,

> everywhere was a sense of loss, and of change. The long voyage in the quiet home was over; we had crossed the bright sea of our youth, and already Lettie had landed and was travelling to a strange destination in a foreign land. It was time for us all to go, to leave the valley of Nethermere whose waters and whose woods were distilled in the essence of our veins. We were the children of the valley of Nethermere, a small nation with language and blood of our own, and to cast ourselves each one into separate exile was painful to us. (p. 259)

The voyage leads from youth to maturity, from the pastoral valley to the world of urban masses and machinery and money. When it is time for them to go forth out of the valley, ". . . we all felt very keenly our exile from Nethermere" (p. 276).

Soon after Lettie's marriage, George too yearns "to venture into the foreign places of life" (p. 269). The Saxtons, including George, are gradually driven out of Nethermere by the squire's refusal to let them protect their farm from rabbits. But more important, Lettie and Cyril have made George restless, and he yearns "to taste the towns" and "get rich" (p. 204). They stimulate George to develop "the aspiring mind" so antithetical to pastoral happiness. Earlier, George had been unaware and unconscious, in his "good living and heavy sleeping," that he possessed the ideal pastoral condition of the contented mind. But ambition and what Lawrence later called "prostitution to the bitch-goddess, Success"[22] destroy that innocent contentment. George crosses the borders of the valley of Nethermere and replaces "the glamour of our yesterdays" on the farm, which had come over him "like an intoxicant" (p. 262), with the artificial glamour of alcoholic intoxicants in the world outside Nethermere. Yet he "could not get over the feeling that he was trespassing" (p. 269). When he goes to Nottingham to marry Meg, he realizes that "he had begun to trespass that day outside his own estates of Nethermere" (p. 271 ). The suggestion of trespass or sin and of consequent exile from Eden dominates the opening pages of Part 3. As soon as George trespasses, he too is faced with the penalty of exile.

Although coming later to love the town, Cyril suffers most "the sickness of exile" in a London suburb:

> For weeks I wandered the streets of the suburb, haunted by the spirit of some part of Nethermere. As I went along the quiet roads where the lamps in yellow loneliness stood among the leafless trees of the night I would feel the feeling of the dark, wet bit of path between the wood meadow and the brooks. The spirit of that wild little slope to the Mill would come upon me, and there in the suburb of London I would walk wrapt in the sense of a small wet place in the valley of Nethermere. A strange voice within me rose and called for the hill path; again I could feel the wood waiting for me, calling, and calling, and I crying for the wood, yet the space of many miles was between us. Since I left the valley of home I have not much feared any other loss. The hills of Nethermere had been my walls, and the sky of Nethermere my roof overhead. It seemed almost as if, at home, I might lift my hand to the ceiling of the valley, and touch my own beloved sky, whose familiar clouds came again and again

to visit me, whose stars were constant to me, born when I was born, whose sun had been all my father to me. (pp.283-284)

The tone of the passage suggests a yearning for the Golden Age, for the recovery of the innocence and happiness found in all traditional forms of pastoral. In part, the novel can be regarded as a pastoral of innocence—of a world that has not discovered the bitterness of maturity or experience. The pastoral world of the novel is essentially a world of childhood. With maturity, that world vanishes. Yet it is not so much time that breaks up the pastoral world of innocence as it is outside influences, the yearning for money and success. It is because Cyril and George both trespass permanently beyond the limits of the Nethermere valley that they are unhappy. The novel is therefore closer than we might have guessed to Hardy's pastoral novels, where, generally, those who remain within the agricultural boundaries of their home communities are happy, but where those who leave, as in *The White Peacock,* come either to ruin or to despair.

Only Emily, by marrying a young farmer and returning to the rural world, "had escaped from the torture of strange, complex modern life" (p. 349) that the other characters must endure. Because George has been most sharply uprooted from his attachment to the land, he succumbs most quickly to the torture of modern life and deteriorates rapidly into an incurable alcoholic. Thus Lawrence tolls the death bell of the old agricultural order with its pastoral beauty and pastoral peace. *The Rainbow*, like *The White Peacock*, progresses also from rural idyll to urban nihilism, to a critical view of society and of the potential for fulfillment that society offers. In its pastoralism *The White Peacock* anticipates the opening third of *The Rainbow*, which Ford calls "a pastoral movernent";[23] it further anticipates *The Rainbow* in that both novels delineate an older, happier generation (Mr. Saxton and Tom Brangwen) being replaced by a dissatisfied, rootless generation (George Saxton and Ursula Brangwen) that can no longer enjoy the case and simplicity of filling a traditional role in rural society.[24] As a result, the pastoral world in both novels quickly becomes remote and distant in time, like a memory.

When, near the close, Cyril returns to Nethermere from London, he takes what would appear to be a pastoral journey—from city to rural oasis—only to find that Nethermere "had now forgotten me" and that "I was a stranger, an intruder" (p. 334). The journey becomes an inverted pastoral journey: "I had done with the valley of Nethermere. The valley of Nethermere had cast me out many years before, while I had fondly believed it cherished me in memory" (p. 335). The pastoral journey is unsuccessful because the narrator, now fully urbanized by his life in London and Paris, has no longer any true need of the pastoral world. Wishfully he wants to return, but cannot, because both he and Nethermere have changed. Urban culture and his success as a painter have outwardly fulfilled the emotional need that Nethermere once supplied and there can be no return to innocence and happiness, for experience and maturity bar the way. In addition, the decline of agriculture has made the traditional pastoral journey—the retreat from urban complexity to rural simplicity—an impossibility. The pastoral people Nethermere, the Saxtons, have fled the forces that encroached upon them.

The novel shows, therefore, the decline of an old agricultural way of life. But more important, it can be read as an inverted pastoral novel—a modern form of pastoral that, as Renato Poggioli points out, embodies "the bucolic aspiration only to deny it."[25]  A picture of beauty and loveliness is created, then destroyed; an idyll is transformed into ugliness.  Thus the final pages of *The White Peacock* shatter the illusion of Nethermere that the novel has so patiently built up.  What makes it a very modern  form of the pastoral novel is its ambiguous and ironic ending.

## V

*The White Peacock* is, then, a prose mutation of traditional pastoral, characterized by richly sensuous evocations of the natural world, intense concentration on a small circumscribed valley, nostalgia for this pastoral valley, praise of country life, a re-creation of what was for Lawrence a  Golden Age, tension between urban and rural values, the inclusion of a  pastoral picnic among the Strelley hayfields, and the inverted pastoral of  the final pages. Harsh realism manifests itself largely outside the valley of Nethermere and in the third part, written as an afterthought.[26] For the most part, the valley of Nethermere was "a complete, wonderful little world that held us charmed inhabitants" (p. 291)— however much the disillusion of adulthood may qualify this judgment of the narrator.  Graham Hough remarks that "in *The White Peacock* the human failures are almost absorbed in the quivering joy of earth, the vibration of the non-human world that surrounds them"[27] and that, paradoxically, "the prevailing impression it leaves behind is one of tenderness, freshness and young growth."[28]   The naturalistic details, such as those surrounding Mr. Beardsall's death, were in Lawrence's words only "fading phrases of the untruth. That yellow blaze of little sunflowers was true, and the shadow from the sun-dial on the warm old almshouses—that was real"; with the heavy afternoon sunlight, "the untruth went out of our veins" (p. 47). Nature, and man amid nature, are the "true" and the "real" in the novel. They are what live in the novel with greatest independent life and with greatest impact on the imagination. The harsh realism functions chiefly as an antidote to the charge of sentimentality and is not the primary ingredient. The primary ingredient is the marvellous evocation of the pastoral valley, of its people and its landscape, capturing the music  of larks,  the scent of violets and ripening corn, or the slow rhythm of the harvest.

The novel is not a masterpiece. It is not internally consistent, and its logical failures are frequent: the pretentious dialogue, the gamekeeper digression, the failure to integrate the various conflicts and episodes into a coherent whole, and the unsatisfying final portion. But its lyrical beauty creates a pastoral mood that dominates the novel because of the intensity with which the lyrical passages capturing landscape and human character are executed. Yet this world and its fragile pastoral beauty hover just at the brink of dissolution. A French critic reminds us that we are given in *The White Peacock* a "picture of an agricultural community in its last breath of life, with the acute human problems this dissoludon involves."[29] Beyond the pastoral world of Nethermere, the industrial forces of destruction and defeat crowd closer and closer, ushering in the new era:

outside the valley, far away in Derbyshire, away towards Nottingham, on every hand the distant hooters and buzzers of mines and ironworks crowed small on the borders of the night, like so many strange, low voices of cockerels bursting forth at different pitch, with different tone, warning us of the dawn of the New Year. (p. 280)

Industrial England blots out agricultural England, and the New Year, leaving the lyrical pastoral World behind, is a harbinger of modern industrialism.

*Texas Studies in Literature and Language: A Journal of the Humanities*, 13, March, 1972.

## Notes

[1] Harry T. Moore, ed., *The Collected Letters of D.H. Lawrence* (New York, 1962), I, 67.

[2] *The Dark Sun: A Study of D. H. Lawrence* (NewYork, 1957), p. 27. Although Claude M. Sinzelle's *The Geographical Background of the Early Works of D. H. Lawrence* (Paris, 1964) is the fullest (and most inaccurate) study of *The White Peacock*, Hough's remains the most perceptive. Other worthwhile studies of the novel include Robert E. Gajdusek, "A Reading of *The White Peacock*," in *A D. H. Lawrence Miscellany,* ed. Harry T. Moore (Carbondale, Ill., 1959);    Julian Moynahan, *The Deed of Life: The Novels and Tales of D. H. Lawrence* (Princeton, 1963); George H. Ford, *Double Measure: A Study of the Novels and Stories of D. H. Lawrence* (New York, 1965); Keith Sagar, *The Art of D. H. Lawrence* (Cambridge, Eng., 1966); W. J. Keith, "D. H. Lawrence's *The White Peacock*: An Essay in Criticism," University of Toronto Quarterly, XXXVII (April, 1968), 230-247; and Robert E. Gajdusek,    "A Reading  of 'A Poem of Friendship,' A chapter in Lawrence's *The White Peacock"*,  The D. H. Lawrence Review, III (Spring, 1970), 47-62.

[3] *George Eliot*  (New York, 1967), p. 183. We have Lawrence's own statement  to Jessie Chambers that when he was ready to write a novel, it was with George  Eliot's novels in mind: "'The usual plan is to take two couples and develop their relationships,' he said. 'Most of George Eliot's are on that plan.'"(E T. [Jessie  Chambers], *D.H. Lawrence: A Personal Record*, 2nd edition, ed. J.D. Chambers, London, 1965 ., p. 103).

[4] The idea was suggested by Frank O'Connor's remark that *Sons and Lovers*  "is particularly interesting because, though it ends as a novel of the modern type, it begins as one of the classical kind, made familiar to us by nineteenth-century novelists" (*The Mirror in the Roadway* [New York, 1956] p. 270).

[5] W. J. Keith argues (incorrectly, I think), "Although I am convinced that the influence of Hardy upon Lawrence was profound and has not been sufficiently discussed, I believe that, in the case of *The White Peacock,* comparison with Hardy is more of a hindrance than help" ("*The White Peacock:* An Essay in Criticism," p. 231)  Raney Stanford asserts in "Thomas Hardy and Lawrence's *The White Peacock," Modern Fiction Studies*, V (Spring, 1959), 19-28, that the points of similarity are two: "using symbolic scenes as structural devices; and the interest, even the obsession, that both writers display for feminine psychology embodied in uprooted or distressed heroines" (p. 20). Keith adds three more similarities: "the fictional adaptation of an actual landscape, the introduction of alien outside elements into a hitherto unchanging scene, the underlying feeling for the economic realities of rural life" (p. 231). Though Hough has noted that "George Saxton owes a little to Gabriel Oak" (*The Dark Sun,* p.24) and though Eugene Goodheart, in *The Utopian Vision of D. H. Lawrence*  (Chicago, 1963), p. 80, has said that both novelists share the "vivid apprehension of man and nature as a living continuum," no one else seems to have probed the matter of influence with any depth.

[6] F. R. Leavis, *D. H. Lawrence: Novelist* (New York, 1956), p. 6.

[7] *The Art of D. H. Lawrence*, p. 9. In *D. H. Lawrence: The Failure and the Triumph of Art* (Bloomington, Ind., 1964), p. xi, Eliseo Vivas adds: "His first two novels I have not examined at all. The work of a talented beginner, they can have only biographical interest. Had they not been written by Lawrence they probably would not be kept in print." But George H. Ford makes perhaps a fairer statement of the novel's merit: "It is, however, worth discussing like an early Shakespeare play or Hardy novel, both for its charm in its own right and for its interest as forecasting Lawrence's characteristic preoccupations as a writer of fiction" (*Double Measure*, p. 48).

[8] Introduction to *Lady Chatterley's Lover*, Modern Library Edition (New York, n.d.), pp. ix-x.

[9] *Double Measure*, p. 47.

[10] "*The White Peacock*: An Essay in Criticism," p. 240.

[11] For Moynahan, *The White Peacock* "depicts in a series of loosely repetitive episodes the spiritual ruin or actual physical destruction of several male characters" (*The Deed of Life*, p. 5).

[12] Cf. Claude M. Sinzelle's remarks: "The paradox of *The White Peacock* is that, though the treatment of the human plot is pessimistic, the general impression left is one of brightness and hope. . . . This prevailing impression of brightness is not easy to account for, but it permeates subtly every description and it is the out-of-doors scenes which impress the mind most in *The White Peacock*" (*Geographical Background of the Early Works,* p. 57).

[13] Parenthetical page numbers in my text refer to D. H. Lawrence, *The White Peacock*, ed. Harry T. Moore and Matthew J. Bruccoli (Carbondale, Ill., 1966). Inconsistencies have been silently corrected in the following lines of the novel: 54.35, 171.12, 177.38, 250.21, 250.41, 251.27.

[14] "Fromentin and Jewett: Pastoral Narrative in the Nineteenth Cenbtury," *Comparative Literature*, XVI (Fall, 1964), 334.

[15] Walter R. Davis, *A Map of Arcadia* (New Haven, 1965), p. 28.

[16] Magowan, "Fromentin and Jewett: Pastoral Narrative," p. 334. The same point is made in his article "Pastoral and the Art of Landscape in *The Country of the Pointed Firs*, The New England Quarterly, XXXVI (June, 1963), 230.

[17] Although it forms a digression from the central thread of the novel, an outgrowth of the novel's emphasis on flowers is the near-pastoral elegy for Annable, the gamekeeper. In the pastoral mode, grief conventionally expresses itself in the form of a pastoral elegy, employing among its many characteristics a personal exression of sorrow, a procession of mourners, the pathetic fallacy, flower symbolism, and a joyous consolation. These all occur in the variation of the pastoral elegy found in *The White Peacock*, where the natural world—especially the birds and flowers—laments vicariously the death of the gamekeeper:

> Till the heralds come—till the heralds wave like shadows in the bright air, crying, lamenting, fretting for ever. Rising and falling and circling round and round, the slow-waving peewits cry and complain, and lift their broad wings in sorrow. They stoop suddenly to the ground, the lapwings, then in another throb of anguish and protest, they swing up again, offering a glistening white breast to the sunlight, to deny it in black shadow, then a glisten of green, and all the time crying and crying in despair (p. 171). After the pallbearers pause for a rest, they "lift up the burden again, and the elm-boughs rattle along the hollow white wood, and the pitiful red clusters of elm-flowers sweep along it as if they whispered in sympathy—'We are so sorry, so sorry—'; always the

compassionate buds in their fulness of life bend down to comfort the dark man shut up there" (p. 172).

Although the funeral procession is perhaps a set piece, it bears a significant relation to the pastoral tradition, particularly in nature's lamentation over a human death. Renato Poggioli thinks, in fact, that the pathetic fallacy "may well be a variant" of the pastoral fallacy ("The Oaten Flute," *Harvard Library Bulletin*, XI [Spring, 1957], 184). Because Lawrence's elegy is written in prose and because it does not follow closely the conventions of the pastoral elegy, it should be considered a free variation of the traditional form.

18 Paggioli, p. 161.

19 *D.H. Lawrence: Novelist*, p. 6.

20 In *The Rainbow,* published only four years after *The White Peacock*, Lawrence has high praise for *As You Like It*. Of Ursula's studies, he says: "Most tedious was the close study of English literature.. . . . Only in odd streaks did she get a poignant sense of acquisition and enrichment and enlarging from her studies; one afternoon, reading *As You Like It;* once when with her blood, she heard a passage of Latin, and she knew how the blood beat in a Roman's body; so that ever after she felt she knew the Romans by contact" (Phoenix Edition [London, 1955], pp. 333-334).

21 *The Collected Letters of D.H. Lawrence*, I, 57.

22 *Lady Chatterley's Lover*, Modern Library Edition (New York, n.d.), p. 79.

23 *Double Measure*, p. 145.

24 In a number of ways *The Rainbow* is a rewritten and expanded version of *The White Peacock*, especially of its final chapters. Just as George Saxton marries a woman outside of Nethermere (Meg), so Tom Brangwen marries an outsider when he chooses Lydia Lensky. Cyril, the bachelor who is unable to love fully any character in *The White Peacock,* becomes in *The Rainbow* Uncle Tom, flawed and corrupt, who is equally unable to love and whose marriage to Winifred Inger is only a marriage of convenience. Lettie (strong) and Leslie (weak) become Ursula and Skrebensky: both women defeat the men they attempt to love. And Strelley Mill farm has as its equivalent Marsh farm. In both novels Lawrence focuses on three couples and one outsider. The essential difference is that in *The Rainbow* the couples represent three generations rather than one and are connected by family ties. In both novels, moreover, the dominant impression is one of lyrical intensity: in *The White Peacock* the stimulus for the lyrical intensity is nature; in *The Rainbow,* the emotion of love.

25 "The Oaten Flute," p. 177.

26 It is indicative of the shift from the nineteenth to the twentieth century that in an early draft of the novel, Lettie married George in the same way that Fancy Day marries Dick Dewy or that Bathsheba Everdene marries Gabriel Oak in Hardy's pastoral novels. Lawrence's revision of this early draft shows him to be much closer to the Hardy of *The Woodlanders,* another novel that was rewritten toward a negative conclusion. Although it cannot be discussed here, the explanation probably lies in the swift social and economic changes that affected the late nineteenth and very early twentieth centuries.

27 *The Dark Sun*, p. 53.

28 Ibid., p. 31.

29 Sinzelle, *Geographical Background of the Early Works*, p. 45.

# II

# SONS AND LOVERS

## Lascelles Abercrombie

'Odi et amo' should have been on the title page of Mr. D.H. Lawrence's *Sons and Lovers*. On the whole, the book may be said to contrast filial and maternal love with the kind of love which is called amour. A good many amours are described, involving several markedly diverse persons; but all the affairs and all the persons are unanimous in one matter—whatever kind of love it may be, some kind of hate is mixed up in it. A simultaneous passion of love and hatred is, of course, a well-known psychological fact; and certainly Mr. Lawrence makes its unfailing appearance in his story curiously credible. But it is not a very pleasant fact; is it not essentially a weakness of vitality, a kind of failure—life failing to appreciate itself, hating itself because it cannot appreciate the splendour of its own fate? Whether or no, it is a fact one can easily have too much of. If Mr. Lawrence thought to give intensity to the whole length (the very considerable length) of his story by this mingling of contrary passions, he miscalculated seriously. The constant juxtaposition of love and hatred looks like an obsession; and, like all obsessions, soon becomes tiresome. You begin to look out for the word 'hate' as soon as you have read the word 'love', like a sort of tedious game. 'Odi et amo' does marvellous well in an epigram; in a novel of four hundred odd pages it is a bore. The book has other faults. It has no particular shape and no recognizable plot; themes are casually taken up, and then as casually dropped, and there seems no reason why they should have been taken up unless they were to be kept up. Everything that happens is an extraordinarily long time about it, and sometimes it takes a very long time for nothing at all to happen. Faults like these ought to swamp any virtues the book may possess; set them down in this abstract fashion, and it seems incredible that *Sons and Lovers* can be anything but a dull success of cleverness. So, perhaps, it would be, if Mr. Lawrence were simply a novelist. But he is a poet, one of the most remarkable poets of the day; and these faults of his are actually of no more account than the soot of a brilliant, vehement flame. Indeed, you do not realize how astonishingly interesting the whole book is until you find yourself protesting that this thing or that thing bores you, and eagerly reading on in spite of your protestations. You decide that the old collier, the father, is a dirty brute; and then perceive that he profoundly has your sympathy. The mother is a creature of superb and lovable heroism; and yet there is no doubt that she is sometimes downright disagreeable. You think you are reading through an unimportant scene; and then find that it has burnt itself on your mind. The 'Odi et amo' of the main theme, in fact, is only an exaggerated instance of the quality which runs through the whole book, which may be best described as contrary, in the sense the word has when it rhymes with Mary. Life, for Mr. Lawrence, is a coin which has both obverse and reverse; so it is for most people, but his unusual art consists in his surprising ability to illuminate both sides simultaneously. The scope and variety of the life he describes, his understanding and vivid realizing of circumstance and his insight into character, and chiefly his power of lighting a train of ordinary events to blaze up into singular significance, make *Sons and Lovers* stand out from the fiction of the day as an achievement of the first quality.

*Manchester Guardian*, 2 July 1913.


# Mark Schorer, "Technique as Discovery"

Modern criticism, through its exacting scrutiny of literary texts, has demonstrated with finality that in art beauty and truth are indivisible and one. The Keatsian overtones of these terms are mitigated and an old dilemma solved if for beauty we substitute form, and for truth, content. We may, without risk of loss, narrow them even more, and speak of technique and subject matter. Modern criticism has shown us that to speak of content as such is not to speak of art at all, but of experience; and that it is only when we speak of the *achieved* content, the form, the work of art as a work of art, that we speak as critics. The difference between content, or experience, and achieved content, or art, is technique.

When we speak of technique, then, we speak of nearly everything. For technique is the means by which the writer's experience, which is his subject matter, compels him to attend to it; technique is the only means he has of discovering, exploring, developing his subject, of conveying its meaning, and, finally, of evaluating it. And surely it follows that certain techniques are sharper tools than others, and will discover more; that the writer capable of the most exacting technical scrutiny of his subject matter, will produce works with the most satisfying content, works with thickness and resonance, works which reverberate, works with maximum meaning.

We are no longer able to regard as seriously intended criticism of poetry which does not assume these generalizations; but the case for fiction has not yet been established. The novel is still read as though its content has some value in itself, as though the subject matter of fiction has greater or lesser value in itself, and as though technique were not a primary but a supplementary element, capable perhaps of not unattractive embellishments upon the surface of the subject, but hardly of its essence. Or technique is thought of in blunter terms from those which one associates with poetry, as such relatively obvious matters as the arrangement of events to create plot; or, within plot, of suspense and climax; or as the means of revealing character motivation, relationship, and development; or as the use of point of view, but point of view as some nearly arbitrary device for the heightening of dramatic interest through the narrowing or broadening of perspective upon the material, rather than as a means toward the positive definition of theme. As for the resources of language, these, somehow, we almost never think of as a part of the technique of fiction—language as used to create a certain texture and tone which in themselves state and define themes and meanings; or language, the counters of our ordinary speech, as forced, through conscious manipulation, into all those larger meanings which our ordinary speech almost never intends. Technique in fiction, all this is a way of saying, we somehow continue to regard as merely a means to organizing material which is "given" rather than as the means of exploring and defining the values in an area of experience which, for the first time *then*, are being given.

Is fiction still regarded in this odd, divided way because it is really less tractable before the critical suppositions which now seem inevitable to poetry? Let us look at some examples: two well-known novels of the past, both by writers who may be described as "primitive," although their relative innocence of technique is of a different sort—Defoe's *Moll Flanders* and Emily Bronte's *Wuthering Heights*; and three well-known novels of this century—*Tono Bungay,* by a writer who claimed to eschew technique: *Sons and Lovers*, by a novelist who, because his ideal of subject matter ("the poetry of the immediate present") led him at last into the fallacy of spontaneous and unchangeable composition, in effect eschewed technique; and *A Portrait of the Artist as a Young Man,* by a novelist whose practice made claims for the supremacy of technique beyond those made by anyone in the past or by anyone else in this century.

Technique in fiction is, of course, all those obvious forms of it which are usually taken to be the whole of it, and many others; but for the present purposes, let it be thought of in two respects particularly: the uses to which language, as language, is put to express the quality of the experience in question; and the uses of point of view not only as a mode of dramatic delimitation, but more particularly, of thematic definition. Technique is really what T. S. Eliot means by "convention"—any selection, structure, or distortion, any form or rhythm imposed upon the world of action; by rneans of which—it should be added—our apprehension of the world of action is enriched or renewed: In this sense, everything is technique which is not the lump of experience itself and one cannot properly say that a writer has no technique or that he eschews technique, for, being a writer, he cannot do so. We can speak of good and bad technique, of adequate and inadequate, of technique which serves the novel's purpose, or disserves.

## II

In the prefatory remarks to *Moll Flanders*, Defoe tells us that he is not writing fiction at all, but editing the journals of a woman of notorious character, and rather to instruct us in the necessities and the joys of virtue than to please us. We do not, of course, take these professions seriously, since nothing in the conduct of the narrative indicates that virtue is either more necessary or more enjoyable than vice. On the contrary, we discover that Moll turns virtuous only after a life of vice has enabled her to do so with security; yet it is precisely for this reason that Defoe's profession of didactic purpose has interest. For the actual morality which the novel enforces is the morality of any commercial culture, the belief that Virtue pays—in worldly goods. It is a morality somewhat less than skin deep, having no relation to motives arising from a sense of good and evil, least of all, of evil-*in*-good, but exclusively from the presence or absence of food, drink, linen, damask, silver, and time-pieces. It is the morality of measurement, and without in the least intending it, *Moll Flanders* is our classic revelation of the mercantile mind: the morality of measurement, which Defoe has completely neglected to measure. He fails not only to evaluate this material in his announced way, but to evaluate it at all. His announced purpose is, we admit, a pious humbug, and he meant us to read the book as a series of scandalous events; and thanks to his inexhaustible pleasure in excess and exaggeration, this element in the book continues to amuse us. Long before the book has been finished, however, this element has also become an absurdity; but not half the absurdity as that which Defoe did not intend at all—the notion that Moll could live a rich and full life of crime, and yet, repenting, emerge spotless in the end. The point is, of course, that she has no moral being, nor has the book any moral life. Everything is external. Everything can be weighed, measured, handled, paid for in gold, or expiated by a prison term. To this, the whole texture of the novel testifies: the bolts of goods, the inventories, the itemized accounts, the landlady's bills, the lists, the ledgers: all this, which taken together comprises what we call Defoe's method of circumstantial realism.

He did not come upon that method by any deliberation: it represents precisely his own world of value, the importance of external circumstance to Defoe. The point of view of Moll is indistinguishable from the point of view of her creator. We discover the meaning of the novel (at unnecessary length, without economy, without emphasis, with almost none of the distortions or the advantages of art) in spite of Defoe, not because of him. Thus the book is not the true chronicle of a disreputable female, but the true allegory of an impoverished soul—the author's; not an anatomy of the criminal class, but of the middle class. And we read it as an unintended comic revelation of self and of a social mode. Because he had no adequate resources of technique to separate himself from his material, thereby to discover and to define the meanings of his material, his contribution is not to fiction but to the history of fiction, and to social history.

The situation in *Wuthering Heights* is at once somewhat the same and yet very different. Here, too, the whole novel turns upon itself, but this time to its estimable advantage; here, too, is a revelation of what is perhaps the author's secret world of value, but this time, through what may be an accident of technique, the revelation is meaningfully accomplished. Emily Bronte may merely have stumbled upon the perspectives which define the form and the theme of her book. Whether she knew from the outset, or even at the end, what she was doing, we may doubt; but what she did and did superbly we can see.

We can assume, without at all becoming involved in the author's life but merely from the tone of somnambulistic excess which is generated by the writing itself that this world of monstrous passion, of dark and gigantic emotional and nervous energy, is for the author, or was in the first place, a world of ideal value; and that the book sets out to persuade us of the moral magnificence of such unmoral passion. We are, I think, expected, in the first place, to take at their own valuation these demonic beings, Heathcliff and Cathy: as special creatures, set apart from the cloddish world about them by their heightened capacity for feeling, set apart, even, from the ordinary objects of human passion as, in their transcendental, sexless relationship, they identify themselves with an uncompromising landscape and cosmic force. Yet this is absurd, as much of the detail that surrounds it ("Other dogs lurked in other recesses") is absurd. The novelist Emily Bronte had to discover these absurdities to the girl Emily; her technique had to evaluate them for what they were, so that we are persuaded that it is not Emily who is mistaken in her estimate of her characters, but they who are mistaken in their estimate of themselves. The theme of the moral magnificence of unmoral passion is an impossible theme to sustain, and what interests us is that it was device—and this time, mere, mechanical device—which taught Emily Bronte that, the needs of her temperament to the contrary, all personal longing and reverie to the contrary, perhaps—that this was indeed not at all what her material must mean as art. Technique objectifies.

To lay before us the full character of this passion, to show us how it first comes into being and then comes to dominate the world about it and the life that follows upon it, Emily Bronte gives her material a broad scope in time, lets it, in fact, cut across three generations. And to manage material which is so extensive, she must find a means of narration, points of view, which can encompass that material, and, in her somewhat crude concept of motive, justify its telling. So she chooses a foppish traveller who stumbles into this world of passionate violence, a traveller representing the thin and conventional emotional life of the far world of fashion, who wishes to hear the tale: and for her teller she chooses, almost inevitably, the old family retainer who knows everything, a character as conventional as the other, but this one representing not the conventions of fashion, but the conventions of the humblest moralism. What has happened is, first, that she has chosen as her narrative perspective those very elements, conventional emotion and conventional morality, which her hero and heroine are meant to transcend with such spectacular magnificence; and second, that she has permitted this perspective to operate throughout a long period of time. And these two elements compel the novelist to see what her unmoral passions come to. Moral magnificence? Not at all; rather, a devastating spectacle of human waste; ashes. For the time of the novel is carried on long enough to show Heathcliff at last an emptied man, burned out by his fever ragings, exhausted and will-less, his passion meaningless at last. And it goes even a little further, to Lockwood, the fop, in the graveyard, sententiously contemplating headstones. Thus in the end the triumph is all on the side of the cloddish world, which survives.

Perhaps not all on that side. For, like Densher at the end of *The Wings of the Dove*, we say, and surely Hareton and the second Cathy say, "We shall never be again as we were!" But there is more point in observing that a certain body of materials, a girl's romantic daydreams, have, through the most conventional devices of fiction, been pushed beyond their inception in fancy to their meanings, their conception as a written book—that they, that is, are not at all as they were.

## III

Technique alone objectifies the materials of art; hence technique alone evaluates those materials. This is the axiom which demonstrates itself so devastatingly whenever a writer declares, under the urgent sense of the importance of his materials (whether these are autobiography, or social ideas, or personal passions)—whenever such a writer declares that he cannot linger with technical refinements. That art will not tolerate such a writer H. G. Wells handsomely proves. His enormous literary energy included no respect for the techniques of his medium, and his medium takes its revenge upon his bumptiousness. "I have never taken any very great pains about writing. I am outside the hierarchy of conscious and deliberate writers. altogether. I am the absolute antithesis of Mr. James Joyce. . . . Long ago, living in close conversational proximity to Henry James, Joseph Conrad, and Mr. Ford Madox Hueffer, I escaped from under their immense artistic preoccupations by calling myself a journalist." Precisely. And he escaped—he disappeared—from literature into the annals of an era.

Yet what confidence! "Literature," Wells said, "is not jewelry, it has quite other aims than perfection, and the more one thinks of 'how it is done' the less one gets it done. These critical indulgences lead along a fatal path, away from every natural interest towards a preposterous emptiness of technical effort, a monstrous egotism of artistry, of which the later work of Henry James is the monumental warning. 'It,' the subject, the thing or the thought, has long since disappeared in these amazing works; nothing remains but the way it has been 'manipulated.'" Seldom has a literary theorist been so totally wrong; for what we learn as James grows for us and Wells disappears, is that without what he calls "manipulation," there *is* no "it," no "subject" in art. There is again only social history.

The virtue of the modern novelist—from James and Conrad down—is not only that he pays so much attention to his medium, but that, when he pays most, he discovers through it a new subject matter, and a greater one. Under the "immense artistic preoccupations" of James and Conrad and Joyce, the form of the novel changed, and with the technical change, analogous changes took place in substance, in point of view, in the whole conception of fiction. And the final lesson of the modern novel is that technique is not the secondary thing that it seemed to Wells, some external machination, a mechanical affair, but a deep and primary operation; not only that technique *contains* intellectual and moral implications, but that it *discovers* them. For a writer like Wells, who wished to give us the intellectual and the moral history of our times, the lesson is a hard one: it tells us that the order of intellect and the order of morality do not exist at all, in art, except as they are organized in the order of art.

Wells's ambitions were very large. "Before we have done, we will have all life within the scope of the novel." But that is where life already is, within the scope of the novel; where it needs to be brought is into novels. In Wells we have all the important topics in life, but no good novels. He was not asking too much of art, or asking that it include more than it happily can; he was not asking anything of it—as art, which is all that it can give, and that is everything.

A novel like *Tono Bungay,* generally thought to be Wells's best, is therefore instructive. "I want to tell—*myself*," says George, the hero, "and my impressions of the thing as a whole"—the thing as a whole being the collapse of traditional British institutions in the twentieth century. George "tells himself" in terms of three stages in his life which have rough equivalents in modern British social history, and this is, to be sure, a plan, a framework; but it is the framework of Wells's abstract thinking, not of his craftsmanship, and the primary demand which one makes of such a book as this, that means be discovered whereby the dimensions of the hero contain the experiences he recounts, is never met. The novelist flounders through a series of literary imitations—from an early Dickensian episode, through a kind of Shavian interlude, through a Conradian episode, to a Jules Vernes vision at the end. The significant failure is in that end, and in the way that it defeats not only the entire social analysis of the bulk of the novel, but Wells's own ends as a thinker. For at last George finds a purpose in science. "I decided that in power and knowledge lay the salvation of my life, the secret that would fill my need; that to these things I would give myself."

But science, power and knowledge, are summed up at last in a destroyer. As far as one can tell Wells intends no irony, although he may here have come upon the essence of the major irony in modern history. The novel ends in a kind of meditative rhapsody which denies every value that the book had been aiming toward. For of all the kinds of social waste which Wells has been describing, this is the most inclusive, the final waste. Thus he gives us in the end not a novel, but a hypothesis; not an individual destiny, but a theory of the future; and not his theory of the future, but a nihilistic vision quite opposite from everything that he meant to represent. With a minimum of attention to the virtues of technique, Wells might still not have written a good novel; but he would at any rate have established a point of view and a tone which would have told us what he meant.

To say what one means in art is never easy, and the more intimately one is implicated in one's material, the more difficult it is. If, besides, one commits fiction to a therapeutic function which is to be operative not on the audience but on the author, declaring, as D.H. Lawrence did, that "One sheds one's sicknesses in books, repeats and presents again one's emotions to be master of them," the difficulty is vast. It is an acceptable theory only with the qualification that technique, which objectifies, is under no other circumstances so imperative. For merely to repeat one's emotions, merely to look into one's heart and write, is also merely to repeat the round of emotional bondage. If our books are to be exercises in self-analysis, then technique must—and alone can—take the place of the absent analyst.

Lawrence, in the relatively late Introduction to his *Collected Poems*, made that distinction of the amateur between his "real" poems and his "composed" poems, between the poems which expressed his demon directly and created their own form "willy-nilly," and the poems which, through the hocus pocus of technique, he spuriously put together and could, if necessary, revise. His belief in a "poetry of the immediate present," poetry in which nothing is fixed, static or final, where all is shimmeriness and impermanence and vitalistic essence, arose from this mistaken notion of technique. And from this notion, an unsympathetic critic like D. S. Savage can construct a case which shows Lawrence driven "concurrently to the dissolution of personality and the dissolution of art." The argument suggests that Lawrence's early, crucial novel, *Sons and Lovers,* is another example of meanings confused by an impatience with technical resources.

The novel has two themes: the crippling effects of a mother's love on the emotional development of her son; and the "split" between kinds of love, physical and spiritual, which the son develops, the kinds represented by two young women, Clara and Miriam. The two themes should, of course, work together, the second being, actually, the result of the first: this "split" is the "crippling." So one would expect to see the novel developed, and so Lawrence, in his famous letter to Edward Garnett,  where he says that Paul is left at the end with the "drift towards death," apparently thought he had developed it. Yet in the last few sentences of the novel, Paul rejects his desire for extinction and turns towards "the faintly humming, glowing town," to life—as nothing in his previous history persuades us that he could unfalteringly do.

The discrepancy suggests that the book may reveal certain confusions between intention and performance.

The first of these is the contradiction between Lawrence's explicit characterizations of the mother and father and his tonal evaluations of them.  It is a problem not only of style (of the contradiction between expressed moral epithets and the more general texture of the prose which applies to them) but of point of view. Morel and Lawrence are never separated, which is a way of saying that Lawrence maintains for himself in this book the confused attitude of his character. The mother is a "proud, *honorable* soul," but the father has a "small, *mean* head."  his is the sustained contrast; the epithets are characteristic of the whole; and they represent half of Lawrence's feelings.  But what is the is the other half? Which of these characters is given his real sympathy—the hard, self-righteous, aggressive, demanding mother who comes through to us, or the simple, direct, gentle, downright, fumbling, ruined father?  There are two attitudes here. Lawrence (and Morel) loves his mother, but he also hates her for compelling his love; and he hates his father with the true Freudian jealousy, but he also loves him for what he is in himself, and he sympathizes more deeply with him because his wholeness has been destroyed by the mother's domination, just as his, Lawrence-Morel's, has been.

This is a psychological tension which disrupts the form of the novel and obscures its meaning, because neither the contradiction in style nor the confusion in point of view is made to right itself. Lawrence is merely repeating his emotions, and he avoids an austerer technical scrutiny of his material because it would compel him to master them. He would not let the artist be stronger than the man.

The result is that, at the same time that the book condemns the mother, it justifies her; at the same time that it shows Paul's failure, it offers rationalizations which place the failure elsewhere. The handling of the girl, Miriam, if viewed closely, is pathetic in what it signifies for Lawrence, both as man and artist. For Miriam is made the mother's scapegoat, and in a different way from the way that she was in life. The central section of the novel is shot through with alternate statements as to the source of the difficulty: Paul is unable to love Miriam wholly, and Miriam can love only his spirit. The contradictions appear sometimes within single paragraphs, and the point of view is never adequately objectified and sustained to tell us which is true. The material is never seen as material; the writer is caught in it exactly as firmly as he was caught in his experience of it. "That's how women are with me," said Paul. "They want me like mad, but they don't want to belong to me." So he might have said, and believed it; but at the end of the novel, Lawrence is still saying that, and himself believing it.

For the full history of this technical failure, one must read *Sons and Lovers* carefully and then learn the history of the manuscript from the book called *D.H. Lawrence: A Personal Record,* by one E. T., who was Miriam in life. The basic situation is clear enough. The first theme—the crippling effects of the mother's love—is developed right through to the end; and then suddenly, in the last few sentences, turns on itself, and Paul gives himself to life, not death. But all the way through, the insidious rationalizations of the second theme have crept in to destroy the artistic coherence of the work. A "split" would occur in Paul; but as the split is treated, it is superimposed upon rather than developed in support of the first theme. It is a rationalization made from it. If Miriam is made to insist on spiritual love, the meaning and the power of theme one are reduced; yet Paul's weakness is disguised. Lawrence could not separate the investigating analyst, who must be objective, from Lawrence, the subject of the book; and the sickness was not healed, the emotion not mastered, the novel not perfected. All this, and the character of a whole career, would have been altered if Lawrence had allowed his technique to discover the fullest meaning of his subject.

*A Portrait of the Artist as a Young Man*, like *Tono Bungay* and *Sons and Lovers*, is autobiographical, but unlike these it analyzes its material rigorously, and it defines the value and the quality of its experience not by appended comment or moral epithet, but by the texture of the style. The theme of *A Portrait*, a young artist's alienation from his environment, is explored and evaluated through three different styles and methods as Stephen Dedalus moves from childhood through boyhood into maturity. The opening pages are written in something like the stream of consciousness of *Ulysses*. as the environment impinges directly on the consciousness of the infant and the child, a strange, opening world which the mind does not yet subject to questioning, selection, or judgment. But this style changes very soon, as the boy begins to explore his surroundings, and as his sensuous experience of the world is enlarged, it takes on heavier and heavier rhythms and a fuller and fuller body of sensuous detail, until it reaches a crescendo of romantic opulence in the emotional climaxes which mark Stephen's rejection of domestic and religious values. Then gradually the style subsides into the austerer intellectuality of the final sections, as he defines to himself the outlines of the artistic task which is to usurp his maturity.

A highly self-conscious use of style and method defines the quality of experience in each of these sections, and, it is worth pointing out in connection with the third and concluding section, the style and method evaluate the experience. What has happened to Stephen is, of course, a progressive alienation from the life around him as he progressed in his initiation into it, and by the end of the novel, the alienation is complete. The final portion of the novel, fascinating as it may be for the developing aesthetic creed of Stephen-Joyce, is peculiarly bare. The life experience was not bare, as we know from *Stephen Hero*; but Joyce is forcing technique to comment. In essence, Stephen's alienation is a denial of the human environment; it is a loss; and the austere discourse of the final section, abstract and almost wholly without sensuous detail or strong rhythm, tells us of that loss. It is a loss so great that.the texture of the notation-like prose here suggests that the end is really all an illusion, that when Stephen tells us and himself that he is going forth to forge in the smithy of his soul the uncreated conscience of his race, we are to infer from the very quality of the icy, abstract void he now inhabits, the implausibility of his aim. For *Ulysses* does not create the conscience of the race; it creates our consciousness.

In the very last two or three paragraphs of the novel, the style changes once more, reverts from the bare, notative kind to the romantic prose of Stephen's adolescence. "Away! Away! The spell of arms and voices: the white arms of roads, their promise of close embraces and the black arms of tall ships that stand against the moon, their tale of distant nations. They are held out to say: We are alone—come." Might one not say that the austere ambition is founded on adolescent longing? That the excessive intellectual severity of one style is the counterpart of the excessive lyric relaxation of the other? And that the final passage of *A Portrait* punctuates the illusory nature of the whole ambition?

For *Ulysses* does not create a conscience. Stephen, in *Ulysses,* is a little older, and gripped now by guilt, but he is still the cold young man divorced from the human no less than the institutional environment. The environment of urban life finds a separate embodiment in the character of Bloom, and Bloom is as lost as Stephen, though touchingly groping for moorings. Each of the two is weakened by his inability to reach out, or to do more than reach out to the other. Here, then, is the theme again, more fully stated, as it were in counterpoint.

But if Stephen is not much older, Joyce is. He is older as an artist not only because he can create and lavish his Godlike pity on a Leopold Bloom, but. also because he knows now what both Stephen and Bloom mean, and *how much,* through the most brilliant technical operation ever made in fiction, they can be made to mean. Thus *Ulysses*, through the'imaginative force which its techniques direct, is like a pattern of concentric circles, with the immediate human situation at its center, this passing on and out to the whole dilemma of modern life, this passing on and out beyond that to a vision of the cosmos, and this to the mythical limits of our experience. If we read *Ulysses* with more satisfaction than any other novel of this century, it is because its author held an attitude toward technique and the technical scrutiny of subject matter which enabled him to order, within a single work and with superb coherence, the greatest amount of our experience.

## IV

In the United States during the last twenty-five years, we have had many big novels but few good ones. A writer like James T. Farrell apparently assumes that by endless redundancy in the description of the surface of American Life, he will somehow write a book with the scope of *Ulysses*. ThomasWolfe apparently assumed that by the mere disgorging of the raw material of his experience he would give us at last our epic. But except in a physical sense, these men have hardly written novels at all.

The books of Thomas Wolfe were, of course, journals, and the primary role of his publisher in transforming these journals into the semblance of novels is notorious. For the crucial act of the artist, the unique act which is composition, a sympathetic editorial blue pencil and scissors were substituted. The result has excited many people, especially the young, and the ostensibly critical have observed the prodigal talent with the wish that it might have been controlled. Talent there was, if one means by talent inexhaustible verbal energy, excessive response to personal experience, and a great capacity for auditory imitativeness, yet all of this has nothing to do with the novelistic quality of the written result; until the talent is controlled, the material organized, the content achieved, there is simply the man and his life. It remains to be demonstrated that Wolfe's conversations were any less interesting as novels than his books, which is to say that his books are without interest as novels. As with Lawrence, our response to the books is determined; not by their qualities as novels, but by our response to him and his qualities as a temperament.

This is another way of saying that Thomas Wolfe never really knew what he was writing *about*. Of Time and the River is merely a euphemism for Of a Man and his Ego. It is possible that had his conception of himself and of art included an adequate respect for technique and the capacity to pursue it, Wolfe would have written a great novel on his true subject—the dilemma of romantic genius; it was his true subject, but it remains his undiscovered subject, it is the subject which we must dig out for him, because he himself had neither the lamp nor the pick to find it in and mine it out of the labyrinths of his experience. Like Emily Bronte, Wolfe needed a point of view beyond his own which would separate his material and its effect.

With Farrell, the situation is opposite. He knows quite well what his subject is and what he wishes to tell us about it, but he hardly needs the novel to do so. It is significant that in sheer clumsiness of style, no living writer exceeds him, for his prose is asked to perform no service beyond communication of the most rudimentary kind of fact. For his ambitions, the style of the newspaper and the lens of the documentary camera would be quite adequate, yet consider the diminution which Leopold Bloom, for example, would suffer, if he were to be viewed from these, the technical perspectives of James Farrell. Under the eye of this technique, the material does not yield up enough; indeed, it shrinks.

More and more writers in this century have felt that naturalism as a method imposes on them strictures which prevent them from exploring through all the resources of technique the full amplifications of their subjects, and that thus it seriously limits the possible breadth of aesthetic meaning and response. James Farrell is almost unique in the complacency with which he submits to the blunt techniques of naturalism; and his fiction is correspondingly repetitive and flat.

That naturalism had a sociological and disciplinary value in the nineteenth century is obvious; it enabled the novel to grasp materials and make analyses which had eluded it in the past, and to grasp them boldly; but even then it did not tell us enough of what, in Virginia Woolf's phrase, is "really real," nor did it provide the means to the maximum of reality coherently, contained. Even the Flaubertian ideal of objectivity seems, today, an unnecessarily limited view of objectivity, for as almost every good writer of this century shows us, it is quite as possible to be objective about subjective states as it is to be objective about the circumstantial, surfaces of life. Dublin, in *Ulysses,* is a moral setting: not only a city portrayed in the naturalistic fashion of Dickens' London, but also a map of the modern psyche with its oblique and baffled purposes. The second level of reality in no way invalidates the first, and a writer like Joyce shows us that, if the artist truly respects his medium, he can be objective about both at once. What we need in fiction is a devoted fidelity to every technique which will help us to discover and to evaluate our subject matter, and more than that, to discover the amplifications of meaning of which our subject matter is capable.

Most modern novelists have felt this demand upon them. André Gide allowed one of his artist-heroes to make an observation which considerably resembles an observation we have quoted from Wells. "My novel hasn't got a subject.... Let's say, if you prefer it, it hasn't got *one* subject. . . . 'A slice of life,' the naturalist school said. The great defect of that school is that it always cuts its slice in the same direction; in time, lengthwise. Why not in breadth? Or in depth? As for me I should like not to cut at all. Please understand; I should like to put everything into my novel." Wells, with his equally large blob of potential material, did not know how to cut it to the novel's taste; Gide cut, of course—in every possible direction. Gide and others. And those "cuts" are all the new techniques which modern fiction has given us. None, perhaps, is more important than that inheritance from French symbolism which Huxley in the gittering wake of Gide, called "the musicalization of fiction." Conrad anticipated both when he wrote that the novel "must strenuously aspire to the plasticity of sculpture, to the colour of painting, and to the magic suggestiveness of music—which is the art of arts," and when he said of that early but wonderful piece of symbolist fiction, *Heart of Darkness,* "It was like another art altogether. That sombre theme had to be given a sinister resonance, a tonality of its own, a continued vibration that, I hoped, would hang in the air and dwell on the ear after the last note had been struck."" The analogy with music, except as a metaphor, is inexact, and except as it points to techniques which fiction can employ as fiction, not very useful to our sense of craftsmanship. It has had an approximate exactness in only one work, Joyce's final effort, and an effort unique in literary history, *Finnegan's Wake*, and here, of course, those readers willing to ap roach the "ideal" effort Joyce demands, discovering an inexhaustible wealth and scope, are most forcibly reminded of the primary importance of technique to subject, and of their indivisibility.

The techniques of naturalism inevitably curtail subject and often leave it in its original area, that of undefined social experience. Those of our writers who, stemming from this tradition, yet, at their best, achieve a novelistic definition of social experience—writers like the occasional Sherwood Anderson, William Carlos Williams, the occasional Erskine Caldwell, Nathaniel West, and Ira Wolfert in *Tucker's People* have done so by pressing naturalism far beyond itself, into positively gothic distortions. The structural machinations of Dos Passos and the lyrical interruptions of Steinbeck are the desperate maneuvers of men committed to a method of whose limitations they despair. They are our symbolists *manqué,* who end as allegorists.

Our most accomplished novels leave no such impression of desperate and intentional struggle, yet their precise technique and their determination to make their prose work in the service of their subjects have been the measure of their accomplishmer Hemingway's *The Sun Also Rises* and Wescott's *The Pilgrim Hawk* are works of art not because they may be measured by some external, neoclassic notion of form, but because their forms are so exactly equivalent with their subjects, and because the evaluation of their subjects exists in their styles.

Hemingway has recently said that his contribution to younger writers lay in a certain necessary purification of the language; but the claim has doubtful value. The contribution of his prose was to his subject, and the terseness of style for which his early work is justly celebrated is no more valuable, as an end in itself, than the baroque involutedness of Faulkner's prose, or the cold elegance of Wescott's. Hemingway's early subject, the exhaustion of value, was perfectly investigated and invested by his bare style, and in story after story, no meaning at all is to be inferred from the fiction except as the style itself suggests that there is no meaning in life. This style, more than that, was the perfect technical substitute for the conventional commentator; it expresses and it measures that peculiar morality of the stiff lip which Hemingway borrowed from athletes. It is an instructive lesson, furthermore, to observe how the style breaks down when Hemingway moves into the less congenial subject matter of social affirmation: how the style breaks down, the effect of verbal economy as mute suffering is lost, the personality of the writer, no longer protected by the objectification of an adequate technique, begins its offensive intrusion, and the entire structural integrity slackens. Inversely, in the stories and the early novels, the technique was the perfect embodiment of the subject and it gave that subject its astonishing largeness of effect and of meaning.

One should correct Buffon and say that style is the subject. In Wescott's *Pilgrim Hawk*, a novel which bewildered its many friendly critics by the apparent absence of subject, the subject, the story, is again in the style itself. This novel, which is a triumph of the sustained point of view, is only bewildering if we try to make a story out of the narrator's observations upon others; but if we read his observations as oblique and unrecognized observations upon himself the story emerges with perfect coherence, and it reverberates with meaning, is as suited to continuing reflection as the greatest lyrics.

The rewards of such respect for the medium as the early Hemingway and the occasional Wescott have shown may be observed in every good writer we have. The involutions of Faulkner's style are the perfect equivalent of his involved structures, and the two together are the perfect representation of the moral labyrinths he explores, and of the ruined world which his novels repeatedly invoke and in which these labyrinths exist. The cultivated sensuosity of Katherine Anne Porter's style has charm in itself, of course, but no more than with these others does it have aesthetic value in itself; its values lie in the subtle means by which sensuous details become symbols, and in the way that the symbols provide a network which is the story, and which at the same time provides the writer and us with a refined moral insight by means of which to test it. When we put such writers against a writer like William Saroyan, whose respect is reserved for his own temperament, we are appalled by the stylistic irresponsibility we find in him, and by the almost total absence of theme, or defined subject matter, and the abundance of unwarranted feeling. Such a writer inevitably becomes a sentimentalist because he has no means by which to measure his emotion. Technique, at last, is measure.

These writers, from Defoe to Porter, are of unequal and very different talent, and technique and talent are, of course, after a point, two different things. What Joyce gives us in one direction, Lawrence, for all his imperfections as a technician, gives us in another, even though it is not usually the direction of art. Only in some of his stories and in a few of his poems, where the demands of technique are less sustained and the subject matter is not autobiographical, Lawrence, in a different way from Joyce, comes to the same aesthetic fulfilment. Emily Bronte, with what was perhaps her intuitive grasp of the need to establish a tension between her subject matter and her perspective upon it, achieves a similar fulfilment; and, curiously, in the same way and certainly by intuition alone, Hemingway's early work makes a moving splendor from nothingness.

And yet, whatever one must allow to talent and forgive in technique, one risks no generalization in saying that modern fiction at its best has been peculiarly conscious of itself and of its tools. The technique of modern fiction, at once greedy and fastidious, achieves as its subject matter not some singleness, some topic or thesis, but the whole of the modern consciousness. It discovers the complexity of the modern spirit, the difficulty of personal morality, and the fact of evil—all the untractable elements under the surface which a technique of the surface alone can not approach. It shows us—in Conrad's words, from *Victory* —that we all live in an "age in which we are camped like bewildered travellers in a garish, unrestful hotel," and while it puts its hard light on our environment, it penetrates, with its sharp weapons, the depths of our bewilderment. These are not two things, but only an adequate technique can show them as one. In a realist like Farrell, we have the environment only, which we know from the newspapers; in a subjectivist like Wolfe we have the bewilderment only, which we record in our own diaries and letters. But the true novelist gives them to us together, and thereby increases the effect of each, and reveals each in its full significance.

Elizabeth Bowen, writing of Lawrence, said of modern fiction, "We want the naturalistic surface, but with a kind of internal burning. In Lawrence every bush burns." But the bush burns brighter in some places than in others, and it burns brightest when a passionate private vision finds its objectification in exacting technical search. If the vision finds no such objectification, as in Wolfe and Saroyan, there is a burning without a bush. In our committed realists, who deny the resources of art for the sake of life, whose technique forgives both innocence and slovenliness—in Defoe and Wells and Farrell there is a bush but it does not burn. There, at first glance, the bush is only a bush; and then, when we look again, we see that, really, the thing is dead.

*The Hudson Review* I, Spring, 1948

## Colin Holmes, "A Study of D.H. Lawrence's Social Origins"

What were the social origins of D.H. Lawrence? Was he from a proletarian background? Or was this a myth which at times he found convenient to cultivate? Have we believed too much of what he said about these matters? And has the time come to demolish the views which are held regarding his social background?[1]

My interest in this is not accidental. I know Lawrence country. For me, as for him, it constitutes 'the country of my heart'[2] and, like Lawrence, I went to University in Nottingham, 'that dismal town'.[3] Not to the 'ugly neo-Gothic building' in Shakespeare Street[4] which opened its doors in 1881 but to that lighter University on the hill, 'Nottingham's New University' built 'grand and cakeily'[5] above its lake and near to Jesse Boot's Beeston. In my years there the memory of Lawrence and his stature as a writer were in the process of being revived. The scandal of the elopement with Frieda Weekly had disappeared into the realms of the past and Vivian de Sola Pinto was trying to re-establish Lawrence's literary importance in the University free from such personal considerations. It was in fact a time of considerable activity in Lawrence studies. In 1960 the University held its Lawrence Exhibition[6] and in the same year Professor Pinto gave evidence at the prosecution over *Lady Chatterley's Lover* when, with other critics, he testified to Lawrence's literary genius and played a part in releasing the author's work from the problems of censorship which had bedevilled it since *The Rainbow* case in 1915.[7] Throughout the late 1950s and early 1960s, in line with this growing interest, there seemed to be a procession of research students making a pilgrimage to the English Department at Nottingham, anxious to discuss central, interstitial and vestigial aspects of Lawrence's life and thought. To us, the undergraduates, it seemed that an enthusiastic industry was at work.

Most thinking students were aware of all this but in the Sub-Department of Economic and Social History there was a link of a different kind with this activity. The head of the Sub-Department—Departmental status came in 1960— was J. D. Chambers.[8] At this time Chambers was in charge of a small, energetic school which was rapidly establishing its name in the growing discipline of economic and social history. But there was more to Chambers than the academic historian. He was the brother of Jessie Chambers, the Miriam of *Sons and Lovers*. The small, round-faced, booted child on the family photographs, the Hubert of *Sons and Lovers,* was now lecturing to us on the Industrial Revolution. And in the course of his lectures he suggested that it would be rewarding for an economic and social historian to analyse Lawrence's work, to test it with the rigour which might be applied to any other historical source.[9] Lawrence had a great deal to say about the processes of industrialisation and the social consequences of the transformation of England from an agrarian to a 'mechanical disintegrated, amorphous'[10] industrial society. Growing up in Eastwood he saw every day a blend of the old and the new. The blackened pit-tips where the earth's core accumulated on the surface and the iron headstocks below which men were taken into an underground world rose stark and sudden among stretching woodlands and country fields. Through the clash of such visual symbols Lawrence could hardly fail to be aware of the impact of industrialisation. On a more animate level the sight of colliers in their pit dust spilling into Eastwood when their shift was over was another permanent feature of the industrial landscape.[11] But familiarity does not necessarily lead to accuracy and in 1960 Chambers made it clear in his seminars on the Industrial Revolution—a course for third-year undergraduates— that he was deeply dissatisfied with the analysis presented by Raymond Williams in *Culture and Society,* in which Lawrence was described as a perceptive critic of industrialisation.[12]

Any attempt to discuss Lawrence's critique of industrialisation would be a formidable undertaking and is best left for another occasion. Instead, as I indicated at the beginning, I want to restrict myself to a study of Lawrence's social origins; and to discuss, in particular, George Watson's recent opinions on this, in the course of which he draws upon Chambers's knowledge and recollections of Lawrence's early life.[13]    Watson's work has shown a clear tendency to cross traditional academic boundaries in pursuit of the past and his peppery, iconoclastic raids are concerned to overturn current orthodoxies, particularly those derived from the writings of the political Left.[14]   As a historian I want to question his argument on Lawrence's origins and, at the same time, to indicate some of the dangers which arise when academic boundaries are crossed.

There is a classical view about Lawrence's background which derives from Lawrence himself who wrote, 'I was born among the working classes and brought up among them': he went on to comment that he was in fact 'a man from the working class'.[15] Such a view has become widely accepted. While Marxist critics of the inter-war years like Christopher Caudwell could refer to Lawrence as a bourgeois artist, this constituted an attack upon his ideas rather than a reference to his social origins.[16] Indeed, the belief that Lawrence had a working-class background became part of the accepted version of his life. E. M. Forster could refer to him as of the working class in an obituary notice in 1930[17], and a similar belief was apparent at a later date in F. R. Leavis's discussion of Keynes and Lawrence in Cambridge.[18]  Indeed, 'By the 1950s', Watson has written, 'the myth had taken up its lodging in academe'.[19]   Richard Hoggart in *The Uses of Literacy*[20] and Raymond Williams in *Culture and Society*[21] both viewed Lawrence's origins in this light and, still more recently, Terry Eagleton in *Criticism and Ideology* has referred to Lawrence as 'of proletarian origin'.[22] It is this strand of opinion which Watson attempts to overturn.

Watson's argument can be summarised in the following terms. Lawrence was 'the son of a contractor in a Nottinghamshire coal mine and of a former schoolmistress of some cultivation and social standing'. Consequently, it is argued, 'The common assertion that his father was a miner, though not false, is misleading in context; he was not by the period of Lawrence's upbringing dependent upon wages, being in charge of a group of miners, and his income was good'.[23] Furthermore, it is argued, 'If his manners were rough and at times even wild, this needs to be measured against the superior existence his wife created at Eastwood for the sons who, as she successfully resolved, would never work in a mine'. This is the first salvo of the counter attack.

The next barrage comes via J. D. Chambers, described as 'the brother of Jessie Chambers and himself a social historian' who knew Lawrence 'intimately in his youth'.[24] According to Chambers—and Watson uses this in his evidence—it was simply untrue to say that the Lawrence family had lived in poverty. Lawrence's father was:

> a highly skilled man, bringing home good money, occupying a house with a big window and separate 'entry' of which the Lawrences were immensely proud, and handing over to his wife enough money to give three of their five children a good education.[25]

In view of this the working-class origins of Lawrence are regarded by Watson as without foundation and he is particularly keen to emphasise that after the age of six Lawrence left 'the mean terraced house marked as his birthplace' and 'lived in a superior residence on the hill until he was eighteen'.[26] And going to Nottingham High School for the best type of local education, to the University in Nottingham, to a schoolnaster's post in Croydon, and marrying the daughter of a German aristocrat, were all, in a sense, part of a progression away from the wage earners, whose lives, it is argued, he had observed rather than experienced.

According to Watson, therefore, Lawrence was never outside the middle class, although at no point is any clear indication given of what Watson regards as the determinants of class position. And in order to explain why the myth of Lawrence's social origins should have arisen, Watson refers to the possibility that in his later years 'the humbler status of his father came to look disputatiously convenient' to Lawrence. Indeed, 'men sometimes discover in their middle years that an origin they once found disadvantageous can be turned to an unlooked-for account'.[27]

In considering this counter-interpretation it has to be admitted straightaway that Arthur Lawrence was not just a day-wage collier and any account which has assumed that he was, is undoubtedly mistaken. In that sense alone we need to take Watson's argument seriously. But Watson's own position is unsatisfactory both with regard to his discussion of the nature of Arthur Lawrence's work and his suggested wage-earning capacity.

Lawrence's father, we are told by Watson, was a contractor, in charge of men and not dependent upon wages.[28] In more conventional terms, he was a 'butty'. Butty work, which is still in need of close academic study, was subject to great regional variations and different practices prevailed between and within pits in the same area. But oral historians, using collective memories of miners, are in the process of reconstructing the historical patterns of the butty system and the essential features it contained. From this work it becomes clear that there were broadly two kinds of butty. There was the sub-contractor or 'big butty' who contracted with the owners to get a certain amount of coal in return for an agreed payment, and who then proceeded to recruit workers and provide the working capital to achieve this. In this case we are referring to a self-employed man who also employed wage labour. But in the course of the nineteenth century this type of man became less significant as mining life became increasingly regulated and responsibility for working conditions became more centralised and organised. In such circumstances the contractor or the 'little butty' remained important, but his role was significantly different from that of the sub-contractor. The 'little butty' was a type of boss-workman who oversaw the working of a stall, a place of work at the coalface, and was responsible for getting out the coal. For this he collected the wages for the coal filled by the stall and proceeded to distribute part of such payment to the men who worked under him and who were, like himself, employees of the coal owners. Whichever system operated it allowed for corruption. Details of the financial arrangements which butties, big and little, had with the owners were often secret and a source of tension and suspicion. Good, or in other words, docile butties would be favoured with stalls which guaranteed high productivity, while recalcitrant men like Arthur Lawrence could be given difficult parts of the pit to work. Furthermore, an inevitable consequence of so splitting the workforce—with men working under butties, while the butties also encountered managerial discrimination—was that the butty system generally operated as an agency of management control.[29]

So much for the general picture. But what of Brinsley? As yet we have no detailed study of this particular pit. But Alan Griffin, who has had access to the papers of this Barber, Walker pit, is prepared to say that 'D.H. Lawrence's father was a "little" Butty at Brinsley Colliery', who worked his stall in conjunction with another butty and two or three day-wage workers, and was in fact 'dependent entirely upon wages'. This is quite different from the image of the self-employed Lawrence that Watson, Georgeis keen to stress.[30] Moreover, being an independent-spirited man, Arthur Lawrence was seldom guaranteed a good stall. Evidence suggests that he gave no inch to the owners; he showed no signs of bowing before authority, even if docility held out the prospect of material benefits. He did not share a consciousness with the pit owners; nor did he find it with his family. His sense of belonging came when he was with his fellow colliers. In view of all this, how much remains of the new image of Arthur Lawrence in which we are asked to believe?[31]

However, in trying to establish a new image of Lawrence's background, Watson also contends that Arthur Lawrence earned 'good money'. Such a remark runs counter to that made by Ada Lawrence; one that is more in line with the traditional or classical view of the Lawrence household. Her comment on the family situation was as follows:

> We were always conscious of poverty and the endless struggle for bread. Perhaps many other children of mining folk knew frequently enough that they had not enough to eat. We were conscious of more. The anxieties of our mother were shared by us. She never concealed the fact that she had not enough money to clothe and feed us as adequately as she wished. The sight of father coming up the field at midday took all the pleasure from our games. It meant that on Friday night he would be short on half a day's pay. I don't remember him giving mother more than thirty-five shillings a week. So much was rare. The usual amount was twenty-five. The rent was five shillings and the rates were extra. She baked the bread, made what clothes she could

for us and schemed day and night so that we should have enough to eat. It was the terrible indignity of such poverty that embittered my brother so much.[32]

But we do not know if Arthur Lawrence handed over all his wages and, since his earnings would be cyclical, trusting to Ada Lawrence's impressions, in this case, could be dangerous. Thus we should be cautious about accepting her statement. However, we are equally unable to accept uncritically Watson's claim that Lawrence's father earned good money. This claim is derived from Chambers and for a historian it is a surprisingly vague statement. We simply do not know whether it is the relative or absolute level of earnings to which reference is being made. In fact, we are unable to make any positive statement about the earnings of Lawrence's father until the wage sheets at Brinsley have been examined and earnings compared both with those elsewhere in the Nottinghamshire coalfield and with other occupations. Until then everybody should stay his/her hand in discussing the kind of money earned by Arthur Lawrence.[33]

Nevertheless, it might further be argued that the change of houses in which the Lawrence family was involved could hardly have occurred in the absence of Arthur Lawrence's considerable earning power. And Watson does in fact make this point. In reply it should be said that if anyone wishes to develop this kind of argument the first requirement is to provide accurate information on the moves undertaken by the Lawrences—and this Watson fails to do. The moves during Mrs Lawrence's life were from Victoria Street down to the Breach, up to Walker Street and then, after the death of Ernest Lawrence, in 1902, to Lynn Croft. Watson's account, which implies that movement was from the Breach—where he seems to believe that Lawrence was born—up the hill towards better property, is a simplification of events.[34] Nevertheless, the fact remains that Lawrence did move over the course of time into a better type of property. But this does not necessarily have the implications for Arthur Lawrence's earning power that some might suppose. For instance, there is evidence, of a personal kind, which would indicate that the journey up the hill was achieved by engaging in a good deal of sacrifice. Mabel Collishaw, one of Lawrence's contemporaries in Eastwood, unsuspectingly provides evidence on this when she writes:

> Mr Lawrence was a very boastful man and a very careless one when working in the mine. As a direct consequence, he had many accidents. My father was the sick visitor for the Foresters lodge, and it was a part of his duty to pay benefits and take care that the miner's wife and children had food if the husband was seriously injured. On one occasion, Mr Lawrence broke his leg and had to be taken to the hospital in Nottingham. As they were carrying him out of the house he said to his wife:-'Don't let the children starve. Cut that large ham behind the pantry door'.
> Father opened the door to see if they had meat but the only food was bread.[35]

This was written to provide an insight into the psychology of Lawrence's father. But it reveals more than that. It suggests that the Lawrences could have their 'superior residences' (anyone who has seen them will recognise that there are overtones in this which should be resisted) at a cost of doing without certain other needs. In this instance it seems that food was skimped for the sake of a house. In this connection it is also worth recalling the following—the evidence again comes from Collishaw.

> When his parents moved from the Breach to Walker Street, it was a great lift for the family, for we who lived on Lynn Croft never, as a rule, mixed with the children of the Breach. The first thing Mrs Lawrence did was to buy new lace curtains for the bay windowed 'parlour' . . . My sister and I were passing as she was hanging up the curtains threaded on a tape and Bertie stood proudly beside her. When he saw me coming, he held the curtain for the side window high up. His looks said, 'You boast about your curtains on a bamboo pole. Now we have some too!' He nearly cried when he came out to play and said, 'I don't care! We will have a proper pole some day!'[36]

Collishaw's recollection illustrates the social distinctions which existed in Eastwood—and these clearly stayed with her—and also aims to throw light on Lawrence's character. But once again it is also revealing in a different sense. One could move to Walker Street and have the house but, at the same time, it became necessary to economise on the bamboo pole.

Apart from moving into better types of property, the drive towards respectability was also evident within the Lawrence household. This is presumably part of the 'superior existence' to which Watson refers, attributing an influence here to Lydia Lawrence. Although it is not clearly spelt out, the assumption behind such a statement is that it could occur because Mrs Lawrence was the wife of a high earning miner and had the resources with which to continue her earlier refined tastes. But we need to be careful in jumping to such conclusions and should bear in mind the well-known Northern saying about 'lace curtains and nothing for breakfast'. In other words, it was not unusual for a home to be built up through careful husbandry and sacrifice rather than a high level of earnings, and there is evidence that such forces were present in the Lawrence family. In describing the home Ada Lawrence recalled:

> We were proud of our front room or parlour with its well-made mahogany and horse-hair suite of furniture—the little mahogany chiffonier and the oval Spanish mahogany table which my mother insisted on covering with a fawn and green tapestry tablecloth to match the Brussels carpet.  Here again were oleographs heavily framed in gilt, and the family portrait in the place of honour over the mantelpiece.
> Although so unpretentious there was something about our house which made it different from those of our neighbours. Perhaps this was because mother would have nothing cheap or tawdry, preferring bareness.[37]

Further confirmation that the 'superior existence' of the Lawrences came through self-help and sacrifice rather than earning power is provided by the careers of the Lawrence children. The drive towards respectability held by Mrs Lawrence was reflected in the ambitions which she nourished for them, which resulted in all of them being placed in clerical or teaching careers. In this instance there is firm evidence that the economic foundations for this came through sacrifice rather than the 'good money' earned by Lawrence's father—whatever that is intended to mean.[38]

So where does this leave us? 'There is no real evidence', Watson has written, 'that Lawrence was ever outside the middle class as that phrase is most commonly understood, at any time in his life'.[39] In this view Lawrence's father was a self-employed contractor; he earned good money; on the basis of this the Lawrences could enjoy a 'superior existence' in Eastwood. In reply to this it has been argued that Watson has misunderstood the kind of work in which Arthur Lawrence was engaged. Lawrence's father was an employee of the Barber, Walker Company and it is Watson's ignorance of the butty system which has resulted in his major misjudgment. Furthermore, Watson has produced no evidence, other than Chambers's comment, made without access to any wage sheets, to substantiate his claim that Lawrence's father earned good money, which by itself anyway is a vague comment. He has also failed to recognise that the moves of the Lawrence family to better properties within Eastwood—a place with which Watson is clearly unfamiliar—and other aspects of their 'superior existence' can be accounted for on the basis of quite different influences from those which he suggests. Thus, each point of Watson's argument can be refuted or contested.

But it would be unwise, having countered Watson's argument to stress that Lawrence's social background was typically working class. Lawrence's father, even though he enjoyed some status in the mining community as a result of his role as a little butty, was working class. His market situation was that he was a miner in receipt of wages—on which the family was solely dependent—and that he was reliant upon the pit owners for employment. He could read only with difficulty and could only just sign his name. His culture was of a non-literate kind. In terms of such economic and cultural indices he could hardly be described as other than working class. It would strain the bounds of social analysis to argue otherwise. But the Lawrence family was made up of more than Arthur Lawrence. It is also necessary to take account of the strong mother figure, Lydia Lawrence, who played a critical role in the family and upon the development of the children. We have already noticed her commitment to respectability, her striving to 'get on' and her consequent worship of the lean goddess, abstinence. In this she was displaying her attachment to the virtues worshipped in Samuel Smiles's catechism and such qualities helped to secure her children against a working-class future. But these were not the only values she brought to the household. She also injected into it other cultural strands. She read a good deal,wrote poetry, insisted on standard English, and refused to make any concession to the local dialect. The result was that the home contained the culture of Lawrence's father, which D.H.L. came to regard as 'the old instinctive, sensuous life of pre-industrial England' and that of 'a woman of intellectual attainments'.[40]

In other words, colliding planes of consciousness were present and Lawrence was tossed between both sets of influences. And, as Lydia Lawrence took a grip on the family, as the children were turned against their father, Arthur Lawrence expressed himself increasingly in the company of his fellow miners in the local public houses. Consequently, the gap in the family widened. This was the crucible in which D.H. Lawrence was born, through which he lived and which he immortalised in his poem, 'Red Herring', which appeared in 1929 in *Pansies*. Watson's interpretation of this work is that it provides further evidence for his case that Lawrence was 'outside the working class'. But it is a mistaken insistence upon this view, based mainly upon his distorted conception of the work of Lawrence's father, which prevents Watson from making the poem a central feature in his analysis of Lawrence's social origins. 'Red Herring' is in fact a hymn to social and psychological marginality, to the in-between. What is being suggested here—and Lawrence's poem is about this—is that Lawrence was born into a working-class home, in terms of his father's occupation, but it was one full of aspirations derived from Lydia Lawrence. In other words it was a household in which the children were orientated towards a future life outside the working class. It was because of this that the Lawrence children experienced problems of ultimate social identification. 'Red Herring' stands as the clearest testimony of this, and consequently it is worth extracting from it its salient message:

> My father was a working man
>     and a collier was he . . .
> My mother was a superior soul
>     a superior soul was she,
> cut out to play a superior role
>     in the god-damn bourgeoisie
>
> We children were the in-betweens
>     little non descripts were we,
> indoors we called each other *you,*
>     outside, it was *tha* and *thee.*
>
> But time has fled, our parents are dead
>     we've risen in the world all three;
> but still we are in-betweens, we tread
>     between the devil and the deep sad sea.[41]

This consideration of Lawrence's social origins has turned principally upon a discussion of Watson's *Encounter* article and, in the final stages of my discussion, I want to set his work in a wider context. Watson's writing is patently ideological in character. His pen has been used to label Marx and Engels as racialists and in the course of a number of writings he has displayed a clear relish in taking an intellectual swipe at anything socialist.[42] It is no surprise that he finds *Encounter* a congenial home for his material and, in pursuit of Lawrence's origins, his reliance upon the testimony of J. D. Chambers has brought about an interesting fusion of academic forces. Chambers himself was a leading representative of the optimistic school of economic and social history which exercised a powerful influence upon the academic history world of the 1950s and 1960s. As a young man he had been a near convert to Marxism under the influence of Maurice Dobb's 1925 publication *Capitalist Enterprise and Socialist Progress* —he once described its author as probably the cleverest man of his generation—and devoted the rest of his life, after the trauma of near conversion, to an attack upon the Marxist historical position while simultaneously having the highest regard for individual Marxists.[43] In general terms the consequence of this was an emphasis upon certain positive favourable trends within the process of industrialisation and a minimising of the conflict inherent in such a traumatic change.[44] What we have, then, in the *Encounter* article is the merging of two strands of thought drawn from literature and history which are hostile to socialist opinion, in an attempt to construct a different picture of Lawrence's origins from that which has been widely accepted—particularly on the Left.[45] But, it has been argued, it is a picture which is ultimately unconvincing.

A failure along these lines is not a cause for rejoicing. In spite of all the attention which has been lavished upon Lawrence much yet remains to be done. If we restrict ourselves to the kind of work which would benefit from an inter-communion of the disciplines of history and literature, the opportunity still exists for a full scale examination of his writing in the light of what we know about the economic and social history of the time through which Lawrence lived and the area where he was born. Furthermore, there is still historical evidence as yet unused and, indeed, unseen on Lawrence's problems with the censor.[46] There is also, I suspect, a need for a re-evaluation of Lawrence's social-political philosophy, free from the distortions to which it has been subjected by the categorisation of his thought outside its appropriate context.[47] In all these instances a cross fertilisation of history and literature is capable of yielding fresh insights into Lawrence's life and work. But the rigours and pitfalls of inter-disciplinary work need to be constantly kept in mind and in this respect the *Encounter* analysis of Lawrence's origins is a reminder not only of the potential, but also of the actual dangers, which can arise when academic boundaries are crossed in the reconstruction of the past. However, a failure should not deter us; we should press ahead seeking for the illuminating inter-connections between history and literature, confident that the fruits, still largely unpicked can be considerable.[48]

*Literature and History: A New Journal for the Humanities*, 6, 1980

## Notes

[1] As suggested by George Watson in 'D.H. Lawrence's Own Myth', *Encounter*, December 1976, pp. 29-34, reprinted in his book, *Politics and Literature in Modern Britain*, (1977), pp. 110-19, as 'The Politics of D.H. Lawrence'. The reviewer of Watson's book in *The Times Literary Supplement*, 21 July 1978, p.826 found the chapter on Lawrence unconvincing but was unable to bring evidence to bear in order to support his disquiet.

[2] Letter to Rolf Gardiner, 3 December 1926, in Aldous Huxley (ed.), *The Letters of D. H. Lawrence*, 1932), p. 674.

[3] See 'Nottingham's New University', in D.H. Lawrence, *Selected Poems*, (Harmondsworth, 1972), p. 204.

[4] V. de S. Pinto, *Reginald Mainwaring Hewitt (1887-1948), a Selection from his Literary Remains*, (Oxford, 1955), p. 18.

[5] See 'Nottingham's New University' in *Selected Poems*, pp. 204-5.

[6] V. de S. Pinto, *D. H. Lawrence after Thirty Years*, (Nottingham, 1960). For an earlier appreciation by Pinto of Lawrence see *Prophet of the Midlands*, (Nottingham, 1951).

[7] C.H. Rolph, *The Trial of Lady Chatterley* etc., (Harmondsworth, 1961), pp. 73-83.

[8] On Chambers see the obituary in *The Times*, 15 April 1970. He provides some background on his family in Edward Nehls (ed.), *D. H. Lawrence. A Composite Biography*, 3 vols, (Madison, Wisconsin, 1957-9), III, pp. 531-629.

[9] A theme he developed in his seminars on the Industrial Revolution with third year undergraduates in 1960.

[10] Raymond Williams, *Culture and Society*, (Harmondsworth, 1961), p. 201.

[11] Such scenes are captured in the works set in the area, in particular *The White Peacock*, (1911), *Sons and Lovers*, (1913) and *Lady Chatterley's Lover*, (1928). See also his essay, 'Nottingham and the Mining Countryside', *New Adelphi*, June-August 1930, 255-63.

[12] Although the standard of living debate generated considerable interest in the late 1950s, there was very little discussion of literary evidence. For some later critical comment on literary sources as aids in understanding the industrialisation process in Britain, see J. M. Jefferson, 'Industrialisation and Poverty: In Fact and Fiction', in the Institute of Economic Affairs publication, *The Long Debate on Poverty*, (1972), pp. 189-238.

[13] See the introduction to ET (Jessie Chambers), *D.H. Lawrence, A Personal Record* (2 ed., 1965), and J. D. Chambers, 'Memories of D.H. Lawrence', *Renaissance and Modern Studies*, vol. XVI, (1972), pp. 5-17.

[14] A selection of his work; is collected together in *Politics and Literature in Modern Britain* etc. For an earlier attempt of his to blend history and literature see *The English Ideology*, (1973).

[15] This remark appeared in Lawrence's autobiographical sketch and can be found in A. Beal (ed.), *D. H. Lawrence, Selected Literary Criticism*, (1963).

[16] C. Caudwell, 'D. H. Lawrence: A Study of the Bourgeois Artist', reprinted in S. E. Hyman, *The Critical Performance*, (New York, 1956), pp. 153-73.

[17] R.P. Draper (ed.), *D. H. Lawrence: The Critical Heritage*, (1970), pp. 332 ff.

[18] F. R. Leavis, 'Keynes, Lawrence and Cambridge', *Scrutiny*, vol. XVI, (1949), reprinted in *The Common Pursuit*, (1952), p. 258.

[19] Watson, *Encounter*, p. 32.

[20] Richard Hoggart, *The Uses of Literacy*, (Harmondsworth, 1959), p. 33.

[21] Williams, *op. cit.,* p. 205.

[22] Terry Eagleton, *Criticism and Ideology* (1976), p. 157.

[23] Watson, *Encounter*, p. 30.

[24] *Ibid*.

[25] See the introduction by J.D. Chambers to ET (Jessie Chambers), *D H. Lawrence*, p. xv. In *Renaissance and Modern Studies*, p. 7. Chambers placed greater emphasis depending upon whether the butty obtained a good stall i.e., section of the coal face, on which to work. Watson does not stress this qualification and his work does not recognise this change of emphasis.

[26] Watson, *Encounter*, p. 30.

[27] *Ibid.*, p. 33.

[28] *Ibid*.

[29] R. Goffee, 'The Butty System in the Kent Coalfield', *Bulletin of the Society for the Study of Labour History,* No.34 (Spring 1977), p.42, notes the need for further research into the butty system. Alan R. Griffin, *Mining in the East Midlands 1550-1947*, (1971), pp.111, 117, 163, 192, refers to the generally diminishing role of butties in the Nottinghamshire pits in the course of the nineteenth century, the variations within the region in the butty system  and the retention of butties in Barber, Walker pits, including Brinsley, until nationalisation in 1947. See also his earlier publication, T*he Miners of Nottinghamshire*, vol 1, 1881 to 1914 (Nottingham, 1955), pp.137-8, and particularly p.178. ET (Jessie Chambers) *D. H. Lawrence*, p.16 mentions that a contribution to the

Congregational chapel in Eastwood could secure a better type of stall. Hence the chapel's nickname, the 'Butty's Lump'. A recent, as yet unpublished study of the butty system, which provides a useful general background to the situation in the Notts-Derbys coalfields is: Paul Turner, 'The Butty System in the Notts-Derbys Coalfields and its Contribution to the 1926 Strike'. Available in the Department of Economic and Social History at Sheffield University.

[30] Letter Alan R. Griffin to author, 22 March 1977. Griffin has had sight of a large number of pay slips at Brinsley.

[31] Nehls, *op.cit.*, vot 1, p.21 (evidence of Hopkin) and *ibid.*, p.10 (evidence of Ada Lawrence) together provide evidence on Arthur Lawrence which supports my argument.

[32] *Ibid.*, pp. 16-7.

[33] Earnings at Brinsley were generally low in relation to other pits in Nottinghamshire. Griffin to author 22 March 1977. For a recent loose acceptance of the Lawrences' evidence see Phillip Callow, *Son and Lover,* (1975), pp.26-7.

[34] Watson, *Encounter*, p. 30.

[35] Quoted in Nehls, *op. cit.,* I, p. 31.

[36] *Ibid.,* p 30.

[37] Quoted in *ibid.*, p.9. See G. D. H. Cole *A Short History of the British Working Class Movement, 1789-1937*, (1960), pp.152 ff. for the ambience of self-improvement after the mid-nineteenth century.

[38] Harry Moore, *The Intelligent Heart*, (Harmondsworth, 1960), pp.43 and 46, and Nehls, *op.cit.*, vol 3, p.605. See ET (Jessie Chambers), *D. H. Lawrence* p.75, for evidence of Lawrence saving up to pay for himself at University College, Nottingham. Ada Lawrence in *ibid.*, vol 1, pp.16-7, comments upon her mother's careful management.

[39] Watson, *Encounter*, p. 32.

[40] Pinto, *Prophet,* pp. 7-8 refers to cultural differences.

[41] On marginality see, *inter alia*, H. F. Dickie Clark, *The Marginal Situation*, (1966). 'Red Herring' appears in *Selected Poems,* pp.205-6. Although Mrs Lawrence had well authenticated interests in literature, this does not mean that she would have approved of the precarious financial literary life which D.H.L. pursued. Her concern was for the children to acquire professional respectability and security. In fact, Lawrence defied the career expectations of both his parents. See Graham Holderness, 'Lawrence, Leavis and Culture', in *Working Papers in Cultural Studies*, No.5, Spring 1974, (University of Birmingham), pp.94-6. Lawrence's marginality is hinted at but not directly mentioned in Graham Hough, *The Dark Sun,* (1956), p.90. Most of the themes referred to in this categorisation of Lawrence are touched upon in Brian Jackson, *Working Class Community*, (1968), pp.15-7. For Watson's passing reference to 'Red Herring', see *Encounter*, pp.32-3. Moore, *op.cit.*, p.27 argues that Lawrence exaggerates the class differences within his family, noting that Arthur Lawrence had 'no genuine seasoned proletarian heritage'. But this underplays the fact that for D.H.L. the crucial issue was the immediate one, that his father and mother represented opposing cultures derived from their different occupational backgrounds

[42] See his article 'Race and the Socialists', *Encounter*, November 1976.

[43] Referred to in 1960 in his third year seminars on General Economic History. The major fruit of this research was his paper, 'Enclosure and Labour Supply in the Industrial Revolution', *Economic History Review,* vol V, (1952-3), pp.319-43. On Dobb, see the obituary in *The Times,* 19 August 1976.

44 A point emphasised by a former Nottingham student, G. E. Mingay, in 'The Contribution of a Regional Historian: J. D. Chambers 1898-1970', in *Studies in Burke and His Time*, vol XIII, (1971), p.2007. The same point is made but from a differing ideological viewpoint by F. K. Donnelly in 'Ideology and Early English Working Class History: Edward Thompson and his Critics', *Social History*, No. 2, May 1976, pp. 219-38.

45 In the words of Watson, *Encounter*, p. 32 the belief that Lawrence had working class origins amounted to 'a standard intellectual socialist myth by the 1950s'.

46 Nehls, *op. cit.* III, p. XXI, refers to the withholding of Metropolitan Police material on the exhibition of Lawrence paintings which was raided in London in 1929.

47 J. R. Harrison, *The Reactionaries*, (1966) needs careful watching in this connection. See the wise and cautionary general remarks in Hough, *op. cit.,* p. 239.

48 For an affirmative general comment on the inter-communion of the disciplines and the need to perceive society as an interconnecting totality, see R. H. Tawney, 'Social History and Literature', in Rita Hinden, (ed.), *The Radical Tradition*, (1964), pp. 183-4. Watson in *Politics and Literature* p.9 acknowledges the risks of any enterprise which defies conventional boundaries.

## Earl G. Ingersoll, "Gender and Language in *Sons and Lovers*"

*Sons and Lovers* occupies an ambivalent position in the canon of D.H. Lawrence. Scholars rank it below his masterpieces—*The Rainbow* and *Women in Love*—and yet it has been particularly attractive to the "common reader." It has the clearly autobiographical elements we expect in a writer's first novel, even though it is Lawrence's third. In addition, it pays its respects to the realist tradition of such essentially English novelists as George Eliot and Thomas Hardy. *Sons and Lovers* has also appealed to some because it was Lawrence's last novel before the controversies surrounding *The Rainbow* in his lifetime and those surrounding a novel like *The Plumed Serpent* in ours.

More than anything else he wrote, *Sons and Lovers* has opened Lawrence's work to traditional psychoanalytic readings. When the novel appeared in 1913, the English psychoanalyst Barbara Low, for example, urged her friends to read it as an expression of Freud's Oedipus theory. Lawrence had written the penultimate version of the novel before he met Frieda and learned from her what she knew of "Freud," as it was filtered through his disciple Otto Gross, her lover of just four years before. Frederick J. Hoffman, who interviewed Frieda in 1942, argues that Lawrence was almost immediately resistant to Frieda's Freudian reading of his text; however, he probably focused more fully on the relationship between Paul and his mother in the final revision. Paul Morel's sexual dysfunction was based on Lawrence's, even though the narrator attempts to find similarities in a "good many of the nicest men he knew" (279).

Traditional psychoanalytic readings of *Sons and Lovers*, initiated by Lawrence's associates like Barbara Low and by Frieda herself, were given a boost by John Middleton Murry in his biography of Lawrence, subtitled *Son of Woman*. "Freudian" readings of Lawrence and *Sons* have persisted in our own time in the work of Mark Spilka, Daniel Weiss (*Oedipus in Nottingham*), and as recently as James Cowan's *D.H. Lawrence and the Trembling Balance* (1990). Cowan speaks for a traditional "psychoanalytic" approach in arguing:

> If critical reading may be seen as analogous to the analytic situation, then the text projected by the author corresponds to the patient's projective identification. The critical reader is then in the position of the analyst, who receives, internally processes, and responds to the communication, reflecting understanding and appropriate interpretation of what has been communicated. (10)

This kind of simplistic reduction of the literary text to the unmediated ramblings of a patient on the analyst's couch can only end by privileging the critic over the artist and by perpetuating the misguided notion of an encoded text whose "hidden meanings" can be deciphered only by the sleuthing critic for the astonished reader's edification.

To replace such "Freudian" readings, I would propose a "new psychoanalytic criticism." Unlike earlier varieties, this psychoanalytic criticism of literature, as practiced by theorists like Shoshana Felman and Peter Brooks, is not intent upon the "psychoanalatic study of authors, readers, or fictional characters" (Brooks, xiv). This "narratology" attempts to apply psychoanalytic insights to narrative and intersubjectivity, or the interchange between "subjects"—the traditional term "individuals" having been dismissed for its suggestion of autonomous, integrated "selves." Such practice owes an immense debt to Freud's most astute reader—Jacques Lacan.

Like Freud's, the psychology associated with Lacan's writings is grounded in a notion of the unconscious. For Lacan, the unconscious was not Freud's romantically dark and chaotic underworld of irrational drives or instincts but a fabric or text woven from the infant's reception of auditory and visual images, virtually from birth. The unconscious is a structure of words (even before those words are "understood") as well as auditory and visual images that the infant receives through the ear and eye, but especially the eye. Because it is born "premature," the infant is absolutely dependent upon its female care-giver and spends its first six months restricted to hearing and gazing at what is closest to it. In this stage, the maternal body and objects, as well as the objects of hearing and gazing, become confused: as the French psychoanalyst Michelle Montrelay says, "hearing is very close to the eye, which is seen by the child as an eye-ear, an open hole" (qtd. by Ragland-Sullivan, 20). In this way, the unconscious becomes associated with all those early images and sensory experiences taken in by the eye and ear. This visual-verbal construct forms the abstract signifiers, or what Lacan calls the "letters" of the body, the effects of outside phenomena through touch, the gaze, sounds, and images. The body is thus eroticized, as these external signifiers become associated with the "letters" of the body, or the erotogenic zones, which Freud termed "mouth, anus, phallus, genitals." As "letters" or erotogenic zones of the (m)Other, voice and eye become erotic organs, or part objects of Desire.

Lacan's focus upon infancy led to his theory of the "mirror stage." Between the ages six and eighteen months, Lacan hypothesizes a literal encounter with the mirror in which the infant discovers difference in the the reverse mirror image. That image is the first expression of an "other" as totalized unity, distinct from the subject's perception of itself as fragmented and dispersed. In contrast to the subject's humbling movements, the mirror image is static, symmetrical, statue-like, as an ideal unity. The subject's jubilation in discovering an ideal outside itself is the beginning of alienation, a movement away from a natural fusion with the (m)other, the first step toward dependence upon culture. Lacan also understood the mirror as metaphor, as the subject's identification with the (m)other before eighteen months, a kind of Edenic fusion with the other before the fall into language and individuation. This stage of unity and harmony is, however, fraught with anxiety since the other cannot be possessed. Indeed, when the eighteen-month-old discovers that its parents do not uniformly respond to its demands, it is ready to move from the Imaginary to the Symbolic.

At eighteen months, the subject also has achieved some mastery of motor coordination, and its psychic energies can now be directed toward mastery of this "foreign language" that has had its impact upon the subject since birth. The father intrudes upon the mother-child dyad as a representation of the *"Nom-du-Pere,"* or the Name-of-the-Father, Lacan punning on the French homonyms "nom" and "non," or "name" and "no." For Lacan, the Oedipal impulse is not the infant's desire to possess the mother sexually, but the impulse to preserve symbiotic unity with the (m)other even though that unity has been paid for with the repression of difference. At the very time, then, that the infant is learning to represent things as words, the Name-of-the-Father (represented by the literal father or some other adult male) is intervening with its "no" to the desire for unity, a prohibition commensurate with the subject's recognition of its own psychic boundaries. In this way, the subject's development from nature to culture, from symbiotic unity to individuation, is inevitably implicated in language and the threat of castration. For Lacan, castration is clearly not a physical emasculation but the metaphorical representation of the trauma of loss, the separation from the mother, the acknowledgment of difference and individuation, experienced by the female child as well as the male. From this point the Phallus is forever a metaphor, a "phallic signifier" in the Symbolic register, rather than the penis, clitoris, or genitalia as a whole.

Lacan also draws on the modern linguistic notion of language as both *langue*, or "linguistic and informational meaning," from the conscious, and *parole*, or "truth value meaning," from the unconscious. The former is associated with the Law and the Name-of-the-Father, with culture and reason, with metaphor and the Symbolic; the latter, with Desire and the mother, with nature, with metonymy and the Imaginary. Thus, the conscious and unconscious cannot be separated; both are involved in an inevitable interchange. The conscious, as it is implicated in language, represents the repressed text of the unconscious. Since the unconscious is structured like a language, and metaphor is the means by which a signifier replaces another signifier repressed beneath the bar separating off the unconscious, metaphor both indicates that repression and the possibility for the language of the unconscious to "cross the bar," surfacing veiled within the conscious.

The Oedipal stage, then, for Lacan is the male or female infant, submitting its sexuality to the Name-of-the-Father as the Symbolic order requires accession to language and individuation. Rather being innate, gender is the result of an alignment with sameness—the mother, primary Desire, the female—or with difference—the law of the Name-of-the-Father, the male. A subject assumes maleness or femaleness by identifying or not identifying with the phallic signifier. The father stands for the Symbolic order mediating between the Imaginary, associated with the mother, and the Real. The biological father is the presence signifying the effects of the Real, while the mother is the first real Other, a signifier of primordial unconscious.

Ellie Ragland-Sullivan proceeds from her reading of Lacan to speculate on the effects of contemporary research on the shaping of gender from the completion of the mirror stage to the age of five. As we now know, concrete and verbal functions are the province of the left hemisphere of the brain, while abstract and spatial functions are the province of the right. The "lateralizing," or specializing, of these left-brain, right-brain functions is not completed, however, until the subject is five, the very age at which "grammar is acquired and a primary sexual identity fixed" (291). In this way, identification with the natural, with the female principle, structures the left brain as concrete and verbal, while identification with the male principle and a movement away from loss, structures the right brain as the result of the association with the abstract phallic signifier. Thus, during these years, gender is coming into being physiologically as the hemispheres of the brain are being specialized as more "female," i.e., concrete and verbal, or "male," i.e., abstract and spatial. Can this hypothesis help to explain, Ragland-Sullivan speculates, the concrete and verbal tendencies of men who frequently identify themselves with their mothers rather than their lower-class (and often absent) fathers?

It is Ellie Ragland-Sullivan's provocative question about gender orientations of lower-class sons who identify themselves with their mothers that opens the text of *Sons and Lovers*. Paul Morel becomes the focal consciousness of the narrative only belatedly, after an extensive description of his parents' courtship and marriage. Dominant in the descriptions of the courting parents are the "erotic organs" of the voice and eye. It is through Gertrude's eyes that Walter is introduced with his "wavy black hair," "vigorous black beard," his "ruddy" cheeks, and "red, moist mouth," the latter noticeable because "he laughed so often and so heartily" (17). Through repetition, the narrative stresses how she "watched him, fascinated." Other than perhaps "her blue eyes . . . very straight, honest and searching," she is not described as she appeared in his eyes. He is "melted away before her," not because of her physical appearance but because she speaks "with a southern pronunciation and a purity of English which thrilled him to hear." From the beginning, it is her voice which "fascinates" him, while it is the "dusky, golden softness of this man's sensuous flame of life" which fascinates her eyes. Although he initiates their relationship by inviting her to dance, it is she who pursues him visually, her eyes ensnared by his beauty—and inversion of the male gaze—while he is fascinated by her voice and the power of language. Years later, when Paul as a young man experiences "strife in love," the narrator allows him to view his father's half-naked body through his mother's still-passionate gaze and to complain to Miriam that she lacks Mrs. Morel's response of fascinated looking. Thus, even before Paul is born, we are introduced to his parents as inversions of conventional gender associations—she is the fascinating speaker, and he, the sensuous object of her fascinated gaze.

The infancies of the Morel children are notably disparate. William's infancy is memorable for the episode of his father's shearing the golden locks which have ensnared his mother's loving gaze. One can only wonder at the effect on William of this intrusive, prohibiting father holding those shears like the sword of the archangel Michael casting him out from the Eden of harmony with the mother's body, especially in conjunction with the mother's rare sobbing as she buries her face in his shorn hair. The scene seems almost a parody of popularized Freudian "castration." At the same time, it foregrounds the particularly Lacanian notion of castration, since William at a year old cannot conceivably wish to remove his father as a rival in order to appropriate his mother sexually. On the other hand, we can conceive of a pre-conscious but sentient subject who experiences this threat to the *jouissance,* the sheer physical ecstasy of connection with the mother's body. Much as she will eventually claim to have been silly, admitting that William's hair would have needed cutting anyway, she remembers the event for the rest of her life, "as one in which she suffered the most intensely." The birth of Annie, the next Morel child, is not even "announced": she is first referred to in this pre-Paul retrospective when William is old enough to swim naked in the "dipping hole" and Annie to play under the hedge. It is as though Annie materializes like the adult Athena from the forehead of Zeus. Paul's infancy, on the other hand, is "special"—even pre-natally.

The "primal scene" of Paul's being is the famous moonlight-and-lilies episode, an aftermath of his parents' row when the drunken Walter shuts Gertrude out in the garden. Appropriately, the reader learns of her pregnancy only after she has been ejected from her husband's house. Paul "boiled within her." Granted this "boiling" takes place in the context of the "shock to her inflamed soul," "seared with passion" and subjected to the cold shower of "great white light." Still, the narrative allows this subject-to-be-Paul the experience of a world beyond the womb, as that phenomenal world has an impact on the mother's body—a body not yet different from its own. The mother "lost herself awhile. She did not know what she thought. Except for a slight feeling of sickness, and her consciousness in the child, her self melted out like scent into the shiny, pale air." Eventually, "the child, too, melted in her in the mixing-pot of moonlight, and she rested with the hills and lilies and houses, all swum together in a kind of swoon" (34). In this way, the narrative offers an attempt to recover the experience of *jouissance,* resulting from a memory of limitless joy in the paradise lost of the subject's harmony with the body of the mother. Nowhere in literature does one find such a transposition of that *jouissance* from infancy back to its pre-natal antecedent. In that "swoon" from which "she came to herself" again, Gertrude remembers her own unnamed mother whom she loved "best of all," the "gentle, humorous, kindly-soul mother" toward whom Gertrude's father was "overbearing."

With Paul, Mrs. Morel has recuperated the joyful connection with her own mother, as that loss is replicated in her joy of intense connectedness with him. In the key scene of her holding Paul up to the sun, his heavenly father, Gertrude "felt as if the navel string that had connected its frail little body with hers bad not been broken. A wave of hot love went over her to the infant. She held it close to her face and breast" (51). What follows seems straight from Lacan: "Its clear, knowing eyes gave her pain and fear. Did it know all about her? When it lay under her heart, had it been listening then? Was there a reproach in the look?" (51). Yes, we are encouraged to answer these rhetorical questions: the pre-natal Paul did, indeed, *listen* under her heart, and after birth as well, to the wash of auditory images from without. But even more appropriately, Mrs. Morel's consciousness marks the presence of the gaze of her infant's "knowing eyes." The text foregrounds in the clearest manner the centrality of the Lacanian gaze in the mother-infant relationship: "Its deep blue eyes, always looking up at her unblinking, seemed to draw her innermost thoughts out of her" (50-51). That gaze has already been able to read her as co-extensive with the infant subject's being, to know a *jouissance* that it will ultimately lose and seek futilely to recuperate in all later relationships. It is at this point that she thrusts him up toward the sun, as if it were her infant's true progenitor, mimicking some primitive ritual in which the newborn's father introduces it to the cosmos. *She* names the subject, as a forestalling of the later Oedipal scene in which the Name-of-the-Father will initiate the subject into individuation and subjectivity with the prohibitory *Nom/non* of movement into the Symbolic register of language.

This scene ends with a counterpart to the pre-natal moon-light-and-lilies scene. The dispute between the Morels ends in Walter's flinging a drawer at Gertrude and wounding her brow. The blood drips first into Paul's shawl, and then into his "fragile, glistening hair." Walter watches "fascinated" while "his manhood broke" (55). The focus on his "fascinated" gaze at the blood dripping into Paul's hair re-inscribes the earlier scene of William's hair-clipping. Once again, well before the Lacanian 'castration' scene in which the subject is forced to acknowledge the Name/No-of-the-Father and thereby be initiated into the Symbolic register of language and culture, Walter has proved to be ineffectual in fulfilling that function.

The engendering of language foregrounds the parents' conflict. It is through verbal impotence rather than drunken violence that the father breaks his manhood. Gertrude might have felt sorry for him if he had apologized. She expects him to fulfill his responsibility as the Law of the Name-of-the-Father, to be a master of language, but he cannot: "He had hurt himself most. And he was the more damaged, because he would never say a word to her, or express his sorrow" (55). His gestures, action, even his physical bearing may "express his sorrow," but she insists upon representation of meaning in language, in the signifiers associated with her own father, and the Name-of-the-Father. "And so he broke himself" (56). Appropriately, for our concern with gender and language, Paul will represent his own accession to masculinity in the "baptism of fire in passion" in the dialect of his father.

At this point, however, the mother controls the language in the household. When Morel comes down from the bedroom to Sunday tea, he eats in a silence that shuts him out from his family. Literally and figuratively, the mother and children speak another language. As the dialogue in the text indicates, Morel speaks the broad Midlands dialect, while the children are learning their mother's tongue, the Queen's English. Several days later, when Morel compounds his alienation by getting caught "stealing" from his wife's purse and threatens to abandon the family, William uses the most "proper English" to ask, "What shall we do?" When Morel returns, he tells his wife: "You may thank your stars I've come back tonight," and as the narrator indicates he was "trying to be impressive" (60). In this way, Gertrude confirms her mastery through the control of language, coercing Morel into adopting her tongue to be "impressive." Paul may be an infant, but these auditory images, and perhaps the sensations and feelings associated with them, have begun to inscribe themselves in the text of his unconscious.

Central to that text is the bilingual context of the Morel home. From infancy Paul has "heard" the *language* of his father's dialect and *parole* of his mother even before he could consciously distinguish what the signifiers meant. He has heard William and Annie using standard English. Because Lawrence is aware that his audience is used to reading texts in the dominant dialect, the text foregrounds Walter's language, indeed to such an extent that when he struggles to be "impressive" verbally we hear the difference. We are insistently reminded of the children's approximation of standard English until they launch out into their father's world outside the home. A case in point is Gertrude's defense of William against the mother of a schoolmate with whom he has been scuffling. In contrast to Mrs. Anthony's dialect, reminiscent of Walter's, Mrs. Morel's tongue allows her to enjoy mastery over those who are "beneath" her. The struggle for power in the family, as in Lawrence's culture, represents itself in part as difference in dialects:

> "What" cried Mrs. Morel, panting with rage. "You shall not touch him for *her* telling, you shall notl"
> "Shonna I?" shouted Morel. "Shonna I?". . .
> "Only dare!" she said in a loud, ringing voice. "Only dare, milord, to lay a finger on that child! You'll regret it for ever." (68)

Tangential as this concern with the young life of William may seem, it is not, since he is Paul's forerunner and these battles are being pre-fought for the younger son.

Unlike William who can negotiate the linguistic realms of both parents, Paul functions with great difficulty in the world of his father. Perhaps the best example of that difficulty is the scene of anguish and humiliation when Paul collects his father's "pay" and is gently teased by the men who fault his grasp of arithmetic. When Paul goes home "glowering" to tell his mother that he will never go again, he accuses the men of being "hateful, and common," focusing upon their *language*: "Mr. Braithwaite drops his 'h's, and Mr. Winterbottom says, 'You was'" (97). In this way, Paul acknowledges the effects of inversions of Lacan's notions of the mother and the Name-of-the-Father. "Proper English" is associated consistently with the mother's tongue, as *she* learned her father's. It is his mother who speaks with the authority of patriarchy, not his father. In the hierarchy of dialects, the Queen's English is privileged. Walter's dialect, then, is "feminized" by its position of powerlessness: it is speech marginalized by the "proper" dialect spoken by the middle and upper classes, a written language.

The scene is repeated on Paul's first day of work when he must confront new figures of male authority alone this time, without the comfort of even his mother's submissive presence. In addition to Jordan, he must deal with Pappleworth, the chief of the Spiral department, who ridicules him for his "execrable handwriting." Like the men in the cashier's office where he collects his father's earnings, Jordan and Pappleworth lament the deficiencies of modern education: "lads learn nothing nowadays, but how to recite poetry and play the fiddle" (132). Pappleworth embarrasses Paul by asking him yet another time, "Let's see, *what's* your name?" The narrator adds: "It's curious that children suffer so much at having to pronounce their own names." A child like Paul suffers because in supplying his name to these embodiments of the Name-of-the-Father he acknowledges their hegemony over the Symbolic. His only relief from that embarrassment once again is gloating to remind himself that Jordan is lacking as a gentlemen: "he spoke bad English" (132).

These issues of gender and language come together in the memorable scene in Clifton Grove. As has been so frequently noted, Paul lapses for the first time into his father's dialect, perhaps as an acknowledgment of the Law of the Name-of-the-Father. He begins with merely a shade of his father's language—"Why dost look so heavy?"—but moves to "'Yea, tha does! Dunna thee worrit,' he implored *caressing*" (356; emphasis added). Tellingly, he later says nothing until they have completed their fifteen-minute climb to top of the riverbank, returning to his mother's tongue: "Now we're back at the ordinary level" (356).

When Paul's "baptism of fire in passion" comes in the scene of the peewits, the narrative breaks out of its conventional realism and offers a foretaste of Lawrence's technique in *The Rainbow*. The narrator struggles to move beneath the surface of consciousness into a realm of desire suggestive of the garden scene in which the unborn Paul "boils" in Gertrude's womb. Indeed, one senses that this realm outside consciousness parallels the lost *jouissance* of infant and mother: "The naked hunger and inevitability of his loving her [Clara], something strong and blind and ruthless in its primitiveness, made the hour terrible to her"(397). "When he came to," Paul's consciousness is allowed the language to translate this baptism into the metaphors of immersion in the life force, to recognize "in their meeting the first of the manifold grass stems, the cry of the peewit, the wheel of the stars" (398).

Admittedly, the language here is the narrator's, not Paul's; its function, however, is to provide equivalents for the empowerment of metaphoricity, the sense of Paul's coming to consciousness as an acknowledgment of the Law of the Name-of-the-Father. Paul must recognize both the irrevocable loss of *jouissance*—the joyful, preconscious harmony with the mother's body—and the inevitable movement into the symbolic register of language. The passage is crucial because its central metaphors are repeated in the novel's ambivalent ending:

To know their own nothingness, to know the tremendous living flood which carried them always, gave them rest within themselves. If so great a magnificent power could overwhelm them, identify them altogether with itself, so that they knew they were only grains in the tremendous heave that lifted every grass-blade its little height, and every tree, and living thing, then why fret about themselves. . . . (398)

Thus, it is only through metaphor that Paul can be empowered.

Riding the train back to town after having abandoned his relationships with first Clara and then Miriam, Paul is overwhelmed by the immense darkness: "In the country all was dead still. Little stars shone high up; little stars spread far away in the floodwaters. . . . the vastness and terror of the immense night" (464). He feels like a "tiny upright speck of flesh, less than an ear of wheat lost in the field," a "spark" being pressed into extinction. The body of the mother, now forever relinquished, equates here with the ultimate castration, the total alienation of the subject for the first time. At the same time, however, the narrative is foregrounding the metaphors of the life force, metaphors associated with Walter Morel—the "flame of life"—and the Paul who came through the baptism of fire in passion—the kernel of wheat and the flood.

These metaphors are central to Paul's entry into the symbolic register, into language and culture. Through these metaphors, the narrative offers us Paul's final accession to the realm of the Name-of-the-Father, the movement from darkness into "the faintly humming, glowing town." Paul moves finally from the text of the unconscious associated with the mother to the empowerment of metaphor associated with the Name-of-the-Father.

## Bibliography

Brooks, Peter. *Reading for the Plot: Design and Intention in Narrative.* New York: Knopf, 1984.

Cowan, James. *D.H. Lawrence and the Trembling Balance.* University Park and London: Pennsylvania State University Press, 1990.

Felman, Shoshana ed. *Literature and Psychoanalysis: The Question of Reading: Otherwise.* Baltimore and London: Johns Hopkins University Press, 1982.

Hoffman, Frederick J. *Freudianism and the Literary Mind.* Baton Rouge: Louisiana State University Press, 1957.

Lacan, Jacques. *Écrits: A Selection.* Trans. Alan Sheridan. New York: Norton, 1977.

Lawrence, D. H. *Sons and Lovers.* Eds. Helen Baron and Carol Baron. Cambridge: Cambridge University Press, 1992.

Murry, John Middleton. *D.H. Lawrence: Son of Woman.* London: Jonathan Cape, 1954.

Ragland-Sullivan, Ellie. *Jacques Lacan and the Philosophy of Psychoanalysis.* Urbana and Chicago: University of Illinois Press, 1986.

Spilka, Mark. *The Love Ethic of D.H. Lawrence.* Bloomington: Indiana University Press, 1986.

Weiss, Daniel A. *Oedipus in Nottingham: D.H. Lawrence.* Seattle: University of Washington Press, 1962.

*Midwest Quarterly : A Journal of Contemporary Thought,* 37:4, 1996.

# III

# THE RAINBOW

**Seymour Lainoff, "*The Rainbow*: The Shaping of Modern Man"**

---

D.H. Lawrence's *The Rainbow* tells of three generations of Brangwens— Tom
and Lydia, Anna and Will, Ursula and Anton Skrebensky—and also of their
ancestors, whose unchanging way of life is described in the first five pages of the
novel. Tom and Lydia think and live somewhat the same as did Tom's ancestors,
but Anna and Will think and live differently; and Ursula and Anton still more so.
*The Rainbow* intends in part to reveal how the modern outlook has evolved, that
mind-set belonging to the generation of Ursula and Anton. The evolution is one
of decline; a deadening of man's response to nature, a weakened relationship
between men and women, a paralyzing of action.

Lawrence's prose is itself a comment upon this evolution. At the beginning of
the novel, it is expository, with little dialogue; his characters do not possess, or
are not concerned with, the articulation or discrimination needed for dialogue.
The point of view (as Lubbock uses the phrase) is the author's, viewing his
characters with a bard-like reverence and also remoteness; the characters have a
non-conscious communion with the world around them. Since the human
situation approximates the ideal, the characters behave truly and objectively. The
point of view of no one character, no matter how sensitive or intelligent, is as
important as the general mold of things, as the behavior of the inarticulate but
completely integrated characters. They have achieved what the Rainbow, the
central symbol of the book, stands for—the harmony of vertical and horizontal
impulses for which men must always strive.

In contrast, the events of the last section are described largely as they are seen
by Ursula. This section consists mostly of Ursula's experience as a school teacher
at Cossethay. The school-room at Cossethay serves as a specimen of modern

industrial society, possessing its facelessness, its insentience, its brutality. Men have grown so mechanical or ineffectual that the human scene can be made significant for fiction only if perceived by a growing intelligence. If the author spoke in his own right, he could do little but preach. This last section is rendered not only by Ursula's strongly sensitive and individual point of view, but also by a close and particularized description of setting, by a sharp etching of several characters in the tradition of realistic fiction. The scene has shifted from the Eden of yeoman England to the grimy colliery and the grimy schoolroom; the style must shift from Parnassus to the streets of social criticism.

To examine further the spiritual life of the Brangwen ancestors, we might look at the famous fifth paragraph of the book, in which their unchanging life is described:

> So the Brangwens came and went without fear of necessity, working hard because of the life that was in them, not for want of the money. Neither were they thriftless. They were aware of the last half-penny, and instinct made them not waste the peeling of their apple, for it would help to feed the cattle. But heaven and earth was teeming around them, and how should this cease? They felt the rush of the sap in spring, they knew the wave which cannot halt, but every year throws forward the seed to begetting, and, falling back, leaves the young-born on earth. They knew the intercourse between heaven and earth, sunshine drawn into the breast and bowels, the rain sucked up in the day time, nakedness that comes under the wind in autumn, showing the birds' nests no longer worth hiding. Their life and inter-relationships were such; feeling the pulse and body of the soil, that opened to their furrow for the grain, and became smooth and supple after their plowing, and hung to their feet with a weight that pulled like desire, lying hard and unresponsive when the crops were to be shorn away. The young corn waved and was silken and the lustre slid along the limbs of the men who saw it. They took the udders of the cows, the cows yielded milk and pulse against the hands of the men, the pulse of the blood of the teats of the cows beat into the pulse of the hands of the men. They mounted their horses, and held life between the grip of their knees, they harnessed their horses at the wagon, and, with hand on the bridle-rings, drew the heaving of the horses after their will.

The Biblical diction reminds us that here described is an Eden, timeless, perfect, before the Fall. The personifications reveal the vivacity of this Eden, and the sexual images its internal physical intimacy, its reciprocity of influence and beneficence among men, beasts, and plants. The word Lawrence stresses is "life"; life is complete sympathy between man and nature. Men live without the conscious assertion of will, for will and impulse are united in seemingly instinctive gesture.

These Brangwens live without ritual, without "mysteries," for when man's sympathy with nature is complete, the need for ritual does not exist. Ritual arises only after the Flood. In the Foreword to *Fantasia of the Unconscious*, translating the suggested Biblical imagery of the first section of *The Rainbow* into scientific terms Lawrence identifies the Flood as the Glacial Period. After the Glacial Period, man lost his pristine knowledge of nature, and only fragments of that knowledge survived. These remnants took the shape of myths or symbols. The Foreword continues:

Then came the melting of the glaciers, and the world flood. The refugees from the drowned continents fled to the high places of America, Europe, Asia, and the Pacific Isles. . . . some, like Druids or Etruscans or Chaldeans or Amerindians or Chinese, refused to forget, but taught the old wisdom, only in its half-forgotten, symbolic forms. More or less forgotten as knowledge; remembered as ritual, gesture, and myth-story.

And so, the intense potency of symbols is part at least memory. And so it is that all the great symbols and myths which dominated the world when our history first begins, are very much the same in every country and every people, the great myths all relate to one another.

The symbol implies perfect knowledge. Accordingly, Lawrence in this first section does not employ the symbol, but a device more suitable to the way his characters apprehend the world—a device pecularily his and the source of much of this section's strength. An illustration follows:

He had her in his arms, and, obliterated, was kissing her. And it was sheer, blenched agony to him, to break away from himself. She was there so small and light and accepting in his arms, like a child, and yet with such an insinuation of embrace, that he could not bear it, he could not stand.

He turned and looked for a chair, and keeping her still in his arms, sat down with her close to him, to his breast. Then, for a few seconds, he went utterly to sleep, asleep and sealed in the darkest sleep, utter extreme oblivion.

From which he came to gradually, always holding her warm and close upon him, and she as utterly silent as he, involved in the same oblivion, the fecund darkness.

He returned gradually, but newly created. . . . And she sat utterly still with him, as if in the same.

This technique fuses the physical, mental, and sensory into one. To understand the passage, one must perhaps examine its context: the history of the relationship between Tom and Lydia. Tom Brangwen has inherited the Brangwen capacity to establish the Edenic *rapport* with nature, to establish "blood-intimacy." But because the Brangwen women ate of the Apple of Knowledge, Tom is dissatisifed with the farm, and veers indecisively to and from the farm, in an effort to escape his Brangwen destiny. The Brangwen women prefer men like the Vicar——"dark, dry, and small," and Tom's final security and happiness on Marsh Farm are established only when he decides to marry an outsider, the Polish Lydia Lensky. Lydia's chief trait is her "remoteness," her withdrawal from "life" or "being," after her first husband in his intellectual passion and reforming zeal had incurred the death of two children and a wrecked marriage. Tom is attracted to Lydia's remoteness, for he feels her need to re-establish a fundamental association with a man. Her need throws Tom back upon his own origins, where he most deeply wishes to return; Lydia, in turn, feels Tom's mastery in his Marsh Farm surroundings, is attracted to his closeness to "life."

The selection above describes a new start for Tom and Lydia. Lydia responds to this first embrace with the freshness of a child, with "candid, newly-opened" eyes. Tom falls asleep, entering into an oblivion to his former restlessness, and awakens "newly created." Now, by the tenets of most fiction, this sleep a few seconds long is most unusual. The death-and-rebirth pattern is physically embodied in this sleep, part of an embrace itself of not too long a duration. The experience the passage describes is not physical, mental, nor spiritual alone, but all three.

Most events of the first section are rendered this way, perhaps most skillfully in the description of Anna and Will among the sheaves. Lawrence's technique attests to the unified response his characters make to the world, a response which makes ritual and the imperfect knowledge of the symbol unnecessary.

It becomes even more apparent, upon reading the second section of *The Rainbow* , that the novel is not only a social history of England, but Lawrence's parable of the history of the human race. Will and Anna possess only fragments of the complete knowledge, the sympathy with nature, held by their forbears, even by Tom and Lydia. Their generation institutionalizes "blood-intimacy" in the forms of religion, that creates ritual and dance from which sophisticated arts later emerge, that expresses itself in symbols. Its *rapport* with nature is partial. The unified personality begins to disintegrate; the single vision is lost: one man becomes a rationalist; the second, an esthete; the third, a religious mystic. One part of personality becomes a dominant and threatens to submerge the other parts; as a result, self-conflict and conflict between persons arise. At the same time, articulation increases, for articulation is the product of human differences and is sharpened through controversy just as the tusk of a boar is sharpened through combat.

The second section is full of references to the Church and to church architecture, and its pivotal chapter is called "The Cathedral." The pointed arch, more vertical than horizontal, has superseded the rounded arch of the rainbow. To illustrate, we have the following passage, in which Anna listens to Will's discourse on church architecture:

> The influence of Ruskin had stimulated him to a pleasure in the medieval forms. His talk was fragmentary, he was only half articulate. But listening to him, as he spoke of church after church, of nave and chancel and transept . . . speaking always with close passion of particular things, particular places, there gathered in her heart a pregnant hush of churches, a mystery, a ponderous significance of bowed stone, a dim-coloured light through which something took place obscurely passing into darkness.

In contrast to the clarity of "blood-intimacy" is the opaqueness, the occultness, of religious institutions. Knowledge through intuition has become an appreciation of "mystery." Will's power of articulation is not yet fully developed. Later, the exchanges of dialogue between Anna and Will, growing in number, rarely reveal an understanding between them; rather, they signify a failure to arrive at common terms.

Will is a person half-realized. He has replaced the original Brangwen relationship with life with a vague and specialized mysticism. His physical appearance suggests a hidden nature, a lurking, misguided vitality: "He had . . . a very curious head. . . . It reminded her she knew not of what: of some animal, some mysterious animal that lived in the darkness under the leaves and never came out, but which lived vividly, swift and intense." Anna is alternately attracted and repelled by Will's religion. Although he loves church services, she is offended by the verbalizing of religious feeling. She feels the incompleteness of Will's religious response: his is a Sunday worship, and has no relation to his work the other days of the week. In her attempt to combat Will's incompleteness, she resorts to the destructive strategies of modern rationalism.

> "And I think the Lamb in Church," she said, "is the biggest joke in the parish—"
> She burst into a "Pouf" of ridiculing laughter.
> "It might be, to those that see nothing in it," he said. "You know it's a symbol of Christ, of his innocence and sacrifice.
> "Whatever it means, it's a lamb," she said.

Will is the maker of symbols, also the artist working on the woodcarvings of Adam and Eve: Anna, too, has her rituals, for example, the rite in which she celebrates the forthcoming birth of her child, thereby separating herself from Will.

The second section poses a mixture of two styles, the bardic and the realistic. But the bardic style is put to the employment of the private ecstasies of Will and Anna: neither is sympathetic to the ecstasy of the other, and a process of attrition ensues, of which the weapon is the ironic comment, the lashing tongue. The Cathedral must have its gargoyle.

The third and longest section, concerned with Ursula Brangwen, traces her journey to self-discovery. We follow the progress of her thinking and feeling closely and sympathetically. From the beginning Ursula insists on her own individuality. She contrasts the hurly-burly of her own home to the "hushed, paradisal" peace of her grandmother's, Lydia's. She revolts against her parents, against her mother's babies and muddled domesticity, against her father's now mechanical and non-vital religiosity. She asserts the value of courage over brains, rejects the authority of her schoolmistresses, thereby winning the enmity of her teachers and fellow pupils. "This strange sense of cruelty and ugliness always imminent . . . this feeling of the grudging power of the mob lying in wait for her, who was the exception, formed one of the deepest influences of her life." But in rejecting her parents she has also rejected their "vision world." As Ursula moves through events without these visions, Lawrence describes her experience in a style more realistic than heretofore, with small reliance on symbol or on the special technique of his first section. The style is graphic, the characterization more conventional. Lawrence appropriates traditional approaches excellently; the schoolroom sequence is executed with great vividness and speed.

Without even the "vision world" of her parents, Ursula is thrown upon her own resources and finds them empty: "So she wrestled through her dark days of confusion, soulless, uncreated, unformed." She has lost all sight of the original Brangwen *rapport*. At church one morning she listens to the reading from the Book of Genesis in boredom: "Multipying and replenishing the earth bored her. Altogether it seemed merely a vulgar and stock-raising sort of business."

What characterizes the modern most in *The Rainbow* is vacancy of spirit and barrenness of instinct. Ursula is attracted to Anton, the soldier, and Winifred, the woman athlete, because of their ostensible self-sufficiency, but she does not suspect until later that theirs is the sufficiency of loose comets flying free of any orbit. Her disillusionment with these two, together with her trial in the schoolroom at Cossethay, gives her some measure of self-knowledge and of an awareness of what has been generally lost:

> That which she was, positively, was dark and unrevealed, it could not come forth. It was like a seed buried in dry ash. This world in which she lived was like a circle lighted by a lamp. This lighted area, lit up by man's completest consciousness, she thought was all the world; that here wall was disclosed for ever. Yet all the time, within the darkness she had been aware of points of light, like the eyes of wild beasts, gleaming, penetrating, vanishing.

*Modern Fiction Studies*, 1 May 1955

## Edward Engelberg, "Escape from the Circles of Experience: D.H. Lawrence's *The Rainbow* as a Modern *Bildungsroman*"

Late in his life, in 1933, Yeats read *Sons and Lovers, The Rainbow,* and *Women in Love* "with excitement," and found the love story of *Lady Chatterley's Lover* "noble." In Lawrence he found an ally "directed against modern abstraction;" and he considered that, with Joyce, Lawrence had "almost restored to us the Eastern simplicity."[1] A hatred of Abstraction; a fearless plunge into the mire of human existence; an anti-intellectual stance (which was almost at times a pose); and a mythopoeic conception of art and life: these Yeats and Lawrence shared, whatever their differences—which were considerable. And what they shared accounts in part for their similar response to Goethe's *Wilhelm Meister* and that hero's search for experience: it was, they felt, guided too dominantly by intellectual choices. In 1928 Lawrence wrote to Aldous Huxley that he thought "*Wilhelm Meister . . .* amazing as a book of peculiar immorality, the perversity of intellectualised sex, and the utter incapacity for any development of contact with any other human being, which is peculiarly bourgeois and Goethian."[2] Yeats remarked that Goethe, a man "in whom objectivity and subjectivity were intermixed," could "but seek . . . [Unity of Being] as Wilhelm Meister seeks it intellectually, critically, and through a multitude of deliberately chosen experiences." He insisted that "true Unity of Being . . . is found emotionally, instinctively, by the rejection of all experience not of the right quality, and by the limitation of its quantity."[3] But for Yeats, the poet, it was less problematic than for Lawrence, the novelist, to crusade against Abstraction and Intellection: the poem had its gnomic power to snap meaning at you in an instant of time; the novel had somehow to have people and a story—and a world in which both could occur.

The problem for Lawrence, as for most of the novelists of the nineteenth century, was the meaning of experience. For Goethe, who established the prototype of the *Bildungsroman,* the question was simpler. Wilhelm Meister must endure two trials of experience: the first would consist of *Lehrjahre* (apprenticeship), the tilt with experience, high and low, elevating and degrading; the second would then be a reaping of the rewards, for the *Wanderjahre* are the years when the *Lehrjahre* are tested in the large world, and at the end of which the hero emerges as a man of some wisdom who has found his place on the horizontal plane of worldly existence. Such a path through life made it necessary for the hero to adapt his inner self, in some degree, to the outer reality he faced, for the ultimate goal was selfhood within society: to attain it certainly involved the hero in intellectual discriminations and abstract values—though it was also an act of free will. The inability to engage the world on these terms led, in Goethe's conception, to the subjective weakness of a Werther who, unable to endure experience *except* emotionally, can only shoot himself. "It is justly said," Goethe told Eckermann, "that the communal cultivation of all human powers is desirable and excellent. But the individual is not born for this; everyone must form himself as a particular being—seeking, however, to attain that general idea of which all mankind are constituents."[4] Although Lawrence would not have quarreled with the notion of man forming his "particular being," he would hardly have gone so far as to require that being to adjust his identity to the "general idea" of "all mankind."

It is not surprising that nineteenth-century fiction nourished itself on the *Bildungsroman*, particularly in England, though it encountered problems with the form that Fielding and Smollett were spared. After all, the Victorians were *engagé* in a brave new world, and one had much to experience, and to learn from that experience, in order to come to terms with hard times in a hard world. Orphans and waifs, like David Copperfield and Heathcliff, Becky Sharp and Jane Eyre, serve their apprenticeship in countless novels; but the *Wanderjahre* are not always so neatly apportioned to a second volume—in equal balance to the first— as Goethe had been able to manage it (in *David Copperfield* three *Wanderjahre* are compressed into one short chapter). A novelist like Dickens became increasingly uncertain what the hero ought to do at the end of his experience, or perhaps what he, the author, ought to do with his hero's experience. If David Copperfield finally achieves his patriarchal peace by the familiar hearth, in spite of the harrowing experiences from which Dickens spares neither his hero nor us, the case of Pip was harder to solve. We know of the two endings to *Great Expectations*, the happy and the unhappy: and was not Dickens' problem to decide how—or whether—to reward his heroes? In the happy ending Pip reaps his benefits as an exchange of values: suffering and wisdom are educative, and a pitying Pip rescues a pitiable Stella. But the unhappy ending is quite a different matter: Pip's expectations remain as unfulfilled as Stella's, whose face, voice, and touch at their final interview assured Pip that "suffering had been stronger than Miss Havisham's teaching." Experience on either side leaves both wiser, sadder, and—on the level of immediate attainment or "adjustment"—unrewarded. Experience had indeed taught both what the world can be like, but it provided no guarantees that one could, or proscriptions that one ought, to live in it. Pater's notorious remark, "Not the fruit of experience, but experience itself, is the end," seemed a logical conclusion by 1873: *Lehrjahre* and *Wanderjahre* had become merged in the instantaneous time-present; the future could not be relied upon to preserve either the meaning or intensity of experience, and the notion that wisdom was the fruit of experience was becoming as passé as the idea that emotion could be recollected in tranquility. *The Picture of Dorian Gray* is also a *Bildungsroman* in which the "Bild" after all is the central character; but Wilde had stood *Wilhelm Meister* on its head, fictionalizing Pater's doctrine of experience: *Wanderjahre* precede *Lehrjahre*, though time hardly separates them. While Dorian Gray experiences, his portrait learns: true suffering had been (almost) successfully projected onto a canvas in the attic.

Of course the *Bildungsroman* did not die; it merely changed some of its organizing principles, for the novelist still faced his problem: what was the hero to make of his experience? Was it to lead him to know the world in order to reject what was evil in it, or to accept what he found worth saving? And what if that find was, after all, not in the world but in the soul or psyche? Joyce's hero flies his nets, but then be was an artist and the case was therefore special. When Lawrence came of literary age with *Sons and Lovers* and *The Rainbow*, the *Bildungsroman* in English fiction was, if not moribund, in a state of suspension. The hero still learned and he still wandered, but be did less of both; and his education was as likely to lead him to the fate of Wells's Mr. Polly as to have, like Galsworthy's young Jolyon, the door slammed in his face, or to end like Conrad's Heyst in a funeral pyre of his own making. Experience was proving to be a fairly ineffectual method of coping with the world.

Lawrence hated all enclosures, whether Marxian, Darwinian, or Freudian, and he had his quarrels with all three. But in particular, as be wrote in his essay on Franklin, he hated that kind of "barbed wire moral enclosure that Poor Richard rigged up." Barbed wire: the metaphor is aptly commensurate with Lawrence's conception of life as struggle. To break through enclosures took not only a passionate will but the endurance to drive through all entanglements toward the periphery—and then beyond it. Unlike Daedalus you could not make your escape from the labyrinth merely by making a pair of wings: you had first to "come through" (to use Lawrence's language) on foot and bleed in the process. And that was truly to experience the world before you earned the *right* to reject it for what you found wanting in it.

Lawrence, of course, lived his own *Bildungsroman—Lehrjahre* and *Wanderjahre*: he would go his own ways. Toward his contemporary novelists he had little but contempt, ranging from mere petulance to hatred. One finds scattered in his writings condemnations of almost all the great novelists whom we consider today the giants of modern fiction: Flaubert, Proust, Gide, Mann, Joyce, Conrad (nor did he like Bennett, Galsworthy, Gertrude Stein, or Dorothy Richardson). He wanted no part, either of their subject or form: as innovators from whom he might learn he rejected them absolutely. In what sense, then, is Lawrence really modern, speaking of him as a novelist, not a philosopher or myth-maker? His modernity—like Yeats's—seems to be inherent in his apparent isolation from his contemporaries, an isolation that permitted him to solve (or attempt to solve) his aesthetic problems outside the great revolutionary innovations, from a position where it was still possible—because he ignored the experiments that lay between him and the past—to attach oneself to tradition by dint of one's own originality.

"The free moral and the slave moral," he wrote in an essay on Galsworthy, "the human moral and the social moral: these are the abiding antitheses."[5] And these antitheses he would attempt to resolve in at least three novels—*Sons and Lovers*, *The Rainbow*, and *Women in Love*. In some fashion all three novels were variations of the *Bildungsroman*, but only in one—*The Rainbow*—did Lawrence fully succeed in achieving the kind of balance leaving him visibly aligned to a tradition and yet marking out a solution that defined what a modern *Bildungsroman* could be like—what the relation of the hero to his experience had become in the twentieth century.[6]

## II

Like all of Lawrence's novels, *The Rainbow* has suffered its share of abuse, but even admirers have attacked its ending—as they have that of *Sons and Lovers* and, to a lesser degree *Women in Love*. This disaffection with the conclusions of novels otherwise highly regarded constitutes a serious charge: it calls in doubt not only the coherence of Lawrence's ideology but, more damaging, Lawrence's capacity as an artist to sustain his work and bring it to a proper end. With respect to *Sons and Lovers* and *The Rainbow* the question raised is the same: does the hero earn the rewards which the novelist bestows at the end? Or are Paul Morel's rather sudden determination to live purposefully and Ursula Brangwen's dramatic vision of the rainbow mere curtain-drops, the impatient gestures of a novelist already hurrying on to his next work? And what of Birkin's final disagreement with Ursula at the end of *Women in Love*—does it not sabotage the "star equilibrium" toward which the novel seems to be shaped? It is difficult to defend the ending of *Sons and Lovers* without reservations; the conclusion to *Women in Love* is more defensible; but with *The Rainbow* the problem seems crucial: to call in doubt that novel's resolution is to question the structure and meaning of the whole book, and to undercut the vision of the rainbow is to undercut all that precedes it. The risks are so high because the structure of the novel and the meaning that it carries forward depend on the validity of the rainbow image. Without the rainbow we would have something radically different from what Lawrence in fact has achieved, and this novel, which occupies the central position between *Sons and Lovers* and *Women in Love,* could not be—as I think it is—a higher achievement than its predecessor or successor.[7]

The major clue to the success of Lawrence's conclusion to *The Rainbow* [8] lies in the criticism of the failure in *Sons and Lovers*. "The trouble" with that novel, complains one critic, "is that the characterization is too flat and that the contest is over too soon. As a consequence, no changes—either developmental or disintegrative—can take place. . . . This is not a finished book."[9] Such a criticism, of course, assumes certain conventions, about both the novel and this novel in particular. One of them is that a novel like *Sons and Lovers* is intended to show growth of character, growth which leads to change, and precisely to such change, such "resolution of tensions," that makes the final achievement of the hero both believable and earned. It is also assumed that growth and change emerge out of "contest," and that in order to convince the reader that the fruits of such a contest are legitimate the struggle must be worthy of its rewards. If, then, *Sons and Lovers* fails in part because character remains static and contest is too inconclusive, it is precisely on those points that *The Rainbow* succeeds.

Tested against the criteria of character-growth and significant struggle *Sons and Lovers* fails as a *Bildungsroman* where, traditionally, the hero meets the experiences of life by trial and error, by suffering and failure, and at the end is rewarded for his trials by faith and for his errors by knowledge. Whatever one says about the ending of *Sons and Lovers,* one fact is abundantly clear: Paul Morel's experience of the world has made him neither wise nor foolish but rather helpless. And the sudden shift in direction at the close betrays confusion and a poor sense of timing more than impatience: Lawrence had not yet solved what his hero was to do with his experience—if, indeed, it had been experience at all. Yet, in spite of the faltering at the end, Lawrence intuitively, I think, meant to have the sudden turn, just as later he fully intended to give us (and his heroine)—at the right moment—the image of the rainbow. Lawrence insisted with vigor that the novel had form: "I tell you it has got form—*form*,"[10] he wrote to Garnett, and one supposes he meant chiefly that *Sons and Lovers* was well constructed (which it was), unaware perhaps that it lacked the sort of form that goes beyond construction to attain a dimension of psychological truth. When Lawrence wrote to Garnett about his intentions in *The Rainbow* he spoke of gaining that dimension in what he considered a new way altogether: "I don't care about physiology of matter—but somehow—that which is physic—non-human, in humanity, is more interesting to me than the old-fashioned human element— which causes one to conceive a character in a certain moral scheme and make him consistent. . . . You musn't look in my novel for the old stable *ego* of the character. There is another *ego*."[11]

Since Ursula is after all the heroine of *The Rainbow*, it is to her that we look for the book's texture. And—Lawrence to the contrary—Ursula is really more human than non-human, more a stable ego than a plastic psyche; old-fashioned she may not be, but she is both consistent (to her inner self) and inescapably committed to a "moral scheme," if such commitment implies an honest confrontation of life in the search for truth. The consistent—and human—character within a moral scheme: that has always been the traditional framework of the *Bildungsroman*; and a careful reading of *The Rainbow* reveals not a less traditional novel than *Sons and Lovers* (as Lawrence thought) but a traditional novel which has made its own space in the continuum. What Lawrence could not solve in *Sons and Lovers* he did solve in *The Rainbow*. This is not to imply that the novel is entirely conventional, or that Ursula is wholly a stable ego, for the timely ritual scenes— the moon episodes, the cathedral tableau—do attempt to convey some sense of a plastic psyche being molded beneath the character's secondary ego.

In rejecting the Proustian and Joycean techniques of projecting their characters' inner life, Lawrence substituted a real persona whose psyche would operate as a kind of anti-self. In that way the hero's journey through experience would become a sort of dialogue of self and soul, a dialectic between the character's objective experience and his subjective assimilation of it. This provided the novel with a realism without depriving it of the psychological subtleties that Joyce or Virginia Woolf achieved by different routes. But the ritual scenes occur less frequently in *The Rainbow* than they do in *Women in Love* where, it is fair to say, they form the very choreography of the novel, holding it in place with delicately interlaced continuity. On close inspection, the letter to Garnett more accurately applies to *Women in Love*. In *The Rainbow,* the ritual scenes arrest, at crucial points, the more traditional narrative of the hero's pilgrimage toward knowledge; but, from each of these climactic pictorial dramas, Lawrence moves back to the central motion of his story. So that in the end, the stable ego is somehow made to accommodate the plastic ego. Ursula remains a fully realized character, whose inner life has been almost completely appropriated by her outer. Pared to the bone of her Being as she is at the end, we think of her, as we leave the novel, as character rather than psyche. And we feel, as we do not always feel in Lawrence, that the author has cared for that character: it makes for a unique accomplishment of integration—perhaps correlation is a better term— between the intentional direction of the artist and the demands that his character seems to have made against them. It is a triumph which Lawrence failed to repeat, not because his powers declined but because by the time he wrote *Women in Love*, he had truly achieved another—and radically different—dimension, from which there was no turning back.

## III

*The Rainbow,* as we know, was scheduled at one point in its writing—when *Women in Love* was not yet conceived of as a separate novel—to be entitled *The Wedding Ring*; that title proved to be unsuitable for both novels. Lawrence probably rejected the title for *The Rainbow,* in spite of its apparent aptness to the marriage theme traced through several generations, because the ring image, wrongly conceived, might contradict an essential element of meaning in the novel. For it is Ursula's express triumph over her experience to break through all circles, all encircling hindrances, and among them, particularly, the circle of the wedding ring. Even in *Women in Love* she still rejects the ring, flinging Birkin's gift of three rings into the mud; and she can only accept the rings when they are joined by the flower, which she brings to her reconciliation with Birkin as a symbol of continuing growth. It is growth, indeed, that *The Rainbow* is centrally occupied with: two long chapters in the novel are headed "The Widening Circle," and both circles—the first leading from childhood to adolescence, the second from adolescence to adulthood—as they increase in circumference increase in the threat of enclosing and arresting Ursula's growth. Paradoxically, the widening circles cannot keep pace with the widening of Ursula's aspiring soul, and the larger her world becomes, the more acute is her realization of its limitations. Growth is Ursula's emblem; at times, as in the moon scene, it is a frightening, inhuman vitality, saved only by the humanness of character which Lawrence succeeds in building into her. Experience may be a teacher, but to Ursula it is more than that—it is the very motive of life, something she hunts out as an end in itself (though the rainbow is at the end of it) until, in *Women in Love*, Lawrence, through Birkin, teaches her its limitations. At the beginning of *Women in Love*, when Gudrun and Ursula talk discursively about marriage, Gudrun suggests that the experience of wifehood may, after all, be a necessary treasure in one's life. But Ursula is skeptical that marriage *is* an experience: "More likely," she says, "to be the end of experience."

This voracious appetite for experience is not unique with Ursula: her mother, Anna, possessed it in its barest state, and her grandmother, Lydia, had merely disguised it under her aristocratic pretensions, her "foreignness." One aim in tracing the three generations of women is to demonstrate the progressive shades of meaning in their appetites for experience: in Lydia it is partially subdued by convention, only to stir underneath as melancholia and frustration; in Anna it is wild and undirected and self-consuming. Only in Ursula does this appetite become truly attached to a conscious being, become, ultimately, directed and civilized. Therefore, the striving—and the failure of achievement—of the earlier generations prepares us for the vital center of the novel: the education of Ursula, through whom the preceding, and partial, impulses are carried to successful completion.

In the opening pages of *The Rainbow* we are told that the women looked to the "spoken world beyond," to the Word within the World. Facing outward, just as the men face inward, the women seek to fulfill their "range of motion" by searching for "knowledge," "education," and "experience." Only Ursula finds all three—and finds them wanting. Anna is a primitive version of Ursula, and her experiences so often resemble Ursula's that Lawrence at times seems almost to be straining the point. But the differences are more significant than the similarities, for Anna remains unconscious, to the end, of the full meaning of her experiences. Her main defense against the encircling world and the roofed-in arch of the church is multiplication of self: by producing scores of children she erects a kind of shield around herself. But children remain at best unwilling ambassadors and cannot negotiate for her. Ursula realizes this almost from the start as she chooses the opposite way: not padding the self protectively but stripping it to the core.

In the harvest scene between Will and Anna, the latter reveals the doomed nature of her relationship with life which consists in trying to achieve the impossible simultaneity of isolation and relatedness, the repulsion of being within the ring (of marriage) and the passionate necessity to possess its very center. There is no Birkin here who can explain the complex "star equilibrium" in which a man and a woman find separateness in union. Anna is torn between what she fears most and craves most, and it is this scene which clearly presages her future. It is a ritual, very Lawrentian with its moon and mood of incantation. Anna is always first in returning her harvest to the stocks. As Will comes with his bundle Anna leaves: it is a "rhythm" in which she "drift[s] and ebb[s] like a wave." But the rhythm that keeps them together keeps them apart: "As he came, she drew away, as he drew away, she came. Were they never to meet?" Always there remains the "space between them" until at last they meet and make love—until, that is, Anna, with her Brangwen passion, subdues her opposing Will.

Now the point of this scene is, in part, to convey Anna's violation of the rhythm that had kept her apart from intimacy; or, to put it differently, to show how she chooses one way, though committed to another. The intimacy is all too temporary, severed during the fortnight of honeymoon. And the "space between them" is never finally breached. Anna's pursuit of experience is therefore always blinded by the insistent demands of an inner resistance to accept experience, to go through with it to the end in order to test its validity. Ursula commits herself to experience in the full knowledge of risk and is willing to taste—again and again—the ashen fruits of the experiences that fail her—religion, education, knowledge, passion. Anna's incomplete and arrested tilt with experience rewards her with only an incomplete and arrested vision of the rainbow, and Lawrence could not be clearer about his meaning:

> Dawn and sunset were the feet of the rainbow that spanned the day, and she saw the hope, the promise. Why should she travel any further?
>
> Yet she always asked the question. As the sun went down . . . she faced the blazing close of the affair, in which she *had not played her fullest part,* and she made her demand still: "What are you doing, making this big shining commotion?"
>
> . . . With satisfaction *she relinquished the adventure to the unknown.*
>
> . . . If she were not the wayfarer to the unknown, she were arrived now, settled in her builded house, a rich woman, still her doors opened under the arch of the rainbow, her threshold reflected the passing of the sun and moon, the great travellers, her house was full of the echo of journeying. [Italics mine]

Were Anna content with the "echo of journeying" as a fit substitute for the journey itself, her attainment of family, house, and children would be well enough for creative life. But she is not content. And since she has no way of working out her discontent other than yearning for that in which she is unwilling, always, to play her full part—the experience of life measured to its ends—she is left with a finite vision after all, a rainbow whose two ends bind her to the rising and setting sun, to the limited existence of an everyday world.

It is a mistake Ursula does not make because she has the courage to face the annihilating, but paradoxically freedom-giving moment of having journeyed fully committed to the end of experience. In the central Cathedral scene, Anna "claimed the right to freedom above her, higher than the roof. She had always a sense of being roofed in"; yet her claim is undercut by her incapacity to approach anything beyond the roof. She turns immediately to the gargoyles which she reduces, defensively, to human shapes, an act of reassurance, not of faith. Ursula's struggle for the beyond is differently shaped. To each new experience she brings the whole of herself. Her encounter with religion is total: she even plays out, against her intuition, the practical results of offering the other cheek, and only rejects the act after her cheeks burn with the slap of her sister's hand. Failing in religious faith she puts next her faith in love, though she enacts it, at first, amidst the ruins of her old faith, in the interior of the church which, with its fallen stones, its ruined plaster, its scaffolding, is all too symbolically under constant repair.

Always, with Ursula, there is yearning followed by enactment: she never retreats, she always chooses. Three quarters through the novel we find her amidst an emblematic landscape, which aptly projects her state of being constantly on the verge of setting foot into another world, of widening her circle:

> The blue way of the canal wound softly between the autumn hedges, on towards the greenness of a small hill. On the left was the whole black agitation of colliery and railway and the town which rose on its hill, the church tower topping all. The round white dot of the clock of the tower was distinct in the evening light.
>
> That way, Ursula felt, was the way to London, through the grim, alluring seethe of the town. On the other hand was the evening, mellow over the green watermeadows.
>
> . . .

> Ursula and Anton Skrebensky, walked along the ridge of the canal between. . . . The glow of evening and the wheeling of the solitary pee-wit and the faint cry of the birds came to meet the shuffling noise of the pits, the dark, fuming stress of the town opposite, and they two walked the blue strip of water-way, the ribbon of sky between.[12]

The canal divides the two shores which together form the whole of Ursula's potential world and, incidentally, the whole of the world which she experiences in the novel. On the right lie the fields of her birth, the fecund earth on which she and Skrebensky first consummate their love; on the left lie the colliery, the town, the church, and London, each of which is once tested and discarded. She rejects the fecund earth when she renounces the blood-prescient nature of Anthony for the sake of the journey onwards: "But she was a traveller, she was a traveller on the face of the earth, and he was an isolated creature living in the fulfilment of his own senses." The refusal of the church we have already pointed to; with Winifred Inger, Ursula pushes away the colliery of her uncle Tom—"impure abstraction, the mechanisms of matter"—and London as well, the London of Miss Inger, sophisticated perversion. And the town, where Ursula is so brutally initiated into the man's world is gladly forsaken too: "The stupid, artificial, exaggerated town. . . . What is it?—nothing, just nothing." She will have to walk through the town, not towards it, like Paul Morel, and the transcendence can only occur vertically toward a vision, since on the horizontal plane—where Anna was always condemned to move—the landscape of the world is, at the end of the novel, fully exhausted of possibilities.

To say that Ursula searches for selfhood is descriptive but not very profoundly interpretive, for that fact is of lesser importance by far than the manner of her search. I have already said that the growth of Ursula's world coincides with the diminishing possibilities of her functioning creatively within it. From that point of view the novel is largely negative, consisting of a number of refusals and rejections without any corresponding affirmations. But the search for self, in the fitting image of husk and kernel at the end of the book, is a process of stripping away all layers that disguise and protect self from the truth of self (it resembles Lear's stripping process). So while the circle of the world widens, the circle of the self narrows in inverse proportion: the larger the one, the smaller—and the nearer to the core—the other. Ursula's annihilation of Skrebensky under the moon is no mere repetition of Anna's subjugation of Will under the same moon: it is, indeed, a far more violent and total act, but one with more results as well, and more motive. Ursula has the ability—which Anna lacked—to convert experience into knowledge: she masters the economics of experiencing to perfection. What she discovers is Skrebensky's lack of self and through it she is illumined on the nature of self—her own and in the abstract. She triumphs—not as Anna had, in order to subdue Will, but to create a self of her own. There under the moon she is awakened for the first time to the awful power of self—and its dangers; and it frightens her, enough to prevent her from severing her relationship with Skrebensky. It is true that her lust motivates her to "tear him and make him into nothing," but that impulse itself spells out the nature of a ceaselessly moving self. After she destroys Skrebensky, her soul is, understandably enough, "empty and finished": destruction has not come without its price. When he leaves she feels that emptiness even more acutely. Although she has seen the power of self she has not gained control of it by far, "since she *had* no self." Only after turning with shame and hatred on Winifred Inger and uncle Tom does she get any closer to it, and that double rejection makes way for her final struggles.

The last episodes with Skrebensky have puzzled a good many readers and some, like Hough, have suggested that Lawrence himself was not clear on the subject.[13] Yet if Lawrence was not, Ursula was, for she predicts the failure of her resumed affair before she ever embarks on it: "Passion is only part of love. And it seems so much because it can't last. That is why passion is never happy." Yet, in the tradition of the hero undergoing the education of life, knowledge—of a kind—often precedes the experience that will confirm it. The true hero must always experience before he can truly know: he never substitutes intuitional wisdom for the living through itself. Often, as with Ursula, this is a conscious sacrifice at the altar of life's suffering, and it is consciousness, as I have said, that distinguishes Ursula as the kind of hero she is. "Ursula suffered bitterly at the hands of life": and that is proper for the hero whom life educates in its bitter school. But consciousness makes such suffering even more intense and makes it so precisely because it injects and maintains some ideal toward which all action gravitates with certainty and direction. When she and Anthony face a beautiful sunset, it is Ursula's consciousness of its beauty that gives her the capacity for feeling pain—the pain that comes with recognizing the inevitable disparity between the achieved and the achievable. "All this so beautiful, all this so lovely! He did not see it. He was one with it. But she saw it, and was one with it. Her seeing separated them infinitely." Sight precedes perception; acknowledgment precedes knowledge.

It is this aspect of conscious perception in the pursuit of experience that I have earlier called civilized; but the cost of such awareness is very high and makes for the awful negation that burdens the whole novel. Ursula is hardly unaware of it: the pressure is always there, to seek out life, to encounter it in battle, to discard and to be defeated, and to move on again:

> She had the ash of disillusion gritting under her teeth. Would the next move turn out the same? Always the shining doorway ahead; and then, upon approach, always the shining doorway was a gate into another ugly yard . . . .
> No matter! Every hill-top was a little different, every valley was somehow new. . . .
>
> But what did it mean, Ursula Brangwen? She did not know what she was. Only she was full of rejection, of refusal. Always, always she was spitting out of her mouth the ash and grit of disillusion. . . . She could only stiffen in rejection, in rejection. She seemed always negative in her action.

Such is her state as Lawrence moves into the final pages of his story, and to extricate Ursula from her negation, to provide her with an earned vision at the close was, as is apparent, no easy task. At this point Ursula begins to perceive, dimly, a world outside experience, a world outside the "circle lighted by a lamp," a world dark and mysterious where "she saw the eyes of the wild beast gleaming." Towards that world she must move, out of the circle of the lighted lamp, from the illumination of familiarity into the shadows of the unknown, truly the unknown. This constitutes the search beyond the finite self, the personal self.[14]

One day, watching the sea roll in, she comes to know that through the self-consciousness of seeking life one is heir to the shocks of recognition which reveal what one has not attained, an exercise of the imagination which presupposes fulfillment of things the other side of the present. Touched by the beauty of the rhythmically moving sea—as she was by the sunset—she laughs and weeps from a single impulse. Then she follows "a big wave running unnoticed, to burst in a shock of foam against a rock . . . leaving the rock emerged black and teeming." Her wish for the fate of the wave is symbolic: "Oh, and if, when the wave burst into whiteness, it were only set free!" If, that is, the wave, making its climactic collision with the rock of the opposing world, could only be liberated from its flux of experience, prevented somehow from falling into the sea again, only to become water for another wave. If only Ursula could fly the flux of her experience and bear away her trophy, the fruits of experience, to the safety of some timeless region that would not condemn her to this ceaseless repetition of battle with life. The image of the liberated wave resembles the circle lighted by a lamp, and both resemble the encircling horde of stallions at the end.

Ursula's final experience with the lighted circle of the world is her futile passion with Skrebensky, and it is preceded by the botany classroom scene in which Ursula makes her penultimate leap. She sees the speck under her microscope moving and it appears vitally alive, but Ursula questions its beingness, its teleology, if it has one: "She only knew that it was not limited mechanical energy, nor mere purpose of self-preservation and self-assertion. It was a consummation, a being infinite." By being a fully realized self, one could in fact fly the circle into a "oneness with the infinite": "To be oneself was a supreme, gleaming triumph of infinity." To capture the wave out of the sea was to catapult it into the infinite reaches, where it might be preserved with wholeness. Such an insight followed by yet another disillusionment is not meaningless. The affair with Skrebensky, aside from providing proof of what she has perceived, serves also to clarify the contours of the circle which Ursula must flee. Already as a school teacher she had felt increasingly the "prison . . . round her"; and the sense of wishing to break out of the enclosing and binding circles becomes sharply defined in the penultimate chapter in which, on two occasions, the final rainbow image is clearly prefigured. "This inner circle of light in which she lived and moved" has become too much to bear; and finally she would "not love [Skrebensky] in a house any more." "She must go to the downs, into the open spaces, where in the darkness of night she experiences the final "bitterness of ecstasy." They await the dawn: "She watched a pale rim on the sky . . . The darkness became bluer . . . The light grew stronger, gushing up against the dark . . . night. The light grew stronger, whiter, then over it hovered a flush of rose. A flush of rose, and then yellow . . . poising momentarily over the fountain on the sky's rim." Here the spectrum of colors certainly suggests the rainbow—the rose burns, then turns to red; "great waves of yellow" are flung over the sky, "scattering its spray over the darkness, which became bluer and bluer . . . till soon it would itself be a radiance." And finally the sun breaks through, "too powerful to look at." Some pages earlier appeared another image, also suggestive of the rainbow, and again Ursula and her lover were in the open: "And in the roaring circle under the tree . . . they lay a moment looking at the twinkling lights on the darkness opposite, saw the sweeping brand of a train past the edge of their darkened field." Such deliberate preparation hardly suggests haste and impatience when Lawrence came to the final pages of his novel.

## IV

That Ursula's journey through the widening circles of experience, and her ultimate flight beyond those circles into the arches of heaven, may be limited acts after all is a question Lawrence does not raise until *Women in Love*. There, in retrospect, Ursula sees at one point the possibility that even the exhaustion of experience may bring one only to the threshold of death. Socrates was right: the unexamined life was not worth living; but the modern novelist had to ask whether the examined life was worth living: "She had travelled all her life along the line of fulfilment, and it was nearly concluded. She knew all she had to know, she had experienced all she had to experience, she was fulfilled in a kind of bitter ripeness, there remained only to fall from the tree into death."

But in *The Rainbow* it is not the falling into death but the falling away from it which dominates as an image. In the scene with the stallions Ursula finally accomplishes her transcendence of the circles, precisely by letting herself drop from a tree. In doing so she fulfills the wish given us in an earlier image: "She saw herself travelling round a circle, only an arc of which remained to complete. Then, she was in the open, like a bird tossed into mid-air, a bird that had learned in some measure to fly." Repeatedly the horses come to ring her—"Like circles of lightning came the flash of hoofs"; "They had gone by, brandishing themselves thunderously about her, enclosing her." As the circle closes, every horizontal route of escape "to the highroad and the ordered world of man" is cut off. There is only one way she can move—up: "She might climb into the boughs of that oak tree, and so round and drop on the other side of the hedge." So she proceeds; and her symbolic drop liberates her—as such drops often do in literature—into a consciousness of separateness done with temporal and spatial dimensions of world: "time and the flux of change passed away from her, she lay as if unconscious . . . like a stone . . . unchanging . . . whilst everything rolled by in transcience . . . [she was] sunk to the bottom of all change." Now may the kernel shed the enclosing husk and "take itself the bed of a new sky"; only the child remains: "[it] bound her ... like a bond round her brain, tightened on her brain." But when that bond is loosened she is ready for her rainbow—ready because free at last from the perpetuity of experience which had victimized her for so long. There is no taking the past away, for it had to be; only the full commitment to the circles of experience allows one to escape them. Ursula has escaped the fate of her father, who had gained "knowledge and skill without vision."

At the end of the novel there is no doubt that the reader has earned a vision of the rainbow, for he, unlike Ursula, has been subjected to the struggle of not one but three generations. But, if we look upon *The Rainbow* as a modern *Bildungsroman*, a trial and error warfare with experience, which allows finally a glimpse of an ideal that rises inevitably out of experience, then there can be little doubt that Ursula too has earned the right to her open, semi-circular rainbow, leaving her free like a bird "that has learned in some measure to fly."[15]

In none of the three major novels—*Sons and Lovers, The Rainbow, Women in Love*—does Lawrence resolve his ending as the logical, inevitable conclusion to a single ruling passion. Had he done so Paul Morel should have committed suicide; Ursula should have died of her heavy losses; and *Women in Love* should have been altogether an impossible book to write. Those who accuse Lawrence of a sleight of hand at the end of these novels fail to see the intuition and later the consciousness of his purpose, for he was quite aware that his conclusions were not the neat, conventional climaxes that satisfy a reader's expectations because they are coincident with his prophecies. Such endings he would have considered "immoral":

> Because *no* emotion is supreme, or exclusively worth living for [or dying for, he might have added]. *All* emotions go to the achieving of a living relationship between a human being and the other human being or creature or thing he becomes purely related to . . . If the novelist puts his thumb in the pan, for love, tenderness, sweetness, peace, then he commits an immoral act: he presents the possibility of a pure relationship, a pure relatedness . . . and he makes inevitable the horrible reaction, when he lets his thumb go, towards hate and brutality, cruelty and destruction.[16]

No one emotion carried to its end tells the whole truth, because it obstructs the basic complexity of the human psyche, its multifarious potential to act, to fulfill, at many levels, its inner needs in balance with the outer demands of the world. "The business of art is to reveal the relation between man and his circumambient universe, at the living moment." Lawrence goes on to call this "living moment" a "fourth dimension," "a revelation of the perfected relation, at a certain moment, between a man" and his object. And that "which exists in the non-dimensional space of pure relationship is deathless, lifeless, and eternal . . . beyond life, and therefore beyond death."[17] So precisely does Ursula exist at the conclusion of *The Rainbow*. Here Lawrence succeeded in capturing the "momentaneous" (it is a favorite word) in the midst of timelessness: this is the essential meaning of the rainbow. Ursula's "living moment" is therefore beyond life or death, in the fourth dimension where neither hope nor despair has any business.

In its demand that the hero experience—indeed, that he seek out experience —and suffer for it, *The Rainbow* remains an entirely conventional *Bildungsroman,* a type of novel naturally suited to a man of Lawrence's passionate pedagogic temperament. But in rejecting, at the end, both the hero who is a helpless victim of experience and the hero whom experience transforms into a malcontent, Lawrence achieved a new dimension for the novel of education in the twentieth century: the hero has been "*emotionally* educated [which] is rare as a phoenix."[18] Here lies the true originality of form in *The Rainbow:* at the end of experience the hero has gained the privilege of release from it; and the *Lehrjahre*—post-apprenticesbip learning—really lie ahead in the *Wanderjahre,* in the inconclusiveness of *Women in Love*, where experience is not tested against the world but against one's self. The end of experience, in the modern world, is only the beginning of selfhood. Life is no longer just a school nor experience a mere teacher: both have become antagonists to conquer in exchange for freedom.

It is a fair war since Lawrence never refuses to exact the price of suffering. The "human moral," having fully tested the "social moral," is at liberty to discriminate. Such a view of experience has influenced a writer like Hemingway (one of the few modern novelists Lawrence admired),[19]whose heroes—despite their hunger for experience—wish finally to become educated "emotionally" and thereby be liberated from the compulsive tests of experience, Hemingway going Lawrence one better by suggesting a "fifth dimension" in which this might be achieved. Certainly the ending of *The Old Man and the Sea* owes something in spirit to that of *The Rainbow*: after the worst that experience can inflict the old man comes home to dream of the lions on the beach.

"While a man remains a man, a true human individual," Lawrence insisted, "there is at the core of him a certain innocence or naïveté. . . . This does not mean that the human being is nothing but naïve or innocent. He is Mr. Worldly Wiseman also to his own degree. But in his essential core he is naïve."[20] Here surely is an account of Ursula as we find her at the end of the novel: worldly-wise but purged, and at the core innocent. For Goethe the end of experience was also the end of innocence, for in his world the hero's path was still clearly marked so that, in proportion as the hero grew wise, he would choose the right way: the flux of experience gave way to the steadiness of wisdom. For Lawrence—as, for others, of course—the modern world offered no such clear topography, and experience had indeed become, in a way, as Pater had said, an end in itself. *Wilhelm Meister,* Goethe told Eckermann, "seems to say nothing more than that man, despite all his follies and errors, being led by a higher hand, reaches some happy goal at last."[21] Love, Lawrence said, "travels heavenwards": "Love is not a goal; it is only a travelling, death is not a goal; it is a travelling. . . . There is a goal . . . absolved from time and space, perfected in the realm of the absolute."[22] For a moment Ursula and the rainbow merge to chart that absolute—vertical, not horizontal; and in that merging they objectify what Lawrence set down as a definition of art: "the relation between man and his circumambient universe." But Ursula reaches no "happy goal" at the end of her experience in *The Rainbow,* and the novelist, like his heroine, had to begin again, from a different perspective, where Goethe could contentedly end.[23]

*PMLA: Publications of the Modern Language Association of America*, 78, 1963

## Notes

[1] *The Letters of W. B. Yeats* , ed. Allan Wade (London 1954), pp. 803, 807, 810.

[2] D. H. Lawrence, *Selected Literary Criticism*, ed. Anthony Beal (London, 1955), p. 148.

[3]*The Autobiography of William Butler Yeats* (New York, 1953), p. 212. It is relevant to record young Henry James's remarks on *Wilhelm Meister* (he was twenty-two) in his review of "Carlyle's Translation of Goethe's *Wilhelm Meister*," first published in *The North American Review*, July 1865, and reprinted in *Literary Reviews and Essays,* ed. Albert Mordell (New York, 1957), pp. 267-271. James regarded the book as a "great novel" (p. 267), recognizing, however, its intellectualized stance: "It is, indeed, to the understanding exclusively, and never, except in the episode of Mignon, to the imagination, that the author appeals"; "Was there ever a book so dispassionate, or, as some persons prefer to call it, cold-blooded? [But] Goethe's plan was *non flere, non indignari, sed*

*intelligere"* (p. 271). It was finally the 'reality' of Goethe that most impressed James: "Goethe's persons are not lifelike they are life itself. They *live,*—and assuredly, a figure cannot do more than that" (p. 269).

[4] *Conversations of Goethe with Eckermann,* tr. John Oxenford, ed. J. K. Moorhead, Everyman's Library, 1951, p. 103.

[5] *Selected Literary Criticism*, p. 120.

[6] Since I am now prepared to treat *The Rainbow* as a *Bildungsroman,* I should make clear that I am not forgetting that the novel is also a family chronicle. But Lawrence's interest is clearly in Ursula—in her education. And the novel is shaped toward that end from the beginning, since Ursula learns—and profits—from the failures of the generations that precede her. Thomas Mann's *Buddenbrooks* is also a family chronicle, but the fourth generation, represented by Hanno, never has a chance. Hanno is trapped by heredity and destroyed by his forebears. *The Rainbow,* unlike *Buddenbrooks*, leads toward a progressive strengthening, toward life, not toward decline and death. Here, too, Lawrence reversed a trend of his time. Marvin Mudrick has written a fine appreciative and interpretive essay on *The Rainbow*: "The Originality of *The Rainbow*," reprinted in *A. D. H. Lawrence Miscellany,* 1959), ed. Harry T. Moore (Carbondale, Ill., 1959), pp. 56-82. His essay is shaped toward different ends than mine, which is ultimately an examination of Ursula's experience, the validity of the rainbow image (which Mudrick defends), and the tradition of the *Bildungsroman.* I cannot agree that the "last half of *The Rainbow* seems to have been written with a slackening of Lawrence's attention to proportion and detail" (p. 78). The words "originality" and "tradition," as Mudrick uses them, carry rather special meanings: I argue that *The Rainbow* is more within a tradition than Lawrence thought and that its structure is defensible in these terms. The originality lies in Lawrence's special conception of the hero's education. Mudrick is, of course, right in insisting that part of the "originality" of the novel was its treatment of themes hitherto less boldly explored in English fiction.

[7] F. R. Leavis thinks otherwise. See *D. H. Lawrence: Novelist* (New York, 1956), p. 111.

[8] Two strong objections to the conclusion of *The Rainbow* are raised by Leavis and Graham Hough. Although he admires *The Rainbow* and thinks it a unique book, Leavis feels that there are "signs of too great a tentativeness in the development and organization of the later part; signs of a growing sense in the writer of an absence of any conclusion in view" (p. 172). He also feels that the rainbow vision is "a note wholly unprepared and unsupported, defying the preceding pages" (p. 170). This position is supported by Graham Hough, *The Dark Sun, A Study of D. H. Lawrence* (London, 1956), p. 71: "the book can have no proper ending . . . we can only feel that . . . [the rainbow vision] is quite insufficiently based, nothing in the book up to now has led up to it." Arnold Kettle, in an otherwise useful essay, concludes with a strong social indictment of Lawrence and of the rainbow image: "the final image of the rainbow, upon which almost everything, artistically, must depend, is not a triumphant image resolving in itself the half-clarified contradictions brought into play throughout the book, but a misty, vague and unrealized vision which gives us no more than the general sense that Lawrence is, after all, on the side of life" (*An Introduction to the English Novel,* London, 1953, II, 131). The most recent attack on *The Rainbow* (though it is not a total condemnation) was published after the present essay was completed. S. L. Goldberg, in *"The Rainbow*: Fiddle-Bow and Sand," *Essays in Criticism,* XI (October 1961), finds, in general, that the ideology and the artistry of the novel are unresolved. He underscores the "emotional falsity of the last few pages" (p. 427); finds the second half of the novel weaker than the first; accuses Lawrence of "romantic assumptions . . . impatience and vagueness . . . in the last pages" (pp. 431-

432); and sees the rainbow image as a culminating "weakness that is obviously more than stylistic and is also more than local" (pp. 426-427).

9 Louis Fraiberg, "The Unattainable Self: D. H. Lawrence's *Sons and Lovers,*" in *Twelve Original Essays on Great English Novels,* ed. Charles Shapiro (Detroit, 1960), pp. 200-201. Mark Spilka is willing to grant Paul "a kind of half-realized, or jigsaw success . . ." (*The Love Ethic of D. H. Lawrence,* Bloomington, Ind., 1955, p. 85). Graham Hough can say no more than that Paul sbows himself "capable of a regenerating spark" (p. 52). Leavis devotes no space to this novel at all. Eliseo Vivas feels that the ending is there "simply to wind up the book and enable[s] the novelist to write 'The End'" (*D. H. Lawrence, The Failure and the Triumph of Art,* Evanston, Ill., 1960, p. 175).

10 *Selected Literary Criticism,* p. 13.

11 Ibid., pp. 17-18.

12 Leavis admires this passage and feels it to be symbolic, but only of the world which lies before them, not also of the world which in the end will lie behind them—at least behind Ursula (p. 165).

13 Pp. 69-71.

14 Spilka discusses this perceptively and in greater detail, pp. 111-112. See also Leavis, p. 118 ff.

15 Like Lear, Ursula is freed from the "wheel of fire," "the rack of this tough world"; Lawrence felt that "Lear was essentially happy, even in his greatest misery" (*Selected Literary Criticism,* p. 123), just as Yeats considered Lear "gay" in "Lapis Lazuli." Lawrence might have entitled his penultimate chapter "The Ecstasy of Bitterness," instead of "The Bitterness of Ecstasy": at any rate, release makes way for vision: "the moment of [Ursula's] vision," writes Harry T. Moore, "is the moment of her relase" (*The Rainbow, The Achievement of D. H. Lawrence,* ed. Frederick J. Hoffman and Harry T. Moore, Norman, Okla., 1953, p. 156).

16 "The Morality of the Novel," *Selected Literary Criticism,* p. 11.

17 Ibid., pp. 108-109.

18 Ibid., p. 118. Lawrence considered Flaubert, Ibsen, and Hardy "nihilist" and wrote, after reading Bennett's *Anna of the Five Towns*: "I hate Bennett's resignation . . . [the book] seems like an acceptance—so does all the modem stuff since Flaubert" (pp. 72, 131). Emotional education would resist both annihilation and resignation. The schoolroom section of *The Rainbow,* with Ursula in the frustrating position as teacher, ironically counterpoints her education in the world: just as she must fail—in the ordinary sense—to learn from experience, so she must fail to impart such wisdom in the schoolroom, society's microcosmic experience-chamber. The effect of the schoolroom's inadequacy is thematically suggestive in projecting—often through ironic parallel to the school of life— the educative theme of nineteenth-century fiction. The schoolroom appears often, of course, in Dickens; but it plays its role in a good many books—*Jane Eyre, Madame Bovary, Le Rouge et le Noir,* and, to reach into our own century, in *Buddenbrooks* and *A Portrait of the Artist as a Young Man,* to cite only a few instances.

19 See his review of *In Our Time* (ibid., pp. 427-428): "Don't get connected up. If you get held by anything, break it. Don't be held. Break it, and get away. . . . Beat it! 'Well, boy, I guess I'll beat it.' Ah, the pleasure in saying that!" (p. 427). The review is dated 1927.

20 Ibid., p. 120.

21 *Conversations with Eckermann,* p. 84.

22 "Love," *Phoenix, The Posthumous Papers of D. H. Lawrence,* ed. with an Introduction by Edward D. McDonald (London, 1961), pp. 152-153.

[23]The rainbow does not suggest denial of life, nor is it a permanent lure from the real world. As Spilka (who approves of the ending) says, Ursula must learn to have a "conjunction" with life (p. 112); the full possibilities of such a conjunction are explored in *Women in Love*. One has finally to meet the objection—implicit in most critiques of the rainbow symbol—that, on the literal level, the rainbow is a temporary, transitory image: rainbows give way to different weather. But Lawrence was fully aware of this: *The Rainbow* gave way to a different novel. The very transitoriness of the rainbow makes it a proper and significant symbol for, at the end of the novel, Ursula is meant to be projected into that fourth dimension, suspended between an end and a beginning. It is a position of respite from which 'she will later re-enter the world; though neither she nor the world will be the same.

# James Twitchell, "Lawrence's Lamias: Predatory Women in *The Rainbow* and *Women in Love*"

One of D.H. Lawrence's most repeated literary devices is repetition. He repeats words, phrases, images, allusions, characters, and situations as few artists have ever dared to do. In *The Rainbow* and *Women in Love* (both derived from his proto-novel *The Sisters*), words like "blood," "flux," and "convulsive," phrases like "he wanted death," "she must know," "he seemed to have passed into a dream world," images of horses, drive wheels, and hawks, and allusions to the phoenix, the Flood, and the rainbow, are repeated so often as to have an almost incantative rhythm of their own. But they have an important structural purpose as well: they are both leitmotifs carrying the story forward and independent variations on subthemes adding depth.[1] For in a sense Lawrence tells his story both straight ahead and sideways at the same time. First he tells the story; then he tells variations of it. He must have realized that this incremental repetition would be a problem for readers accustomed to the traditional novel's rising action, climax, and resolution, for he wrote in the Foreword to *Women in Love* that "fault is often found with the continual slightly modified repeition," but exculpated himself in a most Lawrentian way: "The only answer is that it is natural to the author: and that every natural crisis in emotion or passion or understanding comes from this pulsing, frictional to-and-fro which works up to culmination" (*WL*, viii).[2]

The concern of this paper is to detail part of a scene that Lawrence repeats again and again throughout *The Rainbow* and *Women in Love*. The scene itself is a central melody: two young people meet and enter into what is described as a "battle for life itself." This struggle to evolve a lasting relationship is completed early on in the novels with the marriage of Tom Brangwen and Lydia Lensky, but variations of it form a kind of Wagnerian attempt at chromatic harmony.[3] As in Wagner's musical dramas, we are led through Lawrence's "Ring of the Brangwen" by a strange expectation of returning to the tonic key, a hope of reachieving stasis. It is the absence of such a stopping place, or cadence point, that gives these novels their eerie sense of unendingness as well as their seamless quality. Or in another musical metaphor of infinitely smaller scale, Lawrence is here writing a fugue with Lydia and Tom's relationship as the subject melody and the relationship of Anna and Will, Ursula and Anton, Hermione and Birkin, Gudrun and Gerald, as contrapuntally discordant. We are kept listening in expectation of the return of subject melody, which we almost but do not quite hear in the relationship of Ursula and Birkin.[4]

To explain why these later relationships are not harmonious is what the novels are about. These couples fail to strike chords because, now in Birkin's analogy, the partners do not orbit around each other like stars, but rather collide like meteors. We hear no "music of the spheres" because of a flaw in character, and that flaw in each instance is the same—the desires of the females to know, to control, and finally to possess her man have become inordinate. Lawrence's females in these novels are primal passions, fields of force whose surge and recoil, if not directed by the male, will overwhelm their mates. I admit it seems unfairly reductive to place the blame for human incompleteness, or human discontinuity, primarily on the female, but Lawrence does, and in these days of heightened sensitivity to sex roles it may be especially instructive to examine Lawrence's predatory women closely.[5]

Admittedly the men are weak (Will is rigid, Anton is spineless, Birkin is initially homosexual, and Gerald is power misdirected), but they are not killers, only pathetic victims.[6] They are the male praying mantises waiting to be devoured by the female after she has used them. They are weak because they are, in Lawrence's pandect, the results of the movement of male and female away from "primal unity" toward separateness. And this separateness implies opposition: machine versus man, law versus love, working versus living, self-preservation versus self-fulfillment, centripetal versus centrifugal, or, in the "modern" world, female versus male. Again I should make it clear that the male is culpable (although blame is hard to assess, for in Lawrence's work it is almost axiomatic that characters are unable to change), but he is culpable in the sense that, as Birkin says, "every murder has a murderee [who] in a profound if hidden lust desires to be murdered" (*WL*, 27). The male is the murderee, the female is the murderer, and although they participate in the same crime their culpabilities differ.[7]

Near the end of *Women in Love* Lawrence postulates four kinds of human relationships based on "sensational experience": repetition, separation, subjugation, or death (*WL*, 443). A relationship can achieve repetitive stasis (the "harmonious flux" of Tom and Lydia), it can split apart (Birkin and Hermione), it can have one member dominate (Ursula and Anton), or it can cause death (Gudrun and Gerald). Again and again Lawrence repeats the last three of these relationships, changing only the cast of characters. However, the dominant character in each remains the man-devouring female. Biographically Lawrence knew the most constant of his character types firsthand from his mother, but in his artistic reconstruction of her, Hardy's females seem to provide the literary template.[8] By the time Lawrence was ready to cast this *femme fatale* into *The Rainbow*, he had already etched in his own mythic overlay (perhaps with the help of Poe)—the female as vampire.[9]  And this female, after some initial variation, becomes almost a stereotype—from Gertrude Morel to Miriam Leivers, then to Anna, Ursula, Hermione, and finally to Gudrun.[10]

Ironically we know too much about the vampire to appreciate Lawrence's deft use of the myth.[11] For today vampires teach our children the numbers on "Sesame Street" (Count Count), are the name of a breakfast cereal ("Count Chocula"), were the subject of a soap opera ("Dark Shadows"), comic books ("Vampirella"), and of seemingly endless Hollywood films (1931: *Dracula*, 1936: *Dracula's Daughter*, 1943: *Son of Dracula*, 1960: *Brides of Dracula*, 1966: *Billy the Kid vs. Dracula* . . . ). In the first quarter of this century, however, the vampire was not the boring cultural menace he has become. In fact the vampire Lawrence inherited from literature and lore is not one we would easily recognize.[12] For Lawrence the vampire was simply a demon who had taken over the body of a sinner and who was using that body to prey on unsuspecting yet unconsciously willing victims. He was technically known as a "revenant"— literally come back from the dead, and was distinct from a ghoul in that he was controlled by no external force. The vampire in Lawrence's time was mercifully without the red eyes, horrid laugh, Bela Lugosi accent, extended incisors tipped with blood—he was in fact, as Bram Stoker pictured him in *Dracula* (1897), something of an English country gentleman. In folklore he was not so polite. In contradistinction to the celluloid vampire who is positively photophobic, the vampire Lawrence knew from Midland superstition and English literature preferred to work at night but could also function by day. Also the vampire did not immediately kill his victim, as does his Hollywood descendant, but rather slowly enervated her by repeated visits until she became "walking dead" herself, looking for victims of her own. And most importantly, the vampire was never happy about being involved in this heinous process, but was hopelessly trapped by the need for life, the need for blood. The vampire was thus an apt image for fate—eternally trapped in an endless process.

The victim's character was almost as prescribed as the fiend's. The victim was almost always someone young and of the opposite sex, who must in some way initiate the rapprochement.[13] For the vampire would never attack wantonly, but first singled out a victim who had expressed some subtle desire for a love that went beyond mortality. The innocent need not fear, for the vampire could be warded off simply by inattention or, if the individual wanted protection, by the display of ecclesiastical icons—the Bible, the cross, or holy water.[14]

If the vampire's victim is female, she eventually becomes a lamia, and to be precise, this is the appropriate term for Lawrence's man-consuming women. The lamia is mythically mixed into the Christian tradition as Lilith, the supposed first wife of Adam, who turned to blood-sucking only after she had been spurned by her husband. Although called Lilith in Christian lore, Lamia descended from Greek myth, where she was a lover of Zeus, and was condemned to madness (which led to child-devouring) by jealous Hera.[15] Lawrence could not have cared less. His interest is in adaptation, not history. So just as Gudrun is by turns Daphne (*WL*, 108), or Medusa (*WL*, 440), and Gerald is Dionysus (*WL*, 94), or Cain (*WL*, 20), so too are Lawrence's destructive females partially—never completely—lamias.[16]

The vampire's central act has remained unchanged regardless of cultural medium: it is the kiss. It is with the kiss that the vampire makes contact, drains the lifeblood, thereby enervating the victim and starting the process of possession. The kiss is as crucial as it is oxymoronic—it is awful and sensuous, hideous and exciting. Since the publication of *Dracula* and the movie adaptations the fiend usually makes contact on the neck just below the ear, but previously the vampire was thought to literally suck the lifeblood out of his victim by kissing on the mouth. The kiss, as it is the only contact between demon and victim, is fraught with sexual connotations, for it provides a sublimated way to combine pleasure with sin, sucking with devouring, kissing with biting. On the surface, it is an apt image of energy transfer, referring back to such innocent pleasures as the nursing babe drawing in his mother's life through his mouth. In fact Lawrence describes the process at its most acceptable level—Anna Brangwen is nursing her daughter Ursula:

> It was enough that she had milk and could suckle her child: Oh, Oh, the bliss of the little life sucking milk of her body! Oh, Oh, Oh the bliss, as the infant grew stronger, of the two tiny hands clutching, catching blindly yet passionately at knowledge, of the sudden consummate peace as the little body sank, the mouth and throat sucking, sucking, sucking, drinking life from her to make a new life, almost sobbing with passionate joy of receiving its own existence, the tiny hands clutching frantically as the nipple was drawn back, not to be gainsaid (*R*, 210).

Lawrence applies this principle of mutual energy exchange to all the relationships described in *The Rainbow* and *Women in Love*; it is only when one of his Miriamesque characters is described in one of the later stages of "sensational experience" that the process becomes vampiric. The best explanation of this process outside these novels occurs in a piece he wrote on Edgar Allan Poe which he was working on in Cornwall after the publication of *The Rainbow* and during the revisions of *Women in Love*.[17] First he explains the psychology of human interaction:

> The central law of all organic life is that each organism is intrinsically isolate and single in itself.
> The moment its isolation breaks down, and there comes an actual mixing and confusion, death sets in.
> This is true of every individual organism, from man to amoeba.
> But the secondary law of all organic life is that each organism only lives through contact with other matter, assimilation, and contact with other life, which means assimilation of new vibrations, non-material. Each individual organism is vivified by intimate contact with fellow organisms: up to a certain point. (*SCAL*, 331)

But if that "certain point" is passed, if the struggle for contact becomes too frenetic, then one lover may seek to dominate or, in Lawrence's terms, to "know" the other. When this happens, the life membranes of the weaker begin to rupture as the lovers vibrate to such a pitch that "the nerves begin to break, to bleed as it were, and a form of death sets in." (*SCAL*, 331) As with Lawrence, Poe usually has the female (Morella, Ligeia, Berenice) acting as the devourer, although she is often introduced to the demonic pleasures of eccentric love by her male consort. Lawrence explains what happens when the lovers lose their balance:

> It is easy to see why each man kills the thing he loves. To know a living thing is to kill it. You have to kill a thing to know it satisfactorily. For this reason, the desirous consciousness, the *spirit*, is a vampire.
>
> One should be sufficiently intelligent and interested to know a good deal *about* any person one comes into close contact with. *About* her. Or *about* him.
>
> But to try to *know* any living being is to try to suck the life out of that being. . . . It is the temptation of a vampire fiend, is this knowledge. (*SCAL*, 335)

## II

> As a matter of fact, unless a woman is held, by man, safe within the bounds of belief, she becomes inevitably a destructive force. She can't help herself. . . . But let a woman loose from the bounds and restraints of man's fierce belief, in his gods and in himself, and she becomes a gentle devil. She becomes subtly diabolic . . . [18]

From the very first Anna Lensky is described in terms that while not precisely vampiric are nonetheless in the Gothic tradition of the possessed child. She has "unblinking" (*R*, 38) "resentful black eyes," (*R*, 27, 38) "wild fierce hair," (*R*, 37) is called a "changeling," "bewitched," (*R*, 28) "a wild thing," (*R*, 93) "a savage," (*R*, 80) and although she goes to church she cannot abide the rosary (*R*, 100) or for that matter the service itself. (*R*, 93) It is with her stepfather, Tom, that she initiates the first of her lamiaesque encounters. One of the characteristics of folklore demons is that they are able to metamorphose into animals, and the vampire is no exception. The male vampire is able to turn himself into a wolf or a bat while the lamia can change at will into a snake.[19] Anna is described with all the lamia's serpentine attributes: "a little darting forward of the head, something like a viper;" (*R*, 62) "she hissed forward her head," (*R*, 65) yet she is also her father's darling, loving to cuddle up next to him in his chair or on the gig.

In two scenes Lawrence hints of her potentially demonic nature and the weird symbiosis between father and daughter. First he mentions that Anna never sleeps with her eyes completely shut, which is also a trait of the vampire: "The little Anna clung around her mother's neck. The fair, strange face of the child looked over the shoulder of the mother, all asleep but the eyes, and these wide and dark. . . ." (*R*, 38) "The child was asleep, the eyelids not quite shut, showing a slight film of black pupil between. Why did she not shut her eyes?" (*R*, 75)[20] But more revealing is her response to her father's death, for here Lawrence seems to be pulling out all stops to show the vampiric nature of all human relationships, even subtly incestuous ones.[21] "When Anna heard the news [that her stepfather was dead], she pressed back her head and rolled her eyes, as if something were reaching forward to bite at her throat." (*R*, 247) Are we to believe that there may be some diabolical relationship between them, some sublimated energy flow between father and daughter? The analogy, if indeed I am reading this correctly, is as bold as it is apt, and prepares us to understand the other masculine relationship Anna has, namely with her stepcousin Will.

The Anna/Will relationship is both a condensation and a prefiguring of male-female interactions to come. It starts abruptly: they meet, become spellbound, and kiss. Here is their first kiss (as it will later be repeated), with the male as aggressor.

> Her breast was near him; his head lifted like an eagle's. She did not move. Suddenly, with an incredibly quick, delicate movement, he put his arms round her and drew her to him. It was quick, cleanly done, like a bird that swoops and sinks close, closer.
> He was kissing her throat. She turned and looked at him. Her eyes were dark and flowing with fire (*R*, 112).

Paradoxically it is Will, the eagle/vampire who is being caught in Anna's Circesque web, for the participants will soon reverse roles. Slowly she takes control, slowly he wastes away, becoming dependent on her for life itself until she realizes she must cast him off.

> His hovering near her, wanting her to be with him, the futility of him, the way his hands hung, irritated her beyond bearing. She turned on him blindly and destructively, he became a mad creature, black and electric with fury. The dark storms rose in him, his eyes glowed black and evil, he was fiendish in his thwarted soul.
> There followed two black and ghastly days, when she was set in anguish against him, and he felt as if he were in a black, violent underworld, and his wrists quivered murderously. And she resisted him. He seemed a dark, almost evil thing, pursuing her, hanging on to her, burdening her. She would give anything to have him removed. (*R*, 148)

Yet when she needs his energy he is there and willing. "He could not bear to think of her tears—he could not bear it. He wanted to go to her and pour out his heart's blood to her. He wanted to give everything to her. He wanted to give everything to her, all his blood; to the last dregs, pour everything away to her. He yearned with passionate desire to offer himself to her, utterly." (*R*, 151)

His death wish comes to fruition before even he is aware of what has happened. In "Anna Victrix" she finally literally has her man; "He did not understand, he had yielded, given away. There was no understanding. There could be only acquiescence and submission, and tremulous wonder of consummation." (*R*, 153) But in her victory, like the praying mantis, she has destroyed her mate. He fights back, but too late: "Dark and destroyed, his soul running with blood, he tasted of death." (*R*, 168) He has become subservient to her. She has made him bleed (*R*, 166) and as with the vampire of lore, he has been consumed in fire.[22] Now with the male docile, submissive, enervated, and bled, the new female generation can begin.

Ursula, the result of their dark union, draws life and energy from her battling parents, and in so doing pacifies them as Anna had done for Tom and Lydia. Here starts the first variation on the theme, for Ursula will replay that role, with some modification, that her mother and grandmother had played before her. She must now find a man, a livelihood of her own. The man she finds is much like Lydia Brangwen's first husband, Paul Lensky, for Anton Skrebensky is a slight, indolent, intellectual, aristocratic Middle European.

Ursula is as "fated" to meet Anton as her mother had been to meet Will. But Anton is not the man Ursula's father finally became. He is spineless from the start, pallid, already enervated, and it is not long before we see what is becoming the central act of the male-female relationship, the infamous kiss.

> This his mouth drew near, pressing open her mouth, a hot, drenching surge rose within her, she opened her lips to him, in pained, poignant eddies she drew him nearer, she let him come farther, his lips came and surging, surging, soft, oh soft, yet oh, like the powerful surge of water, irresistible, till with a little blind cry, she broke away.
>
> She heard him breathing heavily, strangely, beside her. A terrible and magnificent sense of his strangeness possessed her. (*R*, 297-98)

Ursula soon realizes he is in her power, realizes she can "live off" him and indeed proceeds to do so: "she reached him her mouth and drank his full kiss, drank it fuller and fuller." (*R*, 302)

> Looking at him, at his shadowy, unreal, wavering presence a sudden lust seized her, to lay hold of her and tear him and make him into nothing. Her hands and wrists felt immeasurably hard and strong, like blades. He waited there beside her like a shadow which she wanted to dissipate, destroy as the moonlight destroys a darkness, annihilate, have done with. (*R*, 319)

> She seemed to be destroying him. He was reeling, summoning all his strength to keep his kiss upon her, to keep himself in the kiss.
>
> But hard and fierce she had fastened upon him . . . destroying him, destroying him in the kiss. And her soul crystallised with triumph, and his soul was dissoved with agony and annihilation. So she held him there, the victim, consumed, annihilated. She had triumphed; he was not any more. (*R*, 320)

Finally, as a sign of complete mastery she is able not just to annihilate but resurrect as well:

> Her heart was warm, her blood was dark and warm and soft. She laid her hand caressively on Anton's shoulder.
>
> "Isn't it lovely?" she said, softly coaxingly, caressingly. And she began to caress him to life again. For he was dead. And she intended that he should never know, never become aware of what had been. She would bring him back from the dead without leaving him one trace of fact to remember his annihilation by . (*R*, 321)

She has drained him and revived him, made him a coreless, bloodless initiate of the walking dead ("To his own intrinsic life, he was dead. And he could not rise again from the dead. His soul lay in the tomb.") (*R*, 326) Since he is enervated, he can no longer furnish her life, and so she turns, as Lawrence's characters will later do in *Women in Love*, elsewhere.[23]

Six years pass before Anton returns. Away from Ursula in Africa he has been revived, but it will prove a short, unhappy revival:

> He kissed her, with his soft, enveloping kisses, and she responded to them completely, her mind, her soul gone out. Darkness cleaving to darkness, she hung

close to him, pressed herself into soft flow of his kiss, pressed herself down, down to the source and core of his kiss, herself covered and enveloped in the warm, fecund flow of his kiss, that travelled over her, flowed over her, covered her, flowed over the last fibre of her, so they were one stream, one dark fecundity, and she clung at the core of him, with her lips holding open the very bottommost source of him. (*R*, 447)

What little life he has regenerated flows here to Ursula as she, the predator, consumes him. Once again we watch his slow demise:

She waited, every moment of the day, for his next kiss. She admitted it to herself in shame and bliss. Almost consciously, she waited. He waited, but, until the time came, more unconsciously. When the time came that he should kiss her again, a prevention was an annihilation to him. He felt his flesh go grey, he was heavy with a corpse-like inanition, he did not exist, if the time passed unfulfilled. (*R*, 450) . . .

He felt like a corpse that is inhabited with just enough life to make it appear as any other of the spectral, unliving beings which we call people in our dead language. . . . He felt as if his life were dead. His soul extinct. The whole being of him had become sterile, he was a spectre, divorced from life. He had no fullness, he was just a flat shape. (*R*, 457)

Then, finally, he is shattered:

His drawn, strangled face watched her blankly for a few moments, then a strange sound took place in his throat. She started, came to herself, and, horrified, saw him. His head made a queer motion, the chin jerked back against the throat, the curious, crowing, hiccupping sound came again, his face twisted like insanity, and he was crying, crying blind and twisted as if something were broken which kept him in control.
"Tony—don't," she cried, starting up. (*R*, 466-67)

In keeping with the vampire myth, the victim does not physically die, but rather becomes an active participant in the process that destroys him. She, the lamia, the devourer, has made him party to her appetites, only to have the balance of horror reverse as he now turns on her. At last Skrebensky becomes "an incubus upon her," (*R*, 471) desperately attacking back.

This is a situation that cannot endure. This is the situation where, in Lawrence's words, the lovers' vibration has risen to such a pitch that the nervous membranes must break, and indeed they do. In a scene that could come from Lewis's *Monk,* Maturin's *Melmoth the Wanderer,* or Stoker's *Dracula*, Lawrence has Ursula, like a hideous Goya character, devour her mate.[24] On the moonlit Lincolnshire coast among the dunes, she consumes him:

She prowled, ranging on the edge of the water like a possessed creature, and he followed her. . . . And she seized hold of his arm, held him fast, as if captive, and walked him a little way by the edge of the dazzling, dazing water.
Then there in the great flare of light, she clinched hold of him, hard, as if suddenly she had the strength of destruction, she fastened her arms round him and tightened him in her grip, whilst her mouth sought his in a hard, rending, ever-increasing kiss, till his body was powerless in her grip, his heart melted in fear from the fierce, beaked, harpy's kiss. The water washed again over their feet, but she took no notice

till she had the heart of him. Then, at last, she drew away and looked at him—looked at him. He knew what she wanted. (*R*, 478-80) . . .

"Have you done with me?" he asked her at length, lifting his head.
"It isn't me," she said. "You have done with me—we have done with each other."
(*R*, 480)

And indeed they have. She has had her fill. There is no more love between them, no energy flow, no possibility for flux, no life, no blood.

This then is the circle at its greatest circumference—just at the moment of bursting. It is the discordant codetta that ends this movement of Lawrence's symphony of human affairs. The rhetoric of horror has reached a wondrous percussive crescendo. As with all such scenes, the horror is not actual but metaphorical. We realize, of course, that no actual bloodletting is going on here, instead something worse is happening: the process of enervation is undetectable to the observer yet the results are real. We may well hope for some reversal of this psychological "draining," at least some resolution between the characters, but there is none. We expect, for instance, that Ursula will carry Anton's child to term (if indeed she is really pregnant), that it will be born female, and that this new female will be able to return to the balanced world of her maternal grandmother.[25] But no, there is to be no child. Instead we are given Ursula's vision of the rainbow, an epiphany of sorts, a fain half-hope for new generation. Here biographical reality dashed fictional resolution, for *The Rainbow* was banned as obscene, World War I was more than a year old, Lawrence was dejected, quarrelsome, and despondent, and what seemed Ursula's hopeful vision was to prove possibly an illusion. For in *Women in Love* the cycle simply continues, the same themes are recapitulated until with Birkin there is at last the faint hint of genuine resolution.

Human relationships begin in *Women in Love* by precisely repeating the one that concluded *The Rainbow*, namely predatory female attempting to devour debilitated male. We know from the Wagnerian pattern of composition that Lawrence invented Ursula's affair with Skrebensky to prepare us for her success with Birkin; it was then Lawrence's task to prepare Birkin for Ursula.[26] He did this by introducing an Ursula figure without redeeming features, almost an Elizabethan humor character, in the figure of Hermione. To rearrange Lawrence's own analogy of describing characters on a continuum or as allotropic states of the same ego, Hermione is one extreme, coal dust to what will become Ursula's future diamond.[27] In both cases however, the theme is carbon—the man-destroying woman.

To understand the interactions between Hermione and Birkin it may be helpful, although critically dangerous, to consult Lawrence's discarded "Prologue." For here we can see Lawrence most obviously, perhaps blatantly, building the psychological analogy between powerful female/weak male and vampire/victim. However we must also remember that Lawrence ultimately deletes this chapter. Still for purposes of exposition of imagery and motifs the "Prologue" contains a wealth of information. For instance, when we first meet Birkin in the "Prologue," he is remarkably like Skrebensky—"hollow and ghastly to look at," while Hermione has become "fulfilled and rich." ("Prol.," 97) Again, like Ursula,

Hermione is waging the inner battle between Eros and Thanatos, on one hand wanting to consume, on the other wanting to be consumed, but never wanting to consummate. While she lusts for Birkin she also

> "wanted him to take her. She wanted him to take her, to break her with his passion, to destroy her with his desire, so long as he got satisfaction. She looked forward, tremulous, to a kind of death at his hands, she gave herself up. She would be broken and dying, destroyed, if only he would rise fulfilled .And she hated him, and despised him, for his incapacity to wreak his desire upon her, his lack of strength to crush his satisfaction from her. If only he could have taken her, destroyed her, used her all up, and been satisfied, she would be at last free. She might be killed, but it would be the death which gave her consummation. ("Prol.," 100)

Even before *Women in Love* opens, Birkin is just at the moment of collapse; her "deadly half-love" has almost drained him dry. "He became more hollow and deathly, more like a spectre with hollow bones. He knew that he was not very far from dissolution." ("Prol.," 103) This is of course the precise description of Skrebensky and we may well have the feeling we have met him before. It is here, however, that Ursula enters—Ursula who has blood and strength sufficient to revive Birkin from Hermione's deathly onslaught.

All this formulaic recapitulation of the vampire motif is lost in Lawrence's final version, for this chapter never made it to print. It is understandable why Lawrence excised this "Prologue"—the rhapsodic descriptions of homosexuality are maudlin and unsubstantiated, and Birkin is such a fop as to be unsympathetic, but the deletion, I think, is nonetheless unfortunate.[28] For this chapter is an important causeway between *The Rainbow* and *Women in Love*, preparing us for Birkin's battle with Hermione by reminding us of Skrebensky's duel with Ursula. It reminds us how truly dangerous Lawrence felt the predatory female could become if not resisted.

Hermione is not merely as Julian Moynahan has asserted in passing, "like a kind of vampire figure:" Of all Lawrence's females she is *most* like a vampire.[29] In no characterization so far has Lawrence been more insistent on the analogy. Hermione is serpentine: "coiled to strike," (*WL*, 10) "like a pythoness;" (*WL*, 35, 290) she is the "spectre" (*WL*, 289) with the "phosphorescent face," (*WL*, 131) literally "craving" (*WL*, 11) Birkin, attempting first to transfix him with her hypnotic stare (*WL*, 16) and then possess him. (pass.) She is indeed, as Birkin diagnoses, "the woman wailing for her demon lover;" (*WL*, 36) Lawrence here may be depending on our ability to recall possible vampiric allusions in "Kubla Khan," as he earlier in *The Rainbow* referred to the Lamia myth in "Christabel."[30]

Although at the beginning of *Women in Love* Hermione is full-fleshed and healthy, Birkin's refusal to enter any sort of rapprochement soon deprives her of his vitality. She becomes pale and weak, now all the more desperate for his strength. In descriptions almost as Gothic as Ursula's sucking life from Skrebensky, Lawrence pictures Hermione's death-agonies:

> Hermione looked at him along her narrow, pallid cheeks. Her eyes were strange and drugged, heavy under their heavy, drooping lids. Her thin bosom shrugged convulsively. He stared back at her, devilish and unchanging. With another strange,

sick convulsion, she turned away, as if she were sick, could feel dissolution setting-in her body. . . .
She suffered the ghastliness of dissolution, broken and gone in a horrible corruption. And he stood and looked at her unmoved. She strayed out pallid and preyed-upon like a ghost, like one attacked by the tomb-influences which dog us. And she was gone like a corpse. (*WL*, 82)

She is literally wasting away, "sick, like a *revenant*," (*WL*, 83) almost "unconscious, sunk in a heavy half-trance," (*WL*, 83) until finally "she suffered sheer dissolution like a corpse, and was unconscious of everything save the horrible sickness of dissolution that was taking place within her body and soul." (*WL*, 85) All sustenance denied her, she even "seemed to grip the hours by the throat, to force her life from them." (*WL*, 91) Lawrence thankfully did not pursue the temporal applications of the vampire myth, as it could only produce imagery beyond even his ability to sustain it; but still the reader gets the point—Hermione bleeds everything, not just organic life, but life in the abstract as well.

The analogy of energy flow and blood transfer is by no means circumscribed by the vampire imagery. In fact Lawrence is so intent on describing the interactive process between overly demanding female and weak male that he makes it part of the fugal organization of many subsidiary scenes. Thus although they have blood in common, the metaphorical vehicle has been slightly altered so that the vampirism is blurred while the tenor remains the same. Minette's fascination with the bleeding hand, (*WL*, 63-64) the "Blutbruderschaft" or the intermingling of Birkin and Gerald's blood, (*WL*, 198) or the hemorrhaging death of Mr. Crich (*WL*, 209-10) are variations on this theme of human interaction with blood as common image.[31] So too in a sense is the macabre death scene of Diana Crich and her rescuer at the "Water-Party." For here in an imagistic epitome is the predatory female not draining blood but rather throttling life from the male: "These bodies of the dead were not recovered till towards dawn. Diana had her arms round the neck of the young man, choking him. 'She killed him,' said Gerald." (*WL*, 181)

All of these scenes, scenes that appear at first so extraneous, are included to prepare for us, and provide accompaniment to, the major vampiric action of the novel—the battle for life between Gerald and Gudrun. Early on we are introduced to Gerald as a man's man, unlike Skrebensky or Will or even Birkin. Throughout the novel he exerts this power over both man (the colliers) and beast (the mare at the railroad tracks, the rabbit). But from the outset he is no match for Gudrun: "he would be helpless in the association with her." (*WL*, 114) The more he struggles for domination, the more potent she becomes, the more lamia like, the more fatal: "Gudrun looked at Gerald with strange, darkened eyes, strained with underworld knowledge, almost supplicating, like those of a creature which is at his mercy, yet which is his ultimate victor." (*WL*, 234) Ironically his power makes him all the more vulnerable, as Lawrence details in another controlling analogy for interpersonal dynamics—current, like blood flow, cannot be stopped up, and especially cannot be redirected back against itself without disastrous consequences.

The battle for this current becomes most intense, as we have seen before, in the kiss, the kiss of death. In a scene reminiscent of Ursula's and Skrebensky's seaside death embrace, Gudrun and Gerald meet under the colliery railroad bridge. It is here that Gerald, like Will Brangwen and Anton Skrebensky, initiates the perverse Eucharist.[32]

> His arms were fast around her, he seemed to be gathering her into himself, her warmth, her softness, her adorable weight, drinking in the suffusion of her physical being, avidly. He lifted her, and seemed to pour her into himself, like wine into a cup.
>
> "This is worth everything," he said in a strange, penetrating voice.
>
> So she relaxed, and seemed to melt, to flow into him, as if she were some infinitely warm and precious suffusion filling into his veins, like an intoxicant. Her arms were round his neck, he kissed her and held her perfectly suspended, she was all slack and flowing into him, and he was the firm, strong cup that receives the wine of her life. (*WL*, 323)

From this encounter Gerald first draws strength, gains access to reserves of energy otherwise unknown. But to do so he becomes "possessed," he becomes a creature of the night, endowed with "senses . . . almost supernaturally keen," (*WL*, 333) travelling through the darkness to his lover with "occult carefulness." (*WL*, 334) In the chapter "Death and Love," which Mark Schorer aptly retitled "Love as Death," Gerald, the night stalker, sneaks into the sleeping Brangwen household. He makes his way to Gudrun; once he is by her bedside, Gudrun realizes that his mysterious powers have flowed from her, and that somehow she must stop the flow before he drains her. "He was inevitable as a supernatural being. When she had seen him, she knew. She knew there was something fatal in the situation, and she must accept it. Yet she must challenge him." (*WL*, 335) And challenge him she does, with all the wiles of her sister, all the inherited cunning of her mother and grandmother. She has given him appetites for energy that will never be sated. She has made him dependent on her for his life:

> As he drew nearer to her, he plunged deeper into her enveloping soft warmth, a wonderful creative heat that penetrated his veins and gave him life again. . . . All his veins, that were murdered and lacerated, healed softly as life came pulsing in, stealing invisibly into him as if it were the all-powerful effluence of the sun. His blood, which seemed to have been drawn back into death, came ebbing on the return, surely, beautifully, powerfully.
>
> He felt his limbs growing fuller and flexible with life, his body gained an unknown strength. (*WL*, 337)

By the time they arrive in the Tyrolean Alps, however, Gudrun has almost been destroyed by the obscene monster she helped create. Gerald has become too demanding, too dependent. Finally with the "bat-like" (*WL*, 413) Loerke's assistance, she "turned aside, breaking the spell, (*WL*, 404) refusing Gerald her life. Then one night he is sent to bed—in Lawrence's rather horrid pun—without his dinner: "When he slept he seemed to crouch down in his bed, lapped up in his own strength, that yet was hollow. And Gudrun slept strongly, a victorious sleep." (*WL*, 407)

It is now all over but the actual dying. Deprived of his life support, Gerald physically shrivels up, as had his predecessor Anton Skrebensky. But Anton was made lucky by his own weaknesses; he was able to escape his own appetites for blood energy by separating himself from Ursula. Gerald the mechanical man, is not so resourceful. He cannot escape; he is so brittle he cannot bend, only break. Death is the only choice, and so like his literary predecessor, Emily Bronte's Heathcliff, he burns himself out, he consumes himself; he dies, in a sense, of starvation.[33]

In the end only Ursula and Birkin remain. They are the only ones in this generation who have achieved the literal and figurative marriage of opposites. They have "struggled into being" primarily because Birkin has refused to mix blood with Ursula. She has been bled, (*WL*, 183) but she has never bled him.

> He knew that Ursula was referred back to him. He knew his life rested with her. But he would rather not live than accept the love she proffered.The old way of love seemed a dreadful bondage, a sort of conscription. What it was in him he did not know, but the thought of love, marriage, and children, and a life lived together, in the horrible privacy of domestic and connubial satisfaction, was repulsive. He wanted something clearer, more open, cooler, as it were. The hot narrow intimacy between man and wife was abhorrent. The way they shut their doors, these married people, and shut themselves into their own exclusive alliance with each other, even in love, disgusted him (*WL*, 191).

So they battle it out, not for control but for balance, to become "like two poles of one force, like two angels, or two demons." (*WL*, 191) Even though Ursula wants "to drink him down—ah, like a lifedraught," (*WL*, 257) to quaff him "to the dregs," (*WL*, 258) he will never give in. Ursula in a scene of ironic description furiously calls him an "eater of corpses," (*WL*, 299) but the description better fits her. For Birkin is neither eater nor eaten; he is the unfusable, unmergeable, unconsumable, independent man. Birkin is the hero of the piece, and as such he sets the pattern for a masculine figure that will become dominant in Lawrence's fiction from here on. As Charles Rossman has noted, *Women in Love* is a decisive turning point in Lawrence's treatment of character, for in it he makes a transition from strong women who destroy men to positive men who destroy women.[34] The male, starting with Birkin, wins the "fight for phallic reality" and the women become not the destroyers but (at best) the source of his strength, not lamias but acolytes. The female role is still not one of equality; as a matter of fact with the exception of Connie Chatterley it is still lopsided, but now in the other direction.[35]

Lawrence never returns to the lamia myth again, for he never returns to this view of the female. He has taken both the character-type and the myth about as far as they can go before disintegrating into self-parody. Still when the analogy works, as I think it does best with Ursula and Skrebensky, it is marvelously effective, and readers who have complained about Lawrence's excessive hyperbole may simply have misunderstood his mythopoetic design. For Lawrence defanged and otherwise temporized the macabre aspects of the vampire while still asserting the validity of the process of energy transfer, and it is this psychological process, minus the Gothic machinery, that he repeats again and again in *The Rainbow* and *Women in Love* to show what happens when the "struggle into being through love" goes awry.

*Studies in the Novel*, 11, 1979.

## Notes

[1] For an investigation of Lawrence's almost "obsessive repetition," see Robert B. Hailman, "Nomad, Monads, and the Mystique of the Soma," *Sewanee Review*, 68 (1960), 650, and for the forward/sideways progression see, among others, F. R. Leavis, *D. H. Lawrence: Novelist* (New York: Alfred A. Knopf, 1956), p. 122, and E. K. Brown, *Rhythm in the Novel* (Toronto: Univ. of Toronto Press, 1950), chap. 2.

[2] Lawrence's works are cited parenthetically in the text by abbreviated title and page numbers from the following editions: *R, The Rainbow* (New York: Viking Press, Compass Books, 1961); *WL, Women in Love* (New York: Viking Press, Compass Books, 1960); *SCAL, Studies in Classic American Literature* as included in *D. H. Lawrence: Selected Literary Criticism*, ed. Anthony Beal (New York: Viking Press, Compass Books, 1966), and "Prol.," "Prologue to *Women in Love*" in *Phoenix II: Uncollected, Unpublished and Other Prose Works by D. H. Lawrence*, ed. Warren Roberts and Harry T. Moore (New York: Viking Press, 1968).

[3] For a study of Lawrence's interest in Wagner see William Blissett, "D. H. Lawrence, D'Annunzio, Wagner," *Contemporary Literature*, 7 (1966), 21-46. William York Tindall is less enthusiastic: "Lawrence appears to have adored [Wagner] as much as he detested eighteenth-century composers, Lawrence had no understanding of music." (*D. H. Lawrence & Susan His Cow* [New York: Columbia Univ. Press, 1939], p. 170).

[4] I belabor this musical analogy in part because it seems most productive to discuss Lawrence's literary forms in nonliterary terms. For instance, Mark Schorer ("*Women in Love* and Death," rpt. in *The Achievement of D. H. Lawrence*, eds., Frederick J. Hoffman and Harry T. Moore [Norman: Univ. of Oklahoma Press, 1953] pp. 169-70) discusses the work in terms of choreography. But I suspect music is the more comprehensive metaphor—see Angus Wilson and others who have likened *Women in Love* to a quartet or two duets.

[5] Lawrence's reductive view of women has of late been examined and reexamined, often more to prove sociological arguments than to provide literary insight: see Simone de Beauvoir, *The Second Sex* (New York: Bantam Books, 1961), p. 204; Kate Millett, *Sexual Politics* (Garden City, N.Y.: Doubleday, 1970), and Norman Mailer, "The Prisoner of Sex," *Harper's Magazine*, 242 (March 1971), 70. For an examination of this type of female in Lawrence's short stories see Kinglsey Widmer, *The Art of Perversity* (Seattle: Univ. of Washington Press, 1962), chap. 2, "The Destructive Woman."

[6] Birkin's initial homosexuality is obvious in Lawrence's deleted first chapter. This chapter belongs with *Women in Love* if we are to understand the Birkin/Hermione and especially the Birkin/Gerald relationships. See George H. Ford, "An Introductory Note to D. H. Lawrence's 'Prologue' to *Women in Love*," *The Texas Quarterly*, 6 (Spring 1963), 92-97.

[7] This argument is made today in a slightly different context, namely, that the victim of a rape attack has secretly invited her own defilement. And while there may be some truth in this in isolated instances, the raped is hardly as guilty as the raper. In these novels by Lawrence the male victim is hardly as guilty as the female attacker. Mark Schorer, "*Women in Love* and Death," attempts an interepretation of *Woman in Love* in terms of such invited oppositions.

[8] The influence of Hardy seems obvious, especially when one realizes that Lawrence wrote his "Study of Thomas Hardy" just before writing *The Rainbow*. For more on the possible importance of Hardy on Lawrence's negative female characterizations see, among

others, Frank Kermode, *D. H. Lawrence* (New York: Viking Press, 1973), pp. 43-45, and Richard Swigg, *Lawrence, Hardy and American Literature* (London: Oxford Univ. Press, 1972).

9 For more of Poe's use of the vampire see Lee J. Richmond, "Edgar Allan Poe's 'Morella': Vampire of Volition," *Studies in Short Fiction*, 9 (Winter 1972), 93-94; Lyle H. Kendall, Jr., "The Vampire Motif in 'The Fall of the House of Usher,'" *College English* 24 (March 1963), 450-53; and my forthcoming article, "Poe and the Vampire Motif," *Studies in Short Fiction*.

10 For a more complete view of the destructive female in Lawrence's fiction before *The Rainbow* see Charles Rossman, "'You are the call and I am the answer': D. H. Lawrence and Women," *The D. H. Lawrence Review*, 8 (Fall, 1975), 258-68. To the best of my knowledge Lawrence first uses the lamia motif in *Sons and Lovers* with the characterization of Miriam Leivers, who is described by Mrs. Morel as "one of those who will want to suck man's soul out till he has none of his own left." Here is a typical scene:

> She seemed to want him, and he resisted. He resisted all the time. He wanted now to give her passion and tenderness, and he could not. He felt that she wanted the soul out of his body, and not him. All his strength and energy she drew into herself through some channel which united them. She did not want to meet him, so that there were two of them, man and woman together. She wanted to draw all of him into her (chap. 8).

11 Although the vampire had long been a subject in folklore, the first vampires in serious literature were in English Romantic poetry—in Coleridge's "Christabel" Southey's *Thalaba the Destroyer*, and Keats's "Lamia." The vampire's first appearance in the novel was in John Polidori's *Vampyre* (1819), famous more because it was published under Byron's name than for any literary merit. From this auspicious beginning the vampire degenerated into the hero of "penny dreadfuls" surfacing at midcentury to be incorporated into the mythic detail of Emily Bronte's Heathcliff, then submerged again until revived in the best of all vampire novels, Bram Stoker's *Dracula*. (1897)

12 The pioneering work on vampires was Montague Summers, *The Vampire: His Kith and Kin* (1929; rpt. New Hyde Park, N.Y.; University Books, 1960), which has since been followed by a spate of paperbook works in part based on it; Gabriel Ronay, *The Truth about Dracula* (New York; Stein and Day, 1974); Douglass Hill, *The History of Ghosts, Vampires and Werewolves* (New York: Harper and Row, 1973); Leonard Wolf, *A Dream of Dracula: In Search of the Living Dead* (New York: Popular Library, 1972); Anthony Masters, *The Natural History of the Vampire* (London: Mayflower Books, 1974); Nancy Garden, *Vampires* (New York: J.B. Lippincott, 1973); Raymond T. McNally and Radu Florescu, *In Search of Dracula* (New York: Warner Paperback, 1973); and Basil Cooper *The Vampire in Legend Fact and Art* (Secaucus, N.J.: The Citadel Press, 1974).

13 The role of the victim is glossed in Masters, Pt. II; Wolf, chap. 4; Ronay, Pt. I; McNally and Florescu, chap. 7; Summers, chap. 3; and Garden, chap. 2. The fact that Anton and Gerald initiate the affair seems clear; with Will it is not so; however, they all initiate the kiss. More perplexing is the interaction of Tom and Lydia. I am especially puzzled by Lawrence's use of the threshold, as this is an important barrier for any demon to cross. Lydia, of Polish birth (alas, not Transylvanian), seems to need no invitation:

> Another day, at tea-time, as he sat alone at table, there came a knock at the front door. It startled him like a portent. No one ever knocked at the front door. He rose and began slotting back the bolts, turning the big key. When he

had opened the door, the strange woman stood on the threshold. . . . what was there, in her very standing motionless, which affected him?

He stepped aside and she at once entered the house, as if the door had been opened to admit her. That startled him. It was the custom for everybody to wait on the doorstep till asked inside (*R*, 29).

It should also be remembered that the man-consuming women (Anna, Ursula, Gudrun) are not really Brangwen women at all—they are closer genetically to Paul Lensky than to Tom Brangwen. Lawrence may have intended these initial scenes as a kind of explanation for the second and third generation's behavior. Perhaps Lydia should be seen as a kind of ur-lamia.

[14] The vampire superstition was revived in the Middle Ages, ironically by the Catholic church, which used it as a lever to keep in line those faltering in faith. The sinner, the apostate, the suicide, the excommunicate, the unbaptized all could become vampires after death. The priest was both the vampire killer and expert on vampire lore; see Masters, Part IV, and Ronay, chap. 2.

[15] For more on the lamia myth see, among others, Garden, chap. 8, and Summers, pp. 226-29.

[16] For more on Lawrence's mixing of mythic allusions and the development of character see Donald R. Eastman, "Myth and Fate in the Characters of *Women in Love*," *D.H. Lawrence Review*, 9 (Summer 1976), 177-93.

[17] Lawrence was reading and writing about Poe during the composition of *Women in Love* and possibly *The Rainbow* as well. His first essay on Poe was written between 1917-18 in Cornwall and appeared in the *English Review* for 1919. It does not include the references to Poe's lovers as vampires. However the 1923 book version does, so it seems reasonable to assume that between 1918 and 1922 Lawrence is thinking about the specific analogy of the lover as vampire, perhaps as a result of his own fiction. For the 1919 version see *The Symbolic Meaning* ed. Armin Arnold (New York: Viking Press, 1964), pp. 105-20.

[18] This is Lawrence's view just after *Women in Love*, as expressed in the 1924 version of "Nathanial Hawthorne and *The Scarlet Letter* (*SCAL*, 356). In the earlier version he was not so stridently antifeminist.

[19] The relationship between the lamia and the snake is clear in literature (cf. Coleridge's "Christabel," Keats's "Lamia") and based on folklore; see n. 15 above.

[20] That vampires sleep with their eyes open, see, for instance, Garden, p. 64; Summers, chap. 3; and Cooper, chap. 3. This is a crucial bit of lore, for since the vampire is always seeing he will know who is attempting to destroy him.

[21] While it is true that Tom and Anna are not related by blood, their relationship is psychologically incestuous. Lawrence believed that neurosis was primarily caused by incestuous desires. Incest is also part of the vampire superstition. Since vampires first attack those whom they loved best, usually the first victim is a spouse or relative. For Lawrence's views on incest, see "Parent Love" in *Fantasia of the Unconscious*.

[22] Will's death by fire is implied in his reaction to Anna's victory (*R*, 181). After this, Will is "born again" and now, like the vampire of folklore, he prowls the evenings for victims of his own. He finds one, a shopgirl, Jeannie, and the process of eccentric love continues. As they are walking into the dark night,

He was alert in every sense and fibre, and yet quite sure and steady, and lit up, as if transfused. He had a free sensation of walking in his own darkness, not in anybody else's world at all. He was purely a world to himself, he had nothing

to do with any general consciousness. Just his own senses were supreme. All
the rest was external, insignificant, leaving him alone with this girl whom he
wanted to absorb. He did not care about her except that he wanted to overcome
her resistance, to have her in his power, fully and exhaustively to enjoy her (*R*,
227).

Once their eyes meet, "he seemed to hold her in his will". (*R*, 227) Then the inevitable
kiss:

> So he came at length to kiss her, and she was almost betrayed by his insidious
> kiss. Her open mouth was too helpless and unguarded. He knew this, and his
> first kiss was very gentle, and soft, and assuring, so assuring. So that her soft,
> defenceless mouth became assured, even bold, seeking upon his mouth. And he
> answered her gradually, gradually, his soft kiss sinking in softly, softly, but
> ever more heavily, more heavily yet, till it was too heavy for her to meet, and
> she began to sink under it.  She was sinking, sinking, his smile of latent
> gratification was becoming more tense, he was sure of her. (*R*, 228)

She escapes, leaving him both despondent and exhilarated, to turn like his uncle Tom to
his work and to his daughter for sustenance.

23 Ursula's relationship with Winifred Inger is also desultory. Lawrence realized the
rightful opponent of all love struggles is the opposite sex, just as it almost always is in the
vampire myth—the exception being Coleridge's "Christabel." Yet he also realized that
there is an onanistic desire to regenerate without opposition, without passing the confines
of one's own sex. In one almost throwaway scene that occurs between Ursula and the
melancholy Maggie Schofield, Lawrence hints of a possible symbiosis growing between
them. Maggie, jealous for Ursula's attention, tries to separate Ursula from her brother
Anthony, by inviting her for a walk in the woods.  They wander off into the park at
Belcote. They settle beneath "a big tree with a thick trunk twisted with ivy [where] Maggie
took out a book, and sitting lower down the trunk began to read Coleridge's 'Christabel.'
Ursula half listened.  She was wildly thrilled" (*R*, 415). Why "Christabel" and why is she
'thrilled' ? Because, I suspect, Lawrence knew what A. H. Nethercot has to remind the
twentieth-century reader, namely that Geraldine was a lamia preying on Christabel (cf. A.
H. Nethercot, *The Road to Tryermaine* [1939; rpt. New York: Russell & Russell, 1962]).
Lawrence here uses the literary allusion to show the possible similarity of the affairs, for in
Coleridge's poem Christabel meets Geraldine under an old oak tree covered with ivy. But
unlike Christabel, Ursula escapes for the moment at least, as Anthony, the noble knight of
the piece, arrives to break the spell.

24 This omophagic scene is more ghoulish than vampiric. The ghoul preys upon living
people, sucking brains and spinal fluid as well as blood. The ghoul has never been human
and usually acts in response to some external command. Often in folklore the two are
mixed, so that the vampire drinks the blood and eats the flesh, as is metaphorically
happening here with Ursula and Anton.

25 I am not alone in believing this: see Mark Kinkead-Weekes, "Eros and Metaphor:
Sexual Relationship in the Fiction of D. H. Lawrence," *Twentieth Century Studies*, I
(1969),11.  Lawrence's problems with endings, both in *The Rainbow* and *Women in Love*,
has been much discussed, nost notably in David Daiches, *The Novel and the Modern
World*, rec. ed. (Chicago: Univ. of Chicago Press, 1960), pp. 168 ff.; F. R. Leavis, *D. H.
Lawrence: Novelist*, p. 172; Alan Friedman, "Suspended Form: Lawrence's Theory of

Fiction in *Women in Love*" in *Twentieth Century Interpretations of Women in Love* (Englewood Cliffs, N.J.: Prentice-Hall, 1969), pp. 40-42.

[26] For an explanation of the composition of *The Rainbow* and *Women in Love* see Mark Kinkead-Weekes, "The Marble and the Statue," in *Imagined Worlds. Essays on Some English Novels and Novelists in Honor of John Butt,* eds., Maynard Mack and Ian Gregor (London: Methuen, 1968), pp. 371-418.

[27] "Letter to Edward Garnett, June 5, 1914," in *The Collected Letters of D. H. Lawrence*, ed. H. T. Moore (New York" Viking Press, 1962), p. 282.

[28] See George Ford, "An Introductory Note to D. H. Lawrence's 'Prologue' to *Women in Love*," pp. 96-97.

[29] Julian Moynahan, *The Deed of Life: The Novels and Tales of D. H. Lawrence* (Princeton: Princeton Univ. Press, 1963), p. 72.

[30] The demon lover in "Kubla Khan" has caused considerable critical investigation, of which the vampiric explanation is only one of many. See Nicolas K. Kiessling, "Demonic Dread: The Incubus Figure in British Literature" in *The Gothic Imagination*, ed. G. R. Thompson (Pullman, Wash.: Washington State Univ. Press, 1974), p. 37. For more on Lawrence's use of "Christabel" see n. 23.

[31] There is also the suggestion of a blood bond—almost a marriage ritual performed by the clawing rabbit—between Gerald and Gudrun in chap. 18; see Eliseo Vivas, *D. H. Lawrence: The Failure and Triumph of Art* (Evanston: Northwestern Univ. Press, 1960), pp. 250-54.

[32] The image of drinking the blood-red wine to partake of the energy of another is part of both Christian and folk traditions. These traditions met in the Middle Ages with the introduction of the newest sacrament in the Catholic church. The Eucharist was the most abstract of the sacraments, depending on the metaphorical understanding of Christ's words:

> Whoso eateth my flesh, and drinketh my blood, hath eternal life, and I will raise him up at the last day. For my flesh is meat indeed, and my blood is drink indeed. He that eateth my flesh, and drinketh my blood, dwelleth in me, and I in him. As the living Father hath sent me, and I live by the Father: so he that eateth me, even he shall live by me. (John 6:53-57)

Was it not equally sensible that this transubstantiation process could be reversed by the devil, who would celebrate a diabolical eucharist by drinking the blood of the sinner? For more see note 14 above.

[33] Lawrence had first read Bronte's *Wuthering Heights* in 1906 (Rose Marie Burwell, "A Catalogue of D. H. Lawrence's Reading from Early Childhood," *D. H. Lawrence Review*, 3 [Fall 1970], 204). Anton buys a copy of it for Ursula soon after they meet (*R*, 293). This may be Lawrence's ironic joke, for Heathcliff is described as if he were a vampire sucking life from the Earnshaws and Lintons. The final kiss scene at Thrushcross Grange, Heathcliff's digging up of Catherine's grave, his offer to drink Edgar's blood for her sake, and his strange death (almost a kind of suicide) all reinforce Nelly Dean's final question: "Was he a ghoul or a vampire?" (chap. 34) Gerald acts like Heathcliff—powerful, clingingly devoted, heroically demonic, and perhaps Lawrence is comparing his death to Heathcliff's.

[34] Charles Rossman, "'You are the call and I am the answer': D. H. Lawrence and Women," p. 273.

35 Rossman charts the rise of the Birkin type of male and catalogues his female helpmates, pp. 282-306.

# IV

# WOMEN IN LOVE

## Rebecca West, "Notes on Novels"

Many of us are cleverer than Mr. D.H. Lawrence and nearly all of us save an incarcerated few are much saner, but this does not affect the fact that he is a genius. It does, of course, affect the fact of his being an artist. *Women in Love* is flawed in innumerable places by Mr. Lawrence's limitations and excesses. His general ideas are poor and uncorrected, apparently, by any wide reading or much discussion; when he wants to represent Birkin, who is supposed to be the brilliant thinker of the book, as confounding the shallow Hermione with his power over reality, he puts into his mouth a collection of platitudes on the subject of democracy which would have drawn nothing from any woman of that intellectual level, except perhaps the remark that these things had been dealt with more thoroughly by Havelock Ellis in his essay on the spheres of individualism and Socialism. He is madly irritable. "The porter came up. 'A Bâle—deuxième classe?—Voilà!' And he clambered into the high train. They followed. The compartments were already some of them taken. But many were dim and empty. The luggage was stowed, the porter was tipped. 'Nous avons encore?' said Birkin, looking at his watch and at the porter. 'Encore une demi-heure,' with which, in his blue blouse, he disappeared. He was ugly and insolent." We are not told anything more about this porter. This is the full span of his tenuous existence in Mr. Lawrence's imagination. He has been called out of the everywhere into the here simply in order that for these two minutes he may be ugly and insolent. This is typical of Mr. Lawrence's indifference to that quality of serenity which is the highest form of decency. He thinks it natural that everybody should take their own Grand Guignol about with them in the form of an irritable nervous system and that it should give continuous performances. This prejudices his work in two ways. It makes him represent the characters whom he wishes to be regarded as normal as existing permanently in the throes of hyper-aesthesia. When Gerald Crich and Gudrun stay in London on their way to the Tyrol, her reactions to London, which she does not appear to like, are so extreme that one anticipates that Gerald will have to spend all his time abroad nursing her through a nervous breakdown, which is in fact not what happened. It also shatters the author's nerves so that his fingers are often too clumsy and tremulous to deal with the subtleties which his mind insists on handing them as subjects. There is, for example, a scene in an inn at Southwell, where Ursula has an extraordinary crisis of delight at some physical aspect of Birkin. At first reading it appears that this is simply a sexual crisis which Mr. Lawrence is describing according to his own well-worn formula, and one reflects with fatigue that Mr. Lawrence's heroines suffer from molten veins as inveterately as Sarah Gamp suffered from spasms, and that they demand as insistently just a thimbleful of union with reality. But then if one is a conscientious reader one perceives that this is wrong. There is something else. Ursula seems to have caught sight of some physical oddity about him, to have noticed for the first time that he was really Siamese twins. One thinks crossly, "Unobservant girl." But if one has a decent sense of awe one realises that the author of *Sons and Lovers* is probably trying to say something worth hearing, and one reads it over again, and in the end perceives that Mr. Lawrence is simply trying to convey that mystical sense of the sacredness of physical structure, quite apart from its aesthetic or sexual significance, which is within the experience of nearly all of us. Ursula, contemplating her lover's body, had a sudden realisation that flesh is blessed above all other substances because it is informed by life, that force of which there is such a stupendous abundance on this earth, which has such divine attributes as will and consciousness, which has so dark a past and so mysterious a future. It is a reasonable enough emotion, but Mr. Lawrence is so nerve-shattered by these extravagant leaps, which suggest that somebody has lit a little gunpowder under his sensorium, that he is unable to convey the spiritual incident save as a hot geyser of sensation.

But *Women in Love* is a work of genius. It contains characters which are masterpieces of pure creation. Birkin is not. The character whom an author designs as the mouthpiece of truth never is; always he is patronising and knowing, like "Our London Correspondent" writing his weekly letter in a provincial newspaper. But here is Hermione Roddice, the woman who stood beyond all vulgar judgment, yet could be reduced to misery by the slightest gesture of contempt from any servant because she had no real self and, though she could know, could not be. Mr. Lawrence could always conjure imaginary things into the world of the eye, and he makes visible the unhappy physical presence of Hermione, with her long face and her weight of heavy dull hair, her queer clothes, her strange appearance that made people want to jeer yet held them silent till she passed. In the scene where she sits at Birkin's table with Ursula and plays with the cat and coos Italian to it, and scores a barren victory by making the girl feel raw and vulgar and excluded by exercise of that static impressiveness which she has cultivated to conceal her dynamic nullity, he discloses the pathetic secret of her aching egotism with a marvellous appropriateness. He has found there the incident and the conversation that perfectly illustrate the spiritual fact he wishes to convey. There are also Mr. and Mrs. Crich, the mineowner and his wife, though their creation is not so indisputably pure as that of Hermione. One suspects that they were called into being in consequence of Mr. Lawrence's readings in German philosophy, that they are not only post but propter Nietzsche and Max Stirner. But they are great figures: the father, who loved to give to the poor out of his faith that "they through poverty and labour were nearer to God than he," until in time he became "some subtle funeral bird, feeding on the miseries of the people," a creature damp with continual pity; the mother, like a hawk, loathing the rusty black, cringing figures of his parasites, despising him for his perpetual indulgence in the laxer, gentler emotions, and bending over his dead body at the last in bitter contempt because his face was so beautiful, so unmarked by pride or the lordlier emotions. The persons who are most intimately concerned in the development of the main thesis of the book are not so satisfactory because that thesis deals with love. It is in itself an excellent thesis. It is a stern answer to the human cry, "I can endure the hatred the world bears me, and the hate I bear the world, if only there is one whom I love and who loves me." It declares: "No, that is not how it is. There shall be no one who loves you and no one whom you love, unless you first get in on loving terms with the world." Gerald Crich refuses to enter into an alliance of friendship with Birkin. He, the materialist, has no use for an expenditure of affection in a quarter where there is no chance of physical pleasure, and stakes his all on his union with Gudrun. This concentration itself wrecks that union. She finds him empty of everything but desire for her; he has had no schooling in altruistic love; he does not help her out of her own fatigued desire for corruption and decay, the peace of dissolution; and she breaks away from him. Thereby, because he has staked everything on her, he is destroyed. It is not really very abstruse, nor very revolutionary, nor very morbid. In *Antony and Cleopatra* Shakespeare permitted himself to say much the same sort of thing about the quality of love that arises between highly sexual people. But when Mr. Lawrence writes of love he always spoils his matter by his violent style. In an exquisite phrase Mrs. Mary Baker Eddy once remarked that the purpose of the relationship between the sexes is to "happify existence." There are times when Mr. Lawrence writes as if he thought its purpose was to give existence a black eye. His lovers are the Yahoos of Eros, and though Beauty may be in their spirits, it is certainly not in their manners. This is not represented as incidental to their characters, but as a necessary condition of love. It is a real flaw in Mr. Lawrence's temperament; but it is so marked and so apart from the rest of him that it no more spoils the book than a crack in the canvas spoils a beautiful picture.

There are, of course, many obvious distortions of life in *Women in Love* which it is easiest to consider as sheer meaningless craziness. There are, for instance, the extraordinary descriptions of the women's clothes, especially of Gudrun's stockings. She was more decorative about the legs than anybody has ever been except a flamingo. There are also incidents that flout probability or even possibility. There is that amazing scene when Hermione, who is supposed to be an effete aristocrat of unimpeachable manners, comes up behind Birkin, who is sitting on the sofa reading Thucydides as good as gold, and hits him on the head with a paperweight of lapis lazuli. This is certainly not the done thing. All this is without doubt not life as we know it, but the smallest reflection shows that it is not crazy and it has a meaning. The trouble is with Mr. Lawrence that he is so much of a poet that it is difficult for him to express himself in prose, and in particular in the prose required of a novel, and that he finds it impossible to express what he wants save by desperately devised symbols. He has felt that there is a quality about many women which makes them wear gay clothes and go actively yet not purposively about the world, and promote events that are never of the highest importance yet often interfere with others that are, which makes them, in fact, build a dome of many-coloured glass to stain the white light of eternity. He feels that every time that Gudrun appeared she was this quality made manifest to the eye, and he is at a loss how to convey it. In sheer desperation he ascribes to her these astonishing stockings. When one visualises those shapely, coloured ankles moving swiftly on those restless errands of destruction, one perceives that the touch is not meaningless at all, though it is clumsy. And the incident of Hermione and the paperweight also is a desperately devised symbol. He has wanted to express that a woman like her, bitter with a sense of spiritual insufficiency, would in the end turn against the lover whom she had wooed because of his extreme sufficiency, and become envious because she could not steal his sufficiency, and try to destroy him. In his impatience he has dragged into his novel this very dark scene which, though it is a distortion of life's physical appearances, nevertheless succeeds in conveying the spiritual truth with which he is concerned at the moment. To object to this on the ground that an author has no right to distort life's appearances for his own ends is to subject literature to an unreasonable restriction. It is not imposed on the art of painting. The greatest artists, such as Velasquez and Michaelangelo, have managed to express their vision of reality without tampering with appearances, but there is also El Greco, whose right to manipulate form for his own purposes no sane person would now dispute. Those who deny Mr. Lawrence's right to be an El Greco of literature had better not plume themselves that they are actuated by admiration for Michaelangelos's and Velasquez's fidelity to true form; if they can remain unmoved by Mr. Lawrence's genius it is much more likely that they are actuated by a longing for the realism of Mr. John Collier.

*The New Statesman*, XVII, 9 July, 1921

# John Middleton Murry, "Dr Leavis on D.H. Lawrence"

Dr Leavis's study of D.H. Lawrence's novels opens with the words: "This book carries on from *The Great Tradition.*" Readers of that book will regard the statement as something of a warning. For the treatment of the novelists dealt with in it was highly selective. Dickens barely scraped his second class, and that solely on the strength of *Hard Times.* And only portions of the three placed in the first class—George Eliot, James and Conrad—were awarded highest honours.

Lawrence is now admitted among them, and only Lawrence among their successors. But his entry is triumphal. Though Dr. Leavis does not say so in so many words, from his tone it is evident that he regards him as the greatest of them all. Never has he been so prodigal of eulogy; never quite so pugnacious in downing the opposition, which consists, for Dr. Leavis, not only of those who have been in any way publicly critical of Lawrence's work but even of the novelists who have had the misfortune to be contemporary with him.

Nevertheless, he applies to Lawrence the same selective method. One hundred pages of his book are devoted to *The Rainbow* and *Women in Love*; another fifty to *St. Mawr* and *The Captain's Doll*; and since, excluding two appendices, there are only 300 in all, and many of these are spent on unnecessary polemic, the treatment of the rest of Lawrence's prose fiction is distinctly eclectic. Dr. Leavis has his defence. "I want the stress to fall unambiguously on *The Rainbow, Women in Love*, and the tales." These two novels, according to him, are of a much higher order than the others which Lawrence wrote; and they have had "essentially no recognition at all." But they are, in fact, the "supreme creative achievement" in "the great tradition" of the English novelists since Jane Austen, who are "the successors of Shakespeare."

It is a thankless task to criticize such enthusiasm; but in the interest of a just appreciation of one who, taken all in all, is the most significant English writer of the twentieth century, a caveat must be entered. Lawrence can be made to fit into "the great tradition" of the English novel, as Dr. Leavis understands it only by a great deal of manipulation. Take, for instance, *The Rainbow*. Concerning the earlier part of it, Dr. Leavis has much that is wise and illuminating to say; he makes just and revealing comparisons to Lawrence's advantage with George Eliot. But when he comes to deal with the later and more baffling part of the book—the story of the relations between Ursula and Anton—he passes hurriedly over it.

> A more serious criticism, perhaps, bears on the signs of too great a tentativeness in the development and organization of the later part; signs of a growing sense in the writer of an absence of any conclusion in view. Things very striking in themselves haven't as clear a function as they ought to have. Above all, the sterile deadlock between Ursula and Skrebensky—a theme calling, we can see, for the developments it gets in *Women in Love*, but cannot have here—seems too long drawn out.

Considering the importance of this relation between Ursula and Anton, Dr. Leavis's perfunctory treatment of it amounts to evasion. For the difficulty is not that the sterile deadlock is too long drawn out, but it is presented in terms which, even to the eager and sympathetic reader, are incomprehensible. It may be that what is arcane to them is lucid to Dr. Leavis. But if ever exegesis was required, it is surely here. What is it that happens in the scene in the stackyard in Chapter XI, or on the seashore in Chapter XV? We have Lawrence's word for it that Ursula apparently unwittingly became for Anton "the darkness, the challenge, the horror"; that she "consumed and annihilated" him and that the annihilation was permanent; but the process by which it was accomplished, though described in detail and with vehemence by Lawrence, remains entirely mysterious. Yet this is the major psychological or spiritual happening in the second half of *The Rainbow*. Dr. Leavis does not explain it at all.

Neither does he do so in his detailed exposition of *Women in Love*. In that novel, the theme of Ursula's destructive relation to Skrebensky is taken up again in the relation of Gudrun and Gerald; while Ursula finds a man whom she cannot annihilate and to whom she must surrender, in Rupert. Lawrence's descriptions of the crucial moments in both relations are as mysterious as they were when the book was first published. Again Dr. Leavis passes them over: this time not quite in silence, for he quotes one of them and comments:

> I see here a fault of which I could find worse examples in *Women in Love*, though it is a fault that I do not now see as bulking so large in the book as I used to see it. It seems to me that in these places Lawrence betrays by an insistent and over-emphatic explicitness, running at times to something one can only call jargon, that he is uncertain—uncertain of the value of what he offers;  uncertain whether he really holds it—whether a valid communication has really been defined and conveyed in terms of his creative art.

That is all. The difficulty is dismissed. But it has not been overcome. Consequently Dr. Leavis gives the impression of expounding and exalting a different novel from that which Lawrence actually wrote: a version bowdlerized, or at least mitigated *in usum Delphini*.

It is easy enough to understand Lawrence's intention in *Women in Love*; to present first the contrast between a man who immolates himself to the mechanism of modern civilization and one who is in dynamic revolt against it; and also to present the fatal influence on the man-women relation of the inward sterility of Gerald, and the gleam of hope in the "love" that is based on Ursula's response to the vitality with which Birkin conquers his own despair. The theme is profound and prophetic. But much of its working out is mysterious. Again we ask what it is that happens in the crucial scene where Ursula enters into the "full mystic knowledge" of Birkin's "suave loins of darkness." If it is true, as Dr. Leavis suggests, that Lawrence was uncertain of the value of what he offered, uncertain whether he really held it, it has a vital bearing on the convincingness of the novel: for Ursula's relation to Birkin is certainly offered as the way out of the spiritual impasse of contemporary civilization. It is presented as "normative" to use Dr. Leavis's word.

Dr. Leavis's method of isolating the two novels from their important context does real injustice to Lawrence's achievement: for the subsequent novels are full of implicit and explicit criticism of what he had previously "offered," or at least of readjustment of it to further experience. So that to dispose of the subsequent novels as a preliminary to the consideration of the two that preceded them seems, in the literal sense of the word, preposterous. It is as a whole—as the unique record, and imaginative projection of the life and thought adventure of a man prophetically sensitive to the deep inward decay of a civilization—that Lawrence's achievement is so astonishing. It is at once greater and less than Dr. Leavis represents it. He is understandably indignant with those who merely allow Lawrence a certain magic of style; but in his effort to vindicate for him the position of the supreme artist—let us put it bluntly, since Dr. Leavis plainly implies it—of the same order as Shakespeare, he unduly exaggerates the perfection of some, and unduly depreciates the merit of other of Lawrence's work. Thus he dismisses *The Plumed Serpent* as "a bad book and a regrettable performance." Even if that were a sound judgement (as it is not) the phenomenon would call for explanation, for there is no doubt that Lawrence himself considered it as serious an undertaking as any novel he ever wrote.

Of his contrary tendency to impute perfection to work with serious defects his extreme eulogy of *St.Mawr* is a striking example. *St.Mawr*, it will be remembered, is the story of how a stallion comes to reveal to a woman the utter insufficiency of her husband and her marriage, and the sterility of the polite semi-artistic world in which her life has been caught. Lou, in contemplating the stallion, receives a revelation of the reality of the life-power that has been suppressed and destroyed in men of the modern civilization, and she imagines a "new man" in whom the vivid instinctive life of the animal should be completed by a kindred swift intelligence. Dr. Leavis admits that this ideal is not presented in any character of the story.

> But it is, nevertheless, irresistibly present in *St. Mawr* the dramatic poem; it is no mere abstract postulate. It is present as the marvellous creative intelligence of the author.

Is this argument more than ingenious? Can an author's intelligence, however creative and pervasive, really take the place of a created character of the kind posited? From *The White Peacock* onward Lawrence made many attempts to present such a character, the last being Mellors in *Lady Chatterley's Lover*. But, significantly, none of them has Dr. Leavis's approval. So he subtly, and perhaps unconsciously, shifts his ground. Lou repudiates her mother's cynical insinuation that she wants a cave man.

> He's a brute, a degenerate. A pure animal man would be as lovely as a deer or a leopard, burning like a flame fed straight from underneath. And he'd be part of the unseen, like a mouse is, even. And he'd never cease to wonder, he'd breathe silence and unseen wonder, as the partridges do, running in the stubble. . . Ah no, mother, I want the wonder back again, or I shall die.

On which Dr. Leavis comments:

> Lawrence can make "wonder" . . . seem so much more than a vaguely recoiling romanticism, because for him it is so much more. He can affirm with a power not given to poor Lou, who is not a genius, and there is nothing merely postulated about the positives he affirms.
>
> The power of the affirmation lies, not in any insistence or assertion or argument but in the creative fact, his art; it is that which is an irrefutable witness. What his art *does* is beyond argument or doubt. It is not a question of metaphysics or theology. . . . Great art, something created and *there*, is what Lawrence gives us. And there we undeniably *have* a world of wonder and reverence, where life wells up from mysterious springs.

For all its surface plausibility, this burkes the real issue. In so far as it is relevant to Lou's demand for a "new man," it amounts to no more than implying that Lawrence himself was such a man. And Lawrence himself, in a remarkable sequence of novels with which Dr. Leavis does not really grapple, dealt with astonishing honesty with that possibility, or hypothesis, and demonstrated where it failed. The wonder, which Lawrence the writer felt and so marvellously communicated, of the animal and natural world, does not extend to the human being—except in the case of his fictional presentation of himself.

But that, it might be said, is because the "wonder" is not in civilized man or woman. It has departed. That assuredly was Lawrence's conviction. But Dr. Leavis does not adopt it. Instead he asserts that such figures as Rico and Mrs. Witt are triumphs of creative art. Surely he is hypnotizing himself. He is apparently not quite unaware of the danger.

> Lou's vision is of a flood of evil enveloping the world. Rico "being an artist," and bent on Kudos and "fun," might seem to be too much of a figure of comedy to play the major part assigned to him in so portentous a vision. It is a mark of the wonderful success of the tale in its larger intention that, irresistible as it is in its comedy, we are not moved to anything like that criticism: the significance represented by the visionary role inheres potently in the Rico we have been made to realize. He is, in the first place, we may say, Bloomsbury. . . .

A half-page of denunciation follows. A sense of anti-climax is irrepressible. Whether or not Rico is a plausible embodiment of Bloomsbury—and one would say he was not—he cannot carry the weight of apocalyptic significance with which Dr. Leavis would invest him; neither can Mrs. Witt, with her enjoyment of the churchyard, carry hers. With characteristic gravity Dr. Leavis warns us:

> Mrs. Witt's note is not so much merely light as it sounds. The churchyard, with its funerals, becomes an insistent theme. It isn't, for Mrs. Witt, an obsession with death as the terrifying and inescapable reality, but a fear that death will prove unreal. Reported in this way, the case may not seem to carry much in the way of convincing poignancy. But this is what we are actually given; the thing is *done*, in its inevitability an astonishing triumph of genius; and since the success—the convincing transmutation, in Mrs. Witt, of hard-boiled ironic destructiveness into agonized despair—is crucial to the success of the whole, a long quotation will be in place.

The long quotation cannot be copied; but to the present writer's sense it simply does not substantiate Dr. Leavis's claim. And the shrillness of his superlatives which culminate in the dictum that "one would have said that the kind of thing hadn't been done and couldn't be done, outside Shakespearian dramatic poetry" seems to be a means of drowning the still small voice of critical sanity.

*St.Mawr* is a significant story; but not a supreme one. Dr. Leavis's criticism of it has been dealt with in some detail, because his method of intense and highly selective concentration on parts of Lawrence's prose fiction admits no other mode of questioning. To account for his aberration—and his emphatic endorsement of Rico as a convincing apocalyptic character can be reckoned no less—we should invoke his unnecessary divagation against Bloomsbury, and his previous invective against the successors of Bloomsbury.

> In the period in which Auden was so rapidly established as a major poet and remained one for so long, and Spender became overnight the modern Shelley, it was not to be expected that the portrayer of Rico would receive the sympathetic attention denied him in the emancipated twenties.

Dr. Leavis has, in fact, made Rico a symbol of his critical detestations. Rico's illusory magnitude and convincingness as a character are a function of his own private universe. They are not intrinsic to the character presented by Lawrence. Here we touch upon a real and pervasive weakness of Dr. Leavis's championship of Lawrence. For all his genuine reverence for Lawrence's genius, he cannot refrain from using him as a weapon of offence against those whom he regards as literary enemies. What in Lawrence himself was light-hearted becomes weighted with a deadly seriousness in Dr. Leavis's commentary: Lawrence's casual dismissals are transmuted into excommunications.

It is an exaggeration to represent Lawrence as neglected since his death. He has been continually in the consciousness and on the conscience of literate England for at least twenty-five years. And if he has not yet been accepted as the only inheritor of "the great tradition" of the English novel, it is largely because he was, essentially, something more important than that—more revolutionary, more truly new, more challenging, more disturbing—which refuses to be accommodated in our conventional categories. Dr. Leavis, by virtue of his profession, has made a heroic effort to subsume all that he can of this unique being under the category of "supreme artistic intelligence." He has made a brave and stimulating effort to separate Lawrence's art from his doctrine; but in order to do it he has been compelled to a tacit expurgation. The doctrine is always there.

*Times Literary Supplement*, 28 October 1955 (review of F. R. Leavis, *D.H. Lawrence: Novelist*)


## Jack F. Stewart, "Primitivism in *Women in Love*"

Lawrence has been considered a representative primitivist,[1] but the nature and value of primitivism in general, and of the primitive in Lawrence's works, have been the subject of wide disagreement. Arthur 0. Lovejoy and George Boas[2] distinguish between "chronological" and "cultural," "soft" and "hard" primitivism, and their historical work provides background for Kingsley Widmer's and Jascha Kessler's [3] contrasting views of Lawrence. My own point of view is indebted to Michael Bell's *Primitivism*, [4] with its more literary-critical approach. Bell, who illustrates the pervasive quality of primitivism in *The Rainbow*, distinguishes between "primitive sensibility" and "conscious primitivism," and argues that "it is precisely at the point in his career at which the romantic faith of *The Rainbow* gives way to the bitterness of *Women in Love* that Lawrence begins to make overtly primitive use of his anthropological reading" (Bell, p. 60). As Bell indicates, the primitive animism of *The Rainbow* modulates into more explicit and critical reflections on the primitive in *Women in Love*.[5] Primitivism, in the latter novel, becomes a complex interplay of unconscious ritual (the language of symbolism) and conscious reflection (the language of prophecy). This inter-play, with its focus on primitive art, is the subject of the present study.

Lawrence read Frazer's *Golden Bough* and *Totemism and Exogamy*, Tylor's *Primitive Culture* (which he preferred to Frazer), and Frobenius's *Voice of Africa*,[6] and became interested in the decline and degeneration theories of the anthropologists. He was enthusiastic about Jane Harrison's *Ancient Art and Ritual:* [7] "It just fascinates me to see art coming out of religious yearning—one's presentation of what one wants to feel again deeply."[8] But he did not romanticize the primitives or share the progressive theory that saw them as simply an earlier phase of cultural development.[9] Lawrence denied the theory of evolution because he did not feel it in his solar plexus (*Letters* xv)—a properly primitivist attitude. Culture, to him, was not a continuum, but a series of experiments along parallel lines:

> The savages, we may say *all* savages, are remnants of the once civilised world-people, who had their splendour and their being for countless centuries in the way of sensual knowledge, that conservative way which Egypt shows us at its conclusion, mysterious and long-enduring. It is we from the North, starting new centers of life in ourselves, who have become young. The savages have grown older and older. No man can look at the African grotesque carvings, for example, or the decoration patterns of the Oceanic islanders, without seeing in them the infinitely sophisticated soul which produces distortion from its own distorted psyche, a psyche distorted through myriad generations of degeneration.[10]

This critique, written shortly after Lawrence had completed *Women in Love*, paraphrases central themes in the novel. The primitives have gone further on the road to degeneration than the white race.

The distortions of primitive sculpture have a particular *frisson* for the modern artist-intellectual, who feels this process of reduction imminent in himself or his society. André Malraux suggests some reasons why primitive sculpture and carving were of such compelling interest to European artists in the first two decades of this century: "The artist feels that he can make use of some of these forms, but is less aware that the gods lurking behind them are seeking to make use of him. For fetishes . . . are not just quaint museum-pieces; they are indictments . . . The diabolical principle—from war, that major devil, to its train of minor devils, fears and complexes—which is more or less subtly present in all savage art, was coming to the fore again."[11] Malraux penetrates beyond the aesthetic surface of primitive religious art to the dark savage gods within.

Robert Goldwater's description of Henry Moore's work stresses primitive qualities similar to those in Lawrence's totem: "African inspiration can be seen in the heavy, squared-off bent legs and buttocks, the enlarged feet, and the general proportions of *Standing Woman* ( 1923); they are related to the 'heavy bent legs' by which African sculpture, rising upward like the tree it comes from, still is 'rooted in the earth.'"[12] Birkin, who is knowledgeable about African art, also "admir[es] the almost wizard, sensuous apprehension of the earth" in Picasso's art (*WL* 247).

The art-historian, Paul S. Wingert, approves the term "primitive" for certain cultures, "not because they represent the fumbling early beginnings of civilization . . . [but] because [they] show developments more closely alled to the fundamental, basic, and essential drives of life that have not been buried under a multitude of parasitical, non-essential desires."[13]Harry T. Moore[14] notes the cult of primitivism in Europe at the outset of Lawrence's career, with reference to African and Melanesian art, Gauguin, Kirchner, Die Brücke, the Fauves, Picasso, Stravinsky, and Roger Fry's essays. Fry, in "The Art of Bushmen" and "Negro Sculpture,"[15] discusses the distortions of primitive art[16] from an aesthetic viewpoint, and concludes: "It is for want of a conscious critical sense and the intellectual powers of classification that the Negro has failed to create one of the great cultures of the world, and not from any lack of the creative aesthetic impulse, nor from lack of the most exquisite sensibility and the finest taste" (Fry, p. 89). Much as he scorned Fry's emphasis on "plastic values"—and dissatisfied as he was with civilization—Lawrence, too, was crucially concerned with the balance of intellect and sensuality that makes for creative culture. Birkin is no simple primitivist; Gerald, for whom, as a boy, "Life was a condition of savage freedom" (*WL* 214), might be considered closer to that extreme.[17] Indeed, Birkin sees the entropic extremes of primitivism and civilization, raised to a high level of "abstraction," as dialectical counterparts (see *WL* 246). He himself oscillates between conscious primitivism and allotropic animism. His dark ritual of stoning the moon's image closely precedes his enlightened meditation on the totem. C.R. Aldrich has said that the totem as symbol "acts as a focus for the interest, the libido, of both consciousness and the unconscious."[18] Thus primitive art casts its magnetic spell on Birkin's psyche, and the image of the totem resurfaces as the focus of his religious musings. Up to this point, there has been little integration of the allotropic and prophetic, animistic and intellectual aspects of his experience. But in recognizing Ursula as his anima ("'There is a golden light in you, which I wish you would give me'" [*WL* 241]), he begins to move toward equilibrium. The novel, however, like Birkin's reactions to primitive art, remains a volatile combination of empathy and abstraction.[19]

Primitivism is generally considered to be a symptom of cultural crisis.[20] Among the severest critics of modern primitivism is Jascha Kessler, who sees it as an atavistic impulse for destruction, that "attacks the historical sense and manifests concomitantly a terrific urge toward Psychological regression" (Kessler, p. 470).[21] But there is a vital difference between merely destructive regression—the "Gadarene swine" complex that Lawrence saw in the War—and the "destructive creation" Birkin explores in "Water-Party". Whereas Widmer regards the *primitivistic* as an amoral aesthetic force, Kessler clearly associates it with demonic (and political) evil.[22] He even "[goes] so far as to claim that primitivism in its modern incarnation is the servant of Ananke, and that the extraordinary work of D.H. Lawrence shows him to have been wholly in its grip" (Kessler, p. 471). Undoubtedly, Birkin suffers at times from the death-wish that is consuming his society, and would like to see civilization swept away. But knowing psychic death is not necessarily succumbing to it; it may, indeed, be the first step towards transcending it. It is ridiculous to say that Lawrence, as a primitivist, is wholly in the grip of Ananke, when he is actively diagnosing it. Norman O. Brown, like Lawrence, stresses that Eros and Ananke are interdependent forces, and that there can be no fulfilment of life as long as knowledge of death is repressed. Brown, following Nietzsche, says of the Dionysian artist: "Instead of negating, he affirms the dialectical unity of the great instinctual opposites: Dionysus reunites male and female, Self and Other, life and death" (Brown, p.175). The Dionysian strain in Lawrence's art is an overflowing of cultural barriers, an imaginative transcendence of the civilization that preached love and made war. Yet Birkin advocates a reunion of Apollo and Dionysus,[23] of "the senses and the outspoken mind," rather than a simple resurrection of the "Savage God." Michael Bell acutely summarizes some of the central issues here:

> Primitivism, then, is born of the interplay between the civilized self and the desire to reject or transform it. This interplay . . . may take a positive or creative direction. In Lawrence, for example, there is a recreation within the civilized consciousness of very primary levels of feeling; a mingling of both to produce that spontaneity and emotional fullness so superbly embodied in his best works. Primitivism, we might say, is the projection by the civilized sensibility of an inverted image of the self. Its characteristic focus is the gap or tension that subsists between these two selves and its most characteristic resultant is impasse. (Bell, p. 80)

This "sense of impasse, the recognition of the contradictory nature of the primitivist impulse" (Bell, pp. 80-81) provides a useful point of departure for a study of Birkin's—and Lawrence's—cultural dilemma in *Women in Love*.

The central themes of the novel are brought into focus by the totem that Birkin and Gerald confront in Halliday's rooms:

> . . . there were several statues, wood-carvings from the West Pacific, strange and disturbing, the carved natives looked almost like the foetus of a human being. One was a woman sitting naked in a strange posture, and looking tortured, her abdomen stuck out . . . she was sitting in child-birth, clutching the ends of the band that hung from her neck, one in each hand, so that she could bear down and help labour. The strange, transfixed, rudimentary face of the woman again reminded Gerald of a foetus, it was also rather wonderful conveying the suggestion of the extreme of physical sensation, beyond the limits of mental consciousness. (*WL* 67)

At this point, the vital questions of blood-brotherhood and marriage have not yet come up for Gerald and Birkin, so their paths have not yet diverged. But their contrasting attitudes to bohemianism and primitivism show the form that this divergence will take. Gerald is simultaneously attracted and repelled by the "absolute" sensation in the totem.[24] Sensation, for Gerald himself, is vitiated by escapism, will-to-power, or conscious demonism. This willed sensation reduces being to the nothingness that he so much dreads, and his "go" to the mechanical energy of the death process. He is attracted to the totem, and wants to wrest its secrets from it, because he senses in it the counterpart of his own monomania. Indeed, the resemblance becomes almost physical, when Gerald nearing the end of his corrosive course, "[looks] like a mask used in ghastly religions of the barbarians" (*WL* 430).

Birkin, who oscillates "between animalism and spiritual truth" (*WL* 289), at first seems to cultivate primitivism, but later rejects primitive and civilized extremes to seek wholeness in duality.[25] Ironically, Gerald lectures Birkin: "'You like the wrong things . . . things against yourself.'" (*WL* 72), because he cannot see that Birkin is trying to restore the balance in himself of a civilization gone wrong. Culture, for Birkin (the "changer") is a search for homeostasis in a constantly shifting world. "White and somehow evanescent" (*WL* 71), he nevertheless has an intuitive understanding of the black totem as a symbol of "culture in the physical consciousness." His primitivism fits Bell's formula of a "projection by the civilized sensibility of an inverted image of the self." His concentration on the totem as dream-opposite stimulates that "passionate struggle into conscious being" (*WL* viii) that produces a clearcut dialectic. Thus Birkin's "conscious critical sense" (to echo Fry) gradually overcomes the "megalomania" that isolates him in "An Island," until he achieves a standpoint of cultural objectivity and independence that contrasts with Gerald's increasing monomania.

Gerald fears and resents the abandonment to sensation he sees in the totem:

> "Why is it art?" Gerald asked, shocked, resentful.
> "It conveys a complete truth," said Birkin. "It contains the whole truth of that state, whatever you feel about it."
> "But you can't call it high art," said Gerald.
> "High! There are centuries and hundreds of centuries of development in a straight line, behind that carving; it is an awful pitch of culture, of a definite sort."
> "What culture?" Gerald asked in opposition. He hated the sheer barbaric thing.
> "Pure culture in sensation, culture in the physical consciousness, mindless, utterly sensual. It is so sensual as to be final, supreme." (*WL* 71-72)

In the "terrible face, void, peaked, abstracted almost into meaninglessness by the weight of sensation beneath" (*WL* 71), Gerald suddenly sees Minette, masochistically yielded to him as "the passive substance of his will" (*WL* 72). Here is utter disequilibrium, foreshadowing the sado-masochistic relationship with Gudrun. Exploitation, possession, violation link African and Nordic extremes, in contrast with the way of mutual freedom. The connection between Minette's vulnerable sensuality and the absolute sensation of the totem becomes clearer: "Her face was like a small, fine mask, sinister too, masked with unwilling suffering" (*WL* 73). These masks of primitive and civilized degeneration are twin faces of a single Janus-figure. (An intermediary figure is the culturally degraded Arab servant, whose "aristocratic inscrutability of expression" suggests "a nauseating, bestial stupidity" [*WL* 73].) Birkin's understanding of primitive art shows up the shallowness of "the whole Bohemian set," in which he is ironically included by Minette. The fact that Halliday, a decadent connoisseur "like a Christ in a Pieta" (*WL* 70), possesses a totem and poses nude by the fireplace allows Lawrence to satirize the inherent contradictions of self-conscious primitivism.

The conscious primitivism of "Totem" is the key to many scenes of primitive sensibility in the novel, as well as to explicit themes of cultural hypertrophy, crisis, and decline. The most over-civilized character in the novel, and the most corrupted by mental consciousness, is Hermione. Like the totem, Minette, and later Gerald, she is characterized by a mask of suffering: "Her long, pale face, that she carried lifted up, somewhat in the Rossetti fashion, seemed almost drugged, as if a strange mass of thoughts coiled in the darkness within her, and she was never allowed to escape" (*WL* 10). The fashionable manner of this *Kulturträger* masks a chaos of passion and intellect. In "Classroom" (*WL* 32), she extols "primitive passion," but Birkin tears her self-conscious primitivism to shreds: ". . . knowledge means everything to you. Even your animalism, you want it in your head . . . If one cracked your skull perhaps one might get a spontaneous, passionate woman out of you, with real sensuality" (*WL* 35-36). The mirror and Lady of Shalott images are central in Birkin's harangue: to shatter skull or mirror is to destroy the grip of mental consciousness over primal sensation. Maddeningly for Birkin, his own ideas are reflected in the distorting mirror of Hermione's "hidebound intellectualism" while his intellectual rage is transformed into her physical violence. The scene in which she strikes him is a catharsis for both that shatters civilized repressions. Birkin has to condone her libidinous outburst, because it fulfills, with a vengeance, the lesson of "Classroom." His words are doubly prophetic, for after she has cracked *him* over the head with a symbolic art-object, *he* experiences a pantheistic return to nature, with a reflux of spontaneous, passionate feeling.

This Rousseauian primitivism clearly issues from the impasse of Birkin's relationship with Hermione: his primroses and fir-trees are the antidote to her *willed* daffodils. It is a flight back to simple sensation without human commitment, in the mood of Marvell's "Garden." Idyllic as such pantheism may seem, it is regressive by Birkin's own standards, for he later realizes he is "damned and doomed to the old effort at serious living" (*WL* 294). His momentary retreat into primitive isolation (the Alexander Selkirk theme of "The Man Who Loved Islands") comes from despair of finding equilibrium with others. At least his nudity is spontaneous and refreshing, unlike Halliday's fireside cult. Despite his idyll in the pine-grove, Birkin never becomes a whole-hearted romantic primitivist like Gauguin: neither did Lawrence who preferred to seek *mana* in trees, animals, and sun, rather than in actual savages. Lawrence feels the attraction of the primitive, but resists the plunge into atavism.[26]

Primitive rituals play a central role in *Women in Love,* but space does not permit me to discuss the "Rabbit"—"Moony"—"Gladiatorial" sequence here. Instead, I shall briefly consider animism in one of these scenes. Maud Bodkin[27] first pointed to the role of the archetypal unconscious in "Moony." Unconscious identification and projection by the characters give the moon-stoning ritual a strange quality of primitive animism. As Tylor observes:

> First and foremost among the causes which transfigure into myths the facts of daily experience, is the belief in the animation of all nature, rising at its highest point to personification. This . . . is inextricably bound up with that primitive mental state where man recognizes in every detail of his world the operation of personal life and will . . . The basis on which such ideas are built is not to be narrowed down to poetic fancy and transformed metaphor. They rest upon a broad philosophy of nature . . . (Tylor, I p. 285)

He adds: "In early philosophy throughout the world, the Sun and Moon are alive and as it were human in nature" (Tylor, I p. 288). Thus Gauguin adapts Maori myth to his own enigmatic vision in "The Moon and the Earth"[28] (I 893), with its giant female and male figures. Lawrence, however, rejects anthropomorphism, celebrating Sun and Moon as polarized sources of living energy, and incorporating them into his own myths of death and renewal. In "Moony," the Cybele myth is secondary to the startling revival of animism, whereby the moon comes to life as a psychic force. Lawrence strives to recover that "primitive mental state", that unites man's psyche with nature. In "Moony," animism, ritual, myth and symbol, together with rhythmic language, recreate a primitive sensibility that is pre-cognitive, rapturous, and instinctual. Just as ritual precedes myth, so the moon scene has little need of classical allusion. It appeals, as Bodkin (Bodkin, p. 291) shows, to a complex of "obscure mingled feelings" of a sexual nature, that does not yield easily to knowledge. The conscious primitivist is immersed in the archetypal unconscious, as Birkin's acts take on the compulsive quality of a dream. The substance of the scene is animistic, whatever shadow of meaning we assign to it. The image of the moon on dark water reflects the image of the female anima in Birkin's psyche. Yet, by enlargement, it may also reflect mental consciousness superimposed on the primitive unconscious—thus providing a tenuous link with the cultural reflections that arise later in the chapter. Birkin's revolutionary aim is to shatter the pale cast of thought, with its superficial appearance of wholeness, and "to drive it off the surface of the pool." This constitutes a ritual enactment of his earlier attack on mental mirrors. But, despite his violence, he is unable to disperse the moon's image, which keeps re-forming like a mandala on the dark pool.

Birkin's symbolic action leads to his profound reflection on African and Nordic ways. He is led to see the fatal incompleteness that causes degeneration in each of these systems. Cultivation "all in one kind" leads to entropy, not equilibrium. Birkin despairs of mass culture and looks to some "other way" for individual being, which must struggle against the false essence and deathward drag that society imposes. A preconditioned tendency is to conspire with the reductive process and take unconscious delight in destruction of self and others. This is the way of Hermione, Gudrun, Gerald, and Loerke, of sex-in-the-head, of animal movements in mirrors, of mechanical organization, of war—in short, of civilization in chaos. The creative individual must resist inertia, and struggle to make existential choices that determine his own being. That is why Birkin needs to be a conscious primitivist, as well as developing primitive sensibility: "Any man of real individuality tries to know and to understand what is happening, even in himself, as he goes along. This struggle for verbal consciousness should not be left out in art" (*WL* viii). Birkin must resist the tide of his own culture, which seems set for destruction, and choose from other cultures those aspects that will help to restore the balance in himself. While Hermione suffers the living-death of hypertrophied consciousness, and Gerald dies of an atrophied will, Birkin (would-be Salvator Mundi) saves himself by making a bond beyond love with the life-force in Ursula. The "star equilibrium" they achieve is more than an existential resolution of personal and cultural crisis; it is a spiritual state that surpasses reason.

Birkin explores the primitive as a clue to the vital unconscious and comes to realize the contradiction between his conscious primitivism ("he was always talking about sensual fulfilment" [*WL* 245]) and the totem's silent sensuality. As a conscious primitivist, he is fascinated by unconscious primitive sensibility. But once he becomes aware of the implications of that downward drift in himself, he decides "he [does] not want a further sensual experience. . . deeper, darker, than ordinary life could give" (*WL* 245). He rejects atavism and the knowledge that Kurtz finds in the heart of darkness, which is death to the soul. In his long reflection on fetishes,[29] he strives to grasp the inner orientation of primitive culture, and to isolate the contrasting dynamic of European civilization:

> He remembered the African fetishes he had seen at Halliday's so often. There came back to him one, a statuette about two feet high, a tall, slim, elegant figure from West Africa, in dark wood, glossy and suave. It was a woman, with hair dressed high, like a melon-shaped dome. He remembered it vividly; she was one of his soul's intimates. Her body was long and elegant, her face was crushed tiny like a beetle's, she had rows of round, heavy collars, like a column of quoits on her neck. He remembered her: her astonishing cultured elegance, her diminished, beetle face, the astounding long elegant body on short, ugly legs, with such protuberant buttocks, so weighty and unexpected below her slim long loins.      (*WL* 245)

Despite apparent confusion,[30] this is surely a different carving from the one of the woman in labor in "Totem." The description is detailed, with an eye for those distortions in West African art that are most. striking to European sensibility. The most evident of these is the disproportion of upper to lower body. Birkin, in reaction against his own culture, feels a deep affinity with that of the statuette; he is simultaneously fascinated and repelled. Indeed, there is a certain fetishism of loins and buttocks. Gudrun watches "the movement of [Gerald's] white loins" (*WL* 112) as he rows the boat, and has a "fatal" vision of "the beauty of the subjection of his loins, white and dimly luminous" (*WL* 173), as he climbs back into another boat after his sister's drowning. The comparison of black and white loins is a significant part of the African-Nordic dialectic. Thus a further attraction of the fetish for Birkin is its grotesque, but highly formalized, emphasis on lower centres of the body which are the locus of unconscious libidinal energy (*FU* 74-75)—and of his own sexual-religious preoccupations. According to H.L B. Moody (Moody, p. 76), Birkin's attitude is "remarkably like that of a worshipper before the image of a deity (which of course is probably the purpose for which the statuette was originally created) . . ." Thus, through a mixture of empathy and introspection (he *senses* what the fetish symbolizes and knows what is imminent in himself), Birkin re-discovers a savage consciousness rooted in the solar plexus and exclusive of mind. But he draws back from the brink of atavism, desiring to integrate physical consciousness with spiritual intelligence in a new wholeness of being. This rite of fusion is provisionally enacted with Gerald in "Gladiatorial," and consummated with Ursula in "Excurse."

Birkin's reflection on primitivism enables him to see the price exacted by all high culture. Instead of lapsing into mindless ecstasy (as Kessler accuses Lawrence of doing), Birkin clings to "the goodness, the holiness, the desire for creation and productive happiness"—Apollonian qualities that represent psychic integration and finer culture. Meanwhile, the war-torn civilization to which he belongs is seen to merge with its opposite pole of barbarism, insofar as both lapse from duality into limiting, destructive "singleness of vision." The overdevelopment of certain faculties at the expense of others causes entropy and decline. Indeed, Birkin sees all cultural organization as stemming from, and perpetuating, the individual's failure to find harmony within himself. The fetish is more than an art-object; it is a racial and cultural icon. As Birkin's contemplation of it shifts from aesthetic to philosophic, his attitude shifts from admiration to horror:

> She knew what he himself did not know. She had thousands of years of purely sensual, purely unspiritual knowledge behind her. It must have been thousands of years since her race had died, mystically: that is, since the relation between the senses and the outspoken mind had broken, leaving the experience all in one sort, mystically sensual. Thousands of years ago, that which was imminent in himself must have taken place in these Africans: the goodness, the holiness, the desire for creation and productive happiness must have lapsed, leaving the single impulse for knowledge in one sort, mindless progressive knowledge through the senses, knowledge arrested and ending in the senses. mystic knowledge in disintegration and dissolution, knowledge such as the beetles have, which live purely within the world of corruption and cold dissolution. (*WL* 245-46)

The beetle, despite its associations with the apocalyptic scarab (cf. "The Ladybird"), is a negative symbol that plainly shows Birkin's rejection of unmodified blood-consciousness. He tells Ursula of a "silver river of life" and a "dark river of dissolution" (*WL* 164) in the body. Creative energy involves the symbiotic flow of these opposing streams:[31] "'When the stream of synthetic creation lapses,'" says Birkin, "'we find ourselves part of the inverse process, the blood of destructive creation'"[32] (*WL* 164). Uncontrolled acceleration of energies in a single direction— a process that might be symbolized by Yeats's gyres— leads to increasing entropy within the cultural or psychic system. Every system directs and channels energy; thus certain faculties are developed at the expense of others. This tendency of one pole to draw energy away from its opposite, instead of exchanging energy with it, is ultimately self-negating. If those (like Gerald) who are trapped within a closed system, could learn to embrace their opposite (like Birkin) they might be saved. The irony of not liking "things against yourself" becomes evident.

Birkin is not about to trade one form of cultural conditioning for another. He has reached that high level of abstraction at which the content of a culture is less significant than its potential for fulfilment or desruction. The root of evil is "the single impulse for knowledge in one sort," which prevents the flow of energy between opposing poles. Thus the African fetish is just as extreme an instance of primitive unconsciousness as Hermione is of civilized consciousness. Her mental contortions are caused by displacement of energy upward: if the fetish is bottom heavy, she is top-heavy. Thus the radical otherness of primitive culture provides a touchstone for the distortions of civilized being.

As a cultural prophet, Birkin has the capacity to take things to visionary extremes. He explores his own psychosexual imbalance, not only to shed his own sickness, but to diagnose the sickness of society. A dose of primitive blood-consciousness might seem the proper antidote for civilized hyper-consciousness, yet wilful "primitivism" merely corrupts, as in Halliday's bohemian circle or Hermione's "false self system."[33] The point is that culture, civilized or primitive, exacts its price. And to the rebel or visionary the social contract involves more sacrificess than benefits.[34] A decade before Freud, Lawrence linked repression with war and the death-wish.

Birkin's interpretation of the African fetish is amazing in its scope; it opens up a whole metaphysic of death-in-life, with its secrets of atrophy and disintegration: "There is a long way we can travel after the death-break: after that point when the soul in intense suffering breaks, breaks away from its organic hold like a leaf that falls. We fall from the connection with life and hope, we lapse from pure integral being, from creation and liberty, and we fall into the long, long African process of purely sensual understanding, knowledge in the mystery of dissolution" (*WL* 246). Birkin is the prophet of this Fall, as well as of "paradisal entry"—which might be renamed "paradisal re-entry," after Lawrence's painting, "Flight Back into Paradise"[35] (1927). This large canvas, formally awkward in its disposition of figures, is interesting for the light it throws on Lawrence's post-Christian mythology. It shows "Eve dodging back into Paradise, between Adam and the Angel at the gate, who are having a fight about it—and leaving the world in flames in the far corner behind her" (*Letters* 678). The world from which Eve is escaping is at once industrial landscape and smouldering inferno. Birkin (like Lawrence) sees primitive and industrial cultures as dual versions of the Fall:

> He realised that there were great mysteries to be unsealed, sensual, mindless, dreadful mysteries, far beyond the phallic cult. How far, in their inverted culture, had these West Africans gone beyond phallic knowledge? . . . There remained this way, this awful African process, to be fulfilled. It would be done differently by the white races. The white races, having the Arctic north behind them, the vast abstraction of ice and snow, would fulfil a mystery of ice-destructive knowledge, snow-abstract annihilation. Whereas the West Africans controlled by the burning death-abstraction of the Sahara, had been fulfilled in sun-destruction, the putrescent mystery of sun-rays. (*WL* 246)

Lawrence's climatological symbolism points forward to the apocalyptic metaphors of the German expressionist, Gottfried Benn, who speaks of "this white race with its compulsive pursuit of a downward path of no return, a lost, icy, heat-baked, weather-ravaged *anabasis* not held in the embrace of any *thalassa*."[36] The driving-force of civilization, for Birkin as for Benn, is Thanatos: Eros is the liberation from culture into paradisal being.[37] The history of cultures, their rise, decline, and fall tends to repeat itself. As if by the Second Law of Thermodynamics, those very elements that bring about efficiency in a closed cultural system, also cause its disintegration. The theme of equilibrium versus reduction suggests that Lawrence, who had been reading Gibbon and Frobenius (*Letters* 439), also had entropy theory in mind. Science may have given him motifs for fiction: "The second law states that for an isolated system which cannot interact with other systems, the entropy cannot decrease."[38] This is clearly the fate of Gerald, who "cannot love," and of Gudrun, who is obsessed with the ticking of the clock. Birkin and Ursula, conversely, share "a rich new circuit, a new current of passionate electric energy . . . released from the darkest poles of the body . . ."(*WL* 305-6).

The lovers' entry into "paradisal unknowing" invokes the myth of Edenic return—"[Ursula] recalled again the magic of the Book of Genesis, where the sons of God saw the daughters of men that they were fair" (*WL* 304)—and thus relates the scene in "Excurse" to idyllic or millennial motifs of chronological primitivism. The rediscovery of innocence (in Northrop Frye's terms) or renewal of being (in Lawrence's) gives the world the primal radiance of a Golden Age. There is a complete washing away of civilized consciousness, and a baptismal re-immersion in the living body (see imagery, *WL* 306). After the complexity and strife of their relationship have passed a crisis, Birkin and Ursula suddenly come through to a simpler, freer, more joyful existence. This quest and its consummation—to which *The Rainbow* is a long prelude—superficially resemble romantic (or "soft") primitivism. In *Women in Love*, however, the idyll is complicated by dialectics of "destructive creation," by conscious primitivism, and by the bitter background of war.

Whereas *The Rainbow* ends with a millennial vision of blood and spirit fused in radiant new being, *Women in Love* offers no such visionary transcendence of psychic and social crisis. Interaction between the given thesis of civilization and the imagined antithesis of primitivism leads to no universal synthesis. "Excurse," as the title indicates, lies out side ordinary reality. Birkin and Ursula do find a way out, one that involves reconciliation of upper and lower, mental and sensual, centres of being. But it remains a way out for them alone—not a solution for the dying culture from which they must extricate themselves. In his *Movements in European History* [39] (written shortly after the novel), Lawrence rejects socio-economic causation, which, for a Marxist like Caudwell, holds the keys to disintegration and reconstruction.[40] Lawrence's view of history is passional and mystical—the creative and destructive forces that well up from the unconscious group-soul are unknowable. Man can only respond to these forces by becoming aware of what is taking place in himself. Thus Birkin's empathy with primitive blood-consciousness stimulates his understanding of cultural growth and decline. His response to totem and fetish releases "that other basic mind, the deepest physical mind" (*WL* 310) that is the complement of the critical intellect. The "Egyptian" state of "Excurse" is one of holistic being, not of savage reversion. Neither Birkin nor Lawrence is a primitivist in the simple chronological or cultural senses of the term. Yet, in *Women in Love*, primitive art and experience play crucial roles in the unending quest for total being.

*The D.H. Lawrence Review*, 13, 1980

## Notes

[1] M. H. Abrams, "Primitivism," *A Glossary of Literary Terms* (New York: Holt, Rinehart and Winston, 1957), p. 74.

[2] *Primitivism and Related Ideas in Antiquity* (New York: Octagon Books, 1965).

[3] Widmer, "The Primitivistic Aesthetic: D. H. Lawrence," *The Journal of Aesthetics and Art History*, 17, No. 3 (March 1959), 344-53; Kessler, "D. H. Lawrence's Primitivism," *Texas Studies in Literature and Language*, 5, No. 4 (Winter 1964), 467-88. The following also deal centrally with Lawrence's primitivism: K. K. Ruthven, "The Savage God: Conrad and Lawrence," *Critical Quarterly*, 10, Nos. 1-2 (Spring and Summer 1968), 39-54; H. L. B. Moody, "African Sculpture Symbols in a Novel by D. H. Lawrence," *Ibadan*, 26 (1969), 73-77; George H, Ford, *Double Measure* (New York: Holt, Rinehart and Winston, 1965), pp. 184-207; Robert L. Chamberlain, "Pussum, Minette, and the Africo-Nordic Symbol in Lawrence's *Women in Love*," PMLA, 78, No. 4 (September 1963), 407-

16. See also Jack Lindsay, "The Impact of Modernism on Lawrence," *Paintings of D. H. Lawrence*, ed. Mervyn Levy (London: Cory, Adams and Mackay, pp. 47-48. Subsequent references to these works will be cited parenthetically in the text by author's surname and page number(s).

[4](London: Methuen, 1972). Subsequent references to this work will be cited parenthetically in the text by author's surname and page number(s).

[5] (1920; rpt. New York: Viking Press, 1964). Subsequent references to this work will be cited parenthetically in the text by abbreviated title, *WL*, and page number(s).

[6] G. Frazer, *The Golden Bough*, 3rd ed., 12 vols. (London: MacMillan, 1911), *Totemism and Exogamy*, 4 vols. (London: Macmillan, 1910); Edward B. Tylor, *Primitive Culture* (1871), 6th ed., 2 vols. (London: Murray, 1920); Leo Frobenius, *The Voice of Africa*, trans. Rudolf Blind, 2 vols. (1913; rpt. New York: Blom, 1968). Subsequent references to these works will be cited parenthetically in the text by author's surname, volume number, and page number(s).

[7] (1913; rpt. London: Butterworth, 1927).

[8] *The Letters of D. H. Lawrence*, ed. Aldous Huxley (London: Heinemann, 1932), p. 149. Subsequent references to this work will be cited parenthetically in the text by abbreviated title, *Letters*, and page number(s).

[9]Frazer, *Totemism and Exogamy*, 1, 95, speaks of "the slow evolution of civilization and savagery," while the Freudian view also involves oversimplification. Norman O. Brown, *Life Against Death* (New York: Vintage, 1959), p. 37, for instance, writes: "Primitive is that level of culture in which the rhythm of what Freud calls the primary process—the rhythm of dreams and childhood play—is predominant. Civilized is that level of culture which effectively represses the rhythm of the primary process in favor of rationality and the reality-principle." Subsequent references to these works will be cited parenthetically in the text by author's surname and page number(s).

[10] Lawrence, "Herman Melville's *Typee* and *Omoo*," *The Symbolic Meaning*, ed. Armin Arnold (Fontwell, Arundel: Centaur Press, 1962), p. 223.

[11] *The Voices of Silence*, trans. Stuart Gilbert (St. Albans, Herts.: Paladin, 1974), p. 538, 541.

[12] *Primitivism in Modern Art* (1938); rev. ed. (New York: Vintage, 1967), p. 242.

[13] *Primitive Art: Its Traditions and Styles* (New York: Oxford Univ. Press, 1962), p. 7.

[14] *The Priest of Love: A Life of D. H. Lawrence*, rev. ed. (New York: Farrar, Straus and Giroux, 1974), pp. 266-67.

[15] *Vision and Design* (1920: rpt. Harmondsworth, Middlesex: Penguin, 1961), pp. 74-85, 85-89. Subsequent references to this work will be cited parenthetically by author's surname and page number(s). See also Herbert Read, *The Meaning of Art* (1931: rpt. London: Faber and Faber, 1977), pp. 71-76; Christopher Heywood, "African Art and the Work of Roger Fry and D. H. Lawrence," *SheffieldPapers on Literature and Society*, I (1976), 102-13.

[16] According to R. E. Pritchard, *D. H. Lawrence: Body of Darkness* (London: Hutchinson Univ. Library, 1971), p. 112, n. 13, "Lawrence saw primitivist art . . . as a distortion of the intuitive understanding, equivalent to the perversion of true male sensuality." This comment is based on the Melville essay, but it would be misleading to apply it to the wood-carvings in the novel, whose "absolute sensuality" contrasts with the self-conscious fetishism of Halliday or Loerke. A distortion of another kind of that of Horace Gregory, *D. H. Lawrence: Pilgrim of the Apocalypse* (1933; rpt. New York: Grove Press, 1957), who takes the totem as a norm of primitive sensibility against which to measure the

characters and their culture. (Gregory's thesis is criticized by Ford, pp. 192-93, and discussed by Colin Clarke, *River of Dissolution* [London: Routledge & Kegan Paul, 1969], pp. 81-82.)

[17] Gerald has explored the Amazon (*WL* 57), and reads "books about the primitive man, books of anthropology" (*WL* 225).

[18] *The Primitive Mind and Modern Civilization* (London: Kegan Paul, 1931), p. 93.

[19] Scott Sanders, *D. H. Lawrence: The World of the Five Major Novels* (New York: Viking, 1974), p. 103, discusses the relation of Wilhelm Worringer's modes to primitive art and to Lawrence's novels.

[20] Lovejoy and Boas, p. 7, observe: "Cultural primitivism is the discontent of the civilized with civilization. . . . It is the belief of men living in a relatively highly evolved and complex cultural condition that a life far simpler and less sophisticated. . . is a more desirable life." Jane Harrison, p. 235, gives summary statement to the negative view: "The cult of savagery, and even of simplicity, in every form, simply spells complex civilization and diminished vitality"; while Harry Levin, *The Myth of the Golden Age in the Renaissance* (London: Faber & Faber, 1970), p. 5, points out: "The positive thrust of this [primitivist] attitude has been provoked by a negativistic recoil. . . ."

[21] Cf. Christopher Caudwell, *Studies in a Dying Culture* (1938; rpt. London: Bodley Head, 1949), pp. 44-72, who sees Lawrence's primitivism, from a Freudian-Marxist point-of-view, as regression to the womb and repression of history.

[22] Cf. K. K. Ruthven, p. 39: "Savage primitivism. . . is a destructive hatred of civilization; the savage primitivist envisages destruction as the only solution to the problems of a hypercivilized Europe, and . . . generally takes a compensatory interest in primitive peoples, particularly in primitive Africans." Kessley, p. 472, although he finds primitivism in *The Rainbow* and *Women in Love*, considers Lawrence wholly a primitivist only in his post-European phase.

[23] Chamberlain, p. 414, observes that "Birkin's task . . . includes the leashing of delirium . . . and the revitalizing of analysis. He must reconcile man's darkness and his light." Birkin rejects "Dionysic ecstasy" (*WL* 243), shortly before rejecting the "African process" of mystic sensuality (*WL* 245-46).

[24] Read, p. 78, sees African art, in its totemic aspect, as "a visible expression of the absolute."

[25] See Lawrence, "The Two Principles," *Symbolic Meaning*, pp. 175-89.

[26] Cf. Mary Freeman, *D. H. Lawrence: A Basic Study of His Ideas* (Gainsville: Univ. of Florida Press, 1955), p. 5; also Clarke, p. 134: "There is no espousing of Utopian primitivism in this novel, no crude flight from reason." Lawrence, "Indians and an Englishman," *Phoenix*, ed. Edward D. McDonald (1936; rpt. New York: Viking, 1972), p. 99, writes: "Our darkest tissues are twisted in this old tribal experience, our warmest blood comes out of the old tribal fire. And they vibrate still in answer . . . But me, the conscious me, I have gone a long road since then . . . My way is my own, old red father; I can't cluster at the drum any more."

[27] *Archetypal Patterns in Poetry* (1934; rpt. London: Oxford Press, 1965), pp. 290-91. Subsequent references to this work will be cited parenthetically in the text by author's surname and page number(s).

[28] See Robert Goldwater, *Paul Gauguin* (New York: Abrams, n.d.), p. 122.

[29] Birkin uses the terms "fetish" and "totem" somewhat loosely. Frazer, *Totemism and Exogamy*, I, 3-4, defines *totem* as "a class of material objects which a savage regards with superstitious respect, believing that there exists between him and every member of the

class an intimate and altogether special relation. . . . As distinguished from a fetich [sic], a totem is never an isolated individual. . . ." Tylor, I, 144, stresses the religious aspect of totemism, but neither Frazer nor Tylor have much to say about totemic art. Wingert, p. 24, defines *fetish* as a "[magical] object that had an indwelling power, when properly invoked, of curing disease, causing destruction, or giving protection." The objects Wingert describes are mostly decorated masks or statuettes. See also Franz Boas, *Primitive Art* (1927; rpt. New York: Dover, 1955), pp. 280-81. (I cannot attempt to document here the varying uses of "Totemism" from Freud to Levi-Strauss).

[30] After Philip Heseltine (prototype of Halliday) had threatened a libel suit, Lawrence changed the provenance of the totem from West Africa to West Pacific, but did not carry through the change to "Moony." Yet this is hardly a significant slip (if it is one at all). While the reference should obviously be to the same *group* of scultpures, the "rudimentary" woman in labor, and the "tall, slim elegant figure" seem quite distinct, and could belong to different cultures (cf. Moody, pp. 74-75).  Chamberlain shows extensively how Lawrence took artistic advantage of the forced changes (See also Ruthven, p. 52).

[31] Clarke, *River of Dissolution*, pp. 70-87, demonstrates the paradoxical fusion in *Women in Love* of creative and destructive processes.

[32] Cf. C. G. Jung, "The Spiritual Problem of Modern Man" (1928), *Collected Works*, trans. R. F. C. Hull (London: Routledge & Kegan Paul, 1964), 10:81: ". . . modern man is thrown back on himself; his energies flow towards their source, and the collision washes to the surface those psychic contents which are at all times there, but lie hidden in the silt so long as the stream flows smoothly in its course."

[33] See R. D. Laing, *The Divided Self* (Harmondsworth, Middlesex: Penguin, 1970), pp. 94-105.

[34] Freud, *Civilization and Its Discontents* (1930), trans. James Strachey (New York: Norton, 1962), pp. 44, 34, stresses "the extent to which civilization is built upon a renunciation of instinct, how much it presupposes precisely the non-satisfaction . . . of powerful instincts," and he attributes the rise of primitivism to "a deep and long-standing dissatisfaction with . . . civilization. . . . " Cf. Lawrence, *Psychoanalysis and the Unconscious*, p. 45: "The tortures of psychic starvation which civilized people proceed to suffer, once they have solved for themselves the bread-and-butter problem of alimentation, will not bear thought." Like Birkin ("In the Train"), Lawrence rejects materialistic solutions; his viewpoint (which is comparable to Freud's in all but emphasis) is the converse of Caudwell's Marxism.

[35] See Lindsay, p. 45.

[36] *Primal Vision*, ed. E. B. Ashton (Norfold, Conn.: New Directions, n.d.), p. 66.

[37] Cf. Herbert Marcuse, *Eros and Civilization* (1955; rpt. New York: Vintage, 1962); Brown, *Life Against Death. Geza Roheim, *The Origin and Function of Culture* (New York: Nervous and Mental Disease Monographs, 1943), p. 79, regards culture from the standpoint of the Id as "neurosis." (Freud, of course, saw sublimation of Eros—not its negation—as the motive force of civilization.)

[38] R[ichard] S. T[horsen], "Thermodynamics," *Funk & Wagnall's New Encyclopedia*, 1973.  See also Rudulf Arnheim, *Entropy and Art* (Berkeley: Univ. of California Press, 1970).

[39] (Oxford: Oxford Univ. Press, 1921, 1925), pp. xi-xiii.

[40] Lawrence was fully aware that erotic drives do not terminate in sexual relations, but reach out toward ever-increasing transformations of society. In a letter to Dr. Trigant Burrow, he writes: "What ails me is the absolute frustration of my primeval societal instinct" (*Letters*, 685). Outside his novels, Lawrence's primitivism took the form of

wanting to sail away from a decadent, complex civilization to found a community of likeminded beings. Caudwell brands this impulse as regressive, although Lawrence does posit a sort of pre-politicial, primitive "communism," based on "goodness in the members" (*Letters* 215).

# V

# THE PLUMED SERPENT

## Judith Ruderman: "Rekindling the 'Father-Spark': Lawrence's Ideal of Leadership in *The Lost Girl* and *The Plumed Serpent*"

D.H. Lawrence's third writing phase, the so-called leadership period, is commonly discussed in terms of large social and political issues, as an anomaly in Lawrence's career. Yet, it may be argued, the central character in these works is the same domineering mother who figures so importantly in *Sons and Lovers* and elsewhere, the "smother mother" who, hovering anxiously over her child as he grows, leaves him no room to breathe. The central issue is likewise domestic: the maintenance into adulthood of an infantile dependency of the child upon the mother, fostered through covert means that play subtly upon the child's feelings of shame and guilt and that keep him feeling "small."

One work of this period, *Fantasia of the Unconscious* (1922), shows clearly that Lawrence's strictures about leadership of society by a strong man are based on his beliefs about the proper relationships among family members. His purpose in this treatise on psychology is to show how the problems of society at large begin in the mother-centered first society of most individuals in this modern age. Lawrence points to what he considers biological facts to explain, and also to counteract, maternal dominance:

> The connection with the mother may be more obvious [than that with the father]. Is there not your ostensible navel, where the rupture between you and her took place? But because the mother-child relation is more plausible and flagrant, is that any reason for supposing it deeper, more vital, more intrinsic? Not a bit. Because if the large parent mother-germ still lives and acts vividly and mysteriously in the great fused nucleus of your solar plexus, does the smaller, brilliant male-spark that derived from your father act any less vividly? By no means. It is different—it is less ostensible. It may be even in magnitude smaller. But it may be even more vivid, even

more intrinsic. So beware if you deny the father-quick of yourself. You may be denying the most intrinsic quick of all.[1]

It is the child's connection with the father, or the child's acceptance of the "father-quick" in himself, that Lawrence offers as the salvation of humankind: this is what he meant by the principle of lordship that his leadership novels are all about. Because the dire consequences of the mother-dominated household are the springboard from which Lawrence produced the works of his leadership period, one may trace a direct path from *The Lost Girl* (1920), which depicts the invidious rule of the Magna Mater, to *The Plumed Serpent* (1926), which retaliates against the Magna Mater and restores the rightful leader—that is, the father—to his throne.

Chapter One of *The Lost Girl* is a kind of prolegomenon to that novel, for it suggests how the heroine, Alvina Houghton, came to be lost in the first place. The reasons for Alvina's "lostness" vary with one's perspective; and, in fact, alternative explanations are offered in the novel.[2] But neither fictional character nor literary critic has pointed to a most important cause of Alvina's troubles: her lack of a father.

To be sure, Alvina has a nominal father, James Houghton, and in a certain sense the author shows a wry affection toward him. However, the first chapter— "The Decline of Manchester House"—records the many ways in which Alvina's father abdicates his leadship responsibilities and, in effect, abandons his daughter from early babyhood. Because James is always busy with one impractical financial scheme or another, Miss Frost, the governess, "imperceptibly [takes] into her hands the reins of domestic government" (*LG* 14); and Miss Pinnegar, the manageress of Houghton's work-girls, develops "a curious ascendancy" over her boss in matters of business (*LG* 19). James says little about his lack of status, seemingly indifferent or resigned to it, until, in his seventies, he lashes out at Alvina when she tries to take charge of him in his last illness: "Leave me alone! Will you leave me alone! Hectored by women all my life—hectored by women— first one, then another. I won't stand it—I won't stand it—" (*LG* 194). James Houghton's belated self-assertion does little to help either himself or his daughter: he dies the following day, leaving Alvina unprovided for in the psychological as well as the financial sense. For she, too, has been "hectored by women" all her life. Even the most passive woman in the household—Alvina's mother, Clariss—has in her invalidism manifested a hectoring feminine willfulness. Suffering from heart trouble, she cannot tolerate violence of any sort or degree, and she cultivates daintiness and gentility in her only child. Lawrence shows greater harshness toward Alvina's mother than toward her father, having created Clariss's illness to express her "obstinate self-importance" and her unfulfilled expectations of being made happy (*LG* 53). Clariss effectively rules the roost from her sick bed, for she has a kindred spirit in the governess, Miss Frost; and James in his dream world allows Miss Frost to take a parent's charge of Alvina.

Miss Frost's characteristic mode of parenting is forcefully illustrated when Alvina tries to make up her mind about marrying Alexander Graham and going with him to Australia. The matter is of central importance, for in Lawrence's fiction a common test of a child's maturity is the decision not merely to leave the nest but also to go off with a mate to a foreign land. Everyone in the Houghton household opposes the union, but it is Miss Frost who effectively circumvents it by arousing Alvina's feelings of guilt:

> "I feel you don't love him, dear. I'm almost sure you don't. So now you have to choose. Your mother dreads your going—she dreads it. I am certain you would never see her again. She says she can't bear it—she can't bear the thought of you put there with Alexander. It makes her shudder. She suffers dreadfully, you know. So you will have to choose, dear. You will have to choose for the best. . . . Don't trust me, dear, don't trust what I say," poor Miss Frost ejaculated hurriedly, even wildly. "Don't notice what I have said. Act for yourself, dear. Act for yourself entirely. I am sure I am wrong in trying to influence you. I know I am wrong. It is wrong and foolish of me. Act just for yourself, dear—the rest doesn't matter. The rest doesn't matter. Don't take *any* notice of what I have said. I know I am wrong." (*LG* 32-33)

After this "piece of indecent trickery of the spiritual will," as Lawrence calls it in *Fantasia* (*FU* 91), Alvina certainly cannot act for herself; instead she acts for her mother and for Miss Frost, who require her dependence on them for their own sense of identity.

If Alvina had had a father worth his salt, she could have resisted Miss Frost's maternal bullying; for the father's role in the child's development, according to *Fantasia*, is to stimulate the urge toward independence (partly through spanking, which activates certain nerve centers at the base of the spine) and thus to counteract the smothering effects of a mother's love. Lawrence characterizes the sort of love shown by Miss Frost as the "Northern" mode, arising from over-activity of the cardiac plexus and involving devotional worship. Miss Frost's name unsubtly hints at the "northern" aspects of her motherliness; but in case there is any doubt about the matter, Lawrence spells out that "her very breeding had that Protestant, northern quality, which assumes that we have all . . . the same divine nature" (*LG* 55). This northern quality is an enormous burden to Alvina: "It is doubtful which shadow was greater over the child: that of Manchester House, gloomy and a little sinister, or that of Miss Frost, benevolent and protective. Sufficient that the girl herself worshipped Miss Frost: or believed she did" (*LG* 27). Alexander Graham—with his "cruel, compact teeth," his dark skin and "dark blood," and the probability "that never, never would he make any woman's life happy" (*LG* 29)—offers Alvina what Lawrence in *Fantasia* calls the "Southern" mode of love, a "lower" kind, arising from the solar plexus. As the governess herself recognizes, "it was a question of heart against sensuality. Miss Frost tried and tried to wake again the girl's loving heart" (*LG* 31); and, with the weight of twenty-odd years of instruction behind her, she necessarily succeeds.

Miss Frost's seemingly benevolent protectiveness seduces Alvina into the view that Alexander is only a "little man, . . . a terrible outsider, an inferior, to tell the truth" (*LG* 31)—a situation repeated in *The Fox* (1921), when Banford convinces March that Henry Grenfel is just a boy, and an intruder into their cozy domestic relationship.[3] But Alvina has more spunk than March, and her force of will propels her out of Manchester House and into a six-month training period as a maternity nurse in Islington. Once she is geographically separated from Miss Frost, and engaged in an occupation that focuses her attention on the mother-child connection, Alvina seeks complete emotional separation and decides that it is "time for Miss Frost to die" (*LG* 45). Thereafter she appears to maintain with Miss Frost their old, loving relations, but in actuality Alvina is "almost coldly independent" (*LG* 54). Miss Frost, who has always been subject to bronchitis, finally develops pneumonia and dies, a victim of ailments that, according to *Fantasia*, result from an overactive cardiac plexus: a too-loving heart. It is as if she has been willed to death by Alvina, as Grenfel in *The Fox* wills that Banford be crushed by a tree.

But domineering mothers abound in *The Lost Girl*, as in a nightmare; no sooner is one slain than another arises to take her place. Alvina's dependency problem has not been solved, for gradually Miss Pinnegar takes over Miss Frost's role. Alvina had believed that Miss Pinnegar was different from Miss Frost, since "she never made you feel for an instant that she was one with you. She was never even near. She kept quietly on her own ground, and left you on yours. And across the space came her quiet commonplaces—but fraught with space" (*LG* 55). Yet, when Alvina is so stunned by her father's acquisition of a cinema that she cannot eat her dinner, Miss Pinnegar bids her eat in a way that makes her sound "short, almost like Miss Frost. Oddly like Miss Frost" (*LG* 113); and thirty-year old Alvina dutifully picks up her fork. Miss Pinnegar only *seems* to leave space; as far back as the maternity nurse episode, when she says in Alvina's defense, "Well really, if she wants to do it,why, she might as well try," Lawrence comments ominously, "And, as often with Miss Pinnegar, this speech seemed to contain a veiled threat" (*LG* 38). From years of tutelage in a mother-dominated household, Lawrence was extremely well-schooled in niceties of speech that mask hostile and aggressive inter-dependencies. Miss Pinnegar unmasks herself when, James having died, Alvina decides to join a traveling stage show as pianist, a rather compromising endeavor for a proper Woodhouse spinster, Miss Pinnegar simply assumes that Alvina is out of her mind and needs someone—namely, Miss Pinnegar—to take charge of her life: "You need to be looked after," she says (*LG* 242). Alvina flees the benevolent despotism of her mother-friend, and with it the cocoon-like protection of Woodhouse as a whole.

But Alvina merely exchanges one matriarchal society for another when she joins the traveling company. Madame Rochard, who heads the troupe, acts like a "wonderful mother" to the actors, busily sewing and cooking for them and generally looking after their needs. When Alvina first meets her, called in to diagnose her illness before her scheduled performance at James Houghton's theatre, Madame is being attended by two of her "boys," Max and Louis, who are devastated to the point of tears by her fever. Advised to take to her bed, Madame worries about fulfilling her matronly duties: "'Tonight,'" she moaned, "'I shan't be able to see that the boys' rooms are well in order. They are not to be trusted, no. They need an overseeing eye'" (*LG* 144). She worries, too, that their Indian act, in which she plays the part of the squaw Kishwégin, will fail without her: "'Children—they are all children!' wailed Madame, 'All children! and so, what will they do without their ould *gouvernante*? My poor *braves*. What will they do without Kishwégin?'" (*LG* 151). Her "wonderful" motherliness, therefore, has as its negative aspect the belief that these grown men are singularly incapable of acting on their own. Like the other *gouvernante*, Miss Frost, and like Miss Frost's doubles, Clariss Houghton and Miss Pinnegar, Madame Rochard is what *Fantasia* labels "queen of the earth, and inwardly a fearsome tyrant. She keepts pity and tenderness emblazoned on her banners. But God help the man whom she pities. Ultimately she tears him to bits" (*FU* 134).

Of the troupe, Max and Louis are so devoted to Madame that they may be said to worship her:

> Max watched her [sleeping] for some moments. Then suddenly he . . . crossed himself, dropping his knees as before an altar; crossed himself and dropped his knee once more; and then a third time crossed himself and inclined before the altar . . . .
> Louis also crossed himself. His tears burst out. He bowed and took the edge of the blanket to his lips, kissing it reverently. Then he covered his face with his hand.
> (*LG* 147)

Like Mr. May, the manager of Houghton's Picture Palace, Max and Louis take their places in the long procession of Lawrence's male characters who adore the Madonna figure: Mr. May is said to like "the *angel*, and particularly the angel-mother in woman. Oh—that he worshipped" (*LG* 120). This kind of "northern" love renders Mr. May unfit for a normal, sexual relationship with a woman, and even though Lawrence treats this gentleman's marital problems somewhat comically (*LG* 118-19), the repetitiveness of the issue in Lawrence's novels and the factual discussion of it in *Fantasia of the Unconscious* indicate the seriousness with which Lawrence considered it.[4]

The alternative to Max and Louis' devotion to Madame is offered by the two other members of the troupe, Geoffrey and Ciccio, especially the latter. While Max and Louis hover anxiously over their sainted mother-figure, Geoffrey sits "blowing the smoke down his nose, while Ciccio callously [lights] another cigarette"; when Madame's fever mounts, 'the young men [are] all extremely uncomfortable. . . . Only Ciccio [keeps] the thin smile on his lips, and [adds] to Madame's annoyance and pain' (*LG* 142-43). Madame is extremely sensitive to Ciccio's recalcitrance and tells Alvina that of all her boys, Ciccio especially needs her "over-seeing eye" (*LG* 144). Ciccio, in turn, is "on" to Madame's maternal dictatorship. He notes, in answer to Alvina's question about what Madame does, that "she does it all, really. The others—they are nothing—what they are Madame has made them" (*LG* 156). In answer to the question about why the troupe loves Madame so intensely, Ciccio responds simply, "We like her—we love her—as if she were a mother" (*LG* 157). Exactly how much Ciccio himself likes this relationship is made clear a moment later, when the seemingly dull-witted man waxes suddenly profound on this issue:

> "Have you a mother and father?" [Alvina asked.]
> "I? No! . . . They are dead."
> "And you wander about the world—" she said.
> He looked at her, and made a slight, sad gesture, indifferent also.
> "But you have Madame for a mother," she said. He made another gesture this time: pressed down the corners of his mouth as if he didn't like it. Then he turned with the slow, fine smile.
> "Does a man want two mothers? Eh?" he said. . . .
> "I shouldn't think so," laughed Alvina.

He glanced at her to see what she meant, what she understood.

'My mother is dead, see!" he said. "Frenchwomen—Frenchwomen—they have their babies till they are a hundred—"

"What do you mean?" said Alvina, laughing.

"A Frenchman is a little man when he's seven years old—and if his mother comes, he is a little baby boy when he's seventy. Do you know that?"

"I didn't *know* it," said Alvina.

"But now—you do."                                                                   (*LG* 158-59)

Alvina, of course, has spent a lifetime of conflict between her desire to please the women she has been devoted to and her desire to cut free from these women and assert her independence. Her life's pattern repeats itself when, in spite of Ciccio's tacit warning, she attaches herself to yet another domineering mother-figure by accepting initiation into the theatrical "tribe" of the Natcha-Kee-Tawara Indians. The ceremony is a farce: the participants have been drinking large quantities of wine and Alvina's "Indian" name of Allaye is a ribald joke—which she does not comprehend—referring to Ciccio's sexual access to her. But Madame is deadly serious when she has her followers repeat certain key concepts: WE HAVE NO LAWGIVER EXCEPT KISHWÉGIN. WE HAVE NO HOME BUT THE TENT OF KISHWÉGIN (*LG* 224). After holding her customary court, requiring her troupe to come forward and kiss her fingers, Madame units Alvina-Allaye and Ciccio-Pacohuila in tribal marriage. But Alvina is unable to find her home "beneath the wings of Pacohuila" as long as she and Ciccio live like babies beneath the smothering wings of Kishwegin. As she had once fled Manchester House, Alvina now flees the Natcha-Kee-Tawara, taking again a position as maternity nurse in another town.

Here begins an affair that curiously and ironically seems to invert the pattern of mother-child relationships established in the novel: no longer is Alvina the child dependent upon a mother whom she seeks to please; instead, she herself becomes the divine mother adored by a child-slave. The child in question is an unlikely one indeed: a fifty-four year old doctor, tall and beefy, with a blustering manner. Dr. Mitchell bullies his patients by insisting that he and he alone knows what is good for them, but his dominating and willful behavior is soon revealed as an attempt to cover up, or perhaps to compensate for, his inner lack of security. The doctor's stomach is said to be "as weak as a baby's" (*LG* 285), and thus he provides in this novel another physical manifestation of a psychic impairment. Before long, Dr.Mitchell begins to dote on Alvina. When he shows Alvina his grand home he is so delighted by her admiration that he feels himself capable of falling at her feet and kissing them ecstatically (*LG* 290). He contemplates "the treat of his life: hanging around the woman he had made his wife, following her about, feeling proud of her and his house, talking to her from morning till night, really finding himself in her" (*LG* 291). His first thought at the idea of having children with Alvina is that "a child would take her away from him." His pathetic relationship with Alvina therefore fits the definition of incest that Lawrence offered in a 1918 letter, in reference to Middleton Murry's relationship with Katherine Mansfield and to his own with Frieda: "At certain periods the man has a desire and a tendency to return into the woman, make her his goal and end, find his justification in her. In this way he as it were casts himself into her womb, and she, the Magna Mater, receives him with gratification."[5]

On the one hand, Alvina does receive Dr. Mitchell with gratification. At first she had disliked him, but when he begins to fawn on her she "liked him much better, and even saw graceful, boyish attractions in him. There was really something childish about him. And this something childish, since it looked up to her as if she were the saving grace, naturally flattered her and made her feel gentler toward him" (*LG* 288). But if Alvina is tempted by the knowledge that "of course he'd adore her" (*LG* 294), she also feels Dr. Mitchell's demanding love as a kind of weight upon her. Their relationship reaches its crisis when the doctor, incensed by Alvina's obstinate refusal to say yes or no to his marriage offer, shoves her violently against a wall, then falls on his knees before her "like a child" and begs over and over again, "Love me! Love me!" (*LG* 198-99). The incident shows clearly his immature need for Alvina's nurturing as well as his hostility toward her because of the power over him that his very need grants her. It is only to extricate herself from this painful situation, and from his smothering embrace, that Alvina accepts Dr. Mitchell's ring, which Lawrence has him place symbolically above the mourning-ring that had been Miss Frost's. Both Dr. Mitchell and Miss Frost wish to engage Alvina in a mother-child dependency that stifles growth; Dr. Mitchell's desires are the complement to Miss Frost's:

> He wanted her to be there. That was his greatest craving. He wanted her to be always there. And so he craved for marriage: to possess her entirely, and to have her always there with him, so that he was never alone. . . . She could see the hysterical little boy under the great authoritative man.  (*LG* 301)

Obviously Dr. Mitchell is not the "Dark Master" upon whom Alvina had ruminated some years earlier, in Woodhouse (*LG* 58). Although she connects up again with the swarthy Ciccio, marries him and goes off to live in a primitive region of southern Italy, surrounded by the ancient gods, one doubts whether Alvina has found her Dark Master to look up to. Certainly she occupies a tenuous position among the people of Pescocalascio, almost as tenuous as among the tribe of the Natcha-Kee-Tawara. She is pregnant as the story ends, and therefore "revered," Madonna-like, by Ciccio and his uncle; yet their reverence, Lawrence notes perceptively, contains elements of fear and hatred, and Alvina feels that Ciccio's benevolent sentimentalism toward her masks his unconscious desire for her death (*LG* 368, 374). Having always "banked hard on her independence" (*LG* 267), Alvina feels herself annihilated by Ciccio's love, and he in turn needs to keep a part of his life separate from her. The central problem in the novel—the tension between the desire for merger or union and the desire for separation or independence—remains unresolved. The decline of Manchester House as outlined in Chapter One, caused by the father's dropping the reins of leadership, is expanded upon in course of the novel and comes to symbolize the decline of England—even Europe—itself. But Lawrence ends his story on a note of hope: Alvina's unborn child and a projected journey to America after Ciccio's return from war offers promise for a future life in which the proper balance in human relations will be achieved. It is Kate Leslie, another lost girl, who makes that journey in *The Plumed Serpent*, which may be read as a sequel to *The Lost Girl*.

On 3 October 1924, from his ranch in New Mexico, Lawrence wrote to Murry of his strong desire to return to old Mexico (where he had written a first draft of *The Plumed Serpent* some months earlier): "It is time to go south.—Did I tell you that my father died on Sept. 10th, the day before my birthday?—The autumn always gets me badly . . . I want to go south" (*CL* 812). The placement of Lawrence's aside about his father's death is surely of some significance: the lack of a father is associated in Lawrence's mind with autumn and the north, and the search after a father, as well as after life and health, takes him off in a southerly direction. Moreover, the seemingly offhand notation of this death is belied by the mention of its proximity to Lawrence's own birthday (his thirty-ninth). In fact, the letter to Murry begins with—was perhaps promted by—Lawrence's reaction to Murry's news about his wife's expecting a baby: "Frieda says every woman hopes her BABY will become the Messiah. It takes a man, not a baby. I'm afraid there'll be no more Son Saviours. One was almost too much, in my opinion" (*CL* 812). What Lawrence presented to the world in his Mexican novel, the final version of which he completed a few months after writing this letter, was a Father Saviour rather than a Son Saviour—"a man, not a baby." The religion of Quetzalcoatl signifies the overthrow of the Magna Mater and the ascension of the Pater Magnus to the throne.

The role of the Magna Mater in *The Plumed Serpent* has not yet received its due, even though many note that, for all its sociological, political, and religious trappings, this novel is concerned in the main with the male-female relationship. The postures that men and women must take in the church of the living Quetzalcoatl, and that Kate Leslie and Cipriano assume in their marriage ceremony, require the woman to stoop and kneel, the man to stand erect; these ritualized positions invert the positions of the characters in *The Lost Girl* and are meant to correct the modern-day ascendancy of the Magna Mater that *The Lost Girl* depicts. For it is not simply woman who has assumed the power role but woman qua Mary or Queen of the World: she is the real target of Lawrence's spleen in this novel. Kate has been worshipped as a queen by her previous husbands, blue-eyed, ineffectual men like Basil in *The Ladybird*; now, the black-eyed men, like Count Dionys in that novella, are ready to re-assume their proper leadership role after pulling woman down from her pedestal. The Madonna figures in the Sayula church are literally ripped down and burned in preparation for the rededication of the church to Quetzalcoatl.[6] For what is wrong with the Jesus of Mexican Catholicism is not only that he personifies meekness and death but also that he has a mother; what is right with Quetzalcoatl, among other things, is that "he has not mother, he!"[7]

The central figure in *The Plumed Serpent*, that which initiates the action of the novel, is "the pretty white woman in a blue mantle, with her little doll's face under her crown, Mary, the doll of dolls, Niña of Niñas" (*PS* 302)—virginal girl-child-mother, who needs no human male partner. Kate Leslie, her imposing size and sexual aura notwithstanding, is a human representation of the white Madonna: her servant Juana makes this connection when she points to Kate's feet and tells her children to "look! Look at the feet of the Niña! Pure feet of the Santisima! . . . And She, the Holy Mary, is a gringita. She came over the sea, like you, Niña?" (*PS* 246). In Kate's Maryhood lies one reason for Cipriano's attraction to her:

> He looked at [Kate's] soft, wet white hands over her face . . . in a sort of wonder. The wonder, the mystery, the magic that used to flood over him as a boy . . . when he kneeled before the babyish figure of the Santa Maria de la Soledad, flooded him again. He was in the presence of the goddess, white-handed, mysterious, gleaming with a moon-like power. . . . He watched [Kate] continually, with a kind of fascination: the same spell that the absurd little figures of the doll Madonna had cast over him as a boy. She was the mystery, and he the adorer, under the semi-ecstatic spell of the mystery. But once he rose from his knees, he rose in the same strutting conceit of himself as before he knelt: with all his adoration in his pocket again.
>
> (*PS* 75, 88)

The novel records both Cipriano's desire for Kate and his struggles to rise from his knees, arm thrust upward in the Quetzalcoatl salute, asserting himself as an adult male, while she, the queen dethroned, kneels or lies prone at his feet.

The purest example of the Magna Mater in *The Plumed Serpent* is, of course, the woman who commits her life absolutely to the Madonna-principle: Carlota, Ramón's first wife. Miss Frost was a governess in *The Lost Girl*, and in this novel Carlota runs a Cuna or foundling home: both "northern" women are mother figures who live by the Christian ideal of charity that Lawrence terms "that cruel kindness" (*PS* 228). Their kindness is cruel because it presumes the recipient to be a child in need of their protection (even if the recipient is an adult), robs the individual of his human dignity, and delays or stifles his maturity. Miss Frost and Carlota are but two in the long line of mother figures that includes, to name only a few, Hermione in *Women in Love*, who continually attempts to take charge of Birkin and who treats his revolutionary ideas like some sort of little-boy whim; Banford in *The Fox*, whose hospitality toward the man she regards as a younger brother ends when he threatens her domination of March; and Tanny Lilly in *Aaron's Rod*, who remarks to her would-be prophet of a husband, in front of company, that he more than most men needs to hold a woman's hand.

Carlota in her turn denigrates Ramón's attempts to bring back pre-Christian gods by reducing her husband to a child—her child:

> Ah, it is terrible! terrible! And foolish like a little boy! Ah, what is a man but a little boy who needs a nurse and a mother! . . . He-he-he wants to be worshipped! A God! He, whom I've held, I've held in my arms! He is a child, as all men are children. And now he wants to be worshipped. (*PS* 181)

Horrified by Ramón's success, Carlota asks Kate, "Could you follow Ramón? Could *you* give up the Blessed Virgin?—I could sooner die!" (*PS* 207). And she does die—must die, for she is the greatest enemy of the phallic mystery, and Ramón, unlike impotent Clifford Chatterley in Lawrence's last novel, refuses to be nursed and mothered. The rededicatiojn of the church to Quetzalcoatl signifies the end of Madonna worship and therefore the end of Carlota: from her death bed Carlota accuses Ramón of murdering her, while Cipriano, Ramón's spokesman, heaps invectives on her and calls upon her to die (*PS* 381). At dawn—the dawn of a new era, Lawrence would have it—she obliges.

Ramón's second wife, Teresa, provides a stark contrast to the first. A brown-skinned Indian, she parrots Ramón's philosophy of parenthood and provides Kate with a corrective to the white-northern-Christian kind of mothering: "I, if I have any children, . . . I shall try to cast my bread upon the waters, so my children come to me that way. . . . I hope I shall not try to fish them out of life for myself, with a net. I have a very great fear of love. It is so personal" (*PS* 453). Kate's smothering relationship with her own children across the seas is only hinted at in this novel, but it is her wish to re-establish contact with them that prompts her to make plans to abandon her husband Cipriano and her new way of life. Carlota herself has over-protected Ramón's sons to the point of crushing out their life spark and turning them into ninnies. One of the boys wishes to become a priest, the other a doctor—to Ramón, and thus to Lawrence, both boys would be slaves to their mother's ideal of love. In Carlota Lawrence offers a prime example of what he lambastes, in *Fantasia*, as "this scorpion of maternal nourishment. Always this infernal self-conscious Madonna starving our living guts and bullying us to death with her love" (*PS* 173).

Ramón, in contrast, refuses to bully his children with love. When they repudiate him he tells them, in disgust, "You had better say to everybody: Oh, no! we have no father! Our mother died but we never had a father. We are children of an immaculate conception" [Lawrence means, of couorse, virgin birth] (*PS* 590). Yet if his sons should ever wish of their own accord to return to their father, Ramón will be ready to receive them, "to be a stronghold to them" (*PS* 392). Lawrence would have him offer protection without suffocation, authority without authoritarianism. To many readers, however, Ramón may not appear to be a good father; for he has allowed Carlota to smother the boys, retreating into himself in times of conflict with his wife (see *PS* 187). But Ramón's unwillingness to do battle with Carlota for possession of the children is not to Lawrence the equivalent of James Houghton's evasion of parental responsibility in *The Lost Girl*. To use Lawrence's own terms, set forth in the essay called "Master in His Own House" (1928), James Houghton shows indifference, Ramón, insouciance.[8] Ramón's retreat is meant to be born of strength rather than of weakness, indicating his belief in the inviolability of each individual soul and setting an example to his children that he can only hope they will choose to follow in later years. To Cyprian's cry that only his mother has loved him, Ramón answers that "she called thee her own. I do not call thee mine own. Thou art thyself" (*PS* 391).

Significantly, Ramón's son and Ramón's best friend are similarly named: if Cyprian is Ramón's biological son, Cipriano is his spiritual heir. Cipriano's godfather was a bishop, a Catholic father; but Cipriano believes that Ramón is better attuned to the needs of Mexico as a whole and Cipriano in particular. He explains that he worships Ramón in a sense because Ramón "can compel me to. When I grew up, and my godfather could not compel me to believe, I was very unhappy. . . . But Ramón *compels* me, and that is very good" (*PS* 88, 224). This compulsion is presumably "very good" because it translates into Ramón's helping to realize the beliefs that he already possesses; that is to say, Ramón can bring out the best in Cipriano, rather than imposing something on him. When Cipriano and Ramón meet on the terrace, having convened for tea at Ramón's home, Cipriano gazes "into the other man's face with black, wondering, childlike, searching eyes, as if he, Cipriano, were searching for *himself*, in Ramón's face. Ramón looked back . . . with a faint, kind smile of recognition, and Cipriano hung his head as if to hide his face" (*PS* 200). Sometimes at moments of great revelation between two characters, Lawrence heightens the impact of the scene by having it witnessed by a third party, in *The Lost Girl*, for instance, the pathetic confrontation between Dr. Mitchell and Alvina, at which he blubbers at her knees, is watched by a matron at the hospital, and the shock value for the reader is duly increased. In *The Plumed Serpent*, Lawrence has Carlota and Kate witness the tender scene between Ramón and Cipriano precisely in order for them—and, beyond them, the reader—to see that a new relationship has supplanted the unsatisfactory one between man and woman: as Lawrence urges in *Fantasia*,"wait, quietly, in possession of your own soul, till you meet another man who has made the choice and kept it. Then you will know him by the look on his face. . . . Then you two will make the nucleus of a new society" (*PS* 178).

The importance of the relationship between Ramón and Cipriano—as of that between the other blood-brothers in Lawrence's works—lies in what it reacts against: the Magna Mater and her smothering love. The novels ends with Kate's realization that, so far as Ramón and Cipriano are concerned, "a woman is really *de trop* "(*PS* 486). Kate's feeling of exclusion is mitigated somewhat by the remaining lines of the novel, in which Cipriano indicates to Kate that he desires her and wants her to stay. Yet according to L.D. Clark, the final line of the novel—Kate's "You won't let me go!"—was probably not decided on until Lawrence corrected the galleys in England in October 1925; as Lawrence wrote the scene some months earlier, the concluding sentence reads, "'Le gueux m'a plantée là!" she said to herself in the words of an old song."[9] Translated as "the scoundrel has jilted me," Kate's thought reiterates her feeling of exclusion, whether the French lyric refers in her mind to Ramón, who has just left the scene, or to Cipriano, who has just spoken. In *The Lost Girl*, the friendship between Ciccio and Giorgio arouses similar feelings of exclusion in Alvina, especially as the two men use French, a language that Alvina does not understand, as a secret code of communication; but Giorgio drops out of the story after Ciccio's commitment to Alvina, and Lawrence makes no political point of the love between the two men. In *The Plumed Serpent*, Ramón and Cipriano speak the language of the Quetzalcoatl movement, a language foreign to Kate, and their relationship, forming "the nucleus of a new society," is a love beyond woman.

*Fantasia of the Unconscious* offers an explanation of why "a woman is really *de trop*" to Ramón and Cipriano. According to the Introduction to that work, in which Lawrence sets forth his major criticisms of Freudian theory, a greater urge than that toward sexual intercourse—and often in direct antagonism to it—is "the desire of the human male to build a world: . . . to build up out of his own self and his own belief and his own effort something wonderful" (*PS* 60). By the time of his leadership period, Lawrence, the self-proclaimed "priest of love" (*CL* 173), preaches a subordination of heterosexual love—if only by a hair's breadth—to "the desire of the human male to build a world." Ramón, as founder of the Quetzalcoatl movement, has built a world animated by the patriarchal principle. The "essential quickening dark rays" that Lawrence speaks of in *Fantasia* (*FU* 70, 73)—those that pass from father to child in the family unit, meeting the "unquenched father spark" in the child—form the basis of a religion in which the dark sun, called the Father, supersedes the Magna Mater-Mary-moon goddess of both Protestantism (à la Miss Frost) and Catholicism (à la Carlota). Ramón composes the hymns and stories in which, as the Mexican peasants recognize, "there spoke a new voice, the voice of a master and authority. And though they were slow to trust . . . they seized upon the new-old thrill, with a certain fear, and joy, and relief" (*PS* 286).

What Lawrence advocates in *The Plumed Serpent*, then, is the sort of father-leadership, in all realms of life, that is shown by Don Ramón When Ramón speaks, Kate recognizes "a certain vulnerable kindliness about him, which made her wonder, startled, if she had ever realized what real fatherliness meant. The mystery, the nobility, the inaccessibility, and the vulnerable compassion of man in his separate fatherhood" (*PS* 206). Kate has been searching after a man worthy to take the lead in a relationship with her, and although Cipriano may seem at times "the supreme god-demon . . . the Master" (*PS* 343), Ramón is the true Dark Master that all of Lawrence's lost girls (and boys) seek. Cipriano without Ramón is "just an instrument, and not ultimately interesting" to Kate (*PS* 447). Moreoever, Kate, who banks just as hard on her independence as Alvina Houghton does, believes that "Ramón would never encroach on her, he would never seek any close contact. It was the incompleteness in Cipriano that sought her out, and seemed to trespass on her" (*PS* 207). Lawrence seems not to have been fully aware of this unattractive aspect of Cipriano's personality. Incidents like the aforementioned meeting for tea, at which Ramón and Cipriano greet each other tenderly, suggest what Lawrence did not intend: that Cipriano is as dependent upon Ramón, whom he calls "my Lord," as he refuses to be on "my Lady." Herman Daleski notes that Lawrence "generally castigates a childlike dependence in adult relationships, whether between man and man or man and woman; but Cipriano's eyes are 'childlike,' and *his* dependence is apparently acceptable not only to Ramón. [The relationship] . . . is subversive of what Lawrence would seem to contend it is—an ideal relation between two men, each of whom has consummated a self and one of whom, while maintaining his independence, willingly submits to the greater soul of the other."[10] Indeed, Lawrence gives the reader no grounds for believing that Cipriano after his incarnation as Huitzilopochtli is any more of a man than he was before, when he worshipped at the feet of the Madonna. And Cipriano's crucial lack of independence does more than make Kate wary of establishing a permanent relationship with him; it also causes the reader to cast a critical eye on Ramón, who, like Miss Pinnegar, only *seems* to leave space.

In the first version (1919) of his essay on Fenimore Cooper's Leatherstocking novels, Lawrence states that "a race falls when men begin to worship the Great Mother, when they are eveloped within the woman, as a child in the womb."[11] In his leadership period, Lawrence's hatred of the domineering mother-type caused him to oversimplify the options open to society: he says in *Fantasia* that "it is a choice between serving *man*, or woman. It is a choice between yielding the soul to a leader, leaders, or yielding only to the woman, wife, mistress, or mother" (*FU* 145). *The Plumed Serpent* represents the social and political corollary to Lawrence's emphasis, during this period, on the necessity for a father's leadership in the family. Even the supposedly just physical punishment meted out by Cipriano in his role as Quetzalcoatl's warrior aspect may be seen as a mere extension into society as a whole of the father's corporal punishment in the family group. The novel presents in fictional form the kinds of relationships that Lawrence believed would lift up the race after the cataclysmic reign of the Magna Mater: obedience of the masses to a supreme male leader; love between man and woman that is necessary for, but subordinate to, the man's larger mission in society. Was it Lawrence's recognition of the difficulty in establishing these relationships that caused him to counterweight the Quetzalcoatl movement with Kate Leslie's resistance to its precepts, and to give the novel a characteristic "open" ending . . . or was it Lawrence's inability to give his own full allegiance to the novel's strictures about sacrificing one's independence in allegiance to another (male) human being and to the mission he represents? *The Plumed Serpent* takes *The Lost Girl* one step further toward realizing the goals that Lawrence set forth clearly in *Fantasia of the Unconscious*. But the promising note on which the earlier novel ends is still unfulfilled in 1926.

It is now a commonplace in Lawrence criticism that Lawrence repudiated the ideal of leadership after *The Plumed Serpent*, adopting instead the mode of tenderness. Yet it may be argued that Lawrence retained to the end his belief in the patriarchal ideal and gave up only the search for its embodiment in a social, political, or religious system. A late story entitled "Mother and Daughter," written some time between November 1928 and February 1929, presents in capsule form the major concerns of *The Plumed Serpent*. In this story the Ramón figure, Arnault, is physically an unlikely marriage candidate for the heroine, Virginia Bodoin: he is sixty years old, grey haired, and fat. Yet he is a powerful antagonist to Virgina's dominating mother, and in the course of the story he succeeds in overthrowing the matriarchal ideal that she represents. Arnault's power lies in the fact that "his whole consciousness was patriarchal and tribal. And somehow, he was humble, but he was indestructible."[12] He recognizes that Virginia has led an unsatisfactory life because she is her mother's daughter (Virginia's father has been summarily dismissed—as Mrs. Bodoin had no doubt summarily dismissed him—in the first paragraph of the story, in the mere phrase, "since the effacement of a never very important husband" [*CSS* 805]). Arnault seeks to rescue this lost girl from her mother and to assert himself as the proper authority:

> He was in love with Virginia. He saw, first and foremost, the child in her, as if she were a lost child in the gutter, a waif with a faint, fascinating cast in her brown eyes, waiting till someone would pick her up. A fatherless waif! And he was the tribal father, father through all the ages. (*CSS* 820)

When Virginia commits herself to Arnault her mother sarcastically voices to her the sentiments that Kate Leslie entertains about Teresa's marriage to Ramón: "You're just the harem type, after all" (*CSS* 826). But if Kate feels that she cannot bear Ramón's "pasha satisfaction" and Teresa's "harem" mentality, she also admits to herself that she envies Teresa and begins to question whether Teresa is not the greater woman (*PS* 452, 449). Similarly, "Mother and Daughter" ends on a note of pity for Mrs. Bodoin, who has never been the "harem type."

It is ironic and sad that the patriarchal ideal—the Great Father—requires the same abnegation of individual personality as the mother-worship it replaces—the same envelopment of the smaller soul by the larger, the same losing of one's soul in order to gain it. The effects are presumably different, but the differences are hard sometimes for the reader to ascertain. Jeffrey Meyers, in his reading of "Mother and Daughter," understandably concludes that Virginia has merely exchanged "her deadly existence with her mother for a kind of death-in-life with the horrible yet attractive Arnault."[13] Meyers trusts the tale rather than the artist: Lawrence's depiction of the patriarch Arnault is fraught with the same ambiguities that surround the savior males in his other works, with the result that readers are as uncomfortable with Lawrence's notion of the Great Father as he would have them be with the Great Mother. Lawrence meant to show that, like the male-spark itself, a father's love is less showy than a mother's, but deeper and more important to the child's development. In trying to ignite this father-spark, Lawrence let the blaze get out of hand.

Lawrence's logic falters when he places woman securely in her domestic realm (as in the essay "Matriarchy") and then blames her for getting overly involved in her children; or when he attributes to woman the innate, biological urge toward connection (as in his treatises on psychology) and then blasts her for her unwillingness to let go. Occasionally Lawrence does portray a strong (as opposed to domineering) mother—Juliet in "Sun" comes to mind. But it is the sun, the male principle, that has taught Juliet how to parent: under its influence she takes "the strain of her anxiety and her will from off [her son]. And he thrived all the more for it" (*CSS*, II, 532). Instinctual, good mothering seems to abound for Lawrence only in the wild animal kingdom. In "Education of the People," contemporaneous with *The Lost Girl*, he laments that "there isn't a wild she-wolf in the length and breadth of Britain."[14] The one human mother who seems to live by she-wolf principles is Mrs. Barlow in *Touch and Go* (1920), but she is too sketchily drawn, and her son too weak, for her to exemplify model motherhood. On the whole the animal kingdom provided Lawrence with role models for fathers rather than for mothers, especially in his leadership period, with its herds of foxes and plumed serpents (its kangaroo, large of foot and thigh, shows promise of fatherhood, but his smothering pouch is suspiciously maternal). Although Lawrence credited both male and female children with a "father-spark" he was largely unwilling to credit females with the ability to use theirs wisely. Unfortunately, the rigidity of Lawrence's mother-father dichotomy and his idealization of the "father-spark" led to the dangerous idolization of particular males.

Yet if Lawrence's solution to the problem of maternal domination is suspect, his analysis of the problem is no less significant and the problem itself is no less real. Because of his particular family constellation in its particular Victorian setting, Lawrence was fixated on the parent-child relation—indeed, it is more central to his canon than the male-female sexual relation for which he is more commonly known; but Lawrence's statements on good parenting have value beyond auto- and cultural biography. Psychoanalytic thinking since Freud has emphasized the early dependence of the child upon the mother and the centrality of the preoedipal conflict between dependency and autonomy to the child's psychological development.[15] When the mother is over-protective and unable to let go, the father is in an ideal position to "rescue" the child, for the father stands outside the mother-child symbiosis but not so far outside as to be unfamiliar and frightening. Even if the mother does not feel the need to live through her children, having enough independent life of her own, a strong father figure is still desirable in providing the child a way to get beyond the primary caretaker. For the father and the mother both, good parenting as Lawrence forcefully and helpfully defines it includes the wisdom and the self-control to leave the child space or growing room. Lawrence's lifelong emphasis on striking the proper belance between protectiveness and respect for the integrity of each individual tempers somewhat his shrill excesses and remains the emphasis that ensures his works' lasting value.

*The D.H. Lawrence Review, 13:3 Fall, 1980*

## Notes

[1] *Fantasia of the Unconscious*, in *Psychoanalysis and the Unconscious and Fantasia of the Unconscious* (New York: Viking Press, Compass Books, 1960), p.70. Subsequent references to *Fantasia of the Unconscious* refer to this edition and will be cited parenthetically in the text using the abbreviated title, *FU*, and page number(s).

[2] Miss Pinnegar voices (and Mr.May implies) the conventional view that Alvina is morally lost. Alvina realizes that by her relationship with Ciccio she has cut herself off from society and also that she has lost one aspect of her self in order to gain another. *The Lost Girl* (New York: Viking Press, Compass Books, 1968), pp. 243, 254, 341, 350, 352, 197. Subsequent references to *The Lost Girl* refer to this edition and will be cited parenthetically using the abbreviated title, *LG*, and page number(s).

[3] For a discussion of *The Fox* in terms of the domineering mother see Judith Ruderman, "*The Fox* and the 'Devouring Mother,'" *DHLR* 10 (Fall, 1977), 251-69.

[4] Even when a character's relationship with a woman includes genital sex, the relationship is shown to be unsatisfactory if the male depends on the female for his feeling of self-worth and centers his life on her. Siegmund in *The Trespasser* and Gerald in *Women in Love* actually commit suicide when the maternal figures to whom they cling cannot (or will not) sustain them any longer. Many others (like Egbert in "England, My England" and Maurice in "The Blind Man") feel unbearably excluded when "real" children threaten to steal their share of the attention. To some degree, most of Lawrence's fiction is concerned with fixation on the mother.

[5] *The Collected Letters of D.H. Lawrence*, 2 vols., ed. Harry T. Moore (New York: Viking Press, 1962),I, 565. Subsequent references to Lawrence's letters refer to these volumes and will be cited parenthetically using the abbreviated title, *CL*, and page number(s).

[6] In *Sons and Lovers*, the young Paul and his sister burn the doll, called the Missus, that stands in for the mother. An interesting sidelight on the subject of doll-burning is provided by an August 1924 letter to Clarence Thompson, one of the hangers-on at Mabel Luhan's ranch: "I burned that hideous Indian doll—seriously set fire to her. She was too ugly . . . I feel it's a new phase altogether. The old idols put in the kitchen stove, like that doll" (*CL* 805).

[7] *The Plumed Serpent* (New York: Random House, Vintage Books, 1954), p.247. Subsequent references to *The Plumed Serpent* refer to this edition and will be cited parenthetically using the abbreviated title, *PS*, and page number(s).

According to tradition, Quetzalcoatl does indeed have a mother—a virgin mother, to boot! Laurette Sejourné, *Burning Water: Thought and Religion in Ancient Mexico* (London and New York: Thames and Hudson, 1956), p. 56.

8 In *Phoenix: Uncollected, Unpublished, and Other Prose Works by D.H. Lawrence*, ed. Warren Roberts and Harry T. Moore (New York: Viking Press, Compass Books, 1970), pp.548:

> Insouciance means not caring about things that don't concern you; it also means not being pinched by anziety. But indifference is inability to care; it is the result of a certain deadness or numbness. And it is nearly always accompanied by a pinch of anxiety. Men who can't care any more, feel anxious about it. They have no insouciance. They are thankful if the woman will care. And at the same time they resent the woman's caring and running the show.
>
> The trouble is not in the woman's bossiness, but in the men's indifference.

9 L D. Clark, *Dark Night of the Body: D. H. Lawrence's "The Plumed Serpent"* (Austin: University of Texas Press, 1964), p. 47. Clark believes that the French lyric is an inappropriate closing line because, "suggesting desertion, it is a long way from the circumstances".

10 Herman Daleski, *The Forked Flame: A Study of D.H. Lawrence* (Evanston, Ill.: Northwestern University Press, 1965), p.239.

11 *The Symbolic Meaning: The Uncollected Versions of "Studies in Classic American Literature,"* ed. Armin Arnold (Arundel: Centaur Press, Ltd., 1962), p. 109.

12 "Mother and Daughter," in *The Complete Short Stories of D.H. Lawrence*, 3 vols. (New York: Viking Press, Compass Books, 1961), III, 820. Subsequent references to Lawrence's short stories refer to these volumes and will be cited parenthetically in the text using the abbreviated title, *CSS*, and page number(s).

13 Jeffrey Meyers, "Katherine Mansfield, Gurdjieff, and Lawrence's 'Mother and Daughter,'" *Twentieth Century Literature*, 22 (December 1976), 452.

14 In *Phoenix: The Posthumous Papers of D.H. Lawrence*, ed. Edward D. McDonald (New York: Viking Press, Compass Books, 1972), p. 633. Lawrence wishes that, like Romulus and Remus, he had been suckled by a she-wolf: "It might have made a man of me" (p. 623).

15 See, for example, Margaret Mahler, Fred Pine, and Anni Bergman, *The Psychological Birth of the Human Infant* (New York: Basic Books, Inc., 1975). My thanks to Drs. Allen and Susan Dyer for bringing this book to my attention and for discussing with me the "separation-individuation" stage of psychological development.

## John Humma, "The Imagery of *The Plumed Serpent*: The Going-Under of Organicism"

*The Plumed Serpent* has this distinction: it is D.H. Lawrence's most ambitious failure. William York Tindall, who, at any rate, hardly admired Lawrence, is very nearly alone in believing the work to be his best.[1] Other readers, including Katherine Anne Porter,[2] praise the writing in the novel—or portions of it—and perhaps a very few, most notably L. D. Clark, would prefer to think of it as a qualified success rather than as an interesting failure.[3] The great majority, however, take this latter view—or worse. Eliseo Vivas, though he allows that the book has several "virtues," thinks its central situations "silly."[4] David Cavitch considers them 'offensive.'[5] Julian Moynahan calls its rituals "bathetic."[6] Graham Hough believes that the novel simply "goes to pieces."[7] Even F. R. Leavis finds the book hard to stomach; he speaks of it as the only one of Lawrence's novels "difficult to read through."[8] James C. Cowan, finally, speaks for most of these critics when he criticizes *The Plumed Serpent* for its failure of "unity."[9] The central defect of the book, according to the overwhelming majority of the critics, is that its parts simply do not hang together organically. Thus, Leavis says that it is "willed and mechanical"; Vivas, that it is not an "organic work of art."[10] Of these critics, only Cowan and Clark concern themselves with the imagery. Neither, however, discusses the imagery in relation to the novel's problems. Like the others, they trace its failure largely to implausibilities in plot, character, and meaning—and to Lawrence's lack of success in integrating these elements. Though so much is true, I believe that the best clue to why *The Plumed Serpent* goes wrong lies in Lawrence's handling of its imagery. The contention of this article is that when the imagery begins to go wrong, so does the novel.

In speaking of Lawrence's descriptive powers, Clark makes a useful if awkward distinction between what he calls "ordinary description" and "organic description": "Organic description, as I am using the term, includes the body and spirit of the principal character involved: both in his individual and in his allegorical capacity, and the spirit of religious awareness embodied in the landscape—in 'nature' if you will."[11] According to Clark, Chapter V, "The Lake," contains several instances of organic description, in which "the dominant force of Lawrence's genius expresses itself." Any image deserving to be called organic must have, of course, the appearance, at least, of having participated in a lived experience. It is true that the talented author can make us believe that a scene in which a character participates had to have been one which he himself must have similarly experienced—*whether he did so or not*. Thus, the incidents involving the snake near the end of the novel and the urchin and waterfowl earlier give the impression of having happened. The images grow out of the action; they do not appear merely to have been superimposed upon it. The problem is that these scenes of "organic description," as Clark speaks of them, are more nearly incidental than central: the principal imagery, nearly all of it symbolic, is, though brilliant in conception, of the "ordinary" sort. And here we may see that Lawrence's failure to make the characterizations of Don Ramón and Cipriano and their actions plausible has its corollary failure in imagery. Because we finally cannot believe in the imagery, which is made to carry much of the meaning of the novel, we cannot believe in the characters and their deeds. And the novel caves in on itself. Nonetheless, Lawrence is working with an exceedingly ambitious imagery, and for a long while our fascination with its symbolic configurations and with its complex and largely successful interconnections is sufficient to distract us from the growing problems of character and action. The first part of this article will consider the extension to which this central imagery *is* successful and will also consider one very likely source for the imagery. The second part will investigate what goes wrong. We will be considering, in short, why the first half or so of the novel seems to work, why the second half does not.

I

There are, of course, two central actions in *The Plumed Serpent*: the re-establishment of primitive religion and culture in Mexico and the realization of what we might call a Lawrentian womanhood for Kate. Lawrence works hard to bring these two actions within one frame; given the effort that he must have put into it, we should not find it difficult to see why he thought it, at one stage of its composition, the novel which "lies nearer my heart than any other work of mine."[12] These two actions, integrated through Kate's relationship with and ultimate marriage to Cipriano together with her assumption of the role of the green goddess Malintzi, parallel a third "action," that of the developing symbolic imagery of the novel. One of the problems is Lawrence's failure to synchronize properly the imagery and the two principal actions of the plot. But purely in terms of how much he gave himself to do and how intricate the apparatus necessarily became, we cannot but admire the ambitiousness of the undertaking, if not the final product itself.

As with just about all of Lawrence's later works, *The Plumed Serpent* has its source and being in myth. The best examinations of the mythic dimensions are Clark's and Cowan's (though John B. Vickery's and Jascha Kessler's studies are both valuable, Vickery's in demonstrating the influence of Frazer upon the symbology and structure of the novel and Kessler's in demonstrating the presence in *The Plumed Serpent* of the monomythic pattern which Campbell delineated in *The Hero With a Thousand Faces*[13]). Cowan and Clark directly confront the way in which the central symbol, the circle, either synthesizes or embodies Lawrence's principal thematic concern of integration, or "creative being."[14] If one statement from the novel succeeds in connecting the two actions, it is Kate's (it will also be Constance Chatterley's): "Ye must be born again."[15] Kate, of course, is born again, as is Quetzalcoatl.Kate's effort for herself, as well as Don Ramón's for the Mexican people, is nothing less than an attempt to come *full circle* to the lost condition of integrated being. The circle, then, in addition to emblematizing wholeness, as I shall be attempting to show, also structurally embraces the central actions of the novel.

The most important images involved in Lawrence's circling symbolism either are themselves not circles or have symbolic meanings which extend beyond their "circular" meanings. To this first category belong the snake, the eagle, the 'Tree of Life.' To the second belong the sun, the morning star, the eye. Related also to several of these is associative, subordinate imagery which reinforces and amplifies the meanings of the main symbols. So rich (if finally incoherent) are the parts which make up the whole of *The Plumed Serpent* that, for all the critical attention paid to the novel, much remains to be said, especially about the imagery. To consider, as I am doing here, Lawrence's strategy regarding several of the images is merely to scratch the overall surface. The question is why, if this novel is a failure, should we wish further to irritate that surface. The answer, of course, is that we often have as much to learn about an author and his technique from his failures—especially when they are ambitious ones—as from his successes. Certainly, this novel tells us a lot about Lawrence's method in his later novels. Clark's analysis of the way the symbolic conclusion of the novel plays against the beginning at the bull ring and the way that the symbol of the lake throughout establishes a texture and a reference point[16] reveals that Lawrence, though not so meticulous a novelist as some, certainly devised on occasion impressive strategies when it came to the coordination of details. Consequently, his efforts along these lines deserve our consideration. To be sure, *The Plumed Serpent* is a much more meticulously composed novel than his previous novels, *Aaron's Rod* and *Kangaroo*. If, in the former, he sometimes forgets in the second half what he had written almost two years before in the first half; and, if the latter is largely breezy (if sometimes brilliant) improvisational writing (Lawrence wrote the bulk of the novel in about five weeks), the evidence of the two drafts of *The Plumed Serpent* indicates that it is, to use Richard Aldington's phrase, one of Lawrence's more "worked-over novels."[17]

The symbols of the eagle and the snake, which in the Quetzalcoatl emblem form the eye-like circle, recall for us, as Julian Moynahan has remarked, the lion-unicorn opposition of "The Crown" and the iris symbol of *The Rainbow*.[18] The one is our higher, the other our lower consciousness. Don Ramón Carrasco, although the "representative" of Quetzalcoatl, whose symbols *both* eagle and snake serve, is the eagle (with his European, "white" consciousness) to Cipriano's snake (with his Indian, "dark" consciousness). One of Cowan's criticisms—it is one, I think, generally valid for most of Lawrence's work—is that, although Lawrence suggests balance as the ideal, he generally subordinates the one to the other. Here is Cowan: "This duo-mythic pattern, through the metaphorical function of contrasting characters, is employed in differentiating between white consciousness and dark consciousness as opposite modes of being. The effect of the contrast, however, rather than to reconcile the two, is to elevate the latter at the expense of the former."[19] Cowan's contrasts are Ramón-Cipriano vs. Owen Rhysbud Villiers, Teresa vs. Carlota, Ramon vs. the Bishop. But when we view the opposition in terms of the eagle (bird) and the snake, this criticism, though probably still valid for a good portion of the book, is not quite so easy to make. *The Plumed Serpent* contains much genuine criticism of the dark, instinctual self. Again and again we read of the "serpent-like," "reptilian" oppression of the spirit of Mexico. Kate thinks with revulsion of the "reptilian," "half-created women": "Something lurking, where the womanly centre should have been; lurking snake-like. Fear! The fear of not being able to find full creation, . . . insolent against a higher creation, the same thing that is in the striking of a snake" (pp. 82-83). Cipriano, despite his education, has a "barbarian consciousness," which is like an "intolerable weight" upon Kate. Clearly, he needs Kate, as he needs Don Ramón, to complete his being. For, unlike Ramon, he is all snake-like darkness.

In general, however, the novel vigorously posits blood-instinct and not mind-spirit as the way through. The tenor of nearly all of Don Ramón's screeds is that we must throw off the Christian, spiritual ethic by submerging ourselves in the instinctual life. Implicit in this descent is an ultimate reconciliation, but the novel's pronouncements, whether we view them in Don Ramón's or in Cipriano's statements or in Kate's attempt to symthesize these with her own more cautionary attitudes, are heavily on the side of "blood knowledge." This much is evident in Lawrence's selection of the two creatures which together take on the shape of the novel's central symbol. Lawrence, of course, is more or less stuck with the snake if he is going to give the myth of Quetzalcoatl primary status in the novel. His selection of the eagle as complement to the snake is considerably more arbitrary. The fact that he chose the fiercest, most rapacious of the avians (when he might have chosen, say, the dove) makes the novel's sentiments quite clear. Clark, who has much to say about both images, assumes that Lawrence's selection of the eagle, since it figures in the Mexican flag, was practically automatic. I would suggest as amplification to Clark, and not in contradiction of him, that Lawrence was also thinking of Nietzsche, who figures importantly in Lawrence's attitudes during this period.[20] To be precise, the snake and the eagle, which are the emblems of Quetzalcoatl, are also the emblems—and companions—of Nietzsche's Zarathustra.

Before we pursue this association further, we should look at the way in which Lawrence conflates eagle and snake and eye into *one* artistically complete symbol. In "The Plaza," before the participants form the inner and outer dance rings (symbolizing among other things the dark sun within the outer sun), Lawrence describes the leaflet upon which Kate and we encounter the first of the many poems of Quetzalcoatl:

> At the top of the leaflet was a rough print of an eagle within the ring of a serpent that had its tail in its mouth; a curious deviation from the Mexican emblem, which is an eagle standing on an opal, a cactus with great flat leaves, and holding in its beak and claws a writhing snake.
>
> This eagle stood slim upon the serpent, within the circle of the snake, that had black markings round its back, like short black rays pointing inwards. At a little distance, the emblem suggested an eye.   [p. 129]

Then follows the poem:

> In the place of the west
> In peace, beyond the lashing of the sun's bright tail,
> In the stillness where waters are born
> Slept I, Quetzalcoatl.
>
> In the cave which is called Dark Eye,
> Behind the sun, looking through him as a window
> Is the place. There the waters rise,
> There the winds are born.
> On the waters of the after-life
> I rose again to see a star falling, and feel a breath on my face.
> The breath said: Go! And lo!
> I am coming.                                    [pp. 129-30]

The rest of the poem concerns the withdrawal of Jesus to make way for the reemergence of Quetzalcoatl. Of concern to us here, however, is the way that Lawrence forges the four images into one comprehensive symbol of the higher (or here deeper) vision celebrated by the Romantics. Addressing the assemblage, Ramón tells of Quetzalcoatl's emergence from the lake and what he said to the thirsty men who came to hear him. Having assured them that he brings moisture for their dry mouths, he says: "When the snake of your body lifts its head, beware! It is I, Quetzalcoatl, rearing up . . . and reaching . . . to the sun of darkness beyond, where is your home at last." He tells them, "Without me you are nothing. Just as I, without the sun that is back of the sun, am nothing" (p. 134). Lawrence provides a number of reinforcing scenes and incidents. Earlier Kate, feeling the 'old reality' starting to give way, experiences "a soft world of potency . . . in its place. . . . Behind the fierce sun the dark eyes of a deeper sun were watching, and between the bluish ribs of the mountains a powerful heart was secretly beating, the heart of the earth" (p. 119). Here Lawrence is taking the image beyond itself, as he will do elsewhere, to suggest the organic connection possible when we see with more than what Blake calls "single Vision and Newton's sleep." Later, at his house, Ramón, backgrounded by the sun, appears to Kate dressed as Quetzalcoatl. On his hat is a round crest 'like an eye, or sun' (p. 187). The emblem devised by Ramón's blacksmith is of a bird within the sun, whose circle, of course, replicates the snake. The sail of Ramón's *canoa* "had the great sign of Quetzalcoatl, the circling blue snake and blue eagle upon a yellow field, at the centre, like a great eye" (p. 312). Kate is never of one mind about the movement, though her doubts do diminish and her acceptance grows—enough certainly for her to marry Cipriano and to take on the brideship of Malintzi. But early in the novel she had felt "like a bird round whose body [the Mexican] snake had coiled itself" (p. 77). But as Ramón had told her, in a metaphor we shall examine later, "It may be you need to be drawn down, down, till you can send roots into the deep places again. Then you can send up the sap, and the leaves back to the sky, later" (p. 86).

This passage leads nicely into Nietzsche and into the remarkable analogies between *The Plumed Serpent* and *Thus Spoke Zarathustra*. The title character of Nietzsche's eccentric work is a figure who in special regards is rather like Kate herself and also like Ramón-Quetzalcoatl. Like Kate (and like other Lawrentian heroes), he has an almost obsessive fear of and loathing for humanity. He urges the higher types to "flee into your solitude! You have lived too close to the small and miserable. Flee their invisible revenge!" Humanity is so many "poisonous flies," and it is "far from the market place that the inventors of new values have always dwelt."[21] And yet, like Kate and like Ramón Carrasco also, he needs companions:

> For a long time Zarathustra slept, and not only dawn passed over his face but the morning too. At last, however, his eyes opened: amazed, Zarathustra looked into the woods and the silence; amazed, he looked into himself. Then he rose quickly, like a seafarer who suddenly sees land, and jubilated, for he saw a new truth. And thus he spoke to his heart:
> 'An insight has come to me: companions I need, living ones—not dead companions and corpses whom I carry with myself wherever I want to. Living companions I need, who follow me because they want to follow themselves—wherever I want. . . . '
> [p. 135]

The similarities here to the Quetzalcoatl situation in *The Plumed Serpent* are intriguing to say the least. Like Quetzalcoatl, Zarathustra returns to the world after a considerable absence. In his instance, to be sure, it is not an age but a decade; nonetheless, like Quetzalcoatl, he arises after a lengthy sleep to urge a renewal upon the world. Again, like Quetzalcoatl, he will restore by pulling down the old values: "The man who breaks their tables of values, the breaker, the lawbreaker; yet he is the creator" (p. 135). Quetzalcoatl, of course, is a deity of pre-Christian origins whose vitality as a god lies deep within the primitive roots of Mexican-Indian culture; Zarathustra, similarly, is rooted in the ancient pre-Christian past. Under his more common name, he is the Persian prophet whose teachings became the foundation for Zoroastrianism. In seeking an ethic, or religion, in opposition to Christianity, both authors significantly located its source in primitive civilizations. The prophet (Zarathustra) and the god (Quetzalcoatl) predictably preach a human, earth-based religion. Here is Zarathustra:

> Behold, I teach you the overman. The overman is the meaning of the earth. Let your will say: the overman *shall be* the meaning of the earth! I beseech you, my brothers, *remain faithful to the earth*, and do not believe those who speak to you of otherworldly hopes! Poison-mixers are they, whether they know it or not. Despisers of life are they, decaying and poisoned themselves, of whom the earth is weary: so let them go.
>
> Once the sin against God was the greatest sin; but God died, and these sinners died with him. To sin against the earth is now the most dreadful thing, and to esteem the entrails of the unknowable higher than the meaning of the earth.    [p. 125]

To acquire what is needed, he, like the sun, must "go under": "I must descend to the depths, as you do in the evening when    ou go behind the sea and still bring light to the underworld, you overrich star. Like you I must *go under* [Nietzsche's italics]—go down. As is said by man, to whom I want to descent" (p. 122)

The "overman," of course, is Kaufmann's translation of *Ubermensch*, a more accurate rendering than "superman" in that it preserves the over/under tenor of Nietzsche's ethic. As Quetzalcoatl, Don Ramón's efforts are to create his own cadre of overmen. He tells Cipriano, "I would like to be one of the Initiates of the Earth. One of the Initiators. Every country its own savior. . . . And the First Men of every people forming a Natural Aristocracy of the World. One must have aristocrats, that we know. But natural ones, not artificial" (p. 272). Nietzsche's attack upon Christianity centered on *its* artificiality. It was, in his view, an anti-natural religion. Precisely the same is true for Lawrence. Thus, Zarathustra's 'God is dead' has its analogue in the retirement from Mexico of the moribund Christ. And the reborn deity, like his followers, must as Zarathustra says, "go under." As Don Ramón had told Kate, "It may be you need to be drawn down, down, down, till you send roots into the deep places again" (p. 86). There is even a hint of Nietzsche's notion of eternal recurrence in *The Plumed Serpent* in the alternation of Quetzalcoatl and Jesus as Mexico's deities, for centuries earlier a worn-out Quetzalcoatl had withdrawn as quietly and resignedly as Jesus does now. "*Quetzalcoatl said*: It is very good. I am old. I could not do so much. I must go now. Farewell, people of Mexico. Farewell, strange brother called Jesus. Farewell, woman called Mary. It is time for me to go" (p. 245). The rhythms of life dictate the rise and fall of religions. The implication is that Quetzalcoatl's present emergent triumph is subject to the same.

All of this has been preamble to an examination of the "Prologue" of *Thus Spoke Zarathustra*, a line or two of which I have just quoted above. The Prologue contains the basic shape of the Quetzalcoatl development in *The Plumed Serpent*, and it contains *all* of the core images of that novel:

> When Zarathustra was thirty years old he left his home and the lake of his home and went into the mountains. Here he enjoyed his spirit and his solitude, and for ten years he did not tire of it. But at last a change came over his heart, and one morning he rose with the dawn, stepped before the sun, and spoke to it thus:
> 'You great star, what would your happiness be had you not those for whom you shine?
> 'For ten years you have climbed to my cave: you would have tired of your light and of the journey had it not been for me and my eagle and my serpent.
> 'But we waited for you every morning, took your overflow from you, and blessed you for it.
> 'Behold I am weary of my wisdom, like a bee that has gathered too much honey; I need hands outstretched to receive it.
> 'I would give away and distribute until the wise among men find joy once again in their folly, and the poor in their riches.
> 'For that I must descend to the depths, as you do in the evening when you go behind the sea and still bring light to the underworld, you overrich star.
> 'Like you I must *go under*—go down, as is said by man, to whom I want to descend.
> 'So bless me then, you quiet eye that can look even upon an all-too-great happiness without envy!
> 'Bless the cup that wants to overflow, that the water may flow from it golden and carry everywhere the reflection of your delight.
> 'Behold, this cup wants to become empty again, and Zarathustra wants to become man again.'
> Thus Zarathustra began to go under.    [pp. 121-22]

Like Ramón's Quetzalcoatl, Zarathustra must take up a *human* existence if his influence is to be vital. Quite remarkable is the appearance here of the images that in *The Plumed Serpent* become the central symbols: the eagle and the snake, the sun-star, the rendering of the sun as an eye, even the lake and the image of restorative water. To be sure, Nietzsche does not develop these images as Lawrence is to do. But they signal, nonetheless, vitality. Eagle and snake, as in Lawrence, effect the reconciliation between transcendence (spirit) and descendence (instincts). In Lawrence, of course, the morning star further establishes the notion of a balance between the two ways. The sun here has no "dark" counterpart, but Nietzsche insinuates much the same idea when he speaks of its nightly descent "to the depth" of the sea "underworld." If the sun, like an "eye," has by a day a "vision," so to speak, so by night, through its "going-under," it takes on the property of a further, deeper vision. Nietzsche, like Lawrence, is insistent that if man is to achieve an organic relation to the universe, he must see with more than the purely rational eye. Finally, Zarathustra speaks of the lake he had left and the waters with which he once again would like to refill his cup for the regeneration of others. Quetzalcoatl returns to earth from a lake, and water throughout the novel signals regeneration. Certainly it is no surprise to discover that water symbolizes life or renewal (it would be surprising if it did not). What is surprising is to find these conjunctions of images in such a short space in a work otherwise so similar in meaning to another. If Lawrence was not consciously or unconsciously influenced by *Zarathustra*, then we have, I think, a remarkable coincidence. One wishes, indeed, that this were the case insofar as it would attest to the theories of Frazer, Jung, and others who have worked with mythic and archetypal figures that an elemental presence in our subconscious selves informs our conscious way of seeing the world. It may be that artists do not so much choose among what there is in what they work with as that they have no choice in what they "choose." The important consideration then becomes not so much what they write about as how they write about it. This question, as it concerns these images and others in *The Plumed Serpent*, will be the focus of the second part of this paper.

## II

The central thematic opposition in *The Plumed Serpent*, as in some sense it is in all of Lawrence's fiction, is the opposition between organic connection and mechanical fragmentation. We have observed Kate as she realized that she must break with the "sterility of nothingness which was the world, and into which her life was drifting," that she must free herself from her "mechanical connections" with people like Villiers, who were "widdershins, unwinding the sensations of disintegration and anti-life" (p. 113). Her new life is to be bound up on Don Ramón, who speaks for and leads the cause of vital religion, and in Don Cipriano, whose dark, Pan-like nature is the fleshly embodiment of Ramón's speeches. The language of these speeches, as we have seen, puts a high premium upon symbol. But there is a satellite imagery present in the speeches and conversations and also present in the language of the novel which never becomes symbol. The function of this imagery is to reinforce the theme of organicism in the novel. The central images are bird (flight, flock), tree or plant (forest, leaf, sap), heart (blood), and water (lake, ocean, rain). We get an idea of how Lawrence intends this imagery to serve from this passage from a Ramón speech:

> 'Put yesterday's body from off you, and have a new body. Even as your God who is coming. Quetzalcoatl is coming with a new body, like a star, from the shadows of death.
>
> 'Yes, even as you sit upon the earth this moment, with the round of your body touching the round of the earth, say: Earth! Earth! you are alive as the globes of my body are alive. Breathe the kiss of the inner earth upon me, even as I sit upon you.
>
> 'And so, it is said. The earth is stirring beneath you, the sky is rushing its wings above. Go home to your homes, in front of the waters that will fall and cut you off forever from your yesterdays.
>
> 'Go home, and hope to be men of the Morning Star, Women of the Star of Dawn.
>
> 'You are not yet men and women—'
>
> He rose up and waved to the people to be gone.    [p. 220]

Or "Ye must be born again." But it is the imagery as well as the meaning which concerns us here. Just about all of the imagery of this passage conveys a vitalistic picture of the surrounding world. But the principal image, it seems to me, is not that of the earth in vegetable stir or the sky "rushing" like a bird or even the purifying rains. Rather it is the image of the earth and body as globes. These images serve the novel's central symbol, the circle. Lawrence has Ramón speak of the "round of your body touching the round of the earth." And then "Earth! Earth! you are alive as the globes of my body are alive." The globe is a wonderful image in the way that it connects the two things between which there must be an organic relation. Moreover, it does so through an image that unobtrusively suggests fruit, which, of course, in one form or another is the climax and goal of the entire system of organic life. Our perception of what Lawrence has done here is not so much rational as it is imaginative or intuitive. If Ramón's speeches usually are prose, this one is poetry. Finally, the passage combines in some way or other each of the central images I have spoken of above, taking on the character of a synechdoche for the vast organic relationship toward which its speaker is striving.

Lawrence's chief image of organicism is hardly original: the Tree of Life. In the first ceremony which takes place in the plaza, Kate thinks of what is happening to her as "a sort of fate" which she cannot resist. She thinks, "Like fate, like doom. Faith is the Tree of Life itself, and the apples are upon us," the apples of the eye, chin, heart, breast, belly "with its deep core," loins, knees, even "the little, side-by-side apples of the toes." She perceives that change and evolution do not matter: "We are the Tree with the fruit forever upon it. And we are the faith forever. Verbus Sap" (p. 138). Only Kate in this novel is capable of thinking these words; Ramón, except by fluke or authorial lapse, would be incapable of them. There is a certain whimsy, if not humor exactly, about them, which relieves them of the sententiousness they might otherwise have. The word plays—"apples of the eye," "apple of the belly, with its deep core"—and the inclusion of chin, knees, and 'little, side-by-side apples of the toes" give the paragraph a kind of charm. Here are the great and small—heart and loins, but also chin and knees and toes. These globes are all a part of the fine organic "round" which is Man Living.

This paragraph is followed by one which combines the myriad satellite images in a manner similar to the "globe" passage:

> The one singer had finished, and the drum kept on, touching the sensitive membrane of the night subtly and knowingly. Then a voice in the circle rose again on the song, and like birds flying from a tree, one after the other, the individual voices arose, till there was a strong, intense, curiously weighty soaring and sweeping of male voices, like a dark flock of birds flying and dipping in unison. And all the dark birds seemed to have launched out of the heart, in the inner forest of the masculine chest. [p. 138]

The extended avian metaphor commences with a description of the birds (voices) taking off separately, alone ("one after the other") and concludes with a description of them as one (a "flock"). The last sentence of the paragraph in which the many voices come as if from a singular chest presages the union of men which is to come with the renewal of the myth of Quetzalcoatl in the hearts of the people. But the people will have *one* heart then, just as the disparate images—bird, heart, trees ("inner forest")—are fused here in one trope. This is an alert piece of writing, the images quietly but efficiently encapsuling the larger meaning of the book.

Lawrence's vegetable imagery strategically parallels the dualistic animal imagery of eagle and snake. Each is intended to signify the necessity of a balance between the higher and lower, or the spiritual and physical (sexual, instinctive), faculties of man. Ramón-Quetzalcoatl says, "My stem is in the air, my roots are in all the dark" (p. 249). Kate, when she is dancing in the revolving circles, begins "to learn softly to loosen her weight, to loosen the uplift of all her life, and let it pour slowly, darkly, with an ebbing gush, rhythmical in soft, rhythmic gushes from her feet into the dark body of the earth." The "ebbing gush" suggests the elements both of water and of blood. These images then fuse with the vegetative in the next sentence. "Erect, strong like a staff of life, yet to loosen all the sap of her strength and let it flow down into the roots of the earth" (pp. 143-44). This imagery replicates the meaning of the eagle-snake imagery. But in the merging of imagery from different elements, Lawrence accomplishes something further, as we have observed: he reinforces our sense of the organicism of the cosmos. It *is* a vitalistic earth that Lawrence wants to convey. When he has Ramón-Quetzalcoatl say of the "snake of the world" that "only his living keeps the soil sweet, that grows you maize" and that "the trees have root in him, as the hair of my face has root in my lips" (p. 216), he is once again epitomizing the relation among all living things (vegetable animal, human) through the merging relations of these images themselves.

So far so good. Our problem (as readers) and Lawrence's problem is that it does not go very much further. To be sure, there are a number of nice touches we can admire, as Clark, Cowan, and others have pointed out. The snake and the foal episodes in the last two chapters both are brilliantly concrete dramatizations of Kate's wishes first to submit and then not to submit. The difficulty is that these scenes, and others, finally do not carry the weight of the meaning but are subordinate or incidental to it. It is ironic, I suppose, that a novel which works so hard for the cause of organicism finally fails, according to the charges of Vivas and others, because its own parts do not themselves achieve an artistic organic relation.

I remarked early that the novel's failure is attributable to Lawrence's failure to sustain a consistent imagery. The second half of *The Plumed Serpent* has going for it several instances of fine descriptive writing, which we expect from Lawrence, together with the tension, what there is of it, achieved through Kate's indecisiveness. Nonetheless, the latter portion is, by common consent, a bore. The most glaring defects are, first, the extremes to which Ramón and Cipriano take their ideas and, second, the finally stale repetitiveness of Ramón's oratory and ideas. The extravagances which occur in the second half of the novel—the ritual executions and the "marriage" of Kate-Malintzi to Cipriano-Huitzilopochtli being the chief but not the only instances of these—impair if not destroy our confidence not only in the characters and the narrative but also in the novel's larger meaning and purpose. Moreover, the novel's lame credibility by this point is not bolstered by the later poems and speeches. For, if we have not heard them before, we *think* we have heard them before. And the new development in the plot—the marriage between Malintzi and Huitzilopochtli—is really an anticlimax or, worse, a serious derangement in the coherence of the novel's central tension and attendant imagery.

What happens, I believe, is that Lawrence fails to synchronize the imagery and the action. Thus, while symbol (eagle and snake) and metaphor (tree-stem and roots) assert a balance à la "The Crown" between mind-spirit and blood-instincts, the action is already moving along a logic insistent upon the superiority of the dark forces of the primitive self. Though "Quetzalcoatl" claims that he is "lord of two ways," the "master of up and down," whereas Christ had been lord but "of the one way" (p. 250), more and more it appears that Ramón-Quetzalcoatl is the lord of the *other* way: the down one. No synthesis is allowed Carlota's Europeanized-Christian "way" with Ramón's primitive-pagan way. Lawrence has madness kill her off. Teresa, who replaces Carlota, is a Ramón look-alike. Ramón, who had seemed the eagle complement to Cipriano's snake, becomes Cipriano's look-alike. He may wear, as Quetzalcoatl, the blue of the sky as opposed to the red and black and earth colors which Cipriano wears as Huitzilopochtli, but it is the moral colors of Huitzilopochtli's serpent code which Ramón actually wears. In the strange ceremony in which Cipriano becomes "the living Huitzilopochtli" late in the novel, the priest, or conductor, who initiates him is Ramón. Over and over he asks Cipriano, "Is it dark?" (pp. 402-03) until, of course, fully initiated, Cipriano sees that it is "all dark," "perfect." All that remains is for Ramón and Cipriano to conduct Kate, as the "green Malintzi," to her marriage-in-darkness with Cipriano-Huitzilopochtli. To be sure, green is her color, and grass the product of both blue air and yellow sun, on the one hand, and the dark "under-earth" (p. 412) on the other. But her allegiance must be utterly to the latter. She is, in fact, Persephone to Cipriano's Pluto, as in "Bavarian Gentians"; though Lawrence connects Cipriano with Pan and not Dis, he is, nonetheless, her demon lover; and, as his wife, she must have as her realm the darkness "of the ancient Pan world, where the soul of woman was dumb, to be foreever unspoken" (p. 342). Hardly a synthesis, then: mind, soul, light—extinguished, gone "dumb" in the gravitational pull of Cipriano's 'demon-power' (p. 341).

Had Lawrence not established the logic of another imagery, another symbology, our fault-finding here would be of little weight. As it is, we are struck by a glaring inconsistency between design and execution. Moreover, Lawrence's orchestration of his main symbolism climaxes prematurely. In the first half of the book, the skill with which he introduces and then develops the imagery is fascinating. We are, indeed, witnessing a master hand at it, that of one of the twentieth century's finer poets. (Certainly the real poetry in the novel is in the prose, not in the "poems.") The problem is that he brings the development of this imagery to its crisis before the main actions in the plot even take place. This point is what I mean when I say that the failure of the novel can be blamed upon a failure in the management of the imagery, a failure to coordinate imagery and action. Had Lawrence been successful in pacing his imagery and in embodying the action in the images (and vice-versa), the result might have been the artistic whole promised by the early chapters. By contrast, in *Aaron's Rod*, imperfect as that novel is, Lawrence, nonetheless, orchestrates his imagery with the action. Aaron does not throw his rod into the river halfway through the narrative. When he does, it comes with appropriate symbolic significance, as does Lilly's remark near the end that the broken rod (also Aaron by extension), having organic properties (it is said to "blossom"), can regenerate. In *Lady Chatterley's Lover*, Lawrence's imagery does not reach its climax until the penultimate love scene, in which Constance "becomes a woman" fully for the first time. The late story "The Woman Who Rode Away," which has some of the same disturbing tone and extremes as *The Plumed Serpent*, satisfies us, nonetheless, as a unified work of art, a whole. The extremes of heat and chill, which Lawrence carefully develops in the story, culminate in the epitomizing symbols of the sinking sun and the shaft of ice, which "was like a shadow between her and it."[22] In each of these later works, a pleasing integration of imagery and narrative results in a unity we may call organic. These same elements in *The Plumed Serpent*, without this integration, become merely mechanical.

Lawrence could scarcely write an uninteresting work. And certainly *The Plumed Serpent* is interesting throughout most of its first half and sporadically in its second half. But when Lawrence allows the central action to divorce itself from the controlling imagery, he loses the novel. If there is a lesson in this, it is that a novelist who works as extensively through a texture of imagery as Lawrence does creates a difficulty—and a danger—requiring intricate navigation. It may be that very often a novel's imagery is the (nearly) spontaneous development of the novelist's ideas or preoccupations. If so, it requires him to have good instincts. What may have happened in *The Plumed Serpent* is that Lawrence lost his good instincts for a time, as happens to most novelists at one time or another. Lawrence's ill health and his frequent despondency (reflected in the sentiment of *noli me tangere* of his protagonists of this period) had to be a distraction as the plot, with its harsh and violent extravagances, would appear to indicate. The shorter works of this time could more nearly resist the distractions which the longer work could not. Nonetheless, *The Plumed Serpent* bruises us into a sort of attention—not entirely in spite of its being a failure but in some small measure, at least, because it *is* a failure. About Lawrence's craft in particular, especially the light it sheds upon the virtues of his more successful works and about novel-writing in general, *The Plumed Serpent* still has things to teach us.

*The D.H. Lawrence Review*, Fall, 1982

## Notes

[1] William York Tindall, *D.H. Lawrence & Susan His Cow* (New York: Columbia University Press, 1939), p. 13.

[2] Katherine Anne Porter, "Quetzalcoatl," collected in *The Days Before* (New York: Harcourt, Brace, 1952), pp. 262-67. In this review, Porter praises Lawrence's 'immense and prodigal feeling for the background,' for making 'every minute detail' appear as though 'seen with the eyes of a poet.' Her objections are the usual ones, however: the hymns of Quetzalcoatl are mainly 'hollow phrases' and his principal characters 'mouthpieces.' Reading *Sons and Lovers* again, she says, will make us 'realize the catastrophe that has overtaken Lawrence.'

3 L. D. Clark, *The Dark Night of the Body: D.H. Lawrence's "The Plumed Serpent"* (Austin: University of Texas Press, 1964), pp. 3-13. Clark, however, is not reticent about the book's problems.

4 Eliseo Vivas, *D.H. Lawrence: The Failure and the Triumph of Art* (Bloomington: University of Indiana Press, 1960), p. 70.

5 David Cavitch, *D.H. Lawrence and the New World* (New York: Oxford University Press, 1963), p. 109.

6 Julian Moynahan, *The Deed of Life: The Novels and Tales of D.H. Lawrence* (Princeton, New Jersey: Princeton University Press, 1963), p. 109.

7 Graham Hough, *The Dark Sun: A Study of D.H. Lawrence* (London: Duckworth, 1956), p. 129.

8 F. R. Leavis, *D.H. Lawrence: Novelist* (New York: Knopf, 1968), p. 69.

9 James C. Cowan, *D.H. Lawrence's American Journey* (Cleveland: Case Western Reserve University Press, 1970), p. 120.

10 Leavis, p. 69; Vivas, p. 72.

11 Clark, p. 56.

12 *The Collected Letters of D.H. Lawrence*, ed. Harry T. Moore (London: Heinemann, 1962), p. 844.

13 Vickery in *"The Plumed Serpent* and the Renewing God," *Journal of Modern Literature*, 2 (1971-72, 505-32; and Kessler in "Descent into Darkness: The Myth of The Plumed Serpent" in *A D.H. Lawrence Miscellany*, ed. Harry T. Moore (Carbondale: Southern Illinois University Press, 1959), pp. 239-61.

14 Cowan, p. 103.

15 *The Plumed Serpent* (New York: Knopf and Random House), p. 61. Subsequent references to this Vintage Book edition are cited parenthetically within the text and indicated by page numbers.

16 Clark, pp. 72-73, 140-43.

17 Richard Aldington, from the Introduction to *Kangaroo* (New York: Viking, 1900), p. viii.

18 Moynahan, pp. 108-09.

19 Cowan, p. 100.

20 In this regard, see John B. Humma, "D.H. Lawrence as Friedrich Nietzsche," *Philological Quarterly*, 53 (1974), 110-20.

21 *The Portable Nietzsche* ed. Walter Kaufmann (New York: Viking, 1970), pp. 164-65.

22 *The Complete Short Stories*, II (New York: Penguin, 1978), p. 580.

# Kimberley VanHoosier-Carey, "Struggling with the Master: The Position of Kate and the Reader in Lawrence's 'Quetzalcoatl' and *The Plumed Serpent*"

Critical discussion of *The Plumed Serpent* too often confines itself to the discussion of Lawrence's "male leadership" theme. Even L.D. Clark, one of the novel's most sympathetic critics, in his 1987 introduction to the Cambridge edition of the novel, makes a connection between *The Plumed Serpent* and *Kangaroo* since both "explore magnetism and loyalty between men, most of all male leadership by blood authority" (xxi). Yet the changes made in the revision from the 1923 "Quetzalcoatl" manuscript (held by the University of Texas' Harry Ransom Humanities Research Center) to the 1926 published version of the novel[1] indicate that "male leadership" was becoming less central to Lawrence as his conception of the novel progressed. The focus is not solely on the "magnetism and loyalty between men" as it most certainly was in the manuscript. Ramón and Cipriano are less dominant characters in the published version in that Lawrence no longer reserves the experience of the Quetzalcoatl movement for them alone to the exclusion of Kate and the reader. Therefore, rather than simply examining the text in terms of male leadership, comparing the manuscript to the published version allows us to read the text through the lens of the changes made to Kate's character, changes which indicate a renewed interest in representing female experience.

The development of Kate's character is one of the most drastic changes from the "Quetzalcoatl" manuscript to the published version of the novel. In the published version Kate has a larger, more participatory role within the Quetzalcoatl movement and within the narrative itself than she did in the manuscript. The scope and focus of the revisions indicate that Kate's character is central to the cohesion evident in the published version of the novel in contrast to the manuscript. The manuscript version of the novel contains several structural problems, most of which are resolved in the published version through an increased focus on Kate and through the integration of the hymns and other elements of the Quetzalcoatl movement into the narrative structure. The changes in the characterization of Kate, particularly the emphasis on her participation in the revival of the Quetzalcoatl movement, parallel and provide a focal point for the changes in the representation of the Quetzalcoatl movement and its integration into the narrative structure. Her increased integration into the movement and narrative also creates a space for participation and an experiential understanding on the part of the reader.

In the manuscript version, on the other hand, Kate, like the reader, is a somewhat obtuse student of Ramón and Cipriano, someone to whom they can explain the goals of their movement, someone they can convince of the need for a revival of the ancient form of consciousness and connection with the universe. Many of the plot elements of the published version are not yet included, particularly those elements that mark her participation in the Quetzalcoatl movement and Kate's connection with other characters. For example, she has little contact with Cipriano, she does not marry him or have a sexual relationship with him, she does not take on the role of Malintzi, and in general, she has little connection to the other characters except that of a convenient repository for explanations of their ideas and symbols. Her character becomes much more developed in the published version of the novel; she becomes a full participant in the movement and in her relations with Ramón and Cipriano.

Ramón makes Kate his disciple in the manuscript, the recipient of his lengthy abstract explanations of the symbols he is trying to recreate—symbols such as the cross and the circle which are the basis for his mystical and Christian explanations of the creation of the universe. Throughout the narrative, especially the last fifty pages, Ramón spends most of his time explaining the goals and symbols of the Quetzalcoatl movement as he envisions it. He continually theorizes and lectures Kate about the ideas themselves; he does not develop the symbolism much beyond laying out his revised creation myths[2] in order to initiate Kate into the ancient mysteries underlying the Quetzalcoatl movement. However, he primarily wants to initiate her into an understanding of the ideas rather than participation in the movement itself. Throughout his explanations, he tries to reclaim the symbolism of the ancient mysteries in order to reestablish the "semi-barbaric method of thinking in images" that was "once supposed to be the finest and purest form of thinking" (ms.II: 430). But he never moves beyond thinking to recreating or reestablishing the ideas behind the images. The symbols are presented simply in verbal terms; they are never used in any ceremonies. Thus they convey no meaning and evoke no emotional response on the part of Kate, those involved in the movement, or the reader.

Kate has difficulty understanding any of the images or symbols that Ramón explains to her before her initiation.[3] For example, his very explanation of the new rituals that he does want to reestablish is so abstract that even Kate proclaims it "a bit feeble":

> the cross is again enclosed in the circle of the unity. And the foot of the Cross is in the House of Life, not in the grave. It is the Lower Root from which everything proceeds, and has proceeded, in genesis. . . . And at the head of the cross is the Ram with Golden Horns. The passion of the Lamb is consummated, the blood of Sacrifice has done its work and ceased to flow. At the summit of the cross is the Ram with the horns of power, and thunder is in his forehead when the earth once more marries the heavens. (ms.II: 429)

Continuing in this vein, Ramón explains that 'the soul recovers her wholeness' within "the rosy cross" that is his primary symbol (ms.II: 429). Not surprisingly, Kate does not understand what Ramón means here. In contrast to the published version in which Kate is moved by the rhythm of the words, here she is confused and overwhelmed. Whereas Ramón expounds at length on the creation of the cosmos and of humanity and explicates the symbol of the cross and the tree of life, Kate can only repeat "I don't understand" three times. More importantly, she protests that she "never cared for mysticism and New Jerusalems and Rosy Crosses and Ankhs" because to her they seem "a bit feeble" (ms.II: 430). Ramón accuses her of not wanting to understand; he claims throughout the initiation rite that if only Kate would drink the ceremonial wine he offers her, she would understand the mysteries and the mystical symbols that he uses. Ramón's response suggests that a complete understanding of these ancient ideas will occur only through participation in the rituals, not through abstract discussions of the signs. Yet he still focuses on explaining the symbols rather than allowing Kate to participate fully.

The emptiness of the abstract symbols as Ramón represents them in the manuscript is directly related to Kate's lack of understanding and sense of connection with the movement. Because he keeps the explanations on a cerebral level, Kate is excluded from participation throughout much of the manuscript.

She participates in only one ritual in the manuscript and that ceremony is rather repulsive and fairly violent—she is still a student being forced to undergo a ritual she does not understand and is not sure she likes. Although Ramón asks Kate to drink with him so that she can understand the "language of the old symbols" (ms.II: 429) through which he explains the purpose of his movement to revitalize Quetzalcoatl and the old Mexican gods, she undergoes the initiation rite only because her presumed Master commands her to do so. She remains so frightened and unsure of what she is doing that she trembles and spills the wine.

> Kate picked up her glass, and it spilled over her fingers. Ramón . . . was looking at her with black eyes of judgment. Hastily she put her glass to her lips, spilling the wine down her, and in eagerness and in fear she drank, looking over the rim of her glass with her golden frightened eyes, at Ramón. But she was able only to swallow three mouthfuls. (ms.II: 440)

She is "agonised with terror" at the thought that Cipriano is now "her doom" and that the two men will *make* her participate in their movement by becoming a goddess or taking on some other equally repugnant role.

The thought of Kate taking on any role is as threatening to the narrator (which Lawrence seems to align with Ramón in this section) as it is to her. The description of Kate spilling her wine recalls Ramón's description of the serpent who invades Eden after his journey through Ramón's spheres of creation. The serpent is "ever-unsatisfied," envious, and cowardly because he trembled and spilled his wine in an earlier sphere of creation and so forfeited a chance of perfect existence on the earthly plane. As Kate trembles, she realizes that "perhaps the snake felt that [terror], in the sphere of the sun," a recognition which prompts "a great understanding and a great sympathy with the snake [to] enter her heart" (ms.II: 440). The sympathetic connection suggests that Kate has forged a connection with the natural world despite her lack of understanding of the symbols Ramón has explicated. However, the comparison of Kate with the poisonous, cowardly snake obviously has rather menacing overtones. As both Eve and the serpent here, Kate represents a potential threat to the fledgling Quetzalcoatl movement and thus Ramón and Cipriano cannot allow her and she cannot allow herself the same degree of participation that she achieves in the novel.

Ramón's response to Kate's terror in the manuscript seems to indicate that he, too, perceives her as a poisonous threat rather than a potential participant in the movement—he tells her ominously and threateningly that she has pledged herself. When she fearfully asks, "What to?" (ms.II: 440), she demonstrates that she still does not understand the actions she is taking. She is worried that they will make her marry Cipriano immediately, but Ramón calmly asks her to drink again. She quickly drinks on Ramón's command but instantly rebels. When Ramón explains that her trembling had rocked the wine in her glass so that it was "slowly forming into a vortex" (ms.II: 441), she responds with understanding for the first time in the manuscript:

> In spite of herself the words and the act had magic for her: the magic of the ancient blood, before men had learned to think in words, and thought in images and in acts

(ms.II: 443). Her initiation is complete and she can now comprehend fully the symbols Ramón has been using. She still doubts but she is at the same time deeply drawn. Something in her nature responded to this symbolic language. It was a great rest from the endless strain of reason. It was like the blood flowing released, instead of knotted back in thought. (ms.II: 443)

This passage marks the climax of the early manuscript: Kate finally understands the language and symbols on a level beneath merely verbal or mental consciousness by reacting intuitively instead of cerebrally; she is able to move beyond the level of the spirit and the mind to that of the blood. Significantly, this is the only point in the manuscript where Kate experiences comprehension of or sympathy with the Quetzalcoatl movement. Thus, taking part in the "mystery" is essential to any sort of understanding; it becomes even more central in the published version, as Kate becomes more involved in the ceremonies and dances.

Yet, in the manuscript, Kate remains unsure of her actions and her participation in the ritual. Rather than encourage that participation and understanding as they do in the published version, Ramón and Cipriano make her even more unsure as they continue to insist that she take part in their plan of initiation and to view their ritual according to their terms. When Cipriano takes over the role of master, the ceremony becomes even more coercive. Cipriano tells Kate that the wine is the "serpent of desire" (ms.II: 444) and insists that she recognize it as part of herself. More explicitly, he says his wine is his own blood, as her wine is her blood. Combining the wine of their glasses, he announces fiercely, "I am the man with the sword. You are the woman bound" and orders her to drink (ms.II: 445). Doing so rather meekly, she tastes the warmth and thickness of the wine and smells the scent of blood. She is understandably disgusted and repulsed. Quickly withdrawing from contact with the two men, Kate proclaims "I can't! . . . I can't! I can't! I can't!" Instantly "she felt something had turned to iron inside her, and it would never soften again. This iron resistance inside her would prevent her living" (ms.II: 447-48) but it also prevents her from becoming "the woman bound." Her willful, mental consciousness returns and reacts violently against her instinctive response to Ramón and the potency of the mystical symbols as well as to Cipriano's harsh commands. She may understand the language and submit to *its* power but she will not submit to the control of another will (whether Cipriano's or Ramón's). Though her refusal is presented as the result of her stubbornness and wilfulness, it is also a sign that Kate seeks to retain control of herself and her body. She refuses connection with the others involved in the movement because she is afraid of losing her own voice and disgusted at their insistence that she recognize what they call her desire as represented by the serpent. Though she has briefly responded to the ritual's power with Ramón, she is still unsure of its relevance to herself and fears its overwhelming force and potential violence.

Although throughout the published version Kate continues to question the Quetzalcoatl movement, especially its violence, and balks at submitting her will to that of Ramón and Cipriano, she nevertheless has a larger role in the movement of Quetzalcoatl in this version of the text. She participates in the mysteries that she only vaguely understood in the first manuscript. Her participation in fact helps unify the ceremonies and the movement as well as their integration into the narrative. Kate becomes an integral part of the movement by remaining in Mexico with Cipriano and Ramón and by taking on the role of Malintzi.[4]

This integration begins to happen early in the novel. Kate meets and feels sympathy with individual members of the Quetzalcoatl movement and begins to be associated with the movement even before she completely understands it when the men rowing her to the hotel at Sayula tell her she has "the morning star in [her] eyes" (*PS* 92). They recognize something sympathetic in Kate and recognize something that she, as an individual, can bring to the movement. In this version, she is more open to the movement and to contact with the followers of Quetzalcoatl whereas in the manuscript, she is uneasy and a bit rude when accosted by the man in the lake (ms.I: 95-97). In the published version, she sympathizes even before Ramón and Cipriano explain the goals and elements of the movement. Thus her understanding is not limited to what they tell her; what they do tell her means something to her and affects her only because she has met some of the people and has sympathized with them.

Throughout the published version, then, Kate is not merely the student of Ramón and Cipriano as she was in the manuscript; the explanations they give her concerning the movement take place *because* she is already drawn to the symbol of Quetzalcoatl while in the manuscript she was supposedly drawn because of the explanations provided by Ramón. Kate first uses the language of mysticism even before participating in the ritual dances in the plaza. Upon feeling the power of the lake and the thick air, she speaks to the silent vitality of the universe, declaring "Come then!" Clearly she is already in tune with the stirrings of the universe:

> in her soul she cried aloud to the greater mystery, the higher power that hovered in the interstices of the hot air, rich and potent. . . . 'Come then!' she said, drawing a long slow breath, and addressing the silent life-breath which hung unrevealed in the atmosphere, waiting. (*PS* 106)

Without Ramón's assistance, she can already breathe in the mystery and spirit of the land and the vital universe. Kate recognizes something alive in the land as she does in the people, a vital something to which she responds unconsciously. This feeling of the mystery of the lake and the desire of the people to "breathe" (*PS* 108) comes upon Kate spontaneously when she is tired and, therefore, less cerebrally active. Thus she responds to the vital breath of the cosmos before she is exposed to the rituals of Quetzalcoatl, so that the revival of the ancient gods and ancient ways of experiencing the universe embodied by the movement seems necessary and significant to Kate as well as to the native people who surround her.

Her instinctive response to the men in the lake and the atmosphere of the land sets the stage for her particpation in the plaza dance of the Quetzalcoatl men where she learns the treading, bird-like step of the dance. Instead of hearing Ramón's protracted explanations of the movement, in this later version Kate hears the beating of drums and the singing of songs—the enactment of the movement rather than its abstract explanation. The drums affect Kate "like a spell on the mind, making the heart burst each stroke, and darkening the will" (*PS* 120), and drawing the blood down into connection with the earth. In response to this beat, which produces a throbbing in the blood, the people listening begin to sing, "soaring" and "sweeping" with their voices as their minds (and blood) soar and sweep (*PS* 127). The melody of the song is unimportant; so, too, the

> words did not matter. Any verse, any words, no words, the song remained the same: a strong, deep wind rushing from the caverns of the breast, from the everlasting soul! (*PS* 127)

The crucial activity is the reproduction of the rhythm. While Kate does not sing, she does feel the rhythm working inside her, "sound[ing] in the innermost far-off place of the human core" (*PS* 126). She never felt the rhythm or power of the words in the manuscript, despite Ramón's long lectures on the power of his symbols and her eventual forced initiation. Here, the words and the rhythm are able to act on her without any intervening explanations.

Instead of being forced to drink Cipriano's blood and the vortex in the wine, Kate experiences and helps create the vortex herself. When Kate dances the rhythmic treading dance of the novel's native Americans, she merges into "non-individual," "abstract" contact with the other dancers and into "the slowly revolving ocean of nascent life" (*PS* 131). By participating in the ritual on her own initiative, she has responded fully to the sounds and rhythms of the cosmos. In the manuscript version, Kate merely obeys Ramón's command to drink the vortex in the wine; here, she has become an integral part of the vortex, "wheeling" in the dance of the cosmos (*PS* 131). Kate experiences being caught up in the

> slow, vast, soft-touching revolution of the ocean above upon ocean below, with no vestige of rustling or foam. . . . Herself gone into the greater self, her womanhood consummated in the greater womanhood. And where her fingers touched the fingers of the man, the quiet spark, like the dawn-star, shining between her and the greater manhood of men. (131)

Within the wheeling of the dance, she is able to connect with the universe as well as with the people around her. The dance makes her feel young and vibrant again, foreshadowing what she will feel later with Cipriano in the church. In both the plaza and the church, Kate allows herself to respond to the mythic language and ritual that Lawrence has recreated in his revival of the ancient gods. She is fully a participant in the ceremony rather than just an observer as she is in the corresponding scene in the manuscript.

In contrast, in the manuscript scene, Kate does not participate in the dancing at the plaza—she and Owen *see* the people singing there but they cannot understand the words, both because of the softness of the murmuring voices and because they are being sung in a native American dialect. More importantly, Kate cannot understand the song primarily because she is focusing on the words themselves and their meanings; she tries to connect the words with their definitions, with the abstract, cerebral, or exoteric aspects of the ideas. She is therefore unable to respond to the mystical quality of the sounds and the rhythms, and decides only that "there was something intense and inhuman in the sound" (ms.I: 124). Owen's presence prevents her from responding freely, and a tight circle of men makes it impossible for her to move closer. Thus the manuscript and its male characters exclude Kate's participation in the rituals which would further her understanding of the movement's symbols.

Whereas in the manuscript Ramón was simply preaching concepts and symbols to Kate in the published version she comes to her own understanding of the concepts based on her experience. In "Night in the House," for example, she contemplates her past life and the life she has experienced in Mexico and decides that "We must take up the old, broken impulse that will connect us with the mystery of the cosmos again, now we are at the end of our own tether" (*PS* 138), echoing what Ramón has explained to her near the beginning of the novel. She asserts that Ramón was right in telling her of Mexico's need to make this connection, yet instantly great bursts of lightning and thunder "smash" down outside; "the bolts of thunder seemed to fall on her heart" and "she lay absolutely crushed, in a kind of quiescent hysterics" (*PS* 138). The storm is a not-so-subtle hint that her connection with Ramón will not be as peaceful and easy as it was in the earlier manuscript. Neither Kate nor the storm submits to his will entirely; the universe that Ramón tries to gain a connection with will not be ruled any more than Kate will.

Kate's lack of submission to Ramón, along with her increased participation in the movement's ceremonies as she becomes less of a student to Ramón, is also reflected in her relationship to Cipriano in the published version. Kate becomes more an equal than a disciple or student in her relationship to Cipriano as she has in her relationship to Ramón and the Quetzalcoatl movement. Even in the published version, though, problems in Kate's character and the amount of control over her own will remain; these problems occur primarily in her relationship to Cipriano. In the manuscript, Kate and Cipriano never come together in any sort of union because Kate always puts Cipriano off when he mentions marriage. She feels only repulsion and fear toward him and exclaims at the end: "The change is too great. I can't make it. I can't change my race. And I can't betray my blood" (ms.II: 458). Kate fears that mixing her blood with his will make her only half a person, only part of him. Although she takes this attitude at times in the published edition, she is able to connect with him more fully despite the problematical nature of that connection.

Soon after the published text's 'Auto da Fé,' in which the Christian, white European images are removed from the church, Kate agrees to similarly abandon her old self and her old language which isolates her in this culture, and to marry Cipriano. She and Cipriano both put off their old lives in order to take on the new clothing of Quetzalcoatl. They exchange tokens, symbols of Quetzalcoatl, that represent the morning star or union between them. Yet the union between Kate and Cipriano is still not exactly balanced. She is the earth beneath his feet, he is the sky above her. Kate puts on Cipriano's shoes for him while he puts on her sash "so that he shall never leave [her], and [she] will always be in his spell" (*PS* 363). Thus Kate is still partially "the woman bound" as she was in the manuscript, yet they have moved away considerably from Cipriano's harsh commands to drink his blood.

A similar movement towards equal participation in the relationship occurs within the context of their sexual union, yet this union is just as problematical as their marriage. Kate is no longer simply the disciple but Cipriano often continues to play the role of mentor or leader. Once Kate agrees to legally marry and live with Cipriano in order to achieve social and sexual union with him, Cipriano begins to teach her a new experience by showing her the "worthlessness of foam-effervescence" in their sexual activity, bringing her instead to the "soft, heavy, hot flow" of "circles of phosphorescent ecstasy" that are beyond knowing (*PS* 422). Though he says he cannot be fully godlike without her (*PS* 391), he still desires to establish his superiority over her by insisting that she adopt his notion of sexual experience rather than adopting or adapting to hers; he also tries to teach her supposedly better ways of connecting and combining themselves.

The problematical nature of Kate's relationship to Cipriano is at least part of the motivation behind her reversion to ambivalence and "willfulness" in the last chapter of the published novel. She fears she is losing herself too quickly and tries to hold on to two kinds of consciousness or being at once, an impossible task in the narrator's eyes. Kate's inability to bridge the two modes of consciousness is presented as her problem at the end of the novel. She thinks she must choose one mode of being or the other: that of Mexico or that of Europe. She feels her vital connection with the Quetzalcoatl movement and Cipriano, but knows that this connection means she must give up her own European ego. She is 'aware of a duality in herself" and "suffer[s] from it," because she is unable to "definitely commit herself, either to the old way of life, or to the new" (*PS* 429). So she feels something similar to what she felt at the end of the manuscript version of the novel; "she was on the brink of her own being. But she did not want to be pushed over a precipice" (ms.II: 450). There, she had little control over her position—she might or might not be "pushed" by Ramón and Cipriano to a new sort of "being." In the published version, she is in control of whether she commits herself or not. Thus the endings are reflective of the overall changes from the manuscript to the published versions since they demonstrate the different amounts of control that Kate has over her role and position in the movement.

In contrast to her ambivalence and repulsion in the manuscript, then, Kate responds completely and honestly to the drums and hymns of Quetzalcoatl without Ramón's lengthy explanations of the underlying symbolism. She fully recognizes the problems with the movement and her union with Cipriano because she has participated in both completely. She is convinced that she must break with the European way of experiencing the universe in order to connect with Cipriano and the Quetzalcoatl movement, but she wants to be sure of the connection before she chooses to submit herself to it completely. Despite her choice and control, though, her final act must be either a submission or a refusal to submit.

The reader also faces this choice; s/he experiences both ambivalence about the movement and Kate's representation as well as an aversion to submitting to the novel's rather insistent didacticism which appears in both versions, though more strongly in the manuscript. As Kate becomes stronger and more central to the structure of the novel, Lawrence's desire to affect the reader becomes more evident. In fact, the revulsion Kate feels at the bullfight in the published version as well as her attraction and repulsion toward the dance in the plaza prefigure the response of the reader throughout the novel. Michael Bell suggests that the bullfight, and Kate's abhorrence to it, set up a basis for the reader's identification with Kate; if the reader "does not participate in the Lawrencean response, as highlighted in Kate, then such a reader cannot significantly 'read' the book at all" (195).

The effect of the manuscript on the reader is almost totally negative due to the neglect of Kate's character, the ubiquitous lectures by Ramón, and a lack of connection between most of the major elements of the manuscript. Clark admits that the "Quetzalcoatl" manuscript "resists all that the author can do to give it form and meaning." In this version, Clark adds, "Lawrence paid little heed to structure. Both what happens and the order in which it happens are often ill-considered and ill-executed"(*Dark Night* 100-101). The primary structural problem in the manuscript is that there is little connection between the hymns of Quetzalcoatl and the rest of the narrative. The hymns and stories that Ramón creates, as well as his explanations to Kate as the manuscript ends, are too detached from the narrative structure. Accounts of the Quetzalcoatl movement are rare in the manuscript version—the first mention of the movement is an abbreviated newspaper account in chapter three. In chapter five, Kate and Owen observe men singing ancient songs, but they do not hear the words, and Kate does no dancing in the plaza. Suddenly, in chapter nine, halfway through the manuscript, the first three hymns of Quetzalcoatl are written out, in prose, for the reader (not for Kate), without introductory material to explain their function or importance. They are then sung, accompanied by guitar, and explained to Kate by the men of the Mexican family acting as her servants. She likes the songs but does not understand them, since she has not yet been initiated into the Quetzalcoatl movement and, in fact, has had little contact with it up to this point. So, too, the reader probably has little understanding of or interest in the movement at this point because s/he has had little contact with it.

The lack of integration between the hymns and narrative structure is also evident in that Kate and the reader see little of the preparation behind the movement's revival in the manuscript. For example, neither of them sees Ramón making the iron symbol of the serpent encircling the eagle, nor Ramón posing for the statue of Quetzalcoatl as they do in the published chapter eleven, "Lords of the Day and Night." Hence neither Kate nor the reader sees Ramón's connection with and participation in the revival and its symbols—they simply see his abstract explanations of its importance. The explanations remain almost completely separate from the movement—the reader sees some evidence of men singing and dancing but rarely in connection with Ramón or his lectures to Kate. This lack of connection between the explanations of the symbols and goals of the movement and its activities demonstrate the powerlessness of the explanations themselves. In contrast, in the published version, Ramón tries to reestablish an ancient way of *experiencing* the mysteries of the universe and consequently to reenact the ancient mysteries and their power—thus the characters' participation in the activities is central to the novel's purpose.

The published version of *The Plumed Serpent*, in contrast to the manuscript, integrates the hymns and stories into the narrative in terms of both plot and the Quetzalcoatl movement's ability to revive the old forms of consciousness; the focus is on the means by which the movement reintegrates individuals—

particularly Kate—into the universe and restores the connection between the microcosm and the macrocosm. Every chapter except the first contains either a discussion of the ideas and symbols underlying the revival of the ancient gods or an account of the reenactment of those ideas through ceremonies, dancing, and singing of the hymns. The hymns are interspersed with the narrative and the sequence of the hymns moves logically from a discussion of the creation of the universe and Quetzalcoatl, to his weariness and Christ's arrival in and subsequent departure from Mexico, to Quetzalcoatl's return and reintegration in Mexican society. The ceremonies follow a similar pattern. First, Ramón removes the Christian images from the Sayula church, then he installs the image of Quetzalcoatl in their place, and finally he revives Huitzilopochtli and Malintzi in order to complete the pantheon of gods. Louis Martz points out that the entire focus of the religious movement in the manuscript "develops . . . with the songs and hymns that seem part of an oral, musical culture" while that of *The Plumed Serpent* unfolds from the "printed hymns distributed by soldiers throughout the land" and included within the text for the reader (291). Consequently, the revival of Quetzalcoatl is connected to the movement of the plot and the development of the characters and themes of the novel. That connection centers around Kate. Just as Kate moves from her role as disciple and receptor of Ramón's expositions and becomes a participant in the reenactment itself, so too the text itself moves away from straight exposition of the images and goals of the movement towards reenactment. As Kate is integrated more fully into the movement and the text, the hymns and ceremonies become integrated more fully into the narrative of the text. The effect of this integration is that, in the published version, the reader has the opportunity to respond to the scenes depicted as Kate does rather than being forced to childishly and somewhat violently submit with her to Ramón's abstract ideas in the manuscript version.

To evoke a response from the reader, the published narrative works to draw her/him in using rhythmic language for passages describing the dances and ceremonies of Quetzalcoatl. As the symbols and rituals of Quetzalcoatl gain prominence in the published version, the language becomes more rhythmic in order to embody those rituals in language. The question of the representational efficacy of language is important in both versions, particularly when they are seen in relation to one another. In contrast to the manuscript in which abstract language is used unquestioningly throughout to represent cerebral explanation, in the published version Lawrence works to overcome the difficulty of the verbal representation of non-verbal experience. Michael Bell points out that Lawrence's "increased insistence on the sub-conscious realm accompanies a heightened need for conscious articulacy" (167). He seeks to achieve the articulation of "the sub-conscious realm" by emphasizing the sound and rhythm of the narrative language in the descriptions of the ceremonies; he thus reproduces the mystical experience of the ceremonies themselves rather than articulating the ideas behind them and consequently draws the reader into the experience of those ceremonies.

As Kate dances to the drums in the plaza and experiences a connection with the cosmos, a part of the song of the dance is included so that the reader, too, can feel the rhythm of the music:

As the bird of the sun treads the earth at the dawn of the day like a brown hen under his feet, like a hen and the branches of her belly droop with the apples of birth, with the eggs of gold, with the eggs that hide the globe of the sun in the waters of heaven, in the purse of the shell of earth that is white from the fire of the blood, tread the earth, and the earth will conceive like the hen 'neath the feet of the bird of the sun; 'neath the feet of the heart, 'neath the heart's twin feet. Tread the earth, tread the earth. . . . (*PS* 130-31)

This passage is paradigmatic of the language in which the rituals and ceremonies are reported. Lawrence deliberately provides "no recognisable rhythm" (*PS* 126) that remains constant throughout the passage. Yet it achieves a rhythmic quality by using strings of prepositional phrases of the same length, moving from three to four to five syllables, then returning to three syllables. The language thus seems to replicate the movement of Kate's consciousness outward into the "wheeling" of the cosmos and so reenacts Kate's mystical experience in the scene itself.

The pulsating quality that draws the reader into particpation in the rhythm of the dance also authenticates Kate's experience and serves to prepare the reader for the later ceremonies. Paired with the shift in focus from oral to written texts for the hymns, the use of rhythmic language in descriptions of the dance and other ceremonies suggests that the effect the language has on the reader assumes primary importance in the published version. Lawrence attempts to draw the reader into the narrative as he draws Kate into the rhythm of the movement. So the enactment of the mystical ideas and rituals of the published version serve not only to integrate many elements of the novel but also to make it more effective rhetorically. Part of the response by readers is most likely, however, ambivalence and a reluctance to submit entirely to the will of Ramón, or Lawrence.

While most readers of the manuscript are probably repulsed (I certainly was) by the abstract, self-righteous sermons that dominate the text much as Kate is repulsed by Cipriano's dominance over her will, readers of the published version are more likely to be at least willing to enter into a struggle with the narrator and the narrative much as Kate struggles with Cipriano. On the one hand, this struggle indicates the successful integration of the Quetzalcoatl revival with the plot structure which provides a reasonable motivation for the ceremonies and activities of the movement. The fuller development of Kate's character allows readers to identify and sympathize with her more fully and thus join her in being somewhat more sympathetic to the Quetzalcoatl movement itself. Therefore, both the readers and Kate struggle more fully with the text since they are on slightly more equal footing due to their greater inclusion in the ceremonies and rituals. On the other hand, the problems in Kate's relationship to Cipriano mirror the problems of readers in relation to Lawrence—the element of control or didacticism is still there. In the end, Kate still refuses to give herself up to the will of the movement; so, too, most readers refuse to give themselves up to the will of the text.

Perhaps, though, Lawrence experienced a similar refusal which caused his own ambivalence about the novel. In letters written soon after the completion of the final version's manuscript, he wrote that the novel "scares [him] a bit" and that "at the bottom of [his] heart, [he'd] rather not have it published at all" (*Letters*, 196, 207). His response to Witter Bynner's comments on the novel further indicates his ambivalence as well as his recognition that he was moving away from the original focus in the "Quetzalcoatl" manuscript on Ramón, Cipriano, and the abstract ideas of the movment:

> On the whole, I think you're right. The hero is obsolete, and the leader of men is a back number . . . the leader-cum-follower relationship is a bore. And the new relationship will be some sort of tenderness, sensitive, between men and men and men and women, and not the one up one down. . . . (*Letters VI* 321)

The sentiments expressed in the letters, read in conjunction with the changes made from the manuscript to the final version, indicate that he was moving toward something beyond even the published version of the novel, something which allowed Kate to become as central to the Quetzalcoatl movement as she does to the plot and to the experience of the reader.

The move from the manuscript to the published version of *The Plumed Serpent*, then, allows us to view the novel as part of a trajectory which begins with *Women in Love* and ends with *Lady Chatterley's Lover*, a trajectory focused on Lawrence's concerns with both male-male and male-female relationships and each partner's participation in the various levels (emotion, sexual, and spiritual) of the relationship. That is, like *Women in Love*, the novel is equally interested in reexamining male-male and male-female relationships; like *Lady Chatterley's Lover*, it is concerned with more fully representing female experience and the full range of male-female relationships. Because the move from manuscript to published version of *The Plumed Serpent* indicates the increasing importance of Kate and also the increasing importance of conveying the experience to the reader, the novel no longer has to be grouped only with Lawrence's other novels of the early twenties, *Aaron's Rod* and *Kangaroo*, novels marked by a consideration of male leadership and male experience. Instead, Kate becomes a transitional figure standing between Ursula and Constance and demonstrating Lawrence's concern with representing a female as well as male experience.

*The D.H. Lawrence Review*, 25, 1993-94

## Works Cited

Bell, Michael. *D.H. Lawrence: Language and Being*. Cambridge: Cambridge UP, 1992.

Clark, L.D. *Dark Night of the Body: D.H. Lawrence' The Plumed Serpent*. Austin: U of Texas P, 1988.

_____. Introduction. *The Plumed Serpent*, by D.H. Lawrence. Cambridge: Cambridge UP, 1987.

Lawrence, D. H. *The Plumed Serpent,* Ed. L. D. Clark. Cambridge: Cambridge UP, 1987.

_____. *The Letters of D.H. Lawrence: Volume V: March 1924-March 1927*. Ed. James T. Boulton and Lindeth Vasey. Cambridge: Cambridge UP, 1989.

_____. *The Letters of D.H. Lawrence: Volume VI: March 1927-November 1928*. Ed. James T. Boulton and Margaret H. Boulton with Gerald M. Lacy. Cambridge: Cambridge UP, 1989.

_____. "Quetzalcoatl." Unpublished manuscript. 2 notebooks. Harry Ransom Center. University of Texas, Austin.

Martz, Louis L. *"Quetzalcoatl:* The Early Version of *The Plumed Serpent." D.H. Lawrence Review* 22 (Fall 1990): 287-298.

## Notes

1 For a complete discussion of the circumstances surrounding the production of and changes to the manuscript, see Louis L. Martz, *"Quetzalcoatl:* The Early Version of *The Plumed Serpent."*

2 Briefly, Ramón's creation myth starts with the human soul journeying down through seven spheres of creation to reach the sphere of matter and incarnation, the earth. As *she* moves down through the various creations, 'seeking a husband to cover her nakedness,' the soul becomes 'intoxicated' as she experiences each new form of being and forgets the previous stages. She receives fire in the sphere of the sun, blood in the sphere of the moon, and becomes flesh in the 'realm of the earth,' becoming 'the perfect Adam, and the perfect Eve' (ms.II: 431-32). The soul is followed by the serpent who goes through the spheres too quickly; because of his haste and cowardice, the serpent fails and is 'never perfected' and 'never able to forget' his previous perfection. Thus he makes Eve eat of the Tree of Knowledge, which brings back memory of the previous spheres and makes all humans desire to return to their previous state of perfection (ms.II: 433-34).

3 Not only does she understand little about mystical matters, she literally has problems with the language in the early manuscript, especially with understanding Ramón's speech. Oddly enough, she can understand Carlota much more easily than Ramón because Carlota speaks more slowly and because of the supposed natural sympathy between the two women.

4 In a second version of the manuscript (which corresponds almost completely with the published version and deviates only in the last chapter), she moves on to understanding and internalizing the symbols presented and to beginning to participate in the rituals. Using her knowledge and understanding, Kate prepares to leave for Ireland to spread the ideas of the movement before returning to assume her full role in the pantheon of gods. Ramón explains to her that, as the time has come for Mexico to return to its old gods, so, too, the Irish need to find their ancient myths and symbols in order to revive their society; Kate is to show them how to do so. (See the Textual Apparatus of the 1987 Cambridge edition of the novel for the complete passage.)

# VI

# LADY CHATTERLEY'S LOVER

## Aldous Huxley, "The Censor"

Mrs Grundy resembles the King and that infernal worm of the Bible—she cannot die. *La Grundy est morte. Vive la Grundy!* There is no getting rid of her; she is immortal and succumbs only to be re-born. Disguised as Sir William Joynson-Hicks (for she frequently wears trousers), the dreadful old female has been very active in England during the last few years. When the General Election put an end to Jix (Sir W. J. H.) and his party, the optimists hoped that an end had been put to Mrs. Grundy. But the optimists, as usual, were wrong. In the sphere of sexual behaviour the new government is as rigidly orthodox as the old, and as actively intolerant. Almost the latest acts of the departing Jix were to ban D.H. Lawrence's new novel and to confiscate the registered letter containing the manuscript of his poems, *Pansies*. (And we poor innocents who thought that the official opening and stealing of registered letters were only done by Russians and such like!) One of the first acts of Jix's successor has been to set the police on to the same D.H. Lawrence's exhibition of paintings. Thirteen of the paintings were confiscated and just escaped being burnt. *La Grundy est morte. Vive la Grundy!*

Sexual orthodoxy preserves not only its Athanasian Creed, but also its Grand Inquisitor. "I believe in one Love, monogamous and indissoluble. And I believe in Respectability. And above all in Silence." Against the heretics who will not accept this profession of sexual faith, the Grand Inquisitors are permanently at war. At the beginning of the last century, English Catholics and Jews had no political rights; atheists were expelled from English universities; blasphemers were severely punished. To-day a man is free to have any or no religion; about the Established Church and its divinities he can say almost anything he likes. But woe to him if he deviates from the narrow path of sexual orthodoxy! For writing certain forbidden words and the description or representation of certain acts which everyone performs—the penalty ranges from confiscation of the offending picture or writing to a fine and, possibly, in certain cases, imprisonment. It will thus be seen that, as things stand at present, the Holy Trinity may be insulted with almost perfect impunity. But do, or say, or draw anything to offend Mrs. Grundy, and the avenging Inquisitor will immediately swoop down on you. Mrs. Grundy, in a word, is the only deity officially recognized by the English State. Men are free not to worship the God of Anglicanism; but the law compels them to bow down before the divine Grundy.

To argue the case against Grundyism would be easy, but wholly unprofitable. For these matters, it is obvious, argument is perfectly useless. Argument appeals to reason, and there is no reason in Grundyism. There are at best only rationalizations of prejudices—prejudices that, in most individual Grundyites, date back to the teaching received in childhood. Those who accept the creed of sexual orthodoxy do so because, in Pavlov's phrase, their reflexes have been conditioned at an impressionable period. It would be absurd to doubt the sincerity of people like Jix and Mr. Sumner. They are obviously quite genuinely shocked by such things as Lawrence's paintings. Such things *really* disgust and outrage them.   Given their upbringing it is inevitable; just as it is inevitable that Pavlov's dogs, after have been regularly fed to the sound of a bell, should start to dribble with hungry anticipation each time, in the future, that the bell is rung. Jix (or Lord Brentford, as we must now style him) was doubtless brought up in surroundings where an improper word, an over-frank reference in Saxon phrases to such matters as the processes of reproduction (notice how perfectly respectable all this sounds when shrouded in the decent obscurity of a learned language!) was accompanied, not by anything so mild as the tinkling of a bell, but by appalling silences, by the blushing or swooning away of maiden aunts, by the sadly pious horror of Jehovahistic indignation of clergymen and schoolmasters. So that to this day Jix and his fellows cannot hear these words or read these descriptions without at once recapturing (the process is as automatic as the salivation of Pavlov's dogs) the painful emotions aroused in them during childhood by the portentous accompaniments and consequences of what I have called sexual blasphemy. At present, most of those old enough to be occupying positions of power and responsibility were brought up in environments which conditioned their reflexes into the form of Grundyism. A time may come, perhaps, when these posts will be filled by men whose reflexes have not been so conditioned. When the contemporary child takes a normal, healthy interest in sex and such matters, the majority of young parents do not weep over him, or beat him, or tell him that his soul will roast in hell-fire. It follows, therefore, that his future reactions to sex will be less violently painful than the reactions of those who were children in the high old days of Podsnapian respectability. We are thus justified in cherishing a mild hope for the future. For when I said that Mrs. Grundy was immortal, I was exaggerating. She may, old cat that she is, possess nine lives; but she is not everlasting. That a time may come when she will be, if not stone dead, at least enfeebled, chronically moribund, is, as we have seen, quite possible. Moreover, it is perfectly certain that during long periods of history she hardly existed at all. If we throw our eyes over the whole expanse of historical time, we perceive that active Grundyism is an entirely abnormal phenomenon. During the longest periods of recorded history puritanism has been, if not absolutely inexistent, at least without significance or power. The epochs of highest civilization have been conspicuously un-puritanical. It was to the naked Aphrodite that the Greeks of the fifth and sixth centuries B.C. made sacrifice, not to the much-petticoated divinity worshipped by the Pilgrim Fathers, by the later Podsnap, and by our contemporary Jixes and Sumners. Seen through the eyes of the philosophic historian, the Puritan reveals himself as the most abnormal sexual pervert of whom we have record, while Grundyism stands out as a supremely unnatural vice.

It is against this unnatural vice and the life-hating perverts who practise it that Mr. D.H. Lawrence appears to be fighting. A militant, crusading author, he hurls himself on what he calls "the evil thing, the wicked people." But the evil thing is sacred in our modern world and the wicked people are precisely those Good Citizens who wield the powers of the State. Mr. Lawrence is often discomfited. The giant Grundy props her huge crinoline over him and extinguishes him by force. But not for long; his zeal and his energy are inextinguishable and, in spite of the Jixes, the dangerous flame of his art breaks out again, the warning voice is heard once more.

Cultured and tolerant people often ask: What is the point of this crusading? What is the point of shocking the Jixes into legal retaliation? What is the point of using the brief Saxon words that people shudder at, when you can express the same meaning by means of circumlocutions and Graeco-Roman polysyllables? Might not Grundyism be attacked without ringing those particular alarm bells which cause the mouths of the smut-hounds, not indeed to water, like those of Pavlov's dogs, but to foam with righteous indignation? In a word, might not as good or even better results be obtained if the crusade were conducted with tact and circumspection?

The answer to all these questions seems, to Mr. Lawrence, to be No. What he is crusading for is, apparently, the admission by the conscious spirit of the right of the body and the instincts, not merely to a begrudged existence, but to an equal honour with itself. Man is an animal that thinks. To be a first-rate human being, a man must be both a first-rate animal and a first-rate thinker. (And, incidentally, he cannot be a first-rate thinker, at any rate about human affairs, unless he is also a first-rate animal.) From the time of Plato onwards there has been a tendency to exalt the thinking, spiritual man at the expense of the animal. Christianity confirmed Platonism; and now, in its turn, what I may call Fordism, or the philosophy of industrialism, confirms, though with important modifications, the spiritualizing doctrines of Christianity. Of all the ascetic religions, Fordism is that which demands the cruellest mutilations of the human psyche—demands the cruellest mutilations and offers the smallest spiritual returns. Rigorously practised for a few generations, this dreadful religion of the machine will end by destroying the human race.

If humanity is to be saved there must be reforms, not merely in the social and economic spheres, but also within the individual psyche. Mr. Lawrence concerns himself primarily with these psychological reforms. The problem, for him, is to bring the animal and the thinker together again, is to make them co-operate (as they always have co-operated in the finest human beings of whom we have record) in the building up of consummate manhood. In order to effect this bringing together, certain barriers must be broken down. They are strong barriers; for the conscious mind has taken extraordinary precautions to keep itself out of contact with the body and its instincts. The spirit refuses to be livingly aware of the animal man. Early training has so conditioned the reflexes of the normal bourgeois and his wife that they shudder whenever one of these words is pronounced. For these words bring the mind into direct contact with the physical reality which it is so desperately anxious to ignore. It shrinks with horror. But it ought not to shrink with horror. Among the ancient Greeks, when civilization was in most respects higher than it has ever been since, the conscious mind did not so shrink. What men have once achieved they can achieve again. Admittedly, the task of re-capturing anything like the Hellenic attitude towards life is now incredibly difficult. But it can be done—at least, one hopes it can. A reuniting of animal and thinker is possible. D.H. Lawrence is a crusader for this reuinion. And the use of forbidden words, the describing and portraying of decorously veiled acts are, he thinks, essential tactics in this crusade. The mind must be made conscious of the physical reality; it must be brought into living, intimate contact with the body. And it is only in this way that the desired end can be achieved. The fact that we are shocked is good proof that we require shocking. Our reflexes have been wrongly conditioned; let us get used to being shocked, until the conditioning is undone. But meanwhile, at every ringing of the "obscene" and "pornographic" bell, the smut-hounds furiously foam at the mouth. And unfortunately they are in a position to do more than foam. They are in a position to open and steal Lawrence's letters, to confiscate his books and burn his pictures. And the rest of us can only sit by and impotently look on, and from time to time relieve our feelings by registering a protest, a perfectly useless protest, as I do now.

*Vanity Fair*, November 1929.

## Mark Spilka, "Lawrence's Quarrel with Tenderness"

---

### I

Late in *Lady Chatterley's Lover* the heroine compliments the hero for a quality which other men lack, the courage of his own tenderness, which will 'make the future'. The tenderness she has in mind is frankly physical, as when he puts his hand upon her 'tail' and says she has a 'pretty tail'. Her lover accepts and expands upon her sentiments: 'natural physical tenderness', even between men, means bodily awareness and aliveness, means keeping literally 'in touch' with others; sex itself is only the closest touch, the closest form of natural communion—

And it's touch we're afraid of. We're only half-conscious and half-alive. We've got to come alive and aware. Especially the English have got to get into touch with one another, a bit delicate and a bit tender. It's our crying need.[1]

This connection of tenderness with wholeness and aliveness, awareness and communion, is new in Larence's fiction. Tenderness implies personal feelings, affections, soft sentiments from the conscious heart; and Lawrence usually speaks for dark impersonal passions from unconscious depths. Tenderness is, moreover, a conventionally romantic feeling, an aspect of romantic love; and Lawrence usually speaks against conventional romance. Yet *Tenderness* was his first title for *Lady Chatterley's Lover*, and courage for it his lasting theme. That tenderness should require courage is the telling point; it means that tenderness inspires fear, that tender feelings are somehow frightening and difficult to express. Such fear is not uncommon. I. A. Richards speaks of the 'wide-spread general inhibition of all the simpler expansive developments of emotion . . . among our educated population'; Ian Suttie speaks, more broadly, of 'the taboo on tenderness' throughout our Puritan culture.[2] It was this general social condition which Lawrence was confronting. But he was also confronting his own deepseated fear of 'simple' and 'expansive' feelings. The courage to confront them came late in life, too late perhaps for consequential change: and yet he did make a place for tenderness in his fiction. How he made it, and what he actually made, are questions which may accordingly tell us much about Lawrence, and something more about ourselves, if we can agree that Lawrence explores and clarifies pervasive modern problems.

## II

His quarrel with conventional romance may be illustrated by a late story, aptly called "In Love", where he deals with modish attitudes of the 1920's. Hester and Joe, the engaged couple in the tale, are to spend a weekend together on the little farm Joe has started. Though Hester likes the farm, she is upset by the prospect of making love to Joe. Before their engagement she liked him well enough; there had never been 'anything messy to fear from him. Nor from herself'. But now that cuddling and petting have started, 'she couldn't stand him'. To be stroked and cuddled was, she felt, humiliating, insulting, awful, ridiculous; to be 'in love' was to lose self-respect: it was SPOONING, it was Rudolph Valentino, it was messy and rather sickening, 'As if one were a perfectly priceless meatpie, and the dog licked it tenderly before he gobbled it up'. Thus, when Joe begins his doggy business on the sofa, Hester sickens:

> She endured his arm round her waist, and a certain pressure of his biceps which she presumed was cuddling. He had carefully knocked his pipe out. But she thought how smug and silly his face looked, all its natural frankness and straightforwardness gone. How ridiculous of him to stroke the back of her neck! How idiotic he was, trying to be lovey-dovey! She wondered what sort of sweet nothings Lord Byron, for example, had murmured to his various ladies. Surely not so blithering, not so incompetent! And how monstrous of him, to kiss her like that.

'I'd infinitely rather you'd play to me, Joe,' she snapped . . . 'I'd love to hear some Tchaikowsky, something to stir me up a bit.'[3]

While Joe plays stirring music, Hester slips out of the house, climbs a tree to elude her lover, and questions her normality: 'Because the majority of girls must like this in'love business, or men wouldn't do it. And the majority must be normal. So I'm abnormal, and I'm up a tree.' When she climbs down, however, Joe confesses that he never was 'in love. . . that way'; he merely thought it was 'expected'. He sees his error now, and she too sees more deeply:

> Why had he tried that silly love-making game on her? It was a betrayal of their simple intimacy. He saw it plainly, and repented.
> And she saw the honest, patient love for her in his eyes, and the queer, quiet central desire. It was the first time she had seen it, that quiet, patient, central desire of a young man who had suffered during his youth, and seeks now almost with the slowness of age. A hot flush went over her heart. She felt herself responding to him . . . 'You know, Joe,' she said, 'I don't mind what you do, if you love me *really.*'[4]

To be 'in love,' then, in a conventionally romantic way, is to obstruct the deepest feelings, to insult the deepest self. To feel *real* love is to reach 'that quiet, patient, central desire' which makes 'simple intimacy' possible. Personal closeness depends here on release of deeper, more impersonal feelings. In the modish '20's, after artifical 'spooning', it takes a healthy quarrel to release them. Or so the story argues.

## III

The difficulties of pre-modern lovers are another matter. In the early novel, *Sons and Lovers*, Paul Morel and Miriam Leivers are late-Victorians, intensely spiritual mates whose chaste relations proceed on a high plane of consciousness. They share intellectual and aesthetic interests; they love old churches and medieval ruins; they commune soulfully with nature and each other. But when love becomes physical, their communion stops:

> He courted her now like a lover. Often, when he grew hot, she put his face from her, held it between her hands, and looked in his eyes. He could not meet her gaze. Her dark eyes, full of love, earnest and searching, made him turn away. Not for an instant would she let him forget. Back again he had to torture himself into a sense of his responsibility and hers. Never any relaxing, never any leaving himself to the great hunger and impersonality of passion; he must be brought back to a deliberate, reflective creature. As if from a swoon of passion she called him back to the littleness, the personal relationship. He could not bear it. "Leave me alone—leave me alone!" he wanted to cry; but she wanted him to look at her with eyes full of love. His eyes, full of the dark, impersonal fire of desire, did not belong to her.[5]

When she finally submits to passion, as if to a sacrifice, Paul realizes

> that she had not been with him all the time, that her soul had stood apart, in a sort of horror. He was physically at rest, but no more. Very dreary at heart, very sad, and

very tender, his fingers wandered over her face pitifully. Now again she loved him deeply. He was tender and beautiful.[6]

But his tenderness becomes a 'gentle reaching-out to death'. Miriam has tried to keep their love intensely personal, has been unable to join him spiritually in 'dark, impersonal' desire, unable to respond in kind. There has been no exchange, no communion, and though she responds now to his 'tenderness', he accepts her 'love' as death.

Miriam is clearly a spiritual vampire, one who 'wheedles the soul out of things', as Paul observes. Though he joins her at first in absorbing intimacy, he also resists suffocation and rightly seeks release. In his affair with Clara Dawes he seems to find release in 'dark, impersonal' passion. Clara is an early version of the 'lost girl', the modern feminist who denies the womanhood she desires. Paul sees through her aloofness, responds to her defiance with pagan flower dance and carnation-smashing love in wooded groves. After their first 'baptism of fire in passion' their warmth and gaiety affect their tearoom hostess, who gives them benedictive flowers. Later, in Clara's rooms, Paul affirms her womanhood, heals her hurt pride 'with an infinite tenderness of caress'; and their ensuing gaiety pleases Clara's mother. Yet aside from these moments their love remains impersonal. When Clara pursues him at work Paul becomes extremely vexed:

'But what do you always want to be kissing and embracing for!' he said. 'Surely there's a time for everything.' . . .
'Do I always want to be kissing you?' she said.
'Always, even if I come to ask you about the work. Work's work—'
'And what is love?' she asked. 'Has it to have special hours?'
'Yes; out of work hours.'
'And you'll regulate it according to Mr. Jordan's closing time?'
'Yes; and according to the freedom from business of any sort.'
'It is only to exist in spare time?'
'That's all, and not always then—not the kissing sort of love.'[7]

Paul may be right about love and work, but even on holiday he sets the night aside for love and keeps the day free: 'Love-making stifles me in the daytime', he complains, and deliberately pushes Clara towards her estranged husband. Her possessiveness, and her inability to give him balance, are immediate causes for his discontent; but as he sees himself, his mother's hold is the ultimate cause. Though I have elsewhere argued that Clara, like Miriam, defeats herself, and that Mrs. Morel remains 'the most vital woman in the novel', she is also the most destructive sweetheart.[8] Paul feels that he cannot give himself in marriage while his mother lives; he might have said, more appropriately, that he cannot *be* himself, express his passions and affections freely, because his mother has usurped his ego. The murkiness and confusion which many critics find in *Sons and Lovers* may be traced, I think, to Lawrence's failure to define Paul's egocentric needs. We can see how Clara and Miriam fail him, and how his mother almost kills him, but why he almost fails himself remains obscure.

Significantly enough, Paul's career as an artist is vaguely presented. Though Lawrence knew something about painting, he seems to have faked Paul's talent for it. We see no development in Paul's style; we see few examples of his art.

Painting seems more like a hobby than a career for Paul; it engrosses him less vividly than his work at the factory. What we do see, however, is his artistic dedication to his mother. When he wins prizes in a student exhibition, his mother takes them as her own achievement: 'And Paul felt he had done something for her, if only a trifle. All his work was hers'. When, at 23, he wins first prize and twenty guineas for a landscape, his mother responds so wildly that Paul is 'shocked and frightened':

> She flew to him, flung her arms round him for a moment, then waved the letter, crying:
> 'Hurrah, my boy! I knew we should do it!'
> He was afraid of her—the small, severe woman with greying hair suddenly bursting out in such frenzy . . . [He] was afraid [too] lest she might have misread the letter, and might be disappointed after all.   He scrutinised it once, twice. Yes, he became convinced it was true. Then he sat down, his heart beating with joy.
> 'Mother!' he exclaimed.
> 'Didn't I *say* we should do it!' she said, pretending she was not crying . . .
> 'You didn't think, mother—' he began tentatively.
> 'No, my son—not so much—but I expected a good deal.'
> 'But not so much,' he said.
> 'No—no—but I knew we should do it.'[9]

They get over the 'stress of emotion' by quarreling about the money. Then Paul's father enters, and though he shares their excitement and pride, he also indicates its cost:

> His black arm, with the hand all gnarled with work lay on the table. His wife pretended not to see him rub the back of his hand across his eyes, nor the smear in the coal-dust on his black face.
> 'Yes, an' the other lad 'ud 'a done as much if they hadna ha' killed 'im,' he said quietly.
> The thought of William went through Mrs. Morel like a cold blade. It left her feeling she was tired, and wanted rest.[10]

William, the older son, had been Mrs. Morel's 'knight who wore *her* favour in the battle'. Her hold on his spirit had split and killed him; her selection of that son as lover, and her rejection of her husband and his distasteful work, are repeated now as Paul is rewarded for his prize with the gift of William's evening suit. The living son in the dead son's clothes aptly signifies usurped identity; and the intense emotion, undercut by the cold blade of death, amply clarifies Paul's fear of tender love.

Early in childhood Paul had sensed his mother's suffering as that of a brave woman deprived of vital rights: 'It hurt the boy keenly, this feeling about her that she had never had her life's fulfilment: and his own incapability to make up to her hurt him with a sense of impotence, yet made him patiently dogged inside.   It was his 'childish aim'. Plainly his 'childish aim' comes straight from his mother, though she does not enforce it until William dies and she takes Paul as the favored son. In the years that follow there is abundant gaiety between them, and her fresh responsiveness contrasts with Miriam's cloying ways: yet their close affection, born of intense suffering, is always mixed with her own driving needs. Thus she proves a jealous and demanding sweetheart. With Miriam, her rival for Paul's soul, she disapproves of tender love; with Clara she approves only of passion. Paul's tenderness comes through, significantly, with permissive older women like the tea-room hostess and Clara's mother, or in safe arenas like the factory, where he plays the foreman's role. But under pressure his affections flag and his ego wobbles or collapses. Thus Clara is unable to 'keep his soul steady'. to keep him balanced and intact, as their affair progresses; and Miriam is unable to pull him together, to mother him into selfhood, when his mother dies. His supineness with Miriam is revealing:

> She felt that now he lay at her mercy. If she could arise, take him, put her arms around him, and say, 'You are mine', then he would leave himself to her . . . She was aware of his dark-clothed, slender body, that seemed one stroke of life, sprawled in the chair close to her . . . It called to all her woman's instinct . . . She knew she ought to take it up and claim it, and claim every right to it. But—could she do it? Her impotence before him, before the strong demand of some unknown thing in him, was her extremity . . .
>
> 'Will you have  me, to marry me?' he said very low . . . She pleaded to him with all her love not to make it *her* choice. She could not cope with it, with him, she knew not with what . . .
>
> 'Do you want it?' she asked, very gravely.
>
> 'Not much,' he replied, with pain.
>
> She turned her face aside; then, raising herself with dignity, she took his head to her bosom, and rocked him softly. She was not to have him, then!  So she could comfort him. She put her fingers through his hair.  For her, the anguished sweetness of self-sacrifice. For him, the hate and misery of another failure. He could not bear it—that breast which was warm and which cradled him without taking the burden of him. So much he wanted to rest on her that the feint of rest only tortured him.  He drew away. . . .
>
> It was the end then between them. She could not take him and relieve him of the responsibility of himself.[11]

Yet why should Miriam relieve him of self-responsibility? What 'unknown thing' speaks *strongly* for such privileged weakness? Lawrence's lapse into special pleading reveals Paul's lapse into infantilism and self-negation. His mother has appropriated more than his prizes and affections: she has appropriated his ego, has knighted him in love as well as battle, has given him fatherhood without selfhood and without real self-assurance. No wonder, then, that Lawrence would oppose love with individuality, not hate, in later works, and would move to an extreme defense of individuality, an extreme separation too of tender and impersonal modes of love.

## IV

He defined these extremes most sharply in *Women in Love*.  In this novel there are again two women, spiritual and sensual, in the hero's life. Hermione Roddice is the spiritual vampire, the upper-class intellectual who resembles Miriam Leivers in hyper-conscious intimacy. Ursula Brangwen is sensual and emotional, like Clara Dawes, an uprooted independent woman with romantic predilections. The hero, Rupert Birkin, is articulate and insightful, like Paul Morel, but more messianic, and more consciously concerned with selfhood. Thus he rails against depleting modes of intimacy in Hermione and Ursula; he sees both women as Great Mothers, horrible and clutching, lusting for possession, viewing men as appendages rather than independent beings, and insisting on 'horrible' fusion:

> Hermione saw herself as the perfect Idea, to which all men must come: and Ursula was the perfect Womb, the bath of birth, to which all men must come! And both were horrible.  Why could they not remain individuals, limited by their own limits? Why this dreadful all-comprehensiveness, this hateful tyranny? Why not leave the other being free, why try to absorb, or melt, or merge? One might abandon oneself utterly to the *moments*, but not to any other being.[12]

Birkin has come a long way from Paul's regressive lapse. He links lusting mothers with depleting intimacy;  he links robust selfhood with enriching love. Indeed, he calls for 'paradisal entry into pure, single being, the individual soul taking precedence over love', accepting permanent connection with others, but never losing 'its own proud singleness, even while it loves and yields'. The attempt to preserve the self from absorbing intimacy, yet still allow for love, is clear.

Birkin must literally preserve himself from Hermione's destructive love. He is almost killed when she bashes his head with a ball of lapis lazuli. The destructive potential in Ursula's love is less obvious. Its romantic basis is suggested, in the chapter called 'Island', by the paper boats she makes from purple wrappings for chocolates. The island itself is a romantic site, a place where Chateaubriand's lovers, Paul and Virginia, might hold 'Watteau picnics'. Birkin rejects this pleasant view, however, and makes 'island' stand for selfhood.  He fashions a flotilla of daisies, individualistic flowers, for which Ursula's paper boats provide romantic escort. The precedence of daisies over purple boats, of individuality over love, is eventually conceptualized by Birkin. But Ursula believes meanwhile in 'unspeakable intimacies' and 'complete self-abandon'; she believes that love surpasses individuality and calls for 'absolute surrender to love'. The results of such surrender are conveyed, in the chapter called 'Water-Party', by the drowning of Diana Crich and her boyfriend, the young man choked by Diana's arms around his neck. Birkin eludes that fate by pressing for impersonal union.  'There is', he tells Ursula, 'a real impersonal me, that is beyond love, beyond any emotional relationship. So it is with you . . . And it is there I would want to meet you—not in the emotional, loving plane, but there beyond', in the unknown plane where each acts in accord with 'primal desire'. Here Birkin wants the 'quiet, patient, central desire' of the tale, 'In Love'. But he defines it as a 'strange conjunction', an equilibrium which avoids merging and fusing, 'a pure balance of two single beings:—as the stars balance each other'. His views are modified, ultimately, to allow for 'the yoke and leash of love', which he accepts in the chapter called 'Excurse', where Ursula accepts the primacy of selfhood. But it is love as a bond, a binding yoke, which Birkin acknowledges, and his stress on impersonal desire prevails.

The same stress informs his brotherhood rites with Gerald Crich. Again he wants 'An impersonal union that leaves one free' and avoids 'sloppy emotionalism'. That affection should be primary, in a male relationship, and sensual warmth secondary, seems self-evident; it accords, moreover, with the purposive or spiritual role which Lawrence assigns to brotherhood: yet Lawrence relies on sensual relations and draws away from feared affections; he creates blood rites for brotherhood, strange wrestling scenes, from which each character turns, more plausibly, toward heterosexual affairs.

Gerald is oddly like Paul Morel in his relations with Ursula's sister, Gudrun Brangwen; he reaches finally an infantile dependency which resembles Paul's relapse with Miriam. But Lawrence now sees that state as one of helpless self-exposure:

> A strange rent had been torn in him; like a victim that is torn open and given to the heavens, so he had been torn apart and given to Gudrun. How should he close again? This wound, this strange, infinitely-sensitive opening of his soul, where he was exposed, like an open flower, to all the universe, . . . this disclosure, this unfolding of his own covering, leaving him incomplete, limited, unfinished, . . . this was his cruelest joy. Why then should he forego it? Why should he close up and become impervious, immune, like a partial thing in a sheath, when he had broken forth, like a seed that has germinated, to issue forth in being, embracing the unrealised heavens.[13]

But it is death toward which Gerald yearns, the mystery of his own destruction and annihilation; the open flower, the vulnerable and dependent self, invites extinction. Still, his resemblance to Paul suggests how Lawrence divides himself between his heroes and makes of their affinity a dramatization of his own dilemmas. Birkin is his older self, seeking singleness of being; Gerald, his youthful self, seeking annihilation in dependent love: and Birkin oddly cannot save his friend. Not so oddly, though, if dependence is a necessary part of married love, and if Birkin's stress on selfhood and otherness, on polarization of impersonal selves, is too extreme. The affections find no free release, only grudging acceptance, in this radical scheme, and emotional dependence—which threatens Paul and destroys Gerald—finds only dramatic expression. Lawrence would not compose his famous essay, 'We Need One Another', for some years to come. But at this stage he could at least assert his 'central law' of isolate selfhood, whereby 'each organism is intrinsically isolate and single in itself;' and in stressing *impersonal* singleness, in defining a second ego at impersonal planes of being, he could give metaphysical expression to that unthinking process by which we do accept ourselves.

## V

Alfred Kazin traces Lawrence's sense of authority, his pride in his own powers, his prevailing righteousness, to his mother's love. Agreeing with Freud that the mother's favorite becomes a 'conqueror', he sees Lawrence as the favored son who confidently assays the world, and who recreates his mother's love in all his works.[14] It seems more plausible, however, to see Lawrence's career as a *reaction* to his mother's love, an attempt to reclaim the masculine heritage which she denied him and the selfhood she absorbed. Certainly Lawrence did gain confidence from his mother; his moral sureness, his spiritual strength, owe much to her Congregational firmness. But righteousness is a dubious asset, as Lawrence came to know. In describing Rupert Birkin, in *Women in Love*, as 'a Sunday-school teacher, a prig of the stiffest type', he was criticizing his maternal heritage. In decrying self-importance, in "The Man Who Died", he was castigating the moral egoism of his mother's son.   This correlation is made openly in "The Real Thing", a late essay in which righteous mothers are said to produce sons incapable of feeling, animated by self-will and by secret ambition to impose themselves on the world and other people. Lawrence calls their condition 'the final state of egoism', as opposed to 'the real thing', by which he means a man's faith in himself, his belief 'in his own life-flow'. Quite clearly it is egoism which derives from mothers and faith in self which sons and fathers alike must find. In other words, Lawrence consciously discredits his maternal sense of authority, and consciously affirms his lost masculine heritage. Indeed, he speaks directly of his childhood, of that early 'fight for righteousness' 'our mothers' made, as they tried to improve 'our fathers' and make life 'better' for the children:

> We know now that our fathers were fought and beaten by our mothers, not because our mothers really knew what was 'better', but because our fathers had lost their instinctive hold on the life-flow and the life-reality, that therefore the female had to fight them at any cost, blind and doomed. We saw it going on as tiny children, the battle. We believed the moral excuse.   But we lived to be men, and to be fought in turn. And now we know there is no excuse, moral or immoral. It is just phenomenal. And our mothers, who asserted such a belief in 'goodness', were tired of that self-same goodness even before their death.[15]

Plainly Lawrence too is tired of maternal righteousness. He speaks of the need for men to die, to be born again with 'a different courage', if the fight between the sexes is to cease. In the meantime young men cling desperately to their wives, hate them with the cold hate of ill-treated children, the egoistic sons of egoistic mothers:

> The young men know that most of the 'benevolence' and 'motherly love' of their adoring mothers was simply egoism again, and an extension of self, and a love of having absolute power over another creature. Oh, these women who secretly lust to have absolute power over their own children—for their own good!   Do they think the children are deceived? Not for a moment! You can read in the eyes of the small modern child: 'My mother is trying to bully me with every breath she draws, but though I am only six, I can really resist her . . .[16]

The personal note is unmistakable. Lawrence too resists his mother's egoism, resists it in tales and essays of his middle and final years, resists it in himself and seeks rebirth into 'a different courage' and a different faith. Paul Morel's disguised aggression, in hastening his mother's death, emerges sharply now in tales like "The Rocking-Horse Winner", "Rawdon's Roof", "Mother and Daughter", where usurping mothers are deftly satirized for destroying or enslaving children. At the same time men like Lawrence's father emerge as sensual and unruly heroes—grooms, gypsies, gamekeepers, in whom the 'life-flow', the old masculine warmth and wildness, is still intact, while the old unmanliness, the old brutality and cravenness, is shorn away. In *Oedipus in Nottingham* Daniel Weiss sees the culmination of this process in *Lady Chatterley's Lover*:

> The shift from the parricidal Paul Morel running to his mother's arms while the father whines in the kitchen, to the 'great blond child-man', Clifford Chatterley, fondling the housekeeper's breasts while the gamekeeper waits in the Park, represents the total dilapidation of Lawrence's Oedipal longings and the perfection of his reactive anti-Oedipal vision of life. Along with the heroic contempt for the mother image in absolute decay comes the full identification with the once-despised father.[17]

The reaction is thematic as well as psychological. In *Women in Love* Lawrence had affirmed isolate selfhood as 'the central law of life' and had established star-equilibrium, or polarization, to preserve it from engulfing love. With selfhood affirmed, he could attend more confidently to his 'secondary law of life', that individual fulfillment comes through contact and communion with others. This law operates even in early works: but in the late period there comes a remarkable relaxation and shift of emphasis. In "The Real Thing" Lawrence blithely contradicts his early views on selfhood: 'Man and woman are not two separate and complete entities', he argues; they 'are not even two separate persons: not even two separate consciousnesses, or minds. In spite of vehement cries to the contrary, it is so. Man is connected with woman for ever, in connexions visible and invisible, in a complicated life-flow that can never be analysed'. This from the creator of star-equilibrium, for whom merging and fusing seemed horrible! In "We Need One Another" the contradiction is more openly acknowledged:

> We may as well admit it: men and women need one another. We may as well, after all our kicking against the pricks, our revolting and our sulking, give in and be graceful about it. We are all individualists: we are all egoists: we all believe intensely in freedom, our own at all events. We all want to be absolute, and sufficient unto ourselves. And it is a great blow to our self-esteem that we simply *need* another human being. . . . [It] is terribly humiliating to our isolated conceit.[18]

From isolate selfhood to isolate conceit, from proud singleness to overweening individualism, from impersonal union to the greatest fraud of all, reduction 'to our . . . elemental selves'. The extremes of *Women in Love* have been abandoned. The new goal is relationship, through which we have 'our very individuality'. Lawrence has recovered his father's masculine warmth and wildness, has rejected his mother's egoism and relaxed his own defensive individualism; he is ready now for contact, for sprays and vibrations from living fountains, for outflow and inflow, for true human relationship. And so he writes a novel called *Tenderness*.

## VI

Oliver Mellors, the gamekeeper in that novel, is by profession a keeper or protector of life; he lapses frequently into vernacular speech, the dialect of the lower classes; he goes about his work 'solitary and intent, like an animal that works alone'; he speaks for and conveys warmhearted love. In his work, in his dialect, in his love-making he resembles Paul Morel's father in *Sons and Lovers*, the man whose 'sensuous flame of life' attracts Mrs. Morel, whose children love him when he works dexterously in the home or tells animal tales of the pit-horse Taffy and the mouse who climbed his arm. He had 'a warm way of telling a story', Lawrence writes, and was 'peculiarly lavish' at such times 'of endearments to his second son', i.e. Paul. The warmness of Morel's father, his attractive masculine traits, seem present now in Mellors, and Lady Chattterley likes them. When she comes upon him washing himself behind his cottage, she has what Lawrence calls 'a visionary experience':

> He was naked to the hips, his velveteen breeches slipping down over his slender loins. And his white slim back was curved over a big bowl of soapy water, in which he ducked his head, shaking his head with a queer, quick little motion, lifting his slender white arms, and pressing the soapy water from his ears, quick, subtle as a weasel playing with water, and utterly alone . . . She saw the clumsy breeches slipping down over the pure, delicate, white loins, the bones showing a little, and the sense of aloneness, of a creature purely alone, overwhelmed her. Perfect, white, solitary nudity of a creature that lives alone, and inwardly alone. And beyond that, a certain beauty . . . a lambency, the warm, white flame of a single life, revealing itself in contours that one might touch: a body![19]

Mellors' aloneness here, his sensuous flame of life, his animal quickness and singleness, are qualities of the father. The same qualities are reflected as Mellors builds coops for the coming chicks and Connie, watching him, is again touched by his aloneness, quickness and intentness. His animal singleness differs from Birkin's proud singleness, in *Women in Love*, in visual immediacy, in sensuous appeal, and more than this, in vulnerability, as hinted by the exposed loins and bones; it contrasts, moreover, with that spiritual sense of authority which leads, for Lawrence, to egoism and self-importance. Mellors has his share of maternal egoism; his occasionally shrill preachments suggest that kind of false sufficiency to many readers: but his immediate appeal for Connie is that of masculine integrity and warmth. She turns in spring from the coldheartedness of Wragby Hall to the new life, the hatching chicks, the promise of creative love, at Mellors' hut. And new life comes as Mellors fetches a chick for her, with 'sure gentle fingers', from under the pecking mother hen:

> 'There!' he said, holding out his hand to her. She took the little drab thing between her hands, and there it stood, on its impossible little stalks of legs, its atom of balancing life trembling through its almost weightless feet into Connie's hands. But it lifted its handsome, clean-shaped little head boldly, and looked sharply round, and gave a little 'peep'.
> 'So adorable! So cheeky!' she said softly.
> The keeper, squatting beside her, was also watching with an amused face the bold little bird in her hands. Suddenly he saw a tear fall on to her wrist . . . She was kneeling and holding her two hands slowly forward, blindly, so that the chicken should run in to the mother-hen again. And there was something so mute and forlorn in her, compassion flamed in his bowels for her . . . Her face was averted, and she was crying blindly, in all the anguish of her generation's forlornness. His heart melted suddenly, like a drop of fire, and he put out his hand and laid his fingers on her knee.
> 'You shouldn't cry', he said softly.[20]

Connie's 'crying need', like that of her generation, is for tender love. Mellors responds to it out of that sexual sympathy which, for Lawrence, 'is just a form of warmheartedness and compassionateness, the most natural life-flow in the world'. That Mellors can speak for such compassion is important. His feelings are no different from Paul Morel's in *Sons and Lovers*, as he watches Clara Dawes kneeling among the flowers and suddenly scatters benedictive cowslips over her arching neck and body. But Paul's tenderness is not an articulated value, and in the works that follow, only the heroines speak for tender love; as we have seen, the heroes accept it grudgingly as the lesser part of equilibrium. That grudging compromise is replaced now by Mellors' open affirmation. The man speaks for warmheartedness; he is able to accept it as part of his masculine strength; he is even able to accept connection, or dependence on another, as a heartfelt need.

Lawrence shows this effectively as an artist; yet, ironically, he fails to see it in essays of this period. In "The State of Funk", for instance, he claims that accepting sexuality releases natural 'blood-sympathy', makes us warmer and more sympathetic toward others; and in "A Propos of *Lady Chatterley's Lover*", he holds that freeing the mind from 'fear of the body' releases tender love.[21] It would seem more relevant, however, to free the self from maternal dominance, or from fear of feelings which the mother once usurped. If men must renew faith in themselves, and if Lawrence renewed that faith, in *Lady Chatterley*, through identification with his father, then his affections were released through strengthened masculinity and selfhood, not through sexuality. He had long accepted the body and its sexual needs; now he accepts his masculine heritage, accepts himself as vernacular spokesman for warmhearted love. The sensual and unruly father has finally displaced the righteous mother: thus Mellors can love warmly without fear.

Yet not entirely. Mellors shies away when Connie describes their union as 'just love'; and he hates 'mouth kisses' as too personal. He also wants support from other men in the fight 'to preserve the tenderness of life, the tenderness of women, and the natural riches of desire'. His tenderness takes courage, as Connie says. There is also something limited or limiting about it. Ideally his love for Connie should radiate outward and enrich relations with the world; actually it stops more or less with Connie. These lovers touch each other, but do not reach beyond themselves. Perhaps they ask too much of warmth, of touch, to rest the future on it. Or perhaps they ask too little about its nature, to rest so much upon it. Elsewhere Lawrence argues, for instance, that 'All the emotions belong to the body', including even 'the higher emotions'.

And by the higher emotions we mean love in all its manifestations, from genuine desire to tender love, love of our fellow-men, and love of God: we mean love, joy, delight, hope, true indignant anger, passionate sense of justice and injustice, truth and untruth, honour and dishonour, and real belief in *anything*: for belief is a profound emotion that has the mind's connivance.[22]

## VII

What Lawrence wants, apparently, is to release a whole range of spiritual possibilities by accepting the sensual basis of emotion. The aim is laudable; but when he tries to reach that wider range, in *Lady Chatterley*, he releases only tender love. It may be that the emotions themselves must be accepted, and not merely their sensual basis. It is one thing, after all, to accept the flesh, another to be bound by it; and Lawrence does seem bound at times by fleshly warmth. It may be, too, that 'touch' itself must be accepted on emotional grounds which Lawrence cannot quite acknowledge. Thus Ian Suttie argues that 'love in all its manifestations' begins not simply with the body, but with the body's history, with the nurturing process in infancy, when the body first responds to love, and we learn to distinguish self from other. If this is true, then 'touch' begins with maternal and presexual relations, and 'sexual sympathy' becomes a late development of such relations.[23] There exists, in other words, an original maternal heritage which Lawrence only partially reclaims.

This hypothesis helps to explain, at any rate, why Lawrence stops short of his apparent goals. He sees, wisely enough, that sex is only 'the closest of all touch', that touch is a continuum, sensual rather than sexual, which runs through close relations; but he does not see that touch, as the medium for tender feelings, originates with the mother who usurped his selfhood and his manhood. One critic argues that Lawrence returns to the female principle in *Lady Chatterley's Lover*, that the body and its emotions are feminine in his psychology, while the spirit and its drives are masculine.[24] The trouble with this formula is that Lawrence took his spiritual cues from his mother, his sensual cues from his father. In *Lady Chatterley* he breaks his mother's spiritual hold, accepts his father's role in work and love, and asserts his masculine selfhood. It remains true, however, that the love he accepts is tender, warm, gentle, and in that sense maternal; it is nurturing love, released by masculine strength and confidence—the return of the repressed affections of childhood which a strong man may indulge. Its contrast, in the novel, is Clifford Chatterley's infantile love with Nurse Bolton, his complete abject dependence and regression. Mellors can be tender, even dependent, without regressing; he can indulge the sensual sympathies which Clifford paradoxically denies while wallowing in maternal love. But Lawrence's reaction to such love is so intense he cannot see its bearing on Mellors' courage; his understandable bitterness against usurping mothers leaves him, finally, on the threshold of discovery, unable to cross. He sees only Clifford's weakness, his infantile dependence on nurturing love; he cannot see that Mellors' strength converts the same conditions into masculine warmth, by which a man may offer nurturing love without losing male identity; nor can he see finally, that tenderness, founded in touch, is the true maternal heritage by which—according to Suttie—we claim the deepest love and release the highest feelings: consequently he cannot quite release those wider possibilities which his views entail.[25] But it is enough perhaps that he widens love to include the tender and dependent feelings, enriches love with newfound masculine warmth, and deepens it with genuine desire. Certainly no other modern writer has portrayed love's sensual and emotional range so vividly, nor, finally, with so much courage.

*Critical Quarterly*, 9, 1968.

## Notes

1 D. H. Lawrence, *Lady Chatterley's Lover* (New York: Grove Press, 1959), p. 334.

2 I. A. Richards, *Practical Criticism* (New York: Harvest, n.d.), pp. 253-254; Ian D. Suttie, *The Origins of Love and Hate* (New York: Agora, 1966), pp. 63-77.

3 Lawrence, *The Woman Who Rode Away and Other Stories* (New York: Berkley, 1956), p. 96.

4 *Ibid.*, pp. 105-106.

5 Lawrence, *Sons and Lovers* (New York: Compass, 1958), p. 284.

6 *Ibid.*, p. 286.

7 *Ibid.*, p. 355.

8 Mark Spilka, *The Love Ethic of D. H. Lawrence* (Bloomington: Indiana University Press, 1955), p. 74.

9 *Sons and Lovers*, p. 253.

10 *Ibid.*, p. 254.

11 *Ibid.*, pp. 417-418.

12 Lawrence, *Women in Love* (New York: Compass, 1960), p. 301.

13 *Ibid.*, p. 437.

14 Alfred Kazin, "Sons, Lovers and Mothers," *D. H. Lawrence and Sons and Lovers: Sources and Criticism*, ed. E. W. Tedlock, Jr. (New York: New York University Press, 1965), pp. 238-250.

15 Lawrence, "The Real Thing," *Phoenix: The Posthumous Papers of D. H. Lawrence*, ed. Edward D. McDonald (New York: Viking, 1936), p. 198.

16 *Ibid.*, pp. 199-200.

17 Daniel A. Weiss, *Oedipus in Nottingham: D. H. Lawrence* (Seattle: University of Washington Press, 1962), p. 109.

18 Lawrence, "We Need One Another," *Phoenix*, p. 188.

19 *Lady Chatterley's Lover*, pp. 75-76.

20 Ibid., pp. 134-135.

21 Lawrence, *Sex, Literature and Censorship*, ed. Harry T. Moore (New York: Twayne, 1953), pp. 66-67, 94.

22 Ibid., p. 96.

23 Suttie, *The Origins of Love and Hate*, especially pp. 7-8. 20-21.

24 H. M. Daleski, *The Forked Flame: A Study of D. H. Lawrence* (London: Faber and Faber, 1965), p. 15.

25 Here I contradict my early views on the role of touch, in *The Love Ethic of D. H. Lawrence*, pp. 192-193; but then this whole essay is hopefully an advance beyond such views.

# David Ellis, "D.H. Lawrence and the Female Body"

Although Lawrence's attitude to sexual matters is very important, given the kind of novelist he chose to be, serious discussion of it is still in the early stages. This becomes evident if we compare two passages, one biographical and the other fictional, each of which is startling enough on its own account but even more startling when placed alongside the other. The first can be found in a memoir written in the 1930s by George Neville. Along with Alan Chambers (the brother of Jessie), George Neville was Lawrence's closest male friend during his Eastwood days. Popular as well as enterprising with women, the difficulties Neville experienced as a school-master when he was obliged to acknowledge responsibility for the pregnancy of a girlfriend later provided Lawrence with material for the first half of his unfinished novel *Mr Noon*. By the time these young men were in their late teens and early twenties, Neville was experienced in ways in which he is anxious in his memoir to make clear that his friend was certainly not. He describes the period when Lawrence, who in his youth was always busy drawing or painting, 'turned his attention to the female form'. The faces he began with (Neville reports) were always of women with 'incipient moustaches'. This allowed Neville to tease Lawrence about his obvious fondness for Louie Burrows, the woman whom Lawrence himself was to describe as 'swarthy', once he had become engaged to her.[1]

From faces Lawrence apparently proceeded to 'busts, back views of the nude etc., and then to whole figures'. Neville describes how he called on Lawrence one evening and found him examining critically the sketch of a nude which he had just finished. Asking whether he intended this sketch to be 'a real woman or just a statue', Neville took the pencil from his friend and 'dashed in the shadings under the armpits and on the body'. When Lawrence asked what these shadings were for, Neville replied,

> That . . . is just the difference between your living, breathing woman, full of life and the statue I mentioned. That's HAIR!'

According to Neville, Lawrence's response to this information was suddenly and frantically violent. He leapt from his chair and began pommelling his bigger or at least more athletic companion, calling Neville a 'dirty little devil' and insisting three times that what he had said could not be true. 'Course it's true', Neville insisted, 'and more than ever true in the case of a woman like that one—a woman who's got Nature enough in her to grow a little moustache'. But Lawrence refused to believe him.[2]

The second passage comes from the second version of *Lady Chatterley's Lover*, the one published by Penguin in England as *John Thomas and Lady Jane*. At this stage in the evolution of the novel Lawrence's gamekeeper is still called Parkin (rather than Mellors). Connie Chatterley is puzzled as to how Parkin came to marry a woman like Bertha Coutts, and her curiosity leads to an account of his sexual history which is substantially different from what we learn about Mellors's previous experiences of women in *Lady Chatterley's Lover*. In *John Thomas and*

*Lady Jane*, Parkin has remained a virgin until his marriage with Bertha, and for a very specific reason. When he was eleven or twelve he had gone to the Coutts's house and found the sixteen year old Bertha on her own. She had lifted up her skirts—'They wore them split drawers then, girls did'—and shown him her genitals.

> 'She wanted me to come an' feel. But I never knowed afore then as women had hair there. Black hair! An' I don't know why, it upset me an' made me hate the thoughts of women from that day.'

Later on, Parkin and Bertha nevertheless marry but he finds he is unable to make love to her. When he is eventually persuaded to explain to his wife where the trouble lies, Bertha cries all night but then, in the morning, invites Parkin to shave off her pubic hair. 'An' so I did, an' she laid there so still. An' then it come up in me, an' I wanted her.'[3]

These passages should startle anyone who retains even the vestiges of the old idea of Lawrence as the 'Priest of Love', the enthusiastic celebrant of 'healthy', normative, sexual relationships (whatever they are). It would be helpful in discussing them if one could be absolutely clear about their status. What difference does it make that one is fiction and the other an extract from a memoir? Like most memoirs, Neville's book is demonstrably inaccurate in several of its details but there is no reason to think that he either would or could have invented such a bizarre episode. If it is therefore likely to have been true in substance, there might then be more grounds for suspecting that the incident in the novel was derived from Lawrence's personal experience and that he objected to Neville's addition of body hair to his sketch because it was associated, in however indirect a way, with a painful, repressed episode in his boyhood. This assumption would make it easier to discuss the two passages together because both would then be linked directly to biography: it would remove the awkwardness of talking at one moment about Lawrence himself and at another about a character he created. However, in the absence of any evidence that the young Lawrence did in fact have an experience similar to Parkin's, it will be best in the first instance to consider these two passages as no more than illustrations of a particular kind of phobic dismay at the reality of the female body, and to ask what they mean and how they can be interpreted.

The reasons why a boy or man should be both surprised and alarmed by a feature all female bodies share are not immediately evident. The most highly developed as well as the most popular body of doctrine which offers to explain them is of course Freud's, so that to ignore him, in the present cultural climate, would seem irresponsible. Freud often refers to male fear of the female genitalia but perhaps most directly in two pages he wrote in 1922 about the Medusa's head, in both Greek mythology and as subsequently represented in Western art. Notes for an essay he never completed, these pages illustrate two of the major difficulties of relying on Freud's interpretative method: he carries with him a dictionary of fixed symbolic values, and he is prone to invoke speculations about the usual course of all human development as if they were scientific laws. The fixed symbolic value in this case is that (as Freud here puts it), 'To decapitate = to castrate'. This equation sets the terms of reference for his discussion of the

Medusa's head which he sees as terrifying both because it is detached from the body and because it represents the female genitals. For him, it is associated with that moment in male development when 'a boy, who has hitherto been unwilling to believe the threat of castration, catches sight of the female genitals, probably those of an adult, surrounded by hair, and essentially those of his mother'. What has the force of law for Freud is that no boy is likely to grow up without experiencing such a moment and therefore some such encounter with the castration complex. For the virgin goddess Athena to have carried the Medusa's head on her shield was appropriate because she thus became a woman who 'is unapproachable and repels all sexual desire—since she displays the terrifying genitals of the Mother. Since the Greeks were in the main strongly homosexual', Freud goes on, 'it was inevitable that we should find [in their mythology] a representation of woman as a being who frightens and repels because she is castrated'. Now the aspect of the female organ which repels Parkin and Neville's Lawrence is its hair, but the Freud of these pages would have read that reaction as compensatory displacement. Although he notes that what makes the Medusa's head so frightening is the representation of her hair as snakes (as in the famous painting by Carravaggio, for example), he suggests that—snakes being what we all know they are—this is in fact a mitigation. 'The multiplication of penis symbols' (that is) he sees as a compensatory act to replace the penis itself, 'the absence of which is the cause of the horror'.[4]

Unavoidably sketchy and unclear though it is, Freud's reading of the Medusa's head has had (like all his readings) a good deal of influence on modern criticism. A long essay in Nell Hertz's *The End of the Line*, for example, accepts without question its premises and begins by applying them to Victor Hugo's account of how, during the troubles in France in 1848, two prostitutes stood on their barricade one after the other and exposed their genitals to the enemy—only to be promptly shot for their pains. Freud had recalled in his notes on the Medusa's head that in Rabelais 'the Devil took to flight when the woman showed him her vulva'. The members of the French National Guard were apparently less intimidated but Hertz is concerned to show that in their response, or rather in Hugo's account of their response, the castration fear which sight of the vulva provokes in men is also a fear of losing political rights and privileges.

Hertz's 'Medusa's Head: Male Hysteria under Political Pressure' was first published in 1983,[5] but the continuing popularity of the Freudian hypotheses is demonstrated in Peter Brooks's *Body Work*, a book which appeared in 1993 and which no-one could accuse of being deaf to current intellectual trends. Brooks's enquiry into what his sub-title terms 'objects of desire in modern narrative' could not have proceeded had he not accepted more or less *en bloc* the various myths of origin which accompany Freud's accounts of the castration complex, including the notion that our thirst for knowledge, with all that it implies for an understanding of the history of culture, can be derived from the young male's desire to see his parents copulating, or his mother's genitals. What makes him nervous is not so much that these Freudian beliefs might be shown to be untrue by a mass of enquiries in disciplines more empirically inclined than psychoanalysis, but that several of them at least might have come to seem old-fashioned or objectionable. As he writes in the part of his introduction where he is dealing directly with Freud's castration complex (and its corollary in woman's 'penis envy'), 'although we may reject the Freudian concept in its more naive and anecdotal forms, and in its patriarchal assumption that the development of the male is the norm, the more sophisticated view, associated especially with Jacques Lacan's rereading of Freud, cannot easily be dismissed'. Brooks has no intention of dismissing this more sophisticated view even if, as often as not, it is Freud in his more familiar guises whom one encounters. In a discussion of the scene in chapter 7 of Zola's *Nana* where Count Muffat de Beuville watches the heroine undressing in front of a mirror, for example, he endorses the view of 'some of Zola's best critics' who 'have noted that this passage forcibly reminds us of scenarios sketched by Freud . . . which both affirm and deny the absence of the phallus, and don't know what to see in its place'.[6]

Like Neil Hertz, Peter Brooks is interested in the representation of the female body in painting as well as literature. He notes the powerful taboo in the European tradition against the depiction of pubic hair and, with the help of T. J. Clark, speculates on why Manet's 'Olympia' should have been controversial. The more 'realistic' concept of relations between the sexes implied by this painting derives in part from the defiant way Manet's model stares back at the viewer; but it is also dependent on the impression which the hand covering her genitals gives of clutching—rather than merely hiding in the half protective, half-alluring gesture of 'Olympia's prototype: Titian's "Venus of Urbino"'. The positioning of this hand obviates the problem of pubic hair whose representation, according to Clark, has been displaced onto the 'frothing yellow sheet which hangs down the fold between pillow and sheet' at the front of the picture.[7] Even in such a revolutionary painting the taboo is circumvented rather than transgressed.

As George Neville rightly implies, it was a taboo stronger in statuary than in pictorial art, but consideration of it raises what is obviously a major problem in appealing to Freud in any attempt to understand Neville's account of Lawrence's behaviour. If it really is some form of castration anxiety which explains why Lawrence reacted so violently when Neville added body hair to his drawing, why had he been so relatively comfortable before in sketching female figures which were hairless? Should not a female nude in the manner of (say) Ingres have been even more frightening to a sensitive and inexperienced young man like him because, without either the camouflage of hair or the opportunity it provides for compensatory displacement, there would be even more awareness of the horrifying absence or lack? More generally, why should the French public have been so apparently comfortable with the smooth bodies of the models in paintings by Ingres, Cabanel, Bouguereau, and so apparently uncomfortable with 'Olympia', when the absence of a penis is so much more evident in the former than the latter?

The same problem comes up in a more acute form with episode from *John Thomas and Lady Jane*. At first sight it might seem as if Lawrence, having provided Freudian psychology with so much apparent exemplification of the Oedipus complex in *Sons and Lovers*, was now dramatizing a classic castration trauma which he had dredged up from his own experience or had simply invented—if it is possible to associate such a strange incident with 'simple' invention. It is true Parkin explicitly states that what repelled him about Bertha when he was eleven or twelve was her pubic hair and that ought, according to the schemata Freud offers in discussing the Medusa's head, to have been a mitigating circumstance. But everyone knows that, in the Freudian system, the mechanisms of repression and displacement mean that the declarations of the subject, whether the subject is conceived here as Parkin or his creator, can be discounted. Harder to discount is that Parkin's sexual desire is described as being kindled once Bertha's hair has been shaved off. The virgin Athena wears Medusa's head on her shield because it inhibits sexual desire. Why should Parkin only discover it when Bertha is shaved and he can see more clearly the absence which, in the orthodox Freudian reading, must have been at the origin of his terror as a young boy?

No-one even remotely familiar with Freudian thinking could be simple-minded enough to imagine that problems like these would trouble experienced practitioners for long. One of many reasons for the remarkable success of Freud's procedures is their flexibility. A very simple illustration of this would be that the case for believing members of the French National Guard affected in 1848 by the same fears made Rabelais' devil take flight, would receive just as much support had they held their fire as it does from the fact that they chose to shoot the prostitutes who exposed themselves on the barricades. Both actions could be cited with equal plausibility as evidence of a particular form of terror. Such a degree ratiocinative freedom is hardly character-building. As Frank Cioffi has suggested,[8] the complaint against Freud is not so much that he puts forward theories which are non-testable, but rather that his choices amongst the sets of logical alternatives with which he is habitually faced are too often determined less by what at any one moment he finds before him than a shrewd sense of personal or professional advantage. ('Personal' here largely means the implications of one choice rather than another for the elaborate system he is always seeking either to establish or defend.) In a word, he is often in intellectual bad faith. This is what makes him such a dangerous model for literary intellectuals who work in an environment where there is not even the spectre of a sick mind or body to impose some sense of responsibility, and where what they say hardly matters to anyone but themselves. Neil Hertz's ingenious application of Freudian castration theory to the 1848 revolution in France interestingly reflects his model's own ambivalent shifting between a concern for historical truth (what really happened in the past?), and for narrative coherence. Yet the notes to Freud's 'Wolf Man' case show him to have been genuinely concerned with the implications of abandoning any claim to be describing what had actually happened to his patient whereas Hertz knows that, for the constituency he is addressing, whether what he recounts could ever be established as a true explanation for certain episodes in the past is immaterial in comparison with whether all the parts in an elaborate intellectual jigsaw can be made to fit.

For Freudians, both Parkin's sharing of the pubic hair and Lawrence's omission of it in his drawing, are going to be related in some way to castration anxiety, because that is what every human male inevitably experiences as a normal part of his development. The more vehemently any particular individual wants to deny this truth, the more it is confirmed. Although this is intimidating (and no system of thought can become fashionable without some degree of intellectual intimidation), the difficulties of fitting the Lawrence case into the

Freudian framework must nevertheless be sufficient in this instance to make at least some readers wonder why it is necessary to go so far afield for an explanation of either Lawrence's behaviour or Parkin's, when a satisfactory interpretation is already to hand. This is apparent in the collocation Neville himself suggests between hair and 'Nature'.

Neville's implied enthusiasm is for hair as a sign of vigorous natural functioning, bodily warmth, and he suggests that to see hair on the body in this way can in certain circumstances make it a source of erotic appeal. In the course of a general study of the transformations of the female body in the eighteenth and nineteenth centuries, Phillippe Perrot comments briefly on depilation and cites Victor Leca ('viveur patenté'): 'Not many of our dear friends ("chères amies") want to be the bearded lady but a good number of them are nevertheless happy to show us the "dark forest", without the costs of travel, merely by lifting up their arm'.[9] Perrot has ensured that we shall hear the salacious note in this remark by recalling in his previous sentence Zola's claim, in the first chapter of *Nana*, that when his heroine appeared naked on the stage it was the golden hairs under her arms as well as her plump white thighs which so excited her male public. Neville, one might say, is attempting to lift the erotic appeal of body hair out of a pornographic context and display it as a wholesome, 'natural' feature of sexual attraction. As a man of the world, he wants to teach his inexperienced friend the real meaning and promise of Louie Burrows's slight moustache.

But if hair can excite it can also disgust, however much a part of 'Nature' it may be. 'La femme est *naturelle*, c'est à dire abominable' Baudelaire famously wrote;[10] and in Zola's description of Count Muffat's observation of Nana's nakedness (not on the stage but in the privacy of her apartment) we find that: 'He thought of his former dread of Woman, of the Beast of the Scriptures, a lewd creature of the jungle. Nana's body was covered with fine hair, reddish down which turned her skin into velvet . . .' The inhibited Muffat is both fascinated and repelled by what he perceives as the animality of Nana (whose skin is both hairy and soft). The down on her body is as much responsible for his perception that in her 'il y avait de la bête' as what Zola's Penguin translator immediately goes on to describe as 'her equine crupper and flanks ['sa croupe et ses cuisses de cavale'] . . . the fleshy curves and deep hollows of her body, which veiled her sex in the suggestive mystery of their shadows'.[11] The last words in this quotation show that the great Naturalist is no more able to depict the vulva than most of the painters of his time, but if in them the depiction of body hair is also taboo, one of the reasons is surely the association between hair and animal nature which Muffat's responses reveal. The representation of female bodies as smooth and glossy would thus be a sign of both censorship and idealization, censorship working through idealization. If hair could excite certain kinds of men and, for much the same reasons, disgust others, then it would be better if it were not there. Lawrence's shock at having it added to his drawing can be attributed to his never having had sufficient opportunity to observe at leisure women without their clothes, even in the proximities of a working-class household, as well as to his having derived from European painting and sculpture an idealized notion of the female body. (If there had been in his background an incident equivalent to Parkin's encounter with the young Bertha, factors such as these might have helped to ensure it was repressed.) One could therefore say that for him hair on the female body was objectionable because it indicated that women did not after all operate in a higher, ethereal sphere but on the same, so often unsatisfactory level of natural functioning as men. The fear that is undoubtedly present in his response would then not be one of castration but of having suddenly to come to terms with the idea of a woman with as much animal nature as himself—or rather, since Neville presents him to us as physically unsure and timid, with possibly much more.

Neville's implicit explanation for Lawrence's dismay is less obviously appropriate to the eleven or twelve year old that Parkin is supposed to be when Bertha exposes herself to him. One might ask why there should be any need to attribute special significance to what the young Parkin might actually have seen. For a boy of that age to have a sixteen year old girl display her genitals and invite him to come and feel, could be an experience so disturbing that whatever he saw would then become a mnemonic for the fear associated with the occasion. Black pubic hair would then have no importance in itself but simply be a reminder of what had been a form of sexual assault. Yet in that case one would need to explain why its shaving off could represent such an immediately effective method of coming to terms with the past; and also account for Parkin's own statement that 'I never knowed afore then as women had hair there'. This does not sound as if Lawrence meant us to regard the hair as incidental or the particularity of what Parkin sees as without significance. His shock at its discovery implies an idealization process already in course but eleven is not too early for that, nor for the kind of internalized dichotomy between hairy men and hairless women made explicit in a handbook on feminine beauty from which Alain Roger quotes in an informative article on the representation of the female genitals in art.

> If an abundant head of hair is an asset for a woman, a hairy body is just the opposite. The latter is more a male attribute and in general one can say that the most beautiful women are those who least resemble men. The hairs on a woman's body ought to be soft and infrequent. Their colour usually differs a great deal from the hairs on the head: more often that not it is much darker.[12]

The young Parkin's response to Bertha's black hair is of course that of a character in a novel. The impression he conveys of not merely being shocked but also seeing something he did not expect to see could therefore be thought of as a novelist's error. It could also be attributed to Parkin's own retrospective revision of an early memory. Yet given the amount of socialization any young person has gone through by the age of eleven or twelve, there seems to me also no reason why the response should not be regarded as appropriately attributed.

Bertha's black pubic hair so disturbs Parkin that in later life he cannot make love to her without its removal. What is particularly significant in this action is that Bertha does not shave herself but allows Parkin to do it for her. 'An' she laid there so still'. Her passivity parallels the symbolic removal of those signs which testify to at least as much body heat as Parkin himself possesses; yet as *John Thomas* shows, and *Lady Chatterley's Lover* even more clearly, her initial acquiescence in the passive role has to be paid for by the gamekeeper later. In both versions of the novel, Bertha has become the personification of ravening female desire, a *vagina dentata,* whereas, with Connie, Lawrence could be said to acknowledge and accept woman's full right to a physicality equivalent to a man's but at the same time devise ways—less drastic and temporary than Parkin's—for making it no longer fearsome and threatening.

One of Lawrence's principal aims in the *Lady Chatterley* enterprise seems to have been to exorcise fear of the female body. That fear had rarely been expressed directly in his previous writing career, but it is often apparent in his descriptions of landscape. A particularly striking example occurs in the second half of *Mr Noon* where Lawrence is remembering the trip over the Alps into Italy which he and Frieda made in 1912.

> The valley began to depress him. The great slopes shelving upwards, far overhead: the sudden dark, hairy ravines in which he was trapped: all made him feel he was caught, shut in down below there. He felt tiny, like a dwarf among the great thighs and ravines of the mountains. There is a Baudelaire poem which tells of Nature, like a vast woman lying spread, and man, a tiny insect, creeping between her knees and under her thighs, fascinated. Gilbert felt a powerful revulsion against the great slopes and particularly against the tree-dark, hairy ravines in which he was caught.[13]

This reference to Baudelaire's 'La Géante', which Lawrence reads far more in accordance with his own preoccupation with 'hairy ravines' than its author's, can be associated with a phrase in a letter he had written to Ernest Weekley a few months before the Alpine excursion: 'All women in their natures are like giantesses'.[14] It seems to have taken him a long time to overcome the more fearful implications of this belief. A stage in the process might well be recorded in a short story called 'Glad Ghosts' when the narrator is introduced to a female character with 'the hint of a dark moustache' and later thinks appreciatively of 'the sparse black hairs there would be on her strong-skinned dusky thighs'.[15] Here is Lawrence, one could say, taking George Neville's advice, although perhaps with a suggestion of that same wilfulness and over-insistence which critics so often complain of when they discuss the scene in *Lady Chatterley's Lover* where Mellors and Connie decorate their naked bodies with flowers. In both its extended versions, this episode begins with the gamekeeper threading flowers through Connie's pubic hair.[16] Neville had insisted that body hair was a welcome part of 'Nature'. In *Lady Chatterley's Lover* Lawrence attempted to devise his own, symbolic means of naturalization.

It was in the final version of *Lady Chatterley's Lover* only that Lawrence added to the flower scene Mellors's satisfaction in the fact that Connie shits and pisses.[17] Here an important aspect of the fear inspired by having to recognize that a woman also belongs to Nature, which Neville's Lawrence betrays, is being out-faced. Another aspect of that fear seems to be that a woman is likely to make 'natural' demands of a sexual kind. That there are these two aspects makes especially complicated any interpretation of a particularly disputed episode in *Lady Chatterley's Lover,* the 'night of sensual passion' before Connie leaves the Wragsby area for Venice. On the one hand, the easily decipherable references to anal intercourse in that episode can be read in the context Lawrence himself offers and insists upon: the need to burn out shame even as regards 'the most secret places'. On the other, since anal intercourse is described as imposing a certain degree of passivity on Connie, it can also be seen in relation to a continuing debate in the novel about power relations within sexual intercourse, especially as—in a phrase which justifies at least some of the hostility feminist critics have expressed—Lawrence at one moment writes of Connie's response, 'And how, in fear, she had hated it! But how she had really wanted it!'.[18]

It might also be said that *Lady Chatterley's Lover* is to other novels by men which attempt to deal frankly with the female body what Courbet's 'L'Origine du Monde' is to Manet's 'Olympia'. In Courbet's painting—reproduced in both Hertz and Brooks and once owned (apparently) by Lacan[19]—the whole space is occupied by that part of a naked female body which stretches from the top of the thighs to the bottom of the breasts, seen from an angle which makes the genitals clearly visible. But the comparison breaks down when one thinks how relatively unusual that angle is—bodies in *Lady Chatterley's Lover* are viewed in ways which require no special peculiarities of posture. It also breaks down once we know that the Turkish diplomat who bought this painting kept it hidden behind a locked panel in his room and commissioned other paintings from Courbet of an obviously pornographic nature.[20]  This could be taken merely as an illustration of the truism that no artist can ever control how their work will be received (one thinks of all those dog-eared copies of *Lady Chatterley's Lover* handed round in English class-rooms), but its lesson is rather that to be explicit is not in itself a solution. As the conversation of Sir Clifford's cronies in *Lady Chatterley's Lover* often makes clear, Lawrence understood as well as anyone that the move from the Victorian secrecy in which he had been brought up to the new freedoms centred (for example) around Garsington might still be an evasion. The nature of those freedoms is suggested in a startling form when one finds Lytton Strachey writing to his brother James in 1916 (about Dora Carrington), 'when it comes to a creature with a cunt one seems to be immediately désorienté. Perhaps it's because cunts don't particularly appeal to one'.[21] The passages I have been considering indicate that early in his life they did not appeal to Lawrence either, but he would no more have been able to manage all that is implied by Strachey's fastidious use of 'particularly', a French word and the impersonal pronoun than he seems, as a young man, to have been comfortable with George Neville's hearty, man-of-the-world approach.

To mention Strachey is to be reminded of a third possible reading of the 'night of sensual passion' in *Lady Chatterley's Lover*: that it, along with many other episodes in Lawrence's work, is a sign of his 'latent' or 'repressed' homosexuality. The intellectual crudity with which this position has been argued in recent times is partly a consequence of the refusal of many of Lawrence's admirers to look closely at the unusualness of some of his dealings with sexual matters (so that a split develops in which the two opposing sides adopt extreme positions). Those who refuse close inspection, however, may not always be prudes but sometimes only people who recognize the extreme difficulty of striking the right note in these matters. That it does remain so difficult is an indication of how thoroughly *Lady Chatterley's Lover* must have failed in certain respects, and of how fallacious was Lawrence's belief (even more popular in our time than his) that major cultural change can be effected through an adjustment in language. Lawrence's own defence to the charge of wilfulness in "A Propos of

*Lady Chatterley's Lover*" was that we are at a stage in our culture where we need to make a conscious effort to realise, to know; and that this realization is largely a question of an appropriate vocabulary.[22] The lack of such a vocabulary is acutely brought home to anyone who feels that Lawrence's dealings with pubic hair are both significant and neglected enough to merit close attention and then finds himself driven back, as I have been, on awkward terms such as vulva and genitals. Lawrence's own preferred alternative in his last novel was of course cunt, the meaning of which Mellors explains to Connie with a disconcerting explicitness. Yet the demand that we should call things by their proper names begs the question as well as suggesting too much unthinking optimism as to the effect that will have. We still need to propose terms for serious debate. Had my title been 'Lawrence and Pubic Hair' those not offended might well have taken it as some kind of joke. It was no joke for Lawrence, as it would not have been for Louie Burrows if she and he had been more intimate at the time Neville describes—nor can one imagine Parkin or, more particularly perhaps, Bertha Coutts, finding it very funny.

*Essays in Criticism: A Quarterly Journal of Literary Criticism*, 46:2, April 1996.

**Notes**

---

[1] This was in December 1911. See *The Letters of D. H. Lawrence*, vol. i, ed. James T. Boulton, (Cambridge, 1979), p. 343.

[2] G. H. Neville, *A Memoir of D. H. Lawrence (The Betrayal)*, ed. Carl Baron, (Cambridge, 1981), pp. 81-3.

[3] *John Thomas and Lady Jane*, (Harmondsworth, 1973), pp. 228-231.

[4] See *The Complete Works of Sigmund Freud*, (Standard Edition), vol. 18, pp. 273-4.

[5] In *Representations*, (Fall 1983). See Neil Hertz, *The End of the Line: Essays on Psychoanalysis and the Sublime*, (New York, 1985), p. vii.

[6] Peter Brooks, *Body Work: Objects of Desire in Modern Literature*, (Cambridge, Mass., 1993), pp. 12 & 141.

[7] T. J. Clark, *The Painting of Modern Life: Paris in the Art of Manet and his Followers*, (New York, 1985), p. 136.

[8] See especially 'Freud and the idea of a psuedo-science' in *Explanation in the Behavioural Sciences*, eds. Bolger and Cioffi, (Cambridge, 1970) and 'Wittgenstein's Freud' in *Elective Affinities*, ed. J. Canfield, (New York, 1986).

[9] Philippe Perrot, *Le travail des apparences, ou les tranformations du corps féminin XVIII$^e$-XIX$^e$*(Paris, 1984), pp. 151-2.

[10] Charles Baudelaire, 'Mon coeur mis à nu', *Oeuvres Complètes*, (Paris, Pléiade edition, 1961), p. 1272.

[11] Emile Zola, *Nana*, translated by George Holden, (Harmondsworth, 1972), p. 223.

[12] See Alain Roger, 'Vulva, Vultus, Phallus' in *Communications*, vol. 46 (1987), p. 189 (my translation). Alain Roger, who goes on to show that until the 1970s the taboo against the representation of body hair was as powerful in photography as it was in painting, is quoting from *La Beauté féminine* by E. de Chavannes. Neither he nor the Bibliothèque Nationale's catalogue can give a date for this work but its manner strongly suggests the first decades of this century.

[13] *Mr Noon*, ed. Lindeth Vasey, (Cambridge, 1974), p. 251.

[14] *Letters*, vol. i, p. 392.

[15] *The Collected Stories of D. H. Lawrence*, (1974), pp. 623 & 251.

[16] See *John Thomas and Lady Jane*, pp. 258-9 and *Lady Chatterley's Lover*, ed. Michael Squires (Cambridge, 1993), p. 223.   There is a hint for the flower scene on p. 174 of *The First Lady Chatterley*, (Harmondsworth, 1972), but it is not developed.

[17] *Lady Chatterley's Lover*, p. 223.

[18] Ibid, p. 247.   It is easier to understand why anal intercourse might liberate Connie from certain feelings of shame about her body than what Mellors could gain from it (in the context Lawrence is offering).

[19] 'M. Pleynet nous apprend que ce tableau faisait récemment partie de la collection de Lacan qui, dit-on, le conservait lui aussi derrière un petit rideau'.  Alain Roger, p. 187.

[20] Ibid.  For details of Courbet's Turkish patron (Khalil Bey), see Francis Haskell, *Past and Present in Art and Taste: Selected Essays*, (New Haven, 1987), pp. 175-185 ('A Turk and his Pictures in Nineteenth Century Paris').

[21] See Michael Holroyd, *Lytton Strachey*, vol. II, (1968), p. 198.

[22] 'A Propos of *Lady Chatterley's Lover*' is reprinted in the Cambridge edition of the novel (pp. 305-335).

# VII
# Plays

**Edward Garnett, "Introduction" to *A Collier's Friday Night***

His first play, *A Collier's Friday Night*, Lawrence tells us, in a note pencilled on the MS., "was written when I was twenty-one, almost before I'd done anything. It is most horribly green." From the biographical details contributed by D. H. L. to the American edition of *The Widowing of Mrs. Holroyd* (New York, 1914) we learn that "at twenty-three he left the [Nottingham Day Training] College and went to London to teach school, to study French and German and to write." So, *A Collier's Friday Night* was written at Eastwood, 1906-7. When, five years or so later, April 1912, he sent me the MS., looking back at his provincial inexperience it was natural that both the piece and the youth who wrote it should seem to him "horribly green." But what strikes one critically is the sureness of touch and penetrating directness of this dramatic chronicle of family life. As a theatre piece it is a bit too artless and diffuse, too lacking in concentration and surprise, and its interest lies in the strongly drawn characters, their relations and the clash of their personalities. The life of this household warring within itself is, of course, a transcript of the life of the Lawrence family. The situation is the same that D. H. L. handled later in *Sons and Lovers*, viz. the enmity between the father and the mother, and the latter's jealousy of her son's sweetheart. If "greenness" there be, it lies in the cocksureness of the author's tone and not in the delineation of the situation and characters. The opening scene between Nellie, the mother, and the father, exposes admirably the latter's stormy bitterness against his family, who despise him. And the closing scene between the parents and Ernest (pp. 70-76) is as dramatically powerful as the passage following between mother and son (pp. 77-82) is delicate and poignant. Whether the psychological veracity of these characters and their behaviour can offset the discursiveness of the play will be interesting to watch. The warp and woof of the drama out of which the situations are spun are the bitterness between the parents and Ernest's relations with the women round him. At twenty-one Lawrence had not yet evolved his philosophical doctrines about sex, nor had he developed the "inner conflict" between his selves. But his uncanny clairvoyance about women and the sex duel generally is declared in every scene of *A Collier's Friday Night*, as when Ernest says sadly to Maggie (p. 45):

> "You know you think too much of me—you do, you know." (She looks at him with a proud, sceptical smile.)
> (He waxes suddenly wroth)—"It's just like a woman, always aching to believe in somebody or other, or something or other." (She smiles.)

Then you have the difference between the attitude of the sexes. And later (p. 72) woman's secret is declared in the mother's cry:

> "No, my boy, because she doesn't mean the same to me. She has never understood—she has not been like you. And now—you seem to care nothing—you care for *any*thing more than home: you tell me nothing but the little things: you used to tell me everything; you used to come to me with everything; but now—I don't *do* for you now. You have to find somebody else."

With what a light dexterous hand D. H. L. has touched off the flirtatious relations between himself and the feminine bevy round him, in the scene between Beatrice, Ernest and Maggie, with the cattish innuendoes about the College girls (pp. 49-51). There is no "greenness" in this scene done straight from the life by a man with a genius for attracting the sex. And if anybody wishes to see the difference in expression between this young author of twenty-one and the D. H. L. of twenty-seven, let him compare the two portraits given in *The Early Life of D.H. Lawrence*. The alertness, directness and stubborn pride in the gaze of the youth who wrote *A Collier's Friday Night* has been enriched by something more speculative and roguishly aware of himself and others in the later photograph of 1911. The latter is a marvellously faithful portrait of D.H. Lawrence as I first knew him when he came to the Cearne and his loveableness, cheekiness, intensity and pride are all there for the discerning eye.

*A Collier's Friday Night*, 1st edition, London: Martin Lecker, 1934.

## Edward Sackville West, "A Modern Isaiah" (Reviews of *Reflections on the Death of a Porcupine* and *David: A Play*)

The first essay, "The Crown," in Mr. Lawrence's book of fantasia, dates from 1915. It was written in the shadow of the author's detestation of the war, which gives it its curious intensity. It was written before Mr. Lawrence had evolved the "yelling" style that so unfortunately characterises his later commentaries on Life, Men and Manners. It is long. It is repetitive. It is over-emphatic. These are the qualities which make it so difficult for the reader to listen to Mr. Lawrence; but it is of great importance to try to understand him, for he is one of the few contemporary men of genius.

His physiological mysticism runs straight up against scientific fact, but Mr. Lawrence is a poet and succeeds, on the whole, in "coming out on the other side" of his blatantly mendacious assertions. His "Idea," if looked at when the light of our imagination is turned off, appears the merest rubbish; but, the moment we allow our minds to admit and deal in the images he so vividly and poetically provides, communication is made and we understand with our hearts. What this Idea is it is risky to describe in words other than Mr. Lawrence's own; the following quotation gives it as clearly and concisely as any single passage can:

> There are the two eternities fighting the fight of Creation, the light projecting itself into the darkness, the darkness enveloping herself within the embrace of light. And then there is the consummation of each in the other, the consummation of light in darkness and darkness in light, which is absolute: our bodies cast up like foam of two meeting waves, but foam which is absolute, complete, beyond the limitation of either infinity, consummate over both eternities. The direct opposites of the Beginning and the End, by their very directness, imply their own supreme relation. And this supreme relation is made absolute in the clash and the foam of the meeting waves. And the clash and the foam are the Crown, the absolute.

Now, two opposite attitudes are possible in face of such a passage as this. Either we may regard it as pure nonsense, Neanderthal; or else the whole elaborate simile grips our minds and makes us *feel* the relation that the writer is striving to explain. He has done it better for us elsewhere—in a story called "The Ladybird," where the agonies of the characters carry this idea over to us more or less implicitly. But it is no good, as Mr. Lawrence says, arguing about it and intellectualising his imaginative appeal. We must let ourselves understand him, as one understands poetry, and let him "incite us to an attitude," as Mr. I. A. Richards would say. For the important point, and one with which we feel entirely in sympathy, is that *the religious state of mind is disappearing from Western Europe*, as a result (by no means necessary) of the progress of scientific knowledge:

> Without God, without some sort of immortality, not necessarily life-everlasting, but without *something* absolute, we are nothing. Yet now, in our spitefulness of self-frustration, we would rather be nothing than listen to our own being.

Again, Mr. Lawrence writes, "Your spirit will be like a dead bee in a cell," if you "set up as absolutes" scientific facts. So, for lack of this religious spirit, this smokeless flame that should burn in every man, modern civilisation is decaying *inside its own shell*, wherein it seeks to reform itself, turning and turning upon itself in a vain effort to bring good out of evil. It is only when we have broken the shell that the new shoots of life will spring up and we shall be born again. As Zarathustra, Mr. Lawrence's spiritual father, beautifully said: "One must still have chaos in one, to be able to bring forth a dancing star." Christianity has exhausted itself and has died a natural death; it is time that the old gods of Power came back to us—of Power that is not the same as Will, but the force that made

Sardanapalus, and Saul, and Caesar. The sense of values, all but destroyed by (1) Scientific Materialism, (2) the War, must once again be cultivated. The Heroic Idea will reappear.

The first criticism that must leap to the mind on reading this is that such a new world does not, on the present showing, contain much to recompense us for the loss of (1) the Intellect and its pleasures, (2) the affections; though no doubt Mr. Lawrence would retort that neither of these is worth having, both being implicit in what he calls the "Flux of Corruption." In for a penny, in for a pound!

The remaining essays in the book, all much shorter, belong to more recent years and exhibit the inequalities already referred to. We cannot but admire the intensity of the writer's conviction and the occasional brilliance of the language in which he expresses it, but he too frequently takes the step which lies between the sublime and the ridiculous. On the subject of the novel he has much to say that is both interesting and original; but, unfortunately, here as elsewhere, strength of feeling leads him, as it often led Swinburne, into vociferation, and our prejudice is aroused at the outset by having our ears assaulted by prose resembling the back-chat of a guttersnipe. A good case can be made out against Tolstoy *the man*, on the ground that his philosophy was unconscious humbug. We may agree that his novels succeed triumphantly in spite of their author's otiose pietism. But there are ways and ways of expressing the attack. This is Mr. Lawrence's way:

> And old Leo tries to make out, it was all because of the phallic sin. Old liar! Because where would any of Leo's books be, without the phallic splendour? And then to blame the column of blood, which really gave him all his life riches. The Judas! Cringe to a mangy, bloodless Society, and try to dress up that dirty old Mother Grundy in a new bonnet and face-powder of Christian Socialism. Brothers indeed! Sons of a castrated Father!

This is sad stuff, which forfeits the reader's serious attention. What is meant is true enough and worth saying, but this sort of vulgar slang weakens the writer's attack immeasurably. All through these later essays we have the deplorable spectacle of Mr. Lawrence trying to get force by violent methods—screaming and yelling into ears that close instinctively in self-protection. Thus, "Him with His Tail in His Mouth" is rendered mere gibberish, and "Love was once a Little Boy" is not much better, though it contains one purely descriptive passage about a cow that is worth all the commentary that succeeds it. The essay that gives its name to the volume begins with an account of the writer trying to extract porcupine quills from a dog's nose and of his subsequent killing of the porcupine—a magnificent piece of narrative such as only Mr. Lawrence could have written. Perhaps the best thing in the whole volume—indeed, one of the best things its author has ever done, is the description in "The Crown" of a wounded soldier on a pier at the seaside. Here the "purpose" has become one with the vision and the result is pathetically, terribly beautiful.

Where Mr. Lawrence is at his best, he is the equal of Blake in his finest prophetic mood; at his worst, we seem to hear a street-arab shrieking abuse at someone who has not given him a large enough tip. But—I repeat it—he is one of the few writers of genius now alive and he has almost all the qualities of a great novelist—lyricism, the power of communicating atmosphere, a gift of dialogue, humour (harsh and exultant), ability to portray character. But he has little or no sense of construction and no restraint whatever. This last fault, grave as it is, only vitiates a page or two at a time of his novels; but it frequently renders an entire essay nugatory.

Mr. Lawrence the playwright is a very different subject. It would be hard to beat *David* for sobriety, for the deliberate and well-managed archaism of its diction, for clarity of thought and beauty of detail. The theory on which the play is based is to be found scattered through the pages of the book of essays discussed above. For Mr. Lawrence Saul is a better man than David. He sees in Saul the possessor of that Power, which we of the modern world have lost; but in David he sees the incarnation of Will, as opposed to the blind Power—the cunning, cautious, foxy ability that is the curse of contemporary civilisation. Mr. Lawrence would say, with Zarathustra: "I love all who are like heavy drops falling one by one out of the dark cloud that lowereth over man; they herald the coming of the lightning, and succumb as heralds." Such was Saul: such is Mr. Lawrence's true aristocrat—the embodiment of the Heroic Idea.

It is interesting to compare this play with another on the same subject, André Gide's *Saül*. M. Gide's conception of the story and its protagonists is a totally different one; he also has his theory, but it is a far more "literary" one. He makes of Saul a sort of feeble Baron de Charlus, assailed by the demons of neurosis (brought on to the stage), and the interest of the play is frankly erotic. Mr. Lawrence's Jonathan is rather a strong character, a "lithe stripling," and in his relations with David he takes the ascendant. M. Gide, on the other hand, sees him as a beautiful, fainting, effeminate creature, in a state of hysterical rapture over David's physical strength. The rivalry between Saul and Jonathan for David's affection makes the central theme of the play. There is a shade of affectation in this point of view, which is conspicuously lacking in Mr. Lawrence's austere drama. Sensuously beautiful as are the David-and-Jonathan scenes in *Saül*, yet they do not compare, in subtlety and depth of restrained feeling, with Scenes V. and VIII. of *David*. Yet we can scarcely imagine the latter play on the stage, whereas *Saül* should be effective enough, with its strange, quasi-modern diction.

Perhaps the best of Mr. Lawrence's play lies in the last two scenes—the abnegation of Saul at the hill of sacrifice, and the scene of the shooting of the arrows and the parting of David and Jonathan. Here the author has cast some of the images, in which he habitually bodies forth his own philosophy, in the biblical mould, and the result is superbly moving. The chorus of prophets and the gradual declension of Saul before the strong voice of the soldier has all the quality of a complex musical crescendo, in which one phrase eventually dominates the whole in a sombre climax.

The final scene is one of great emotional solemnity. To give an idea of the strength and beauty of the prose, one cannot do better than quote a few lines of the last speech of Jonathan:

> Thou goest, David! And the hope of Israel with thee! I remain, with my father, and the star-stone falling to despair. Yet what is it to me? I would not see thy new day, David. For thy wisdom is the wisdom of the subtle, and behind thy passion lies prudence. And naked thou wilt not go into the fire. . . . But in Saul have I known the

magnanimity of man . . . Great men and magnanimous, men of the faceless flame, shall fall from strength, fall before thee, thou David, shrewd whelp of the lion of Judah!

*New Statesman* XXVII, 10 July 1926.

## Alan Rudrum, "Stage Sons, Stage Lovers" (Review of *The Complete Plays of D.H. Lawrence)*

Half of the eight plays in this volume were written in 1912, the year when Lawrence finished *Sons and Lovers* and began life with Frieda. Lawrence was at that time an enthusiastic playwright ('I enjoy so much writing my plays—they come so quick and exciting from the pen') and believed that "just as an audience was found in Russia for Chekhov, so an audience might be found in England for some of my stuff".

The earliest play, *A Collier's Friday Night*, foreshadows the episode in *Sons and Lovers* in which Paul Morel allows the bread to burn, and brings down his mother's wrath on his relationship with Miriam. The atmosphere of the collier's home is beautifully evoked, and some of the dialogue is fine, but the play suffers by comparison with the novel, in which the incident of the loaves is absorbed into the larger, continually developing action so that it does not seem either trivial or inflated. The promise shown here is fulfilled in two other plays with colliery settings. In *The Widowing of Mrs Holroyd*, a collier's wife, on bad terms with her drunken husband, comes to the end of her patience when he brings two bowzy females into the house, and decides to leave him for another man. The next day, surly after her railing, Holroyd refuses to accompany the other miners from the coal-face, and is killed in an accident. There is no sufficient equivalent for the long reverie at the end of the related story "Odour of Chrysanthemums," in which the catastrophe precipitates a truly tragic awareness of the long, blind, dead years of the marriage. It is nevertheless a very good play; the tension between the collier and his wife and her friend really hurts, and the children, half-aware of the situation, pathetic and tough at the same time, ring true. Even better is *The Daughter-in-Law*, in which a newly married collier, in bondage to his mother and consequently despised by his wife, learns to his horror that a girl he went with just before his marriage is pregnant. In the ensuing confrontations the characters burst from their emotional prisons, and all ends happily. Perhaps it was of this play that Lawrence wrote to Edward Garnett, "The whole thing is there, laid out properly, planned and progressive." Everything is beautifully worked out in dramatic terms: for once there is no sense of a disparity between the artist and his medium.

In *The Fight for Barbara* author and subject come too close for full artistic success, though it is compulsively readable. It was written in 1912, out of the difficulties of his first few months with Frieda. Frieda's parents and her husband descend upon the lovers (it seems footling to bother about the different names they are given in the play), and we are shown her agony, torn between the man she loves and the husband to whose love she is unable to respond. Yet Lawrence's love-ethic is presented with a surprisingly robust good humour.

But the great symbolic actions of, say, *Women in Love*, cannot be achieved in the purely visual terms of the stage.One realizes how important to the novels is the continual presence of the author, how much more significant an event described may be than an event seen. So with characterization: detached as they necessarily are from the author, the characters of the plays, for all their vitality, are not explored in depth compared with those of the novels.

An obvious attempt to break new ground is *David*, the latest of the plays, wordy and of ineffable import, written in that slackened biblical rhythm Lawrence employed when his sense of the numinous overcame his sense of humour. Michal glows like a young tree in full flower, flame calls to flame and the flower of Saul's navel is filled. Saul turns out to be the true Lawrentian hero in the end, in spite of David's admirably poetic lust for Michal. Devotees of *The Plumed Serpent* may well find this the best of his plays.

*Listener and BBC Television Review*, LXXV, 10 February 1966.


## Ronald Bryden, "Strindberg in the Midlands"


In the winter of 1912, come to rest at last with Frieda in a villa by Lake Garda, D.H. Lawrence completed his final revision of *Sons and Lovers* and looked round for a way of supporting the woman with whom he had run off the previous May. He had already had a couple of shots at play-writing: now, confident in his novel, he decided that the thing to do was displace Shaw, Galsworthy and Granville Barker in the theatre. 'As an audience was found in Russia for Chekhov,' he wrote to a friend, 'so an audience might be found in England for some of my stuff, if there were a man to whip them in.'

As in his sexual theories, he exaggerated the need for an element of sado-masochism. The astonishing thing about *The Daughter-in-Law*, the best of the three or four plays he dashed off that winter in Italy, is that it's taken 55 years to reach the stage, first at the Traverse in Edinburgh, and now in Peter Gill's fine production at the Royal Court. Lawrence might not have proved an English Chekhov but, on its evidence, he could easily with perseverance have become our Strindberg.

The principal weakness of *The Daughter-in-Law* is its attempt to appeal to the audience of the time for the Manchester school of realism. In form, it's a kind of Nottingham version of *Hobson's Choice*: a dialect comedy about an overpowering parent and a strong-minded young wife. But within that framework it explores much the same emotional territory as *Sons and Lovers* and builds up a charge of sexual antagonism as strong as *Women in Love*. At its best, it's as tensely scarifying as parts of *The Dance of Death*.

The setting is the same as in *Sons and Lovers*: the miners' cottages of Lawrence's own village of Eastwood. And in the marriage of Luther and Minnie Gascoigne, Lawrence draws again partly on the relation between his own parents, partly on his crippling tie to his mother. Minnie, who's been in service, looks down on her miner-husband. Although she finds his mask of grime curiously exciting, she can't stop goading him about his dirt and inarticulacy. When it comes out that he's fathered a child on a neighbour's daughter, she's torn between jealousy and disgust, lashing him with her tongue until he turns on her with a brutality to match her spite.

The scene of their quarrel is powerful, compulsive drama. Had Lawrence sustained its note, he might indeed have achieved the theatrical revolution he planned. Unfortunately, he retreats in his last act, jocosely equating Minnie's revolt with the national coal strike during which the action takes place. What she wants to rouse in Luther is the same possessiveness he shows about the mine, when its owners threaten to bring in black-leg labour. She battles for the inmost emotional core which Luther's dominating mother holds captive. 'How is a woman ever to have a husband,' she cries, 'if all men belong to their mothers?'

The ending's happy, but not frivolously so—Lawrence's character-drawing goes too deep for that. As the mother Ann Dyson is formidably saturnine, a lioness who knows that if she doesn't stop licking her cubs she will eventually eat one, but can't restrain herself. Mike Pratt has just the combination of brute strength and bovine evasiveness for Luther, and Judy Parfitt is exactly right as Minnie, her bone-china intellectual pallor flushed with thwarted sensuality.

But the best-imagined character, though functionally the least necessary to the plot, is the younger son, played by Victor Henry. Clearly, he's what Lawrence thought he might have become—the soft, clever, emasculated favourite of his devouring mother. Henry's performance is imposing: a mild, obscurely malicious observer who embraces his fate with a kind of hard gentleness. It's good to see this young actor back at the Court, growing steadily in power.

In fact, this is the best production the theatre has mounted in a year or two. Gill fills it with telling detail: the clanging back-gate outside, the newspapers stacked ready to spread under grimy elbows, the miner stooping for his brother to sponge coal-dust from his back before an open stove. Lawrence feared, correctly, that his contemporaries would find his plays too naturalistic and slow, but he was right and they were wrong. *The Daugher-in-Law* may not compare with his novels, but it makes most of our post-war essays in working-class drama look flimsy.

*The Observer*, 19 March 1967.


# George A. Panichas, "Lawrence's Biblical Play *David*"

There is no break in the great adventure in consciousness. Throughout the howlingest deluge, some few brave souls are steering the ark under the rainbow. (D.H. Lawrence, "Books," *Phoenix*)

In the Bible the name David is given to no one except the great king of Israel. The Hebrew meaning of the word is "Beloved," and according to one interpretation it was even at one time a title for a sun-god. David has come to signify both kingly and divine qualities, and the name of the youngest son of Jesse, of Bethlehem, is often associated with the celebrated life and exploits of a shepherd, minstrel, courtier, warrior, poet, statesman, prophet, king. Concurrently, it connotes the deeper human feelings of loyalty and kindness and tenderness expressed by a friend and husband and father. David Herbert Lawrence was certainly to be fully aware of the fact that he was to bear a name of ancient and goodly reputation, although from his early days in Eastwood he disliked his first name. To the name "Bert," as used by his family and friends, he responded without hesitation; yet, this "delicate brat with a snuffy nose, whom most people treated quite gently as just an ordinary little lad,"[1] defied and enraged his teachers when he refused to answer to David. Indeed, to the end of his life the English novelist maintained this antipathy against his name, and in most of his letters and all his works he appeared simply as D.H. Lawrence.

Nevertheless, though Lawrence disliked and avoided the name David, he still could not escape, deprecate, or disown its significance. Indeed, the actual figure of David was to represent for him "the pride of life," "the pride of the fulfilled self." And his instinctive admiration of David was not dimmed in any way by his disapproval of the name. This can be seen, for example, in a lovely essay in which he records his impressions of a David in a piazza in Florence. He describes the statue as seen one bleak morning—'Dark, grey, and raining with a perpetual sound of water." In this "great city on Arno's fair river," as Dante once described Florence, the statue of David, according to Lawrence, now represents "the trembling union of southern flame and northern waters," "corpse-white and sensitive." Waiting "with that tense anticipation," he is the perfect embodiment of poetency and vitality, of what Lawrence termed the creative and spontaneous fullness of being. "David, with his knitted brow and full limbs, is unvanquished," Lawrence further asserts. "Livid, maybe, corpse-coloured, quenched with innumerable rains of morality and democracy. Yet deep fountains of fire lurk within him."[2]

The ancient figure of David evoked for Lawrence the most dynamic and positive elements of light and love and life. It would not be far-fetched to claim, in fact, that Lawrence actually identified himself with the Biblical figure of David. In him he may have seen both inner and outer affinities with his own poetic temperament, his humble background, his love of life and nature, his passionate religious fervor and faith.   Moreover, David perhaps mirrored his own problems and conflicts and trials with those forces of life overcome by a "bad spirit," and seeking to "do dirt on life." Like David Lawrence saw himself filled with immortal yearnings, plagued with terrible doubts and contradictions, unsure at times which road to take, a little fearful of the future as he looked out on a sometimes brutally indifferent and hostile world. Lawrence could not but sympathize with David's plight, as the mere shepherd-boy learned the real world with all its hate and torment, its hollow fame and whispering calumnies. David, thus, was not only a mirror of his own storm-tossed soul but also a poignant illustration of the hardship and suffering that try one's strength of purpose and that must, in the end, be endured.Perhaps more than anything else, then, it was the trait of endurance itself that Lawrence envisaged and admired in David.

Surely, it is endurance that is encountered and registered in the life and work of both men.

The fullest extent and degree of Lawrence's response to David is to be seen in his Biblical play of the same name. The history of the composition and the eventual production of the play provide some interesting and revealing aspects of Lawrence's own motives and attitudes. At the same time, it is seen that the play was not a mere dramatized elucidation of a religious and Biblical chronicle, but a definite and experienced phase of the artist's own spiritual autobiography. *David* was to be written not too long after the completion of *The Plumed Serpent*, entitled earlier *Quetzalcoatl*. The Lawrences, at the time, were in Oaxca, Mexico, and in February (1925) Lawrence was to suffer a very serious, nearly fatal illness, which is vividly portrayed in an unfinished novel, the fragment of which is entitled *The Flying Fish*, and which had been dictated to Frieda from Lawrence's sickbed. To read this piece is to see why Lawrence was "so near the borderline of death": "He was ill, and he felt as if the very middle of him, beneath his navel, some membrane were torn, some membrane which had connected him with the world and its day."[3] Medical diagnosis was to reveal that Lawrence had tuberculosis in the third degree, and he was expected to live only a year or two at the most. *The Flying Fish*, unlike *The Plumed Serpent*, is free of the violence and brutality and irksome occultism that abound in Lawrence's Mexican novel (essentially, it belongs to the *ethos* of a thriller). On the other hand, both works show a preoccupation with death as found in the midst of a primeval country. This preoccupation with death is especially felt in the music and Biblical pulse-beat of the language, and the following passage from *The Flying Fish* is an example of this:

> There is no help, O man. Fear gives thee wings like a bird, death comes after thee open-mouthed, and thou soarest on the wind like a fly. But thy flight is not far, and thy flying is not long.    Thou art a fish of the timeless Ocean, and must needs fall back. Take heed lest thou break thyself in the fall!    For death is not in dying, but in the fear. Cease then the struggle of thy flight, and fall back into the deep element where death is and is not, and life is not a fleeing away.    It is a beauteous thing to live and to be alive.    Live then in the Greater Day, and let the waters carry thee, and the flood bear thee along, and live, only live, no more of this hurrying away.[4]

This mood of death and the agony of endurance is clearly reflected in *David*, which doubtlessly was written not too long after the completion of both *The Plumed Serpent* and the fragment, *The Flying Fish*, and after Lawrence's departure from Mexico and his arrival on April 5, 1925, at his Del Monte Ranch, Questa, New Mexico, where he remained until September 10. In the early period of this convalescence, he was to write his Biblical play, completing it May 26. "I did a play—a Bible play—*David*—which I'll send you when it's typed out," he wrote to his agent, Curtis Brown.[5] (The play was eventually published by Martin Secker in London, March, 1926.) In her memoir *Not I, But the Wind . . .*, Frieda Lawrence has recalled that as Lawrence improved in health, he began the writing of *David*, "lying outside his little room on the porch in the sun." "I think in that play he worked off his struggle for life."[6] Without doubt, when one reads the play in the light of *The Flying Fish*, Frieda's words become more meaningful. *The*

*Flying Fish* is written in the terrifying midst of death; *David* is written in a period of convalescence, as a sick man strives to endure and survive a terrible ordeal.

It should also be noted, in this connection, that Lawrence wrote *David* with the express purpose of having it staged. The play was actually performed at The Regent Theatre in London, on May 22 and 23, 1927, produced by the Three Hundred Club. Lawrence even wrote the music for *David*, and noted that "It is very simple—needs only a pipe, tambourines, and a tom-tom drum."[7] The tom-tom drum was undoubtedly a derivation from *The Plumed Serpent*, in which drums were used to accompany some of the bizarre rituals and the chanting of hymns. At one time, as a matter of fact, Lawrence was planning to travel to London to assist in the production, for he wanted to make sure that the religious fervor and meaning of the play would be brought out. "If only one can get that feeling of primitive religious passion across to the London audience," he cried. "If not, it's no good."[8] But, for a variety of reasons, Lawrence did not get to London for this purpose, and remained during this time at the Villa Mirenda, Scandicci, Italy. In the first place, his health was again troubling him. Secondly, in the spring and summer of 1927, he was busily writing the second version of *Lady Chatterley's Lover*. And thirdly, in the early spring, from the end of March to about April 10th, he and his close friend Earl Brewster had toured the ancient Etruscan sites, on which his collection of essays, *Etruscan Places*, is based. In all probability this tour must have taxed Lawrence's strength. There is the additional fact that during this time Lawrence was experiencing one of those black, misanthropic moods that overcame him time and again, especially after World War I. On such occasions, Lawrence was literally "heartsick of life" and "torn off from the body of mankind." Thus, when we compare the following passage from a letter written in the spring of 1918—

> My soul, or whatever it is, feels charged and surcharged with the blackest and most monstrous "temper," a sort of hellish electricity . . . for I am no more a man, but a walking phenomenon of suspended fury—[9]

with this passage from a letter of March 8, 1927—

> It's no good for me the human world becomes more and more unreal, more and more wearisome. I am really happiest when I don't see people and never go to town. Town just lays me out. I won't go to London for *David*. I simply won't go, to have my life spoilt by those people. They can maul and muck the play about as much as they like. They'd do it, anyhow. Why should they suck my life into the bargain?—[10]

we can easily understand the demonic sort of mood that possessed Lawrence and precluded a trip to London.

The reactions to the stage production of Lawrence's *David* were none too satisfactory. In his review of the play for *The Spectator*, for instance, Richard Jennings looked on the play as an unconvincing "adventure." "The result," he noted, "is not necessarily anything dramatic at all." He also noted, in terms very peculiar to irresolute critical estimates of Lawrence's work in the 'twenties and 'thirties, that Lawrence was a man with "intense conviction and so little humour," who had done his work, in connection with the play, "soberly, reverentially, cleaving to tradition."[11] Lawrence, of course, was wounded by the unfavorable reviews of *David*, and his reactions—later to be repeated in his harsh outcries against the criticisms of *Lady Chatterley's Lover*—were immediate and explosive. Those who had found the play dull, he wrote to Earl Brewster, had no pluck and, as a result, could not be expected to appreciate his play:

> My business is a fight, and I've got to keep it up. I'm reminded of the fact by the impudent reviews of the production of *David*. They say it was just dull. I say they are eunuchs. . . . It is a fight. The same old one. *Caro*, don't ask me to pray for peace. I don't want it. I want subtly, but tremendously, to kick the[ir] back-sides. . . . There are so many of them. . . . They must be kicked for it—kicked.[12]

And to Mabel Luhan, he bitterly complained that the critics were mere weaklings, perhaps even representative of the intellectual "youngish Englishmen"—whom he described as a typical pansy, as being "insipid, unsalted, rabbity, endlessly hopping. / They nibble the face of the earth to a desert":[13]

> They produced *David* last week. I heard the audience was really rather enthusiastic, but the press notices are very unfavourable. It's those mangy feeble reviewers; they haven't enough spunk to hear a cow bellow. The worst of the youngish Englishman is, he's such a *baby*; one can't imagine his backside isn't swaddled in a napkin: and such a prig, one imagines he must either be a lady in disguise, or a hermaphrodite.[14]

Based on I Samuel 15-21, *David* is written partly in Lawrence's language and partly in that of the King James version of the Bible, from which he has borrowed liberally. This serves to prove once again how steeped Lawrence was in his knowledge and love of the Bible, how much at home he was in the poetry and music of its language. As a play, it does not have the dramatic and human power and effectiveness of his other plays, *The Widowing of Mrs. Holroyd* (1914) and *Touch and Go* (1920). This is readily understandable in so far as in these two plays he is grappling with the more familiar and immediate social themes and problems that are encountered in the novel *Sons and Lovers* and in some of the early short stories, notably "Odour of Chrysanthemums." In *David*, however, we are a long way from some of the vital and earthy scenes of colliery life, of the Midland dialect, of work and love and marriage and death in a once-beautiful countryside that Lawrence came to see as being brutally subjected to "cold ugliness" and "raw materialism." Indeed, the brooding, questioning spirit of *David* is severely punctuated with abstract and complicated issues. Lawrence seems to be undergoing a great deal of soul-searching and self-questioning.

In utilizing the life of David for his play, Lawrence is not interpreting a Biblical and religious theme anew, nor is he probing theological issues. If anything, he has appropriated a theme and episode that harmonize with his belief that religion is not dogma and sentiment, but feeling and "living life." David, as Lawrence sees him, stands for what is simple and innocent in life, undefiled by the assertions of will, idea, ego. A mere youth, he becomes "Jehovah's anointed," the "ruddy-faced fair youth" and "blithe boy" who goes forth, "naked and unafraid," to slay the Philistine giant Goliath who had "defied the armies of the living God." His every action is free of self-concern and selfishness. He never thinks ill of others; he retains his innocence against all that is brought forth to make him yield. His sincerity and courage and piety are his most powerful weapons, and his actions are inevitably the outgrowth of what Lawrence refers to as a "greater morality." Furthermore, David's subsequent sacrament of friendship with Saul's son, Jonathan, is another factor that must have attracted him to Lawrence. The relationship of David and Jonathan was for Lawrence a reality which he could merely conceptualize and idealize in his works. David's words to Jonathan, when both swear to a covenant of friendship, are not at all unfamiliar to those who recollect some of the conversations between Gerald and Birkin in *Women in Love*, Lilly and Aaron in *Aaron's Rod*, and Don Ramón and Don Cipriano in *The Plumed Serpent:*

> I will trust thee, Jonathan, and cleave to thee till the sun sets on me. Thou are good to me as man never before was good to me, and I have not deserved it. Say thou wilt not repent of thy kindness towards me.[15]

In David's tragic struggle with Saul, Lawrence portrays the eternal quarrel between purity and innocence, on the one side, with treachery and debasement, on the other. Saul, the King of Israel, embodies the breakdown of life, when egotism, self-seeking, and the violation of integrity are ascendant. In effect, he is a fallen leader who has rejected the commandments of the Lord and disobeyed "the Voice from beyond" by not destroying the sinful Amalekites completely and by selfishly saving the best spoil of the beaten enemy. Saul, thus, has capitulated to the "evil spirit" and can no longer be thought of as being God's anointed. He has, in Lawrentian terminology, blasphemed and sinned against the Holy Ghost by upholding the little, personal morality of material concern and self-interest. In juxtaposition to David, Saul increasingly personifies the forces of darkness, hate, and death. The venerable prophet Samuel now informs him: "Because thou hast rejected the word of the Lord the Lord hath also rejected thee from being King." Saul's guilt, then, is the direct result of that vanity and egoism concerning which Lawrence was to write in one of his essays:

> The egoist [is], he who has no more spontaneous feelings, and can be made to suffer humanly no more. He who derives all his life henceforth at second-hand, and is animated by self-will and some sort of secret ambition to *impose* himself, either on the world or another individual.[16]

Without doubt, these words accurately depict and define the blasphemy and disintegration of Saul, and to read them with what Samuel says in the following passage is to grasp more precisely the cause and nature of the King's fallen condition:

> Thou hast turned away from the Hidden Sun, and the gleam is dying from out of thy face. Thou hast disowned the Power that made thee, and the flow is leaving thy limbs, the glisten of oil is waning on thy brow, and the vision is dying in thy breast.[17]

When, therefore, Saul realizes that David is God's newly anointed—a fact that becomes painfully clear to him after the slaying of Goliath—his jealousy and capriciousness begin to turn to a malignant hatred and a relentless animosity. Now he becomes fearfully envious of the vitality and blitheness of the young hero, and his reactions and conduct manifest a purely pathological condition of one who has defied and lost God:

> Blitheness in a man is the Lord in his body. Nay boy, boy! I would not envy thee the head of the Philistine. Nay, I would not envy thee the Kingdom itself. But the blitheness of thy body, that is Lord in thee, I envy it thee with a sore envy. For once my body too was blithe. But it hath left me.[18]

He views David's great accomplishments against the enemies of God as an affront to his own prowess and capability. When he hears the thunderous cries that "Saul hath slain his thousands, and David his ten thousands," he sets out with a hard heart and calculated cruelty to destroy David. His refusal to carry out his earlier promise to permit David to marry his daughter, Merab, his violent but unsuccessful attempts on David's life, his slanders against him—these manifest the slow but unmitigable deterioration of Saul. He is, Lawrence is saying, a God-forsaken man who has now fallen from "the hands of the living God," no longer "a creature in the house of the God of Life." In the words of one of Lawrence's *Last Poems*, "The Hands of God," Saul is experiencing

> That awful and sickening endless sinking, sinking
> through the slow, corruptive levels of disintegrative knowledge
> when the self has fallen from the hands of God
> and sinks, seething and sinking, corrupt
> and sinking still, in depth after depth of disintegrative conciousness
> sinking in the endless undoing, the awful katabolism into the abyss!
> even of the soul, fallen from the hands of God![19]

Just how far Saul has fallen "down the godless plunge of the abyss" is also revealed in his innermost thoughts.

> Yea, David, the pits are digged even under the feet of thy God and thy God shall fall in. Oh, their Gods shall fall into the pit, that the sons of David have digged. Oh, men can dig a pit for the most high God, and He falls in—as they say of the huge elephant in the lands beyond the desert. And the world shall be Godless, there shall no God walk on the mountains, no whirlwind shall stir like a heart in the deeps of the blue firmament. And God shall be gone from the world. Only men there shall be, in myriads, like locusts, clicking and grating upon one another, and crawling over one another. The smell of them shall be as smoke, but it shall rise up into the air, without finding the nostrils of God. For God shall be gone! gone! gone! And men shall inherit the earth! Yea, like locusts and whirring on wings like locusts. . . . Godless the world! Godless the men in myriads even like locusts. No God in the air! No God on the mountains! Even out of the deeps of the sky they lured Him, into their pit! So the world is empty of God, empty, empty, like a blown egg-shell bunged with wax and floating meaninglessness. God shall fall Himself into the pit these men shall dig for Him![20]

In short, Saul incarnates an excessively froward and irreverent spirit that is entirely incommensurable with one who is truly "the lord's anointed." The loss of his own blitheness is concomitant with the willed evil and ruthlessness that accompany his actions and attitudes. His condition becomes so irrevocable that the results are most unfortunate not only for David but also for Saul's own family. Ultimately, then, David must flee like some hunted outlaw amongst pits and snares. Jonathan finds himself torn between his friendship for David and his filial responsibility. And Michal, daughter of Saul and now wife of David, desperately struggles to protect her husband against the schemes and contrivances of her father. Gradually David realizes the full extent of Saul's condition, and his discerning insight underscores the true nature of a consuming evil that becomes a dominant and usurpative force in life. To his wife, Michal, he confides:

> But Saul is slipping backward down the pit of despair, away from God. And each time he strives to come forth, the loose earth yields beneath his feet, and he slides deeper. So the upreach of his love fails him, and the downslide of his hate is great and greater in weight. I cannot hate him—nor love him—but, O Michal, I am oppressed with horror of him.[21]

It is interesting to note that when David fully understands the menace that faces him, he appeals to God for guidance and deliverance. Actually, at this point, Lawrence quotes without alteration the fifth psalm, "A Prayer at the Morning Sacrifice." David's supplication is a pious and simple one, as he asks God to illuminate his way, to declare his enemies guilty, and to bring utter failure to his accusers' machinations and unscrupulousness. The poet, as viewed here, is alone with God: his mood at the beginning is one of lamentation as he invokes God to punish "all workers of iniquity." Throughout, the contrariety of God and evil, of righteousness and unrighteousness, is decidedly evident. When the psalm ends, a confident note prevails, with the poet seeing himself in the "House of God," a phrase that was to occur often in Lawrence's last poems. Indeed, the psalmists's cry, "Lead me, O Lord, in thy righteousness," is later re-echoed in one of Lawrence's finest poems, "Bavarian Gentians," in the words "lead me then, lead me the way. / Reach me a gentian, give me a torch!"[22] When we ponder the fifth psalm, then, we become fully aware as to why Lawrence was drawn by its content and significance. There can be little doubt, in the final analysis, that David's prayer was to capture and reflect Lawrence's own feelings and state of mind:

> Give ear to my words, O Lord, consider my meditation.
> Hearken unto the voice of my cry, my King, and my God: for unto thee will I pray.
> My voice shalt thou hear in the morning, O Lord; in the morning will I direct my prayer unto thee, and will look up.
> For thou art not a God that hath pleasure in wickedness: neither shall evil dwell with thee.
> The foolish shall not stand in thy sight: thou hatest all workers of iniquity.
> Thou shalt destroy them that speak leasing: the Lord will abhor the bloody and deceitful man.
> But as for me, I will come into thy house in the multitude of thy mercy: and in thy fear will I worship toward the holy temple.
> Lead me, O Lord, in thy righteousness, because of mine enemies; make thy way straight before my face.

> For there is no faithfulness in their mouth; their inward part is very wickedness; their throat is an open sepulchre: they flatter with their tongue.
> Destroy thou them, O God; let them fall by their own counsels; cast them out in the multitude of their transgressions; for they have rebelled against thee.
> But let all those that put their trust in thee rejoice: let them ever shout for joy, because thou defendest them: let them also that love thy name be joyful in thee.
> For thou, Lord, wilt bless the righteous; with favour wilt thou compass him, as with a shield.[23]

Lawrence's inclusion of the fifth psalm in *David* illustrates once again the fact that the Bible was of major importance in his art. He had read and re-read it since the days of his youth in the English Midlands, and he was to derive from it some of the basic characteristics of his writing, especially his poetry. Concerning the formative influence of the Bible, Lawrence recalled towards the end of his life:

> From early childhood I have been familiar with Apocalyptic language and Apocalyptic image: not because I was sent to Sunday School and to Chapel, to Band of Hope and to Christian Endeavour, and was always having the Bible read at me or to me. I did not even listen attentively. But language has a power of echoing and re-echoing in my unconscious mind. I can wake up in the night and "hear" things being said—or hear a piece of music—to which I had paid no attention during the day.[24]

This statement helps to explain, likewise, why some of the forms found in the Hebrew poetry of the Old Testament are unmistakably present in Lawrence's poetry, such as the spontaneity of expression, the lack of a specific rhyme pattern, metre or strophe, the stress on emotion, sound and sense, the presence of several forms of parallelism (whereby repetition or co-ordination of a thought takes place in the second clause). The startling descriptive power of Hebrew poetry was inevitably to impress Lawrence, and when, for instance, we compare some of the Biblical descriptions of nature and of animal life with Lawrence's poems in *Birds, Beasts, and Flowers* (e.g. "Bat" and "Snake"), the Biblical influence is incontestable. In the Biblical play *David*, therefore, we realize Lawrence's stress on the emotional and devotional aspects of religious life as opposed to the speculative and abstract. It brings to the fore, in addition, Lawrence's intense spiritual consciousness that, in true nonconformist Puritan tradition, had been saturated with the language and spirit of the Bible, as well as with the "sense of wonder" gained from the hymns that he learned in chapel as a child. Of these he wrote: "They live and glisten in the depths of the man's consciousness in undimmed wonder, because they have not been subjected to any criticism or analysis."[25]

As the play moves to a conclusion, David is undergoing deep terror and pain as he flees from "the shadow of Saul" and from the soldiers who are trying to seize him and bring him prisoner to their wrathful king. All this arouses much sadness and compassion in Lawrence, and there is in this part of the play a severe note of questioning and pain. Lawrence seems to be protesting the fact that the "pristine consciousness" and "godly vitality," which David embodies, is retreating before the compulsion and deceit that characterize Saul. Of course, it may be said that Lawrence's reaction to and dislike of Saul is not entirely conclusive, that Saul's shortcomings—the result of his impetuous and passionate nature—perhaps even provoke (or should provoke) Lawrence's sympathy and admiration. After all, it may be asked, would this not be in accord with Lawrence's own emphasis on the instincts and the passions in response to the issues of life, without inhibition or repression? (And it certainly would be in keeping with the counsel found in *Psychoanalysis and the Unconscious* and *Fantasia of the Unconscious*.) To be sure, in the very last words of the play, the generous and guileless Jonathan makes this quite evident as he weighs the strengths and weaknesses of Saul and David. Jonathan's inner thoughts reveal that Lawrence was no less cognizant of Saul's passionate humanity:

> For thy wisdom is the wisdom of the subtle, and behind thy passion lies prudence. And naked thou wilt go into the fire. Yea, go thou forth, and let me die. For thy virtue is in thy wit, and thy shrewdness. But in Saul have I known the magnanimity of a man. Yea, thou art a smiter down of giants, with a smart stone! Great men and magnanimous, men of the faceless flame, shall fall from strength, fall before thee, thou David, shrewd whelp of the Lion of Judah! Yet my heart yearns hot over thee, as over a tender, quick child. And the heart of my father yearns, even amid its dark wrath.[26]

Still, the fact remains that Lawrence ultimately was to view Saul's crime as a major one that violated "the living man" and resulted from a "self-conscious ego." In short, Saul had pushed his own cravings too far, had become too egoistic and willful in his conscious self. He had, by his actions, debased the inmost meaning of instinct and passion which Lawrence reverenced. Consequently, Lawrence saw Saul as being "lost to life" and no longer "in touch." Above all, he had allowed his "passional soul" to deteriorate into an unhealthy state. And it is precisely this unhealthiness—this "process of derangement by degeneration and decadence"—that Lawrence impassionately inveighs and warns against in his portrayal of Saul's collapse.

With the conclusion of the play it appears that nothing is really resolved. David, who is now in hiding in a rocky place outside Gilgal near the stone Ezel, seems to be totally isolated from the body of life, and there is something pitiable and heart-rending about his fate. He is, at this point, the epitome of the agony of endurance. Even when he meets his friend Jonathan, the cruel sense of his isolation is not alleviated, and it is prophesied that he must flee until "the day of the death of Saul, and the day of the death of Jonathan." John Middleton Murry has observed that in this play, consequently, "all the old and sickening irresolutions are manifest."[27] Still, the ostensible lack of any decisive resolution should not be construed as the predominance of hopelessness and despair, but rather as a realistic apprehension on Lawrence's part of the everlasting "struggle between the endless patience of life and the endless triumph of force." It is, moreover, the profound meaning of endurance that prevails in the life of one who seeks to live by the "glow" of the "living God." In certain respects, too, *David* marks a temporary halt, a "pause of peace," when the artist as seeker strives to catch his breath and to "touch and wonder, and ponder." It can even be said that the mood and feelings that Lawrence discloses here are a prelude to what Oliver Mellors speaks of in his letter to Constance at the end of *Lady Chatterley's Lover* as a man's need "to fend and fettle for the best, and then trust in something beyond himself."[28]

In this play, to be sure, Lawrence like David suffers the "searchings of heart," and the cries that throb in him arise, as it were, from "out of the depths." There is in all this a picture of the suffering man in Lawrence and "the infinite pain of self-realization"—to quote Yeats's apt phrase—that is essential to spiritual maturity and to the struggle for wholeness and the steadiness of vision. In the life and trials of David, Lawrence finally comprehended the astonishing lesson of endurance and, simultaneously, anticipated its ultimate translation to the resilience of adventure in "the unmapped wilderness." For, truly, "Tomorrow is another day."

*Modern Drama*, 6, 1963.

## Notes

[1] See D. H. Lawrence's "Autobiographical Sketch" in *Assorted Articles* (London, 1930).

[2] See "David" in *Phoenix: The Posthumous Papers of D. H. Lawrence*, ed. and with an Introduction by Edward D. McDonald (London, 1936), pp. 60-65.

[3] *Phoenix*, p. 782.

[4] *Phoenix*, p. 788.

[5] *The Letters of D. H. Lawrence*, ed. and with an Introduction by Aldous Huxley (New York, 1932), p. 642.

[6] Frieda Lawrence, *Not I, But the Wind . . .* (New York, 1934), p. 151.

[7] *The Collected Letters of D. H. Lawrence*, Volume II, ed. and with an Introduction by Harry T. Moore (New York, 1962), 941.

[8] *The Collected Letters of D. H. Lawrence*, II, 941.

[9] *The Letters of D. H. Lawrence*, p. 444.

[10] *The Collected Letters of D. H. Lawrence*, II, 968-969.

[11] See Richard Jennings, "The Theatre," *The Spectator*, May 28, 1927, pp. 939-940.

[12] *The Collected Letters of D. H. Lawrence*, II, 980.

[13] "The re Are Too Many People" in *Last Poems*, ed. and with an Introduction by Richard Aldington and Giusèppe Orioli (New York, 1933), p. 98.

[14] *The Collected Letters of D. H. Lawrence*, II, 982.

[15] *The Plays of D. H. Lawrence* (London, 1933), Scene VIII, p. 242.

[16] *Phoenix*, p. 200.

[17] *The Plays of D. H. Lawrence*, Scene I, pp. 192-193.

[18] *The Plays of D. H. Lawrence*, Scene VII, p. 235.

[19] *Last Poems*, p. 26.

[20] *The Plays of D. H. Lawrence*, Scene XI, p. 259.

[21] *The Plays of D. H. Lawrence*, Scene XIII, p. 282.

22*Last Poems*, p. 21.

23*The Plays of D. H. Lawrence*, Scene XIII, pp. 278-279.

24*Phoenix*, pp. 301-302.

25 See "Hymns in a Man's Life" in *Assorted Articles*.

26*The Plays of D. H. Lawrence*, Scene XVI, p. 312.

27 John Midddleton Murry, *Son of Woman*, (New York, 1931), p. 335.

28*Lady Chatterley's Lover* (New York, 1959), p. 364.

## Cecil Davies, "D.H. Lawrence: *The Merry-Go-Round,* A Challenge to the Theatre"

Lawrence the dramatist was virtually unknown until some three decades after his death, and it was ultimately the Royal Court Theatre's productions of *The Daughter-in-Law, The Widowing of Mrs. Holroyd,* and *A Collier's Friday Night* which revealed his talent in this field and led, not unnaturally in the circumstances, to some rather inflated assessments of the plays, Lawrence even being described as "a major English twentieth century dramatist."[1]

These three plays are written and conceived in the style of total naturalism, which was the current theatrical fashion in England in the years immediately preceding the First World War. The degree of naturalism in the settings is as extreme as that which had aroused the scorn of critics against Hauptmann's *Before Sunrise* as early as 1889 but which by then had become commonplace. In so far, then, as Lawrence adopted the current naturalism for his plays, he was neither innovative nor original. Nor does he exhibit in their structure any original sense of dramatic shape. Each play, and each act, is, in Zola's phrase, "a slice of life," cut off at the edges as arbitrarily as an Impressionist painting (the actual parallel drawn by Strindberg as early as 1888 for the setting for his naturalistic tragedy *Miss Julie*). But because of the undoubted power of these three plays—a power similar in quality to that which is found in the great "scenes" in his tales and novels—they have been treated as a measure by which his other plays are to be judged, and critics assume that—except in the much later *David* and the *Noah* fragment—he was always aiming in the same direction. Thus, patently non-naturalistic drama has been wrongly subjected to the naturalistic test. This has led to almost total misunderstanding and serious undervaluation of *The Merry-Go-Round*, in which Lawrence is not attempting to write a conventionally naturalistic play.

Indeed, we must be clear from the very outset that Lawrence actually saw himself in revolt against the current fashions in drama: "We have to hate our immediate predecessors, to get free from their authority."[2] That is the healthy, creative attitude expressed in a letter to Edward Garnett in February 1913. It is the attitude of all truly original and imaginative creative writers—witness

Dryden, Wordsworth, Eliot, or Pound—and it obviously does not lead to "fair" judgements upon these predecessors, as Lawrence fully understood when he wrote in the same letter, "It will seem a bit rough to me, when I am 45, and must see myself and my tradition supplanted. I shall bear it very badly" (*Letters*, I, 509). Who were these predecessors, whom Lawrence must hate? He lumps together Galsworthy, Ibsen, and Strindberg, probably having in mind only Strindberg's naturalistic plays. Earlier in the same paragraph he refers to "Shaw and Galsworthy and Barker and Irishy (except Synge) people" (*Letters*, I, 509). The exception of Synge is significant. For Synge,—and, indeed, for Lawrence— the naturalism of Ibsen was that of his prosaic translators, primarily William Archer, and of the inheritors of that prosaic style, Galsworthy and Harley Granville Barker. Synge castigated Ibsen and Zola (that is, their translators) for "dealing with the reality of life in joyless and pallid words,"[3] a criticism very similar to Lawrence's: "the rather bony, bloodless drama we get nowadays" (*Letters, I*, 509). Synge's response was to use language "as fully flavoured as a nut or apple"[4]—language not elaborated in the study but derived from the real speech of people in western Ireland. And, though he does not explicitly say so, Lawrence's response in his naturalistic plays is the same: to write a stage speech based upon the speech of ordinary Nottinghamshire people. So vital is the language to the quality of reality in these plays that they can no more be performed in other dialects than Synge's could be. When *The Daughter-in-Law* was performed in Sheffield with Yorkshire accents, the whole tone of the play was marred and coarsened. Thus allying himself with Synge, Lawrence saw himself, even at his most naturalistic, as in revolt against the naturalism of most of his contemporaries and immediate predecessors.

It is therefore reasonable to see his dramatic oeuvre as a series of experiments carried out with very different degrees of success; and it is as an experiment, an exploration of the possibilities of the theatre and a rebellion against current fashions, that we shall examine *The Merry-Go-Round*.[5] This was the second play Lawrence wrote. The first had been *A Collier's Friday Night*, perhaps first drafted as early as the autumn of 1906 but certainly (by internal evidence) not finished as we have it until 1909. Its title, with the ironic allusion to Burns's *The Cotter's Saturday Night*, should be sufficient warning that even in this first play, "written when I was 21, almost before I'd done anything, it is most horribly green,"[6] Lawrence aimed at something other than mere straight photographic naturalism.

The circumstances under which Lawrence wrote this, his second play, are important. It was written during December 1910, the month in which his mother died after long suffering from cancer, apparently through euthanasia, if, as seems fairly certain, Lawrence and his sister put an overdose of morphine in her milk. During this same month, he made that extraordinary and apparently impetuous proposal to Louie on the railway train, while his tortured relationship with Jessie continued; even between the death and the funeral of his mother, they were walking together by Moor Green Reservoir, and he was still corresponding with Rachel Annand Taylor, with whom, according to Richard Aldington, he had had an affair. Then there was Alice Dax. According to George Neville, supported by Willie Hopkin, it was Alice Dax who introduced Lawrence to sex, probably,

Keith Sagar suggests, in the summer holidays of 1910—that is to say, exactly at the time that his mother's fatal illness began. (However, Roy Spencer, on what authority is not clear, says, "The relationship was quite innocent.")[7] Here, then, is another essential part of Lawrence's personal "merry-go-round" at the time of his mother's death. Her final illness and death were thus emotionally tied up with at least three love-sex relationships, each of a different nature. There was Louie, as Lawrence saw her, sexy, vital, and physical; Jessie, trying to feel for his soul; and Alice, the married man-hater, who fell in love with Lawrence and afterwards, so it is alleged, never let another man touch her. Add to these his many women correspondents. Is it to be wondered at that his play linked his mother's death with a sexual roundabout?

In his *Calendar* of Lawrence's works, Keith Sagar says, "It was also during this period that Lawrence, to relieve the intolerable weight of pain, wrote a romantic comedy, *The Merry-Go-Round*."[8] The phrase "to relieve the intolerable weight of pain" may well have some truth in it, but the description "a romantic comedy" reveals a failure to appreciate the nature of the play. In his earlier, historically important essay "D.H. Lawrence: Dramatist," Sagar had been even more dismissive:

> It is, in intention, an Eastwood *As You Like It*. "It's 'As You Lump It,'" says the play's last line, and that might have been a better title. But the absence of any real wit, subtlety in characterisation, or even appropriateness in the eventual marital pairings makes it little more than a romp for the local amateur dramatic society.[9]

The play had at that time never been performed, and it is partly the fact of having seen it in performance that has led the present writer to come to disagree profoundly with the judgement here expressed—a judgement doubtless influenced by enthusiasm for the three plays then produced at the Royal Court Theatre and the temptation to use them as a criterion for all Lawrence's plays. Of course, *The Merry-Go-Round* has a relationship with *As You Like It* but not a simple one.

As a further example of such dismissive criticism, Harry T. Moore says, "Lawrence tried in *The Merry-Go-Round*, and tried without much success, to write a lively little folk comedy."[10] "A lively little folk comedy" is somewhat nearer the mark than "a romp for the local amateur dramatic society." In fact, the play makes severe technical demands on actors and designer, and the "local amateurs" would certainly fail with the play. And, though it is "lively," it is certainly not "little" in either scale or scope.

When Peter Gill directed the play at the Royal Court Theatre in November 1973, he funked Lawrence's text and used instead an adaptation he himself had made in 1971. What this adaptation did was to eliminate from the text the broadly farcical Polish vicar, Baron Rudolf von Ruge, and his equally farcical wife, Baroness von Ruge, and to replace them (when the story seemed to preclude their total extinction) with an utterly colorless, virtually characterless, and also anonymous "Vicar" and "Vicar's wife." At the same time, there was wholesale cutting of scenes and parts of scenes (whether or not involving the von Ruges) in which there was any broadly comic action. Patty, the goose, was inevitably sacrificed. The aim, clearly, was to make the play approximate in style to the famous naturalistic triptych of plays. This, of course, failed; for the climaxes of this play are conceived in terms of farce and of deliberate patterning; these climaxes include the conclusion of the play, which Peter Gill had to leave, unless he were going to re-write the whole work.

Predictably, the critics praised the surviving naturalistic scenes and those toned down to an approximation of naturalism, while slamming the concluding scenes as "perhaps written when drunk" (John Barber, in *The Daily Telegraph*) or "tawdry" (Jack Tinker, in *The Daily Mail*). Michael Billington, in *The Guardian*, however, refers to "a comedy laced with pain and passion" and "a rippling sexual mating-game," adding that "amazingly all ends like a Shakespearean comedy with a multiple marriage-ceremony symbolishing the sudden access of harmony."[11] He seems to have seen through the emasculated adaptation to some hint of the original multi-conventional play.

For "multi-conventional" correctly describes it. Instead of resting securely in the straightforward naturalistic convention, Lawrence seeks intensity and contrast by other means, above all by the use of a variety of dramatic styles which themselves are often in strong tension with the material being treated; and, while this variety of styles and this profusion of tensions present a challenge to the theatre, they can with skill be made wholly acceptable to an audience, as has been proved by the production of the full original text by Wilfred Harrison at the Octagon Theatre, Bolton, in April 1980. Over the four-week period of the run, attendances at this almost unknown play were:

| | |
|---|---|
| Week 1: | 53% |
| Week 2: | 64% |
| Week 3: | 75% |
| Week 4: | 81% |

Such growth proves that word-of-mouth publicity approved of the play in this production and dismisses any notions of untheatre-worthiness.

Of course, mere audience approval tells us nothing about artistic worth or genuine value; it tells us only that the play as written really appeals to its audiences and "works" in the theatre. This paper does not set out to prove this play to be a masterpiece but simply to show not only that it is stageworthy but also that it is a progressive, forward-looking, experimental play. It reveals many aspects of its author's imagination and of his ability to exploit the resources and potentialities of theatre which have no chance to be revealed in the naturalistic plays. The tension of the play is established from the very first scene; the play lies, as did its writing, under the shadow of death. From the first moment, Mrs. Hemstock is dying. She dies in the course of the play, which thus moves in the realms of comedy and farce against a background of death. The opening scene sets the death-bed-to-be before our eyes; and then, brilliantly Lawrence never shows us Mrs. Hemstock or takes us into that room again, though it is often just off-stage and vividly present in our imagination. Act I, scene i, is thus a kind of prologue. Nor is it a sombre prologue, for within it the creative tensions exist. Very few writers can treat of illness and death in the comic mode and yet fully humanely, but that is exactly what Lawrence does here. His use of

Nottinghamshire speech and Nottinghamshire expressions in this scene is noticeably different from his use of them in the naturalistic plays. Mrs. Hemstock's vocabulary and speech-style are, when compared with natural speech, overloaded or overcharged with picturesque localisms—that is to say, the expressions are authentic, but in the interests of comic intensity they occur more frequently, are more densely packed in proportion to other words and phrases than they would be in normal speech. In her first thirty speeches (the initial dialogue with the Nurse), we find, "like a beetle on my back," "Tha nedna but gi' me a catlick. I'm as snug as a bug in a rug," "gallivanting," "a ronk 'un," "I 'avena clapped eyes on him," "Summat's gen 'im mulligurles," "I wor like Jonah back'ards," "as white-faced as a flat fish," "like a mackerel's head breeds maggots," "'e'd had ructions wi' Rachel Wilcox," "like a cat lookin' for her kittens," "'er'd run like a pig as 'ears the bucket," "'E'd talk the leg off an iron pot," "it's like pottering to get a penny out of a money box" (Act I, Scene i).

This dying mother, unlike Lydia, speaks broad Nottingham. It is the parish nurse who speaks genteelly and whose mother lives in Kent, where Lydia Beardsall lived from the age of two to nineteen. So, at the root of the play lies a reshaping of the reality of December 1910. Lydia Lawrence, who was dying in the real world, was "undoubtedly speaking a mixture of the Kent accent and middle class standard English."[12] Mrs. Hemstock is given a strong local accent and uses such a wealth of regional expressions as almost to pass the limits of probability, while the unmarried nurse, *associated* with her illness and death, is made to "talk posh." Further evidence that the nurse is a second mother-persona is provided by the fact that, in the course of the play, she seriously considers what it would be like to marry a miner, coal-dirt and all, although she finally chooses the doctor. This initial transformation of the real situation currently overshadowing Lawrence's life shows that if indeed one motive for writing was "to relieve the intolerable weight of pain," he was doing this not simply by means of escapism but by the far more fruitful means of sublimation, employing the very trouble that was oppressing him as the material for relief. It is also a remarkable tribute to his creativity that, though he was already working on *Paul Morel*, his "serious" treatment of the mother-son relationship that was maiming his own relationships with girls, he was able in this play to introduce two mother-fixated sons, the literary doctor (surely a wry image of some aspects of Lawrence himself, the budding writer) and Harry Hemstock (in whom the same theme is treated both more farcically and more violently). His very inhibitions are treated farcically in the use of the goose as a vicarious woman:

> MRS. HEMSTOCK: . . . 'E's scared to death of a wench, so 'e goes about wi' a goose.
> *A goose comes paddling into the room and wanders up to HARRY.* [Act I, Scene i]

But he linked this goose-motif with the extraordinary bondage scene in which Harry binds Rachel in a shawl and straps her to a chair with his own belt. At the end of this scene, Rachel having gone, he fetches Patty out of the cupboard and puts his face "caressingly" among the bird's feathers; and, as he expresses his sense of conquest over Rachel in the words "We'll settle her Pat—eh? We'll stop her gallop. Hey, Pat!," the stage direction tells us that *He tosses the bird into the air wildly.*" It is as if, through the bird, he achieves the liberation of orgasm led up to but unfulfilled in his threats of violence to the girl, helpless in his power. Thus, through Harry, Lawrence finds outlet for fantasies he was psychologically incapable of fulfilling in real life.

It is relevant to this interpretation of the scene that it was on the very night his mother died that Lawrence first began to make a copy of Maurice Greiffenhagen's painting *An Idyll*. This picture, first exhibited in 1891, was reproduced in a glossy magazine, *Black and White*, in January 1901, where Lawrence saw it and at once became fascinated with it. He took the magazine to show to the Chambers family. He praised it in an unpublished version of a talk on "Art and the Individual" sent to Blanche Jennings, to whom he wrote (31 December 1908), "As for Greiffenhagen's *Idyll*, it moves me almost as much as if I were fallen in love myself. Under its intoxication I have flirted madly this Christmas" (*Letters*, I, 103). This "mad flirting" must be seen in the light of his letter a fortnight earlier (15 December 1908) to Blanche, in which he says, "I have kissed dozens of girls—on the cheek—never on the mouth—I could not" (*Letters*, I, 99). So, while it is true that the coloring and technique of the *Idyll* interested him, it seems evident that the picture of "a strong young forester about to ravish a willing maiden"[13] stirred him sexually and gave him some sort of vicarious satisfaction. In *The White Peacock*, the sexually shy George tries to tell Lettie, as they look at this picture together, that he would *like* to play that part. That Lawrence first actually began to copy *An Idyll* on the night when his mother's imminent death seemed to promise release from emotional bondage is surely very revealing. Would the fantasy soon become reality?  In a letter written 3 December to Rachel Annand Taylor, he referred to "Louie—whom I wish I could marry the day after the funeral" (*Letters*, I, 191).   That was because he thought Louie could offer "a fine, warm, healthy natural love" (*Letters*, I, 191), but he was mistaken. As Sagar puts it, "Once again he had underestimated the strength of 'time-long prudery.'"[14] We have now perhaps some indication of the depth and intensity which lie beneath the superficial lightness of the play and which a good production can reveal.

That truth is stranger than fiction is a commonplace whose own truth is often borne out.   That the little Nottinghamshire church of Greasley should have had as vicar in Lawrence's day a certain Rodolph von Hube who claimed to be a Polish patriot whose revolutionary activities had forced him to leave his own country— "I vas a baron in MY country"—is extraordinary enough;   that he should have written and published in 1901 "an Illustrated History from the earliest Times and from Reliable Sources" of what he with quaint archaism calls *Griseleia in Snotingscire*, adds to the oddity. Harry T. Moore calls it "a scramble of history, anecdote, and sycophancy to the vicar's leading parishioners." And the anecdotes associated with von Hube himself are quite as farcical as those invented by Lawrence for his fictional counterpart. Willie Hopkin remembered von Hube as "a rum bloke who wouldn't bury anyone after four in the afternoon."The story goes that once, when a body arrived late because of slippery roads, von Hube refused to bury the body until the next day. But the men who brought the coffin took it out of the cart and propped it against the door of the vicarage, saying loudly, "So we'll leave the old booger 'ere til morning" at which, in Moore's words, "the baron popped out at once to attend to the burial." Even more farcical is the story, which Hopkin also insisted was true, that one foggy night, after dining and wining too well with the Barbers at Lamb Close, von Hube missed his way and found himself up to the knees in Moor Green Reservoir. He began to cry out, "Lost! Lost!" Two passing colliers who heard him said, "Oh, he's not wanted till Sunday," and walked on. (He was eventually rescued by the people of Lamb Close.)[15]

Baron Rudolf von Ruge seems scarcely exaggerated when we read these anecdotes; yet, *in a play*, incidents like those of the real-life Baron belong to the realm of farce. Von Ruge's pompous pseudo-soldiership recalls, "I vas a Baron in MY country." His constant splutterings and fizzlings into Germanic gutterals suggest that, at this time, Lawrence did not distinguish very clearly between Germans and Poles—ironically, in view of his marriage! Von Ruge and the Baroness hunt the countryside for courting couples with the assiduity of any priest in western Ireland. The Baroness's penny-pinching concern with trivia— whether a lantern or a burnt rice pudding—contrasts with the Baron's pathetically ludicrous concern with his own dignity and that of his church. Her nickname, "Throttle-ha'penny," derives, of course, from George Henry Cullen's Throttle Ha'penney mine at Hill Top.

The Baron and Baroness are the peak of all that is most farcical in the play. The most broadly farcical scenes centre upon them; their presence in the play throws this broader, more farcical color upon even the more soberly naturalistic scenes, and Lawrence uses them absolutely crucially in the mechanisms of the plot and the development of the relationships of other characters. Thus, in eliminating them and substituting a pallid, conventional vicar and his wife, Peter Gill destroyed not an excrescence but the theatrical and artistic heart of the play. The Baron's first brief entrance establishes his hostile relationship with the Hemstock family, his inflated notion of his duties as vicar, and, through his encounter with Patty, introduces the first moment of farce.

In Act II, Scene ii, we find Rachel, still drying her tears after Harry's violence, meeting Susy on the road outside the house and the two of them discussing—in all the intensity that has been created in the violent scene with Harry—the shape and qualities of the relationships, the love/sex relationships, of Harry; the Nurse; Rachel's father, Hezekiah; Susy herself; and Job Arthur. (The scene loses all psychological force in Gill's version by being transposed to *before* the tying-up scene.) It is into this tense discussion of man-woman relationships that the Baron and his wife come with lantern and stick "to hunt out lovers," as Rachel puts it. Apart from the absurdity always associated with such sex-hunts, the imperfect English of the Baron and the eccentric speech of his wife are used to add a linguistic twist to the comedy. "They who entice young men into these naughty holes and crannies" carried a meaning certainly not intended by the puritanical Baroness, as also do "linked worms," "you suck at sin," and "You lurk, sir, in a hole like a rat." Harry's intervention in this scene eventually gets him his job at the pit. The following scene, in which the Nurse bathes Harry's wounds, gets its tension and interest from the conspiracy of silence of Harry and the Nurse in front of Mr. Hemstock, as well as the opportunity he gets to be "mothered" by her.

(Peter Gill, having cut out the preceding scene, feebly made Harry fall over a stile.)

Act III, scene i, totally cut at the Royal Court Theatre, is also absolutely vital in the development of the relationships: the "shot-gun" engagement of Rachel and the baker; Harry's emergence as rescuer *and* the complicating conspiracy between both his potential lovers, Rachel and the Nurse, to conceal the fact that the Baron had been scared of two women. Only this scene makes later scenes— "especially the final church porch scenes—dramatic and even intelligible. For those final scenes, pivoted upon the eccentric character and ecclesiastical function of the Baron, arise from this scene and exist only because of it; and, because the Baron is central in them, they are so weighted on the side of the farcical as to make the patterned, almost ritual triple solution acceptable. (It is no wonder that the critics of the heavily cut Royal Court production thought the final scenes were written when Lawrence was drunk, so out of key with the rest of the play were they made to seem.)

The von Ruge element in the play thus constitutes its second challenge to the theatre: that of integrating farce, essential and central to the play, with scenes of varying degrees of naturalism—even to the extreme naturalism of the miner's evening wash scene. Such variety of convention within a play is not, of course, to be dismissed as a fault. Shakespeare's comedies, and also his *Henry IV* plays, show a similar integration of apparently incompatible conventions and tones. Lawrence is not a second Shakespeare; but, as his own *As You Like It* reference suggests, he was aware that what he was attempting had Shakespearean affinities.

We turn now to the structure of the play. Apart from the later and very different *David*, which is presented in sixteen scenes, almost all in different, or slightly different, locations, all Lawrence's other plays are in three or four acts, the usual structure for the naturalistic drama of the period. And the famous "three" have each only one set. Naturalistic drama from the mid-nineteenth century onward had tended to demand fewer and fewer sets so that they could be constructed more and more substantially and realistically. But *The Merry-Go-Round* is in five acts. Not that the theatre audience is likely to feel it as five acts, any more than the theatre audience is conscious of the five-act structure conventionally imposed by editors on Shakespeare's plays. Indeed, Lawrence's five-act structure is probably a gesture toward that Shakespearean convention, a young and inexperienced dramatist's feeling that the kind of play he is writing *ought* to be in five acts. In reality, it is in eleven scenes: two in Act I, three in Act II, two in Act III, one in Act IV, and three in Act V. Peter Gill was probably wise simply to number his scenes (reduced in number by two, of course) from one to nine. Another way of regarding the structure would be by days: the first day occupies the first two acts, and each of the other acts occupies one day. But the time sequence is obvious in practice.

With the multiplicity of scenes comes a multiplicity of locations, seven in all, of which five occur only once, one occurs twice, and the other, the kitchen of the Hemstock's house, four times. In a period of box-sets and naturalistic detail, to present a play in this form was in itself a challenge to contemporary theatre, especially because of the flow of the play and the way in which time and again a scene in a new setting follows immediately upon what has gone before, so that slow scene changes would kill the dramatic effect.

We have no means of knowing how Lawrence himself imagined the staging of the play. Common sense tells us that he did not see it as a series of naturalistically constructed sets, each taking several minutes to dismantle and set up. He might conceivably have expected it to be set with changing backcloths and wings, a system of setting long outmoded for straight plays but still used at that time for musical comedies and the like. But his scene descriptions do not seem to fit this; there are too many three-dimensional naturalistic objects—fireplaces, gates, stiles, etc.—to be adapted happily for that kind of staging.

We are left with the possibility of a multiple set. The multiple set is very old in theatrical history. Many medieval religious plays were so staged, with heaven, hell, Bethlehem, Jerusalem, and so on all simultaneously represented on different parts of a large open stage, the action being focused on each, as was appropriate for the individual scenes. But that old tradition did not last. Shakespeare's stage was non-localized—that is to say, the action took place nowhere in particular unless the text made it plain that it was at a specific place. Ocasionally, as in *Richard III*, Shakespeare represented two places simultaneously, but only for a special effect. The proscenium arch and perspective scenery of the Restoration quite eliminated multiple settings, and the box-set of nineteenth century naturalism also kept them at bay. But by 1910, avant-garde dramatists, especially on the continent, were already in revolt against these restrictions. Within the next five or ten years, the Expressionist movement in Germany would be at the flood; and, in the 1920's, the great directors like Erwin Piscator would be using multiple settings as a matter of course. How far Lawrence at twenty-five was conscious that his own revolt and challenge were in line with the most avant-garde theatrical creators of the period is difficult to judge, but that he *was* in revolt is clear from the letters already quoted. In none of his plays did he express that revolt and that challenge as clearly as in this remarkable play.

Peter Gill evaded the challenge to some extent by cutting two settings—an exterior and an interior—and the reviews suggest that the attempt was made to stage the play naturalistically, in harmony with the emasculated text. Today, however, after the breaking of theatrical fetters (the claims of illusion, the proscenium arch, the imagined need to hide what does not need immediately to be seen), it seems not in the least strange but entirely natural to provide this play with a multiple setting. In a multiple set, there is no delay in moving from one location to another; scene can follow scene in as quick succession as on the Shakespearean stage. As settings do not have to be struck and reset but can remain throughout the play, they can be furnished with firm, three-dimensional, naturalistic detail if wanted; while, at the same time, as the whole of this multiple setting can be looked at simultaneously and is, therefore, plainly and patently a work of art and not a copy of "real life," it can be given additional significance— symbolism, if you will. If this kind of setting is used, the structure of Lawrence's play flows through time and space and presents no aesthetic or theatrical problems—except that, as we have seen, the first scene, Mrs. Hemstock's downstairs bedroom, should not be seen again but should be felt to be off-stage when the setting is that of the Hemstock's kitchen.

The setting used at the Octagon Theatre, Bolton, not only solved this problem but worked excellently in every respect. The play was presented on a wide, open stage on two levels. Central on the lower level was a revolve divided into three sectors: "Downstairs front room of the Hemstocks' cottage," the first scene, never visible again; "The Kitchen of the Hemstocks' cottage," used four times; and "The dining room at the vicarage," used once only. The juxtaposition of the two rooms in the Hemstocks' house as sectors of the revolve meant that the death-bed room *really* was just out of sight off-stage during the kitchen scenes. To the actor's right of the revolve was the Nurse's room at the miner's cottage, and to the actor's left was the vicarage garden wall (Act V, Scene ii). Above this, on the higher level, was the road outside the Hemstocks', used in Act II, Scene ii; while, on the higher level, above the Nurse's room, was a suggestion of the church porch. The whole was topped and dominated by the silhouette of a pit head—in the designer's model, of conventional shape, but in the realized decor, the famous twin headstocks of Brinsley Colliery. Lit with skill and imagination, this multiple setting fulfilled every need of the play's full text.

In moving toward a conclusion, let us now consider some aspects of the play's last act.   We have already remarked that the whole comedy lies under the shadow of death; its last act takes place on the Sunday after Mrs. Hemstock's death, and everyone has attended the post-funeral service. There is a new scene, the church porch, which has not been used earlier; and Lawrence asks for no fewer than five anonymous mourners. He conspicuously does *not* ask for the quite superfluously named *Mr. and Mrs. Heseltine, Polly Goddard,* and *Bill Naylor* of Peter Gill's adaptation but for five *Mourners*—that is, five people heavily dressed in black, thus setting, visually, a funereal mood that contrasts almost grotesquely with the gossip about the banns which fills the mourners' dialogue.

> A wedding or a festival, a mourning or a funeral

Lawrence's beloved Wordsworth brings together in one line about children's play what Lawrence brings together in this fifth act. The anonymous mourners who provide the opening (very briefly, for they have disappeared for good after nineteen short speeches) are as important in their minor way to the tensions of Act V as is the opening scene of the sick and dying Mrs. Hemstock to the tensions of the play as a whole.

The "false" banns arise, we may remember, partly from the "shot-gun" engagement of Rachel to Job Arthur and accepted by her then, under pressure from the Baron, because of her exasperation with Harry. The other banns come as a surprise, though we have in fact been unobtrusively prepared for the explanation when, in Act IV, Rachel quite casually asks the Nurse ". . . will you go an' see what's up with my father?" The "false" banns also neatly tie up the financial deals earlier proposed by the baker; it emerges that he owes Hezekiah £180. The calling of these banns, their concreteness and challenge, reinforced by the attitude of the absurd but sincerely affronted Baron, has the effect of concentrating the minds of the potential mates wonderfully and of making them realize with comic but genuine suddenness whom they *really* want. In Act III, Scene ii, Lawrence consciously played with a "fairy-tale" pattern of three, when each of the Nurse's potential lovers—Hezekiah, Foules, and Harry—comes in turn and is, each in a very different way, apparently rejected in turn, with Foules quoting, or slightly misquoting, Feste ("The third time pays for all") to underline the Shakespearean-comedy element in the play. Now, in the final moments of the last act, the "fairy-tale" three asserts itself again:

> DR. FOULES: . . . Nurse, will you be asked in church with me next Sunday?
> BAKER: Susy, will you be asked in church with me next Sunday?
> HARRY: Rachel, will be axed in church with me next Sunday?
> BARON: Enough, enough! Go away, I will suffer no more of this!
> BARONESS: Such wicked frivolity! Rachel, go home at once to see to that pudding.
> DR. FOULES: We are most deeply serious, Nurse, are we not?
> BAKER: Susy, are we not?
> HARRY: Rachel, are we not?
> RACHEL: Chorus of ladies, "Yes"!
> NURSE AND SUSY: Chorus of ladies, "Yes"!
> DR. FOULES: Millicent Broadbanks—Arthur William Foules.
> BAKER: Job Arthur Bowers—Susy Smalley, née Hemstock, widow.
> HARRY: Rachel Wilcox—Harry Hemstock.                    [Act V, Scene iii]

The "threes" also recall the conclusion of *As You Like It*, with its formalized multiple pairings, while the Baron's impatient, "Away! Away!" echoes and parodies the Duke's

> Proceed, proceed. We will begin these rites,
> As we do trust they'll end, in true delights,

which gives the literary Foules the cue to introduce the "Like it or Lump it" coda.

This patterned ending is not, however, meaningless pattern. On the contrary, Lawrence has brought together his couples in a highly significant way: the Nurse (who has the "posh" and Kentish characteristics of Lydia) marries up rather than down in the social scale and is seen to fit with the *literary* mother-fixated son, the Doctor, one of Lawrence's own personae in the play. It is a marriage that has its roots both in Lawrence's dreams of what his mother might have married and in his own relationship with his mother, whom, he told Jessie as they stood near a colliery railway track the day before the funeral, he had loved "like a lover." The second marriage, of Susy and the baker, stands as an example of the ordinary, not intense marriage of ordinary, average people, who, however, are not "in love" in Lawrence's eyes. The third marriage is of Lawrence's other persona, the persona he dreamed of in his Greiffenhagen-*Idyll* fantasies, the marriage of the mother-fixated miner's son, whose subterranean fires and passions are nevertheless capable of breaking forth, to that non-existent woman, as clinging and spiritually demanding as Jessie and as sensually generous and warm as he still thought the Junoesque but puritanically prim Louie would be. (But it is deeply revealing that it is Rachel who has to say, "Come on here, Harry"—for passionate and true lover as he is, he still cannot take the ultimate initiative.)

Each of these three couplings is given a symbolic kiss: the Doctor kisses the Nurse's hand—the least sensual of kisses and the remotest from loving sexual fulfillment. Job Arthur then kisses Susy's cheek. But Rachel and Harry kiss on the mouth. To understand fully the meaning of these kisses, we return to Lawrence's letter of 15 December 1908, to Blanche Jennings:

> Think—if you kissed a man on the mouth—what it would mean to you. I have kissed dozens of girls—on the cheek—never on the mouth—I could not Such a touch is the connection between the vigorous flow of two lives. Like a positive electricity, a current of creative life runs through two persons, and they are instinct with the same life force—the same vitality—the same I know not what—when they kiss on the mouth—when they kiss as lovers do. Come to think of it and [sic] it is exceedingly rare that two people participate in entirely the same sensation and emotion; but they do when they kiss as lovers, I am sure. Then a certain life-current passes through them which changes them forever. . . . [*Letters*, I, 99]

But even now, when dramatizing some of his keenest feelings about sex and love, Lawrence keeps the seriousness ("We are most deeply serious," says the Doctor) held in suspension in the atmosphere of farce, and the closing lines lightly cover the seriousness which otherwise would threaten to upset the comic balance of the play. So far from being written when Lawrence was drunk, these last scenes, when they conclude the total play which he wrote, are both brilliant and profound—as the best farce should be.

*The Merry-Go-Round*, as Lawrence wrote it, is thoroughly viable in the theatre and successful in its relationship with its audience. So far from being a "romp" for amateurs, it is a play demanding a high degree of professional skill. In it we see Lawrence actually putting into practice his rebellion against much of the contemporary naturalistic drama of the pre-1914 era and experimenting more boldly and successfully than in other plays of his. He deploys a considerable range of possibilities of theatrical language: the heavily charged localism of Mrs. Hemstock, the "normal" localism of the other characters, the literary mannerisms of Dr. Foules, the Nurse's Lydia-like Kentish "poshness," the Germanic-Polish English of the Baron and Baroness's eccentric language, influenced by her husband's. This range of language and speech styles is no greater than we find in a Shakespearean comedy; the skill lies in reconciling and integrating them. The same applies to the closely related question of the range of theatrical styles, the degrees of broadness of comedy—and seriousness—in the play. Again, the skill of the dramatist and the challenge to the theatre are not to be revealed and answered by reducing this range and these contrasts to some imagined norm but to play them for all they are worth, to exploit the variety of tones and colors.

In the structure of the play, we have seen, apart from the conventional gesture toward the Shakespearean five acts, a sequential style using a multiplicity of scenes and settings such as was still unfashionable at that time but towards which the avant-garde in the theatre was already turning. Associated with this is the demand the play makes on the designer to provide a stage setting that permits the rapid flow of action through a number of very different locations conceived with considerable three-dimensional solidity. Whatever solution Lawrence himself had in mind, the simultaneous multiple setting, which was to become popular with forward-looking dramatists and directors within a few years of the writing of this play, is the best solution and shows Lawrence once more ahead of his time.

An examination of the play in the light of the tensions and complexities of Lawrence's life and being at the time the play was written brings the realization that its comic and farcical surface masks great emotional depths so that, in the best tradition of farce, *The Merry-Go-Round*, with all its deliberate absurdities, is concerned with matters lying deep in the hearts of men and women. Therefore, (in common with all the best farce) it must be taken in deadly earnest by the actors. (One of the reasons why amateur productions of farce are often so painful is that the actors either try to be funny or are terribly aware that they are being funny. The true art of farce lies in playing it for real.) Properly and professionally played, then, this play while making us laugh also touches in us vital and often painful emotional depths. Like all the best comedy, it makes serious and deep comments upon the human condition. Bertolt Brecht said that, although the purpose of art is to teach, its *aim* must be to entertain. *The Merry-Go-Round* succeeds on both levels. Whether or not it is Lawrence's best play is very questionable. Most theatre-goers and critics will probably reach the conclusion that the intensity and consistency of the famous three plays still give them pride of place; but, if not his best, *The Merry-Go-Round* is certainly Lawrence's most interestingly experimental and forward-looking play.

[This article is based upon a lecture delivered to the D.H. Lawrence Society at Eastwood on 9 November 1983.]

*The D.H. Lawrence Review*, 16:2, Summer, 1983.

## Notes

1 Keith Sagar, "D. H. Lawrence: Dramatist," *The D. H. Lawrence Review*, 4 (Summer 1971), 155.

2 *The Letters of D. H. Lawrence*, Vol. I: September 1901-May 1913, ed. James T. Boulton (Cambridge: Cambridge University Press, 1979), p. 509. Subsequent references to this book will be cited parenthetically in the text.

3 John Millington Synge, "Preface" to *The Playboy of the Western World* (dated 21 January 1907).

4 Synge, *op. cit.*

5 The texts of *The Merry-go-Round* used are as follows: (1) *The Complete Plays of D. H. Lawrence* (London: William Heinemann, 1965), pp. 387-467. [There are two confusing errors on p. 389 of this edition: a) Act II, Scene ii is omitted, and Scene iii incorrectly numbered as Scene ii, though these scenes are correctly numbered in the text; b) Act V, Scene ii is described as being *Beside the vicarage garden walk*, where *walk* should read *wall*, as in the text.] (2) *The Merry-go-Round*, by D. H. Lawrence (1912). Adapted by Peter Gill (1971). Typescript. (London: Margery Vosper, Ltd., 1971).

6 Quoted in Keith Sagar, *D. H. Lawrence: A Calendar of His Works* (Manchester: Manchester University Press, 1979), p. 5.

7 Roy Spencer, *D. H. Lawrence Country* (London: Cecil Woolf, 1980), p. 39.

8 Sagar, *Calendar*, p. 17.

9 Sagar, "D. H. Lawrence: Dramatist," p. 160.

[10]Harry T. Moore, *The Priest of Love: A Life of D. H. Lawrence*, rev. ed. (London: William Heinemann, 1974), p. 71.

[11]Michael Billington, "*The Merry-go-Round* at the Royal Court," *Guardian* [Manchester], 8 November 1973, p. 12.

[12]Spencer, p. 71.

[13]Spencer, p. 48.

[14]Keith Sagar, *The Life of D. H. Lawrence: An Illustrated Biography* (London: Eyre Methuen, 1980), p. 46.

[15]Moore, *Priest of Love*, pp. 71-72.

# VIII
# The Short Fiction

**George Orwell,  "'The Prussian Officer' and Other Stories"**

---

Reviews ought not to consist of personal reminiscences, but perhaps it is worth recording how I first became acquainted with D.H. Lawrence's work, because it happened that I read him before I had heard of him, and the qualities which then impressed me were probably the essential ones.

In 1919 I went into my schoolmaster's study for some purpose, and, not finding him there, picked up a magazine with a blue cover which was on the table. I was then sixteen and wallowing in Georgian poetry.  My idea of a good poem would have been Rupert Brooke's "Grantchester." As soon as I opened the magazine I was completely overwhelmed by a poem which describes a woman standing in the kitchen and watching her husband approaching across the fields. On the way he takes a rabbit out of a snare and kills it. Then he comes in, throws the dead rabbit on the table, and, his hands still stinking of the rabbit's fur, takes the woman in his arms. In a sense she hates him, but she is utterly swallowed up in him.  More than the sexual encounter, the "beauty of Nature" which Lawrence deeply felt, but which he was also able to turn on and off like a tap, impressed me; and especially the lines (referring to a flower):

> Then her bright breast she will uncover
> And yield her honeydrop to her lover.

But I failed to notice the name of the author, or even of the magazine, which must have been the *English Review*.

Four or five years later, still not having heard of Lawrence, I got hold of the volume of short stories now reprinted as a Penguin.[1] Both "The Prussian Officer" and "The Thorn in the Flesh" impressed me deeply. What struck me was not so much Lawrence's horror and hatred of military discipline, as his understanding of its nature. Something told me that he had never been a soldier, and yet he could project himself into the atmosphere of an army, and the German army at that. He had built all this up, I reflected, from watching a few German soldiers walking about in some garrison town. From another story, "The White Stocking" (also in this collection, though I think I read it later), I deduced the moral that women behave better if they get a sock on the jaw occasionally.

Clearly there is more in Lawrence than this, but I think these first impacts left me with a broadly true picture of him. He was in essence a lyric poet, and an undisciplined enthusiasm for "Nature," i.e. the surface of the earth, was one of his principal qualities, though it has been much less noticed than his preoccupation with sex. And on top of this he had the power of understanding, or seeming to understand, people totally different from himself, such as farmers, gamekeepers, clergymen and soldiers—one might add coalminers, for though Lawrence himself had worked in the pit at the age of thirteen, clearly he was not a typical miner. His stories are a kind of lyric poem, produced by just looking at some alien, inscrutable human being and suddenly experiencing an intense imaginative vision of his inner life.

How true these visions were is debatable. Like some Russian writers of the nineteenth century, Lawrence often seems to by-pass the novelist's problem by making all his characters equally sensitive. All the people in his stories, even those to whom he is hostile, seem to experience the same kind of emotions, everyone can make contact with everyone else, and class barriers, in the form in which we know them, are almost obliterated. Yet he does often seem to have an extraordinary power of knowing imaginatively something that he could not have known by observation. Somewhere in one of his books he remarks that when you shoot at a wild animal, the action is not the same as shooting at a target. You do not look along the sights: you aim by an instinctive movement of the whole body, and it is as though your will were driving the bullet forward. This is quite true, and yet I do not suppose Lawrence had ever shot at a wild animal. Or consider the death scene at the end of "England my England" (which is not in the present collection, unfortunately). Lawrence had never been in circumstances remotely similar to those he was describing. He had merely had a private vision of the feelings of a soldier under fire. Perhaps it is true to experience, perhaps not: but at least it is emotionally true, and therefore convincing.

With few exceptions Lawrence's full-length novels are, it is generally admitted, difficult to get through. In the short stories his faults do not matter so much, because a short story can be purely lyrical, whereas a novel has to take account of probability and has to be cold-bloodedly constructed. In *The Prussian Officer* there is an extraordinarily good, longish story called "Daughters of the Vicar." An Anglican clergyman of the ordinary middle-class type is marooned in a mining village where he and his family are half-starved on a tiny stipend, and where he has no function, the mining folk having no need of him and no sympathy with him. It is the typical impoverished middle-class family in which the children grow up with a false consciousness of social superiority dragging upon them like a ball and fetter. The usual problem arises: how are the daughters to get married? The elder daughter gets the chance to marry a comparatively well-to-do clergyman. He happens to be a dwarf, suffering from some internal disease, and an utterly inhuman creature, more like a precocious and disagreeable child than a man. By the standards of most of the family she has done the right thing: she has married a gentleman. The younger daughter, whose vitality is not to be defeated by snobbishness, throws family prestige overboard and marries a healthy young coalminer.

It will be seen that this story has a close resemblance to *Lady Chatterley's Lover*. But in my opinion it is much better and more convincing than the novel, because the single imaginative impulse is strong enough to sustain it. Probably Lawrence had watched, somewhere or other, the underfed, downtrodden, organ-playing daughter of a clergyman wearing out her youth, and had a sudden vision of her escaping into the warmer world of the working class, where husbands are plentiful. It is a fit subject for a short story, but when drawn out to novel length it raises difficulties to which Lawrence was unequal. In another story in this book, "The Shades of Spring," there is a gamekeeper who is presented as a wild natural creature, the opposite of the over-conscious intellectual. Such figures appear again and again in Lawrence's books, and I think it is true to say that they are more convincing in the short stories, where we do not have to know too much about them, than in the novels (for example, *Lady Chatterley's Lover* or *The Woman Who Rode Away*), where, in order to be set into action, they have to be credited with complex thoughts which destroy their status as unspoiled animals. Another story, "Odour of Chrysanthemums," deals with the death of a miner in a pit accident. He is a drunkard, and up to the moment of his death his wife has wanted nothing so much as to be rid of him. Only when she is washing his dead body does she perceive, as though for the first time, how beautiful he is. That is the kind of thing Lawrence could do, and in the first paragraph of the story there is a wonderful example of his power of visual description. But one could not make a full-length novel out of such an episode, nor, without other more prosaic ingredients, out of a series of such episodes.

This is not quite the best volume of Lawrence's short stories, and it is to be hoped that the Penguin Library will follow it up by reprinting *England My England*. That contains, apart from the name story, "Fannie and Annie," "The Horse-dealers's Daughter," and, above all, *The Fox*. This last story is perhaps the best thing Lawrence ever did, but it has the unusual quality of centring round an idea that might have occurred to anybody, so that one can enjoy the mental exercise of imagining the same story as it might have been told by Tolstoy, Maupassant, Henry James or Edgar Wallace. But the present volume contains at least six stories of the first rank, and only one ("A Fragment of Stained Glass") that is definitely a failure.

*Tribune* , 16 November 1945.

## Notes

---

[1] *The Prussian Officer*. By D.H. Lawrence, (London: Penguin Books., 1945) 9d.

## John B. Vickery, "Myth and Ritual in the Shorter Fiction of D.H. Lawrence"

This essay approaches the subject of myth and ritual in D.H. Lawrence's work in two ways: first, through a sketch of his extensive use of material from anthropology and comparative religion; and second, through the analysis of three stories, "England, My England", "The Virgin and the Gypsy", and *The Fox*. These last were deliberately chosen from those tales less obviously possessed of mythico-ritualistic elements in order better to dramatize the extent of Lawrence's use of such elements while at the same time demonstrating a critical technique for the illumination of structure, theme, and motives.

Of all the stories in *The Tales of D.H. Lawrence* barely half a dozen contain no allusions whatsoever to primitive beliefs, habits of thought, or behavior. The rest through image, scene, action, or allusion embrace virtually every major notion concerning myth and ritual to be found in *The Golden Bough*. The point here is not that Frazer's great study constitutes Lawrence's only source, though it is undeniably one of the most important, but that it is the most encyclopedic treatment of primitive life available to the English-speaking world and the one that lies behind the bulk of current literary interest in the subject. As such it is the most convenient touchstone for gauging Lawrence's interest in anthropology and comparative religion.

Lawrence's stories, like *The Golden Bough*, are filled with a number of different kinds of creatures possessing essentially human forms. Unequivocally anthropological are the names of Isis, Osiris, Adonis, Dionysus, Astarte, Bacchus, Pan, Venus, Persephone, Baal, Ashtaroth, Artemis, Cybele, and Balder. All of these are leading characters in Frazer's drama of the dying and reviving god and his wife-mother-lover so that their frequent mention in stories such as "The Ladybird", *St. Mawr*, and "The Man Who Died" make this drama one of Lawrence's major *leit-motivs*. Nor does he confine himself simply to the major deities and fertility cults of the Semitic, Egyptian, Greek, and Scandinavian worlds. The nature and temperament of his characters are continually being defined with reference to maenads, dryads, fauns, and satyrs, out of whose coalescence the greater deities emerged. Indeed, it is in just such references that we see the anthropological dimension with which Lawrence's concept of the spirit of place is endowed. Thus, in *St. Mawr* the New England woman and Louise Carrington feel that the landscape lives and that it possesses a spirit which senses the sacred nature of the female sex. And in this conviction the spirit of place embodies the interrelation of vegetative and human fertility and the primitive worship of both found in *The Golden Bough*.

Neither Lawrence nor Frazer confines his attention solely to the objects of human veneration and respect. Intensification of mood, clarification of character, and deepening of theme, all are achieved by invoking such creatures as devils, demons, and ghosts. Sometimes they are mentioned only casually, but other times they become central to the story as with the title image of "The Captain's Doll" which is not only magical but is regarded by the Captain as a male devil arousing both fascination and repulsion. In *St. Mawr* Frazer's point about the variety of forms possessed by supernatural beings is illustrated by associating demons, devils, and ghosts with human beings, animals, and vegetation. While many of these metaphoric identifications are of vicious, unpleasant persons, there are others which suggest that Lawrence shares Jane Harrison's view of the spiritual worth of the chthonic powers of the underworld. For Frazer and Lawrence both, they reflect one of man's deepest impulses and one which is fundamentally religious in character. Thus, there is a world of difference between the sadistic Pauline of "The Lovely Lady" or the diabolic Ethel Cane of "None of That" and a representative miner like Mr. Pinnegar of "Jimmy and the Desperate Woman". In this connection, it is particularly interesting to note how often Lawrence's miners—the perfect image of the contemporary underworld—possess that inexpugnable quality of life and personal power that Frazer and Miss Harrison attributed to chthonic deities.

In addition to the miner as chthonic power, Lawrence's stories possess many other characters who function as archetypes. One of the most important of these is the stranger who, as in *The Golden Bough*, is a disturbing figure because of his aura of fertility and his apparently magical powers to influence others. Such stories as "Odor of Chrysanthemums", "Samson and Delilah", *The Fox*, and "The Border Line" testify both to the importance of this figure and also to the variety ascribed to it by Lawrence. The same is true of such anthropologically symbolic figures as the virgin ("The Virgin and the Gypsy" and "The Princess"), the witch or magician ("Wintry Peacock" and "Mother and Daughter"), the hanged man ("The Thorn in the Flesh," "A Fragment of Stained Glass," and "The Man Who Died"), and the scapegoat ("England, My England" and "The Princess"). And back of these figures, bulking large in *The Golden Bough* too, are the warriors, hunters, farmers, peasants, and primitive savages whose social and personal needs give rise to the myths and rituals found in Lawrence and Frazer. Indeed, in "The Man Who Loved Islands" there is even a satiric portrait of the sort of person who was one of Frazer's earliest and most avid readers.

Densely populated as Lawrence's stories are with the figures of comparative religion, this is not their only affinity with the primitive world of *The Golden Bough*. Time and time again the characters exhibit those mental phenomena, those modes of thought and belief that Frazer chronicled with such a wealth of illustration. Levels of consciousness from the rational to the most intuitive are as graphically presented in stories like "Glad Ghosts," *St. Mawr*, "The Rocking-Horse Winner," and "The Blind Man" as they are in *The Golden Bough*. Particularly striking in this connection is the idea of spells and magic in general. Lawrence probably describes more characters as "spell-bound" and does so more repeatedly than any other writer of recent times. Through their recurrent use, especially in contexts of great dramatic intensity and mythopoeic overtones, he refurbishes such time-worn phrases and invests them with some of their original potency. "Daughters of the Vicar," "The Captain's Doll," and "The Border Line," all have characters who exercise and react to spells both deliberately imposed and the casual by-product of the individual's impact as a personality on another human being. These spells usually exist between a man and a woman who are aware of one another as desirable but unknown and therefore dangerous, but they also obtain between parent and child as in "The Christening" and "England, My England". Other aspects of magic used in Lawrence's stories to reveal character relationships as well as the incalculable nature of the human mind are talismans, images, second sight, trances, mediums together with all the other apparatus of spiritualism, and sinister physical transformations.

Nor are their physical and mental qualities all that Lawrence's characters share with Frazer's primitive peoples. Lawrence's work, like *The Golden Bough*, possesses a deep and persistent interest in those human actions whose importance derives as much from their being performed by the majority of people as from their being essential to human existence. Death, marriage, fornication, initiation. dancing, sacrifice, departure and arrival, and many other actions are focused on by Lawrence not merely because the conventions of fiction demand a kind of loose realism but because they are performed, consciously or not, in ritualistic fashion. The very manner of their performance testifies to their connection with the sacred existence, that is, the order in which the mysterious potency of life itself resides. Typical of Lawrence's use of ritual actions are those stories revolving around death or sex. In "The Prussian Officer," for example, the struggle between the two men parallels the ritual combat in the grove at Nemi in which victory entails a new and unknown life that leads to a final defeat. Even more deliberately ritualistic is the sacrificial death undergone by the central figure in "The Woman Who Rode Away," while "The Last Laugh" shows the swift retribution visited upon the man who penetrates the mystery of the god's existence and approaches too close to the divine but dangerous power.

Nor is this power limited to the gods. From the behavior of many of Lawrence's characters it is apparent that they would agree with Ernest Crawley's remark in his study of primitive marriage *The Mystic Rose* that "all persons are potentially dangerous to others, as well as potentially in danger, in virtue simply of the distinction between man and man." "Daughters of the Vicar," "Second Best," and "The Horse Dealer's Daughter" develop with considerable power this feeling of the danger inherent in love and entrance into the marriage state. On the other hand, stories such as "The Shades of Spring" and "Sun" reflect Frazer's emphasis on the beneficent custom of human beings miming the rite of the Sacred Marriage in which male and female fertility deities guarantee the perpetuation and flourishing of all forms of life. Similarly, extra- or pre-marital fornication regarded as a sacred rite rather than a social or moral sin is central to both "The Ladybird" and "The Man Who Died," thereby dramatizing *The Golden Bough's* accounts of women who have considered it an honor and religious obligation to serve the god through participating in sexual relations with him.

Not all the ritualistic actions of Lawrence's characters however, are of such an unusual order; many are concerned with human behavior in the face of practical problems in daily life. Perhaps the best example of this is the miner's method of cleaning himself after a day under ground. The practice of kneeling on the hearthrug, stripped to the waist, and washing in a large basin is one to which Lawrence often refers. "Daughters of the Vicar," "A Sick Collier," and "Jimmy and the Desperate Woman" chart both its recurrence and Lawrence's own developing comprehension of its ritualistic character. The first two stories stress the habitual, unconscious movements involved, the feelings of awe and fear aroused, and the underlying phallic core of object and attitude; while the last emphasizes the hypnotic fascination it generates and defines its anthropological role by repeatedly calling it a ritual.

Complementing the mythic and ritualistic qualities possessed by Lawrence's characters and their actions is their physical background, the natural phenomena with which the author invests their world and to which they respond. Their associations with the fertility deities of the ancient world are accentuated by the images of vegetative fertility which run through many of the tales. In "The Prussian Officer" the woman, the golden wheat, and the green corn coalesce into an image reminiscent of Frazer's Corn Goddess. The gradual revival and awakening of the woman in "Sun" is described in terms of ripening grapes and gourds, while her retreat is guarded by a single cypress tree, which Frazer describes as sacred to the healing god's sanctuary. Similarly, pine trees, which are central to the rites of Attis and Osiris, appear as mythopoeic vegetative forms in *St. Mawr*, "The Border Line," and "The Man Who Died". Equally sacred to primitive Europeans and even more numerous, according to Frazer, are oak trees, which in both "A Fragment of Stained Glass" and "The Shades of Spring" Lawrence associates with the hyacinth, the flower of the divine king. The same sort of symbolic background is provided by recurrent references to anemones, almond blossoms, hyacinths, and ivy, all of which *The Golden Bough* shows to be vegetative signs and representatives of the great fertility deities like Adonis and Dionysus. On the animal level, this mythic dimension of the stories is conveyed through the weight of significance given to such creatures as the horse, the snake, the fox, the rat, the scarab, the pigeon, the dove, the mole, the lamb, and the cock, each of which figures in the myths, rites, and superstitions explored by Frazer. The same sort of stress is placed on the mythical nature and magical properties of such phenomena as the sun, moon, water, and fire. In stories like "Sun," "The Horse Dealer's Daughter," "The Ladybird," "The Women Who Rode Away," and "The Man Who Died" they become central to the meaning of the story and to the behavior of the characters who see in them not so much objects as omens, talismans, ritual modes, and mythical beings that lead them to a further and deeper participation in tht drama of existence.

The foregoing sketch suggests that Lawrence's stories contain a wealth of material drawn from anthropology and comparative religion. Needless to say, however, certain myths and rites play a more important part than others in shaping the theme and structure of the stories. Thus, at the risk of oversimplification we can resolve Lawrence's shorter fiction into six main categories which constitute a progression from the obvious and apparent to the subtle and hidden presence of myth and ritual. At one end of the scale, representing a concealed anthropological dimension, is a story such as "England, My England," which is based on the myth of the scapegoat and the rites of passage leading to his expulsion. Equally interesting is the use to which Lawrence puts these beliefs and observances. Lawrence's penchant for social, cultural, historical, and spiritual jeremiads on modern life, especially that of the middle and upper classes, is as well known as it is important, but not much notice has been taken of the way in which, as in "England, My England," he employs myth as a way of emphasizing his major criticisms. For him myth functions as a satiric device by offering not only a contrast between the mythico-ritualistic life of ancient man and that of contemporary man which is profane because commonplace and ordinary but also a sense of the continuity between the two worlds that shows how the one may be both a degeneration and an adaptation of the other.

The second category deals with myths of the Andromeda type in which a virgin faces a sacrificial death and attains a salvation which, as Lawrence would insist, is only partly secular. The central rites are those of purification and revivification by water and fire, a point made clear by the most obvious representatives of this type, "The Virgin and the Gypsy" and "The Horse Dealer's Daughter". In such stories Lawrence's use of myth and ritual is primarily structural: the myth serves as a concealed pattern which organizes the narrative into a ritual sequence. The third category reveals the presence of myth more directly and also fuses the two uses to which it has been put in the earlier categories. Both *St. Mawr* and *The Fox* exemplify Lawrence's treatment of the animal or totemic myth, whose strangeness has, unfortunately, largely kept it from being taken seriously as an integral part of the tale. In *St. Mawr* the myth is more nearly satiric or critical in function, while in *The Fox* it operates as a concealed pattern, though, to be sure, there are elements of both in each.

With the fourth category, which includes stories like "The Ladybird," "The Princess," and "Sun," myth is neither concealed nor employed as critical instrument. Instead it operates as a kind of second story, almost a double plot which illuminates the basic story by suggesting a link with man's earliest forms of belief and behavior. The relevant myth is that of the Sacred Marriage, while the rites of initiation, taboo or prohibition, and fecundation present serve to define the central characters' reaction toward the myth itself. Consequently, we find here instances of Lawrence's using ritual as mythic reenactment, as a method of telling a past story through what is now being done. A related but distinct use of myth and ritual occurs in the fifth category, where stories like "The Man Who Died" and "The Woman Who Rode Away" deal directly and as part of the narrative with the myth of the reviving god and his worship through rites of separation, initiation, propitiation, and ordination. Lawrence treats myth in these instances as a new version of an old story, a technique that links these stories to Graves's *King Jesus*, Mann's *Joseph* series, Gide's *Theseus*, and Faulkner's *A Fable*. In every case the author takes a well-established myth or legend and in the process of retelling it fleshes it out with his own imaginative extrapolations so that the final product is both a new tale and a commentary on the old one.

While in one sense, these last stories represent the fullest development of myth and ritual in Lawrence's shorter fiction, there is also a sixth category which is important but stands a little to one side of the others. It embraces stories like "The Last Laugh," "Glad Ghosts," and "The Rocking-Horse Winner" that focus on the myth of a supernatural world populated by spirits of the dead, ghosts, and invisible divinities and coped with by human beings through magical rites of propitiation and prediction as well as the hocus-pocus of spiritualism. In these myth is again used to underscore a point, most frequently that of the mystery of existence, though as a by-product there are some satiric asides on human ignorance. Ritual, on the other hand, is equated primarily with contemporary habit patterns and as a result becomes, as it were, a satiric view of itself; for modern man's attempt to deal with the unknown is shown to be largely silly or disastrous. In effect, these "ghost" stories demonstrate a concomitant of the other tales' insistence on the importance of myth and ritual: these show that it is too vital a subject with which to trifle or dabble.

## II

In "England, My England" the gradual transformation of the passionate idyll of Egbert's and Winifred's marriage into a savage combat that culminates with World War I and Egbert's death is Lawrence's version of the myth of the dying god and the rites of expulsion that accompany the scapegoat. He takes great pains at the beginning of the story to stress the ancient, primitive character both of the scene and of the protagonists. Crockham, where the newlyweds settled, "belonged to the old England of hamlets and yeomen" and "it lay there secret, primitive, savage as when the Saxons first came." It is one of those places where "the savage England lingers in patches." Into this by-gone world come Winifred and Egbert to reflect its sense of the past: "She, too, seemed to come out of the old England, ruddy, strong, with a certain crude, passionate quiescence and a hawthorn robustness. And he, he was tall and slim and agile, like an English archer with his long supple legs and fine movements." Egbert enhances this affinity by having "a passion for old folk-music, collecting folk-songs and folk-dances, studying the Morris-dance and the old customs."

The connection with the past demonstrated in the setting, the appearance, and the interests of the characters culminates in their marital behavior. Though the desire is their own, it is intensified by and derives from their immediate physical setting: "The flame of their two bodies burnt again into that old cottage, that was haunted already by so much bygone, physical desire. You could not be in the dark room for an hour without the influences coming over you. The hot blood-desire of bygone yeomen, there in this old den where they had lusted and bred for so many generations." In celebrating so triumphantly what Arnold van Gennep calls the fecundation rites of marriage, the couple not only fuse modern individuals with the medieval world of the yeoman but also suggest the truly primitive character of that world. One of the central rites of ancient times that persisted into more recent ages among the European peasantry is the mimetic observance by human beings of the Sacred Marriage of the god and goddess. It is just such an imitative rite that Egbert and Winifred are unconsciously involved in, as Lawrence intimates by juxtaposing the images of their union and the flourishing vegetation and garden which Egbert is said to have "re-created." Further support for this is found in Winifred's being regarded as "a ruddy fire into which he could cast himself for rejuvenation" since *The Golden Bough* emphasizes the procreative and purificatory powers of fire and its employment in conjunction with the Sacred Marriage ritual.

Lawrence, however, is writing a story of savage irony and despairing anguish, and hence he focuses not on the joyous celebration of renewed life that normally follows the ritual marriage but on the expulsion and death of the protagonist. This is ironically prepared for in the midst of the ritual of erotic ecstasy by the intrusion of the author's mock invocation "Ah, that it might never end, this passion, this marriage!" That it will end is certain not only because Egbert and Winifred prove to be incompatible personalities but also because they are unconsciously miming the ritual existence of the fertility deity who suffers a cyclic rejection and demise. And in the same scene an image of the impersonal yet necessary cruelty inherent in the mythic world is revealed in the snake's endeavor to swallow a frog who is uttering "the strangest scream, like the very soul of the dark past crying aloud." Nor is it accident that this ritual of self-preservation should have been witnessed by Winifred, who is to take the lead in Egbert's expulsion from the marriage, the family, and life itself.

In connection with the growing alienation that develops between Egbert and Winifred it is important to notice that the strain between them is not derived from the contrast of Egbert's indolent dilettantism to her passion for responsibility and duty nor even from his habit of sponging off her father. These are, at the most, contributory factors. The genuine source of their estrangement lies in a virtually inevitable change in the structure of their world. Instructive here is van Gennep's point, made in *Les Rites de Passage*, that the life of the individual passes through certain successive stages and that this is achieved through the intermediary of ceremonies calculated to make the transition a safe one. These *rites de passage* are threefold, consisting of those which van Gennep calls "*separation, marge, et agrégation.*" The crucial change in the world of the two characters comes when they enter the state of parenthood. Here is the beginning of the ritual of separation, of detachment from the old world and the old life. Winifred finds in her child "a new center of interest" so that "without anything happening, he was gradually, unconsciously excluded from the circle." Then, following their second child, she begins to resent and despise that physical love which has already become of secondary importance to her in the role of dutiful and responsible mother. To provide a conscious justification for this attitude, she turns to the issue of money and his failure to earn a living. Having thus articulated her sense of critical detachment from her husband, she at length formulates what it is that really separates them: "It was that he stood for nothing."

With this we come to the central antithesis in the story, that between her husband and her father. The basic desire of the former is "to hold aloof. It was not his season." The latter, on the other hand, plunges into the struggle of existence with "an acrid faith like the sap of some not-to-be-exterminated tree. just a blind acrid faith as sap is blind and acrid, and yet pushes on in growth and in faith." The "stoic and epicurean" husband confronts the hardy vegetative father and succumbs, in the last analysis, because he lacks the father's "will-to-power . . . the single power of his own blind self." Their struggle, however, is not direct but operates through and in the person of Winifred. For her, the basic familial unit is comprised of her parents, herself, and her child; in it she finds the core of life, "the human trinity for her." She does so because her father has maintained "a certain primitive dominion over the souls of his children, the old, almost magic prestige of paternity. There it was, still burning in him, the old smoky torch of parental godhead . . . Fatherhood that had life-and-death authority over the children." The only thing that could have supplanted her father would have been Winifred's finding in her husband a greater male-power and authority. But since

Egbert does not possess this power, Lawrence ironically inverts the mythic formula which calls for the young ruler or deity to succeed the old one. Egbert rejects the possibility of his own divinity as a human being replete with power and becomes in contrast to the father a *tabu*-figure, "the living negative of power." And what he taboos by his very presence is Winifred's attempt to exercise "her dark, silent, passionate authority," "the old blood-power," "the old dark magic of parental authority." To this end he uses his own form of magic and witchcraft not only to transform her parental authority into "a sort of tyranny" but also to steal the children (the image is Lawrence's) from her. His magic is that which most completely captures children, namely, the exercise of complete license in behavior: "They could do as they liked with him."

Out of the two men's indirect struggle for the role of father has come the ritual of separation celebrated by Winifred in her increasing sexual reticence and by Egbert in his denial of her parental authority coupled with his own rejection of responsibility. This, however, is but the first stage in the rites of passage, that of detachment from the old life. It is followed by what van Gennep calls the "*rite de marge*," the behavior that marks the interim stage between the old and the new modes of life. In "England, My England" this is reflected in the incident of the first-born child's being lamed as a result of falling on a sickle left in the grass by Egbert. With this the antithesis between Winifred's passion for duty and authority (a worship of hierarchy) and Egbert's rejection of responsibility and power (a belief in liberty and self-determination) is projected into the visible and external world so forcefully that husband and wife are seen to be completely separated, to be living in different worlds. In the weeks that follow the accident, both are moving toward their new and distinct modes of existence. As a period of physical, emotional, and spiritual transition it is "a dark and bitter time" for all.

Yet this incident and its repercussions are not significant solely as a rite of transition from marriage to legal separation. For in the early part of the story Egbert has been identified as a representative and worshipper of phallic potency who like the primitive divine king rules only so long as he can demonstrate his power as a fertility figure. When Winifred denies him this, she makes him "lock up his own vivid life inside himself" and thereby reduces him to virtual impotence. Both Egbert and the divine king react in the same way: through a sacrifice of the first-born, man may continue to live as he has, to retain a wife as well as a throne, to prolong a marriage as well as a reign. Clearly, such a rite could not be deliberately embarked upon by a member of the civilized world for whom it would be a monstrously evil act. But as Lawrence seems to indicate, it would be quite possible to desire this in the subconscious where the primitive and savage impulses of man linger even yet. Thus, the contemporary consciousness registers this longing for sacrifice literally as "a wicked look" and metaphorically as Egbert's having "seven devils inside his long, slim, white body."

Similarly, Egbert himself, immediately after the accident, seeks to assuage his deep sense of guilt by insisting on the accidental character of the event. What is at the core of this guilt, however, is not his own superficial carelessness but rather his profound and abiding responsibility. In times of great calamity, *The Golden Bough* tells us, it was customary to sacrifice the first-born. And for Egbert there could be no greater calamity than losing Winifred, for, as has been suggested, it is through her that his spirit of fertility is released and his rejuvenation effected. By indirectly attempting to sacrifice the child, Egbert is seeking to acquire a new lease of life, to atone for his sins (especially the denial of parental authority's divinity), and to demonstrate that he, like Winifred's father, "had kept alive the old red flame of fatherhood, the fatherhood that had even the right to sacrifice the child to God, like Isaac." That Egbert is using the child as a substitute for himself is further suggested by the weapon's being a sickle, the instrument employed in harvest rituals to sacrifice the fertility deity. Even more striking is the fact that, according to Frazer, "the corn-spirit is conceived as a child who is separated from its mother by the stroke of the sickle."

It is part, however, of Lawrence's ironic intention that this effort at prolonging a state of existence regarded as fruitful and idyllic should be thwarted. He is concerned not with the revival but with the death of human society and its protagonists. This is borne out by the sacrifice of the child, which as a ritual of transition proves to be "an agony and a long crucifixion." The irony appears in that the sacrifice is not complete, the child does not die, and so the father cannot restore the marriage to its sacred status. A further irony follows from the fact that the ultimate ritual sacrifice is made by Egbert as a result of his being the scapegoat in the accident. It is with his assumption of this role that the final stage of the *"rite de passage"* is reached. Following the marginal, transitional observance there is the absorption into a new world and a new mode of life. For Winifred the child's injury completely ends her passionate attachment to Egbert. The existence into which she is drawn is that of institutional religion, the Roman Catholic Church. Here she finds an alternative to the life of passion, sensuality, and distraction she has known with Egbert.

It is from this that Egbert's own ritual of absorption or assimilation follows. When Winifred becomes "purely the *Mater Dolorata*" he finds that for him "she was closed as a tomb, . . . the tomb of his manhood and his fatherhood," an image which both adumbrates his fate and reveals the degree of her responsibility. Like the primitive scapegoat, he finds that he is shut out forever from the community he has known, compelled "to turn aside," to wander "hither and thither, desultory," possessed of "no real home." Even clearer evidence of his assumption of the role of ritual outcast from society is the hatchet-like cleft in his brow developed since the accident which he bears as his Cain-like "stigma." It is this together with his relation to her and her family that gives him for Winifred "the Ishmael quality." But the scapegoat is not simply the creature who wanders in lonely isolation until overtaken by death. It is also representative of the divinity whose death is preordained as an elaborate ritual of sacrifice. Egbert's divinity is revealed by his appearing to Winifred's now nun-like soul as "an erect, supple symbol of life, the living body" and to her Christianized eyes as "Baal and Ashtaroth," "a supple living idol" that "if she watched him she was damned."

To her he appears godlike, but to himself he is the object of sacrifice. Thus, in the landscape bits of vegetation seem to him "like a sprinkling of sacrificial blood." And from this his imagination comes to be dominated by "the savage old spirit of the place: the desire for old gods, old, lost passions, the passion of the cold-blooded, darting snakes that hissed and shot away from him, the mystery of blood-sacrifices, all the lost, intense sensations of the primeval people of the place, whose passions seethed in the air still, from those long days before the Romans came."

The opportunity for the blood-sacrifice of the scapegoat is provided by the war into which he is projected by his wife and father-in-law. With his enlistment the various rites associated with the scapegoat are performed. The customary inversion of the social hierarchy is reflected in Egbert's awareness that joining the army meant "he was going to put himself into the power of his inferiors. . . . He was going to subjugate himself." Similarly, Winifred's being "so ready to serve the *soldier*, when she repudiated the man" (Lawrence's italics) mirrors the scapegoat's being permitted sexual intercourse with a woman usual forbidden him. And finally, Egbert's being wounded twice before his death approximates the custom of beating and wounding the scapegoat before putting him to death. By these rites he is confirmed in his role; now he is not simply expelled from his family, he has "gone out of life, beyond the pale of life." Nor is it without significance that Lawrence should present Egbert under the image of "a man who is going to take a jump from a height," for the scapegoat commonly met his fate by being hurled from a cliff. Out of these rites comes a feeling of participation in an inescapable experience that sustains him through even his death agonies and permits him to will the completion of the scapegoat ritual by which the myth of the dying god is enacted.

## III

"The Virgin and the Gypsy" elaborates the myth of the virgin whose salvation follows from her exposure to a sacrificial death. Central to this salvation is her meeting the stranger, the gypsy who focusses her resistance to her narrow, hypocritical family and its "rectory morality." When instead of concealing or ignoring "the dark, tremulous potent secret of her virginity" she accepts its power to arouse desire, she is capable of accepting the challenge of the outcast which is none other than to become an outcast oneself, to dare to go one's own way.

The steps by which Yvette comes to this awareness are all designed to underscore the mythical and ritualistic character of the narrative. Thus, the first meeting between the young people and the gypsies is described in only partly ironical fashion as occurring between Christians and pagans. Emerging from her private palm-reading session with the gypsy woman, Yvette maintains a "witch-like silence," a manner that is intensified later at a dance when she suggests a "young virgin *witch*" (Lawrence's italics) who "might metamorphose into something uncanny." This quality appears only after her meeting with the stranger, a figure traditionally thought to cast spells and perform other magical feats. And significantly enough, Lawrence twice repeats that the gypsy-stranger's desire exercises a spell-like power over her. As a result of this, too, she finds her soul stolen from her body and drawn to the world of the gypsies.

Nor is the gypsy simply the stranger as magician; he is also the stranger as the representative of the fertility spirit. This is borne out not only by the sexual power Yvette perceives in him and by his being linked with a kindling fire but also by Yvette's being likened in his presence to a flower about to blossom, an act for which he is responsible. His absorption with "the mysterious fruit of her virginity," Mrs. Fawcett's insistence that for Yvette to have a love affair with him would be prostitution, and Mr. Eastwood's declaration that "he's a resurrected man," all combine to identify him as the fertility figure who appears as a stranger to assist in the ritual defloration of unmarried girls.

Strikingly enough, this ritual itself does not seem to take place in the story, though some readers may feel that the ending of Section IX is discreetly ambiguous on this score. Instead, like Mabel, Yvette participates first in a watery sacrifice of her life and then in a divestiture before a fertility figure that restores her to a full sense of life's significance. Her encounter with the water is both a ritual of purgation or purification and protection. The first of these is borne out not only by the usual purificatory qualities attached to water but also by the presence of the larch and laurel trees, both of which are sacred and one of which forms a part of traditional ceremonies of purification. Yet from its being a raging torment to which Yvette is exposed, it is clear that this rite is more than baptismal in character. It is also the ritual sacrifice that precedes the baptismal introduction into a new existence. The Andromeda aspect of the story is subtly brought out by the image of the water as "*a devouring flood*" (my italics). This image together with the attendant descriptions suggests that the threat to which Yvette is exposed is both that of the folklore monster (it is described as "a shaggy, tawny wave-front of water advancing like a wall of lions") and the universal flood that represents a return to chaos.

As stories like "Daughters of the Vicar" make clear, however, chaos in itself is not an unrewarding prospect for Lawrence. It represents that dissolution of the old existence without which no new life can come into being and acquire form. Thus, when Yvette feels "as if the flood was in her soul," we see that it is a psychological dissolution of universal proportions as well as a terrifying natural event. As a ritual of protection, the torrential stream is linked to flood sagas such as in the Bible. The central point here is that the flood functions as a judgment and punishment whereby only the righteous are preserved from destruction. The death by water of the Mater signifies the final assessment of her evil nature. In effect, then, the scene recapitulates Wundt's point that the universal flood (*Sintflut*) develops into a sin flood (*Sündflut*).

With the removal of Yvette's dress, a "death-gripping thing," her purgation of the old, death-like existence of the family is complete, and as prophesied by the gypsy woman, she comes into contact with the dark man who stirs the flame warming her heart. Her understanding of what he has done for her is seen in her acquiescence to his subsequent departure. Like the fertility figure of myth, he lives the cyclic existence of the nomad so that his disappearance is as inevitable as his appearance. Pointing up this parallel is the comment on the letter from "some unknown place:" "And only then she realized that he had a name." By her belated discovery of the gypsy's name, Lawrence emphasizes the archetypal nature of the entire story. Essentially, then, the two leading characters participate in what T. H. Gaster's *Thespis* regards as the true function of myth, namely, the translation of "the punctual into terms of the durative, the real into those of the ideal." As Yvette Saywell and Joe Boswell, they are characters, human beings; as the virgin and the gypsy, they are archetypes with associations that extend far beyond the rectory and village of Papplewick.

IV

A quite different kind of myth is employed by Lawrence in *The Fox* and *St. Mawr*, namely, the animal or totemic myth. In totemism an intimate relation is assumed between certain human beings and certain natural or artificial objects, the latter being called the totems of the former. The outlines of the totemic myth are most apparent in *The Fox* partly because it is shorter and partly because it is a much less complex story than *St. Mawr*. *The Fox* deals with the development and resolution of a romantic triangle involving two girls and a man. Through the use of psychological associations and prophetic dreams the story gradually brings out its totemic form. At the outset Nellie March and Jill Banford are gentlemen farmers who are rather consistently unsuccessful because of a combination of their disinclination for hard work and of their unfortunate circumstances, the most notable of which is a marauding fox that carries off their hens. The first stage in the development of the totemic myth occurs when Nellie encounters the fox one evening, for as a result "she was spellbound—she knew he knew her. So he looked into her eyes, and her soul failed her." The depth of the impression made on her by this meeting is indicated in part by Lawrence's repetition of the image of the spell and possession five times in the two pages following. Ultimately "it was the fox which somehow dominated her unconsciousness, possessed the blank half of her musing," a state that continues from August to November.

The second stage of the myth is reached with the arrival of Henry Grenfel in search of his grandfather, the former owner of the farm and now dead. The stage of confrontation is succeeded by one of identification. Nellie first finds herself "spellbound" by Henry just as by the fox; then she sees the man as quite literally the animal. This identification is due first to his physical appearance and later to his basic form of behavior, that of a fox-like secret watcher. With this stage the totem moves into her consciousness from her unconscious; with the animal-man "in full presence" she accepts the spell that hitherto has been imposed on her and abandons the attempt "to keep up two planes of consciousness." Now "she could at last lapse into the odor of the fox," for the strangeness of her attraction has been modified by the appearance of the man.

The story then enters on the third or prophetic phase of the myth. For the very night of Henry's arrival Nellie dreams of herself and the fox: "It was the fox singing. He was very yellow and bright, like corn. She went nearer to him, but he ran away and ceased singing. He seemed near, and she wanted to touch him. She stretched out her hand, but suddenly he bit her wrist, and at the same instant, as she drew back, the fox, turning round to bound away, whisked his brush across her face, and it seemed his brush was on fire, for it seared and burned her mouth with a great pain." The prophecy immediately begins to work itself out next morning when Nellie notices that "something about the glint of his khaki reminded her of the brilliance of her dream-fox." It is fulfilled a fortnight later when Henry declares his love to Nellie and asks her to marry him, for as she is about to join Jill upstairs, "quick as lightning he kissed her on the mouth, with a quick brushing kiss."

While prophetic concerning their ultimate relationship, the dream is also revelatory about the nature of the fox and, by extension, Henry. To anyone familiar with *The Golden Bough*, the above description of the fox suggests that he is to be identified with the primitive fertility deity or, more specifically, with Dionysus as the corn-spirit. Significantly enough, during harvest season the man who hits the last corn with his sickle is called the Fox and during the evening dances with all the girls. Thus, in Frazer as well as Lawrence fertility figure, man, and animal are all connected. Nor is it irrelevant that at the beginning of the story, before confronting either the fox or Henry, the two girls regard the fox as "a demon." He moves from devil to god as Nellie becomes increasingly aware of what he represents and of what she desires. At the same time, in its appearing to Nellie that "his brush was on fire," the dream hints too at the fate of the fox. This image recalls the custom of fastening burning torches to foxes' tails as punishment for having destroyed the crops in the past. In this there is perhaps an oblique foreshadowing of the fox's death at the hands of Henry and his gun.

The prophetic phase adumbrates the phallic relation of Nellie and Henry, the death of the fox, and, in a second dream of Nellie's, the death of Jill. In the last stage of the myth, that of the sacrificial action, these events are made real. The story's problem, of course, centers on the human triangle; though Nellie is drawn to Henry, Jill stands resolutely between them, threatening the success of his pursuit. The only resolution can be the removal of Jill herself in some swift, irreversible fashion. Preparatory to this, however, Henry slays the fox, an action that is too heavily emphasized to be merely gratuitous plot embroidery. In point of fact, this reflects that part of the totemic myth in which the divine animal is solemnly sacrificed as part of, an annual ritual.

A clue to the most important reason for Henry's slaying of the fox is Frazer's remark that totemism "appears to be mainly a crude, almost childlike attempt to satisfy the primary wants of man," an attempt that operates through the magical creation of that which is sought. For what Henry clearly wants is Nellie, and to this end he eventually attempts the removal of Jill. What he creates is, in short, the absence of Jill, an event that is magical in the sense that it is apparently uncaused and yet follows from the concentrated will of Henry. The slaying of the fox is both a rehearsal and a primitive adumbration of the human death insofar as it demonstrates Henry's resolve in the face of the sacrificial slaying of the creature most sacred to the society. To observe the totemic sacrifice of the fox is to be able to perform it in connection with the totem of modern society, namely, another human being.

In carrying out this twin sacrifice, Henry employs what van Gennep calls "*le rite positif*" in which the individual's wish is translated into an act. Central here is the ability to focus one's spiritual and emotional energies on a single end: "In his heart he had decided her death. A terrible still force seemed in him, and a power that was just his. If he turned even a hair's breadth in the wrong direction, he would lose the power." This rite of separation by sacrifice is identical with that of assimilation by which Henry draws Nellie to him. In both cases the act is first mimed in the imagination as a magical guarantee of its physical success. Like Frazer's savages, Henry believes that the central feature of the hunt resides in the conquest of the soul: "First of all, even before you come in sight of your quarry, there is a strange battle, like mesmerism. Your own soul, as a hunter, has gone out to fasten on the soul of the deer, even before you see any deer. And the soul of the deer fights to escape. Even before the deer has any wind of you, it is so. It is a subtle, profound battle of wills which takes place in the invisible." And it is in this spirit that Henry stalks, in turn, Nellie, the fox, and finally, Jill.

These rites, however, are not simply isolated events performed for immediate practical ends; they are also the behavioral concomitant of Henry's character and the culmination of his prototypical social function. For just prior to Jill's death Henry is likened to "a huntsman who is watching a flying bird." That this is more than a casual simile is suggested by Jill's having been described as a bird on more than one occasion. Even more, important is the scene that inaugurated the hunt motif, the scene in which Henry first thinks of marrying Nellie. Lawrence here emphasizes Henry's basic nature: "He was a huntsman in spirit, not a farmer, and not a soldier stuck in a regiment. And it was as a young hunter that he wanted to bring down March as his quarry, to make her his wife." With this, we find a broader perspective on the totemic myth and ritual, one which links it to a way of life characteristic of the society itself. Frazer formulates this pattern clearly when he observes that although totemism "probably always originated in the hunting stage of society, it has by no means been confined to that primitive phase of human development but has often survived not only into the pastoral but into the agricultural stage." And as we have seen, in *The Fox* the survival of totemism and the mingling of the two stages of society are both present: in the midst of the agricultural life of the two girls appears both the totemic respectful awe of the fox felt by Nellie and the "stranger-youth" who is a hunter.

Just as the totemic myth and ritual underlies the narrative development, so it also defines the relationships of the characters. For Nellie, Henry is the totem animal to be revered and respected; for Jill, whose own totem is the bird, he is the sinister antagonist, a natural enemy to be feared. For Henry, Nellie March is the game he seeks, while Jill is a bothersome creature whose intrusive demands and influence on Nellie ultimately overcome the taboo on man-slaying. Thus, in a sense, both women are objects of the hunt, the one because she is desired, the other because she is not. Mediating between them is the fox who is also overcome by the hunter. In the case of Jill, as already noted, the fox slaying is a rehearsal for the human death. Nellie, on the other hand, is won over completely following the death of the fox. What is contingent and fortuitous in the realism of the narrative pattern becomes necessary and inevitable in terms of the totemic myth. For Nellie, the fox, her totem, contains what Frazer calls the external soul, that projection of one's life drives into the objective world which keeps one in contact with reality and so alive as an individual. With the slaying of the fox Henry has acquired her soul and so can sway her to his will, an achievement symbolized by her changing from breeches, "strong as armor," to a dress in which she is "accessible." From all of this it is apparent that if, as Malinowski says in *Magic, Science, and Religion*, totemism is "a mode of social grouping and a religious system of beliefs and practices," then it is central to the meaning of *The Fox*. The various attitudes toward the fox obviously produce conflicting groups within the society as a whole. At the same time, Henry's drive to marry Nellie qualifies as religious in Malinowski's sense, that is, as expressing the desire "to control the most important objects" in man's surroundings.

*Modern Fiction Studies*, V, Spring, 1959.

## R.P. Draper: "The Defeat of Feminism: D.H. Lawrence's *The Fox* and 'The Woman Who Rode Away' "

*The Fox* and "The Woman Who Rode Away," tales about the defeat of woman's independence, are part of Lawrence's answer to the suffragettes. Already in *Sons and Lovers* he had shown a militant feminist, Clara Dawes, up in arms against the tyranny of man, when what she really wants, as Paul Morel conveniently discovers, is to be reunited with her husband. More seriously, the histories of Mrs. Morel and Miriam reflect the influence of strong-willed, high-minded women who think they know as well as a man himself what is good for him. What Lawrence thought of such women in later life, when his sympathy for his mother had almost turned sour, is summed up in the essay "Women Are So Cocksure": "As sure as a woman has the whip-hand over her destiny and the destinies of those near her, so sure will she make a mess of her own destiny, and a muddle of the others."

In *The Rainbow* and *Women in Love* his theme is similar—"woman becoming individual, self-responsible, taking her own initiative" (letter of 22 April 1914)—although the treatment is far more sympathetic and intelligently balanced. Despite his anti-feminist attitude, Lawrence possessed a markedly feminine, temperament; and this, aided by a quite considerable amount of self-identification with the character of Ursula, gives a quality of inwardness and sympathetic understanding to his presentation of the modern, independent-minded woman in these two novels. *The Fox* and "The Woman Who Rode Away" are undeniably inferior in this respect. They come much nearer to exemplifying the cruder attitude of "Women Are So Cocksure."  But they also have two very important compensating qualities. Firstly, we see the defeat of woman as a recovery of her lost self, which, even though it is associated with a distorting simplification of the roles of male and or female, releases Lawrence's own feminine awareness in passages of great visionary power. Secondly, Lawrence pushes to an extreme the more reactionary view of woman informing these two stories where he brings out into the open the extravagances and vindictive motivation of this view. This has unpleasant consequences but is a valuable, and fundamentally healthy, process. It is an immersion in the destructive element from which self-knowledge becomes at least a possibility.

*The Fox*, started in 1918 and finished in Taormina in 1921, belongs to the period at the end of the First World War. During the war the suffragette movement was in abeyance, but the shortage of men on the home front was giving far more effective support to the feminist cause than any of the previous agitations had done. The government called upon more and more women to work like men in factories and on the land, to dress like men, to behave like men. Other stories besides *The Fox* show Lawrence's interest in all this. "Tickets, Please," which first appeared in the *Strand* (April 1919), is a story about girls who replaced men tram-conductors and their relationship with a philandering ticket inspector, aptly named John Thomas Raynor—"always called John Thomas, except sometimes in malice, Coddy." His sexual conceit is given a rough tumble when the girls with whom he has played around once too often corner him in their lounge and beat him up. [Harry T. Moore suggests that there might have been a personal experience behind this story. The girls in the surgical firm where Lawrence worked as a young man are said to have "pounced on him, and tried to expose his sex." (*The Intelligent Heart*)]. In another tale, "Monkey Nuts," first published in 1922 but completed before the summer of 1919, Lawrence writes satirically about a land-girl who reverses the customary roles of the sexes and becomes the wooer of a shy young soldier. This story has the same Berkshire setting as *The Fox*, and its land-girl may very well be based on the same person as became March. The war is also an important part of the background of *The Fox*. Lawrence refers to the Daylight Saving Bill, to the food shortage, to soldiering in France and Salonika, and at one point to the specific year 1918. And he describes March, if not Banford, as wearing puttees and breeches, belted coat and loose cap—the semi-military uniform of the land-girl, in which she looks "almost like some graceful, loose-balanced young man."

March and Banford, though not specifically replacing men who have gone to the war, are putting into practice the notion of female independence and equality with the male. They form a "couple" of their own, Banford the woman, March the man. But the union is barren. Their farming is not a success because the two girls cannot put really creative energy into their work. Their hens prove infertile, and they panic when one of the heifers is about to calve. They lack the single-mindedness of men; the cultural frills are as important to them as the business of farming. Above all, ". . . they seemed to have to live too much off themselves." Their feminist self-sufficiency excludes them from the main stream of life.

March, however, is not the "man" that her clothes and her work proclaim her. "But her face was not a man's face ever"; and the false part that she is playing brings an unconsciously "satirical flicker" into her eyes. This is a weakness in the Lesbian ménage that the coming of the fox exploits. March's failure to shoot when she has the opportunity is part of her own vulnerability, merely disguised by the masculine pose she has adopted. The very effort that she has to make to be on the lookout for the fox reveals her unfulfilled condition: she lapses into an "Odd, rapt state, her mouth rather screwed up. It was a question whether she was there, actually consciously present, or not." The fox holds her "spellbound" (the word is one that Lawrence insists upon), against her will, and yet without an effect of arbitrary magic. It is an actual beast out there in the natural world, charged, however, with a poetic aura and conveying a hint of mockery that makes it a creature of special significance for March. Its mesmeric influence does not affect Banford or Henry because its power to influence is dependent upon, and even to some extent created by, the frustration unconsciously existing within March herself. The *mana* is also transferable. When Henry appears on the scene, closely resembling the fox in several physical details, this mesmeric influence becomes his—superficially because of the resemblance, but fundamentally because it is he who can fulfill the unconscious need, the resemblance being more in the nature of an effect than a cause. Not that he is essentially a glamorous person, any more than March is. For all the false ideas that have grown up about the Lawrentian hero—fed, it must be admitted, by Lawrence himself through the creation of such spurious figures as Count Psanek and Don Cipriano—the man who comes to satisfy the unfulfilled woman does not have to be some incredible exotic. If the assumptions involved are romantic, Lawrence is not guilty of a fairy tale, or in its debased form a women's magazine romanticism. Henry exists in the story as a rather ordinary, even vulgar, young man, nothing remotely resembling a Prince Charming. But where Lawrence parts company with other realists is in accepting the transforming glow of sexual desire as an aspect of reality. He even sets up a deliberate opposition between the realism of the enlightened Banford, who sees no more than the vulgarity of Henry, and the kind of vision that descends upon March when she feels the pull of the unconscious "bond" with Henry. And the opposition expresses itself within March as a conflict between the needs of her real self and the false demands and protests of her modern woman's independent self.

The story also involves a reevaluation of realism. Lawrence is careful to preserve a convincingly naturalistic surface. Henry's reason for suddenly turning up at the farm is plausible; the dialogue between the three main characters is prosaically matter-of-fact; and Lawrence keeps the growth of events—Henry's slow winning of March's confidence, for example, counterpointed with rising hostility between him and Banford—from violating the reader's sense of probability. But concurrently with this, the reader feels Henry's presence at a different, and more compelling, level of reality. If we could view the events independently of Lawrence's narrative, it might seem that Henry's power was merely hallucinatory. Within the story, which is the only place where we can in fact view the events, the power is far more real than the commonplace world that the "realism" of the story presents. Lawrence does not belittle the surface, either intentionally or by failure to give it appropriate substance; but as in Wordsworth's "Resolution and Independence," where the old leechgatherer's voice becomes "like a stream/Scarce heard," a visionary awareness supervenes upon the commonplace reality for which in some way it is a source of strength. March struggles against the spell of Henry, her modern feminism being in conflict with the visionary awareness; and this makes an important difference between the experiences recorded in the tale and in the poem. She has to undergo the Wordsworthian experience in spite of herself:

> March was busy in the kitchen preparing another meal. It was seven o'clock. All the time, while she was active, she was attending to the youth in the sitting-room, not so much listening to what he said as feeling the soft run of his voice. She primmed up her mouth tighter and tighter, puckering it as if it were sewed, in her effort to keep her will uppermost. Yet her large eyes dilated and glowed in spite of her; she lost herself.

As a "lost girl," March has many sisters among Lawrence's stories and novels, and like them she loses contact with the world of commonplace reality as the price of finding herself at a deeper level.

In the passage just quoted, Lawrence sets March's strain "to keep her will uppermost" against the dilation and glowing of her eyes. Julian Moynahan has drawn attention (in *The Deed of Life*) to the significance of eye-references in *The Fox*. The responsiveness betrayed in March's eyes, the sharpness and "fixed attention" in Henry's, and the weakness of Banford's sight are details that at once belong to the naturalistic surface of the tale and that also through varied repetition acquire a symbolic status. The purpose of the symbolism thus built up within the story is to give the reader imaginative access to the deeper level of reality where, in spite of their seeming incompatibilities, March and Henry meet. The eye is a symbol traditionally associated in works as various as *King Lear* and "The Hollow Men" with the reevaluation of reality, and it has similar associations in *The Fox*. A striking example occurs in a passage following a more than usually banal conversation among March, Banford, and Henry:

> "Do you get so tired, then?" he asked.
> "So bored," said Banford.
> "Oh" he said gravely. "But why should you be bored?"
> "Who wouldn't be bored?" said Banford. "I'm sorry to hear that," he said gravely.
> "You must be, if you were hoping to have a lively time here," said Banford.
> He looked at her long and gravely.
> "Well," he said, with his odd, young seriousness, "it's quite lively enough for me."
> "I'm glad to hear it," said Banford.
> And she returned to her book. In her thin, frail hair were already many threads of grey, though she was not yet thirty. The boy did not look down, but turned his eyes to March, who was sitting with pursed mouth laboriously crocheting, her eyes wide and absent. She had a warm, pale, fine, skin, and a delicate nose. Her pursed mouth looked shrewish. But the shrewish look was contradicted by the curious lifted arch of her dark brows, and the wideness of her eyes; a look of startled wonder and vagueness. She was listening again for the fox, who seemed to have wandered farther off into the night.

The repetition of *bored* recalls the "I'd be bored. You'd be bored" exchange between Sweeney and Doris in "Sweeney Agonistes." It is symptomatic of a life lived only on the surface level of reality, and there are accompanying suggestions in Banford's premature aging and March's pursed mouth and shrewish look of a withering from within. But these suggestions are "contradicted" in March by her complexion, her dark brows and especially her eyes, which reveal how far she has withdrawn from this surface world and is yielding to the more compelling reality of Henry and the fox.

We can make another comparison between Lawrence and Eliot in their treatment of the deeper level of reality. For both of them it is initially painful. In "Burnt Norton" the vision of the pool "filled with water out of sunlight" is momentary only: "human kind/Cannot bear very much reality." The Birth at last found by the wise men in "Journey of the Magi" was "Hard and bitter agony for us, like Death, our death." There is a similarly double-edged quality in March's dream of the fox:

That night March dreamed vividly. She dreamed she heard a singing outside which she could not understand, a singing that roamed round the house, in the fields, and in the darkness. It moved her so that she felt she must weep. She went out, and suddenly she knew it was the fox singing. He was very yellow and bright, like corn. She went nearer to him, but he ran away and ceased singing. He seemed near, and she wanted to touch him. She stretched out her hand, but suddenly he bit her wrist, and at the same instant, as she drew back, the fox, turning round to bound away, whisked his brush across her face, and it seemed his brush was on fire, for it seared and burned her mouth with a great pain. She awoke with the pain of it, and lay trembling as if she were really seared.

The fox is sweet, desirable, and, through the image of the corn, associated with natural fertility—an intentional contrast with the barrenness of March and Banford's farming. But it is also savage and terribly hurtful. By making this not simply a beautiful but also an extremely painful, vision, Lawrence hints that the reality that attracts March contains the agony of destruction as well as the joy of creative release. The paradox of the dream is realized in Henry, who not only hurts March by destroying her friendship with Banford, but also as an effect upon her that is more like paralysis, or the cauterizing of a wound, than the ecstasy of romantic love. This is, of course, part of a hearing process; the pain and destruction that come with Henry and the fox are counterbalanced by a regenerative process that restores March to her true self and brings appearance and reality into accord. March, for example, puts on a dress one evening instead of her land-girl's uniform, and Henry notices that "Through the crape her woman's form seemed soft and womanly." Passivity and a longing for sleep—appearance and feeling alike indicating the emergence of true femininity as feminist assertion gives way—replaced the feeling of responsibility that had been a "great stimulant" for March, but also a deadly strain. Yet there is something harsh even here, a quality almost of violation in the "helplessness and submission" that is imposed upon March, and Lawrence admits at the end: "Something was missing. Instead of her soul swaying with new life, it seemed to droop, to bleed, as if it were wounded."

The destruction-creation theme is tainted by a strain of vindictiveness in Henry's triumph over Banford, about which Lawrence himself is ambiguous. When Henry announces that he is going to marry March, we read that he is a "bright and gloating youth," the second adjective seeming to evoke a feeling that Lawrence approves rather than condemns. This is unpleasantly confirmed by the later scene in which Henry watches Banford struggle back from the station with her arms full of parcels, and mutters: "You're a nasty little thing, you are." The ambiguity stretches to his wooing of March as well. The paragraph describing his decision to hunt her down like a deer is powerful and psychologically convincing but also repellent in its reduction of March to the status of mere quarry. And because of the symbolic identity of Henry and the fox, it is impossible to isolate from Henry himself the sadistic element in the presentation of the fox. Lawrence may here be attempting to communicate the cruelty inevitable in the Dionysian mixture of savagery and vitality, but Henry's sulkiness and resentment when not getting his own way are not so easily explained. There is some truth in Banford's view of him:

"Oh, Nellie, he'll despise you, he'll despise you, like the awful little beast he is, if you give way to him. I'd no more trust him than I'd trust a cat not to steal. He's deep, he's deep, and he's bossy, and he's selfish through and through, as cold as ice. All he wants is to make use of you. And when you're no more use to him, then I pity you."

As March says, he is not as bad as all that; but it is an old rhetorical trick to undermine a potentially embarrassing view by exaggerating it and putting it in the mouth of a discredited opponent. Something of what Banford says sticks. Henry is, after all, willful and bullying, and the fact that Lawrence is honest enough to present him so is an important piece of authorial self-criticism.

At the end of the story—the "longer tail" that was added, significantly, during the Sicily revision—the domineering insistency of Henry becomes more evident. At the same time he becomes more of a mouthpiece for Lawrence's own theory of the utter separateness of the sexes. (Parts of this last section read almost like an extract from the roughly contemporary *Fantasia of the Unconscious*.) March, too, loses her individuality and becomes an abstraction representing all women who try to usurp male responsibility and imagine that they can find happiness. In all this Lawrence is his worst, tiresomely jeering, self.

The one passage in which he recovers his power to write evocatively and compellingly is a description of the state of mind that Henry demands from the unwilling March:

No, she had to be passive, to acquiesce, and to be submerged under the surface of love. She had to be like the seaweeds she saw as she peered down from the boat, swaying for ever delicately under water, with all their delicate fibrils put tenderly out upon the flood, sensitive, utterly sensitive and receptive within the shadowy sea, and never, never rising and looking forth above water while they lived. Never never looking forth from the water until they died, only then washing, corpses, upon the surface. But while they lived, always submerged, always beneath the wave. Beneath the wave they might have powerful roots, stronger than iron; they might be tenacious and dangerous in their soft waving within the flood. Beneath the water they might be stronger, more indestructible than resistant oak-trees are on land. But it was always under water, always under water. And she, being a woman, must be like that.

This is feminine, but not restrictively female; not so much a statement about the nature of woman as a quality of mind akin to Keats's negative capability or a "Consider the lilies of the field" insouciance. ("Insouciance" is the revised title of a relevant essay by Lawrence, originally called "Over-earnest Ladies.") It is a condition of creative relaxation in which consciousness of self—for Lawrence the peculiarly modern disease—gives way to immersion in the flux of life. The hyper-conscious and strenuously competitive nature of modern life is something that we might metaphorically call "masculine," and then by comparison this "sensitive and receptive" state would be "feminine." Particular men and women, however, are complex beings in whom both active and passive principles exist and need to exist. To simplify them into wholly masculine males and wholly feminine females in accordance with Lawrentian theory would be to destroy them as living human beings. From this point of view March's reluctance to abandon herself unquestioningly to her husband is a sign of health. Lawrence does not explode the theory—and, as later work, including "The Woman Who Rode Away," shows, he continued to be addicted to it—but at least implies a scepticism by the conclusion in which nothing is concluded. Not only March, but also Lawrence "can't tell what it will be like over there."

"The Woman Who Rode Away" repeats on a larger, mythical scale the contradictions and confusions of *The Fox*. What Lawrence muted in the earlier tale, in this story he gives extreme development—though he still balks at the final translation of theory into imagined action. In particular, his attack on modern feminism receives its sharpest and most explicit expression in the woman's thoughts on her own impending death:

> Her kind of womanhood, intensely personal and individual, was to be obliterated again, and the great primeval symbols were to tower once more over the fallen individual independence of woman. The sharpness and the quivering nervous consciousness of the highly-bred white woman was to be destroyed again, womanhood was to be cast once more into the great stream of impersonal sex and impersonal passion.

Lawrence gives greater emphasis to self-consciousness here than in *The Fox* and the theme of the tale is correspondingly more generalized. The annihilation of the entire mode of Western intellectual civilization is at stake, for the sacrifice of the woman will enable the blood-consciousness of the Indians to triumph over the mind-consciousness of the white man. But as in *The Fox*, the fate of the independent modem woman remains the central concern of the tale. And again as in *The Fox* we feel the woman to be the object of compassionate rescue and of vindictive outrage.

The sterility that Lawrence obliquely shows to be the result of the Banford-March relationship is starkly presented at the beginning of "The Woman Who Rode Away" in the surrealistic setting of the woman's home. Lawrence's insistence on its deadness anticipates his description of Tevershall in *Lady Chatterley's Lover*; and Lederman, the woman's husband, is equally an anticipation of Sir Clifford Chatterley. He and the scientists who make an expedition to the Chilchui Indians, but see "nothing extraordinary," are representative of modern indifference to all that evokes mystery and wonder. For Lederman "Savages are savages, and all savages behave more or less alike: rather low-down and dirty, insanitary, with a few cunning tricks, and struggling to get enough to eat." To be able to see the Indians, as the woman does, in a more romantic light is a sign of grace. Though at first she feels it to be a "foolish romanticism more unreal than a girl's," when the woman sets out in search of the Chilchuis, she falls increasingly under its influence. Eventually, like March, she becomes "spell-bound, and as if drugged"; and in this condition she achieves a visionary awareness that is the very opposite of the denial of wonder from which she has fled.

Lawrence, however, makes no simple antithesis between the woman and the deadness she seeks to escape. She is, or has been, as much a meaningless "dynamo of energy" as her husband. As a "rather dazzling Californian girl from Berkeley" she represents an egalitarian, yet intensely competitive, society and a more advanced stage of feminism than we find in *The Fox*. The failure of her marriage has undermined her confidence, but the details of her behaviour show that she is still a woman of that world. She insists on having a horse of her own and dreams of "being free as she bad been as a girl, among the hills of California." Her voice is an "assured, American woman's voice," and in her eyes there is "a half-childish, half-arrogant confidence in her own female power" (though balanced by "a curious look of trance"). Her ride to the Chilchuis is itself an expression of her independence. From the Indians who guide her she expects as a matter of course both social and sexual recognition, and when they rebuff her, "All the passionate anger of the spoilt white woman rose in her." But these are in a sense the twitches of the corpse, evidence that the woman is part of the sterility of her civilization. On her journey she seems to hear "a great crash at the centre of herself, which was the crash of her own death." The whole of the first section of the tale, not only the opening, is thus a prolonged death movement, culminating in a symbolic night of coldness, numbness, and death: "All was silent, mountain-silent, cold, deathly. She slept and woke and slept in a semi-conscious numbness of cold and fatigue. A long, long night, icy and eternal, and she was aware that she had died."

Section II, a life-movement counterpoising the death-movement of Section I, opens with the striking of flint and "a red splutter of fire". With the dawn comes heat, and then "in the full blaze of the mid-morning sun" the woman has her first sight of the Indian village. It is an idealized place, in some ways suggestive of the Utopian Eastwood of Lawrence's "Autobiographical Fragment," neat, glittering with white houses and having gardens "full of flowers and herbs and fruit-trees"; and as against the crude, dehumanized squalor of the mining town this has "a soft narrow track between leaves and grass, a path worn smooth by centuries of human feet, no hoof of horse nor any wheel to disfigure it." The Indians themselves wear the flame colors of red, orange, yellow, and black; their steps are "soft and heavy and swift" and they move rhythmically. Their old chief has the dignity and visionary splendor (he "roused himself like a vision") of an Old Testament prophet. It is astonishing how much of this, inspired as it is by Mexico and the American Southwest, recalls the idealized countryside and chapel-going fervor of Lawrence's youth. The world to which the woman has come is a recovered Eden of warmth and natural human dignity.

But the longing which gives rise to this idyllic, yet vigorous, pastoral is also in Lawrence something bitterly frustrated. As a result, what might have been a simple Golden Age fantasy turns into a weird complex of idealism and vindictiveness. Having persuaded himself that Western civilization is responsible for the strangulation of this ideal, and that the independent-minded white woman is the epitome of the strained consciousness on which Western civilization is based, Lawrence exults in the subjugation of the woman by the Indians and craves the satisfaction of her sacrifice. The matter is further complicated, however, for Lawrence is not content that the woman should die she must also be converted. Her physical death followed a spiritual death that has reduced her to the passivity demanded of woman by the Lawrentian theory. Accordingly, despite her remaining a victim who cannot be said to give more than hallucinated consent to her fate, the woman receives the reward of the "feminine" vision proposed for March at the end of *The Fox*:

> Afterwards she felt a great soothing languor steal over her, her limbs felt strong and loose and full of languor, and she lay on her couch listening to the sounds of the village, watching the yellowing sky, smelling the scent of burning cedar-wood, or pine-wood. So distinctly she heard the yapping of tiny dogs, the shuffle of far-off feet, the murmur of voices, so keenly she detected the smell of smoke, and flowers, and evening falling, so vividly she saw the one bright star infinitely remote, stirring above the sunset, that she felt as if all her senses were diffused on the air, that she could distinguish the sound of evening flowers unfolding, and the actual crystal sound of the heavens, as the vast belts of the world-atmosphere slid past one another, and as if the moisture ascending and the moisture descending in the air resounded like some harp in the cosmos.

The heightened sensitivity described in this passage is matched by other moving descriptions of a state of mind that annihilates self-consciousness, the woman's senses being released "into a sort of heightened, mystic acuteness and a feeling as if she were diffusing out deliciously into the harmony of things." Through such passages Lawrence communicates a feeling of relaxation and renewal that succeeds in making the woman's experience seem the satisfaction of a deep human need. But, as the context reasserts itself, he reminds us, inevitably, and even with something like malevolent purpose, that the woman is a prisoner, that her visions are drug-induced, and that she is being deliberately conditioned to accept the part of victim in a ritual sacrifice. The resulting impression is that Lawrence is wresting his own vision to suit some incompatible end that is more like vengeance than regeneration.

Lawrence's treatment of the Indians involves similar contradictions. When he is describing their dancing in long rhythmic periods of hypnotic repetition, he makes completely convincing their symbolic identification with the sources of natural power. The language vibrates on the mind as immediately as a physical sensation; the Indians seem the very embodiment of vital energy. In this respect they are a mythopoeic extension of the wild regenerative force associated with Henry in *The Fox*. But like Henry, only again on a grander scale, they are also vindictive and treacherous in a peculiarly human way. Lawrence may well have intended the opposite effect—something to be compared with the distinctively animal slyness and bloodthirstiness of the fox. But it is purely human dishonesty that is suggested by the ambiguity in the question ". . . do you bring your heart to the god of the Chilchui?" and again in the answer given to the woman's question about her fate: "Have I got to die and be given to the sun?" she asked.

"Some time," he said, laughing evasively. "Some time we all die." There is more of the animal power that can be represented as inextricably destructive-creative in the description of the priests who watch over the woman just before she is to be sacrificed: ". . . their eyes, with that strange glitter, and their dark, shut mouths that would open to the very broad jaw, the small, strong, white teeth, had something very primitively male and cruel." This is strongly reminiscent of the description of the fox in the earlier tale. But even here the phrase "primitively male and cruel" attaches an ideological animus to what we might otherwise take for a healthy instinctive ferocity.

What distorts Lawrence's treatment both of the woman and of the Indians is the intrusion, as in *The Fox*, of his sexual theory and its accompanying enmity towards the independence of woman. He insists upon the same doctrine of the separateness of the sexes. The Chilchui men have all the colorful glamor and activity—phrases like "darkly and powerfully male" and "storm-like sound of male singing" become almost a cliché. Their women, on the other hand, dress in black and look on passively. And Lawrence invents a somewhat spurious symbolism in which "men are the fire and the daytime" and "women are the spaces between the stars at night," or, alternatively, men are guardians of the sun and women of the moon. Resentment of the woman, not as an individual, but as a representative of her kind, permeates the tale and reveals itself in words like *derision* and *malignancy*, used to describe the Indians' attitude towards her—derogatory, yet seeming to carry Lawrence's approval. This, too, is incorporated in the symbolism as the anger of the moon at being kept in the white woman's cave. And what looks like a reference to cancer (the disease from which Lawrence's mother died) is also incorporated: "'The moon, she bites white women—here inside,' and he pressed his side."

Unpleasant as this element is, it remains in balance with the genuinely visionary element until the time for the ritual sacrifice arrives. Then, in Section III, it dominates the narrative. Lawrence builds up a sickening climax, from the "long, strange, hypnotic massage" that is like a parody of love-making, through the mass-hysteria of the crowd when the woman is shown to them, to the final horrific scene, made the more appalling by the emotions of "glittering eagerness, and awe, and craving" attributed to the Indians. The whole section reads, paradoxical though it may be, like an experiment in deliberate abandonment to the vindictiveness that has been gnawing at the tale throughout.

In *Fantasia of the Unconscious* Lawrence writes of sexual consummation as a thunderstorm that clears the atmosphere, giving release to the "inevitable electric accumulation in the nerves and the blood, an accumulation which weighs there and broods there with intolerable pressure." There is an analogously orgasmic effect in this last section of "The Woman Who Rode Away." Its mounting tension drives towards a final act that is also a consummation, though the real release that can be hoped for is not from the tyranny of mental consciousness, as Lawrence would have us believe, but from the "accumulation in the nerves and the blood" that has manfested itself in the persistent vindictiveness of the tale. The climax, however, remains a suspended one—possibly because the release is there in the writing, and vicariously in the reading, of it; more probably because the clearing of the atmosphere that succeeds it is the subject for a different kind of art. And, as a final speculation, we may find the sequel towards which "The Woman Who Rode Away" points in *Lady Chatterley's Lover* and "The Man Who Died," where Lawrence, though still an opponent of the feminists, is no longer pursued by the demon of his own animosity towards them.

*Studies in Short Fiction*, 3, 1966.

# James C. Cowan, "D.H. Lawrence's 'The Princess' as Ironic Romance"

In D.H. Lawrence's "The Princess," as John B. Vickery has suggested, myth "operates as a kind of second story, almost a double plot which illuminates the basic story by suggesting a link with man's earliest forms of belief and behavior." The basic story, consequently, functions on one level "as a mythic reenactment, as a method of telling a past story through what is now being done."[1] Lawrence employs, as structural and thematic motifs, first, as in *Lady Chatterley's Lover*, the fairy tale of the Sleeping Beauty, and second, as in *The Plumed Serpent*, the "separation—initiation—return" pattern of romance, which Joseph Campbell, using Joyce's term, calls the monomyth. But Lawrence inverts the pattern of quest as the aging princess rejects her would-be prince only to "return" to an even deeper slumber than before. The result is a brilliantly realized ironic romance.

Mary Henrietta Urquhart, whose mother calls her "My Dollie," a name suggesting, as in Ibsen, possession of the plaything rather than love of the person, and whose father calls her "My Princess," a title with multiple allusions to aristocracy of birth, social snobbishness, and the unreality of romance, strikingly resembles her sleeping prototypes. The Germanic Briar Rose falls into her hundred years sleep as the result of a curse laid upon her by the fairy who was not invited to the King's feast honoring her birth. The Norse Brynhild, as punishment for disobeying Odin, is put to sleep until a man shall awaken her. In both, the charm is inculcated by a magic circle: Briar Rose's castle is surrounded by a hedge of thorns, and Brynhild's couch is encircled with fire. As Campbell explains, "This is an image of the magic circle drawn about the personality by the dragon power of the fixating parent," resulting in "an impotence to put off the infantile ego, with its sphere of emotional relationships and ideals." With the parents guarding the threshold, one "fails to make the passage through the door and come to birth in the world without."[2]

Dollie Urquhart's world is defined by the family circle. Lawrence subtly mythicizes her father, Colin, the mad descendent of Scottish kings: "He looked like some old Celtic hero. He looked as if be should have worn a greyish kilt and a sporran, and shown his knees. His voice came direct out of the hushed Ossianic past."[3] Her mother Lawrence disposes of quickly with the omission of particulars that is characteristic of fairy tales. Having "lived three years in the mist and glamour of her husband's presence," "She had no great desire to live. So when the baby was two years old she suddenly died" (pp. 473-474). Dollie herself is characterized by juxtaposed contradictions: "To her father, she was The Princess. To her Boston aunts and uncles she was just *Dollie Urquhart, poor little thing*." Hostesses comment, "She is so quaint and old-fashioned; such a lady, poor little mite!" And the author explains, "She was always grown up; she never really grew up. Always strangely wise, and always childish." (pp. 473-476)

As Dollie develops, or rather fails to develop, under Colin's tutelage, she becomes fixated, as in the extended sleep of her prototypes, at an Oedipal level, suspended in a story-book world in which children pretend to be adults, adults behave like children, and the way to maturity is obstructed for all. Colin early puts Dollie in the ambivalent position of masking fearful distrust with polite condescension. His method of doing so is revealed in his baroque fable of peeling the onion: "You peel everything away from people, and there is a green, upright demon in every man and woman; and this demon is a man's real self, and a woman's real self. It doesn't really care about anybody, it belongs to the demons and the primitive fairies, who never care." Dollie, Colin says, is the last of the "royal fairy women," but she must keep this fact a secret since others, envious of her state, will try to kill her. She must, therefore, treat others with *noblesse oblige* but not, since they are commoners, as her equals (pp. 475-476). Colin is presenting, of course, a version of the "pristine unconscious," which Lawrence defines as "That essential unique nature of every individual creature, which is, by its very nature, unanalysable, undefinable, inconceivable."[4] But when Colin uses the fable only to impose on Dollie his fantasy of aristocratic birth in the privileged class, a far cry from the Laurentian aristocracy of blood consciousness, his perversion of the concept becomes clear. The psychological phenomenon of the *folie à deux*, "the occurrence in two close associates of the same mental disorder at the same time,"[5] may prove instructive. T. Lidz and his associates, on the basis of their study of schizophrenic patients and their families, concluded that parents often transmit their irrational or delusional conceptions directly to their children without elaboration; thus, Lidz enlarges the concept to *folie à famille*.[6] The effect of the Urquharts' *folie à famille* is Dollie's education in basic distrust: "The Princess learned her lesson early—the first lesson, of absolute reticence, the impossibility of intimacy with any other than her father; the second lesson, of naive, slightly benevolent politeness." Illustrations of these generalizations are profuse. In refusing an invitation to live with her grandfather, for example, Dollie says: "You are so very kind. But Papa and I are such an old couple, you see, such a crochety old couple, living in a world of our own." In this world Dollie's potential womanhood sleeps: "She was so exquisite and such a little virgin." Mediterranean cabmen and porters, standing in for Lawrence, sense in her a "sterile impertinence towards the things they *felt* most," "*beauté male*" and "the phallic mystery," and long to crush the "barren flower" of her maidenhood. Dollie senses their hatred, but, as Lawrence puns, "she did not lose her head. She quietly paid out money and turned away" (pp. 476-477). As Sigmund Freud observes, such girls, "to the delight of their parents, retain their full infantile love far beyond puberty. . . ." Even as wives they remain "sexually anesthetic." To Freud, "This shows that the apparently nonsexual love for parents and sexual love are nourished from the same sources, i.e., that the first merely corresponds to an infantile fixation of the libido."[7] In the sleep-like fixity of her personality, Dollie "had that quality of the sexless fairies, she did not change." In contrast to Lawrence's sexual sleepers who are awakened by some phallic representative of the sun god, Dollie is languid, "like a flower that has blossomed in a shadowy place." When she is thirty-eight, her father dies: "She was the Princess, and sardonically she looked out on a princeless world." (p. 479)

Though Dollie retains "the idea of marriage," What Lawrence calls her "passion for her mad father" she now transfers to Colin's nurse-companion, Miss Charlotte Cummins. When the two women move west to a New Mexican dude ranch, the Rancho del Cerro Gordo, the Sleeping Princess encounters there her dispossessed and fragmented Prince, Domingo Romero, the son of an old San Christobal family of Spanish landowners who, as the result of their own inertia and the invasion of the white man, have become mere Mexican peasants. The heir apparent to this ruin works as a guide on the ranch, where the emotionally lifeless tourists "rarely *see* anything, inwardly" of the "spark" in the middle of his eyes. Dollie does see it, however, and promptly concludes that Romero is a "gentleman" with a "fine demon" (pp. 482-483). Not surprisingly, Dollie conceives a desire for Romero to fulfill, in relation to her, both his literal and symbolic functions as guide: "She wanted to look over the mountains into their secret heart" (p.487). In a fictional rendering of a biographical experience, Dollie, Miss Cummins, and Romero set out on a three days' journey to the top of the mountain ridge. The Honorable Dorothy Brett has recorded a day's ride she made with Lawrence and Mrs. Rachel Hawk to the top of the ridge above San Christobal canyon.[8] Dollie Urquhart, in several significant ways, resembles Brett, and Romero, even in his fragmentation, embodies some of Lawrence's key ideas, Yet in "The Princess" Lawrence maintains the aesthetic distance necessary to unity of plot, character, and setting in universal rather than merely personal or local significance.

From this point to the end of the story, the structural and thematic principle is an ironically inverted rendering of the mono-myth. Romero, dressed in Laurentian black and riding a black horse, is the mythic guide, whose function, like that of supernatural helpers as various as the Virgil of Dante's *Inferno* and, the Mephistopheles of Goethe's *Faust*, is to lure "the innocent soul into realms of trial." As the "supernatural principle of guardianship and direction," this figure unites in himself "all the ambiguities of the unconscious," thus demonstrating both the unconscious source of support for the conscious personality and the "inscrutability of the guide that we are following. . . ."[9] Romero as guide has chthonic qualities associated with his negative task of peeling the onion of Dollie's social self. When Miss Cummins turns back, the last support for Dollie's dependent state vanishes. Reaching the ridge with Romero, Dollie gazes down into the primordial core of the Rocky Mountains: "It frightened the Princess, it was *so* inhuman" (p. 496). What frightens Dollie is the vision of independent, amoral, even impersonal self-hood, the cosmic identification of "the first and supreme knowledge that *I am I*."[10] For the "intestinal knot" of the mountains into which she stares is the ultimate green demon of the earth, the solar plexus of the cosmos, the navel of the world. As Campbell explains, the quest of the hero of the monomyth is "the unlocking and release again of the flow of life into the body of the world." The hidden source of this torrent is under the World Navel, "the center of the symbolic circle of the universe": "Beneath this spot is the earth-supporting head of the cosmic serpent, the dragon, symbolical of the waters of the abyss, which are the divine life-creative energy and substance of the demiurge, the world-generative aspect of immortal being."[11]

As Dollie and Romero descend, they move, as if in answer to the mythic summons, out of society and across the threshold into the center of experience. According to Campbell, "the call rings up the curtain, always, on a mystery of transfiguration—a rite, or moment, of spiritual passage, which, when complete, amounts to a dying and a birth."[12] Since such a transfiguring experience is hardly subject to deliberate, conscious control, both Dollie's and Romero's minds are appropriately numb. When they reach the cabin, they find this artifact of civilization all but taken over by nature: "The roof had gone—but Romero had laid on thick spruce boughs" (p.500). But that night, instead of feeling transfigured, Dollie feels trapped: "She dreamed it was snowing, and the snow was falling on her through the roof, . . . and she was going to be buried alive" (p. 503). Lawrence's comment on Poe's premature burial stories, which the dream parallels, is critically appropriate to Dollie's character: "All this underground vault business . . . symbolizes that which takes place *beneath* the consciousness. On top, all is fair-spoken. Beneath, there is awful murderous extremity of burying alive."[13] Dollie's ambivalence about Romero reveals the symbolic value of the dream: "She wanted warmth, protection, she wanted to be taken away from herself. And at the same time, . . . she wanted to keep herself intact, intact, untouched, that no one should have any power over her . . . " (p. 503). When Dollie complains that she is cold, Romero offers to warm her. Contrasting the extremes of heat and cold, they also represent the opposite values of body and mind, blood and nerve, the sensual and the spiritual, the organic and the inorganic. As Lawrence explains in the essay on Poe: "In sensual love, it is the two blood-systems . . . which sweep up into pure contact. . . . In spiritual love, the contact is purely nervous."[14] When Romero comes into Dollie's bed "with a terrible animal warmth that seemed to annihilate her," he pants "like an animal." For Dollie, however, the sexual act is purely mental: "She had never, never wanted to be given over to this. But she had *willed* that it should happen to her" (p. 504). In *Psychoanalysis and the Unconscious,* Lawrence defines Idealism as "the motivizing of the great affective sources by means of ideas mentally derived":[15] "I may have ideals if I like. . . . But I have no right to ask another to have these ideals. And to impose *any* ideals upon a child as it grows is almost criminal. . . . It results in neurasthenia."[16] Dollie's father had imposed upon her his delusional "ideas" of aristocracy. The imbalance thus set up between the opposites of her personality makes impossible any but a willed, mental relationship with Romero, and so leads to his psychic ruin, too. In the face of her obstinate coldness, he alternates ambivalently between wheedling: "You sure won't act mean to me," and despair: "I sure don't mind hell fire. . . . After this." (pp. 506-508)

Dollie, having irrevocably rejected the mythic call to adventure and transfiguration, dissolves in helpless hysterics. According to Campbell, rejection of the summons, essentially, is a refusal to surrender old modes of being for new ones. The future, thus, "is regarded not in terms of an unremitting series of deaths and births, but as though one's present system of ideals, virtues, goals, and advantages were to be fixed and made secure." The refusal, however, results not in conservation but in negation. The hero's "flowering world becomes a wasteland of dry stones and his life feels meaningless. . . . All he can do is create new problems for himself and await the gradual approach of his distintegration."[17] The principle is illustrated brilliantly in the conclusion of "The Princess" Dollie, freed from the cabin by forest rangers, who kill Romero in an exchange of gunfire, remains the prisoner of her own psychic virginity, her sexual sleep. Years later, still fixated in her daughter state of dependency, Dollie infuses her experience at the World Navel with delusion: "Since my accident in the mountains, when a man went mad and shot my horse from under me, and my guide had to shoot him dead, I have never felt quite myself." Symbolically, through her marriage to a much older man, Dollie even gets her father back. (p. 512)

*Studies in Short Fiction* 4, 1967.

## Notes

[1] "Myth and Ritual in the Shorter Fiction of D.H. Lawrence," *Modern Fiction Studies*, V (Spring, 1959), 70.

[2] *The Hero with a Thousand Faces* (New York, 1956), p. 62.

[3] "The Princess," in *The Complete Short Stories of D.H. Lawrence* (Melbourne, London, and Toronto, Heinemann, 1955), II 473. Further citations in my text will be to this edition.

[4] *Psychoanalysis and the Unconscious* and *Fantasia of the Unconscious* (New York, 1960), p. 15.

[5] Horace B. English and Ava Champney English, *A Comprehensive Dictionary of Psychological and Psychoanalytical Terms* (New York, London, and Toronto, 1958), p. 212.

[6] Silvano Arieti, "Schizophrenia: The Manifest Symptomatology, the Psychodynamic and Formal Mechanisms," *American Handbook of Psychiatry* (New York, 1959), I, 469-470.

[7] *Three Essays on the Theory of Sexuality*, in *The Complete Psychological Works of Sigmund Freud*, trans. and ed. James Strachey in collaboration with Anna Freud (London, 1953), VII, 227.

[8] *Lawrence and Brett: A Friendship* (Philadelphia, 1933), pp.149-152.

[9] Campbell, pp. 72-73.

[10] *Psychoanalysis* and *Fantasia*, p. 75.

[11] Campbell, pp. 40-41.

[12] *Ibid.*, p. 51.

[13] *Studies in Classic American Literature* (New York, 1955), pp. 89-90.

[14] *Ibid.*, p. 75.

[15] *Psychoanalysis* and *Fantasia*, p. 11.

[16] *Ibid.*, p. 90.

[17] Campbell, pp. 59-60.

## Leo Gurko, "D.H. Lawrence's Greatest Collection of Short Stories—What Holds It Together"

On January 9, 1922, in a letter from Taormina to the painter Jan Juta, Lawrence announced: "Today thank heaven I have sent off the last of my MSS— three long-short stories, will make a really interesting book those three—*The Fox,* 'The Ladybird,' and 'The Captain's Doll.'" The three were published in London in March, 1923, as "The Ladybird," and a month later in New York as "The Captain's Doll". hey are probably Lawrence's most brilliant single assemblage of tales, and rank with Conrad's *Youth and Two Other Stories* and Joyce's *Dubliners* as the richest of their kind in modern English.

Their aesthetic quality is more evident than Lawrence's reasons for publishing them in the same volume. he did of course write them in the same period: he had begun *The Fox* in 1918 while still in England and had finished "The Ladybird" at the end of 1921 in Sicily. As stories, all three take place in Europe toward the end of the First World War and immediately afterward, the very time in which they were written. Yet the differences among them in tone, atmosphere, and even the social classes to which their characters belong are so striking as to overoverwhelm the surface unity supplied by dates of composition and historical locale.

In tone, they range from the rhapsodic, incantatory style of "The Ladybird," to the impressionistic pathos of *The Fox,* to the worldly comedy of "The Captain's Doll." The atmosphere of "The Ladybird" is mystical, *The Fox* broodingly Freudian, "The Captain's Doll" playfully ironic and sophisticated. There is a spread in social status from the lower-middle-class farm girls of *The Fox* to the established aristocracy of "The Ladybird," from the army private of *The Fox* to the Scottish captain of "The Captain's Doll." "It illustrates Lawrence's range," wrote F. R. Leavis, "that not only 'The Ladybird,' with its exalted incantatory mode, but also one of his best things, 'The Captain's Doll,' the characters of which are upper-middle-class and aristocratic, and the tone of which has a flexibility corresponding to the range and resource of their speech, should have appeared in the same volume."[1]

Yet there they are, between the same covers. In so placing them, Lawrence invites us to do more than be impressed with their range. He challenges us to discover the tie that pulls them together, the shared principle that underlies their vivid differences. Harry T. Moore suggests that "The Ladybird" is based on the Sleeping Beauty motif of folklore.[2] The motif is certainly present here, and in the two companion tales as well. Lady Daphne is emotionally "asleep" until "awakened" by Count Dionys. Her sleep is a disturbed one: she is vaguely conscious of unrealized feelings, of longings that find no outlet; she is oppressed by a sense of being cut off from some deeper self. Her freedom of movement is severely constricted. "She was nailed inside her own fretful self-consciousness," Lawrence says of her in one of the story's great phrases. Thus impaled, she can only wait for the stranger, with his special magic, to free her from the evil spell. The young soldier in *The Fox* does the same for March. Her heterosexual nature, slumbering beneath the lesbian surface, is released from its entombment by the insistent force of his desire for her. The sleeping beauty idea is less overtly present in "The Captain's Doll," but even there the drugged way in which Captain Hepburn moves through the early stages of the story is in striking contrast to the alertness of his actions at the end; he too passes from sleep to wakefulness. The process has its obvious biographical prototype in Frieda Lawrence's well-known statement about the kind of life she was living as Frieda Weekley when Lawrence first appeared: she felt like a sleepwalker, sunk lethargically in a state of spiritual drowsiness, only half-alive. Lawrence, she claimed, released her from this emotional torpor for good and all.

Another theory has been advanced by George Ford. Mr. Ford finds in "The Ladybird"—and in other works by Lawrence—a retelling of the Pluto-Persephone myth.[3] In it the dark man (Pluto, Lawrence, Count Dionys) emerges from the nether world (Hades, the coal mine, Eastern Europe) and compels the blonde woman (Persephone, Frieda, Lady Daphne) to accompany him back to his domain. In the end, the call of the upper region is too strong and he is forced to share her with it. Lady Daphne remains part of the conventional world represented by her English husband and part of the underworld ruled over by the King of Darkness. The black-haired man, incarnating the dark gods that serve for Lawrence as a metaphor of psychic potency, was a standard figure in his fiction. He is plainly present in "The Ladybird." One notes that the German countess in "The Captain's Doll" is blonde and the Scottish captain dark; in the end, he carries her off from the light of Europe to the darkness of Africa. The pattern is not immediately applicable to *The Fox* where March, the Persephone figure, is dark-haired. But one might argue that she is sexually displaced, being presented as a man in the early stages of the story: "She would be a man about the place."[4] "She looked almost like some graceful, loose-balanced young man."[5] And that is the role she plays in her relationship with Banford. Her color is therefore reversed, for perhaps the same reason that Gerald Crich, in *Women in Love*, playing the dependent feminine role in his affair with Gudrun, is intensely blond.

There is no doubt that Lawrence is using these materials from fairy tale and mythology, but the stories have a larger scope and deeper resonance than are accounted for by them. The three principal characters in each set up a triangular relationship too complex to be adequately described by fixed patterns borrowed from the past. The ambience in which they move, unsettled, transitory, richly chaotic, is peculiar to Lawrence's art and not easily explained in schematic terms. "The Captain's Doll," with its sense of deliberate comedy, is especially resistant to definition by traditional romance, whether folk or myth. We are encouraged to look more intently within the stories themselves for clues to their collective meaning.

The element first encountered is the titles, each containing a symbol for a figure within. The ladybird or scarab is the emblem for the Count, the fox for Henry, the doll for the captain. These emblem images are embodiments of some significant quality in the man, but because they represent only the one quality, they are caricatures. They are, in effect, to use one of Lawrence's favorite terms, *reductions* of the men. We see the men in them clearly enough, but in a shrunken way. The problem for each—the problem of the stories—is how to be freed from the emblem into themselves, how to escape from their imprisonment as caricatures and regain their living wholeness.

The liberation process is particularly marked in "The Captain's Doll." The Countess makes a doll of her Scottish lover as a sign of her exasperation with him. The doll is a perfect physical likeness, down to the tight-fitting tartan trews. Seeing it for the first time, the Captain says, "You've got me." But the point of course is that she hasn't got him. All that she has caught of him is his physical self, down to his straight, handsome legs mentioned several times during the course of the story. The visible part of him is all she can take hold of; the invisible side of him—vague, non-thinking, gazing at her with "that other, unseeing look"—eludes her. She is fascinated by it, but cannot pin it down, and in her frustration imprisons in the doll the part of him that she can pin down. The doll expresses her relationship with the Captain when the story opens; it has been sexually satisfactory and emotionally baffling. As long as the doll stands between them, their relationship cannot progress.

The Captain is a doll not only to the Countess but also to his wife. With her "lardy-dardy middle-class English," her sense of ownership and her obsessively feminine determination to "Protect our men," Mrs. Hepburn is triumphantly characterized. On their wedding night, she extracted from her husband a promise, delivered on his knees, to love and adore her. This suppliant position confirms his function as her doll, a possessed subservient object that feeds her emotionally. Even when he ceases to "love" and "adore" her, he continues, willingly and calmly, to make love to her—a fact that shocks the Countess. Paradoxically, she finds it hard to believe that the man of whom she has made a doll has been one for eighteen years to another woman.

With the wife's death, the Captain is freed from his bondage to her. He repudiates the love-adoration posture and sets off in pursuit of the Countess in search of another kind of relationship. But first he must get rid of the doll. He finds it staring at him uncannily in a Munich shop window, and later as part of a fashionable still-life canvas, surrounded by two sun-flowers in a glass jar and a poached egg on toast. The doll disappears, but he buys the still-life, turns it over to the Countess when he finds her, and in the end, when a new and unexpected union between them is created, she burns the painting as a sign that the Captain's phase as a doll is over and his phase as a man has begun.

Something of the same process occurs in the other two novelettes. The fox raids the hen coops, and the women are helpless against his assaults. March is entranced by the fox, whom she encounters but is unable to shoot. He is a kind of demon that invades her unconscious: "She lowered her eyes, and suddenly saw the fox. . . . And he knew her. She was spell-bound—she knew he knew her. So he looked into her eyes, and her soul failed her. . . . For he had lifted his eyes upon her, and his knowing look seemed to have entered her brain. She did not so much think of him: she was possessed by him. She saw his dark, shrewd, unabashed eye looking into her, knowing her. She felt him invisibly master her spirit."[6] The Biblical use of "know" here suggests the sexual elements in the encounter. The fox is young, male, arrogant, and triumphant. Henry, who appears presently, has all these qualities in human form. Inevitably, he slays the fox and replaces it in March's sexual and psychic life.

In "The Ladybird" there is also a movement from the emblem to the man. On a visit to England years before the story opens, the Count had given Lady Daphne a thimble as a present on her seventeenth birthday. The thimble has a beetle in green stone at the top: the beetle is the ladybird, the Count's family crest. Until she uses the thimble, the Count is only a remote, mysterious abstraction to Daphne, a vague emanation from Eastern Europe far from her ken. When she meets him again as a wounded war prisoner, he reminds her of the thimble and asks her to sew him a shirt with it. At this point, the process of his ceasing to be an abstraction and becoming a man gets under way. A shirt touches the skin, and we know that to Lawrence touch was the most sacred and personal of the senses. Daphne, inept at sewing and confused in her feelings, misplaces the thimble, and not until it is found again can her relationship with the Count proceed. As with the doll and the fox, the emblem must be found and disposed of before the man can begin.

The emblem motif underlines Lawrence's conviction that modern life tends to shrink human beings into objects and abstractions, and that it is the mission of art to reverse the process, to restore men to their original individuality and wholeness.

But while this motif powerfully affects the men in these stories, it does not take the women into account. Yet their fate depends on the equilibrium established with the men. This equilibrium had been set forth as a theory not long before by Birkin in *Women in Love*, and emerges as one of the binding elements in these tales at the beginning of the '20's. The Countess is too masculine and "free" at the start of the "The Captain's Doll." Her excessive independence, assertiveness, and desire to get hold of the Captain—his vagueness irritates and disorients her—are as much her response to the unsettled times as to the compulsions of her own nature. The Captain's elusiveness is due to his married subservience. He has yielded too much of himself to his wife. Not until she dies can his balance be regained and can he be free to create a new relationship with the Countess. The equilibrium they finally establish is achieved not through harmony, friendly negotiations, and prudent adjustments, but through argument, angry dialectic, and a period of prolonged tension. They are deeply attracted to one another, but the ground through which they must pass is a minefield of resentments, demands, ultimatums, and mutual rage. The quarrel over the words in the marriage ceremony is characteristic of these collisions. He wants her not to love but to honor and obey him. She is anxious to love him, but is not prepared to honor and obey. It is an outrage, she feels, for an emancipated woman thus to humble herself before a man. So they quarrel, argue, and drive at each other. She finally gives way, grudgingly, reluctantly, not at all in the state of passive radiance typical of the traditional heroine. The equilibrium they reach is an equilibrium of tension. Their opposing male and female selves do work out an understanding, but it is an uneasy truce that prevails, not a stabilized peace.

In his opposition to Christian love, Lawrence repudiated meekness and docility in his lovers. As with himself and Frieda, belligerence and anger led to the promised land much more surely than passivity and non-resistance. He became a great specialist on love that is prickly, tense, bellicose, and quarrelsome, the kind that has its profound satisfactions but never ends "happily." Anti-Christian and anti-chivalrous, it was a nervously modern conception of love, rooted of course in the equality of the sexes, where each lover has, in Joseph Conrad's words, "an amazing sensitiveness to the claims of his own personality."[7] When March is torn away from Banford's orbit and drawn into Henry's, she resists him to the very end of *The Fox*. He wants more of her than she is willing to give; she is fearful of losing herself in him entirely. As they prepare to leave England, the struggle between them is still going on full force, but it is a struggle for equilibrium, Lawrence's ultimate objective in his dramas of personal life. And in "The Ladybird" Daphne's distorted relationship with her adoring husband is pulled into balance by her newly forged, polyandrous connection with the Count.

The search for emotional equilibrium has its geographic analogues. The Captain, after marrying the Countess, will take her off to a farm in East Africa: the contact between sophisticated Europe and primitive Africa reveals Lawrence's instinct for bringing opposites together. Earlier, the Captain had disclosed a passion for astronomy, and he is observed gazing at the moon through a telescope: the crowded earth and the uninhabited moon are another pair of opposites being momentarily joined. In *The Fox* March and Henry are setting off for the New World: England, small and enclosed, is juxtaposed with Canada, vast and open. In "The Ladybird" Eastern and Western Europe meld briefly in the embraces of Daphne and the Count. The development of a new emotion in Lawrence seems to require a change of venue, or at any rate is always accompanied by one. Paul Morel, at the end of *Sons and Lovers*, leaves the countryside and moves toward the glowing town. Birkin and Ursula leave Europe altogether and flee southward. Aaron Sisson abandons England and gropes his way to Italy. So does Alvina Houghton in *The Lost Girl*. In the novels where everyone remains in the same place, like *The White Peacock* and *The Trespasser*, everything relapses in defeat.

The shifts in location, however, are not arranged haphazardly. It is not just a matter of picking oneself up and leaving, where any place will do. The two places in each instance are usually in the same stark contrast to one another as are the man and woman connecting them. Lawrence wishes to make them extraordinarily different from one another to emphasize the necessity of the man and the woman being as different from one another as possible, for only in preserving the purity and absoluteness of that difference can a new relationship between them be possible. Only then can they really come together. A successful fusion is therefore possible only to the degree that they remain distinct. This is the paradox that lies at the heart of Lawrence's psychic-sexual dramas. And it is a paradox reinforced at every point by the geographic arrangements that Lawrence, quite as much as Conrad before him, organizes in the service of his art.

Underneath all the ideas in these stories described so far, underneath the classical and fairy-tale motifs, the emblem-symbols, the equilibrium of opposites, there appears most powerfully and inclusively the theme that absorbed Lawrence during the last ten years of his life: the theme of resurrection. It had been impressed upon him in the non-conformist chapels he had attended as a boy, in the Methodist hymns he loved to sing, in the whole atmosphere of Evangelical Christianity in which he had been reared. The rebirth into Christ he later changed to rebirth into man, the resurrection in heaven he altered to resurrection on earth.

This was the radical surgery he performed on Orthodox Christianity. But the Christian conviction of death as a preface to rebirth he retained intact, and in each of the three novelettes death is not only the preliminary but the prerequisite to new life.

In "The Captain's Doll" it is the death of Mrs. Hepburn that releases the others to a fresh beginning. Though her fall from a hotel window is accidental, there is something deeply purposive about it. The Captain, reporting the event to the Countess, describes his wife as a caged bird trapped in the wrong environment, even speaking a language not native to her soul. Her death, while a physical shock, is a psychic relief. Lawrence wishes to free the event from the burden of contrivance, from being, too baldly, a device manufactured to make the main sequence of his story possible. He does so by endowing Mrs. Hepburn with a complex nature not wholly borne out by the facts. As we see her in action when alive, she is a possessive woman with a will to sexual ownership underlined by her feverish attempt to secure the doll. After she dies, we are told by her husband of her imprisoned side, a side we must take on faith since it is not dramatized but only described. The description, however, is eloquent, and is delivered in that tone of special wisdom, of Delphic emanation from the Captain's remote and hidden self that developed into Lawrence's special "art language". Mrs. Hepburn dies, but she dies from a compelled emotional position and not simply in an arranged moment of plot. Her death removes a relationship which by its devouring character sealed off the Captain's life energies.

The act of death is more deliberately willed in *The Fox*, and is no less decisive. Two living creatures stand in March's way; both are slain by Henry. One is the aggressive male fox that raids the coop, who exercises a spell over March so potent she is unable to lift her gun against him. In the contest between *his* natural maleness and her *assumed* maleness, his is plainly the more powerful. In slaying the fox, Henry absorbs its power and draws March into his psychic field. The other obstacle is of course Banford, with whom March has a lesbian relationship. Henry kills her too, with the exercise of the same force of will that he exhibited over the fox. Warning her to step aside from the path of the tree he is cutting down, Henry knows that the warning is precisely what will stiffen her resolve not to move. The tree falls, crushing the girl, and at the same time freeing March from a tie she is unable to break of her own accord. Again the two deaths are more than episodes in the plot; they are also events in March's emotional life, embodying her defected energies and clearing the way to her rebirth.

In "The Ladybird" death is not specific but generalized. "How many swords had Lady Beveridge in her pierced heart!" is the story's opening sentence. She had lost her sons and brother in the war, and "death seemed to be moving with wide swathes through her family."[8] The war, devouring a whole generation, is the death agent that clears the ground, if horrifyingly, for emotional rebirth, just as the Count's war wounds, from which he is slowly recovering, lead to the purification and intensification of his role as the agent of the healing darkness. "The Ladybird," and the other two stories as well, taking place as they do toward the end of and immediately after the war, exploit the feeling always present at such times that the old ways are shattered as new ones maneuver to be born. Lawrence hated the war, but he exploited it to great advantage in his work.

The three types of death on display here—accidental, deliberate, and generalized—are repeated, with variations, in all of Lawrence's writings from this point on. The accidental killing of Kangaroo is in line with Mrs. Hepburn's fatal fall. The ritualized murder of the young protagonist in "The Woman Who Rode Away" and of the three Mexicans at the hands of Don Cipriano in *The Plumed Serpent* are akin to the slaying of Banford. The shattering effects of the war are taken up once more in *Lady Chatterley's Lover*, and the slowly healing wounds of Count Dionys reappear in the slowly healing wounds of the Christ figure in "The Man Who Died".

Each type of prefatory death presents Lawrence with an artistic problem. Accidental death carries with it the curse of contrivance, the author arranging a haphazard event just to make his plot come out right. The deliberately willed death involves him in something far more serious: the inevitable arousing in the reader of feelings of nausea and horror that run counter to and threaten to destroy the author's channels of sympathy. The murder of Banford, offered to us as a necessary and even humane act, creates a visible chill in the reading air. The story survives the shock of this ruthless event but it never entirely repairs the damage done to our deepest feelings, those very feelings that Lawrence is forever appealing to and proclaiming as the ultimate source of truth. When in *Kangaroo*, Jack Callcott kills three men in a brawl between the socialists and the Diggers, he feels marvelous afterward: "Cripes, there nothing bucks you up sometimes like killing a man—*nothing*. You feel a perfect angel after it." Killing he finds as natural as "lying with a woman."[9] His state of mind is perfectly convincing in itself, but Jack is presented to us as integrated man; we are therefore asked to accept his killer instinct as part of a personality being offered for our admiration. This again does violence to our feelings, and is considerably more damaging to the novel than even Banford's death is to *The Fox*. Lawrence goes over the line altogether with Don Cipriano's Aztec-like butcheries, where the validity of the new religion is at once destroyed by the literal blood-lust of its initiation rites.

In his assault on Christianity, Lawrence believed that hate, violence, and anger, sincerely felt, had as legitimate a right to expression as kindness and love. Whatever may be said for this in theory, it raises formidable problems in the actualities of conduct. Here Lawrence's attempt to reform our sensibilities was probably too radical as a life purpose, while it introduced into his art grave emotional complications that grew progressively more serious and became, at last, unmanageable. Resurrection that depended on murder somehow destroyed itself.

"The Captain's Doll" and its two companion tales are the supreme staging ground for Lawrence's ideas at a turning point in his life. A month after sending off the last of them to his publisher, he left Europe altogether for wanderings in other parts of the world. Like the Captain, like Henry, he abandons the old world and its old forms in search of new resurrections, and, with his belief in the spirit of place, such resurrections were most readily accessible elsewhere. In his fiction, the novel of personal relationships and personal conflicts was behind him for the time being, and the novel of ideas, of programs, of social and political resurrection lay ahead. The stories of this collection contain some of his best and most representative writing. Beyond that, they link the early Lawrence with the later, and thereby serve as a revealing microcosm of his career.

*Modern Fiction Studies*, 18, 1972.

**Notes**

[1] *D.H. Lawrence: Novelist* (New York: Knopf, 1956), p. 235.

[2] *The Intelligent Heart* (New York: Grove, 1962), p. 349.

[3] *Double Measure: A Study of the Novels and Stories of D. H. Lawrence* (New York: W.Norton, 1965), p. 30.

[4] *The Captain's Doll* (New York: Thomas Seltzer, 1923), p. 127.

[5] *The Captain's Doll*, p. 128.

[6] *The Captain's Doll*, pp. 132, 133.

[7] Applied to Massy, in "The End of the Tether."

[8] *The Captain's Doll*, p. 227.

[9] *Kangaroo* (New York: Thomas Seltzer, 1923), pp. 375, 376.


# Volker Schulz, "D.H. Lawrence's Early Masterpiece of Short Fiction: 'Odour of Chrysanthemums'"

D.H. Lawrence is not only a major novelist (if far from a flawless one), but also one of the great masters of the modern short story. H. E. Bates was the first of several critics who have considered his short fiction superior even to his novels: "the short stories will emerge as the more durable achievement"(201).[1] Nevertheless, it was not until 1984 that the first really comprehensive book-length study of Lawrence's short fiction appeared (Harris),[2] and many of the sixty-odd short stories have yet to receive the detailed critical appreciation they deserve. The following interpretation of one of Lawrence's early masterpieces of short fiction, "Odour of Chrysanthemums," is meant to help fill this gap.

The composition history of "Odour of Chrysanthemums" is fascinating, and a close study of it is bound to lead toward understanding a crucial phase of Lawrence's development;[3] nevertheless, I will touch on it only briefly here, mainly because it has already been thoroughly treated by Cushman (47-71) and Harris (25-36). For this discussion, it will be sufficient to note that the first version of "Odour of Chrysanthemums," which seems much more sympathetic to Mrs. Bates (the fictive counterpart of Lawrence's mother), who in the final scene utters "a clear, unadmitted, and shocking confession of pleasure in Walter's death" (Harris 34),[4] was written late in 1909 and published in 1911. When Lawrence was preparing his first collection of stories, *The Prussian Officer and Other Stories* in the summer of 1914, he substantially revised the final scene. The revision seems to reflect some critical distance from the character of Mrs. Bates, perhaps in part due to the author's relationship with Frieda Weekley (born von Richthofen), with whom he had eloped in 1912 and whom he had married in July 1914. That relationship liberated Lawrence from the overpowering influence of his possessive mother. In 1914 "Lawrence has passed beyond the personal question of his mother and father to express an insight into man's fate" (Cushman 69).[5]

In this short story, as in his first great novel, *Sons and Lovers* (written from 1910 to 1912), we find a combination of Lawrence's two main contributions to British fiction. The first of these is the authentic "portrayal of working-class life in a mining district. . . . Lawrence might easily have become . . . the classic novelist of the English workers" (Hough 170).[6] The second is the subtle and unflinching exploration of love relationships. According to Ford:

> his men and women are seekers. What they seek . . . is to establish some transforming relationship which will rouse them to life. . . in Lawrence's writings the drive to love and be loved is the chief preoccupation of mankind, and not to love or be loved is the most destructive of life's frustrations. (16)

In "Odour of Chrysanthemums" Lawrence presents a vivid picture of early twentieth-century life in a Midlands mining-area. It is, as Werner Hüllen has called it, "eine Meisterleistung dichter Wirklichkeitsvergegenwärtigung" ("a paragon of detailed rendering of reality" [80]). By shifting the focus several times between the mining town's environment dominated by the colliery, the mining town with its row of small houses and its pubs, the kitchen and parlor of the Bates's house, and the kitchen of another miner's house, the author succeeds in making the reader visualize many details of setting as well as accentuating the main features of the miners' and their families' lives.

There is the miners' hard, monotonous, and dangerous work. Their exhaustion is suggested by their "trailing" homeward (Lawrence 268); the alienating monotony of their work is indirectly reflected by their habit of drinking; the danger is intimated by Mr. Rigley's "blue scar, caused by a wound got in the pit" (276) and cruelly confirmed by Mr. Bates's fatal accident.

A second ubiquitous feature is poverty, often aggravated by the large number of children (Mrs. Bates catches sight of twelve shoes in the Rigleys' house) and by the men's drinking. Poverty means primitive housing: there are no drains in the Bates's "low cottage" (268) so that Mrs. Bates has to "strain" the potatoes in the yard (271); the yard is "overrun" with rats (275); there is only one "bit of carpet" in the whole house (280). Poverty also means badly fitting old clothes: the son's clothes "were evidently cut down from a man's clothes" (269).

A third feature stressed by Lawrence is industry's disturbance of the natural order. The landscape around the mining-town is spoiled and violated by the concomitant phenomena of mining: noise, smoke, soot, and fire. The animals are upset, the fields "dreary and forsaken" (268), the hill scarred, "flames like red sores licking its ashy sides" (268). The overall impression is that animal as well as human life is overpowered by the mechanical force of industry: "the clanking, jolting, spasmodic sounds of machinery" and "the repetitive movements of locomotive wheels or lift machinery" contrast sharply with the atmosphere of a quiet evening and "the free movement in flight of animals and birds" (Moynahan

182). In this context, the figure in the opening scene of the solitary woman "insignificantly trapped between the jolting black wagons and the hedge" (268) acquires symbolic meaning: like her, all the colliers and their families "are . . . subjects and victims. . . . Men and women, at the mercy . . . of the machine, breathe an atmosphere of death" (Sagar 15).

While horses, fowls and birds can take flight, the human beings cannot escape: "the anomaly of this human entrapment . . . becomes the central . . . motive of the story" (Moynahan 182).[7] Fittingly, the report on Mr. Bates's gruesome death. employs the trap metaphor again: "It *is* the most terrible job I've ever known. Seems as if it was done o'purpose. Clean over him, an' shut 'im in, like a mouse-trap" (281). Whereas the firm's representative tries to put off the responsibility for the accident to some unknown superhuman power ("done o' purpose"), the symbolism of the opening paragraph as well as Mr. Rigley's "blue scar" (276) make it quite clear that such accidents are part and parcel of the industrial system. However, the main emphasis of this story is not on the hardship and death of victims of the industrial system in general and of the mining industry in particular—though Lawrence never tired of attacking modern industrial civilization and its stifling, poisonous impact on human beings. The story does not culminate in the bitter grief that Mr. Bates's mother and wife experience at the news of his death. Rather, the old woman's moaning is used by the author to accentuate, by contrast, Mrs. Bates's much more complex and more shattering reaction when she is confronted with the dead body of her husband. This internal process, which takes the form of a discovery or recognition of truth followed by a radical reorientation, constitutes the story's true climax, whereas the climax of the external action, i.e., the reversal of Mrs. Bates's expectations and the drastic change of the family's situation brought about by Mr. Bates's death, turns out to be only a preliminary to it.

The story's external action has three phases: (1) the family's long wait for Mr. Bates to come home: the "tension of expectancy" (274) becomes hard to bear not only for Mrs. Bates but also for the reader, who is, however, given several unmistakable hints of the kind of homecoming this will be, by way of dramatic irony ("he'll not come now till they bring him" [273]; "They'll bring him when he does come—like a log . . . he'll not go to work tomorrow" [274]); (2) the slowly mounting certainty that Mr. Bates has been killed by a mining disaster: his mother, an angel of death clothed as she is in "a black bonnet and a black woolen shawl" (277), is followed by the miner who reports his death and its particular circumstances and, finally, by the manager dwelling on the "horror" (281) of this accident while the dead body is brought in and put down on the cloths that Mrs. Bates had spread in order "to save her bit of carpet" (280); (3) the laying out and washing of the seemingly unviolated body of the miner by his wife and his mother, both of whom try to come to grips with their loss.

As the shift of point-of-view to Mrs. Bates's consciousness and the extensive presentation of her thoughts and feelings in this final phase of the external action clearly indicate, the author's main objective in this story is to explore the widow's complex response to her husband's death. The sight of his half-naked dead body, the confrontation with "the naive dignity of death" (283), and the awareness of the impossibility of making a "connection" (284) with her husband any more trigger a series of insights in Mrs. Bates that amount to a discovery of the "truth" about her relationship with her husband: "She was grateful to death which restored the truth" (285).

The inescapable realization that the dead man is completely out of her reach, that he is "inviolable," "impregnable" (283), "apart and utterly alien to her" (284), leads to the shocking additional recognition that this had *always* been the case. The familiarity of their living together, even their sexual contacts resulting in a number of children, their "exchanging their nakedness" (284), had been nothing but a superficial "heat of living" obscuring the fact that "they had been two isolated beings, far apart as now" (284). This means that at the core of their two lives there had never been any common ground but "utter, intact separateness" (284); that her assumption of having known him and of being able to judge him had been wrong; her attempts at altering, morally reforming, him ("fighting him" [284]) had been principally and inevitably futile: "his look was other than hers, his way was not her way. She had denied him what he was—she saw it now. She had refused him as himself" (285). What Mrs. Bates recognizes with "shame" (284-85) is that she had always been "wrong" in feeling "familiar with him" (284), that she had been living intimately, for years, with a complete stranger ("this separate stranger with whom she had been living as one flesh" [284]).

However, the tragic failure of this marriage cannot be laid at Mrs. Bates's door, as some critics have insisted.[8] The reader is not meant to arrive at a one-sided moral judgment, but to understand that both of the marital partners were unable to accept each other as they were: "They had denied each other in life" (285). Although Mrs. Bates is shown, above all, to recognize her own share in this mutual failure, the failure had been unmistakably mutual: "He was no more responsible than she" (284).[9] The failure of this marriage is not simply due to the husband's drunkenness or the wife's nagging. These patterns of behavior are rather symptoms of their fundamental incompatibility: "his look was other than hers, his way was not her way" (285). "Odour of Chrysanthemums" is certainly something like "a lesson in human isolation" (Cushman 69), but I wonder whether this isolation is meant to be universal rather than individual, i.e., whether it is actually, as Cushman claims, a "revelation of our [i.e., everyone's] irredeemable loneliness" (69)[10] rather than of the irredeemable loneliness of these particular unsuitable spouses.

Mrs. Bates's confrontation with the death of her husband not only leads her to a penetrating and disillusioning analysis of her married life, which had been a sort of "death in life" (Tedlock 26), but also affects her central orientation and conception of life. "The truth liberates and gives renewed life" to her (Cushman 70). At first the feeling of loss is predominant: "He was dead. . . . Her life was gone like this" (284). Accordingly, "the child within her," representing the essential life force, "was a weight apart from her" (283). Then, with the growing awareness of the complete failure of their married life, which causes Mrs. Bates to feel its product, the unborn child, "like ice in the womb" (284), she slowly becomes aware of the different paths for which she and her husband have been destined: "Life with its smoky burning [has] gone from him" (284) but "she knew she was not dead" (285). With the death of her husband, her own life is not finished: only an "episode of her life closed" (285).[11]

The third step Mrs. Bates takes in the course of her "reverie over the corpse of her husband" (Cushman 57), then, is her consciously and deliberately turning toward life: "There were the children—but the children belonged to life" (285). After the "awful" failure of her marriage she hopes to find a new meaning in life in her role as "a mother": "She knew she submitted to life, which was her immediate master. But from death, her ultimate master, she winced with fear and shame" (285).[12] The dead husband, separated from her by an "infinite . . . gap" (285), represents the force of destruction and death that nobody can ultimately escape, while the unborn child represents that force of life from which Mrs. Bates had been alienated for many years.

That the central symbol of this story, the chrysanthemums, no longer play an important role during Mrs. Bates's analysis of her married life and her slow and hesitant, but determined, reorientation has been called "eine strukturelle Schwäche in dieser künstlerisch sonst so vollendeten Erzählung" ("a structural weakness in this otherwise artistically consummate story" [Broich 169]). Given the complex, yet well-calculated and homogeneous, symbolic meaning of the flowers, it is, on the contrary, quite consistent that they do not figure in the climactic scene of Mrs. Bates's "final discovery" (Ford 70). For the chrysanthemums have represented, from the very start, decay ("disheveled" [268]) and destruction ("dropped the petals in handfuls" [269]); they have been "markers" of the death-in-hfe marriage of Mr. and Mrs. Bates (Amon 224):

> It was chrysanthemums when I married him, and chrysanthemums when you were born, and the first time they ever brought him home drunk, he'd got brown chrysanthemums in his button-hole. (273)[13]

Appropriately, then, when this marriage ends with Mr. Bates's death, one of the men carrying the miner's body knocks off "a vase of chrysanthemums" (281). Mrs. Bates's eagerness to remove "the broken vase and the flowers" (281) and to mop up "the water with a duster" (281) can be taken as a symbol of her subsequent clearing away of the broken pieces of her wrecked marriage. The final scene's very lack of reference to the flowers that have previously played such an important role in the external action subtly corroborates Mrs. Bates's turning away from the irreparable failure of her married life toward a vague hope of finding fulfillment as a mother.

*Studies in Short Fiction* 28, Summer 1991.

## Works Cited

Amon, Frank. "D.H. Lawrence and the Short Story." *The Achievement of D.H. Lawrence.* Ed. P. J. Hoffman and H. T. Moore. Norman: U of Oklahoma P, 1953. 222-34.

Bates, H. E. *The Modern Short Story: A Critical Survey.* London: Michael Joseph, 1972.

Boulton, James T. "D.H. Lawrence's 'Odour of Chrysanthemums': An Early Version." *Renaissance and Modern Studies* 13 (1969): 5-48.

Broich, Ulrich. "Odour of Chrysanthemums." *Die englische Kurzgeschichte* Ed. K. H. Göller and G. Hoffmann, Düsseldorf: Bagel, 1973.162-71.

Cushman, Keith. *D.H. Lawrence at Work: The Emergence of the Prussian Officer Stories.* Hassocks: Harvester Press, 1978.

Ford, George H. *Double Measure: A Study of the Novels and Stories of D.H. Lawrence.* New York: Holt, 1965.

Harris, J. H. *The Short Fiction of D.H. Lawrence.* New Brunswick, NJ: Rutgers UP, 1984.

Hough, Graham. *The Dark Sun: A Study of D.H. Lawrence.* London: Duckworth, 1970.

## Notes

[1] Cf. Moynahan 175 and Hough 168.

[2] Widmer's 1962 study focused on Lawrence's bias toward depicting extreme, self-annihilating experiences, i.e., on a particular thematic cluster.

[3] Cf. Harris: "the Croydon stories [1909-11] are far more autobiographical than anything Lawrence had yet written" (31).

[4] For the first version of the story see Boulton (12-44).

[5] Cf. Littlewood: "'Odour of Chrysanthemums' is in fact, in its final form, an offspring of *The Rainbow* [published in 1915] and of Lawrence's married life, yet it is also in some ways still a product of his earlier life. . . . it consists of first impressions coexisting with revolutionary second thoughts about his childhood and parentage" (15).

[6] By "authentic" I mean "'from his own personal experience' and reflecting an attitude that Leavis justly called 'one of essential reverence, wholly unsentimental and unidealizing'" (257).

[7] According to Harris, the initial "image of a small, dirty mining village late in the afternoon of a raw autumn day . . . foretells the ruined love of Elizabeth and Walter Bates" (33)

[8] For instance, Broich maintains that the failure of the Bates is marriage is grounded in the "geschlecht- und lebensfeindlichen Haltung der Ehefrau" ("the wife's hostile attitude toward sex and life" [168]) and that the gist of the story is "die Diagnose eines persönlichen Versagens" ("the diagnosis of a personal failure" [170]). Cf. Cushman: "the final text contains an impressive statement of the full dimensions of Mrs. Bates's guilt" (70).

[9] Cf. Ford's general observation that Lawrence's "best fiction portrays conflicts, one force pitted against another, in which a dramatic testing is more significant than a simplified evaluation, especially a consistently righteous evaluation of the protagonists" (24).

[10] Cf. Hüllen: "So gestaltet *Odour of Chrysanthemums* schliesslich aus dem Schicksal der in ihren persönlichen, örtlichen und zeitlichen Verhältnissen verfangenen Familie Bates ein allgemeines Bild von dem in seinem *Ego* hilflos eingeschlossenen Menschen unter seinen beiden Herren, dem Leben und dem Tode" (83).

[11] Hudspeth overlooks this aspect, maintaining that "the reader accepts the prior existence of a wasted life and so is compelled to accept its extension into Elizabeth's future" (636).

[12] Mrs. Bates's "shame" does not, I think, refer to.any moral weakness but means "the shame of having been, to such a tune, so confidently wrong" (Littlewood 123).

[13] In my view, Harris's assertion that the chrysanthemums 'suggest both hope and disappointment, past and current experience . . . the complexity of Elizabeth's life" (28) is unwarranted. On the other hand, Hudspeth is right in arguing that for Mrs. Bates, the flowers "have marked moments of heightened passion," but in view of the concluding

scene it is very doubtful, indeed, whether this means that they convey "the *contact*, concrete and definite, with the moments of intense reality" (633).

## Harbour Winn, "Parallel Inward Journeys: *A Passage to India* and *St. Mawr*"

E. M. Forster's satiric depiction of the British enclave desperately holding together the fabric of Empire in *A Passage to India* is a perspective D.H. Lawrence appreciated. The distortion and confusion of Christianity with imperialism and the subsequent condescension toward Islamic and Hindu traditions is a theme he could also have developed himself. In fact, in a letter written shortly after the publication of *A Passage to India* in 1924, Lawrence expresses satisfaction with Forster's repudiation of "our white bunk." In the same letter he also says that "the *Passage to India* interested me very much."[1] His appreciation of Forster becomes even more interesting with the realization that he wrote this letter three days after mailing the manuscript of *St. Mawr*, which was published in 1925, about one year after *A Passage to India*. During the same period in which he was working on *St. Mawr*, then, he was also reading Forster's novel. The parallels between the two novels have been briefly acknowledged but not fully explored. Referring to the same letter, Monroe Engel mentions in a footnote the possibility of comparing Lou Witt's vision on the expedition to the Devil's Chair rock formation with Mrs. Moore's vision on her visit to the Marabar Caves.[2] In a later note, M. L. Raina briefly describes similar word choices in the descriptions of the rocks and caves as well as the symbolic association of evil with both visions through the occurrence of a snake in each excursion[3] More substantive associations exist between the two works, however, regardless of the question of Forster's influence. The path of Mrs. Moore's and Lou's recognizably similar experiences or stages in a mythical journey toward self-knowledge provides a clarifying pattern within each work as well as a comparative link between them.

Both heroines find themselves alienated within their international cast of characters. Mrs. Moore wishes to experience India and move beyond the enclave of British clubs and provincialism; the American Lou finds herself alienated from the artistic façade and cliché-filled world of her Australian husband Rico and their British acquaintances. While Mrs. Moore breaks national and racial barriers by befriending the Islamic Aziz, Lou defies class barriers by developing rapport with the Navaho Phoenix and Welsh Lewis through their care of her horse, St. Mawr. Both women encounter an experience of the sacred beyond the parochial barriers of a superficial Christianity. Mrs. Moore senses a transcendent mystery when she visits a mosque and declares "God is here";[4] Lou senses a vital, dark mystery "almost like a god"[5] in St. Mawr. These experiences suggest the disposition toward an alternative way of seeing that will characterize both women in the major excursion in each novel.

Guided by Aziz, Mrs. Moore visits the ancient Marabar Caves. This threshold-crossing experience, much like the pattern of the hero described by Joseph Campbell in *The Hero with a Thousand Faces*,[6] generates a succession of trials. The caves suggest primitive forces, the primal womb and tomb, the dark labyrinth of self-exploration. In the caves she begins to hear an echo, an echo that reverberates to the depths of her being for the rest of her life. No matter what sound she hears, no matter how evil or praiseworthy, the echo returns the same; all things that exist seem to be identical, and the neat distinctions Mrs. Moore has always made between good and evil, fair and foul, English and Indian, Christian and Hindu, are dissolved. This intense confrontation with a deep sense of evil at the heart of life unnerves her, precipitating a physical and psychological collapse. Her new perceptions lead her inward to confront her mortality, to reassess her whole life.

On the country outing to Devil's Rock, Lou is unnerved when St. Mawr, scared by a snake, falls over on Rico and writhes on its back trying to get up. The timeless quality of the Marabar Caves parallels the fury of the horse that seems "to be seeing legions of ghosts, down the dark avenues of all the centuries that have lapsed since the horse became subject to man" (68).Feeling an "unspeakable weariness" (68), Lou rides alone for help as a vision of evil overcomes her: "She became aware of evil, evil, evil, rolling in great waves over the earth. Always she had thought there was no such thing—only a mere negation of good. Now, like an ocean to whose surface she had risen, she saw the dark-grey waves of evil rearing in a great tide" (68-69). The echoing that reverberates within Mrs. Moore becomes a great tide that sweeps throughout the centuries within Lou. For Mrs. Moore the echo begins "in some indescribable way to *undermine* her hold on life" (149; emphasis added); she feels it murmur to her, "Pathos, piety, courage they exist, but are identical, and so is filth. Everything exists, nothing has value" (149). For Lou, the tide sweeps over mankind with "people performing outward acts of loyalty, piety, self-sacrifice. But inwardly bent on *undermining*, betraying. Directing all their subtle evil will against any positive living thing. Masquerading as the ideal, in order to poison the real" (71; emphasis added). The juxtaposition of the descriptions from the visions illuminates their similarities.

Retreating from society, both women, unable to tolerate contact with others, journey inward, searching for an inviolable sanctuary. In their solitude, each is revulsed by relations between the sexes, what Mrs. Moore thinks of as "centuries of carnal embracement" (135); for Lou, revulsion is related to the Lawrenthian theme of the unavailable "mystic new man" (140). Longing to return home, both begin ocean voyages. Mrs. Moore, of course, becomes ill in the tropical heat and dies at sea. Lou's voyage is symbolically similar; she feels as if all of her life is "passing in a grey curtain of rainy drizzle, like a death, and she with not a feeling left" (126). Whether or not Mrs. Moore emerges from her spiritual muddle in her last hours on the Indian Ocean is unknown; her life and death, however, prove redemptive for others in the remainder of the novel: Adela withdraws her accusation against Aziz, who declines to assert claims against her, and Fielding and Mrs. Moore's children encounter Professor Godbole in a transcending moment inspired by the memory of Mrs. Moore.

In the final section of *St. Mawr,* Lou's retreat extends to the primitive landscape of the deserted goat ranch in northern New Mexico. There, she becomes absorbed in the contemplation of the landscape just as Mrs. Moore had in her train ride across India to Bombay for her voyage home. Both observe the harsh beauty and destructive power of nature that can drain the spirit of man. At the end, Lou is left in contemplation, her future recovery open; the vivid description of the landscape, however, offers an obvious contrast to the superficial European society she has left.

The degree to which the cycle of the hero has been fulfilled remains debatable in both works; each woman, however, has clearly left one way of life in search of another—each has journeyed inward into the self. Amidst these parallel journeys other comparative possibilities abound: the pairing of Mrs. Moore with her anticipated daughter-in-law Adela resembles the pairing of Lou and her mother Rachel; the older Mrs. Witt broods and withdraws from the world just as Mrs. Moore does; Adela eventually rejects the devitalizing masculine dominance of Ronny just as Lou leaves the equivalent in Rico. The associations between the two novels are thus manifold and a study of Lawrence's manuscript could suggest possible direct influences. That the two novelists produced works with comparative elements should not be surprising, though, for Forster and Lawrence, loathing a modern world they regard as devitalized, both quest, like Mrs. Moore and Lou, for spiritual essences in life, sacred places for the self to be.

*English Language Notes*, 31:2, December 1993.

## Notes

---

[1]D.H. Lawrence, *Collected Letters of D.H. Lawrence*, ed. Harry T. Moore (London: Viking, 1962) 811.

[2]Monroe Engel, "The Continuity of Lawrence's Short Novels," *Hudson Review* II (1958): 207.

[3]M.L. Raina, "A Forster Parallel in Lawrence's 'St. Mawr,'" *Notes and Queries* 13 (March 1966): 96-97.

[4]E.M. Forster, *A Passage to India* (New York: Harcourt, Brace, 1924; 1952) 20. Further references are to this edition, and page numbers appear parenthetically.

[5]D.H. Lawrence, *St. Mawr and the Man Who Died* (New York: Random House, 1953) 14. Further references are to this edition, and page numbers appear parenthetically.

[6] Joseph Campbell, *The Hero with a Thousand Faces* (Princeton: Princeton UP, 1949; 1968).

# IX

# Poetry

## A. Williams-Ellis, "Mr D.H. Lawrence's Work" [*Amores: Poems*]

Mr. D.H. Lawrence seems, at any rate for the present, to have come to the end of his poetical utterances. The novelist, and still more the philosopher, was always inclined to shoulder the poet, and now, for the time being, seems to have ousted him. Mr. Lawrence has had a considerable influence upon other modern writers, and it is perhaps not uninteresting in this pause of his career to endeavour to estimate the nature of his contribution to modern lyrical poetry. For reasons of space, I propose to leave out of consideration the long narrative poem, "Look, we have come through." In the first place, on coming back to Mr. Lawrence's poems, we shall probably be struck by their vigour. The emotional stress is often tremendous. We feel that the content is, as it were, always bursting out of the skin of the poem. The inspiration was apparently, as a rule, too white-hot to submit to the bonds of a regular metre. Often there was not even time for any symbolism. he poem is a naked, direct statement. Take the following. It seems devoid of every quality that we expect in verse except emotion, and yet who can deny it the title of poetry?

> "And if I never see her again?
> I think, if they told me so,
> I could convulse the heavens with my horror.
> I think I could alter the frame of things in my agony.
> I think I could break the system with my heart.
> I think, in my convulsion, the skies would break."

This directness often gives to the poems a curious flavour that we associate with very different productions—Mr. Waley's exquisite translations from the Chinese. They have the same naked simplicity, but their writers have come to it not from stress and agony of emotion, but from niceness and satiety, and a taste purged and refined through the centuries.

What do we have to pay for this tensity, this veritable vibration, in Mr. Lawrence? As we should expect, his poems, or rather his mental attitude, seem to be without sense of proportion and his work seems to be done without consciousness. He is struggling so hard to give utterance to some burning emotion that his verse often becomes tortured and harsh—a contortion rather than a poem. The more violent the emotion of which he writes, the more we are conscious of a febrile quality in the verse. He can never stand back from his passion. Therefore we often find that his most passionate love poetry, remarkable as it is, is so feverish, so contorted, as to be pathology, not literature. We have perhaps been moved and duly caught into the swing of the poet's mood, and then Mr. Lawrence lets his fever get the better of him and lets himself slip into what is something very near to delirium—too near, at any rate, to be expressed in half a dozen lines. And so it is that we find the paradox that Mr. Lawrence often writes best upon what are to him emphatically secondary subjects. Two poems about children in *Amores*, for instance, are extraordinarily beautiful and well observed, especially perhaps the one which begins:-

> "When the bare feet of the baby beat across the grass
> The little white feet nod like white flowers in the wind,"

and which ends:-

> "I long for the baby to wander hither to me
> Like a wind-shadow wandering over the water,
> So that she can stand on my knee
> With her little bare feet in my hands,
> Cool like syringa buds,
> Firm and silken like pink your peony flowers."

But whatever may be Mr. Lawrence's faults, this poem illustrates his chief virtue. He is never negligible. His poems have an intense objective existence. To borrow a most repulsive expression from the jargon of the stage, they are always "strong." There appears to be no civilized expression which gives the notion conveyed by the phrase, "Punch back of it." And yet this is a quality of which we are particularly conscious in poetry. There are delightful poets whose works are singularly wraith-like. They may be admirable and charming, but we feel that they are akin to Herrick's daffodils and fade away so fast that we must use a sort of cunning in relation to them—must stalk them. *Per contra*, there are poems which we may like much less; they are often dull or unsubtle, for instance, but they are, as it were, irrevocable. This vigorous life belongs, in a high degree, to Mr. Lawrence's lyrical poetry. It is this lesson of strength that he has to impart to younger writers. Nevertheless, his decision to express himself in prose for the moment may very likely be a wise one.

*Spectator*, CXXVII, 1 October 1921.

# William J. Fisher, "Peace and Passivity: The Poetry of D.H. Lawrence"

To read the poems of D.H. Lawrence after knowing his novels and other prose is to confront the paradox of the romantic. The rebellious individualism which distinguishes Lawrence's fiction is inverted in the poetry into a continuing desire to be merged, to be soothed into some harmonious and self-obliterating whole. In contrast with the turbulent fiction, Lawrence's poetry is generally temperate, expressing a craving for an "oblivion," for an "utter sleep," or for some other quiescent oneness. The passive conception and the passive image prevail: the poet yearns to be taken, touched, folded, enclosed; to be eased into darkness to be immersed softly and unconsciously.

Throughout his life and his writings, Lawrence re-enacted the perennial tragedy of romanticism: proclaiming rebellion ("Certainly with this world I am at war"), he longed for peace and security demanding liberation in behalf of life, he perpetually sought escape from it to deathlike states; urging an unrestrained self-assertion, if not self-indulgence, he kept trying to effect a merging, a self-obliteration. The poetry reflects most clearly and consistently this latter passive side and thereby escapes the dilemma of an unresolved dualism.

The "phallic quest" of the novels was seldom convincing. There was generally an element of "passivity" in the make-up of the dark, goaty heroes. Lawrence tried to free them from the natural demands of their role by enveloping them in his religion of the blood, his idea that true sexuality exists only in the precivilized unconscious, in the dark oblivious depths, independent of will and personality. The result was that these strangely ambivalent characters usually alternated between the desire to be assimilated and the need to triumph over the female. Birkin of *Women in Love* is a typical Lawrencean hero. By turns, he is a noble idealist, a pouting adolescent, a flaming lover, a finicky hermit, and a tedious pseudo-philosopher. In one scene he retreats from the advances of the overcivilized Hermione to the consolation of a dewy hillside, where he strips off his clothes and loses himself in herbaceous intercourse. Saturated with the touch of flowers and shrubs, he discovers that "to lie down, and roll in the sticky, cool hyacinths" is "more delicate and more beautiful than the touch of any woman . . . How fulfilled he was, how happy!" He knew now "where he belonged." But Birkin is the main personage of a novel, and he must stir himself, must arise and return to the world of human beings, where he has his virile role to perform. The novel bloats and and blurs under the strain.

Yet Lawrence was able to use an almost identical episode as the core experience of a poem without running the same risks or committing the same excesses, and without violating the integrity of his conception. "The Wild Common" describes a youth exulting in his discovery of nature, finding in air, earth, and water the elements of an exuberant love. Like Birkin, the "naked lad" takes a passive part, yielding himself into a happy harmony as air and water embrace him and take him into themselves. But by contrast with the novel, the lyric is self-sufficient in its containment of the joyful moment; there is no need in a poem to disturb the equilibrium:

Over my skin in the sunshine, the warm, clinging air
Flushed with the songs of seven larks singing at once, goes kissing me glad.
You are here! You are here! We have found you! Everywhere
We sought you substantial, you touchstone of caresses, you naked lad!
Oh, but the water loves me and folds me,
Plays with me, sways me, lifts me and sinks me, murmurs: oh marvellous stuff !
No longer shadow!—and it holds me
Close, and it rolls me, enfolds me, touches me, as if never it could touch
    me enough.

Thus it was in his poems that Lawrence gave in to the passivity and allowed it to govern his literary design. The poems disclose forthrightly the yearning for an "immersion, " which is immanent both as temper and as subject. The poet can symbolize undisguised goals: a Lethe in which human activity is suspended; a selfless self wholly free from demands; a sanctuary of darkness, silence, warmth, comfort.

In landscapes and other natural surroundings, Lawrence found an ideal way of making things harmonize and of relieving the aching consciousness. Communion with the inanimate was satisfying because it demanded no response. Through identification with the physical world, the poet can experience an untroubled awareness:

So now I know the valley
    Fleshed all like me
With feelings that change and quiver
And clash, and yet seem to tally,
Like all the clash of a river
    Moves on to sea.  ("Renascence")

Frequently the soothing power of nature restores a disturbed peace, as in "First Morning." The night had been a failure, the poet laments; "I could not be free." Yet—

Now in the morning
As we sit in the sunshine on the seat by the little shrine
And look at the mountain-walls,
Walls of blue shadow
And see so near at our feet in the meadow
Myriads of dandelion pappus
Bubbles ravelled in the dark green grass
Held still beneath the sunshine—
It is enough, you are near—
The mountains are balanced,
The dandelion seeds stay half-submerged in the grass.

Sometimes in his merging and submerging the poet identifies himself with specific natural elements or animals, so that he becomes one with the nonvolitive: with sea, wind, trees. "I am the sea, I am the sea!" is the ardent cry of one poem; while another contemplates a more serene absorption:

> Imitate the magnificent trees
> That speak no word of their rapture, but only
> Breathe largely the luminous breeze.

The poet especially envies the fish, because "so little matters" to it; it is free from the awful demands of consciousness, living "utterly without misgiving" in its watery suspension: "To be a fish!" It is equally satisfying for the poet to yield his will to an outside force, abdicating all need to act, in deference to "my best/Soul's naked lightning, which should sure attest/God stepping through our loins in one bright stride"; or simply to disclaim his own volition: "Not I, not I, but the wind that blows through me."

The quintessence of Lawrence's feelings toward nature as expressed in his verse is contained in a single four-stanza poem titled "Nonentity":

> The stars that open and shut
> Fall on my shallow breast
> Like stars on a pool.
>
> The soft wind, blowing cool,
> Laps little crest after crest
> Of ripples across my breast.
>
> And dark grass under my feet
> Seems to dabble in me
> Like grass in a brook.
>
> Oh, and it is sweet
> To be all these things, not to be
> Any more myself.

Ironically, the author of this paean to "Nonentity" later ridiculed Walt Whitman for being one of the "great mergers" and for trying to achieve an "identity," an "Allness," with everything. "There can't be much left of *you* when you've cooked the awful pudding of Identity," Lawrence declared, neglecting to say what might be left of you when you've cooked the pudding of Nonentity. And though he celebrated Whitman's genius and acknowledged a debt to the poet of the Open Road, Lawrence protested that too often "Whitman becomes in his own person the whole world, the whole universe, the whole eternity of time."

Compounding the irony, Lawrence elsewhere used the same objection to decry the kind of "love" which becomes (as in Poe) a "glowing unison with all the universe." Yet Lawrence himself was as great a Merger in his poems of love as in his nature poetry.   Sometimes, indeed, he combined the two themes: The poet-lover and his beloved know bliss when they can diffuse into a setting of pastoral harmony, misery when they and nature cannot coalesce.

In one of his first love lyrics, Lawrence wrote of a wish to "lie quite still, till the green/Sky ceased to quiver, and lost its active sheen./"

> I should like to drop
> On the hay, with my head on her knee,
> And lie dead still, while she

> Breathed quiet above me; and the crop
> Of stars grew silently.
>
> I should like to lie still
> As if I was dead; but feeling
> Her hand go stealing
> Over my face and my head, until
> This ache was shed.

The image expresses the desire for an experience that is unconscious, yet conscious and feeling too; to be free of demands and responsibilities, of pain and struggle, to merge with something warm and comforting in suspended, isolated darkness: that is the recurring prospect of the love poems. Instead of the drive for conquest and exaggerated sexual triumph which we find in the novels, the poetry expresses a desire for nirvana and a sexual yielding.

This love which the poet craves is invoked repeatedly in the mother poems:

> Then I longed for you with your mantle of love to fold
> Me over, and drive from out my body the deep
> Cold that had sunk to my soul, and there kept hold.

And years later, in the poems celebrating his relationship with Frieda, Lawrence was still writing of the love-impulse this way:

> So I hope I shall spend eternity
> With my face down buried between her breasts;
> And my still heart full of security
> And my still hands full of her breasts.

Elsewhere, the poet wishes to blend with the beloved in a fluid harmony, "liquid" frequently becoming the medium of total immersion:

> Ah, drink me up
> That I may be
> Within your cup
> Like a mystery,
> Like wine that is still
> In ecstasy.
>
> Glimmering still
> In ecstasy
> Commingled wines
> Of you and me
> In one fulfill
> The mystery.

And in a common variation of the pattern, the lovers figuratively melt into a flame, "a bonfire of oneness."

The merge-wish appears in still other love poems as a desire to *be* the beloved, to assume the passive role of the woman. "But how lovely to be you!" is the cry in "Wedlock." In "Wedding Morn," the man yields himself to the overpowering love of the woman: "carelessly," "unconsciously," "helplessly," he is "at last laid low" by her. The woman speaks the piece, for the man in his fulfillment sleeps "satiate/with a sunk, unconscious head." In other narrative poems in which the narrator is a woman, the focus is on her experience as she submits to the male's advances. Thus, the final stanza of "Love on the Farm" is a direct evocation of sexual passivity:

> And down his mouth comes to my mouth! and down
> His bright dark eyes come over me, like a hood
> Upon my mind! his lips meet mine, and a flood
> Of sweet fire sweeps across me, so I drown
> Against him, die, and find death good.

"The effect is startling. . . as S. W. Powell has stated. "For one feels that [the poet] is not merely impersonating the woman: he is the woman, and Lawrence the man is deleted."

While the poet craves inactive love, he fears the love which makes demands, which insists on a participation or action. From this love, the poet longs to be free. He hates "the burden of self-accomplishment:/The charge of fulfillment!" and he seeks escape. In "End of Another Home Holiday," a mother-poem contemporaneous with the early love lyrics to Miriam, Love is described as "the great Asker," "the beggar-woman," and is contrasted throughout the poem with the animals and the natural elements, for the latter are happy and peaceful in undisturbed isolation:

> The sun and the rain do not ask the secret
> Of the time when the grain struggles down in the dark . . .
> The moon sets forth o'nights
> To walk the lonely, dusky heights
> Serenely, with steps, unswerving;
> Pursued by no sight of bereavement
> No tears of love unnerving
> Her constant tread.

The heifer seeks a "loneliness"; the grain buries itself in the earth, "to hide."

> Nay, even the slumberous egg, as it labours under the shell
>     Patiently to divide and self-divide,
> Asks to be hidden, and wishes nothing to tell.
> But when I draw the scanty cloak of silence over my eyes
> Piteous love comes peering under the hood. . . .
> With a hoarse, insistent request that falls
>     Unweariedly, unweariedly,
>     Asking something more of me,
>         Yet more of me.

The emotional balance of the poem is thus established between the tired wretchedness of the poet, who is crying in plaintive protest against the beggar-woman, and the peacefulness of nature, which is allowed to go its way unmolested. In his desire for silent serenity, the poet likens himself to nature; it is only "love" which disturbs him, as if a hound were intruding on a sleeping calf.

Lawrence's poems on tortoises reiterate this theme. The poet sympathizes with the male tortoise, the "poor darling" who is the smaller and more delicate of the species, who has to suffer in humiliation the sex demands of the laconic and insensitive female hulk. He is "doomed," "divided into passionate duality,"

> ... now broken into desirous fragmentariness
> Doomed to make an intolerable fool of himself
> In his effort toward completion again.

Meanwhile, the baby tortoise enjoys the perfect freedom of "isolation"; one must envy this creature who thrives alone, untouched by demands of any kind.

> To be a tortoise!
> Think of it, in a garden of inert clods
> A brisk, brindled little tortoise, all to himself—
> Adam!
> . . .
> Moving and being himself,
> Slow, and unquestioned.

And one must grieve that the baby will some day face an adult sex responsibility. For this is the deadly fate of the male:

> Grim, gruesome gallantry, to which he is doomed,
> Dragged out of an eternity of silent isolation,
> And doomed to partiality, partial being,
> Ache, and want of being,
> Want,
> Self-exposure, hard humiliation, need to add himself to her.
> . . .
> And the still more awful need to persist, to follow, follow, continue,
> Driven, after aeons of pristine, fore-god-like singleness and oneness,
> At the end of some mysterious red-hot iron,
> Driven away from himself into her tracks . . .

The consistency in Lawrence's poems of love resides in the poet's yearning for harmony and inactivity. Whether the immediate objective is to merge or to isolate, whether the wish is to be free of a discordant demand or to be folded over in an oblivion, the goal is a passive oneness. There must be no infringement on the poet's "freedom"; there must be no need for action or response. When others come too close, he retreats. Explicitly, "Excursion Train" at once acknowledges the anguish of demanding love and cherishes the peacefulness of an undemanding envelopment:

> You hurt my heart-beat's privacy;
> I wish I could put you away from me;

> I suffocate in this intimacy
>> In which I half love you . . .
> Though surely my soul's best dream is still
> That a new night pouring down shall swill
> Us away in an utter sleep.

We know that in his personal life Lawrence ran into constant conflict with other people. All his life he searched for some "sweet home" of peace, purity, and brotherhood. His plans for a brotherly utopia filled dozens of letters and occupied much fervent conversation, but the dream never approached realization, principally because of Lawrence's perfectionism, his dissatisfaction with each person and place as it became here and now. ("I sort of wish I could go to the moon.") The way in which Lawrence projected into his novels an inadequate resolution of this dilemma is typified by *The Plumed Serpent,* where he contrasts the real, modern Mexico which disgusted him with an ideal reprimitivized culture of his own incredible design. In his poems, he was writing more credibly, without ambivalence:

> I like people quite well at a little distance.
> I like to see them passing and passing
> and going their own way,
>> especially if I see their aloneness alive in them.
>
> Yet I don't want them to come near.
> If they will only leave me alone
> I can still have the illusion that there is
>> room enough in the world.

This way, in the vicinity of people yet undefiled by them, the poet retains the integrity of his quiescence. Otherwise, the discordant world must be shunned. In a verse about misunderstood adolescence, the young Lawrence wrote that he was glad to be "remote":

> I sit absolved, assured I am better off
> Beyond a world I never want to join.

In the poems of his maturity, the world is still oppressive and threatening:

>> Ah, if only
> There were no teeming
> Swarms of mankind in the world, and we were less lonely.

For aloneness can become intolerable too. The harmony can be spoiled by the discord of one's self and its awareness. Knowing per se, the consciousness of existence, can be too active. Whereupon the poet cries out against the demands of his own being:

> And oh—
>> That the man I am
>> Might cease to be.

For, although Lawrence insisted in his mystical psychology on "the deep, rich aloneness" by which a man should "possess his own soul in strength within him, deep and alone," he never portrayed self-sufficiency with conviction. His novels fracture on characters who aggressively declare their independence, yet who unwittingly reveal their dependencies. The poems not only acknowledge the dependencies, but focus especially upon them.

When Lawrence called Whitman "fearfully mistaken" for trying to merge with the whole world, he granted the need for some intimacy, but claimed that Whitman had gone so far in embracing the "All" that he had led himself straight to "Death." Though each organism, including man, is intrinsically "isolate and single," Lawrence explained, it must be continually "vivified" through "contact with other matter." The "blood systems" of man and woman should meet and "almost fuse." But, Lawrence emphasized, they must maintain that final thin barrier. Merging would mean some form of Death. And so, Lawrence charged, apparently unaware of the irony, Whitman the self-styled poet of Life had betrayed his own cause: "Love, and Merging, brought Whitman to the edge of Death! Death! Death!"

> This is strange from the exultant Walt.
> Death!
> Death is now his chant! Death!
> Merging! And Death! Which is the final merge.
> The great merge into the womb. Woman.
> And after that, the merge of comrades: man-for-man love.
> And almost immediately with this, death, the final merge of death.
> There you have the progression of merging. For the great mergers,
>     woman at last becomes inadequate. For those who love to extremes,
>     Woman is inadequate for the last merging. So the next step is the
> merging of the man-for-man Love. And this is on the brink of death.
> It slides over into death.

Lawrence's description of Whitman's "progression" could, of course, stand as a tracing of the cycle in his own works. For death, a subject which hovers about a good deal of Lawrence's poetry, predominates in the *Last Poems*. Images of darkness and oblivion and the silence of waters convey the theme. Praising these poems as among Lawrence's best, Kenneth Rexroth has written, "In the last hours Lawrence seems to have lived in a state of suspended animation, removed from the earth, floating." But whereas Rexroth attributes this state exclusively to the fact that Lawrence was "transfigured by the immediacy of death," these poems actually carry through to their logical conclusion the moods, attitudes, and themes of Lawrence's whole previous body of poetry. Early in his career, Lawrence had written:

> I wish the church had covered me up with the rest
> In the home-place. Why is it she should exclude
> Me so distinctly from sleeping the sleep I'd love best?

And he had often used such images as this one:

> Not sleep, which is grey with dreams,
> nor death, which quivers with birth,
> but heavy, sealing darkness, silence, all immovable . . .

Compare these earlier poems with a typical "last" poem, "The End, The Beginning":

> And if there were not an absolute, utter forgetting
> and a ceasing to know, a perfect ceasing to know
> and a silent, sheer cessation of all awareness
> how terrible life would be!
> how terrible it would be to think and know, to have consciousness!
> But dipped, once dipped in dark oblivion
> the soul has peace, inward and lovely peace.

If there is any change, the quiescence has become an immediate, felt reality rather than a yearning. "The waters of oblivion" are at hand without the seeking for them that had marked many of the earlier poems. Where the younger poet had written, "You know how it rests/ One to be quenched, to be given up, to be gone in the dark;/ To be blown out, to let night douse the spark," the later poet is at peace for the most part. In one version of "The Ship of Death," written during his last days, Lawrence carries through a figure of the "little soul" rowing over the seas on its "longest journey, towards the greatest goal"—"the womb of silence in the living night." And in the same final period, he wrote "The Breath of Life," quoted here in its entirety:

> The breath of life is in the sharp winds of change
> Mingled with the breath of destruction.
> But if you want to breathe deep, sumptuous life,
> Breathe all alone, in silence, in the dark
> and see nothing.

It would be oversimplification to label the impulse a "death wish." For the ideal is still what Lawrence calls "an oblivion of uttermost living." One is "not quite dead"—or more than dead. The poet seeks to be acted upon so that his state of perfect harmony will be perpetuated in sensate consciousness. He shall have only to *be* in the most quiescent sense as he is lulled softly within the darkness. Life is "a cat asleep on a chair, at peace," and the end for which the poet prepares is a goal he has sought all his life: "a long, long journey . . . to the sweet home of pure oblivion."

*South Atlantic Quarterly*, 55:3.July 1956.

All quotations from Lawrence's poems are from the two-volume *Collected Poems* (1928) and the *Last Poems* (1933) edited by Richard Aldington.

## Keith Sagar, "Open Self and Open Poem: The Stages of D.H. Lawrence's Poetic Quest"

What I want to do here is to give an account of Lawrence's spiritual and artistic development in terms of a small number of key poems. I want to follow through these poems the implications of four key symbols representing four stages of growth (or, perhaps, sickness, diagnosis, prescription, and cure): they are womb, wind, fissure, and underworld. These are symbols not only of the content of these and many other poems, but also of their form.

There are not many good poems among those Lawrence chose to call his Rhyming Poems, and their inferiority is not unrelated to the fact that most of them rhyme. Even those that do not are "closed" within straight-jackets of meter, lineation, and stanza which prevent the full flow of his imagination. I am not, of course, suggesting that these formal elements of poetry always constrict imagination. For Donne, for example, or Hopkins, rhyme releases great energies built up by the approaching rhythm. For Yeats, rhyming and the other formal demands of his craft enabled him to focus and concentrate his attention, to clarify his vision and reach the meanings that were in him.   But there are other great poets, among whom Whitman and Lawrence and Ted Hughes are striking examples, for whom rhyming, meter, stanza and so on have nothing to offer. At the stage of his career when Lawrence felt that these were essential elements of poetry, they merely prevented him from getting at the "real naked essence" (*Letters I* 519) of his vision. Hughes has spoken of "the terrible, suffocating, maternal octopus" (Faas 201) of the received poetic tradition (the tradition mediated to Lawrence in his childhood by Palgrave's *Golden Treasury*). And that is just what it was for the mature Lawrence.

After the Rhyming Poems came *Look! We Have Come Through!* The significance of this title has always been taken to be purely biographical. But if Lawrence had had his way, the title of *New Poems* would have been *Coming Awake*, and when we look at this title in conjunction with the title Lawrence gave to the introduction to the American edition, "Poetry of the Present," we see clearly that what he felt himself to be belatedly awakening from was the trance of the past. And this trance seems to have lasted a good deal longer in the context of poetry than of fiction, because it is not simply a matter of cutting the umbilical cord that had tied Lawrence emotionally to his mother for so long, even after her death, but also of making it new, which meant, in the context of poetry, getting out from under that "maternal octopus." What he needed to come through to was not only his marriage, but also a new poetic.

This is very clearly exemplified by the history of the much-discussed poem "Piano." The first version (*Collected Poems* 943) was written during Lawrence's years at Nottingham University College, probably in 1908. Like many other poems of that period, it is purely sentimental, nostalgic.   By the time Lawrence came to revise those poems in January 1916 for *Amores*, he sought a way to record the immature experience faithfully and yet at the same time to escape from it, to consign it to a now-dead past. But the very form of the poem, the kind of poetry it was, resisted any such undermining. Lawrence was still not satisfied with it, and held it back for further revision, to appear finally in *New Poems*, in 1918.

The poem is, of course, about *two* pianos, and two women. It begins and ends with the living woman who sings to him, at first softly, later passionately, at a great black piano. But the poem never realizes her. She is not *there* in the poem at all, just a vague anonymous figure in the dusk. She was not there for the poet. She could not compete, for all her passion and clamor, with the woman he once called the only woman he had ever truly loved—his mother, with the memories her music evokes from the past, a past remembered in vivid loving detail.   The young woman's singing has quite the opposite effect from what she had intended. She is obviously inviting him to take a romantic interest in her, to become emotionally involved. He would like to respond, but "in spite of himself" the song betrays him back to the mother whose memory eclipses all other women. He does not just recapture the past, he has never left it. He is still that child, in a miniature, enclosed world, curled up under the keyboard of a small upright piano, pressing his mother's feet, pressed against the piano so that he feels rather than hears the music; it booms and tingles. Life comes to him through the mother with whom he is in close physical contact. The image is of total warmth, security, and cosiness. It is an image of the womb. But the warmth and security which are necessary and life-giving to a small child have become disabling to the young man in his mid-twenties who should be free to move out into the unknown, into a wider world of mature sexual relationships: "The glamour of childish days is upon me, my manhood is cast / Down in the flood of remembrance, I weep like a child for the past" (*Collected Poems* 48). These closing lines have all the despair of a man behind bars, and the bars are those of the poem as well as of the psychological situation, for the inherited form of the poem is also part of the suffocating, maternal past. The poem is a closed system designed to answer certain expectations. It is a form which is superbly equipped to evoke sentiment and nostalgia, but offers no possibility of escape from them, however aware the poet may be that these are but symptoms of his sickness. The poem in its final form works splendidly as diagnosis, but cannot operate as auto-therapy. The revision transforms the charge of the poem from positive to negative, but the poem is as closed as ever to anything outside its own nostalgic terms of reference. Cosiness simply becomes claustrophobia. Such poetry could speak for the young man, but not for the demon. The young man, in Lawrence's words, is afraid of the demon and puts his hand over the demon's mouth and speaks for him. No amount of revision could allow the voice of the demon to come through.

Within a few weeks of publishing this poem, Lawrence wrote to Katherine Mansfield:

> At certain periods the man has a desire and a tendency to return unto the woman, make her his goal and end, find his justification in her. In this way he casts himself as it were into her womb, and she, the Magna Mater, receives him with gratification. This is a kind of incest. . . . I have done it, and now struggle all my might to get out. In a way, Frieda is the devouring mother.—It is awfully hard, once the sex relation has gone this way, to recover. If we don't recover, we die. (*Letters III* 301-02)

Thus the theme of the poem was still an urgent issue for Lawrence in 1918, but whereas *Women in Love* and some of the best poems from *Look! We Have Come Through!* were part of the struggle to get out, to come awake, to recover from disabling sickness, "Piano," partly because of the kind of poem it was, could make no such contribution.

* * *

The violent break Lawrence made with his past when he left England with Frieda in 1912 immediately affected his poetry. Frieda said, "Any new thing must find a new shape, then afterwards one can call it 'art'" (*Memoirs* 186). Her iconoclasm was catching. In most of the poems of *Look! We Have Come Through!* Lawrence sheds all the formal disciplines which had crippled his earlier verse. His primary concern now is "to get an emotion out in its own course, without altering it. It needs the finest instinct imaginable, much finer than the skill of the craftsmen. . . . Sometimes Whitman is perfect" (*Letters II* 61). Or again: "It is the hidden *emotional* pattern that makes poetry, not the obvious form. . . . It doesn't depend on the ear, particularly, but on the sensitive soul and the ear gets a habit, and becomes master, when the ebbing and lifting emotion should be master, and the ear the transmitter." He was aware of "a constant war" being fought out within him "between new expression and the habituated, mechanical transmitters and receivers of the human constitution" (104-05).

A key poem here is "Song of a Man Who Has Come Through." I have analyzed the poem and its imagery at length elsewhere (*Life into Art* 31-33). Here I will simply point out that the wind to which the poet tries to open himself is the opposite of the claustrophobic womb of "Piano" and most of the earlier poems. It represents the not-self or unknown, imprisoned self; but also what he was later to describe as "the unrestful, ungraspable poetry of the sheer present, poetry whose very permanency lies in its wind-like transit" (*Collected Poems* 183). The rock which must be split is the womb-wall now hardened into a thick shell, the insentient ego which fears to leave the house of its own building, and the inheritance of rigid ideas and forms from the dead past.

But the poem is prayer for such poetry, not yet an example of it. In comparison with the best of the later poems, the language and its rhythms are slightly second-hand. The opening line is lifted from Nietzsche: "Not I! Not I! but a *God* through my instrumentality!" (*Joyful Wisdom* 179), and the whole poem is made up of biblical echoes and time-honored romantic symbols. These symbols are, indeed, archetypes, and Lawrence adapts them well to his purpose, but they are not transformed with the wit and daring with which he uses traditional symbols and myths and literary sources in *Birds, Beasts and Flowers*. Moreover, most of the poem is in the conditional tense—"If only. . . ." One has to have come a long way to know the right things to pray for, but the prayer is not answered within the poem; nor are the angels actually admitted. It would need a different order of awareness and of poetry to describe what would happen if they were. Lawrence still has some way to go before he and his art are ready for such an encounter.

Just a month after writing this poem, Lawrence met the remarkable poet Anna Wickham, who became his neighbor in Hampstead for the latter part of 1915 (see

Pollnitz 137-38). Among the as-yet-unpublished poems she showed Lawrence was this: "Rhymed verse is a wide net / Through which many subtleties escape. / Nor would I take it to capture a strong thing / Such as a whale." Rhymed verse would have been, henceforth for Lawrence, a net to catch the wind.

As early as 1911 Lawrence had registered the way modern poetry was going: "Synge asks for the brutalising of English poetry. Thomas Hardy and George Meredith have, to some extent, answered. But in point of brutality the Germans— and they at the heels of the French and Belgians—are miles ahead of us." ("Two Hitherto Unknown Pieces" 4) But it needed the war to bring him to share Yeats's sense of the impertinence of poetic rhetoric of any kind, of the need to walk naked, to "wither into the truth." In January 1916 he wrote: "The essence of poetry with us in this age of stark and unlovely actualities is a stark directness, without a shadow of a lie, or a shadow of deflection anywhere. Everything can go, but this stark, bare, rocky directness of statement, this alone makes poetry, today" (*Letters II* 503). There is a brutal and naked humanity reminiscent of Brecht in, for example, "After the Opera," which ends: "But when I meet the weary eyes / The reddened aching eyes of the bar-man with thin arms, / I am glad to go back where I came from" (*Collected Poems* 71).

After the war Lawrence's interest in poetry revived. Though he was writing no verse at the time, the summer of 1919 saw the writing of his most important theoretical essay on poetry, "Poetry of the Present," and also the second and earliest surviving version of his essay on Whitman. What Lawrence needed from verse was a means of access to the hidden realities and a means of articulating, bringing into consciousness, the revelations bubbling up from the depths of his being; a means, also, of healing the split psyche of Western man. The answer, he decided was free verse:

> Free verse is, or should be, direct utterance from the instant, whole man. It is the soul and the mind and body surging at once, nothing left out . . . . We can get rid of the stereotyped movements and the old hackneyed associations of sound or sense. We can break down those artifical conduits and canals through which we do so love to force our utterance. We can break the stiff neck of habit. We can be in ourselves spontaneous and flexible as flame, we can see that utterance rushes out without artifical form or artificial smoothness. . . . For such utterance any externally-applied law would be mere shackles and death. The law must come new each time from within. (*Collected Poems* 182-83)

When we try to account for the amazing explosion of great poems which came in Sicily in 1920, we shall have to give some credit to Sicily itself, the transforming effect of exposure to that volcanic climate and spirit of place, and to the sense of release brought by the end of the war and the escape from England and persecution and poverty; but we must also give a great deal of credit to Whitman. When Lawrence had first read Whitman in his youth, he had been impressed, but apart from a few lines in such poems as "The Wild Common" had been unable to assimilate Whitman as a poetic influence. When he reread Whitman in 1918 it was another story. Whitman's verse, in terms of its cadences, met almost all Lawrence's needs; it was the verse equivalent of the wind and the fountain: "It sweeps past for ever, like a wind that is forever in passage, and unchainable. Whitman truly looked before and after. But he did not sigh for what is not. The clue to all his utterance lies in the sheer appreciation of the instant moment, life surging itself into utterance at its very well-head" (*Collected Poems* 183). In the unpublished "Whitman" essay, Lawrence elaborated:

> It springs purely spontaneous from the well-heads of consciousness.  The primal soul utters itself in strange pulsations, gushes and strokes of sound. At his best Whitman gives these throbs naked and vibrating as they emerge from the quick. They follow, pulse after pulse, line after line, each one new and unforeseeable. They are lambent, they are life itself. Such are the lines. But in the whole, moreover, the whole soul speaks at once: sensual impulse instinct with spiritual impulse, and the mind serving, giving pure attention. The lovely blood-lapping sounds of consonants slipping with fruit of vowels is unsurpassed and unsurpassable, in a thousand lines. Take any opening line, almost.—"Out of the cradle endlessly rocking—" . . . Or again "By the bivouac's fitful flame" and "When lilacs last in the dooryard bloom'd"—it goes straight to the soul, nothing intervenes. There is the sheer creative gesture, moving the material world in wonderful swirls. The whole soul follows its own free, spontaneous, inexplicable course, its contradictions and pulsations dictated from nowhere save from the creative quick itself. And each separate line is a pulsation and a contraction. There is nothing measured or mechanical.  This is the greatest poetry.[1]

The next poem I want to draw attention to is "Peach." I can think of three poetic associations of the peach before Lawrence. In Marvell's poem "The Garden," "The Nectaren and curious Peach / Into my hands themselves do reach." This one-ness, atonement, of man and nature is only conceivable in Eden before the creation of Eve and the eating of the apple: "Such was that happy Garden-state, / While Man there walk'd without a Mate." Hopkins admits that he can never sink his teeth into a peach without a sense of sin. And when Eliot's Prufrock tries to think of the wildest, least prudent act, he asks "Do I dare to eat a peach?" Why this association between the peach and sexual sin? "Peach" consists of a series of provocative questions:

> Why so velvety, why so voluptuous heavy?
> Why hanging with such inordinate weight?
> Why so indented?
>
> Why the groove?
> Why the lovely, bivalve roundnesses?
> Why the ripple down the sphere?
> Why the suggestion of incision?
>
> Why was not my peach round and finished liked a billiard ball?
> It would have been if man had made it. (*Collected Poems* 279)

A much later poem, "Whatever Man Makes," contains the lines: "And a Navaho woman, weaving her rug in the pattern of her dream / must run the pattern out in a little break at the end / so that her soul can come out, back to her" (448). And I have heard that the Chinese master potters, if they found they had made too perfect a pot, of "finished beauty and measured symmetry" (185), would gently nudge it with the heel of the hand before the wheel stopped. Or, as Ursula le Guin puts it: "When mind uses itself without the hands it runs the circle and may go too fast. The hand that shapes the mind into clay or written word slows thought to the gait of things and lets it be subject to accident and time. Purity is on the edge of evil, they say" (*Always Coming Home* 175). Nature abhors the billiard ball, the perfect-unto-itself sealed monad, the closed system. Auden claimed that Lawrence's argument in "Poetry of the Present" was invalid because a poem, unlike cyclical organic processes, is "a motion in one direction towards a definite end" (*Dyer's Hand* 283). The interrogative, freewheeling, spontaneous, repetitive, directionless, open style Lawrence is now developing is precisely a technique for enabling the object or experience to escape from the conceptualizing, abstracting, humanizing tyranny of tainted words and closed poems. It was Lawrence's very success in this respect which made him so immeasurably superior to Auden as a poet. Lawrence does not denigrate "the lovely form of metrical verse" and the "unfading timeless gems" produced in it; but he does show some contempt for those who, like the new critics with their insistence on the poem as well-wrought urn, exalt their own fear of mutability into an aesthetic principle: "There is no static perfection, none of that finality which we find so satisfying because we are so frightened" (*Collected Poems* 184). Art, for Lawrence, is not an alternative to transient life, but a means of understanding and accepting it: "There must be the rapid momentaneous association of things which meet and pass on the forever incalculable journey of creation: everything left in its own rapid, fluid relationship with the rest of things" (183).

The attempt to set up the perfection of Art as superior to the imperfection of Nature is characteristic of hubristic Western man. Lawrence's concept of art is increasingly open and natural and therefore female.

The fruit poems with which *Birds, Beasts and Flowers* opens are heavily and overtly sexual: "For fruits are all of them female, in them lies the seed. And so when they break and show the seed, we look into the womb and see its secrets. So it is that the pomegranate is the apple of love to the Arab, and the fig has been a catch-word for the female fissure for ages" (277).

But the fissure in these poems is by no means only "the female part"; that in turn symbolizes any opening to the womb of life, the source, the quick— suffering, for example, as well as sex, as in "Pomegranate":

And, if you dare, the fissure!

Do you mean to tell me you will see no fissure?
Do you prefer to look on the plain side?

For all that, the setting suns are open.
The end cracks open with the beginning:
Rosy, tender, glittering within the fissure.

Do you mean to tell me there should be no fissure?
No glittering, compact drops of dawn?
Do you mean it is wrong, the gold-filmed skin, integument, shown ruptured?

For my part, I prefer my heart to be broken.
It is so lovely, dawn-kaleidoscopic within the crack. (*Collected Poems* 278-79)

In *Lady Chatterley's Lover* Lawrence was to write of "a new flux that would change one away from the old self as a landscape is transfigured by earthquake and lava floods." Sicily changed Lawrence in just this way, providing him with rich imagery of such transformation. What emerges through the fissure in these poems is not angels but streams of red-hot lava, royal snakes, hounds of hell pursuing Persephone. All the flora and fauna of Sicily are but manifestations of a deeper more potent life in the underworld, the world under the world.

Lawrence's creed, which he offers as an alternative to Benjamin Franklin's narrowly anthropocentric creed, focusses on the opening-up of communications between the human and the non-human, the self and the not-self, the conscious and the unconscious. Lawrence believed:

> *"That I am I."*
>
> *"That my soul is a dark forest."*
>
> *"That my known self will never be more than a little clearing in the forest."*
>
> *"That gods, strange gods, come forth from the forest into the clearing of my known self, and then go back."*
>
> *"That I must have the courage to let them come and go."*
>
> *"That I will never let mankind put anything over me, but that I will try always to recognize and submit to the gods in me and the gods in other men and women."* *(Studies* 22).

These strange gods are symbolized in the poems by birds, beasts, and flowers. There are several poems, "Snake" and "Man and Bat," for example, about how difficult it is even to simply let them come and go, to shed all the humanistic assumptions which mankind (the voice of one's education) has been putting over one all one's life. The strong temptation is to anthropomorphize flora and fauna, which is an attempt to accommodate them to that which is known.

Lawrence's misanthropy was in one sense a sickness, but in another a healthy purging of his hitherto anthropocentric vision and of what was left of the anthropomorphic attitude to Nature of his youth. Man now appears on the scene, if at all, as the intruder, the aberration, who, in the presence of the sacred, can think of nothing better to do than to try to kill it (or, in psychological terms, refuse to acknowledge it, drive it into the seething darkness of the unconscious).

For the ancient Greeks the snake was the most sacred of beasts for three reasons. It seemed to them less differentiated from *zoë*, the raw life-force ("Being earth-brown, earth golden from the burning bowels of the earth" . . . "writhed like lightning") than any other creature. Especially when it reared up, it suggested to them the erect phallus, and thus became a male fertility symbol. And its capacity to emerge renewed from its shed skin seemed to them a living testimony of resurrection. So the snake was sacred to the god Aesculapius, god of health and rebirth.

Baring and Cashford testify that "in images of the goddess in every culture the serpent is never far away, behind her, eating from her hand, entwined in her tree, or even, as in Tiamat, the shape of the goddess herself. . . . As the male aspect of the goddess was differentiated, the serpent became the fertilizing phallus, image of the god who was her son and consort, born from her, married with her and dying back into her for rebirth in unending cycle" (499). Pictures of the primal scene in the Garden of Eden are indistinguishable from pictures of the mother goddess with her snake and tree. Only the interpretation has been inverted, the serpent having been the first of beasts to receive Yahweh's curse, transforming him from a lord of life into a lord of death. In "Snake" Lawrence seeks to reverse this transformation. "Snake" re-enacts in a modern setting and a realistic mode, the primal crime, the crime of Marduk, Oedipus, Pentheus, Adonis, and, as the poem itself indicates ("And I thought of the Albatross"), of the Ancient Mariner.

At first the narrator feels something of the wonder with which the snake was seen in the ancient world. But that atavistic response is immediately challenged by the voice of his education telling him that venomous snakes must be killed. But of course this aggression has nothing to do with physical danger. We are now conditioned to respond to the snake as an embodiment of sin and evil. The civilized response is the same whether the snake is venomous or not. Men are also conditioned to measure their manhood by their "courage" in killing monsters, or, indeed, any wild life.

The narrator does not, however, obey that voice until the moment when the snake puts its head "into that horrid black hole . . . the earth-lipped fissure." This act triggers the hysterical and pointless violence. The snake as phallus penetrates the earth mother, and the puritan conditioning of the narrator is such that he cannot respond to that act other than with "a sort of horror" as to the ultimate obscenity.

The narrator is not Lawrence, who had long ago rejected the voice of his education, and had spontaneously welcomed as a "dainty and superb princess" the beautiful brindled adder which visited him in Cornwall in 1916. Yet a year later, thinking of the symbolic significance of snakes for him, he was unable to detach the image from the context of shame, horror, and corruption provided by our culture:

> If there is a serpent of shame and shameful desire in my soul, let me not beat it out of my consciousness with sticks. It will lie beyond, in the marsh of the so-called subconsciousness, where I cannot follow it with my sticks. . . . I must admit the genuineness of my horror, accept it, and not exclude it from my understanding. . . . Then let the serpent of living corruption take his place among us honourably. . . . For the Lord is the lord of all things, not of some only. And everything shall in its proportion drink its own draught of life. (*Phoenix* 677-79)

This is an advance on the voice of his education, but one which takes him not much further than Freud, and by 1920 Lawrence had turned violently against Freud:

> With dilated hearts we watch Freud disappearing into the cavern of darkness, which is sleep and unconsciousness to us. . . . What was there in the cave? Alas that we ever looked! Nothing but a huge slimy serpent of sex, and heaps of excrement, and a myriad repulsive little horrors spawned between sex and excrement. Is it true? Does the great unknown of sleep contain nothing else? No lovely spirits in the anterior regions of our being? (*Fantasia* 203)

Thus in the poem Lawrence castigates the mistakes not only of unregenerate men, but also of his own earlier self, concentrating into a few minutes of poetic time an education in consciousness which had taken him decades. For by the end of the poem the narrator, our representative, has learned that he must expiate the pettiness of the whole perverse rigmarole of sin and guilt which Western Man has allowed to be foisted onto his psyche.

The fissure is, among other things, an image for the creative or mythic imagination, corresponding to Joseph Campbell's description of the myth as "the secret opening through which the inexhaustible energies of the cosmos pour into human cultural manifestation" (*Hero* 13). As early as 1915, Lawrence had used the image in connection with the female, with prophetesses and "some of the great women saints": "the truth came as through a fissure from the depths and the burning darkness that lies out of the depth of time." (According to one version of the myth, Cassandra acquired the gift of prophecy when sacred snakes licked her ears.) The fate of Cassandra at the hands of the male (including Apollo) Lawrence takes to be "symbolic of what mankind has done to her since—raped and despoiled and mocked her, to their own ruin. It is not your brain you trust to, nor your will—but to that fundamental pathetic faculty for receiving the hidden waves that come from the depths of life, and for transferring them to the unreceptive world. It is something which happens below the consciousness, and below the range of the will—it is something which is unrecognized and frustrated and destroyed" (*Letters II* 297-98). In *Kangaroo* we find: "Alone like a pythoness on her tripod, like the oracle alone above the fissure into the unknown. The oracle, the fissure down into the unknown, the strange exhalations from the dark, the strange words that the oracle must utter. Strange cruel, pregnant words: the new term of consciousness" (310). And in a 1926 letter to Rolf Gardiner: "We'll have to establish some spot on earth, that will be the fissure into the under world, like the oracle at Delphos" (*Letters V* 591). We are familiar with the Delphic oracle, through Greek tragedy, as the oracle of Apollo; but Lawrence is clearly thinking of the original Delphic oracle which was the Oracle of Mother Earth. (Cashford and Baring speak of "her priestesses, sitting in the hot sun beside cracks in the earth" [305].) When Apollo wounded Python with his arrows, the serpent fled to the Oracle at Delphi "but Apollo dared follow him into the shrine, and there despatched him beside the sacred chasm" (Graves 76). Zeus demanded expiation, but Apollo, having coaxed the secret of prophesy from Pan, "seized the Delphic Oracle and retained its priestess, called the Pythoness, in his own service."

For Lawrence Etna was such a "fissure into the under world"; and the debate within him between the voice of spontaneous reverence for the creatures of that world, and the voice of his education, is a debate between Dionysos and Apollo, with Apollo, the apotheosis of reason, characteristically resorting to violence. Since the narrator in the poem is not Lawrence but a representative of our civilization, it is essential that Apollo wins, by fair means or foul, leaving the man "accursed." He repents too late, seeing belatedly that the snake is "Like a king in exile, uncrowned in the under world, / Now due to be crowned again" (*Collected Poems* 351). We cannot but think of Lucifer, once brightest of angels, and of what Frederick Carter calls "the mysterious triple communion in the garden between woman and snake and man from which it would seem came the discovery of seed and its purpose" (*Body Mystical* 29).

\* \* \*

The witty, throwaway style of "Peach" or "Figs" will not serve when it is a matter of recognizing and submitting to the gods of snakes, bats, or fishes. What is needed is a technique for shutting out the voices of education and "listening-in to the voices of the honourable beasts that call in the dark paths of the veins of our body, from the God in the heart" (*Phoenix* 759). Description pulls us towards betraying similes. A pike is not, in the last analysis, "like a lout on an obscure pavement." He is not like anything in our world: "I had made a mistake, I didn't know him, / This grey, monotonous soul in the water, / This intense individual in shadow, / Fish-alive. / I didn't know his God. / I didn't know his God" (*Collected Poems* 338).

The god of the flora and fauna and of the human unconscious is, if he can be named, Dionysos or Hades (who, according to Heraclitos, are one). The courage to admit messengers from that realm is only a stage in the journey. Much greater courage is needed to abandon the world of normal human consciousness altogether and follow those messengers back through the fissure into their world. That shamanic journey, is already adumbrated in one or two of the fruit poems, "Grapes" for example:

> And if we sip the wine, we find dreams coming upon us
> Out of the imminent night.
> Nay, we find ourselves crossing the fern-scented frontiers
> Of the world before the floods, where man was dark and evasive
> And the tiny vine-flower rose of all roses, perfumed,
> And all in naked communion communicating as now our clothed
>      vision can never communicate. (286)

Even beyond the journey into "naked communion" is the leave-taking, the "Orphic farewell" of dissolution described in "Medlars and Sorb Apples":

> Going down the strange lanes of hell, more and more intensely alone,
> The fibres of the heart parting one after the other
> And yet the soul continuing, naked-footed, ever more vividly embodied
> Like a flame blown whiter and whiter
> In a deeper and deeper darkness
> Ever more exquisite, distilled in separation. (281)

For the full exploration of that dark region, without benefit of intoxication, we must wait for Lawrence's last poems, when he had to prepare himself in imagination for the "imminent night" of death. The only fully open soul is that of a dying man. Yet even in the magnificent spiritual and poetic achievement of "Bavarian Gentians" and "The Ship of Death," Lawrence found himself betrayed back to the world of that which we can presume to understand, betrayed by the Orphic myths and esoteric oriental doctrines which enable us to invest with attributes whatever lies beyond the life of the body; and that is to violate the tabernacle: "But anyone who shall ascribe attributes to God or oblivion / let him be cast out, for blasphemy. / For God is a deeper forgetting far than sleep / and all description is a blasphemy" (726). Can we imagine poems which would eschew all description? Perhaps they would be like Tamil Vacanas, or some poems by such post-war Eastern European poets as Popa and Pilinszky, or the Epilogue poems in Hughes's *Gaudete* . . . to an English reader still "new, strange flowers" indeed.[2]

*The D.H. Lawrence Review*, 24:1, Spring, 1992.

## Works Cited

Auden, W. H. "D.H. Lawrence." *The Dyer's Hand and Other Essays*. New York: Random House, 1968, 277-95.

Baring, Anne, and Jues Cashford. *The Myth of the Goddess: Evolution of an Image*. London" Viking, 1991.

Campbell, Joseph. *The Hero with a Thousand Faces*. Princeton, NJ: Princeton UP, 1972.

Carter, Frederick. *D.H. Lawrence and the Body Mystical*. London: Archer, 1932.

Faas, Ekbert. *Ted Hughes: The Unaccommodated Universe*. Santa Barbara, CA: Black Sparrow P, 1980.

Graves, Robert. *The Greek Myths*. Harmondsworth, England: Penguin, 1960.

Lawrence, D. H. *The Collected Poems*. Ed. Vivian de Sola Pinto and F. Warren Roberts. Harmondsworth, England: Penguin, 1977.

_____. *Kangaroo*. Harmondsworth, England: Penguin, 1950.

_____. *The Letters of D.H. Lawrence: Volume I: September 1901-May 1913*. Ed. James T. Boulton. Cambridge: Cambridge UP, 1979.

_____. *The Letters of D.H. Lawrence: Volume II: June 1913-October 1916*. Ed. George J. Zytaruk and James T. Boulton. Cambridge: Cambridge UP, 1981.

_____.*The Letters of D.H. Lawrence: Voilume V: March 1924-March 1927*. Ed. James T. Boulton and Lindeth Vasey. Cambridge: Cambridge UP, 1989.

_____. *Phoenix: The Posthumous Papers of D.H. Lawrence*. Ed. Edward D. McDonald. New York: Penguin, 1980.

_____. *Studies in Classic American Literature*. Harmondsworth, England: Penguin, 1971.

_____.*Study of Thomas Hardy and Other Essays*. Ed. Bruce Steele. Cambridge: Cambridge UP, 1985.

_____. "Two Hitherto Unknown Pieces by D.H. Lawrence." Ed. Carl Baron, *Encounter* 33 (August 1969): 3-5.

Lawrence, Freida. *The Memoirs and Correspondence*. Ed. E. W. Tedlock, Jr. London: Heinemann, 1961.

le Guin, Ursula. *Always Coming Home*. London: Grafton, 1988.

Nietzsche, Friedrich. *The Joyful Wisdom*. Trans. Thomas Common. New York: Macmillan, 1924.

Pollnitz, Christopher. "Craftsman before Demon: The Development of Lawrence's Verse Technique." In *Rethinking Lawrence*. Ed. Keith Brown, Milton Keynes, England: Open UP, 1990, 133-50.

Sagar, Keith. *D.H. Lawrence: Life Into Art*. Harmondsworth, England: Viking/Penguin, 1985.

## Notes

1 Quoted with the permission of Laurence Pollinger Ltd. and the Estate of the late Frieda Lawrence.

2 See Nicholas Bishop, *Re-Making Poetry: Ted Hughes and a New Critical Psychology.* Hemel Hempstead, England: Harvester Wheatsheaf, 1991, and Keith Sagar, "The Poetry Does Not Matter," in Leonard M. Seigaj, ed. *Critical Essays on Ted Hughes* (Boston, MA: G. K. Hall, 1992): 99-108.

## Del Ivan Janik, "D.H. Lawrence's 'Future Religion'; The Unity of *Last Poems"*

Several of the poems that D.H. Lawrence wrote in the last months of his life are considered to be among his finest, and among the finest English poems of the century; but it has not been observed that the posthumously published notebook that includes "Bavarian Gentians" and "The Ship of Death" is a unified and cohesively organized work that extends Lawrence's most fundamental religious perceptions into one of his major literary accomplishments. In his introduction to Lawrence's *Last Poems*, first published by Giuseppe Orioli in 1932, Richard Aldington lamented the fact that the poet had not lived to complete his work: "He was too weary, he could not find the strength to build his ship of death and at the same time to build the full whole song of it."[1] But whether or not the sequence of sixty-seven poems that begins with "The Greeks Are Coming!" and ends with "Phoenix" represents Lawrence's final intention, it stands as a coherent and important work. As Tom Marshall has implied and Elizabeth Cipolla and Michael Kirkham have stated, *Last Poems* can and should be read as if it were a single long poem.[2] It is a poem that expresses Lawrence's fervent and very personal religious understanding of life as a preparation for death and ultimate rebirth. *Last Poems* asserts the primary importance of each individual's relationship with the world of experience, so that in the context of Lawrence's whole career it strongly qualifies the collectivistic emphasis of *Apocalypse*, Lawrence's other late religious statement.[3]

It could be maintained that in a loose sense all of Lawrence's mature poetry is religious, but *Last Poems* differs from *Look! We Have Come Through!*, *Birds, Beasts and Flowers*, and the bulk of *Pansies* in that it expresses Lawrence's beliefs in explicitly religious terms, in a sacramental and mythological framework. The sequence deals with the areas of experience that have always been the province of religion: the conduct of life, the nature of evil, the identity of God or the gods, the problem of death and life after death. In *Last Poems* Lawrence gave poetic life to the "Future Religion" that he had outlined in one of his *Pansies*.

The future of religion is in the mystery of touch.
The mind is touchless, so is the will, so is the spirit.

First comes the death, then the pure aloneness, which
                                    is permanent
then the resurrection into touch.  (II, 611)

It is this basic pattern that informs the volume of *Last Poems,* giving it structural and thematic coherence. The opening sequence of some twenty poems deals with the "mystery of touch," exploring the varied possibilities of the world of the senses. The poems from "The Hands of God" to "Departure" evoke the emptiness and horror of a life without touch, a life dominated by the mind and the will. Finally, the sequence that begins with "The Ship of Death" offers Lawrence's vision of the journey of death, oblivion, and bodily resurrections vision that was intensely personal yet was drawn from the distant reaches of human memory.

The personal quality of *Last Poems* is made clear at once by its setting: the Mediterranean as it existed for Lawrence's consciousness as he sat beside its waters at Bandol in the autumn of 1929.[4] The modern Mediterranean was there, with its sunbathers and ocean liners, but for Lawrence the ancient sea of the Argonauts and the Etruscans was also present, just as physically and just as convincingly. The thematic structure of *Last Poems* is analogous to that of symphonic music. Themes, images, and verbal motifs are stated and developed through a series of poems; new themes are introduced and developed in turn, and earlier ones are recapitulated and juxtaposed. The volume begins with a vision of the return of the ancient Greek gods and heroes to the modern Mediterranean. Subsequent poems turn to Judeo-Christian imagery, but "Maximus," "The Man of Tyre," "They Say the Sea is Loveless," and "Bavarian Gentians" return to classical themes; all of these poems express and affirm the importance of the senses—"the mystery of touch." The fall of Lucifer sets the tone for the second sequence of poems, at which is antithetical to the first. Here Lawrence juxtaposes Judeo-Christian formulations with observations about the modern "touchless" world and more poems that draw on the Greek heritage—this time the pre-Socratic philosophers. The concluding "Ship of Death" sequence is founded on Lawrence's understanding of the customs of ancient Egypt and Etruria, expressing through them Lawrence's vision of death, oblivion, and the "resurrection into touch."

The civilizations of the ancient world assert their presence in *Last Poems* not only in the subject matter but also in the form of the poetry, which reflects their modes of consciousness as Lawrence understood them. Mark Spilka has recognized the connection between the primitive concept of theos or mana and Lawrence's manner of writing, in prose as well as verse.[5] For Lawrence as for the ancient peoples of the Mediterranean, spiritual value is immanent in the things of the world, and meaning is not fixed or static but rather shifts constantly among the things that pass through an individual consciousness; this is why the immediacy of touch-intuitive understanding is so important to Lawrence. As Spilka points out, the fluidity and apparent "carelessness" of Lawrence's writing is really a function of his adherence to a different concept of meaning and value than that which governs most modern literature. For Lawrence poetry is not a means of discovering a pre-existent or ideal Truth, but a way of recording the passing physical truths that present themselves to an alert consciousness.

Lawrence enunciated the attitudes that underlie the overall structure of *Last Poems* in his description in *Apocalypse* of the old, sensual "cult-lore" that preceded the more intellectual "culture" of the Hellenic Greeks.

> We have not the faintest conception of the vast range that was covered by the ancient sense-consciousness. We have lost almost entirely the great and intricately developed sense-awareness, and sense-knowledge, of the ancients. It was a great depth of knowledge based not on words but on images. The abstraction was not into generalisations or into qualities, but into symbols. And the connection was not logical but emotional. The word "therefore" did not exist. Images or symbols succeeded one another in a procession of instinctive and arbitrary physical connection—some of the psalms give us examples—and they "get nowhere" because there was nowhere to get to, the desire was to achieve a consummation of a certain state of consciousness, to fulfill a certain state of feeling-awareness.[6]

Similarly, the goal of *Last Poems* is a state of awareness rather than a state of conviction, for the "Future Religion" that Lawrence imagined was basically a process, a way of living, rather than a set of beliefs. The volume moves toward the evocation of that state not through logical connections but through a succession of images, symbols, and contrasting rhythms.

As the critical response to "Bavarian Gentians" and "The Ship of Death" has demonstrated, the individual poems in the volume can be appreciated independently. But as in some of Lawrence's earlier volumes, particularly *Look! We Have Come Through!* and *Tortoises*, the limits of each poem are defined only vaguely. For example, the first four pieces in *Last Poems* are separate and distinct in subject and expression, yet together they form a unit and, in turn, part of a larger cycle of some twenty poems. These patterns of interconnection are not solely thematic; *Last Poems* is given coherence and also variety through a broad formal structure that results from the placement of poems of varied length, diction, and rhythm. More carefully than in any of his earlier poetic works, Lawrence here took advantage of the flexibility of his free-verse medium to create a controlled pattern of emotional peaks, valleys, and plains that underscores the volume's thematic structure. The prosaic flatness of poems like "In the Cities" and "The Evil World-Soul" emphasizes the odiousness of the touchless, will-dominated existence they describe,[7] and contrasts with the lyric intensity of "For the Heroes Are Dipped in Scarlet," "Whales Weep Not," and "The Ship of Death." *Last Poems* has a complexity and at the same time a unity of expression that exceeds anything that Lawrence had accomplished in earlier volumes of poetry.

As I have indicated, the thematic and formal patterns of *Last Poems* follow the outlines of Lawrence's earlier poem, "Future Religion," presenting a way of life, a warning, and finally a new sacrament of death, oblivion, and rebirth. The first cycle or sequence of poems, the poems that explore the "mystery of touch," establishes the physical and emotional setting for the volume as a whole. The first, "The Greeks Are Coming!," is a poem of rebirth and return: the return of the gods and heroes of the Homeric age; yet it is also a poem of the present, in which graceless ocean liners cross the Mediterranean distances once traversed by the Argonauts.

And every time it is ships, it is ships,
It is ships of Cnossos coming, out of the morning end of the sea,
It is Aegean ships, and men with archaic, pointed beards
coming out of the eastern end.

But it is far-off foam.
And an ocean liner, going east, like a small beetle walking the edge
is leaving a long thread of dark smoke
like a bad smell.  (II, 687)

This is poetry of the "immediate, instant moment,"[8] reflecting Lawrence's unstudied response to his changing perceptions of the scene before him. But the apparently spontaneous flow of words is given poetic coherence through the repetition of words and phrases whose significance is amplified as the poem—and the poetic sequence—progresses. In "The Argonauts," the second poem, the waning of day gives the ancient ships new reality, and the poet's excitement mounts in the third poem as the heroes actually assert their physical presence. In "For the Heroes are Dipped in Scarlet" he plainly states the theme that had been developed symbolically in the first three poems.

Before Plato told the great lie of ideas
men slimly went like fishes, and didn't care.  (II, 688)

Before Plato told men that they were nothing and that reality was somewhere outside and beyond them, they simply lived and laughed and fought and danced and were beautiful, like these bearded warriors whose being is so vital and whose *mana* is so strong, that they are still present in the flesh. They are painted red in affirmation of the power of the blood pulsing in their bodies. The poem rises from the quiet assertions of the opening stanzas to a series of excited exclamations that brings the opening sequence of four poems to an end.

So now they come back! Hark!
Hark! the low and shattering laughter of bearded men
with slim waists of warriors, and the long feet
of moon-lit dancers.

Oh, and their faces scarlet, like the dolphin's blood!
Lo! the loveliest is red all over, rippling vermillion
as he ripples upwards!
Laughing in his black beard!

They are dancing! they return, as they went, dancing!
For the thing that is done without the glowing as of God, vermillion,
were best not done at all.
How glistening red they are!  (II, 689)

"Demiurge," the poem that follows, provides a direct contrast to the initial sequence, and thus establishes the volume's overall rhythm. The agitated exclamations and vivid symbols are gone. "Demiurge" and the poems it introduces are further refutations of the "lie of ideals," but their movement is logical rather than imagistic, and their language is more abstract.

> They say that reality exists only in the spirit
> that corporal existence is a kind of death
> that pure being is bodiless
> that the idea of the form precedes the form substantial.

> But what nonsense it is!
> as if any mind could have imagined a lobster
> dozing in the under-deeps, then reaching out a savage and iron claw.

> Even the mind of God can only imagine
> those things that have become themselves:
> Bodies and presences, here and now, creatures with a foot-hold in creation
> even if it is only a lobster on tip-toe. (II, 689)

The succeeding poems also develop the thought and its implications in generally Christian frames of reference, but in varying tones: humorously as in "Red Geranium and Godly Mignonette," or assertively as in "The Body of God." Together, they provide a release from the intensity of the opening sequence, and they contrast with the even greater intensity of the next group of poems, which includes "The Man of Tyre," "Whales Weep Not," and "Bavarian Gentians."

These later poems return the focus of the volume to the sea and to the civilization of the ancient Greeks; they also create a second peak of lyric expression, linking them with the opening sequence and, later, with "The Ship of Death." But within the larger emotional rhythm of *Last Poems* there are subtler movements, and these poems cannot be considered a unit in the same sense as the group of four that opens the volume. "The Body of God" prepares for them thematically by stating that God has many manifestations: "men singing songs, and women brushing their hair in the sun"; and the poem "Maximus," in the calm, ordinary diction of "Demiurge," gives an account of one such manifestation: the god Hermes, warming himself at the poet's hearth.

"The Man of Tyre" also deals with the nature of God, in a scene that parallels Stephen Dedalus' vision in section IV of Joyce's *A Portrait of the Artist.* There is no need to emulate Michael Kirkham's exegesis of the poem in a recent essay,[9] but it should be recognized that the poem is central to Lawrence's exposition of the spiritual significance of physical presences. The man of Tyre walks along the shore pondering the unity of God when he suddenly sees a woman bathing naked in the sea.

> Oh lovely, lovely with the dark hair piled up, as she went
>     deeper, deeper down the channel, then rose
>     shallower, shallower
> With the full thighs slowly lifting of the wader wading
>     shorewards
> and the shoulders pallid with light from the silent sky behind
> both breasts dim and mysterious, with the glorious kindness
>     of twilight between them

and the dim notch of black maidenhair like an indicator,
giving a message to the man—

So in the cane-break he clasped his hands in delight
that could only be god-given, and murmured:
Lo! God is one god! But here in the twilight
godly and lovely comes Aphrodite out of the sea
towards me! (II, 693)

The specificity and physicality of this description as well as its carefully controlled formal structure, contrast sharply with the loose, conversational movement of the poems that precede it. The poet follows every movement as the woman goes "deeper, deeper" into the channel and then "shallower, shallower" to reveal her full godlike beauty to the watcher. The poem exemplifies the delicate balance in Lawrence's diction which lends a quality of spiritual immanence to what is also sensuously physical. The description focuses on the woman's sexuality: her "full thighs" and the "glamorous kindness of twilight," between her breasts; but the vague adjectives—"pallid," "dim," "mysterious"—give her an ethereal quality and invest her with another kind of mystery.

This balance and interpenetration between the spiritual and the physical in Lawrence's sacramental vision of earthly experience receives further expression in "Whales Weep Not," where the mating of the great mammals is described as the movement of "archangels of bliss."

And they rock, and they rock, through the ageless ages
on the depths of the seven seas,
and through the salt they reel with drunk delight
and in the tropics tremble they with love
and roll with massive, strong desire, like gods. (II, 694)

The sensuality of "The Man of Tyre" and the rhythmic drive of "For the Heroes Are Dipped in Scarlet" are both exceeded in this poem as strongly stressed syllables are crowded one upon another in an evocation of the silent thunder of the mating whales.

And over the bridge of the whale's strong phallus, linking the wonder of whales
and burning archangels under the sea keep passing, back and forth,
keep passing archangels of bliss
from him to her, from her to him, great Cherubim
that wait on whales in mid-ocean, suspended in the waves out of the sea
great heaven of whales in the waters, old hierarchies. (II, 694)

This is the climax of the volume's first section, an ultimate manifestation of the wonder and mystery of the world of touch. The poem calls the whole of Lawrence's earlier volume *Birds, Beasts and Flowers* retrospectively into this new context. The hot-blooded, mountainous whales are living manifestations of God; they have a unique and wonderful *mana*—and so by implication do, in their smaller ways, the fishes and tortoises and mountain lions and almond trees of the earlier volume. This is one of the sudden changes in levels of awareness that

Lawrence associated with the ancient "cult-lore" he described in *Apocalypse*: "To appreciate the pagan manner of thought we have to drop our own manner of on-and-on-and-on, from a start to a finish, and allow the mind to move in cycles, or to flit here and there over a cluster of images. . . . One cycle finished, we can drop or rise to another level, and be in a new world at once."[10] Here, Lawrence shifts from the world of the Mediterranean gods and heroes to the "great heaven of whales in the waters," and through them back to the world of *Birds, Beasts and Flowers*, where every living thing is suddenly revealed as a god, a *theos*, in itself.

"Whales Weep Not" is followed by two more poems that present *theoi* in the manner of *Birds, Beasts and Flowers;* but "Butterfly" also reasserts the physical setting of the volume at a villa by the Mediterranean, and "Bavarian Gentians" introduces the theme that will dominate the final section of *Last Poems*. This is the first of the poems that deals directly with death and the preparation for it. The death imagined here follows the pattern of Persephone's descent into the underworld, a place which has a dark beauty that mirrors the daylight beauty of the world under the sky.

> Reach me a gentian, give me a torch!
> let me guide myself with the blue, forked torch of this flower,
> down the dark and darker stairs, where blue is darkened on blueness
> even where Persephone goes, just now, from the frosted September
> to the sightless realm where darkness is awake upon the dark
> and Persephone herself is but a voice
> of a darkness invisible enfolded in the deeper dark
> of the arms Plutonic, and pierced with the passion of dense gloom,
> among the splendour of torches of darkness, shedding darkness on
> the lost bride and her groom. (II, 697)

As the poet imagines himself descending deeper, the repetitions of the calls words "blue" and "blueness," "dark" and "darkness" multiply until there is little else, perhaps prefiguring the "oblivion" of the volume's final sequence. But at the same time "Bavarian Gentians" also brings the poems about the varieties of sensual experience to an appropriate close. The underworld is dim and gloomy, but it is still a world of the senses whose darkness has a certain splendor. Seasonal myths like that of Persephone imply an eventual rebirth, a resurrection in the flesh. This aspect of the pattern of Lawrence's "Future Religion" does not figure directly in "Bavarian Gentians," but the unspoken implication helps to prepare for the affirmations of the "Ship of Death" sequence.

More immediately, however, the myth of Persephone suggests another descent: the fall of Lucifer, with whose story the second major cycle of poems begins. In more than thirty poems Lawrence explores the "touchless" life of mind and will, the negative inversion of the life of the senses. Lucifer's sin—and the sin of any man who "falls from the hands of God"—is willful self-knowledge; and hell is "the turning-down plunge of writing of self-knowledge, self-analysis / which goes further and further, yet never finds an end" (I1, 701 ). As these lines suggest, these poems are abstract rather than imagistic, expository rather than symbolic; and that fact is itself symbolic in the larger scheme of *Last Poems*. A dry, intellectual mode of expression becomes dominant over a long series of poems:

from the plight of Lucifer, Lawrence turns to the errors of the early Greek philosophers who denied the primacy of the senses, and then to the manifestations of "touchless" evil in the modern world. These poems are abstract and argumentative; Richard Aldington has called these meditations on evil "a series of scoldings, which are little better than *Pansies*," the casual satirical verses that Lawrence had published in 1928.[11] Aldington failed to recognize, however, that these admittedly angry and often prosaic verses form an integral part of the thematic and formal movement of *Last Poems*. They are anticipated in the ugly modern steamship of "The Greeks Are Coming!" and they lead directly to the climactic poem, "The Ship of Death." In terms of the volume's poetic texture, their verbal and rhythmic flatness sets off the lyricism of the poems that precede them and of the "Ship of Death" cycle that follows.

Evil, as Lawrence understands it, is the inevitable outcome of the dominance of mind. Man becomes evil when, insisting on the superiority of the mind over the body, he releases his ego from the constraints and checks offered by the rest of the physical world. He becomes a human machine recklessly proceeding toward his own willed ends, and becomes finally the servant of machines.

> When the mind makes a wheel which turns on the hub of the ego
> and the will, the living dynamo, gives the motion and the speed
> and the wheel of the conscious self spins on in absolution, absolute
> absolute, absolved from the sun and the earth and the moon,
> absolute consciousness, absolved from strife and kisses
> absolute self-awareness, absolved from the meddling of creation
> absolute freedom, absolved from the great necessities of being
> then we see evil, pure evil
> and we see it only in man
> and in his machines. (II, 712)

The last several of these poems are progressively fragmented; there is no pretense of sustained thought, but merely a rush to express each angry observation. In "Departure" the poet catalogues the modern manifestations of evil, always returning to the word itself to build up a verbal tension that finds sudden release in "The Ship of Death."

> All forms of abstraction are evil:
> finance is a great evil abstraction
> science has now become an evil abstraction
> education is an evil abstraction.
> Jazz and film and wireless
> are all evil abstractions from life.
> Evil is upon us and has got hold of us.
> Men must depart from it, or all is lost.
> We must make an isle impregnable
> against evil. (II 716)

"Departure" ends with a challenge: evil, mechanical abstraction has conquered the modern world, and the 'only hope is that individuals may turn away from evil and somehow "make an isle impregnable" against it.

Lawrence's response to this challenge comes in "The Ship of Death" and the shorter poems that accompany it. In them he develops the pattern of death and rebirth that he had stated in "Future Religion": first comes death, then the aloneness of oblivion, and finally the resurrection into touch. "The Ship of Death" brings another of the changes in mode and shifts in levels of awareness that characterize *Last Poems*. The invective against abstraction and absolutism is suddenly shut off, as if the poet had closed a door on a room full of noise. The poem does not plunge into the world of the senses like "For the Heroes Are Dipped in Scarlet" and "Whales Weep Not"; it begins quietly and cautiously, proceeding through neatly divided sections with surprising rhythmic regularity. This is still free verse, but it has an iambic core that helps to create a mood of calm determination. Unlike the poems of the volume's second major cycle, "The Ship of Death" is not abstract. It has the same physical immediacy, the same sense of a consciousness reacting directly to experience, that can be found in *Birds, Beasts and Flowers* and in poems like "The Man of Tyre"; but this world of experience is a very different one, and this consciousness proceeds in it with more deliberation.

I

Now it is autumn and the falling fruit
and the long journey towards oblivion.

The apples falling like great drops of dew
to bruise themselves an exit from themselves.

And it is time to go, to bid farewell
to one's own self, and find an exit
from the fallen self.

II

Have you built your ship of death, 0 have you?
0 build your ship of death, for you will need it.

The grim frost is at hand, when the apples will fall
thick, almost thundrous, on the hardened earth.
And death is on the air like a smell of ashes!
Ah! can't you smell it?  (II, 716-17)

Although Lawrence knew when he wrote this that he was fatally ill, the poem's autumnal imagery gives it a more than merely personal significance. The ancient seasonal myths are suggested indirectly (that of Persephone having figured in "Bavarian Gentians"), and with them a hint of the bodily rebirth that will follow death. But this is not a "mythological" poem that solves the problem of the preparation for death for a whole civilization on a symbolic level. It is an invitation to introspection and self-questioning: how can we, in the face of the fact of death, attain "the deep and lovely quiet / of a strong heart at peace"?

Lawrence's answer is put in terms of a ritual suggested by the funerary practices of the ancient Etruscans. Death is seen as a lonely journey for which each man must build a suitable vessel to sustain him.

> Now launch the small ship, now as the body dies
> and life departs, launch out, the fragile soul
> in the fragile ship of courage, the ark of faith
> with its store of food and little cooking pans
> and change of clothes . . .  (II, 719)

The ship of the soul is patterned after the little bronze arks that Lawrence saw in the Etruscan tombs at Cerveteri. He explained in *Etruscan Places* why the Etruscans provided for the physical well-being of their dead: death was more a place than a state of being (or not-being); its boundary with life was not marked by distinctions of flesh and spirit.

> And death, to the Etruscan, was a pleasant continuance of life, with jewels and wine and flutes playing for the dance. It was neither an ecstasy of bliss, a heaven, nor a purgatory of torment. It was just a natural continuance of the fullness of life. Everything was in terms of life, of living.[12]

In Lawrence's poem "the body dies," but the state of the soul after death is never explained, because explanation would be more falsification and dishonesty. Instead, the journey of death is imagined as a real journey, with all the fear and doubt and wonder that would attend a lone mariner on the open sea.

> There is no port, there is nowhere to go
> only the deepening blackness darkening still
> blacker upon the soundless, ungurgling flood
> darkness at one with darkness, up and down
> and sideways utterly dark, so there is no direction any more.
> and the little ship is there: yet she is gone.
> She is not seen, for there is nothing to see her by.
> She is gone! gone! and yet
> somewhere she is there.
> Nowhere!

>                    VIII

> And everything is gone, the body is gone
> completely under, gone, entirely gone.
> The upper darkness is heavy as the lower,
> between them the little ship
> is gone
> she is gone.

> It is the end, it is oblivion.  (II, 719)

What "oblivion" means is not yet clear, nor does it become clear in this one poem. "The Ship of Death" is not an appeal to the rational consciousness; it is an account of a religious experience—"an experience deep down in the senses, inexplicable and inscrutable."[13] It is the sensual detail of Lawrence's description of a dawn at sea, in the poem's final stanzas, that creates an atmosphere of intuitive acceptance for his assertion that the journey of death ends in the resurrection of the body.

> Wait, wait, the little ship
> drifting, beneath the deathly ashy, grey
> of a flood-dawn.
>
> Wait, wait! even so, a flush of yellow
> and strangely, 0 chilled wan soul, a flush of rose.
>
> A flush of rose, and the whole thing starts again.  (II, 720)

Richard Aldington has expressed regret that the final sequence of *Last Poems* was not integrated into a longer version of "The Ship of Death": "As the first draft shows, Lawrence probably meant to make this one long poem, and if this could have been done it would have been his greatest achievement as a poet."[14] As Elizabeth Cipolla has observed,[15] Aldington failed to consider that throughout his poetic career, and certainly in *Last Poems*, Lawrence wrote in extended poetic sequences rather than in sharply delimited individual poems. Each titled poem is an extension of or a commentary upon the others around it, creating a larger unit that reflects the changes of thought and feeling that a man undergoes over a period of time. Furthermore, in the context of *Last Poems* even an extended version of "The Ship of Death" would have been too short, and perhaps too tentative, to balance and resolve the long cycle of negative poems that precedes it. The first draft of "The Ship of Death" which Aldington found in another manuscript probably represents a limited, early attempt at expression, while the long sequence from "The Ship of Death" to "Phoenix" is a more finished and, at least in Lawrence's estimation, a superior work.[16] The shorter poems that follow it explain some of the implications of the journey of "The Ship of Death," and they extend and clarify its symbolic significance. In his own characteristic way Lawrence did write the single long poem that Aldington looked for.

These poems underscore the importance of a conscious preparation for death; living men must learn to see death in proper perspective, as the necessary complement to the fulness of life.

> Sing then the song of death, and the longest journey
> and what the soul takes with him, and what he leaves behind,
> and how he enters fold after fold of deepening darkness
> for the cosmos even in death is like a dark whorled shell
> whose whorls fold round to the core of soundless silence and pivotal oblivion
> where the soul comes at last, and has utter peace.
>
> Sing then the core of dark and absolute
> oblivion where the soul at last is lost
> in utter peace.
> Sing the song of death, 0 sing it!  (II, 724)

The "oblivion" that Lawrence describes is more than mere insensateness; it is the "pure aloneness" of the poem "Future Religion," the death of the ego that must precede the resurrection of the body. Oblivion is not the renunciation of experience but the fulfillment of a life lived in sensual awareness. Only abstract, mechanical knowledge, the kind of touchless self-knowledge that Lawrence rejects in the poems that precede "The Ship of Death," is cast out. Rather than nothingness, oblivion means the renunciation of the personal, self-knowing ego in an opening of the personality to spontaneity and change.

In Lawrence's "Future Religion" the rebirth from oblivion may come after actual, physical death; but "Shadows," one of the last poems in the volume, affirms that the building of the ship of death is also a preparation for life. The "resurrection into touch" can come in the midst of a man's life if he is willing to cease from static knowledge and enter into the universal pattern of vital change.

> And if, as autumn deepens and darkens
> I feel the pain of falling leaves, and stems that break in storms,
> and trouble and dissolution and distress
> and then the softness of deep shadows folding, folding
> around my soul and spirit, around my lips
> so sweet, like a swoon, or more like the drowse of a low, sad song
> singing darker than the nightingale, on, on to the solstice
> and the silence of short days, the silence of the year, the shadow,
> then I shall know that my life is moving still
> with the dark earth, and drenched
> with the deep oblivion of the earth's lapse and renewal. (II, 727)

Thus oblivion means a willingness to be blotted out as a fixed personality again and again in the continuing movement of the universe, and to be made anew by the contingencies of the living world. "Phoenix," the final poem in the sequence of *Last Poems,* is a challenge to face this kind of oblivion and rebirth.

> Are you willing to be sponged out, erased, cancelled,
> made nothing?
> Are you willing to be made nothing?
> dipped into oblivion?
>
> If not, you will never really change.
>
> The phoenix renews her youth
> only when she is burnt, burnt alive, burnt down
> to hot and flocculent ash.
> Then the small stirring of a new small bub in the nest
> with strands of down like floating ash
> Shows that she is renewing her youth like the eagle,
> immortal bird.   (II, 728)

Like almost all of Lawrence's works, his *Last Poems* ends with a beginning. Admittedly, the sequence of poems from "The Greeks Are Coming!" to "Phoenix" is in more than one sense a culmination. It is a mature statement of religious belief, for it presents a summation in symbolic form of Lawrence's approach to life. It exhibits a subtle, confident handling of the free-verse techniques that Lawrence had developed in earlier volumes of poetry. In spite of the fact that it is only a manuscript, never prepared for publication by its author, it is a complex and unified work that embodies Lawrence's spontaneous approach to the world of experience. Yet *Last Poems* is not a completion; there is no ultimate answer for Lawrence, but only a series of explorations, celebrations, warnings, and challenges. The highest and most deserved praise of Lawrence's *Last Poems* is that it is in no sense fixed or complete; like the "Future Religion" that Lawrence imagined, it is spontaneous, open-ended, and vital.

*Texas Studies in Literature and Language: A Journal of the Humanities*, 16:4, 1975.

## Notes

[1] *The Complete Poems of D.H. Lawrence*, ed. Vivian de Sola Pinto and F. Warren Roberts (London: Heinemann, 1967), II, 598. Volume and page references in the text are to this edition.

[2] Tom Marshall, *The Psychic Mariner: A Reading of the Poems of D. H. Lawrence* (New York: Viking, 1970), pp. 195-225; Elizabeth Cipolla, "The *Last Poems* of D. H, Lawrence," *D. H. Lawrence Review* 2 (Summer, 1969), 111; Michael Kirkham, "D. H. Lawrence's *Last Poems*," *D. H. Lawrence Review,* 5 (Summer, 1972), 97-120. Cipolla observes that "the poems show Lawrence's thoughts gradually turning from life to death." As I hope to demonstrate, the structure of *Last Poems* is in fact more complex.

[3] D.H. Lawrence, *Apocalypse* (Florence: G. Orioli, 1931). For a discussion of the development towards communalism in Lawrence's writings, see Baruch Hochman, *Another Ego* (Columbia, S.C.: Univ. of South Carolina Press, 1970 *Texas Studies in Literature and Language* XVI.4 (Winter 1975)

[4] See Lawrence's letter to Else Jaffe, 4 October 1929, *The Collected Letters of D.H. Lawrence*, ed. Harry T. Moore (London: Heinemann, 1962), II, 1206.

[5] Mark Spilka, "Was D. H. Lawrence a Symbolist?" *Accent,* 15, No. I (Winter, 1955), 50-51.

[6] *Apocalypse*, pp. 133-34.

[7] Kirkham (P. 101) observes that in these poems "Lawrence is working within traditional forms of thought and feeling the doctrinal core of which he had disowned." See Lawrence's 1918 essay, "Poetry of the Present" in *Complete Poems*, I 181ff.

[8] "Poetry of the Present," *Complete Poems,* I, 181.

[9] Kirkham, pp. 110-16.

[10] *Apocalypse,* pp. 133-34.

[11] *Complete Poems* , II, 597.

[12] D. H. Lawrence, *Etruscan Places* (London: Martin Secker, 1932), p. 28.

[13] D. H. Lawrence, "New Mexico", (1931) in *Phoenix: The Posthumous Papers of D. H. Lawrence*, ed. Edward McDonald (London: Heinemann, 1936), p. 144.

[14] *Complete Poems*, 11, 598.

[15] Cipolla, p. 111.

[16] For descriptions of these manuscripts, see Aldington's introduction to *Last Poems*, in *Complete Poems*, II, 597.

# X

# The Letters and Prose

John Macy, "The American Spirit" (review of *Studies in Classic American Literature* and Edith Wharton, *A Son at the Front*)

Mr. Lawrence announces himself as the daughter of Pharaoh who is to rescue the Moses of American literature from the bulrushes of ignorance and neglect. He strips the swaddling clouts from eight American writers and in the process he exposes himself in a most penetrating fashion. His book is honest, independent, and eccentric, a thousand miles, or a million light-days, away from most books of critical essays. Mr. Lawrence's philosophy contains strange and apparently unrelated things, though to him the connections are profound and self-evident. His central theme seems to be an attempt to discover in a few American books and American history some characteristics peculiar to the inhabitants of These States. It is an inquiry which has been undertaken by many investigators, foreign and domestic. The result is almost always the same, that is, no final result at all, no conclusion; and the only value of the quest is the interesting observation here and there on the way. America is not homogeneous enough, and was not in the good old days, for any generalization to hold true. And if a generalization holds good for American character, is it anything but a sweeping idea which is more or less true of the whole human race? I am puzzled by the assertions found on almost every page that "this is American," "especially in America," "the essential American soul," "the best Americans," "as in all Americans," "so typically American," "real American logic," in most cases the characteristic in question being more or less universally human. One is tempted to fall back on Mark Twain's dictum that the only distinctively American peculiarity is a liking for ice-water.

Mr. Lawrence despises democracy as it is manifested in America, and many of us who have lived and suffered under it will bitterly agree that our democracy is not liberty. But there seems to be no liberty anywhere from Ireland to China; our bondage differs in no important respect, not an ounce in the weight of the chains, from the bondage of the rest of the world. And Mr. Lawrence's conclusion, his interpretation of Whitman's democracy, "of souls in the Open Road, full of glad recognition, full of fierce readiness, full of the joy of worship, when one soul sees a greater soul," is a rhetorical climax to which the rest of the book does not clearly conduce.

The core of the book is its tinglingly vital challenge not only to America but to all manner of human quackery and puffery. Because it will offend the patriotic and baffle the stupid, I am inclined to insist on its merits, on its essential wisdom, on its insolent courage, and to leave to others the many quarrels which it provokes. But because I feel its strength I feel all the more keenly its weaknesses, many of which the puniest reviewer can light upon and ridicule, or simply misunderstand, as I do. I do not understand the Laurentian physics and anatomy. What in the world is a "polarized circuit" or a "polarized flow" as applied to a storm in the skies or to a storm in the brain? In what other physiology than Mr. Lawrence's is it written that "the poles of the will are the great ganglia of the voluntary nerve system, located beside the spinal column in the back," or that love is the "prime cause of tuberculosis"? Mr. Lawrence's history is shaky. The motives of migration are complicated and may include a spiritual revulsion against political or religious authority and even some mysterious IT (Mr. Lawrence's mystical capitals outdo Whitman or a Hearst editorial). But the main motive for colonization is economic, the desire to get a better living, to exploit new lands, when life is hard in the old ones. It is that desire which has sent races and individuals across continents and seas. The economic motive is the cause also of revolutions. When the colonies rebelled against the mother country they did indulge in oratory and pamphlets, some of them, including Thomas Paine (not "Tom Payne"), eloquent and idealistic. But the motive was simply practical: to kick out a foreign landlord and tax-collector.   Let us alone to manage and exploit this country ourselves. To say that Franklin at the court of France was "contriving the first steps of the overthrow of all Europe, France included," that he was "making a small but very dangerous hole in the side of England, through which Europe has by now almost bled to death," is to rewrite history beyond the legitimate limits of individual interpretation. Mr. Lawrence is not more successful with the earlier history of Europe.   "Mastery, kingship, fatherhood had their power destroyed at the time of the Renaissance." Nothing like that happened in Europe. In France, for example, the power of kingship was at its height long after the Renaissance. Mr. Lawrence's modern history is equally whimsical. "The pattern American, this dry, moral utilitarian little democrat has done more to ruin the old Europe than any Russian nihilist." Which is true only in the sense that the Russian nihilist has done exactly nothing to ruin the old Europe.

But Mr. Lawrence is a literary man, not an historian, and his observations on writers and books are exhilarating.   His subversions of the highly moral maxims of Benjamin Franklin would have delighted A. Ward, an American writer of the old American stock. The remarks on Cooper are illuminating and wise, especially the paragraphs about Natty Bumppo as myth. Dana and Melville Mr. Lawrence heartily appreciates. Poe he dimly understands, and he wraps that already vexed soul in more confusion and mystery. If Poe "told us plainly how it was, so that we should know," why muddle his story with baseless conjecture?"Love killed him." So? That is a purely original contribution on Mr. Lawrence's part to Poe's biography. The two studies of Hawthorne are subtle and mainly just, though marred by irritating trivialities: why should Hawthorne, whose gray eyes were so deeply shadowed that several of his contemporaries called them black, appear in Mr. Lawrence's portrait as "a blue-eyed darling"? The essay on Whitman is least satisfactory, and begins with the strangest of Mr. Lawrence's perversities, that Whitman's effects are "post mortem," like the rest of American literature since 1851 when *Moby Dick* was published, and "the Great White Whale sank the ship of the Great White Soul." Whitman is the poet of "the soul's last shout and shriek, on the confines of death." Let who can make sense of that.

Mr. Lawrence deals only with American classics, with the "old people," and does not mention the living by name, except Sherwood Anderson, "who is so Russian"!  But it would be interesting, if we could, to turn upon an important living American writer one or two reflections from Mr. Lawrence's glancing and erratic lights. . . .

*Nation*, CXVII, 10 October 1923.

# Catherine Carswell, "D.H. Lawrence in His Letters"[1]

It is a measure of D.H. Lawrence's originality that he is so difficult to write about satisfactorily. With most writers we derive at least a degree of what we feel to be legitimate self-congratulation from having set down this or that conclusion. Here, we say, is my finding: differ from it if you must; anyhow, I think I have made myself clear. But with Lawrence, though  clarity is most desirable, a clear statement is no sooner made than it begins to look doubtful, even misleading. The plainest-seeming and best-meaning phrase undergoes a baffling metamorphosis. We become aware that Lawrence himself would have rejected the label with  a vehement or a laughing head-shake. His is a 'bisy ghost, aye flickering to and fro,' and making pronouncements dance a jig in which each hands over the scrap of truth confided in it to its antithesis. Mr. Harold Nicolson has very truly said that the 'correct approach' to Lawrence is 'in terms of the normal, almost of the ordinary.' With no less truth  Mr. Huxley has said that 'it is impossible to write about Lawrence except as an artist.' But Lawrence himself would probably have allowed neither way. For both are hedged abbout with current images of the sort he wished to destroy and pass beyond. In his view the 'ordinary' had ceased to be a living approach and the 'artistic' had become rarefied from vital  experience. Assuredly the ordinary approach has caused at least half the  misunderstanding of this man and his work, and the artistic approach has been as fruitful of mischief. It was part of Lawrence's difficulty that he had to create a new kind of approach between himself and others, and the whole of his aim was to indicate a fresh approach to life. Yet words, even familiar terms, have to be used. He used them himself—the more familiar the better for him. But he safeguarded his intent by maintaining a consciousness within himself that should be 'unbroken, yet storming with oppositons and contradictions.'

'Me, I take no stand on the exception,' he says in an early letter (not in Mr. Huxley's collection), from which I quote from memory. And in a letter of 1926: 'They did make a *tightness* —that peculiar tightness that goes with more or less ordinary people—as if the landscape were shut in, and the air didn't move.' At the same time he was very often a heaper of contempt upon works of art and their makers, and he looked with a sidelong grimace at most persons who claimed to be something above the common. The high solemnities of a Goethe made him want to spit : the 'boiled-down,' aesthetic quality of art master-pieces—'a quality which takes the edge off everything'—bored or revolted him. This, though he had in his early life experienced a disciplined admiration and appreciation of both romantic and classical work. But in his maturity, which came early, he was a merciless picker and chooser. And it was not from the motive of art that he picked and chose and blasted, any more than it was from the motive of morals. It was from a motive of life that is as rare among artists and moralists as among those to whom the language of either is strange. 'If you want uplift,' he writes in his posthumous book on the Etruscans—a book as gay as it is crisply determined—'go to the Greek and the Gothic. If you want mass, go to the Roman.' 'But if you are content with just a sense of the quick ripple of life, then here it is.' So saying he might as well have pointed at himself as at any Etruscan decoration. The fact that the Etruscans were 'lost ' was a large part of their attraction for him. Humanity, with its normal approaches, its noble monuments of art and its massed power, had in his eyes lost the satisfying way of life. Believing that more satisfying, though never perfect, ways had existed at times and in places, and might exist again, he searched about everywhere for ancient clues and for new hints. His Good and True and Beautiful were to be found here, there and everywhere in unexpected manifestations of which the charm was ever of one kind—fugitive. And because of this his own expression must also partake of fugitiveness—must have a sort of careless and transparent imperfection that is in opposition to the aims of the pure artist as we have learned to think of him. For our pure artist becomes enamoured of his special material and strives for a separate perfection in it, inducing us also to detach ourselves from life while we examine his perfect production or criticise it for failing of perfection. But we find Lawrence delighting more in a lizard than in a Laocoon, and he is moved to the quick by the special imperfections of an Etruscan drawing in which the artist—or more likely artisan—has made repeated outlines of a horse, one over the other, without troubling to erase his earlier attempts. Here 'you cannot think of art, but only of life itself.' Mr. Huxley has noted how Lawrence rewrote his books three and four times—not, as most writers do, to polish, correct, improve, with an abstract perfection in mind, but to let through, if it might be, his demonic impulse more richly and clearly.

His pleasure in the Etruscan horse throws light upon his own technique. He desired, not perfect creations, but subtle or agitated indications of what lies behind creation. Before and beyond being an artist he was a diviner. Into a familiar field where we are used to watch men sow and reap there comes a stranger who does neither. He proceeds to make incomprehensible gestures and to move his body into queer postures—intent, mocking, confiding, impassioned, destructive. We find him inappropriate and absurd; until we learn that beneath the field's exhausted surface he has detected a much-wished-for water spring. 'Every real discovery made, every serious and significant decision ever reached, was reached and made by a sort of divination,' says Lawrence. 'Columbus discovered America by a sort of divination. The soul stirs, and makes an act of pure attention, and that is a discovery.' For him, 'there is no other way when you are dealing with life.'

This, of course, does not negative Lawrence as an artist. Rather it should emphasise his achievement in having invented a vehicle suitable for his unique necessity. Though the necessity was not artistic, the vehicle had to be and is. Those who believe they have said something when they say that 'Lawrence was no thinker' have reckoned without the rare order of thought by which a man provides his own medium for the communication to his fellows of something unexpected. In indicating a life that should satisfy Lawrence put desire, in its widest sense, before intellect in the sense of knowledge. But he decried the intellect only in so far as he found the intellectual ideal to be a usurper of spontaneous life. When it came to a demonstration of his findings he knew quite well what he was doing, and his language is the result of much hard, cool, honest thinking. His rejection of the term 'artist' in his work, 'love' in his marriage, 'devotion' in his friendships, 'Christian' in his actions, and 'perfection' in his aims was deliberate and intellectual. How much so will be found by comparing his early letters with those of his prime. In youth he had tested the meaning and accepted the discipline of these things more sensitively than most men. But advancing into life he found that they were devitalised. A 'new-starting reality' was due. For its coming a 'fresh consciousness' was needed. Before this could make itself felt a whole world of 'social images' had to be smashed. Art, love, devotion, perfection, Christianity, were high among the images. Here we have what irritates and antagonises so many people in Lawrence. He was an industrious and incorruptible artist, a faithful husband, a dutiful son and brother, an honest citizen, a scrupulous friend, and a virtuous man. And for those who flouted the common decencies he had a strong distaste. Yet he did his utmost to break down the ideal of a life that is added up in such a description. Is there not something here that is absurd, divided, impossible? Lawrence gives the simple reply in one of these letters: 'Primarily I am a passionately religious man' Who else in our time could have made so simply this confident remark? Certainly not the Pope of Rome or the Archbishop of Canterbury, nor even General Booth or Mr. Gandhi. Thus to expose oneself one must be very sure and very pure.

I began by saying how difficult it is to write satisfactorily about Lawrence. Even more evidently it is impossible to refrain from making the attempt. If the one is a measure of his originality, the other is a measure of his fascination. Those—and they are many—who resent his troublous presence in the literary landscape would gladly see him interred with a few well-chosen words. I imagine Mr. Huxley smiling gently to himself, and to the shade of Lawrence, when he reads this and that reviewer's gracious acceptance of his introduction as a tasteful funeral oration after which anything more said must be regarded as an intrusion on good manners. Tasteful—in the happiest sense of the word—Mr. Huxley has been. His words are chosen wisely, wittily and well, and what he says is the more valuable because it is admittedly a tribute in a language Lawrence did not use. Of Lawrence he notes as early as 1927: 'He is one of the few people I feel real respect and admiration for. Of most other eminent people I have met I feel that at any rate I belong to the same species as they do. But this man has something different and superior in kind, not degree.' Coming from Mr. Huxley, this observation, which experience has not caused him to revise, is received with a fitting respect. Recorded by another it might not be so kindly treated. It might even be designated as hysteria. We say all the better that it comes from him. But Mr. Huxley is the last person to regard a potential originator of species as so easily disposed of, and he knows that Lawrence cannot be susceptible to funeral orations, however moving, just or enlightened. In spite of difficulties from within and discouragements from without, Lawrence will still be written and spoken of and wondered over, often foolishly. Exasperating it may be. The resurgence of a phoenix causes an uncomfortable, sometimes a vulgar, crackle of smoke and flame. But it cannot be helped. It is the way of a phoenix. Throughout much that misses any other point it will become increasingly plain that Lawrence's life and work combine in such a way as to seize upon the common imagination.

In these letters we find the man and may learn the best approach to his work. 'Few men,' as Mr. Huxley says, 'have given more of themselves in their letters,' and 'In them Lawrence has written his own life and painted his own portrait.' It may be added that in doing so Lawrence well knew what he was about. He knew that explanation of this sort was needful in his case, so that letter-writing was as vital a means of expression to him as poetry, fiction, painting, or the essay. In this abridged selection we have some 850 pages from his huge correspondence. Other letters already in print are those to his family and friends of his youth, to be found in his sister's book, *The Young Lorenzo*, and those to Mrs. Luhan, his American hostess, in her book, *Lorenzo in Taos*. Many more exist, and from their intrinsic interest are bound to be published in due time.

To read the letters is—as Mr. Huxley says of being with their author—'a kind of adventure.' And this, even more than their beauty and absorbing interest, gives them their especial quality. But 'beautiful and absorbingly interesting' they are. And they are also exceedingly amusing. For Lawrence had a tongue. The way he used it was his one vice. Gossip he did, and with what fury! To the deadly venom of a wit that might be termed classical was added a vigour of language acquired from labouring men, and directing these was a ferocity of perception that was all his own. He spoke of people behind their backs as Voltaire must have spoken, or Alexander Pope. But there was this difference, that he had no jealousy in his composition and was as incapable of unkindness as of guile. No man ever desired more truly to see everybody happy and vital up to the measure of their beings. 'I hate my enemies,' he writes in one letter, 'but I mostly forget them.' It was true. And he would never grudge any good that might come to an enemy, though this was not in the sense we understand as Christian, but from an overflowing, impatient life. He was never tolerant, but always sensitive, where others were concerned. Frequently his friends of one day were his enemies of the next, and *vice versa*. It was less at the individual than at some lack of spontaneous life he found there—some gloomy or glassy unawareness, or some twist excluding life—that he directed his strokes. But the strokes were many and reckless. Those who heard in talk his wild and wicked sketches of the absent were transported with amazement or with laughter or both. You might be incredulous about the portrait-chart—invariably as well as a portrait he gave a chart claiming to reveal the individual's way of life—or shocked or hilarious. But you had to admit its vigour and its originality. Neither could you afterwards survey the subject of it without reference to the incisive outline which, at the time, had appeared to you as exaggerated or merely fantastic. You might still refuse to believe that what Lawrence had said really told you the essential truth about the individual in question. But remembering what he had said, and looking at the individual, you felt that life, including your own, was elucidated and enriched.

It caused, and will continue to cause, trouble. Remarks came, in a version less innocent of spite, to the ears of the person concerned, who became a resentful victim. Lawrence was often called to account. And if he could sometimes confess that he 'rather liked getting into a bit of a mess with people,' at other times he swerved violently away from the petty or painful revelations he brought about. Then he cursed himself and others. Yet he would maintain that what he had said was both true in its essence and without malevolence in its intent, and that therefore it could not do anything but good in the end.

Opinion here may differ. What is certain is that Lawrence had an unbridled tongue of the kind we more readily associate with a woman than with a man, and that his tongue extended into his letter-writing pen—with one striking difference. He wrote letters as he spoke, so that to those who knew him his voice echoes through these pages. They fairly flash with quick life, presenting us in turn with the writer's malice, insight, plain speaking, shrewdness, loveliness, rage and devastating mockery. And all these come as if without forethought or afterthought, with no other consideration than of the mood and the correspondent of the moment. About the most serious or the most violent passages there is an inherent lightness which argues as superficial the contention that here are the letters of an egoist. Beneath the gayest stretches there is the seriousness of one who detests 'having a good time' as heartily as he thinks the world well lost for happiness. But in direct address the written word forced him to a candour that he did not feel able to observe when face to face with people. In the common exchanges of life he was the reverse of a Carlyle. He liked to please and to be pleased. 'I'm really more good-natured than most people,' he lamented. Socially he was timid, though not nervous. When he first grew his beard he wrote to me beforehand begging me not to smile when I should see him, and before you could get him to tell you in speech anything unwelcome about yourself you had to ask for it. In spoken candour there is an indecency as of physical assault. Besides, it is unfair. The face is too exposed. If it came, as it so often does, to a choice between truth-telling and delicacy, Lawrence was delicate. In company he bore his share of 'pretending.' 'My kindliness makes me sometimes a bit false.'

But when Mr. Huxley, after quoting this admission (which, if I remember aright, occurs, not in a letter, but in one of the *Assorted Articles*), identifies it with Lawrence's ability to adapt himself to each different correspondent, he goes a little beyond its meaning. Lawrence was considerate of his correspondents' interests and moods. But with a pen in his hand he did not evade any truth that seemed relevant to their needs.   '. . . let's not pretend,' he writes to one. 'By pretending a bit, we had some jolly times, in the past.  But we all had to pretend a bit—and we could none of us keep it up. . . . We are a dissonance.' If there be one thing more striking than another in his letter it is this.  Where frankness matters they are shatteringly frank.  Many letters too frank for present publication must still exist in manuscript.  It is stated that passages as well as names have been excised from those here in print.  (Here let me express the only  fault I have to find with Mr. Huxley's editing.  Excised names have necessarily to be represented by a dash ; but apart from that there is no typographical indication of the excision of phrases and sentences; and such excisions are considerable.  This is apt to be misleading, and a general warning that excisions have been made is insufficient.) But there is enough Lawrentian candour to be going on with, and we are indebted to the appreciative courage of some of the correspondents in submitting their letters to so valiant an editor.

> The halfness of your friendship I also hate and between you and me there is no sensual correspondence. . . You're not superior to sex and you  never will be. Only too often you are inferior to it. . . I do *not* want your friendship, till you have a full relation somewhere, a *kindly* relation of both halves, not *in part,* as all your friendships have been. That which is in part is in itself a betrayal. Your 'friendship' for me betrays the essential man and male that I am and makes me ill. Yes, you make me ill, by dragging at one half at the expense of the other half. And I am so much better now you have gone. I refuse any more of this 'delicate friendship' business, because it damages one's wholeness.

So Lawrence, in a characteristic letter to a woman, with a like truth-telling of his special kind in the case of some of his men friends. In talk he had not the sort of courage that says such things. How many have the courage or the capacity to write them? He must have been aware that he could write where he could not speak without wounding and to wound was never his intent. Because of the subtle purity of his truth-telling, these letters do not seem to have wounded their recipients, but rather to have assured them of profound good-will. By any other reckoning it would seem unthinkable that we should find them here for all the world to read. That Lawrence braced himself to write them was an honour rendered by him not to truth alone.

It must be added that this extraordinary directness in some letters does not prevent in others a subtler intimation of Lawrence's opinions any more than it does away with his ruthless remarks to one person about another. Taken in conjunction, the two are highly diverting and deeply informing. Lawrence's manner was governed by the occasion; his matter was inveterate. He was an incorrigible gossip. I repeat that this was the one vice of a man to whom many have been attributed. And it was no excrescence, but a part of the man, of his material and his genius. Without it his letters would not be what they are, either by way of entertainment or enlightenment. Also he was not more ruthless with others than with himself. 'Born' by his own acknowledgment 'in chagrin,' he practised the richest, most casual admissions of his own faults.

And of course the personal is but one, and not the most important, aspect of his letters. For we find in them that highly original being, a gossip who took small interest in 'character' and was bored with 'personality.' The rigidity of the first—in which for a long time he could not bring himself to believe—was a stumbling-block to him, the pretentions of the second an offence. Both interfered with the fluidity of life and brought home the knowledge of 'societal frustration,' a frustration, as Lawrence saw it, 'much deeper and much more devastating' than that of the sex instinct. 'People don't mean much to me.' It goes up like a sigh again and again or is rapped out like a curse. So we turn, sharing the writer's own relief, to his descriptions of what are usually regarded as inanimate objects, to indications of his aims and problems, to sharp pronouncements of his findings, to the tackling of material difficulties, and to the felicitous phrases that seem to fall by accident upon the page at the sight of mountain or of mouse. We see 'Liberty clenching her fist' in New York Harbour, follow with a leap of the heart the tracks of birds and beasts in the snow of Derbyshire, learn to respect the practical plans of this hard-pressed, unaccommodating writer, agree that 'You can convince a man that he lusts after his grandmother—he doesn't mind!—but how are you going to bring him to see that as an individual he's a blown egg!,' discover that 'happiness is a subtle and aristocratic thing,' and at the same time assent to the belief that 'the essential self is so simple and nobody lets it be.'

'The greatest virtue in life is real courage, that knows how to face facts and live beyond them.' 'And the hero is he who touches and transmits the life of the universe.' These are Lawrence's deeply considered definitions of heroism. It is difficult to read his letters without feeling the impulse to hand the palm to him as the hero of modern life—this whether we see him as right or wrong, victorious or a tragic failure, fulfilled or foiled within himself.

Mr. Huxley sees in these letters a curve that is 'splendid' but drooping 'tragically' 'at the end toward the darkness.' This is eloquent, and it is truly felt. But it is not necessarily true. Even if not haunted by a mortal illness which carries him away in pain after darkening years that should have marked his middle age, the letters of a man like Lawrence, extending over a period of twenty years, are not likely to describe either a straight line or an ascending curve. To reinforce his image Mr. Huxley has had to draw attention to the savage mood of "Nettles" and the 'lovely and profoundly moving story' of "The Man Who Died". It may with equal plausibility be argued that a healthy Lawrence could, indeed must, have written "Nettles" after an incident like the condemnation of his pictures. And for "The Man Who Died," the first, most moving, part was written early in 1921. Why omit from the reckoning the gaily slashing *Apocalypse* and the carefree *Etruscan Places*, which were written so much later and were both associated with serious attacks of illness?

Lawrence's illness is important, but its importance may be, and too often is, wrongly stressed. Mr. Huxley was at Vence. It is easy, therefore, to forgive him. He gives expression to his own pain. But Lawrence's response to the defeat that is in mortal illness will probably be found in the forthcoming poems written by him during his last winter at Bandol. Mr. Huxley himself candidly points out that during a middle period—when Lawrence was travelling round the world—the letters notably declined in number and in richness of self-committal. And he offers the explanation that 'for one reason or another Lawrence did not want to feel himself in relationship with anyone.' Further, although 'the stream began again,' it is felt 'that Lawrence no longer wanted to give of himself so fully to his correspondents as in the past.' Well, naturally not. There are, that is to say, more curves than one in the course of a correspondence that covers youth and middle age, and these may be explained as well by the passage of time and the variety of experience as by the darkening of disease. It is not the fulfilled who show a rising curve with middle life in their letter-writing and their 'ability to give themselves,' but the fearful, like Cowper, or the futile, like Fitzgerald. That Lawrence's letters should tail off should be a matter for cheerful rather than tragic musings.

In this connexion, if in contradistinction, when Mr. Huxley hazards the opinion that 'Lawrence's . . . was not a very good philosophy for old age or failing persons,' one might submit that Lawrence's accommodation to these things was inherent and well provided, and that disease alone was the confounder. 'I like being older.' He could say this in all simplicity. And if he might have attained his three-score and ten, no man would more imaginably have been able to say 'I like being old.' Like his Etruscans, his 'philosophy' was 'not a theory or a thesis but if anything an *experience*.' In the trap of illness his courage stayed firm. May he not have been even more nicely adapted to meet the commoner lot of growth and decay? For his findings were directly prompted by life, and he was the enemy of nothing but death in life. Against that, and that only, when he saw it—and he saw it remarkably often—he waged 'the subtlest, most intimate warfare.' 'People are too dead,' he writes, 'and too conceited.' 'One fights and fights for that living something that stirs way down in the blood, and *creates* consciousness'; and between whiles, when the fight looked like deadening something in himself— 'one can but swim, like a trout in a quick stream.' Thus refreshed, he was always claimed once more by the fight. 'I must get in another blow at the lily-livered host,' he wrote me not very long before the end. Had he lived to be a hale hundred, Lawrence would still have had to say 'I am essentially a fighter—to wish me peace is bad luck—except the fighter's peace.'

*Nineteenth Century* , CXII, November 1932.

**Note**

---

[1] *The Letters of D. H. Lawrence*, edited and with an introduction by Aldous Huxley (Heinemann). *Etruscan Places*, by D. H. Lawrence (Secker).

# Frederick J. Hoffman, "From Surrealism to 'The Apocalypse': A Development in Twentieth Century Irrationalism"

## I

In the years since Freud's work was first translated and interpreted for the English speaking world his analysis and description of the unconscious have more and more been adapted to the rhetorical and practical needs of the literary artist. Modern critics have almost invariably drawn upon psychoanalysis for assistance in explaining the modern consciousness; poets have likewise found suggestions in clinical casebooks and in Freud's exploratory work in analysis. Of the many developments in literary theory and practice which took place during the three decades which begin and end in World Wars, I have selected one which, considered as a case history in modern poetics, exemplifies the preoccupation of modern writers with the unconscious. It is both revealing and typical.

Beginning with a brief discussion of dadaism (1914-1922), that temporary and explosive denial of rationalism, I propose to show how many French and English writers have exploited and restated the psychoanalytic "discovery" of the unconscious, and have made what use of it they thought necessary to an adequate definition of the modern spiritual crisis. In general, the view of these writers is that this crisis had been brought about by the failure of the reasoning mind; in varying degrees, all of them felt the heavy weight of the ingenious and inventive intellect as the most serious barrier to a reinstatement of positive values. These values were beyond the power of reason to determine or use; they were discernible only by means of an intuitive realization of that which lay beneath the human consciousness.

Dadaism may be called a gesture of pure denial. Its principal critical weapon was the word "rien," in which it concentrated both its particular views of modern civilization and what might be called its metaphysics. As a means of criticizing the assumptions of the rational, ordering, "civilized" mind—which had met and failed its worst test in the first World War—dada's "rien"was used to deny fixed or static value to anything which the mind of man had thus far created and established. Dada's legacy was this heightened, exaggerated, and forceful denial of conscious values and pretensions; surrealists (many of them former dadaists) retained this attitude, but seriously attempted to go beyond dadaism, to establish a criticism and an art which might successfully state not only the weaknesses of a rational world but also the correctness and value of an alternative set of assumptions. But the surrealism of the 1920's in France eventually proved itself to have been the victim of its own method, and its narrow reading of Freud ultimately provided the excuse for its failure. Surrealists, instead of releasmg the ego from its rational prison, provided another, an irrational, prison for it, from which it could not escape except through a radical revision of surrealist practices. The surrealists explored the caverns of the unconscious, equipped only with a camera; they refused to accept any assistance either from human reason or from intuition. Thus, in turning from the rational to the irrational sphere of the mind, they locked themselves in a prison as strong as the one from which they had escaped.

The young English poets of the early 1940's, who called themselves the poets of "The New Apocalypse" had been introduced to Freud and to the surrealists quite early in their careers. In the essays and books of Herbert Read they learned about the uses of psychoanalysis and about its limitations for art, as these had been proved abundantly by surrealists. Their writing therefore rejected the close confinement of the unconscions and reasserted the value and the power of the ego. This ego was substantially what they called the creative mind, which grasped the meaning of the unconscious but insisted upon organizing its gift to poetry in its own fashion. The most valuable suggestions came to them from D.H. Lawrence, who had criticized Freud and at the same time asserted the importance of irrational thought. The writings of these young English poets stood therefore as a restatement of the twentieth-century protest against tradition, and especially against the tendency toward rigid mechanism which both tradition and its surrealist antagonists revealed. What the poets of the "New Apocalypse" offered to modern writing was an attempt to re-instate the value of the creative mind. This value dadaism had discarded, along with all others; surrealism had destroyed it almost inadvertently, in reducing its function to that of serving rather than dominating the unconscious. In the story of this single development in twentieth-century thought, D.H. Lawrence becomes a key figure; outside the surrealist group, he nevertheless worked and argued for the cause which the surrealists had somehow failed to rescue from the dadist scrap-heap. This paper is an attempt to show the influence of Lawrence upon the work of the young poets of the Apocalypse, who saw the problems of the creative mind and of the unconscious from a point of view quite different from that of the pioneer surrealists. . . .

## III

Both surrealism and dadaism were revolutionary movements in the arts. They expressed in one way or another the restlessness of the post-war artist and intellectual. They were exaggerated protests against the institutions and conventions which were generally being baited and mocked in the 1920's. They were alike in their expression of twentieth century irrationalism, as well as in their desire to hasten the end of the conventional world, to bring about "the revolution." The irrationalism of surrealist preaching and practice was deliberate. Its violation of the psychoanalytic purpose was also a part of the general habit of taking crude advantage of whatever opportunity the age offers for an exploitation of its advances in scientific discovery. In refusing to countenance the purpose of psychoanalysis, the surrealists simply acted in accordance with their revolutionary principles, which were based upon a hatred for and a scorn of the intellect. The world is held in bondage to the intellect, they said in effect; it is victim of the mechanization of the modern intelligence. Modern man can be saved only by his trusting to his instincts, by freeing his instincts from their victimization by the intellect. This opposition to the intellect and the reason, this attempt to break through the conventional protections which the intellect had built against the flood of instinct, was shared by other writers and artists, who were otherwise not comparable with the surrealist group. Chief among these was D.H. Lawrence, and his work provided a bridge from the surrealism of the 1920's to the work of certain British intellectuals of World War II. The crisis in Lawrence's life as a writer and thinker occurred when he rejected the scientific basis of psychoanalysis and substituted his own version of the unconscious; it was a change from a clinical to a mythological point of view.

In his two brief books on the new psychology, Lawrence claimed that psychoanalysis had mapped out the area of the unconscious with the single purpose of putting scientific barriers in the way of its expression. What Freud had described as a vast "reclamation project for the ego" seemed to Lawrence to have been a coordinated plan for preventing the instincts of man from direct and joyful expression. Life must be lived dynamically, he insisted; the psychoanalyst, he said, like any other scientist, wants to control it, to dehumanize it. "Life must be lived from the deep, self-responsible spontaneous centers of every individual, in a vital, *non-ideal* circuit of dynamic relation between individuals,"[1] he said in *Fantasia of the Unconscious.* He discovered nothing in modern civilization but deliberate efforts to cheapen life, to thin it out or to put it in chains fashioned by the intellects of scientist, law-maker, and preacher. All modern demonstrations of the critical intelligence are in effect barriers to life, he argued, and their total effect is to weaken human consciousness and to make it a victim of all forms of insidious moral bacteria. Passions and desires are instinctual and unconscious, Lawrence maintained; to fashion them into *ideals* of conduct, to idealize life, is to threaten it with extinction. "Any particular mode of passion or desire which receives an exclusive ideal sanction at once becomes poisonous."[2] The unconscious is therefore "wiser" than the intellect, for the latter merely fumbles with desires and erects barriers to what it calls their "improper" or "immoral" satisfaction.

Lawrence's book on The Apocalypse provides a clue to what has developed in recent times as the Laurentian tradition in writing and thinking. The book is in part textual criticism, discussing at some length the structure of the Book of Revelation, the tamperings of various scholars and doctrinaires with the original; it is also a discussion of the symbolism of apocalypse. In Lawrence's incidental remarks upon Christianity one finds a statement and a summary of the thoughts which had disturbed him earlier and had roused him to strong opposition to modern civilization. The book expresses Lawrence's opposition to power as that is revealed in modern political expressions. The Apocalyptic religion, said Lawrence, represents that second kind of Christianity which one sees demonstrated in evangelical meetings and in sessions of the Salvation Army, the religion of self-glorification which seeks, by way of compensation, to destroy the power vested in leaders and saints. The mass's fear of power, combined with its resentment of it, is expressed in the apocalyptic fervor of its religious meetings, in which the Lord is represented as an avenging spirit who will restore to men the power they have given away. The Apocalypse is therefore that book of the Bible which provides for "the hidden side of Christianity. . . For the Apocalypse does not worship power. It wants to murder the powerful, to seize the power itself, the weakling."[3]

According to Lawrence, the Christian faith has encouraged a timid withdrawal from individual responsibility, so that today "Society consists of a mass of weak individuals trying to protect themselves, out of fear, from every possible imaginary evil, and, of course, by their very fear, bringing the evil into being."[4] It is in this way that Christianity has developed, in the same manner as civilization, as "one long evasion. It has caused endless lying and misery, misery such as people know today, not of physical want but of far more deadly vital want. Better lack bread than lack life. The long evasion, whose only fruit is the machine!"[5] Modern man is now the victim of this spiritual castration. He has come to rely upon outside authority and advice; his original courage and desire are overwhelmed by the Christianity of thou-shalt-not's and the science of antisepsis. "Men are far more fools today, for stripping themselves of their emotional and imaginative reactions, and feeling nothing."[6]

Lawrence shared at least one point of view with other irrationalists of the 1920's: his opposition to authority and prescription from a non-personal source; that is, opposition to the depersonalizing of the human spirit by mechanical, scientific, and modern religious forces. Like the surrealists, with whom he is otherwise not in sympathy, he spoke with vigor and passion of the danger to modern man caused by a sophistication of his life-processes, the slowly growing domination of the intellect over the body and its instincts. What Lawrence preached is an ancient sermon on an ancient text—the death of the intellect, or rather the death of its power over man. Submission to the agents of the intellect can only lead to a weakening of man's spiritual resources, he insisted. And Lawrence was hostile as well to psychoanalysis; for the secrets which Freud had uncovered and tried to suppress, he maintained, were after all nothing less than the mysteries of man's primitive, whole, healthy life.

## IV

Since Lawrence's death in 1930, his work has had various effects upon his readers and followers. The work of love which Aldous Huxley undertook in the editing of Lawrence's letters and in explaining him to the readers of the 1930's was matched by the attempts of others to introduce Lawrence as a figure of considerable importance for the light he threw upon the problem of modern man. After 1930, in the revaluation of Lawrence, it was the author of *Apocalypse* and of *The Plumed Serpent* who received most attention: the explorer of myth and of ancient religions, the advocate of primitivism in society and of primitive cultism in religion. In these respects Lawrence had opened the door to a realization of the significance of the self, an inquiring and a vigorously healthy and independent self which resisted all pressures from the modern world, all efforts to organize and to "tame" man by reducing his individuality and making him a slave to efficiency.

During the second World War, a number of British poets, who called themselves the "Poets of the Apocalypse," made their appearance in British magazines. The group included such men as Henry Treece, Nicholas Moore, J. F. Hendry and G. S. Fraser. They rejected the precedent of the major British poets, like Auden and Spender, but admired and imitated the work of the young Welsh poet, Dylan Thomas. They were not followers of Lawrence in any strict sense, but they shared with him his opposition to external or impersonal ordering of their minds. The program of the Apocalypse is a restatement of aesthetic anarchism; in 1938 these poets agreed upon a statement of principle:

(1) That Man was in need of greater freedom, economic no less than aesthetic, from machines and mechanistic thinking.
(2) That no existent political system, Left or Right; no artistic ideology, Surrealism or the political school of Auden, was able to provide this freedom.
(3) That the Machine Age had exerted too strong an influence on art, and had prevented the individual development of Man.
(4) That Myth, as a personal means of reintegrating the personality, had been neglected and despised [7]

The four points add up to what the young poets of the Apocalypse called a special form of anarchism, and for both the political meaning of that term and its justification as an aesthetic way of life they have turned to the work of Herbert Read. Read's book *Poetry and Anarchism* (1938) has had an especial influence upon the group. The poet, Read says, "is necessarily an anarchist," and he ought not to trust any idea of the state, whether Marxist or Fascist. The very temperament of the poet is inimical to all external forms of politics: he instinctively rejects any organization of his life imposed from without. Society cannot interfere with. the poet's view, for "no great art is possible unless you have as corresponding and contemporary activities the spontaneous freedom of the individual and the passive coherence of a society."[8]  Where this passive coherence is not possible, the poet must nevertheless remain aloof from "everything temporal and opportunist" and then accept the verdict of society: "stay where you are and suffer if you must."[9]

The poets of the Apocalypse shared Read's political views, and they joined both with him and with Lawrence in condemning modern civilization for its dehumanizing effect upon the individual. As for their attitude toward surrealism, like Read, they praised surrealism for its boldness in revolt against reason, but they insisted strongly upon the right of the poet to give to unconscious imagery his own form and imaginative order. The unconscious is the source of poetic vision, they granted, but it exists for the poet, not the poet for it. Surrealist practice had originally followed the habits of the unconscious almost slavishly, so that at times surrealists had not been much more than reporters of the literal content of the unconscious mind. Read insisted upon the poet's will to order as strongly as he maintained that it can be used only in a condition of privacy. "If a poet describes honestly his private perspective on the world, his private universe," said G. S. Fraser, a spokesman for the Apocalypse, "human minds are sufficiently analogous to each other for that private universe to become (ultimately though certainly not immediately) a generally accessible human property."[10]

In the poetry of the Apocalypse, one discovers a mood of personal resignation to the brutality of modern life, combined with skepticism regarding any confident prophets of world order. The lesson of the second World War seems to have discouraged any whole-hearted sympathy with large, impersonal dogmas. . . .

What these poets of the second World War follow in Lawrence is his steadfast maintenance of the value of the personal consciousness in interpreting and utilizing the resources of the unconscious; so that the impersonal acceptance of the unconscious, which they describe as surrealism's greatest weakness, is replaced by an appeal to the poet to bring to his unconscious all of the resources of his will and imagination. In this respect, the revolutions advocated by dadaism, surrealism, and communism have been rejected for a personal formulation of attitudes and a fundamental trust in the value of the person as the limit of all literary activity. This point of view they accept because, as G. S. Fraser has explained, "To act effectively in this world, one must cease to be a person, and become instead, like so many of the others, a bundle of stock responses and unsatisfied appetites." One discovers in this a reaction quite different from that of the dadaists to World War 1; instead of the very active nihilism of the latter, the poets of the Apocalypse prefer an attitude of resignation and a withdrawal from the hostile society of World War II. "To-day," concludes Fraser, "we feel that we can best serve the general human interest by exercising our specific human function, which is to write poetry: to mount guard over the integrity of the imagination and the completeness of man."[11]

*English Literary History* XV, June 1948.

## Notes

[1] *Fantasia of the Unconscious* (New York, 1930), p. 113.

[2] *Ibid.*

[3] *Apocalypse* (New York, 1932), p. 27. the white horseman of the Apocalypse had an especial attraction for Lawrence, and he is also used as a symbol of the writing of "The New Apocalypse." Lawrence had said in *Apocalypse*, p. 100: "The rider of the white horse! Who is he, then? . . . He is the royal me, he is my very self and his horse is the whole MANA of a man. He is my very me, my sacred ego, called into a new cycle of action by the Lamb and riding forth to conquest, the conquest of the old self for the birth of a new self. . . ." This quotation was used as a prefatory note at the beginning of *The White Horseman: Prose and Verse of the New Apocalypse*, published by Routledge in 1941. Like the poets of the Apocalypse, Lawrence regretted the loss by modern man of his selfness, or personal identity; he called it the "taming" of man. "Man is the only creature who has deliberately tried to tame himself," Lawrence said in a piece called "The Novel and the Feelings," published posthumously in *Phoenix* (1936). The psychoanalysts, he continued, have viewed man as the victim of centuries of taming and have attempted to continue the process by securing him from invasions of primitive desire.

[4] *Ibid.*, p. 33.

[5] *Ibid.*, p. 46.

[6] *Ibid.*, p. 79.

[7] Cited by Francis Scarfe, *Auden and After* (London, 1942), p. 155.

[8] Herbert Read, *Poetry and Anarchism* (London, 1938), p. 20.

[9] *Ibid.*

[10] G. S. Fraser, "Apocalypse in Poetry," *The White Horseman* (London, 1941), p. 29.

[11] *Op. cit.*, p. 31.

# Harry T. Moore, "Some New Volumes of Lawrence's Letters"

Everyone knows that Lawrence was a great letter writer, usually as "creative" in his correspondence as he was in his poetry and fiction. Hence these recent fine collections of letters written by him or to him at different times of his life are a welcome addition to Lawrence scholarship.

When the editor of this journal asked me to discuss these new volumes here, I pointed out that critical ethics would make it difficult for me to review one of them, *Lawrence in Love*, since it is distributed in America by the press of the university where I teach. (It was edited and printed at the University of Nottingham.) But Professor Cowan said that if I simply stated this connection and got it out of the way, I might be able to go on and make some comments about the book, particularly in relation to its background. Its admirably proficient editor, Professor James T. Boulton, of Nottingham, in a very full and well-informed Introduction, as well as in his numerous footnotes, tells us virtually all we need to know about the letters themselves, and the relationship of Lawrence to their recipient. But all he says about the acquisition of the letters by the University of Nottingham (need I add that Lawrence went to college there?) is that they were purchased from the executors of the estate of Mrs. Louisa Burrows Heath,[1] "with the aid of a government grant," in 1966.

I knew of the existence of these letters more than thirty years ago, but didn't have the pleasure of reading them until after the Nottingham acquisition. During various research trips to the Midlands, I didn't meet Mrs. Heath, though in 1950 Lawrence's old friend Bill Hopkin, then nearly ninety and very lively, wanted to have me meet her but said that we hadn't better call because her husband was bitterly resentful of even the remotest reference to Lawrence. About ten years later, when I was editing *The Collected Letters of D.H. Lawrence,* I finally got a letter through to her, requesting use of Lawrence's communications to her. She wrote back to say regretfully that she couldn't let me have them: "What would my family think?" She died in the year that those *Collected Letters* were published, 1962, and not long afterward a friend wrote to me from England saying that her husband wanted to destroy Lawrence's letters to the late Mrs. Heath. The friend added that Mrs. Heath's sister was fighting to preserve them, and he gave me the address of a firm of solicitors to whom he suggested that I write and put in an appeal for the preservation of the documents. With memories of the Aspern Papers burning horribly somewhere at the back of my skull, I composed a passionate appeal in behalf of those Lawrence letters, which, as I pointed out (quite obviously), "belong to the world." I don't know whether or not this had any effect, but at least the letters were preserved, and now all serious readers of Lawrence have the benefit of them.

My books on Lawrence, beginning with *The Life and Works of D.H. Lawrence* in 1951, made the first public mention of Louie Burrows (as she is now generally known) in connection with Lawrence; the picture was more fully filled in with the first edition of *The Intelligent Heart* in 1955; there was information about her family and its relation to the background of *The Rainbow.* But now we have a much more complete portrait, not only because of the appearance of these intimate letters but also because of Professor Boulton's thorough researching into the Burrows background. Incidentally, the photograph he uses as frontispiece shows that Louie was a genuine beauty, and not merely considered so by the young Lawrence, whom that beauty upset over a number of years.

Lawrence probably met Louie Burrows about the time they were attending the Pupil-Teacher Centre at Ilkeston, Derbyshire, beginning in 1902. Louie lived just outside Ilkeston, and although Lawrence perhaps had only a slight acquaintance with her at that time, he met her family, so different from his own over in Eastwood, Nottinghamshire; he made use of the Burrowses as the Brangwens of *The Rainbow* and *Women in Love*. Later, Louie moved to another part of the Midlands, but she and Lawrence once again became fellow students, this time at the University College, Nottingham. Previously published letters by Lawrence describe how he and Louie rather impulsively became engaged just about the time his mother died in 1910. The following year, what he once called his "sick year," he became violently ill with pneumonia and had to give up his teaching position in a London suburb. And, by February 1912, he was asking Louie to release him from the engagement, using his health as only a partial excuse ("I am afraid we are not well suited"). After this the correspondence thins out, with Lawrence writing from Italy in November 1912, "I am living here with a lady whom I love, and whom I shall marry when I come to England, if it is possible." Enter Frieda, exit Louie.

The foregoing sketches out the range of the correspondence, but it can give little idea of its fullness and intensity. Beginning in 1906, it is light enough at first, the friendly young Lawrence writing to an attractive girl acquaintance; the frequent references to "J" in the early letters indicate his close attachment at that time to Jessie Chambers. And through it all we can see Lawrence the writer developing, as he moulds his ideas and as he evolves his highly personalized prose style. The latter doesn't really materialize here until about the time he is completing the final draft of *Sons and Lovers*; a note from Lago di Garda in September 1912 has the color and movement of Lawrence's assured prose style, though something of the same quality appears in a letter to Louie of October 1908 which describes the school and the London suburb he has gone to. And there is one particularly compelling and vivid letter, a long one (March 28, 1909) in which Lawrence describes suffragettes demonstrating during an election campaign. This is true Lawrence.

His letters intensify at the time when his mother is dying, just after he has proposed to Louie. His mother was a wonderful woman, but "You will be the first woman to make the earth glad for me: mother, J—all the rest, have been gates to a very sad world. But you are strong & rosy as the gates of Eden." Then he kept on writing to Louie all through that next "sick year," but most of his letters to her, and indeed to others, don't show him as particularly cast down during most of 1911, though in what was apparently the first draft of the Introduction to his *Collected Poems* (1928), possibly rejected because it was too intimate (but fortunately rescued by E. D. McDonald for the first *Phoenix*, 1936), Lawrence said that "in that year, for me everything collapsed, save the mystery of death, and the haunting of death in life. I was twenty-five, and from the death of my mother [in December 1910], the world began to dissolve around me, beautiful, iridescent, but passing away substanceless. Till I almost dissolved away myself, and was very ill: when I was twenty-six." During that period, beginning with a letter of December 12, 1910, saying that his mother had just been buried, until pneumonia struck him in the following November, he wrote Louie seventy-five letters, far more than he wrote to anyone else at that time; and most of them are at least of medium length. They cheerfully discuss his writings (he often sends manuscripts to her); the appearance of his first novel, *The White Peacock*; his struggles with early versions of *Sons and Lovers,* and the magazine appearances of his poems and stories, as well as writers and editors he meets at parties. Most of the communications are in part love letters, though not fervently so; and he continually refuses to think of marriage until he has a mildly good income. The letters also retrospectively discuss various times he and Louie had been together in those months, in the Midlands, in London, and once, with an excursion party, in Wales. As I suggested before, none of this sounds like the terrible year Lawrence looked back on in his unused Introduction to *The Collected Poems.*

His breaking off of the relationship has already been mentioned. And in the next-to-last among the surviving letters (November 19, 1912), written from Italy and mentioning the "lady" he hoped to marry, he strikes a note of regret and guilt: "I want to say that it grieves me that I was such a rotter to you. You always treated me really well—and I—well, I only knew towards the end we couldn't make a good thing of it. But the wrong was all on my side. I think of you with respect and gratitude, for you were good to me—and I think of myself in the matter with no pleasure, I can tell you . . . . But if we go on writing, I feel I am only doing you more wrong, & it would be easier to stop altogether—wiser perhaps." The last letter, six days later, is a short one, apparently in answer to a letter of hers which had crossed his. He writes in French, neutrally and briefly—and politely. Professor Boulton notes that Lawrence's sister Ada sent Louie his address on February 7, 1913 (as indicated in a holograph letter in the Nottingham University collection); "if Louie then wrote and received a reply it has not survived." Interestingly, February 1913 was the month in which Lawrence's first volume of verse, *Love Poems and Others,* came out.

As I said in *The Intelligent Heart,* "And this was the last of Louie in his life," referring to a couple of letters he wrote to Edward Garnett in February 1912, about a last meeting with Louie in Nottingham, where she giggled and wept; then, about two weeks later, he had a letter from her, "repenting of her horrid behaviour on that Tuesday—beseeching me to take an excursion with her down into the country next Saturday—just to show I forgive her. I daren't accept—and shan't." Again to quote *The Intelligent Heart,* "after his death she rented for years the cottage he had once lived in with his wife, in Cornwall, and Louie made two dramatic visits to his grave in France, with much weeping." In his Introduction, Professor Boulton doesn't mention the Cornwall residence, but he does speak of the two visits to Vence, one of them in 1930, when Frieda Lawrence's daughter, Barbara Weekley Barr, saw her there, leaving some flowers at Lawrence's grave. Sir Herbert Read, who also saw her in Vence, wrote to Professor Boulton that Louie "obviously had never renounced her love and devotion for Lawrence. She was rather a dispirited and sombre kind of person, and I think she felt she had been ill-treated by Lawrence." That last sentence sounds exactly like descriptions of Jessie Chambers in her later years; neither of them seems to have recovered from Lawrence. In the late 1930's Harry K. Wells and his wife told me that they had deduced Louie's address from the Huxley edition of Lawrence's *Letters* and had called on her; she still spoke of Lawrence fondly and kept his letters reverently. For the better luck of all of us, they have been spared; and James T. Boulton has written a most useful Introduction to them, and has edited them with great thoroughness, with perhaps too many annotations (too much material repeated in eye-hurting notes), but he has mastered the subject wonderfully, and certainly no one else in the world could have filled in so much of the background material, identifying so many local references.

George J. Zytaruk has done an equally impressive job with Lawrence's letters to his Russian-émigré friend, Samuel Solomonovich Koteliansky. As Professor Zytaruk points out, that name was so difficult to pronounce that Koteliansky's British friends usually called him Kot. Lawrence at first even misspelled his surname as Kotiliansky.

This volume makes an interesting sequel to the Louie Burrows book, because the letters to Koteliansky begin in 1914, two years after Lawrence's last-known communication to Louie. Koteliansky was then working in London at the Russian Law Bureau, a rather zany office for descriptions of which the editor, in his informative Introduction, draws upon memoirs by two of Koteliansky's friends, Katherine Mansfield and Beatrice Lady Glenavy. Koteliansky (1880-1955) first met Lawrence just as the First World War was breaking out, and across the years he maintained a rather protective attitude toward the frail son of a coal-miner. Frieda, who also outlived Lawrence by a quarter-century, didn't get on well with Koteliansky, and Professor Zytaruk makes an educated guess to the effect that Frieda had blocked Koteliansky as a collaborator with Aldous Huxley on the first collection of Lawrence's *Letters*, which came out in 1932. The Introduction to the present book quotes a 1930 letter to Koteliansky from the painter Mark Gertler, in which he says that he had mentioned his Russian friend as a possible co-editor, and that Huxley was agreeable. It is only reasonable to sunnise that Frieda killed the idea. She wrote unfriendlily about Koteliansky to Middleton Murry as late as 1953, when *Encounter* published a small selection of Lawrence's letters to Koteliansky; Frieda indicated that she was irritated because Koteliansky had withheld all his letters from the Huxley collection.

Throughout most of his life in England (he became a British citizen in 1929), Koteliansky lived poorly, doing a great amount of translating, some of it with Lawrence. In 1932, Lawrence's sister Ada sent me to visit Koteliansky in London, at that famous literary house, 5 Acacia Road, St. John's Wood, where Murry and Katherine Mansfield had once lived. That summer afternoon was an unusual one, since no rain fell, and Koteliansky and I could sit out talking in the garden. Koteliansky (whom Murry compared to an Assyrian bas-relief, Leonard Woolf to Jeremiah, and Lawrence to Jehovah) was fiercely dramatic as he talked about the Lawrence circle. One statement shocked me: "Lawrence didn't die too soon; he wouldn't have been a *good* old man."

Koteliansky willed his letters from Lawrence and others to the British Museum, with a tender note as to the bequest, "made as an acknowledgment of my friendship for England and for the friendship that I have enjoyed with many of her writers and citizens for nearly half a century." In the late 1950's, when I was gathering material for Lawrence's *Collected Letters,* I had access to the 343 of them at the British Museum. I wanted intensely to include every known Lawrence letter, though regrettably (as mentioned earlier) the Louie Burrows items weren't available. As complete a collection as could have been made at that time would have taken three volumes, but the publishers restricted me to two. Of those 343 letters to Koteliansky, only 104 went into the two volumes (the statistics are from the Zytaruk Introduction), of which six had previously appeared in print, in *Encounter.* Professor Zytaruk's book fortunately publishes the 343 from the British Museum as well as three more which he discovered in Oxford. As he points out, this is the largest assemblage of letters from Lawrence to any one person.

A great many of them, however, are brief. just a few lines. And none are really lengthy. But, as Professor Zvtaruk rightly states, "The kind of scholarship which is being applied to Lawrence today makes it imperative to have every authentic document made available for examination." To which all of us can only say "Amen."

The editor of this book assures us of the importance of these letters; and they are important despite the brevity of so many of them. There is no question of the importance of Koteliansky in the Lawrence experience: and this volume is significantly called *The Quest for Rananim*—Rananim was the name Lawrence used for the "ideal colony" he wanted to establish, in Florida, the South Seas, the Andes or, finally, New Mexico. Koteliansky had given Lawrence the word Rananim (its possible derivation is discussed at length in the present Introduction). Yet Koteliansky was one of Lawrence's several friends who didn't join him when New Mexico was at last designated as Rananim. When Lawrence had briefly returned to England in the winter of 1923-24, he staged the grotesque "Last Supper" party in a private room at the Café Royal. Of the seven people who were guests of the Lawrences, only one of them (the Hon. Dorothy Brett) followed him to New Mexico. The party was enlivened by Koteliansky's smashing of wine glasses as he shouted, "No woman here or anywhere else can possibly understand the greatness of Lawrence!" But Koteliansky never went to Rananim.

The early letters from Lawrence to Koteliansky are almost entirely social: in 1914-15, the Lawrences were often in the country, but in and out of London, and most of these first items are little more than arrangements to meet; evidently the two men had a great deal to say to one another when they were together, and Lawrence at least wasn't pouring out his feelings to Koteliansky in letters. Actually, this set the tone of the correspondence, which is for the most part brief and brisk, on Lawrence's side at least;. and it is largely characterized by business discussions, over the translations they worked on, over publishing schemes that never materialized, over Koteliansky's rather frightened assistance, in. 1928, with the English distribution of *Lady Chatterley's Lover*—and so on. But of course a good amount of personal matter thrusts up from these letters, too. There is, for example, the letter tentatively dated February 5, 1915, from Sussex, in which Lawrence says that, after a long numbness that first took possession of him when the war broke out, he is at last coming alive again. Then: "Tomorrow Lady

Ottoline [Morrell] is coming again & bringing Bertrand Russell—the Philosophic-Mathematics man—a Fellow of Cambridge University FRS—Earl Russell's brother. We are going to struggle with my Island idea—Rananim." They struggled, all right.

The letters to Koteliansky from Cornwall later in the War, when the two men were—for residents of England—geographically somewhat far apart, are more intimate in revealing Lawrence's deepest thoughts, and these communications also contain more of the Lawrencean prose landscapes than he usually gave to Koteliansky. And then, after the War, during Lawrence's travel years, the letters to Koteliansky continue to be personal, but they are also heavily factual, full of practical details. There are many sharp judgments of books, particularly Russian (Lawrence *always* disliked Dostoevsky).

An interesting aspect of these communications is what they tell about Lawrence the translator. Here, Professor Zytaruk's notes and comments are especially helpful, for this is a side of Lawrence which has never been fully considered. The Zytaruk Introduction interestingly enough calls Lawrence "an editor of Koteliansky's translations," rather than a co-translator.

Professor Zytaruk notes that "there is a large gap in the correspondence from March 1924 to December 1925." A good deal of that time Lawrence was in New Mexico and Mexico, but he wrote rather full letters to various correspondents. The editor points out, however, that Lawrence's letter of December 6, 1925, written from Italy, "gives no hint of a break in the friendship between the two men"; but he is unable to comprehend why there was a hiatus between the time of this letter and the last previous item in the collection, from New York on March 14, 1924, "unless it is that Lawrence's letters from this period are among those which Koteliansky has designated as not being made available to the public." And there is, in the British Museum Catalogue, a listing, under Lawrence, of "Add. MSS. 48975 (Vol. X.), which is reserved for fifty years." Don't I know it!—in 1958, at the British Museum, this box was delivered by mistake to my desk in one of the auxiliary reading rooms, and just as I started to dig into the material, several librarians appeared who politely but firmly removed it from my grasp. But, back to the question of what possibly caused the possible cessation of Lawrence's letters to Koteliansky: Lawrence said in a letter of September 30, 1925 (quoted in *The Intelligent Heart*), just after he arrived in London, that he intended to see only a few of his old friends: "The Carswells and the Eders, but no more of the old crowd, not Kot." This suggests that there must have been some kind of estrangement between the two men which ended by December 1925. It is interesting to note that Lawrence once stated that Koteliansky wearied him "to extinction." In a letter probably written in 1915, to Gordon Campbell (later Lord Glenavy), Lawrence said, "You exasperate me almost to contempt, still the liking doesn't change. Murry fills me with loathing, still somehow I am fond of him. Kot wearies me to extinction, yet I couldn't forego him." Interestingly, Glenavy, Beatrice [Lady]Lady Glenavy didn't print that part of the letter in her memoir, *Today We Will Only Gossip* (1964), and perhaps she omitted the passage because she was consistently trying to show Koteliansky in the best possible light; but through some mistake that part of the letter was included, along with other sections quoted in her text, on the jacket of her book.

It is necessary to say a few words about the physical appearance of Professor Zytaruk's volume. He is not to blame for the faults in the appearance of the book, which was designed and printed in England, and in such a way that it is difficult to read because of the strain on one's eyes. The texts of the letters, as printed, have what is technically known as the "unjustified right margin," meaning a ragged right margin, with no indentation of paragraphs on the left side and, on the right, the lines of print ending whimsically and unevenly. The penalty on the eyes is intensified by the notes at the ends of the letters, where they are enclosed in black lines (known as "rules") which make for painful reading, particularly when a note is only one line long, and the reader has to fight to get between those "rules." Also, in many cases a short letter will take up an entire page, leaving an enormous blank space. This makes the book longer, and consequently more expensive, than it should have been. And there doesn't seem to be much consistency in the method. For example, on pp. 292–293, Letters 263 and 264 are given a page apiece, although they are brief and have no footnotes and could easily have been fitted together on a single page, in the manner of Letters 64 and 65 on p. 60. There may be some technical reason for this, but it seems just a mystery; and in the printing of so many letters that "unjustified right margin" seems unjustified indeed.

Someone might say that Lawrence didn't bother about such matters; but he did, as his correspondence often shows. Once again, however, Professor Zytaruk isn't to blame for the physical appearance of his book; the point is that, like Professor Boulton, he has made an important contribution to Lawrence scholarship.

The volume of Lawrence's 196 letters to his one-time publisher, Martin Secker, some of which (like those to Koteliansky) have been published before, generally go in a business direction, for the most part discussing publication technicalities, including royalties. This is the fullest presentation of Lawrence's business side, so that it helps fill out our picture of the man. As such, it is extremely useful to all those studying Lawrence in detail (it cleared up a few matters I was in doubt about in working with some Lawrence material, and it can be of help to others). But the letters aren't all commercially slanted, for Lawrence became a good friend of Secker's and went to Spotorno at his suggestion in 1925; Secker also went there at the time. So, toward the end, Lawrence would sometimes put forth a landscape or mention some favorite idea, as in most of his letters to others. Occasionally the editor of this collection put a letter in the wrong place, as in the case of the one numbered CLXXIV. This is dated "3 Dec. 1928," which says, "We left that island—too uncomfortable." Yet number CLXXVII, the third letter afterward, is from the island Lawrence was referring to, Port-Cros (dated only "Sat."). There are several similar mistakes, but they aren't of great importance. The editor, obviously Martin Secker himself, probably also edited the Secker letters to Lawrence and others.

The appearance of that book is something of a miracle, for Lawrence, travelling about so much, usually destroyed letters he received, but these letters from Secker are mainly from office carbons. They are of interest to Lawrence students, both as a counterpoint to the Lawrence-to-Secker volume and as a statement of a publisher's attitude to a writer he welcomed to his list at a time when other firms were rejecting him. Both these books begin with 1911, when Secker wrote to the young author of *The White Peacock* inviting him to submit future manuscripts; Lawrence's reply was cordial, but he explained that William Heinemann had first-refusal rights on Lawrence's next novel (but Edward Garnett eventually wooed Lawrence over to Gerald Duckworth's publishing house).

Secker did bring out Lawrence's *New Poems* in a limited edition in 1918, and in the 1920's became Lawrence's regular publisher in England, undoubtedly at a considerable loss. Lawrence in the letters to Secker points out that his English sales in the 1920's were meager in comparison with those in America. Yet Secker kept on publishing him, except that like everyone else in the trade he refused the unexpurgated *Lady Chatterley's Lover*. Secker also includes in this volume some letters to Lawrence's London agent, Curtis Brown, and one to Robert Bridges, futilely asking him to write a preface to Lawrence's *Collected Poems* (1928). The most important thing these Secker-to-Lawrence letters bring out is Secker's magnanimity in dealing with a somewhat difficult author. His good will and financial aid helped to keep Lawrence going.

Of course, the two limited editions featuring both Lawrence and Secker should be amalgamated in a year or so, after the original editions have been completely sold out, a condition that may come to pass even before the present lines appear in print.

The three volumes of Lawrence's letters show him to be, as always, an absorbing correspondent, using his almost magical gift of language to intensify the *ambiance* of whatever he is writing about; above all, he penetrates all human and inhuman barriers and confronts whatever the subject happens to be. He is earnest, sometimes slyly comic, and never silly in his letters. With the Louie Burrows volume we are able to trace the formation of Lawrence as we could never quite do before; his letters to Koteliansky help us to follow his later development.

And all this is significant because Lawrence spoke so powerfully to our time, to those of us living amid wars and fires and riots forty-one years after his death. Some of his most forceful utterances may be found in that neglected crazyquilt of a book *Kangaroo*, for whose title character Lawrence may have drawn partly upon Koteliansky. Murry, Lawrence's longtime friend and enemy, said in 1932 that *Kangaroo* was "one of the most profound moral treatises of modern times," and that this novel "shows the complete moral demand of conscious politics upon the modern man"; Lawrence "was the first modern Englishman to feel the sternness of the complete demand." In another context, Murry said in 1956, a year before his own death, "Lawrence was alone in the depth of his prescience of the crisis of humanity which has developed since his death." Yes, he speaks to us, but not just to warn us of disaster; essentially he gives us a sense of life. We find all these elements in the new volumes of his letters, so diligently and skillfully edited.

Professional publishers owe students of Lawrence a full edition, or at least a university press should be allowed to bring it out. And, as we all marvel over more letters from Lawrence, we realize that a complete edition, perhaps edited by a group of scholars, is also a distinct necessity. Gerald Lacy of Angelo State University, who is putting together a calendar of Lawrence letters, says there are about 4,000 of them. So let's have that four-volume set of virtually complete letters as soon as possible. Lawrence now so patently "belongs to the world" that those who are clenching his letters or the rights to them should realize their importance to scholars, just plain readers, or newcomers to the Lawrence area of interest.

*The D.H. Lawrence Review*, 4, 1971.

## Note

1 *Lawrence in Love: Letters to Louie Burrows*, edited by James T. Boulton. Carbondale: Southern Illinois University Press. 1969. $7.50. *The Quest for Rananim: D. H. Lawrence's Letters to S. S. Koteliansky, 1914 to 1930.*, edited by George J. Zytaruk. Montreal: McGill-Queen's University Press, 1970. $12.50. *Letters from D. H. Lawrence to Martin Secker, 1911-1930,* edited by Martin Secker. Bridgefoot, Iver, Buckinghamshire, England ("Privately Published"), 1970. 5 guineas. (Limited to 500 copies.) *Letters from a Publisher: Martin Secker to D. H. Lawrence and Others, 1911-1929*. London: Enitharmon Press. 1970. 2 pounds, 10 shillings. (Limited to 350 copies.)

## Evelyn J. Hinz, "The Beginning and the End: D.H. Lawrence's *Psychoanalysis* and *Fantasia*"

*Fantasia of the Unconscious* (1922) is generally viewed as Lawrence's second polemical attempt to denigrate Freudian psychoanalysis and at the same time to systematize the philosophy of the unconscious he had been advancing in his fiction. The reason for the repeated effort, it has been suggested, was the reviewers' ridicule of his first attempt, *Psychoanalysis and the Unconscious* (1921); thus Philip Rieff explains in his introduction to the two works, "When he saw how completely his message had been misunderstood, he immediately tried again—belligerently, even somewhat peevishly. 'I stick to the solar plexus', he announces, and *Fantasia,* published in 1922, is a restatement and elaboration of his doctrine of the Unconscious as it had been stated in *Psychoanalysis*".[1]   To Rieff, the two essays are fundamentally similar and consequently can be treated as a single statement in discussions of Lawrence and psychoanalysis. And in this respect he appears to be representative. In his pioneering exploration of "Lawrence's Quarrel with Freud", Frederick J. Hoffman used both essays in the same way to arrive at his summary of Lawrence's objections to Freudian theory and moved from the early to the later work with the simple observation, "In *Fantasia of the Unconscious* Lawrence carried his disagreement with Freud further".[2]  Similarly, in his recent attempt to explore the mythic dimensions of Lawrence's "theory of human psychology", James C. Cowan shifts from the one essay to the other without specifying from which of the two he is quoting.[3] Whatever their particular approaches or conclusions as to the value of these essays, Lawrence critics share in common the premise that there is no essential difference between *Psychoanalysis* and *Fantasia*.

The purpose of this study is to demonstrate that there is a significant difference between Lawrence's two attempts to answer the challenge science in general and Freudian psychoanalysis in particular seemed to present—the difference between an empirical and a poetic methodology, between an analytic and an archetypal approach to the unconscious. My concern is with the style and structure of the two essays, and my contention, therefore, is not that Lawrence said different things in these two works but that he said things differently in *Fantasia* than he did in *Psychoanalysis,* so differently that not only must *Fantasia* be viewed as a new statement rather than as a re-statement but also that it must be viewed as a different *kind* of work from *Psychoanalysis.*  Specifically, my argument is that while *Psychoanalysis* may appear extremely poetic and consequently unscientific according to absolute standards, in contrast to *Fantasia* and therefore from Lawrence's point of view, it was designed as a scientific answer; and while *Fantasia* cannot be classified as fiction, it demands to be approached as a work of art with its "Foreword" as Lawrence's serious explanation of why he changed his approach. Thus the present study should bring into focus a central document not only in Lawrence's aesthetic development but in the history of the relations between science and art as well.

*Psychoanalysis and the Unconscious* was originally projected as "Six Little Essays on Freudian Unconscious", and a glance at the external structure of the published version indicates that the expository format was carried through. *Psychoanalysis* consists of six chapters: the first two are concerned with a demonstration of the limitations of Freudian theory, the last four with a presentation of Lawrence's own ideas. But if this ratio supports Hoffman's thesis that Lawrence's purpose was to "replace" Freud's explanation of the operations of the unconscious with his own, the language and style of this essay make clear that Lawrence did not view Freud's system as, "sober, scientific", as Hoffman suggests (164), but quite the opposite. "The aim of this little book", Lawrence repeatedly emphasizes, "is merely to establish the smallest foothold in the swamp of vagueness which now goes by the name of the unconscious" (42). Lawrence's basic argument, in short, is not that Freud and his followers are too dispassionate and empirical but that they are not scientific enough. His method in the first two chapters of his little book is to discredit the scientific pretensions of psychoanalysis, and this he does in three ways.

*Psychoanalysis* begins with the insinuation that psychoanalysts are the descendants of the old-fashioned medical charlatan: "No sooner had we got used to the psychiatric quack . . . than lo and behold the psychoanalytic gentleman reappeared on the stage with a theory of pure psychology" (3). And throughout the opening pages he continues to ridicule them because they are pretenders. For example, one might notice Lawrence's use of "as" and words  suggestive of magic: "They have crept in among us  as healers and physicians; growing bolder they have asserted their authority as scientists; two more minutes and they will appear as apostles" (3). It is not because they are medical men but because they are "medicine-men" (4) that they are suspect: "Have we not seen and heard the *ex cathedra* Jung? And does it need a prophet to discern that Freud is on the brink of a Weltanschauung—or at least a Menschenschauung, which is a much more risky affair?" (3). To Lawrence, therefore, psychoanalysis is the enemy of morality not because it operates according to scientific principles but because it does not; science is not concerned with moral issues, psychoanalysis according to Lawrence is.

But simply to label them frauds, to indulge in name-calling and invective, is to prove nothing; and if anything Lawrence's purpose in this essay is to prove that psychoanalysts are wrong. The obvious way to discredit their authority as scientists is to demonstrate that their logic is faulty, and the easiest means to such an end is the classic *reductio ad absurdum*. In Lawrence's discussion of the Oedipal aspects of Freud's theory this technique is everywhere in operation. According to Lawrence, psychoanalysis believes "that at the root of almost every neurosis lies some incest-craving, and that this incest-craving is *not the result of inhibition of normal sex-craving*" (7). But if this is the case, argues Lawrence, then one must view incest as a natural desire: "What remains but to accept it as part of the normal sex-manifestation?" Some psychoanalysts, he then goes on, will go this far, but that is not enough. If their theory is to hold up they must go all the way: if neurosis is caused by repression and if incest is natural, then the cure for neurosis is "to remove all repression of incest itself. In fact, you must admit incest as you now admit sexual marriage, as a duty even" (7).  Of course, if psychoanalysis had minded its own business, had remained a descriptive "physical" science instead of "assuming the role of psychology" (6), its theories could not be brought to this ludicrous end.  But it has not, and therein lies "the moral dilemma of psychoanalysis" (7), and the justification of Lawrence's appeal to morality to discredit it.

A third way in which Lawrence faults psychoanalysts is by pointing out that they do not adhere to the fundamental principles of empirical inquiry: instead of inductively exploring the unconscious, they proceed deductively. Suppose, says Lawrence, the unconscious does contain repressed incest impulses; "But must we inevitably draw the conclusion psychoanalysis draws?" (8)—that this is all the unconscious is? The reason the Freudians come to this conclusion is that they begin with the consciousness, with ideas and ideals, and proceed to interpret the unconscious according to this principle. The unconscious to them is the repressed consciousness, and in thus proceeding they may be making an autonomous and prior thing the effect of a later stage in man's psychic development. For there is one thing "psychoanalysis all along the line fails to determine, and that is the nature of the pristine unconscious in man. The incest-craving is or is not inherent in the pristine psyche" (8). Instead of first making certain that they had found the "rock" (4), the Freudians have built their "doctrine" upon idealistic principles and consequently all of their arguments have an *ex cathedra* rather than an empirical ring.

Lawrence's first purpose in *Psychoanalysis*, therefore, is to denigrate Freudian psychoanalysis by exposing its unscientific methodology; his second purpose is to introduce his own system and a more logical and accurate—in a word, more scientific—procedure.

"There is a whole science of the creative unconscious, the unconscious in it law-abiding activities. And of this science we do not even know the first term" (16). Undoubtedly, the reason critics have tended to appreciate the significance of Lawrence's emphasis upon the scientific aspect of *Psychoanalysis* is (aside from what he might say elsewhere) such statements in the essay as the following: "But it needs a super-scientific grace before we can admit this first new item of knowledge" (16-17). But to repeat, my argument is not that such a statement is scientific but that the context in which it appears indicates that Lawrence did not consider it as antithetical to the scientific method and that in contrast to the way in which such an issue is presented in *Fantasia*, as we shall see, the practice here can be described as "scientific".

With respect to the passage in question, for example, one should notice that the request for "super-scientific grace" is presented not as an alternate or opposite but as the logical solution to the problem that the unconscious presents. The Freudians, he begins, have restricted the unconscious "within certain ideal limits" (16); that is, they have tried to confine the unconscious in terms of consciousness. Clearly such a method is to defeat one's purpose at the outset; but where then can one begin? Lawrence's answer is that one must begin at the beginning—with the unconscious and therefore with the pre-conscious and pre-cognitive sense rather than with the intellectual apprehension. But in a series of four conditional clauses he carefully explains that such a procedure is not to abandon rationality. "Once we can admit the *known*, but incomprehensible, presence of the integral unconscious" is his first statement, and as his italicization indicates, his point is not that we must irrationally accept the concept of the unconscious as an *ex cathedra donnée* but rather that the fact that we know and yet cannot mentally comprehend the unconscious illustrates its pre-cognitive nature. Therefore to understand the unconscious we must begin by utilizing this type of knowledge: "once we can trace it home in ourselves and follow its first revealed movements". But if we must thus by virtue of the nature of the problem begin intuitively, we must proceed methodically: "once we know how it habitually unfolds itself". And this leads directly to the final statement: "once we can scientifically determine its laws and processes in ourselves". In short, while, the phrase "super-scientific grace" may seem to us indicative of a departure from a scientific approach, Lawrence clearly did not consider his method as such. Indeed, he goes on to anticipate objections on these grounds: his method, he says, "means that science abandon its intellectualist position and embraces the religious faculty. But it does not thereby become less scientific it only becomes at last complete in its knowledge" (17).

It is therefore not for a replacement of "the sober, scientific" approach of the Freudians by a "poetic, mystic affirmation" (Hoffman, 163) that Lawrence argues in *Psychoanalysis* but rather for the recognition of a pre-cognitive mode of perception. In this essay it is not the "affirmation of the irrational" (Cowan, 16) that is Lawrence's concern but the rationality of recognizing an uncerebral form of knowledge.

These observations are further supported when one considers the way Lawrence handles the problem of authority in *Psychoanalysis*. "And where in the developed foctus shall we look for this creative-productive quick? Shall we expect it in the brain or in the heart?" he asks in an attempt to locate the physical centre of the integral consciousness.   His answer is typically derived from two sources: "Surely our own subjective wisdom tells us, what science can verify, that it lies beneath the navel of the folded foetus" (19). In short, whenever he resorts to subjectivity in this early essay, he immediately either confirms it with an appeal to science, as in the previous example, or he explicitly denies that he is being unscientific, as in the following anticipation of those who would write off his explanations as poetical: "The nuclei are centres of spontaneous consciousness. It seems as if their bright grain were germ-consciousness, consciousness germinating forever. If that is a mystery, it is not my fault. Certainly it is not mysticism. It is obvious, demonstrable scientific fact, to be verified under the microscope and within the human psyche, subjectively and objectively, both" (43). Whether Lawrence is accurate in his assertion that science can verify his theories is for the present purposes beside the point. The significant issue is Lawrence's determination to be accepted as scientifically respectable and consequently his insistence that his intuitions coincide with and complement scientific fact.

In addition to "subjective wisdom" Lawrence frequently relies upon the wisdom of the past or explores traditional metaphors to explain his theories. For example, in attempting to describe the division of consciousness into subjective (located in the abdominal area) and objective (located in the breast) he observes that his explanation is consistent with an old and traditional attitude. However, instead of simply relying upon its poetic truth, he feels called upon to justify his use of this source by emphasizing that the men of the past were not simply being poetic: "When the ancients located the first seat of the consciousness in the heart, they were neither misguided nor playing with metaphor. For by consciousness they meant, as usual, objective consciousness only" (31). And if one argued that the reason Lawrence insisted upon such a literal interpretation was that he wanted his system to be taken literally, one confirms rather than refutes the argument that *Psychoanalysis* was designed as a scientific exposition.

Similarly, he twice emphasizes that "in calling the heart the sun, the source of light, we are biologically correct even. For the roots of vision are in the cardiac plexus" (36); "It is not merely a metaphor to call the cardiac Plexus the sun, the Light" (37). Instead of giving the essay the quality of "mythic restatement" (Cowan, 16), the metaphors and symbols to be found in *Psychoanalysis* have an opposite effect. In this essay Lawrence's approach to the poetic is comparable to the approach of the Cambridge anthropologists to myth and ritual—they attempted to provide a rational explanation of primitive mysteries; Lawrence is trying to provide a rational basis for his intuitions. "This is the vertical line of division. And the horizontal line and the vertical line form the cross of all existence and being", be observes, and here, as Cowan suggests, he employs "the cosmic image of the cross" (16). But Lawrence does not encourage us to view his system in such mythic terms, for he immediately adds, "And even this is not mysticism—no more than the ancient symbols used in botany or biology" (44). Every poetic usage in *Psychoanalysis* must be defended or justified empirically.

A final way of suggesting the expository design of *Psychoanalysis* is to point out that with one necessary exception (4-5) the entire six chapters utilize the first person plural. On the one hand, this usage enables Lawrence to give his essay an impersonal tone, the tone of critical objectivity: "Now before we can have any sort or scientific, comprehensive psychology we shall have to establish the *nature* of the consciousness" (35). On the other hand, the journalistic "we" characterizes the writer as the spokesman for the majority and thereby enables him to avoid sounding impressionistic: "If however, the unconscious is inconceivable, how do we know it at all?" is the fundamental question in *Psychoanalysis,* and strictly speaking, Lawrence's answer should be "I know it through intuition". But that is a purely subjective answer. "We know it by direct experience" (15) is probably equally subjective but it sounds more scientific. And it is also this use of "we" that makes the speaker's apologies for not employing the specialist's idiom contribute to rather than detract from the tone of critical authority. "We do not pretend to use technical language", Lawrence emphasizes, "But surely our meaning is plain even to correct scientists" (20). The implication here is not that the writer could not, but that because of his role as humanistic spokesman he will not use technical terms. Similarly, when he writes, "We profess no scientific *exactitude*, particularly in terminology. We merely wish intelligibly to open a way" (36) the italicization makes clear that he is not attacking the scientific mode but rather anticipating the charge that because he does not employ the jargon he does not understand the issues involved. The impression would be greatly altered, however, if the statement had read, "I profess no scientific exactitude".

However poetic, mystical, or absurd *Psychoanalysis* may have sounded to his contemporaries and may sound to the modern reader, then, the style of the essay clearly indicates that Lawrence did not view it as such but rather as a scientific piece designed to expose psychoanalysis as a pseudo-science and to introduce a pioneer interpretation of the unconscious. If there are inconsistencies and contradictions in the work it is not because his purpose was to affirm the irrational but because he was too concerned with demonstrating the rationality of his insights. Intuition cannot be bounded by reason and to attempt to do so is to do injustice to either. My concern now is to demonstrate that it was Lawrence's recognition of this situation that prompted him to try again. He wrote *Fantasia,* I suggest not simply because *Psychoanalysis* was unsuccessful but because he realized that he had invited failure because of the method he had chosen. The "Foreword" to *Fantasia* is simultaneously an explanation of why *Psychoananlysis* was a failure—its expository and empirical method—and an introduction to the new methodology and format of the second work—an archetypal perspective and an artistic structure.

"The present book is a continuation from *Psychoanalysis and the Unconscious*", Lawrence announces at the outset of *Fantasia.* "The generality of readers had better just leave it alone. The generality of critics likewise" (53). According to Rieff, this opening may be described as "an unhappy effort to appeal to the snobbishness of his readers" (vii), and generally it is interpreted as evidence of the "companion" nature of the two essays. The style and structure of this introduction and *Fantasia,* however, suggest an alternate interpretation. In the first place, Lawrence does not say that *Fantasia* is a continuation of but a "continuation from" *Psychoanalysis*: the former phrase connotes "restatement and elaboration", but the latter can imply a movement away, a departure from the early essay. While not enough to make a case, it is sufficient to stimulate a reconsideration. Similarly, if one examines the context carefully, the negative appeal to a few fit readers can be viewed as something more than a peevish reaction to the critical fate of *Psychoanalysis.* The dismissal of the "generality", in the first place, is explained in terms of a diagnosis of the ills of Western civilization: "I count it a mistake of our mistaken democracy, that every man who can read print is allowed to believe that he can read everything that is printed. I count it a misfortune that serious books are exposed in the public market, like slaves exposed for sale" (53).

Therefore, if one approaches the "Foreword" simply as Lawrence's peevish reaction to the fate of *Psychoanalysis*, then one must conclude that he is blaming the entire cultural and political system for the failure of his first work. But his argument is not that the majority cannot read, ie., are insensitive, but that the average man *should* not read: the first is the typical defensive complaint of the misunderstood writer, but the second is a statement of principle—furthermore, a principle that constitutes one of the central themes of *Fantasia*. "*The great mass of humanity should never learn to read and write never*" (122), Lawrence writes in the chapter entitled "First Steps in Education"—not because the masses did not appreciate *Psychoanalysis* but because literary education leads to the "disease of idealism" and the death of spontaneity (120). There are, therefore better explanations than the reviewers ridicule of *Psychoanalysis* for Lawrence's *caveat* against the general.

Lawrence's second alleged reason for not seeking a public response, or rather for not seeking a response at all, is that he has no interest in converting anyone to his way of thinking: "I really don't want to convince anybody. It is quite in opposition to my whole nature" (53). Before demonstrating that this seeming petulance is also expressive of a key issue in *Fantasia,* one should recall that *Psychoanalysis* was nothing if it was not an attempt to convince. And therein lay one of the central problems of the work: for the message there, as in *Fantasia*, was that "The mind is the dead end of life" (47), but the method of persuasion there was reason and logic, a direct appeal to the mind. Lawrence's excessive protestations in that essay that he was not being "mystical" may indicate that already he was aware of the conflict between medium and message; however, in *Fantasia* it is evident that he has not only recognized the problem but also knows the solution. "In that little book, *Psychoanalysis and the Unconscious,* I tried rather wistfully to convince you, dear reader, that you had a solar plexus and a lumbar ganglion and a few other things. I don't know why I took the trouble. If a fellow doesn't believe he's got a nose, the best way to convince him is gently to waft a little pepper into his nostrils. And there was I painting my own nose purple, and wistfully inviting you to look and believe. No more, though" (68). His insights into the unconscious, Lawrence suggests, cannot be demonstrated to be accurate; the reader must be made to respond sensually rather than mentally. Therefore, the solution to his problem is that of many anti-intellectualist intellectuals—art, with its dramatic rather than discursive techniques, its poetic rather than rational logic, its connotative rather than denotative language. And again, this reason for turning away from the expository method is not simply thrown up in the "Foreword" as a defensive retort, but is fully explored as another of the central principles of *Fantasia*: "For the mass of people, knowledge *must* be symbolical, mystical, dynamic" (113). But if this is true, then the method of *Psychoanalysis* was wrong, for there Lawrence tried to appeal to the masses in quite an opposite manner. While the failure of *Psychoanalysis,* then, is undoubtedly involved in the writing of *Fantasia,* it is better to describe the latter work as an alternate rather than as a second attempt.

The next directive of the "Foreword" further emphasizes that *Fantasia* is a deliberate departure from the methods of *Psychoanalysis*: "Finally, to the remnants of a remainder, in order to apologize for the sudden lurch into cosmology, or cosmogony, in this book, I wish to say that the whole thing hangs inevitably together" (53). Psychoanalysis, one remembers, tried to hang together logically, its structural format was that of the expository essay; *Fantasia,* Lawrence here announces, will not be governed by the analytic method but will proceed according to the pattern of myth; its coherence will arise from the nature of the subject itself rather than from without. And in the simple statement, "I am not a scientist", Lawrence explains why he has adopted this new procedure. A scientist must prove his assertions, and Lawrence seems to realize that he cannot. Thus when he goes on to say, "you either believe or you don't", he is as much emphasizing the intuitive nature of his material as he is warning his readers not to expect him to prove what he has to say. His apology, therefore, is in the traditional manner—an explanation as much as an admission of a failing.

But technically as well as structurally, *Fantasia* will differ from *Psychoanalysis.* In the latter essay, as we have seen, Lawrence's method was to argue for the empirical validity of intuition and ancient wisdom, to emphasize the correspondence between truths perceived poetically and analytically. In the "Foreword", he now announces that it will be the distinctness of the two modes that will be the premise in *Fantasia:* "Only let me say that to my mind there is a great field of science which is as yet quite closed to us. I refer to the science which proceeds in terms of life and is established on data of living experience and sure intuition. Call it subjective science if you like. Our objective science of modern knowledge concerns itself only with phenomena, and with phenomena as regarded in their cause-and-effect relationship. I have nothing to say against our science. It is perfect as far as it goes" (54). And the point is not that it does not go far enough but that it cannot. Consequently, instead of asserting that science can verify his insights, as he did in *Psychoanalysis,* Lawrence now argues for the independent authority of intuition; subjective and mythological truths are justified not because they can be scientifically verified but because they verify each other.

It is this very recognition of the correspondence between the past and the present, the universal and the individual, that broadly defines *Fantasia* as an archetypal work.[4] Let science proclaim progress and new discoveries, he argues, "Myself, I am not so sure that I am one of the one-and-onlies" (56); to the archetypalist, there is nothing new under the sun. From our "own little dunghill" we see only the present, but from a cosmic perspective one realizes that history continually repeats itself: *eadem sed aliter.* "I do not believe in evolution but in the strangeness and rainbow-change of ever-renewed creative civilizations" (56). Therefore, instead of trying to enunciate a new theory of the unconscious, as he had in *Psychoanalysis,* Lawrence now describes his method as an attempt "to stammer out the first terms of a forgotten knowledge" (56). And not by attempting to "revive dead kings", or "to arrange fossils and decipher hieroglyphic phrases", like the Cambridge anthropologists (one remembers Ludwig Horace Holly's reference in Haggard's *She* to his "fossil friends at

Cambridge"), but by exploring the symbolic significance of "the relics our scientists have so marvelously gathered out of the forgotten past, and from the hint develop a new living utterance" (56). For according to Lawrence, the symbol is the link between the past and the present and "the intense potency of symbols is part memory" (56). Instead of the collective unconscious of Jung, however, Lawrence introduces the myth of Atlantis. as the foundation of his archetypalism. The Atlanteans were our historical ancestors and they developed the science of life (reflected in symbols) and through their wanderings made it universal. Then came the cataclysm, however, and the refugees became the founders of our modern civilizations: "And some degenerated naturally into cave men. . . . and some retained their marvellous innate beauty and life-perfection . . . and some wandered savage . . . and some, like Druids or Etruscans or Chaldeans or Amerindians or Chinese, refused to forget, but taught the old wisdom, only in its half-forgotten, symbolic forms. More or less forgotten as knowledge: remembered as ritual, gesture, and myth-story" (55). In myth and ritual, therefore, will be found the old wisdom, and through myth and ritual the artist is able to make this knowledge available and in doing so to reveal the "inevitable" repetition of the past in the present.

"One last weary little word" (57), adds Lawrence, by way of introducing a comment on the relationship between his fiction and his theories; and this introduction of his creative work indicates a final way in which the "Foreword" points to a difference between *Psychoanalysis* and *Fantasia*. In the former study there was no mention of the fact that the writer was also an artist; indeed, every precaution seemed to be taken to conceal this fact. As was suggested at the outset, most readers do not appreciate this difference but assume that both essays are designed as Lawrence's attempt to systemize the ideas he had formulated. in his art.   But even to view only *Fantasia* in this manner is inaccurate. According to the "Foreword", *Fantasia* was not written with a view to the fiction but as an.answer to "the absolute need which one has for some sort of satisfactory mental attitude toward oneself and things in general" (57), that is the need to formulate a world view on the basis of one's experience. The novels and poems, as Lawrence explicitly states, are part of that experience—part of the material upon which the formulation is based but not necessarily the reason for it. The purpose of *Fantasia* is to answer the need of not only the writer but also of the *man*. Furthermore, while he emphasizes that fiction came before the theory, he goes on to emphasize the Arnoldian idea that criticism is not only the conclusion but also the preparation for art: "Our vision, our belief, our metaphysic is wearing woefully thin, and the art is wearing absolutely threadbare" (57). And since "art is utterly dependent on philosophy", before we can enter a new creative phase we must get new bearings: "We've got to rip the old veil of a vision across, and find out what the heart really believes in, after all. . . . And then go forward again, to the fulfillment in life and art". According to the "Foreword", then, philosophy and criticism are as much the beginning as the end of art, for their function is to "evolve something magnificent out of a renewed chaos" (56). To indicate the ways in which *Fantasia* answers to the polar needs of destruction and revitalization is finally to demonstrate its departure from the purpose and method of *Psychoanalysis*.

Although the many digressions and the encylopedic nature of the work justify the title's suggestion of a formality and spontaneity, *Fantasia* has a very well-defined structure; indeed, two distinct patterns are employed. The first establishes the archetypal dimensions of the work and thus answers to the "Foreword" 's demand that criticism be positive and that it announce "what the heart really wants" (57). *Fantasia* begins, in the "Introduction", literally with The Beginning: "In the beginning—there never was any beginning, but let it pass. We've got to make a start somehow" (63). And *Fantasia* ends, in the "Epilogue", with the announcement that never is there any end: "As it was in the beginning, is now, and ever shall be, World without end.  Amen" (222). The basic structure of *Fantasia* is cyclic, and thus affirmative of the pagan and cosmic perspective.

The second formal pattern of *Fantasia* fulfills the iconoclastic need posited in the "Foreword". Its direction is not cyclic but linear, for it is the Judaic-Christian version of genesis. Following this pattern, we begin not at the top of the turning wheel but on top of a "historical" mountain: "The Moses of Science and the Aaron of Idealism have got the whole bunch of us here on top of Pisgah" (62). And we end, not as in the previous pattern where we began, but at the bottom— "at the foot of the Liberty statue" (222). America becomes the Promised Land, but by evoking the pattern of the fall, Lawrence makes its science and idealism negative rather than positive.

Moreover, in addition to this structural and graphic evocation of the contrast between the archetypal and Hebraic version of genesis, Lawrence also explicitly and strategically invokes the myths that are central to his purposes. In *Psychoanalysis* he suggested that the Edenic fall could be interpreted as a fall from innocent to conscious and therefore guilty sexuality. In *Fantasia*, he *centres* this idea and in thereby making it dramatic makes it doubly effective. Leading up to it are chapters dealing with the birth and development of the child's or the dynamic consciousness; following it are the sections dealing with cerebral consciousness and social problems. Instead of attempting to prove that cognition and its consequent idealism arc steps in the wrong direction, therefore, he simply forces the reader to assent to his conclusion: "Why were we driven out of Paradise? Why did we fall into this gnawing disease of unappeasable dissatisfaction? Not because we sinned. Ah, no. . . . Not because we sinned. But because we got sex into our head" (121). By making the birth of consciousness the "fall", Lawrence simultaneously modernizes the old myth making it available to modern readers and demonstrates the wisdom of the ancients and the eternal validity of myth.

But balancing the Hebraic myth is also a pagan one—a Greek version of the "fall" and the consequent insatiable desire, the legend of Aphrodite. The "sea-born Aphrodite" (212) was the love-goddess born when the Olympians (the mind-gods) castrated Kronus and threw his phallus into the sea. Then history, in the linear sense we envision it, began; and herein according to Lawrence, with this pedestalizing of the woman in the name of an idea, is the prototype for the Statue of Liberty. With her "carrot-sceptre" (223) she is the perfect goddess for a "Moony" nation of "half-born slaves" (225, 71).

*Fantasia* abounds in imagery, but two patterns arc particularly distinct and serve to reinforce the opposing mythic structures. Suggesting the futility and sterility of idealism is a series of machine metaphors, which significantly appear in aggregated force only after the "fall". Our education, for example, turns children into robots triggered to respond automatically to ideals, particularly such sexual ideals as chivalry: "The Windmills spin and spin in a wind of words, Dulcinea del Tobosco beckons round every corner, and our nation of inferior Quixotes jumps on and off tramcars, trains, bicycles, motor cars, in one mad chase of the divine Dulcinea" (118). Suggesting the naturalness and fecundity of the pagan attitude toward life are tree-images, some simply vegetative, some biblical, some Druidical. For example, after attacking our educational process as the hanging of ourselves on a dead tree, he goes on to suggest the corrective: "The idea, the actual idea, must rise ever fresh, ever displaced, like the leaves of a tree, from out of the quickness of the sap, and according to the forever incalculable effluence of the dynamic centres of life. The tree of life is a gay kind of tree that is forever dropping its leaves and budding out afresh quite different ones" (119). But the tree also has an additional thematic importance in *Fantasia*. The book was written, he tells us, in the "Black Forest", symbolic both of the dark unconscious and our ancient past. "That's how I write about these planes and plexuses, between the toes of a tree, forgetting myself against the great ankle of the trunk" (82). As he forgets himself—becomes unconscious—he begins to remember, and also to "understand tree-worship.   All the old Aryans worshipped the tree. My ancestors" (82). By rediscovering his past he recovers his psychic origins. The two thus are one. Perhaps the best way to define the genre of *Fantasia*, therefore, is to follow Lawrence when he describes the work as his "tree-book, really" (82). For his real subject is the tree, "The tree of life and death, of good and evil, tree of abstraction and of immense, mindless life; tree of everything except the spirit, spirituality" (84). Not mystic but mythic is the best way to describe Lawrence's approach.

A final way of demonstrating the artistic nature of *Fantasia* and consequently the way it differs from *Psychoanalysis* is to consider the nature of the speaker. In contrast to the former essay, where as a rule the editorial and critical "we" was employed, here there are three symbolic voices. The first is the first person singular, which has probably contributed to the solipsistic view of the book, but which is demanded by its archetypal premise; the individual experience is a microcosm of the universal one; to look out one must look in. Therefore the second speaker is the cosmic "I" (67). And these come together to constitute the third mode: the plural "we", different from the usage in *Psychoanalysis* in its Whitmanesque implications of camaraderie and in its sense of geographical and temporal unanimity: "Climb down [sic] Pisgah, and go to Jericho. Allons, there is no road yet, but we are all Aarons with rods of our own" (65). The *speaker* in *Fantasia* (the tone of vocal rather than written communication should also be noticed), then, is a *persona*, an artistic creation, and not necessarily Lawrence "coming out from behind the fictional mask to speak directly, in his own person" (Rieff, xx).

The purpose of this study has been to demonstrate that there are significant differences between *Psychoanalysis* and *Fantasia* and that the "Foreword" to the latter work indicates that the change in methodology was a deliberate one occasioned by Lawrence's recognition that his method in the former work was incompatible with the nature of his insights. The "Foreword", therefore, should not be viewed as a peevish appeal to snobbishness; nor should the two essays be considered as a single statement. But neither should either of these essays be considered in isolation; for only in contrasting them does one appreciate their significance, first, with respect to Lawrence's development, and second, with respect to the way they provide a chapter in the history of the artist in in age of science.[5] In *Psychoanalysis* Lawrence attempted to answer what he felt was the challenge of science by meeting it on its own grounds; in *Fantasia* he demonstrates that the artist need not feel challenged but should feel stimulated by the discoveries of science. For science provides the "hints"—the beginning—and art provides the humanistic explanation—the end.[6]

*Dalhousie Review*, 52, 1972.

**Notes**

---

[1] Philip Rieff, *Psychoanalysis and the Unconscious* and *Fantasia of the Unconscious* (New York, 1960), p. vii.   Henceforth all quotations from Lawrence will be from this Compass edition and will be identified by page number in parentheses.

[2] Frederick J. Hoffman, *Freudianism and the Literary Mind* (Louisiana, 1967), p. 165.

[3] James C. Cowan, *D. H. Lawrence's American Journey: A Study in Literature and Myth* (Cleveland, 1970), pp. 15-24.

[4] I am indebted to John J. Teunissen and the group to which I belong, the "Massachusetts Archetypalists", for my definition of the archetypal perspective.   Tentatively, by *archetypal* we imply *the conscious use of mythical patterns and symbols as a ritualistic means of abrogating historical time and its attendant evils and of thereby returning to a cosmic perspective and valuation*.   Because our approach is inductive, however, our premise is always that the work itself must provide the definition; I will, consequently, not introduce our conclusions into the body of this study.

[5] A similar chapter in this history is provided by the work of Otto Rank and N. O. Brown, both of whom began as Freudians and later, finding it impossible to work within the system, repudiated it in favor of the poetic and archetypal.

[6] I wish to express my indebtedness to the Canada Council for the financial assistance which enabled me to explore this subject without pressure.

# Peter Bien, "The Critical Philosophy of D.H. Lawrence"

---

Much has been written on D.H. Lawrence as a literary critic, including an entire book by David J. Gordon[1]—so one wonders if anything else remains to be said.   Probably very little regarding the moral stance that governs Lawrence's criticism,[2] but perhaps something regarding the formal or aesthetic position that—granted—relates to the moral one. This may even by systematic, despite most commentators' inability to reduce Lawrence's criticism, whether moral or aesthetic, to a system. The usual view is that we should accept him on his own terms, valuing him for his idiosyncratic, passionate, unsystematic sincerity.

Gordon does attempt to systematize (halfheartedly), juxtaposing the pre- and post *Rainbow* periods and claiming that a shift can be seen from an earlier critical position to a later one.[3] However, his bottom line is the denial of any system whatsoever. He asserts that Lawrence's fundamental position is articulated in the well-known opening to the piece on John Galsworthy: "Literary criticism can be no more than a reasoned account of the feeling produced upon the critic by the book he is criticizing. Criticism can never be a science. . . . All the critical twiddle-twaddle about style and form . . . is mere impertinence and mostly dull jargon."[4]

Despite this warning, I am going to argue that criticism for Lawrence, precisely in the area of aesthetics, is not just an unsystematic feeling produced upon the critic. As a moralist, he may be too unpredictable and quirky to be contained within a neat system, but I believe that a single theoretical position underlies his aesthetic approach. Not that he himself ever expresses it systematically in one place. However, his scattered shreds of criticism have sufficient consistency to enable us to reassemble them into a more-or-less ordered whole.

I have attempted to do this in a Lawrencean fashion. His mind proceeded from abstract to particular and was fascinated by the conflict between these (and other) opposites. He also liked to define the true negative of any conception. Therefore, I begin abstractly with his ideas of what art should be, ideally; I then proceed to the negative of this—what art should not be, ideally; finally, I go to what art is, actually. Though his formulations sound, and are, moral, they reveal an aesthetic position as well.

## What art should be, ideally

"Art communicates a state of being," says Lawrence.[5] What does he mean by "being" and what by a "state"?

Being presupposes outer and inner wholeness. Outer wholeness is the full person existing in organic relation to the rest of the universe. Inner wholeness is the full person considered in isolation. A person is not "a soul, or a body, or a mind, . . . or any of the rest of these bits. . . . The whole is greater than the part" (*P* 535).

A "state" means "being" at the living moment. Relatedness to the circumambient universe is not a stable equilibrium, but a balance that can easily change. "Everything is true in its own time, place, circumstance, and untrue outside of its own place, time, circumstance" (*P* 528). "And this is the beauty of the novel; everything is true in its own relationship, and no further."[6]

The assertion that art communicates a state of being means, therefore, that art, considered ideally, communicates a fragile moment of life in which the characters enjoy inner and outer wholeness.

## What art should not be, ideally

We know that Lawrence liked to define things by their opposites. When he says that art communicates being, he means that it does not communicate mere existence. "A thing isn't life just because somebody does it. . . . The ordinary bank clerk buying himself a new straw hat isn't 'life' at all; it is just existence . . . If the bank clerk feels really piquant about his hat, if he establishes a lively relation with it, . . . then that is life" (*P* 529-30). The action of hat-buying must involve the whole man—feelings and thought; and the balance of the man's organic relatedness to the universe must shift, if ever so slightly.

Similarly, when he says that art communicates a state, he means that it does not present a fixed balance, either within a man or between a man and the universe. Because art should communicate a relative state of relatedness, the novelist does not put "his thumb in the scale, to pull down the balance to his own predilection" (*P* 528). In other words, he does not distort life in the interests of the intellectual absolute, or "Law," to which he wants life to conform. This is doing dishonor to true, vivid and ever-changing relationships.

But no novel worth considering is either ideally bad or ideally good. We must proceed now from the abstract to the concrete.

### What art is, actually

What art is, actually, is a combination of what it is and is not, ideally. We are coming closer to Lawrence's single theoretical position. This, we shall discover, is a fusion of the abstractly positive and negative positions just explained.

At its best, art, considered actually, is a "revelation of the two principles of Love and Law in a state of conflict and yet reconciled" (*P* 477). Let us not forget this paradox: *in a state of conflict and yet reconciled.* The term "Law" we have already encountered; it signifies everything that is absolute, fixed, and intellectual. "Love" in Lawrence's critical vocabulary means everything that is relative, flexible, and intuitive. Lawrence's fundamental aesthetic position demands that both be present, as we shall see again at the conclusion of this reassembly.

### Problems

Yet Lawrence is so disturbed by the dominance of Law over Love that he often forgets his own formulation about conflict and reconciliation and seems to want instead to rescue Love from Law. We see this in his famous dictum: "An artist is usually a damned liar, but his art, if it be art, will tell you the truth of his day." When he goes on to assert that the critic's proper function "Is to save the tale from the artist who created it,"[7] he means that the critic must penetrate the artist's intellectual absolutes—his Law—and rescue the art-truth—or Love—which is submerged. Needless to say, none of this serves to reinforce the position that art at its best, considered actually, reveals the *two* principles of Love and Law in a state of conflict and yet reconciled.

To complicate matters still further, Lawrence's sensitivity to the dominance of Law over Love leads him often to approach a book in terms of myth and symbol because these, for him, express an author's flexible, non-intellectual side.[8] We are again given the impression that Law ought to be extirpated. When Lawrence says things like "art-speech is . . . a language of pure symbols,"[9] we see him reverting to his conception of an ideal rather than an actual art.

*Practical criticism*

So far, we seem unable to escape Love as Lawrence's chief requirement despite his position that art, considered as actual, reveals the *two* principles of Law and Love in conflict and reconciled, combining what art is, considered ideally, and also what it is not. In his practical criticism, however, Lawrence does not always put his own thumb in the scale to pull down the balance to his predilection, duplicitously applying Law in a campaign against Law. Fortunately, as an actual workaday critic rather than an "ideal critic," Lawrence comes closer to what I think is his fundamental aesthetic position. For example, as a workaday critic he is not interested just in myth and symbol but also in characterization. Let us examine a particular case. In the essay on Galsworthy he sets up the "vivid human being" (*P* 540) as the ideal opposite to the ordinary bank clerk who buys himself a new hat without feeling really piquant about it. He then concentrates on this vivid human being's inner-relatedness. When the human being "becomes too much aware of . . . his own isolation in the face of a universe of objective reality," Lawrence explains, "the core of his identity splits, . . . his innocence . . . perishes, and he becomes only . . . a divided thing hinged together" (*P* 541): a man whose components are no longer related in a proper internal balance.

But the Forsytes' lack of inner-relatedness is not the crux of Galsworthy's problem as far as Lawrence is concerned. Nor is Lawrence so rigidly proscriptive as he appears to be. Indeed, he admits elsewhere that "art has to reveal the palpitating moment or the state of man as it is," even if that state is detestable.[10] In speaking of Hemingway, for instance, he deprecates the attitude of disgust present in the short stories, yet admits that "Mr Hemingway is really good, because he's perfectly straight" (*P* 366).

This is the crux. The trouble with Galsworthy is that he is not perfectly straight. To show this, Lawrence employs three of his most important critical concepts, those of duplicity, negative species, and the social man. Of these, only the last needs definition: the social man is someone whose inner balance has given way so that the weight is now excessively on the side of the spiritual-mental consciousness at the expense of the instinctive-intuitive consciousness—a situation in which an "ideal, social and political oneness" is substituted for a "feeling of physical, flesh-and-blood kinship" (*P* 556). Galsworthy's failing was that he thought he was showing up the social man while he really was not. He pretended that his instinctive self was nauseated by the social man, whereas his supposedly instinctive opposition consisted of an illusion perpetrated by his own spiritual-mental self, an illusion involving a negative species, in this case the person who gives money away or who altruistically wishes to insure people by raising their standard of living. These negative examples of the social species "*want* to have certain feelings: feelings of love, of passionate sex, of kindliness" (*P* 545); but it is this mental wanting itself that confines them within the species they wish to leave. Galsworthy, "setting out to satirize the Forsytes, . . . glorifies the *anti*, who is one worse" (*P* 547). If he had satirized the negative of the social species—the anti-materialist—instead of sentimentalizing it, he would have been a great writer, concludes Lawrence, instead of merely a popular one.

*Lawrence's aesthetic position*

Once again, even when he focuses on characterization instead of myth and symbol, Lawrence seems to be downgrading Law in the interests of Love, by requiring Law's purpose to be "not at outs with the passional inspiration."[11] But what we must realize in the foregoing and similar critiques is that he actually does not wish Law to be eliminated, despite pronouncements that sound one-sidedly in favor of Love. Nor should we be misled by his habitual disparagement of the works he discusses. W. H. Auden was aware of this when he commented that "even when [Lawrence] is violently and quite unfairly attacking an author, he makes him sound far more exciting and worth reading than most critics make one sound whom they are professing to praise."[12] The fact is that the presence of both Law and Love is precisely what makes a work interesting to Lawrence. We return to his position that art, considered actually, is a "revelation of the two principles of Love and Law in a state of conflict and yet reconciled." What we must understand, as well, is that this is just as much an aesthetic position as a moral one.  It is aesthetic, first of all, because it concerns a novel's pattern, quite aside from its subject matter. I feel confident in saying this because Lawrence himself says it, in "Study of Thomas Hardy." The full statement (deliberately withheld by me until now) is: "Artistic form is a revelation of the two principles of Love and Law. . . . It is the conjunction of the two which makes form" (*P* 477). Lawrence's position is aesthetic, secondly, because its center is the imagination. "What we care about," he says, "is the release of the imagination. A real release of the imagination renews our strength and our vitality, makes us feel stronger and happier." Notice that the moral result (increase in strength and happiness) comes from an aesthetic cause: "imaginative release into another vital world" (*P* 294). And the vitality of this other world, in turn, depends, as we saw earlier, on a shift in the balance of a character's—or a reader's—organic relatedness to the universe.

With all this in mind, we can now appreciate that Lawrence's system of aesthetic evaluation depends on the presence and opposition of antagonistic forces.[13] The fun comes because, as Lawrence says in the same previously cited passage from "Study of Thomas Hardy," "since the two [forces] must always meet under fresh conditions, form must always be different. Each work of art has its own form" (*P* 477). In Galsworthy's case, the form derives from secret opposition where the mental self pretends to honor the instinctive self, but makes the cleavage worse; in Tolstoy's it derives from open opposition, and so forth. Lawrence always discovers the nature of the opposing forces—that is his challenge as a practical critic interested in aesthetic analysis. His actual workaday system combines, as I said at the start, his definitions of what art is, ideally, and what it is not, ideally, enabling him to analyze form and also to measure success.

At this point, we must reiterate that Lawrence believes in dynamic opposition as a formal requirement; he does not wish the mental element to be overcome by the instinctive one completely. In his effort to rescue Love from the usual dominance of Law, he often gives the impression that any intrusion by the spiritual-mental is regrettable, but he does not mean this. When he says that a true work of art "must contain the essential criticism on the morality to which it adheres" (*P* 476), he is not saying that the morality—the fixed position called

Law—should disappear. The two great principles of Love and Law "are, in a way, contradictions each of the other," he asserts. "But they are complementary. . . . And nothing is or can be created save by combined effort of the two principles" (*P* 513). Furthermore, although Law often dominates Love, requiring a shift in balance toward the latter, this is not always the case. In the social species of Galsworthy, as we saw, Law outweighs Love, but in the transcendentalist species of a Poe, a Whitman, or a Dostoevsky the reverse is true and the shift required is in the opposite direction, toward the limitation represented by Law.

The remaining problem is how these two principles can be "in a state of conflict and yet reconciled," according to the paradoxical formula I hoped that we would remember. Lawrence sometimes claims that "true balance" is the ideal (*P* 514), but we should be wary of such statements which eliminate the paradox that stands at the heart of his critical philosophy. He helps us when he speaks of a combination of impulses producing "a sum of motion and stability at once, satisfying" (*P* 457). What we must realize is that the motion and stability, or conflict and reconciliation, are not necessarily concurrent. The opposing principles of Law and Love struggle, then reach a momentary balance, then struggle again. We recognize this as the aesthetic pattern of Lawrence's own novels, in which struggle gives way to the temporary stability of union, which then gives way to renewed struggle. However, on a higher level of understanding this dynamic pattern of succession is apprehended statically in a way that allows the opposing forces to be in conflict and yet reconciled at the same time. Lawrence invokes this higher level when he declares that "the aim of man remains to recognize and seek out the Holy Spirit. . . . , He who drives the twin principles of Law and Love across the ages" (*P* 514). And this, I think, is as close as we shall ever come to an articulation of the single theoretical position that underlies the many ideas which appear unsystematized in Lawrence's diverse critical writings, for in this statement Lawrence combines (1) the attention to wholeness that produces his conception of what art should be, ideally,—a vehicle communicating a state of being—with (2) the attention to an ever-readjusting duality that produces both his conception of what art is, actually, and his practice as a workaday critic.

*The D.H. Lawrence Review*, 17:2, Summer, 1984.

## Notes

---

[1] David J. Gordon, *D. H. Lawrence as a Literary Critic* (New Haven: Yale University Press, 1966). A more recent and less valuable book on the subject is Tajindar Singh's *The Literary Criticism of D. H. Lawrence* (New Delhi, India: Sterling Publishers Private Limited, 1984).

[2] For a brief survey, see Debra Journet, "D. H. Lawrence's Criticism of Modern Literature," *The D. H. Lawrence Review*, 17, no. 1 (1984): 29-47. Journet emphasises Lawrence's objections to (a) the autonomy sought by modernist works and (b) modernism's partiality for imaginative rather than direct experience.

[3] Gordon, *D. H. Lawrence as a Literary Critic*, p. 89.

[4]Cited by Gordon, *D. H. Lawrence as a Literary Critic*, p. 17, from D. H. Lawrence, *Phoenix: The Posthumous Papers of D. H. Lawrence*, ed. Edward D. McDonald (London: Heinemann: 1936), p. 539. The pagination of the U.S. *Phoenix* edition (New York: Viking Press, 1936) is identical. Subsequent references to *Phoenix* essays are indicated parenthetically in the text by *P* and the page number(s). Regarding style and especially form, Lawrence has much to say, despite his accusations of twiddle-twaddle. Typically, he accuses modernists of overemphasizing technique, e.g., " . . . we need more looseness. We need an apparent formlessness, definite form is mechanical" (*P* 248); " . . . Germany is now undergoing that craving for form in fiction . . . which is figured to the world in Gustave Flaubert" (*P* 308). Contrariwise, his awareness of the need for form is revealed in remarks such as : "I have read *The House of Ellis* carefully—such good stuff in it: but without unity or harmony. . . . You have a real gift—there is real quality in these scenes. But without form, like the world before creation" (letter to M. L. Skinner, 2 September 1923, in *The Collected Letters of D. H. Lawrence*, ed. Harry T. Moore [New York: Viking Press, 1962], II, 751).

[5] D. H. Lawrence, "The Spirit of Place," *English Review*, 27 (November 1918): 321. This is the first version of the essay printed in revised form in *Studies in Classic American Literature*. The first version is reprinted in D. H. Lawrence, *The Sumbolic Meaning: The Uncollected Versions of "Studies in Classic American Literature"*, ed. Armin Arnold (Fontwell, Arundel: Centaur Press, 1962), p. 19.

[6] D. H. Lawrence, "The Novel," in *Reflections on the Death of a Porcupine and Other Essays* (Philadelphia: Centaur Press, 1925), p. 114.

[7] D. H. Lawrence, *Studies in Classic American Literature* (New York: Viking Press, 1964), p. 2.

[8] Lawrence's most useful definitions of symbol and myth are in his introduction to Frederick Carter's *The Dragon of the Apocalypse*: "Symbols are organic units of consciousness with a life of their own, and you can never explain them away, because their value is .. . . not simply mental" (*P* 295). "Myth . . . is descriptive narrative using images . . . .And the images of myth are symbols. They don't 'mean something.' They stand for units of human *feeling* . . . And the power of the symbol is to arouse the deep emotional self, and the dynamic self, beyond comprehension. Many ages of accumulated experience still throb within a symbol. And we throb in response" (*P* 296).

[9] Lawrence, "The Spirit of Place," *English Review*, 27: 321; also in *The Symbolic Meaning*, p. 19.

[10] Letter to Aldous Huxley, 28 October 1928 [?], in *Collected Letters*, II, 1096.

[11] Lawrence, "The Novel," in *Reflections on the Death of a Porcupine*, p. 104.

[12] W. H. Auden, "Some Notes on D. H. Lawrence," *The Nation*, April 26, 1947, p. 482; reprinted in *Critics on D. H. Lawrence*, ed. W. T. Andrews (Coral Gables, Fla: University of Miami Press, 1971), p. 48.

[13] This is corroborated by many statements. For example:
　　"The rhythm of American art-activity is dual. 1. A distingegrating and sloughing of the old consciousness. 2. The forming of a new consciousness underneath. . . . Poe has only one, only the disintegrative vibration. This makes him alsmost more a scientist than an artist. . . . [I]n true art there is always the double rhythm of creating and destroying." (Lawrence, *Studies in Classic American Literature*, p. 65.)
　　Poets . . . reveal the inward desire of mankind. . . They show the desire for chaos, and the fear of chaos. The desire for chaos is the breath of their poetry. The fear of chaos is in their parade of forms and technique" (*P* 257).

"Life is so made that opposites sway about a trembling centre of balance. . . . And of all the art forms, the novel most of all demands the trembling and oscillating of the balance" (*P* 529).

## Mara Kalnins, "'Terra Incognita': Lawrence's Travel Writings"

Lawrence's travel writings, with his novels, poems and essays, form part of what may be called his *Bildungsroman*, the life-long story of his development as a man and an artist. Chronicling his journeys to other lands, the travel writings not only evoke the artist's response to external landscapes and people, to 'the spirit of place', they also examine themes which are central to nearly all his works: first. a fascination with human psychology which reveals itself in the quest to explore and map the unknown, inner world of man, the 'Terra Incognita', as he called it, of the psyche.

> There are vast realms of consciousness still undreamed of, vast ranges of experience, like the humming of unseen harps, we know nothing of, within us.[1]

And, secondly, the profound and searching criticism of our modern technological age and its effect on the quality of human existence, questions as important for the intellectual and imaginative life of our time as they were for his.

Travel was a necessary part of Lawrence's life. Paul Fussell has suggested that that life 'was virtually a series of impatient acts of travel' following a pattern of self-manufactured illusion and subsequent rejection of places: 'He thus repeatedly took off again, embittered and disillusioned. He is always both escaping and seeking' (*Abroad* [Oxford 1981], p.147). But this is surely to misunderstand the nature of the impulse to travel in Lawrence's life and to diminish the achievement of the travel writings. His journeys around the world were not a form of neurosis nor was the experience of being a stranger in a strange land merely a way of repeating again his feelings of essential alienation, the frustration of his societal self, as he termed it. Neither can those travels and his records of them be seen as simple allegorical accounts of distinct stages in his life. as Mr. Fussell goes on to state:

> Lawrence's travel books ... seem to designate and explore the four stages of everyone's life—youth, whose happiness is inseparable from satisfied sensual love; young adulthood, where happiness derives from social awareness and social self-hood; older adulthood, when vacancy and disillusion trouble the spirit; and old age. the moment for elegy and the wish for peace.*Twilight in Italy*, with its fervours about reconciliation' is about youth; *Sea and Sardinia*, devoted to social comedy, is about young adulthood; *Mornings in Mexico* is about loneliness and disappointment; *Etruscan Places* about dying happily (*Abroad.* pp. 1634).

This is at once to ignore the complexity and organic unity of the travel books which do indeed form a continual record of Lawrence's development and of the maturing of his vision, but not in the linear sense of stages of physical and mental growth and temporal age. Still less can they be categorised neatly by subject matter or single theme. There is as much social comedy in *Twilight in Italy* (consider the *padrone* and the perverse spring-door, the theatre and 'Amleto') or in *Mornings in Mexico* (Corasmin and the parrot, Lawrence's hapless search for oranges, the episode of buying sandals tanned with human excrement) as in *Sea and Sardinia*. And both *Mornings in Mexico* and *Etruscan Places*, ranging over the whole of Lawrence's thought about myth, symbol, religion, the art of living, death and resurrection, are hardly about 'loneliness' or 'dying happily', respectively. On the contrary, the travel writings are complex works, recording Lawrence's continual search to understand the creative and vital forces in nature, man and human civilisation, which he felt could reshape and regenerate our world. Furthermore, the sense of exile, of alienation inherent in visiting and living in new lands, was a necessary condition for Lawrence, a condition without which his greatest works might never have been written. The diversity of external environments and experiences depicted in the travel writings express the diverse and sometimes contradictory impulses and elements of the artist's own psyche. Indeed Lawrence saw these as essential to his writing, for his conception of human existence is based on the notion of creation through conflict, a notion epitomised by Blake's 'Without Contraries is no Progression'. And his travels were a way of generating and altering the condition for those 'contraries', for evolving and creating himself into new being. Like the novels, the travel books express his belief in the fundamental process and purpose of all human life, the creation of self by self, a process which he expressly likened to artistic creation: 'to create oneself . . . create that work of art, the living man, achieve that piece of supreme art, a man's life'.[2] But this creation, this evolution of the self could be achieved only through what Lawrence called 'strife', that is through the continual pressure of conflicting impulses within and without an individual and his environment. Similarly, in Lawrence's fiction, characters are rarely seen as ordinary, stable egos, in the sense of rational personalities whose motives and behaviour can be analysed (or described in stages of development). Rather they are unknown, mysterious beings, caught in a continual process of change and evolution, subject to deep pressures from within and without which destroy or create them into new being.

> You mustn't look in my novel for the old stable ego of the character. There is another ego, according to whose action the individual is unrecognisable, and passes through, as it were allotropic states which it needs a deeper sense than any we've been used to exercise, to discover are states of the same single radically-unchanged element.
> (5 June 1914. *Letters*, 11, 183).

By the same token one should not look in the travel writings for any consistent appreciation and description of places and peoples in the tradition of travel reminiscence—this would be mere reportage and would miss the central importance of travel in Lawrence's life: to create the conditions in which he could continually deepen his understanding of humanity by testing and modifying his beliefs in new environments and cultures. In setting down his responses and thoughts he was not engaged in the superficial acceptance and subsequent rejection of a place or a people, as Paul Fussell suggests, but to record, as Rebecca West has perceptively noted, the manifold workings of the human psyche.

> He was tapping out an article on the state of Florence at that moment without knowing enough about it to make his views of real value. Is that the way I looked at it? Then I was naive. I know now that he was writing about the state of his own soul at that moment, which, since our self-consciousness is incomplete, and since in consequence our vocabulary also is incomplete, he could only render in symbolic terms; and the city of Florence was as good a symbol as any other. If he was foolish in taking the material universe and making allegations about it that were true only of the universe within his own soul, then Rimbaud was a great fool also. Or to go further back, so too was Dante who made a new Heaven and Hell and Purgatory as a symbol of the geography within his own breast, and so too was St. Augustine, when in the *The City of God* he writes an attack on the pagan world, which is unjust so long as it is regarded as an account of events on the material plane, but which is beyond price as an account of the conflict in his soul between that which tended to death and that which tended to life. Lawrence was in fact no different from any other great artist who has felt the urgency to describe the unseen so keenly that he has rifled the seen of its vocabulary and diverted it to that purpose .[3]

Lawrence's travel writings, then, can be seen as a metaphor for his inner development and for his growing understanding of the human psyche and the ways in which human growth or destruction are determined by place and time and culture. The travel metaphor occurs repeatedly in Lawrence's fiction, expressing the spiritual and psychological pilgrimage of his central characters. Thus, at the end of *The Rainbow*, when Ursula has left behind her old self:

> When she looked ahead. into the undiscovered land before her, what was there she could recognise but a fresh glow of light and inscrutable trees going up from the earth like smoke. It was the unknown. the unexplored, the undiscovered upon whose shore she had landed, alone, after crossing the void, the darkness which washed the New World and the Old (*The Rainbow* (Harmondsworth, 1966], p. 494).

And in his poetry, speaking of the mystery of the human psyche, Lawrence uses the image of an unknown continent within man.

> There is the other universe, the heart of man
> that we know nothing of, that we dare not explore.
> A strange grey distance separates
> our pale mind still from the pulsing continent
> of the heart of man.
>
> Fore-runners have barely landed on the shore
> and no man knows, no woman knows
> the mystery of the interior
> when darker still than Congo or Amazon
> flow the heart's rivers of fullness. desire and distress.
>     (*CP*, p. 606)

Similarly, writing about the human consciousness, Aldous Huxley was later to suggest:

> Like the earth of a hundred years ago, our mind still has its darkest Africas, its unmapped Borneos and Amazonian basins . . . A man consists of what I may call an Old World of personal consciousness and beyond a dividing sea, a series of New Worlds—the not too distant Virginias and Carolinas of the personal subconscious and the vegetative soil; the Far West of the collective unconscious, with its flora of symbols. its tribes of aboriginal archetypes; and, across another, vaster ocean, at the antipodes of everyday consciousness, the world of Visionary Experience. (*Heaven and Hell*, [Harmondsworth, 1969] pp. 71-2).

Huxley's description offers an apt analogy to Lawrence's actual travels which formed an ever-widening circle, first to Italy and continental Europe, then in the 1920s to the far east and Australia, widening to include Old and New Mexico and finally, full circle as it were, the return to the Mediterranean, 'the human norm' as he called it. In linking geographical remoteness with the ever deepening exploration of the psyche, Huxley's words suggest Lawrence's own developing vision, a vision which was, nevertheless, always based on the notion of creation through conflict.

The origins of this belief, which was to inform and shape nearly all the works of his maturity, can be found in his first travel book, *Twilight in Italy*. Originally conceived as a series of travel sketches, written variously in the months between the autumn of 1912 and that of 1913, the essays were revised in the summer and early autumn of 1915, significantly at the time when Lawrence was also preparing his long philosophical essay, *The Crown*, for publication. The striking similarities in thought that emerge between *The Crown* and the revised parts of *Twilight in Italy* can be explained by Lawrence's fascination with John Burnet's *Early Greek Philosophy* (London, 1892) which he had read by July 1915. Burnet's account of the pre-Socratic philosophers, in particular the thought of Herakleitos of Ephesus, profoundly influenced Lawrence: 'I shall write all my philosophy again. Last time I came out of the Christian Camp. This time I must come out of these early Greek philosophers' (19 July 1915, *Letters*, 11, 367); and 'I shall write out Herakleitos, on tablets of bronze' (14? July 1915, *Letters*, 11, 364). Several features of Herakleitos' doctrine in particular made a lasting impression on Lawrence and were to influence his thoughts about humanity and the universe. First, Herakleitos' notion that 'strife' or 'conflict' is the creative power which causes all things to rise into being:

> Homer was wrong in saying: 'Would that strife might perish from among gods and men!' He did not see that he was praying for the destruction of the universe; for, if his prayer were heard, all things would pass away. (Burnet, p. 136)[4]

Compare this with similar notions in *The Crown,* for example: 'And there is no rest, no cessation from the conflict. For we are two opposites which exist by virtue of our inter-opposition. Remove the opposition and there is collapse, a sudden crumbling into nothingness' and 'it is the fight of opposites which is holy'.[5]    Central to Herakleitos' teaching was the idea of the world as at once one and many; the notion that the unity of the universe, the Infinite, rests on the opposition or tension between things, without which it could not exist.

> Couples are things whole and things not whole, what is drawn together and what is drawn asunder, the harmonious and the discordant. The one is made up of all things, and all things issue from the one. (Burnet, p. 137)

This concept of 'the one' or 'the Boundless' as Herakleitos calls it elsewhere, out of which all things emerge and into which all things return, became a central tenet of Lawrence's doctrine and is first fully expressed in *The Crown*. But *Twilight in Italy* also formulates this creative tension of opposition as a kind of duality.

> The Infinite is twofold, the Father and the Son, the Dark and the Light. the Senses and the Mind, the Soul and the Spirit, the self and the not-self, the Eagle and the Dove, the Tiger and the Lamb. . . . But that which I may never deny, and which I have denied, is the Holy Ghost which relates the dual Infinities into One Whole, which relates and keeps distinct the dual natures of God. To say that the two are one, this is the inadmissible lie. The two are related, by the intervention of the Third, into a Oneness (*Twilight in Italy* [New York 1962]. pp. 58-9).

Creation, then, is a dialectic; only through contraries can new growth be achieved, can the divisions of the old self be transcended and birth into new being achieved. To the power that brings about this transcendence, Lawrence gave many names in his writing—the Holy Ghost, the Crown, the rainbow, the New Jerusalem are some of them—but in essence it was always a power of creation, as he states in *The Crown*:

> This lovely body of foam, this iris between the two floods, this music between the cymbals, this truth btwecn the surge of facts, this supreme reason between conflicting desires, this holy spirit between the opposite divinities, this is the Absolute made visible between the two Infinities, the Timelessness into which are assumed the two Eternities (*Phoenix 11,* p.373).

Finally, Herakleitos' dictum 'It rests by changing' (Burnet, p. 139) might almost be an epitome for Lawrence himself, whose physical journeys around the globe at once generated the external stimuli and the inner creativity necessary for his art.

Of course the Italian sketches, like all Lawrence's travel writings, are far more than exercises in philosophical speculation. They are also fine evocations of foreign places and peoples, often richly comic, always infused with Lawrence's uncanny ability to sense and transmute into literary art the beauty and spirit of place. Equally, chapters like 'The Lemon Garden' and 'The Return Journey' contain a theme which was to become increasingly important in his work—the fear of encroaching mechanisation and the consequent dehumanisation of the individual. *Twilight in Italy,* completed during the First World War, ends with a bleak vision of a world heading towards the cataclysm of global conflict, a world of hideous rawness and mechanisation descending like an iron weight to crush the heritage of faith and feeling and belief in the beauty of life.

It is the hideous rawness of the world of men. the horrible, desolating harshness of the advance of the industrial world upon the world of nature, that is so painful. It looks as though the industrial spread of mankind were a sort of dry disintegration advancing and advancing, a process of dry disintegration. If only we could learn to take thought for the whole world instead of for merely tiny bits of it  (*Twilight in Italy*, p. 195).

It is as if the whole social form were breaking down. and the human element swarmed within the disintegration, like maggots in cheese. The  roads, the railways are built, the mines and quarries are excavated, but the whole organism of life, the social organism, is slowly crumbling and caving in, in a kind of process of dry rot, most terrifying to see. So that it seems as though we should be left at last with a great system of roads and railways and industries, and a world of utter chaos seething upon these fabrications: as if we had created a steel framework, and the whole body of society were crumbling and rotting in between (*Twilight in Italy*, pp. 210-11).

The outbreak of the war and the carnage of battles like that of the Somme in 1916, confirmed Lawrence in the belief that Europe was caught in a nightmarish death-wish, a destructive and insane hatred of life. For Lawrence, as for many of his generation and time, it seemed as if the end of civilisation had come and that out of the holocaust would emerge a wholly different and unimaginable world like that prophesied by Yeats: 'And what Rough Beast, its hour come round at last, slouches towards Bethlehem to be born'.[6] The letters of the war years are filled with the sense of nightmare and apocalypse: 'So it is the end—our world is gone, and we are like dust in the air' (9 September 1915, *Letters, 11*, 390); and 'Everything has a touch of delirium. . . . It is not a question of me, it is the world of men. The world of men is dreaming, it has gone mad in its sleep, and a snake is strangling it, but it can't wake up' (14 May 1915, *Letters, 11*, 339-40). It is hardly surprising that for a time Lawrence withdrew from humanity and turned to the pristine loveliness and innocence, as he saw it, of the world of nature. Living in Cornwall, in retreat from a world that had 'gone mad', he wrote: 'There is another world, a sort of rarer reality: a world with thin, clean air and untouched skies, that have not been looked at nor covered with smoke. There is another world, which I prefer. And I don't care about any people' (6 January 1916, *Letters 11*, 498).

This is a kind of interval in my life, like a sleep. One only wanders through the dim short days, and reads and cooks, and looks across at the sea. I feel as if I also were hibernating, like the snakes and the dormice,—I saw a most beautiful brindled adder, in the spring. coiled up asleep with her head on her shoulder. She did not hear me till I was very near. Then she must have felt my motion, for she lifted her head like a queen to look, then turned and moved slowly and with delicate pride, into the bushes. She often comes into my mind again, and I think I see her asleep in the sun, like a Princess of the fairy world. It is queer, the intimation of other worlds, which one catches (25 November 1916, *Letters*, III, 40).

And yet it is characteristic of him that even the most despairing of his writings at this time should end with the hope: 'But there must be a new heaven and a new earth, a clearer, eternal moon above, and a clean world below. So it will be. Everything is burst away now, there remains only to take on new being' (9 September 1915 *Letters,* 11, 390). In the autumn of 1919 he left England, never to return to live there, and in the years following the war, in his travels around the world and his eventual return to Europe, he sought for the ways in which mankind could create that new heaven and new earth, that 'new being'. It was a search that was to lead him across the globe to other countries and civilisations and back to old pagan religions and myths in the quest for symbols that would refresh the springs of religious awareness in modern man. Having witnessed the cataclysm of the First World War and perceived the general decay of metropolitan culture around him in England, Germany and Italy, a starving in his time of the deep roots of life, Lawrence sought to discover in the past the sources that fed life then and that therefore must also nourish the present.

His travel writings after the war, like the essays and the fiction, have at their heart a serious purpose: to explore the nature of political and religious power in human societies and to search for the causes of the malaise, as he saw it, of our century. So it is that *Sea and Sardinia,* written in only six weeks after a brief visit to the island in January 1921, contains significantly different levels of response to Italy and her island. There is the artist's delighted recognition of the pristine beauty of the Mediterranean:

> From the islands one of the Mediterranean sailing ships is beating her way, across our track to Trapani . . . on she comes, with her tall ladder of square sails white in the afternoon light, and her lovely prow, curved in with a perfect hollow, running like a wild animal on a scent across the waters. There—the scent leads her north again. She changes her tack from the harbour mouth, and goes coursing away, passing behind us. Lovely she is, nimble and quick and palpitating, with all her sails white and bright and eager (*Sea and Sardinia* [London, 1923], p.62).

Or the fresh appreciation of Sardinia's timelessness in passages such as this:

> A man is ploughing with two small red cattle on a craggy, tree-hanging slope as sharp as a roof-side. He stoops at the small wooden plough, and jerks the ploughlines. The oxen lift their noses to heaven. with a strange and beseeching snakelike movement, and taking tiny steps with their frail feet, move slantingly across the slope-face, between rocks and tree-roots. Little, frail, jerky steps the bullocks take, and again they put their horns back and lift their muzzles snakily to heaven, as the man pulls the line. And he skids his wooden plough round another scoop of earth. It is marvellous how they hang upon the steep, craggy slope. An English labourer's eyes would bolt out of his head at the sight (*Sea and Sardinia* p. 137).

But the book also reveals, as do the Italian chapters of *Aaron's Rod* (also written at this time) Lawrence's shrewd understanding of the mood of Italy and Europe in that era of political unrest which saw the rise of both fascism and communism: 'The era of love and oneness is over . . . The other tide has set in' (*Sea and Sardinia,* p. 142).

And in the journey across Sardinia Lawrence rediscovered his own inner landscape and articulated his sense of the quest which was to occupy him ever more fully in the years to come, the quest for wholeness and integration. Like Jung, Lawrence saw the human psyche balanced between two realities, the outer, objective, material world, and the inner, subjective one, with a profound need to bring the two into harmony, to integrate inner and outer, past and present, for the enrichment and growth of the self. *Sea and Sardinia* recognises this psychological need and expresses Lawrence's renewed commitment to that quest after the disillusionment and bitterness of the war years. It is worth quoting at some length a passage which illustrates this:

> Wherever one is in Italy, either one is conscious of the present, or of the mediaeval influences, or of the far, mysterious gods of the early Mediterranean. Wherever one is, the place has its conscious genius. Man has lived there and brought forth his consciousness there and in some way brought that place to consciousness, given it its expression, and really, finished it. The expression may be Proserpine, or Pan, or even the strange 'shrouded gods' of the Etruscans or the Sikels, none the less it is an expression. The land has been humanised, through and through: and we in our own tissued consciousness bear the results of this humanisation. So that for us to go to Italy and to penetrate into Italy is like a most fascinating act of self-discovery—back, back down the old ways of time. Strange and wonderful chords awake in us, and vibrate again after many hundreds of years of complete forgetfulness.
>
> And then—and then—there is a final feeling of sterility. It is all worked out. It is all known: *connu, connu*!
>
> This Sunday morning, seeing the frost among the tangled, still savage bushes of Sardinia, my soul thrilled again. This was not all known. This was not all worked out. Life was not only a process of rediscovering backwards. It is that, also: and it is that intensely. Italy has given me back I know not what of myself, but a very, very great deal. She has found for me so much that was lost: like a restored Osiris. But this morning in the omnibus I realise that, apart from the great rediscovery backwards, which one must make before one can be whole at all, there is a move forwards. There are unknown, unworked lands where the salt has not lost its savour. But one must have perfected oneself in the great past first. (*Sea and Sardinia*, pp. 185-86).

The passage expresses an inherent paradox found in many of Lawrence's writings: the sense in which the known past is a sterile and finished thing and yet it is that past which also generates the present. So in *The Rainbow* the impulse of each Brangwen generation is to grow beyond the achievement of the previous one, but the vitality for that development comes from the life and the past that are to be transcended. In the chapter 'Breadalby', in *Women in Love*, Birkin muses on 'the lovely accomplished past' which, although static and ultimately 'a delusion', is nevertheless 'better than the sordid scrambling conflict of the present'. And he concludes with the wistful hope that somehow one might integrate past and present—'the simple truth to life' as he calls it—and 'create the future after one's own heart'.

Lawrence's own travels and the travel writings to come were about the 'great past' and its relevance to the present and the future. For Lawrence the question facing every generation was always how to achieve a sense of continuity and wholeness and how to regain the spirit of the human adventure into the unknown. In this quest, of course, he was by no means unique. The image of a lost coherence in the past (and the necessity to regain that coherence in the present) may have little historical basis, but it seems to match a profound psychological and social need in man. With the collapse of old symbols and values precipitated by the Great War, Lawrence felt an imperative drive to search for new symbols which would help his world achieve some kind of regeneration. He therefore sought to understand the nature of political and religious power in past cultures and ancient civilisations—especially the Aztec and American Indian and, towards the end of his life, the Etruscan—not because he advocated a return to primitive forms for modern man, but because he recognised the unchanging qualities of human nature and the validity of laws which had governed man in the past. These, he argued, must also have value for the complex fabric of our century's civilisation. Nowhere is this better seen than in the two late travel books, *Mornings in Mexico* and *Etruscan Places.*

*Mornings in Mexico* was written in the winter of 1924-5 when Lawrence was living in Oaxaca, Mexico, but the proofs were not corrected until April 1927 when he was beginning the essays for *Etruscan Places* so that there is a continuity between the two works and much of the spirit of *Mornings in Mexico* interfuses *Etruscan Places.* Both works describe ancient rituals and ways of life which Lawrence intuitively grasped in his travels through Old and New Mexico and, subsequently, through Etruria in Italy. But beneath the surface concern with describing old civilisations and their customs Lawrence explores the wider concept of man's relation to the universe and seeks to understand humanity's connection with the vast cosmic forces out of which it sprang and into which it will return: 'How is man to get himself into relation with the vast living convulsions of rain and thunder and sun, which are conscious and alive and potent, but like vastness of beasts, inscrutable and incomprehensible?' (*Mornings in Mexico* [Harmondsworth, 1967], p.75). In the Mexican essays, as in *Etruscan Places,* Lawrence gives symbolic value to the Indian dances he witnessed as expressions of that ageless human desire for connection with the universal:

> Man, little man, with his consciousness and his will, must both submit to the great origin powers of his life, and conquer them. Conquered by man who has overcome his fears, the snakes must go back into the earth with his messages of tenderness, of request, and of power. They go back as rays of love to the dark heart of the first of suns. But they go back also as arrows shot clean by man's sapience and courage, into the resistant, malevolent heart of the earth's oldest, stubborn core (*Mornings in Mexico*, p. 87).

Moreover, he found in the dances of the Hopi Indians a form of religion naturally congenial to him and his own conception of God.

> To the Indian there is no conception of a defined God. Creation is a great flood, for ever flowing, in lovely and terrible waves. In everything the shimmer of creation, and never the finality of the created. Never the distinction between God and God's creation, or between Spirit and Matter. Everything, everything is the wonderful shimmer of creation, it may be a deadly shimmer like lightning or the anger in the little eyes of the bear, it may be the beautiful shimmer of the moving deer, or the pine-boughs softly swaying under the snow . . . There is, in our sense of the word, no God. But all is godly. There is no Great Mind directing the universe. Yet the mystery of creation, the wonder and fascination of creation shimmers in every leaf and stone, in every thorn and bud, in the fangs of the rattlesnake, and in the soft eyes of a fawn. Things utterly opposite are still pure wonder of creation, the yell of the mountain-lion, and the breeze in the aspen leaves (*Mornings in Mexico*, p.61).[7]

The passage recalls his own belief, stated in 1911, in God as 'a vast, shimmering impulse which waves on towards some end' (9 April 1911, *Letters*, 1, 256) and expressed again in the last months of his life: that there is that 'in the cosmos which contains the essence, at least, or the potentiality, of all things known and unknown . . . . And . . . this potency I call Almighty God'.[8] In the restated notion of duality, too, we find the subtle influence of his early reading of Herakleitos to whose philosophical writings he was to return in the last year of his life.

In February 1925, however, while in Mexico, Lawrence fell gravely ill and nearly died of malaria. For the first time also his chronic illness was clearly defined as tuberculosis and he was forced to accept that he was a dying man. In March of that year he wrote the beginning of an unfinished novel, *The Flying Fish,* in which the protagonist, ill unto death and weary of years of wandering, returns to his home in England:

> ... in the last years, something in the hard, fierce, finite sun of Mexico, in the dry terrible land, and in the black staring eyes of the suspicious natives, had made the ordinary day lose its reality to him. It had cracked like some great bubble, and to his uneasiness and terror, he had seemed to see through the fissures the deeper blue of that other Greater Day where moved the other sun shaking its dark blue wings. Perhaps it was the malaria; perhaps it was his own inevitable development; perhaps it was the presence of those handsome, dangerous, wide-eyed men left over from the ages before the flood in Mexico, which caused his old connexions and his accustomed world to break for him. He was ill, and be felt as if at the very middle of him. beneath his navel, some membrane were torn, some membrane which had connected him with the world and its day . . . He wanted to go home.[9]

So, too, Lawrence felt compelled to return to Europe and especially to his beloved Italy. The Mediterranean—'so eternally young, the very symbol of youth' as he called it in the final pages of *Mornings in Mexico* (p. 92) —which had been the great inspiration of his early years as a writer was now to become equally important as a source of strength for his last journey into death. Herakleitos' writings again offer a succinct image for Lawrence's return from his travels around the globe: 'In the circumference of a circle the beginning and end are common' (Burnet, p. 138), a kindred vision to Donne's well-known lines:

> As West and East
> In all flatt Maps (and I am one) are one,
> So death doth touch the Resurrection.

One of the great voyagers, in a psychic as well as literal sense, of his time, Lawrence now sought in the joyous myths depicted in the Etruscan tomb paintings for the imaginative and psychologically valid emblems with which to approach that final journey:

> one radical thing the Etruscan people never forgot . . . the mystery of the journey out of life, and into death; the death-journey, and the sojourn in the after-life. The wonder of their soul continued to play round the mystery of this journey and this sojourn.

In the tombs we see it; throes of wonder and vivid feeling throbbing over death. Man moves naked and glowing through the universe. Then comes death: he dives into the sea, he departs into the underworld (*Etruscan Places* [London, 1932], p.94).

Lawrence visited the Etruscan places in April 1927 and began writing his essays at the end of that same month. He had completed only six of them by the end of June and although he planned several more these were never written. The essays record his delighted response (reminiscent of his writings in *Mornings in Mexico*) to what he felt was the essence of the Etruscan religion: 'To the Etruscan all was alive; the whole universe lived; and the business of man was himself to live amid it all. He had to draw life into himself, out of the wandering huge vitalities of the world' (*Etruscan Places,* p. 89). He found the Etruscan conception of death as a natural continuation of this life, congenial and it would have recalled to him the dualistic nature of Herakleitos' teaching: 'Mortals are immortals and immortals are mortals, the one living the others' death and dying the others' life' (Burnet, p.138). And indeed this cyclical idea of life and death as the opposite and necessary scales of existence informs many of the late works. In his preparation for 'the longest journey' as he was to call it in the last poems, however, Lawrence was more than ever concerned to identify and write about all the cosmologies which contribute to man's creation of himself and his world. The lost religion of the Etruscans provided him with the symbols through which to explore those cosmologies: 'the Etruscan religion is concerned with all those physical and creative powers and forces which go to the building up and the destroying of the soul; the soul, the personality, being that which gradually is produced out of chaos, like a flower, only to disappear again into chaos, or the underworld' (*Etruscan Places*, p. 118).

Lawrence had always seen man as a creature of duality, in perpetual conflict with himself, with the claims of emotion and intuition on the one hand and those of the intellect and reason on the other. This is revealed in his two ways of perceiving the cosmos: 'man has two ways of knowing the universe: religious and scientific' (*Apocalypse*, p. 190), by which he meant the poetic and imaginative as against the rational, with a need to bring the two into harmony but often unable to do so, and never less so than in this age of scientific materialism. In the late poems and essays, Lawrence put forward his belief that the way to achieve this integration was through the imagination, through the cultivation of what he called the poetic intelligence: 'the essential act of attention, the essential poetic and vital act' which puts us in touch with the heart of all things, which "discovers" a new world within the known world' (*Phoenix,* pp.261, 255).[10] On the shores of the Mediterranean in the final months of his life, Lawrence wrote a symbolic blueprint, a last testament to the world of that integration of intellect and intuition, of the self and the wider cosmos, of life and death, which he believed in. 'Man is a thought adventurer'—and his last journey was truly a voyage of the imagination through the landscape of visionary experience, a vision recorded in the *Apocalypse* essays and in the last poems where he described that wholeness which he had found and which he was passionately determined to transmit to the world he would shortly leave. It could be argued that the final achievement of the integration was an illusion, a false hope generated by a dying mind; equally that it was a true epiphany, a showing-forth of things as they are. Perhaps it is not given to the human mind to grasp and retain such moments of transcendent insight, as Tolstoy found. Yet through his imaginative, visionary power, a great artist like Lawrence can create those moments of intuitive understanding when we too can glimpse the 'vast realms of consciousness' within man, and recognise afresh the numinous beauty of the created universe, the 'rarer reality' of 'other worlds'.

*Renaissance and Modern Studies*, 29, 1985.

## Notes

[1] V. de Sola Pinto & W. Roberts (eds), *The Complete Poems of D. H. Lawrence* (London, 1964), p. 666.   Hereafter *CP*.

[2] G. Zytaruk & J. T. Boulton (eds). *The Letters of D. H. Lawrence*, Volume II (Cambridge, 1981), p. 299.   Hereafter *Letters*.

[3] R. West, *D. H. Lawrence* (London, 1930), pp. 34-6.

[4] Lawrence quotes this, and several other passages and phrases from Herakleitos, in his later prefatory notes to the poems *Birds, Beasts and Flowers*. See *CP*, p. 348.

[5] W. Roberts & H. T. Moore (eds), *Phoenix II* (London, 1968) pp. 368, 374.   Hereafter *Phoenix II*.

[6] Years later, in December 1924 Lawrence was to write 'Tonight is Christmas Eve, and who knows what sort of a child the Virgin is going to bring forth, this time!' *Phoenix II*, p. 296.

[7] Compare this with the similar passage in *Apocalypse* on the Greek notion of *theos:* "To the ancient consciousness, Matter, Materia, or Substantial things are God. A great rock *is* God. A pool of water is God. And why not? The longer we live the more we return to the oldest of all visions. A great rock is God. I can touch it. It is undeniable. It is God. . . . Today, it is almost impossible for us to realize what the old Greeks meant by god, or *theos*. Everything was *theos*; but even so, not at the same moment. At the moment, whatever struck you was god. If it was a pool of water, the very watery pool might strike you: then that was god: or the blue gleam might suddenly occupy your consciousness: then that was god; or a faint vapour at evening rising might catch the imagination: then that was *theos*,' M. Kalnins (ed.). *Apocalypse and the Writings on Revelation* (Cambridge 1980). p. 95. Hereafter *Apocalypse*.

[8] *Apocalypse*, Fragment 1, p. 175.

[9] E. McDonald (ed.), *Phoenix* (London 1961), pp. 782-83.   Hereafter *Phoenix*.

[10] Cf. *Etruscan Places*: 'The soul stirs, and makes an act of attention, and this is a discovery.' p. 98.

# Selected Bibliography

## Chronologies and Bibliographies—Primary

Aldington, Richard. *D.H. Lawrence, A Complete List of His Works with a Critical Appreciation*. London: Heinemann, 1935.

Bumpus, John, and Edward Bumpus. *D.H. Lawrence: An Exhibition*. London: Bumpus, 1933. (Catalogue of event held April-May 1933)

McDonald, Edward D. *A Bibliography of the Writings of D.H. Lawrence*, Philadelphia: The Centaur Bookshop, 1925.

_____. *The Writings of D.H. Lawrence, 1925-1930: A Bibliographical Supplement*. Philadelphia: The Centaur Bookshop, 1931.

Melvin Rare Books. *A Catalogue of Valuable Books by D.H. Lawrencxe*. Edinburgh: Melvin Rare Books, 1950.

Nottingham University. *Collection of Literary Manuscripts, Typescripts, Proofs and Related Papers of D.H. Lawrence*. Nottingham: University of Nottingham Department of Manuscripts and Special Collections, 1990.

Poplawski, Paul. *The Works of D.H. Lawrence: A Chronological Checklist*. Nottingham: D.H. Lawrence Society, 1995.

Powell, Lawrence Clark. *The Manuscripts of D.H. Lawrence: A Descriptive Catalogue*. Los Angeles: Los Angeles Public Library, 1937.

Preston, Peter. *A. D.H. Lawrence Chronology*. London: Macmillan, 1994.

Rice, Thomas Jackson. *D.H. Lawrence: A Guide to Research* New York and London: Garland, 1983.

Roberts, Warren. *A Bibliography of D.H. Lawrence*, 2nd ed. Cambridge: Cambridge University Press, 1982. (Currently the definitive primary bibliography.)

Sagar, Keith M. *D.H. Lawrence: A calendar of his works with a checklist of the manuscripts of D.H. Lawrence by Lindeth Vasey*. Manchester: Manchester University Press, 1979.

Snyder, Harold Jay. *A Catalogue of English and American First Editions, 1911-32, of D.H. Lawrence*. New York: Privately printed, 1932.

Stoll, John E. *D.H. Lawrence: A Bibliography, 1911-1975*. Troy, N.Y.: Whitston Publishing Co., 1977.

Tarr, Roger L., and Robert Sokon (eds.), *A Bibliography of the D.H. Lawrence Collection at Illinois State University*. Bloomington, Ill.: Scarlet Ibis Press, 1979.

Texas University Humanities Research Center. *The University of New Mexico D.H. Lawrence Fellowship Fund Manuscript Collection.* Austin: University of Texas Humanities Research Center, 1960. (Catalog.)


## Bibliographies—Secondary

Banerjee, Amitava. *D.H. Lawrence's Poetry: Demon Liberated: A Collection of Primary and Secondary Source Material.* London: Macmillan, 1990.

Cowan, James C. *D. H.Lawrence: An Annotated Bibliography of Writings About Him*, Vol.1: 1906-1960, Vol.11: 1961-1975, De Kalb, Illinois, Northern Illinois University Press, 1982, 1985.

*D.H. Lawrence Review.* Checklists of D.H. Lawrence criticism from I, Fall, 1968; III, Spring, 1970; and annually in each Spring issue.

Phillips, Jill M. (ed.), *D.H. Lawrence: A Review of the Biographies and Literary Criticism.* New York: Gordon Press, 1978.

Poplawski, *D.H. Lawrence: a Reference Handbook.* Westport, Conn.: Greenwood Press, 1996.

White, William. *D.H. Lawrence: A Checklist. Writings About D.H. Lawrence, 1931-1950.* Detroit: Wayne State University Press, 1950.


## Biographies, Reminiscences and Recollections

Brett, Dorothy. *Lawrence and Brett, A Friendship.* Philadelphia: J.B. Lippincott, 1933.

Brewster, Earl and Achsah. *D.H. Lawrence: Reminiscences and Correspondence.* London: Secker, 1934.

Burgess, Anthony. *Flame into Being: The Life and Work of D.H. Lawrence.* London: Heinemann, 1985.

Bynner, Witter. *Journey with Genius: Recollections and Reflections concerning the D.H. Lawrences.* New York: Day, 1951; London: Nevill, 1953.

Byrne, Janet. *A Genius for Living: A Biography of Frieda Lawrence.* London: Bloomsbury, 1995.

Callow, Philip. *Son and Lover: the Young Lawrence.* London: The Bodley Head, 1975.

Cambridge Three Volume Biography:

_____. Worthen, John. *D.H. Lawrence: The early years 1885-1912.* Cambridge, New York: Cambridge University Press, 1991b.

_____. Kinkead-Weekes, Mark. *D.H. Lawrence, Triumph to Exile, 1912-1922.* Cambridge, New York: Cambridge University Press, 1996.

_____. Ellis, David. *D.H. Lawrence: Dying Game, 1922-1930.* Cambridge: Cambridge University Press, 1998.

Carswell, Catherine. *The Savage Pilgrimage: A Narrative of D.H. Lawrence.* London: Chatto & Windus, 1932, (New York: Harcourt Brace and Co.,1932.) rev. edn. Secker & Warburg, 1951. Reprinted with a memoir of the author by John Carswell. Cambridge: Cambridge University Press, 1981.

_____. "Reminiscences of D.H. Lawrence" in *New Adelphi* i-v. no.111 (Nov. 1931-Mar. 1932)

Chambers, Jessie (pseudonym E.T.), *D.H. Lawrence, A Personal Record*. London: Jonathan Cape, 1935; with Intro. by Middleton Murry, New York: Knight, 1936. 2nd Edition, with intro. by J. D. Chambers, London: Frank Cass; New York: Barnes and Noble, 1965.

Corke, Helen. *D.H. Lawrence, The Croydon Years*. Austin, Texas: The University of Texas Press, 1965.

_____. *In Our Infancy*, Cambridge: Cambridge UP, 1975.

Daleski, H. M. *The Forked Flame: A Study of D.H. Lawrence*. London and Evanston, Ill: Northwestern University Press, 1965.

Fay, Eliot. *Lorenzo in Search of the Sun: D.H. Lawrence in Italy, Mexico, and the American Southwest*. New York: Bookman, 1953; London: Vision, 1955.

Feinstein, Elaine. *Lawrence's Women: The Intimate Life of D.H. Lawrence*. London: Harper Collins, 1993.

Foster, Joseph. *D.H. Lawrence in Taos*. Albuquerque: University of New Mexico Press, 1972.

Hahn, Emily. *Lorenzo: D.H. Lawrence and the Women Who Loved Him*. Philadelphia and New York: Lippincott, 1975.

Hilton, Enid Hopkin. *More than One Life: A Nottinghamshire Childhood with D.H. Lawrence*. Stroud, Gloucestershire: Alan Sutton, 1993.

Lawrence, Ada, and G. Stuart Gelder. *Early Life of D.H. Lawrence*, Florence: G. Orioli, 1932.

_____. *Young Lorenzo, Early Life of D.H. Lawrence*. London: Martin Secker, 1932; New York: Russell and Russell, 1966.

Lawrence, Frieda, *Not I, But the Wind*, Sante Fe: Rydal Press, 1934; (New York: Viking Press, 1934).

_____. *The Memoirs and Correspondence*, ed. E.W. Tedlock, Jr. London: Heinemann: 1961.

Lucas, Robert. *Frieda Lawrence: The Story of Frieda von Richthofen and D.H. Lawrence* (trans. Geoffrey Skelton), London: Secker & Warburg, 1973.

Luhan, Mabel Dodge. *Lorenzo in Taos*. New York: Alfred Knopf, 1932.

Maddox, Brenda. *The Married Man: A Life of D.H. Lawrence*. London: Sinclair-Stevenson, 1994.

Merrild, Knud. *A Poet and Two Painters: A Memoir of D.H. Lawrence*. London: Routledge, 1938, New York: Viking, 1939. (Reprinted as *With D.H. Lawrence in New Mexico: A Memoir of D.H. Lawrence*. London: Routledge and Kegan Paul, 1964.)

Meyers, Jeffrey. *D.H. Lawrence: A Biography*. New York: Knopf, (dist. Random House), 1990.

Moore, Harry T. *The Life and Works of D.H. Lawrence*. London: Allen & Unwin, New York: Twayne Publishers, 1951. (Revised as *D.H. Lawrence: His Life and Works,* New York: Twayne, 1964).

_____. *The Intelligent Heart: The Story of D.H. Lawrence*. New York: Farrar, Straus, and Cudahy, 1954, rev. ed. Londn: Penguin, 1960. (Revised as *The Priest of Love: A Life of D.H. Lawrence*. Carbondale: Southern Ill. University

Press; London: Heinemann, 1974. Further revised, Harmondsworth: Penguin, 1976.)

_____ and Dale B. Montague (eds.), *Frieda Lawrence and Her Circle: Letters from, to and about Frieda Lawrence*. London: Macmillan: Hamden, Conn.: Shoe String, 1981.

Murry, John Middleton. *D.H. Lawrence*. Cambridge: The Minority Press, 1930.

_____. *Son of Woman.: The Story of D.H. Lawrence*. London: Cape;  New York: J. Cape and H. Smith, 1931.

_____. *Reminiscences of D.H. Lawrence*. London: Cape, 1933.

Nehls, Edward. *D.H. Lawrence, A Composite Biography* (3 vols: 1885-1919, 1919-25, 1925-30), Madison: University of Wisconsin Press, 1957, 1958, 1959.

Neville, G. H. (ed. Carl Baron), *A Memoir of D.H. Lawrence: (The betrayal)*. Cambridge, New York: Cambridge University Press, 1981.

Page, Norman (ed.), *D.H. Lawrence: Interviews and Recollections* (2 vols. London: The Macmillan Press, Ltd., 1981.

Sagar, Keith. *The Life of D.H. Lawrence*. London: Eyre Methuen, 1980.

Schneider, Daniel J. *The Consciousness of D.H. Lawrence: An Intellectual Biography*. Lawrence: University Press of Kansas, 1986.

Schorer, Mark. *D.H. Lawrence*. New York: Dell Publishing Co. Inc., 1968.

Spencer, Roy. *D.H. Lawrence Country: A portrait of his early life and background with illustrations, maps, and guides*. London: C. Woolf, 1979.

Spender, Stephen (ed.), *D.H. Lawrence: Novelist, Poet, Prophet*. London: Weidenfield & Nicholson; NY: Harper & Row, 1973.

Stevens, C.J. *Lawrence at Tregerthen*. Troy, New York: Whitston, 1988.

Tedlock, E. W. (ed.), *Frieda Lawrence, The Memoirs and Correspondence*. London: Heinemann, 1961.

Widdowson, Peter. *D.H. Lawrence*. Longman: 1992.

Worthen, John. *D.H. Lawrence: A Literary Life*. London: Macmillan, 1989.

_____. *D.H. Lawrence*. London: Edward Arnold, 1991a.

## Books

Aiken, Conrad. *Skepticisms: Notes on Contemporary Poetry*. New York: Knopf, 1919b, 91-104.

Alden, Patricia. *Social Mobility in the English Bildungsroman: Gissing, Hardy, Bennett, and Lawrence*.  Ann Arbor, Mich.: UMI Research Press, 1986.

Aldington, Richard. *D.H. Lawrence, An Indiscretion*. Seattle: University of Washington Book Store, 1927.

_____. *D.H. Lawrence*. London: Chatto & Windus, 1930.

_____. *D.H. Lawrence, An Appreciation*, Harmondsworth: Penguin Books, 1950.

_____. *D.H. Lawrence: Portrait of a Genius But . . .*  London: Wm. Heinemann; New York: Duell, Sloan & Pearce, Inc., 1950.

Alldritt, Keith. *Visual Imagination of D.H. Lawrence*.London: Edward Arnold, 1971.

Arnold, Armin. *D.H.  Lawrence in America*, London: Linden Press, 1958.

_____. *D.H. Lawrence and German Literature: With Two Hitherto Unknown Essays by D.H. Lawrence*. Montreal: Mansfield Book Mart, H. Heinemann, 1963

Arrow, John. *J. C. Square v. D.H. Lawrence*. London: E. Lahr, 1930.

Balbert, Peter. *D.H. Lawrence and the Psychology of Rhythm: The Meaning of Form in "The Rainbow."* The Hague: Mouton, 1974.

_____. *D.H. Lawrence and the Phallic Imagination: Essays on Sexual Identity and Feminist Misreading*. London: Macmillan, 1989.

_____, and Phillip L. Marcus, (eds.), *D.H. Lawrence: A Centenary Consideration*. Ithaca, N.Y. and London: Cornell University Press, 1985.

Beal, Anthony, *D.H. Lawrence*, Edinburgh: Oliver & Boyd, 1961.

Beauvoir, Simone de. *The Second Sex*, trans. by H.M. Parshley. London: Cape; New York: Knopf, 1953.

Becket, Fiona. *D.H. Lawrence: the Thinker as Poet*. London: Macmillan, 1997.

Bedient, Calvin. *Architects of the Self: George Eliot, D.H. Lawrence, and E. M. Forster*. Berkeley: University of California Press, 1972.

Bell, Michael. *D.H. Lawrence:Language and Being*. Cambridge: Cambridge UP, 1992.

Ben-Ephraim, Gavriel. *The Moon's Dominion: Narrative Dichotomy and Female Dominance in Lawrence's Earlier Novels*. London and Toronto: Associated University Presses, 1981.

Black, Michael. *D.H. Lawrence: The Early Fiction*. London: Macmillan, 1986.

_____. *D.,H. Lawrence: The Early Philosophical Works: A Commentary*. London: Macmillan, 1991.

_____. *D.H. Lawrence: Sons and Lovers*. Cambridge: Cambridge University Press, 1992.

Bloom, Harold, ed. *D.H. Lawrence: Modern Critical Views*. New York: Chelsea House, 1986.

Bonds, Diane S. *Language and the Self in D.H. Lawrence*. Ann Arbor, Mich.: UMI Research Press, 1987.

Brown, Keith, (ed.), *Rethinking Lawrence*. Milton Keynes and Philadelphia: Open University Press, 1990.

Carswell, Catherine. *Sing a Song of Sixpence, D.H. Lawrence and the Press*. London: The Broadsheet Press, 1930.

Cavitch, David. *D.H. Lawrence and the New World*. New York: Oxford UP, 1969.

Clark, L.D. *Dark Night of the Body: D.H. Lawrence's "The Plumed Serpent."* Austin: University of Texas Press, 1964.

Clarke, Colin, *River of Dissolution: D.H. Lawrence and English Romanticism*. London: Routledge & Kegan Paul, 1969.

Corke, Helen. *Lawrence and Apocalypse*. London: Heinemann, 1933.

_____. *D.H. Lawrence's Princess, A Memory of Jessie Chambers*. Thames Ditton: The Merle Press, 1951.

Cowan, James C., *D.H. Lawrence's American Journey, A Study in Literature and Myth*. Cleveland and London: Case Western Reserve University Press, 1970.

_____. *D.H. Lawrence and the Trembling Balance*, University Park: Pennsylvania State University Press, 1990.

Cushman, Keith, *D.H. Lawrence at Work: The Emergence of the "Prussian Officer" Stories.* Sussex: Harvester, 1978.

_____ and Dennis Jackson (eds.), *D.H. Lawrence's Literary Inheritors.* London: Macmillan, 1991.

Daleski, H.M. *The Forked Flame: A Study of D.H. Lawrence.* Evanston, Ill.: Northwestern UP, 1965.

Darrock, Robert, *D.H. Lawrence in Australia.* South Melbourne: Macmillan, 1981.

Delany, Paul, *D.H. Lawrence's Nightmare: the Writer and his Circle in the Years of the Great War.* New York: Basic Books, 1978.

Delavenay, Emile, *D.H. Lawrence: L'Homme and La Genése de son Oeuvre: Les Annès de Formation, 1885-1919.* 2 vols. Paris: Librarire C. Klincksieck, 1969. (Shorter English edition, translated by Katherine M. Delavenay, *D.H. Lawrence: The Man and His Work: The Formative Years: 1885-1919.* London: Heinemann; Carbondale: Southern Illinois University Press, 1972.)

_____. *D.H. Lawrence and Edward Carpenter: a Study in Edwardian Transition.* London: Heinemann, 1971.

Dix, Carol. *D.H. Lawrence and Women.* London: The Macmillan Press, Ltd., 1980.

Donaldson G. and Kalnins, eds. M. *D.H. Lawrence in Italy and England,* Houndmills: Macmillan; New York: St. Martin's, 1998.

Dorbad, Leo J. *Sexually Balanced Relationships in the Novels of D.H. Lawrence.* New York: Peter Lang, 1991.

Douglas, Norman. *D.H. Lawrence and Maurice Magnus, A Plea for Better Manners.* Privately Printed, 1924.

Draper, R. P. *D.H. Lawrence,* New York: Twayne, 1964. (English Authors Series. Reprinted, London: Macmillan, 1976.)

_____. *D.H. Lawrence.* London: Routledge and Kegan Paul; New York: Humanities Press, 1969. (Profiles in Literature Series.)

_____ (ed.), *D.H. Lawrence, The Critical Heritage.* London: Routledge & Kegan Paul, 1970.

Eagleton, Terry. *Exiles and Emigrés: Studies in Modern Literature.* London: Chatto and Windus; New York: Schocken, 1970, 191-218.

Ebbatson, Roger. *Lawrence and the Nature Tradition: A Theme in English Fiction, 1859-1914.* Sussex: Harvester Press; Atlantic Highlands, N.J.: Humanities Press, 1980.

Eggert, Paul, and John Worthen, (eds.), *D.H. Lawrence and Comedy.* Cambridge: Cambridge University Press, 1996.

Eisenstein, Samuel A. *Boarding the Ship of Death: D H. Lawrence's Quester Heroes.* The Hague: Mouton, 1974.

Eliot, T.S. *After Strange Gods: A Primer of Modern Heresy.* London: Faber and Faber; New York: Harcourt, Brace, 1934.

Ellis, David, and Howard Mills (eds.), *D.H. Lawrence's Non-Fiction: Art, Thought and Genre.* Cambridge: Cambridge University Press, 1988.

Ellis, David and Ornella de Zordo (eds.), *D.H. Lawrence: Critical Assessments* 4 vols. East Sussex: Helm Information, 1992.

Fernihough, Anne. *D.H. Lawrence: Aesthetics and Ideology.* Oxford: Clarendon Press, 1993.

Fjagesund, Peter. *The Apocalyptic World of D.H. Lawrence.* Oslo, Norway: Norwegian University Press, 1991.

Ford, George H. *Double Measure, A Study of the Novels and Stories of D.H. Lawrence.* New York: Holt, Rinehart and Winston, 1965.

Forster, E.M. *Aspects of the Novel.* New York: Harcourt, Brace, 1927.

Freeman, Mary. *D.H. Lawrence: A Basic Study of His Ideas.* New York: Grosset and Dunlop, 1955.

Garcia, Reloy, and J. Karabatsos, (eds.), *A Concordance to the Poetry of D.H. Lawrence.* Lincoln: University of Nebraska Press, 1970.

_____. *A Concordance to the Short Fiction of D.H. Lawrence.* Lincoln: University of Nebrasks Press, 1972.

Gilbert, Sandra M. *D.H. Lawrence's "Sons and Lovers," "The Rainbow," "Women in Love," "The Plumed Serpent."* New York: Monarch Press, 1965.

_____. *Acts of Attention, The Poems of D.H. Lawrence.* Ithaca: Cornell University Press, 1972.

Goodheart, Eugene. *The Utopian Vision of D.H. Lawrence.* Chicago: University of Chicago Press, 1963.

Gordon, David J. *D.H. Lawrence as a Literary Critic.* New Haven and London: Yale University Press, 1966.

Green, Martin Burgess. *The Reputation of D.H. Lawrence in America.* Ann Arbor, Mich.: University of Michigan, 1966.

_____. *The von Richthofen Sisters: The Triumphant and the Tragic Modes of Love: Else and Frieda von Richthofen, Otto Gross, Max Weber, and D.H. Lawrence, in the Years 1870-1970.* London: Weidenfeld and Nicolson, 1974.

_____. *Subject-Object Relations in Wordsworth and Lawrence.* Ann Arbor, Mich.: UMI Research Press, 1987.

Gutierrez, Donald. *Lapsing Out: Embodiments of Death and Rebirth in the Last Writings of D.H. Lawrence.* London and Toronto: Associated University Presses, 1980.

Harris, Janice Hubbard. *The Short Fiction of D.H. Lawrence.* New Brunswick, N.J.: Rutgers University Press, 1984.

Heywood, Christopher (ed.), *D.H. Lawrence: New Studies.* London: Macmillan; New York: St. Martin's Press, 1987.

Hobsbaum, Philip. *A Reader's Guide to D.H. Lawrence.* London: Thames & Hudson, 1981.

Holbrook, David. *The Quest for Love.* London: Methuen, 1964.

_____. *Where D.H. Lawrence Was Wrong about Women.* London and Toronto: Associated University Presses, 1992.

Holderness, Graham. *Who's Who in D.H. Lawrence.* London: Hamish Hamilton; New York: Taplinger, 1976.

_____. *D.H. Lawrence, History, Ideology, and Fiction.* Dublin: Gill & Macmillan; Atlantic Highlands, N.J.: Humanities Press, 1982.

_____. *D.H. Lawrence: Life, Work and Criticism.* Fredricton, N.B., Canada: York Press, 1988.

Hostettler, Maya. *D.H. Lawrence: Travel Books and Fiction*. Berne: Peter Lang, 1985.

Hough, Graham. *The Dark Sun: A Study of D.H. Lawrence*. London, 1956: New York: Macmillan, 1957.

_____. *Two Exiles, Lord Byron and D.H. Lawrence*. Nottingham: University of Nottingham, 1956. (Reprinted in his *Image and Experience: Studies in a Literary Revolution*. London: Duckworth; Lincoln: University of Nebraska Press, 1960, 133-59.)

Hyde, G.M. *D.H. Lawrence and Translation*. London: Macmillan, 1981.

Hyde, H. Montgomery, (ed.), *The "Lady Chatterley's Lover Trial" (Regina v. Penguin Books Limited)*. London: Bodley Head, 1990.

Hyde, Virginia. *The Risen Adam: D.H. Lawrence's Revisionist Typology*. University Park: Pennsylvania State University Press, 1992.

Inniss, Kenneth B. *D.H. Lawrence's Bestiary: A Study of His Use of Animal Trope and Symbol*. The Hague and Paris: Mouton, 1971; New York: Humanities Press, 1972.

Janik, Del Ivan. *The Curve of Return: D.H. Lawrence's Travel Books*. Victoria, B.C.: University of Victoria Press, 1981.

Kalnins, Mara (ed.). *D.H. Lawrence: Centenary Essays*. Bristol: Bristol Classical Press, 1986.

Kelsey, Nigel. *D.H. Lawrence: Sexual Crisis*. London: Macmillan, 1991.

Kermode, Frank. *Lawrence*. London: Fontana, 1973.

Kiely, Robert. *Beyond Egotism: The Fiction of James Joyce, Virginia Woolf, and D.H. Lawrence*. Cambridge, Mass.: Harvard University Press, 1980.

Leavis, F. R. *D.H. Lawrence*. Cambridge: The Minority Press, 1930.

_____. *D.H. Lawrence: Novelist*, London: Chatto & Windus, 1955, New York: Knopf, 1956.

_____. *Thought, Words and Creativity: Art and Thought in D.H. Lawrence*. London: Chatto and Windus, 1976.

Lerner, Laurence. *The Truthtellers: Jane Austen, George Eliot, D.H. Lawrence*. London: Chatto; New York: Schocken, 1967.

Levy, Mervyn, (ed.), *Paintings of D.H. Lawrence*. New York: Viking; London: Cory, Adams, and McKay, 1964.

Lewiecki-Wilson, Cynthia. *Writing Against the Family: Gender in Lawrence and Joyce*. Carbondale: Southern Illinois University Press, 1994.

Lowell, Amy. *Poetry and Poets*, ed. Ferris Greenslet. Boston: Houghton, 1930.

MacLeod, Sheila. *Lawrence's Men and Women*. Heinemann, 1985.

Mailer, Norman. *The Prisoner of Sex*. London: Weidenfeld and Nicolson, 1971.

Malani, Hiran. *D.H. Lawrence: A Study of His Plays*. New Delhi, India: Arnold-Heinemann; Atlantic Highlands, N.J.: Humanities Press, 1982.

Manly, J.M. and Rickert, E.*Contemporary British Literature*. London: Harrap, 1928.

Marshall, Tom. *The Psychic Mariner: A Reading of the Poems of D.H. Lawrence*. New York: Viking, 1970.

May, Keith M. *Nietzsche and Modern Literature: Themes in Yeats, Rilke, Mann and Lawrence*. London: Macmillan, 1988.

Meyers, Jeffrey. *D.H. Lawrence and the Experience of Italy*. Philadelphia: University of Pennsylvania Press, 1982.

_____. (ed.), *D.H. Lawrence and Tradition*. London: Athlone, 1985.

_____. *The Legacy of D.H. Lawrence: New Essays*. London: Macmillan, 1987.

Miko, Stephen J. *Toward "Women in Love": The Emergence of a Lawrentian Aesthetic*. New Haven, Conn. and London: Yale University Press, 1971.

Miliaras, Barbara A. *Pillar of Flame: The Mythological Foundations of D.H. Lawrence's Sexual Philosophy*. New York, Berne, Frankfurt: Peter Lang, 1987.

Miller, Henry. *Notes on "Aaron's Rod" and Other Notes on Lawrence from the Paris Notebooks*. Edited by Seamus Cooney. Santa Barbara, Calif.: Black Sparrow Press, 1980a.

_____. *The World of D.H. Lawrence: A Passionate Appreciation*. Edited with an Introduction and Notes by Evelyn J. Hinz and John J. Teunissen. Santa Barbara, Calif.: Capra Press, 1980b.

Millett, Kate. *Sexual Politics*. New York: Doubleday, 1970.

Montgomery, Robert E. *The Visionary D.H. Lawrence: Beyond Philosophy and Art*. Cambridge: Cambridge University Press, 1994.

Moore, Harry T. and Frederick J. Hoffman (eds.), *The Achievement of D.H. Lawrence*. Noman, Okla.: University of Oklahoma Press, 1953.

_____. (ed.), *Poste Restante, A Lawrence Travel Calendar*. Berkeley and Los Angeles: University of California, 1956.

_____ and Warren Roberts. *D.H. Lawrence and His World*. New York: Viking; London: Thames & Hudson, 1966.

_____ and Robert B. Partlow, Jr. (eds.), *D.H. Lawrence: The Man Who Lived*. Carbondale: Southern Illinois University Press, 1980.

Moore, Oliver. *Further Reflections on the Death of a Porcupine*. London: Blue Moon Press, 1932.

Moynahan, Julian, *The Deed of Life. The Novels and Tales of D.H. Lawrence*. Princeton NJ: Princeton UP, 1963; London: Oxford UP, 19636

Murry, John Middleton, *Love, Freedom and Society. An Analytical Comparison of D.H. Lawrence and Albert Schweitzer*. London: Jonathan Cape, 1957.

Nin, Anais. *D.H. Lawrence: An Unprofessional Study*. Paris: Edward W. Titus, 1932.

Niven, Alastair. *D.H. Lawrence: The Novels*. Cambridge: Cambridge University Press, 1978.

_____. *D.H. Lawrence: The Writer and His Work*. Harlow, Essex: Longman, 1980.

Nixon, Cornelia. *Lawrence's Leadership Politics and the Turn Against Women*. Berkeley: University of California Press, 1986.

Oates, Joyce Carol. *The Hostile Sun: The Poetry of D.H. Lawrence*. Los Angeles: Black Sparrow Press, 1973.

Olson, Charles. *D.H. Lawrence and the High Temptation of the Mind*. Santa Barbara, Calif.: Black Sparrow Press, 1980.

Panichas, George A. *Adventure in Consciousness: The Meaning of D.H. Lawrence's Religious Quest*. The Hague: Mouton, 1964.

Pinto, Vivan de Sola. *D.H. Lawrence: Prophet of the Midlands*. Nottingham: University of Nottingham, 1951. (Twenty-four-page pamphlet of public lecture.)

_____. (ed.), *D.H. Lawrence after Thirty Years, 1930-1960*. Nottingham: Curwen Press, 1960. (Catalog of exhibition held 17 June-30 July, 1960.)

Poplawski, Paul. *Promptings of Desire: Creativity and the Religious Impulse in the Works of D.H. Lawrence*. Westport, Conn.: Greenwood Press, 1993.

Potter, Stephen. *D.H. Lawrence, A First Study*. London: Jonathan Cape, 1930.

Preston, Peter, and Hoare, Peter. (eds.), *D.H. Lawrence in the Modern World*. London: Macmillan, 1989.

Pritchard, R.E. *D.H. Lawrence: Body of Darkness*. London: Hutchinson Univ. Library, 1971.

Rolph, C. H. (ed.), *The Trial of Lady Chatterley: Regina v. Penguin Books Limited. The Transcript of the Trial*. London: Penguin Books, Inc., 1961, 1990. (With a new foreword for this thirtieth anniversary edition by Geoffrey Robinson.)

Rosenfeld, Paul. *Men Seen: Twenty-Four Modern Authors*. New York: Dial Press, 1925.

Ross, Charles L. and Jackson, Dennis, [Eds.]. *Editing Lawrence*. Ann Arbor: University of Michigan Press, 1995.

Ruderman, Judith. *D.H. Lawrence and the Devouring Mother: The Search for a Patriarchal Ideal of Leadership*. Durham, N.C.: Duke University Press, 1984.

Sagar, Keith. *The Art of D.H. Lawrence*. Cambridge: Cambridge University Press, 1966.

_____ (ed.) *A D.H. Lawrence Handbook*. Manchester: Manchester University Press, 1982.

_____. *D.H. Lawrence: Life Into Art*. Harmondsworth, England: Viking Penguin, 1985.

Schorer, Mark. *D.H. Lawrence [An Anthology]*. New York: Dell, 1968a (Contains "The Life of D.H. Lawrence," 3-106.)

_____. *The Phoenix Is My Badge and Sign, Lawrence in the War Years*. Stanford, Calif.: Stanford University, 1968b. (Fifteen-page pamphlet based on a short talk.)

_____. *The World We Imagine: Selected Essays*. New York: Farrar, Straus, 1968.

Seligmann, Herbert J. *D.H. Lawrence, An American Interpretation*. New York: Thomas Seltzer, 1924.

Seltzer, Adele. *D.H. Lawrence, The Man and His Work*. New York: Thomas Seltzer, 1922.

Siegel, Carol. *Lawrence Among the Women: Wavering Boundaries in Women's Literary Traditions*. Charlottesville: University Press of Virginia, 1991.

Simpson, Hilary. *D.H. Lawrence and Feminism*. London and Canberra: Croom Helm, 1982.

Singh, Tajindar. *The Literary Criticism of D.H. Lawrence*. New Delhi: Sterling; New York: Envoy, 1984.

Sinzelle, Claude M. *The Geographical Background of the Early Works of D.H. Lawrence*. Paris: Didier, 1964.

Sklar, Sylvia. *The Plays of D.H. Lawrence*. New York and London, 1975.

Sklenicka, Carol. *D.H. Lawrence and the Child.* Columbia and London: University of Missouri Press, 1991.

Spilka, Mark. *The Love Ethic of D.H. Lawrence.* Bloomington: Indiana University Press, 1955; London: Dennis Dobson, 1958.

_____ (ed). *D.H. Lawrence: Twentieth Century Views*, Englewood Cliffs, N.J.: Prentice Hall Inc., 1963.

_____. *Renewing the Normative D.H. Lawrence: A Personal Progress.* Columbia: University of Missouri Press, 1992.

Squires, Michael. *The Pastoral Novel: Studies in George Eliot, Thomas Hardy and D.H. Lawrence.* Charlottesville: University Press of Virginia, 1974.

_____. *The Creation of "Lady Chatterley's Lover."* Baltimore: Johns Hopkins University Press, 1983.

_____ and Dennis Jackson, (eds.), *D.H. Lawrence's "Lady": A New Look at "Lady Chatterley's Lover."* Athens: University of Georgia Press, 1985.

_____ and Keith Cushman, (eds.), *The Challenge of D.H. Lawrence.* Madison: University of Wisconsin Press, 1990.

_____, (ed.), *D.H. Lawrence's Manuscripts: The Correspondence of Frieda Lawrence, Jake Zeitlin and Others.* New York: St. Martin's;. London: Macmillan, 1991.

Stewart, Jack. *The Vital Art of D.H. Lawrence: Vision and Expression.* Carbondale: Southern Illinois University Press, 1999.

Storch, Margaret. *Sons and Adversaries: Women in William Blake and D.H. Lawrence.* Knoxville: University of Tennessee Press, 1990.

Strachey, John. *The Coming Struggle for Power.* London: Gollancz, 1932.

Swigg, Richard. *Lawrence, Hardy and American Literature.* New York: Oxford University Press, 1972.

Takeo Iida, (ed.), *The Reception of D.H. Lawrence Around the World.* Fukuoka, Japan: Kyushu University Press, 1999.

Tedlock, E. W. *D.H. Lawrence, Artist and Rebell: A Study of Lawrence's Fiction.* Albuquerque: New Mexico UP, 1963.

Tindall, William York. *D.H. Lawrence and Susan His Cow.* New York: Columbia University Press, 1939.

Tiverton, Father William (Martin Jarrett-Kerr). *D.H. Lawrence and Human Existence.* New York: Philosophical Library, Inc., 1951. With a foreword by T.S. Eliot.

Vivas, Eliseo. *D.H. Lawrence, The Failure and Triumph of Art.* Evanston: Northwestern UP, 1960; London: Allen & Unwin, 1961.

Weiss, Daniel. *Oedipus in Nottingham: D.H. Lawrence.* Seattle: University of Washington Press, 1962.

West, Rebecca. *D.H. Lawrence.* London: Martin Secker, 1930.

_____. *Elegy. An in Memoriuam Tribute to D.H. Lawrence.* New York: Phoenix Book Shop; London: Secker, 1930.

Widmer, Kingsley. *The Art of Perversity: D.H. Lawrence's Shorter Fictions.* Seattle: University of Washington Press, 1962.

_____. *Defiant Desire: Some Dialectical Legacies of D.H. Lawrence.* Carbondale: Southern Illinois University Press, 1992.

Williams, Linda Ruth. *D.H. Lawrence: A Literary Life*. London: Macmillan, 1989.

_____. *Sex in the Head: Visions of Feminity and Film in D.H. Lawrence*. Hemel Hempstead: Harvester Wheatsheaf, 1993.

Worthen, John. *D.H. Lawrence and the Idea of the Novel*. London: Macmillan; Totowa, N.J.: Rowman, 1979.

_____. *Cold Hearts and Coronets: Lawrence, the von Richthofens and the Weekleys*. Nottingham: D.H. Lawrence Centre, 1995. (Worthen's inaugural lecture as Professor of D.H. Lawrence Studies at Nottingham.)

Zytaruk, George J. *D.H. Lawrence's Response to Russian Literature*. The Hague: Mouton, 1971.

## Essays and Articles

Abercrombie, Lascelles. "The Poet as Novelist." *Manchester Guardian* (2 July 1913), 7

Aiken, Conrad. "The Melodic Line," in *Dial* 67 (August 1919a), 97-100.

_____. "Disintegration in Modern Poetry," in *Dial* 76 (June 1924), 535-40.

_____. "Mr Lawrence's Prose," in *Dial* 83 (October 1927): 343-46.

Alcorn, Marshall W., Jr. "Lawrence and the Issue of Spontaneity," in *D.H. Laurence Review* 15 (1982), 147-65.

Aldington, Richard. "DHL as Poet," in *Saturday Review of Literature* 2 (1 May 1926), 749-50.

_____. Introduction to *The Spirit of Place*. London: William Heinemann, 1935.

_____. "DHL: Ten Years After," in *Saturday Review of Literature* (20 June 1939), 3-4, 14, 24.

Alexander, Edward. "Thomas Carlyle and DHL: A Parallel," in *University of Toronto Quarterly* 37 (April 1968), 248-67.

Alldritt, Keith. "The Europeans of DHL," in *Etudes Lawrenciennes* 9 (1993), 11-19.

Anderson, Sherwood. "A Man's Mind," in *New Republic* 63 (21 May 1930), 22-23.

_____. "A Man's Song of Life," in *Virginia Quarterly* 9 (January 1933), 108-14.

Anonymous. Unsigned review  [of *The White Peacock*] in *Morning Post*, (9 February 1911), 2.

Arnold, Armin. "DHL and Thomas Mann," in *Comparative Literature* 13 (Winter 1961), 33-38.

_____. "DHL, The Russians, and Giovanni Verga," in *Comparative Literature Studies* 2 (1965), 249-57.

Arvin, Newton. "DHL and Fascism." in *New Republic* 89 (16 December 1936), 219. (Rejoinder to Wells [1936], *op. cit.*)

Atkins, Antony. "Textual Biography: Writing the Lives of Books," in *Writing the Lives of Writers* (eds. Gould-Warwick, Staley-Thomas), Houndmills: Macmillan, 1998, 277-92.

Atkins, John. "Lawrence's Social Landscape," in *Books and Bookmen* 15 (July 1970), 24-26.

Auden, W.H. "Some Notes on DHL," in *Nation* 164 (26 April 1947), 482-84.

_____. "Heretics," in *Literary Opinion in America*. (ed. M.D. Zabel.) New York: Harpers, 1951, 256-59.

Axelrad, Allan M."Wish Fulfillment in the Wilderness: D.H. Lawrence and the Leatherstocking Tales," in *American Quarterly* 39:4, (Winter 1987), 564-585.

Balbert, Peter. "From Hemingway to Lawrence to Mailer: Survival and Sexual Identity in *A Farewell to Arms*," in *Hemingway Review* 3 (Fall 1983), 30-43.

_____. "Silver Spoon to Devil's Fork: Diana Trilling and the Sexual Ethics of *Mr. Noon*," in *The D.H. Lawrence Review* 20 (Summer 1988), 237-50.

_____. "From *Lady Chatterley's Lover* to *The Deer Park*: Lawrence, Mailer, and the Dialectic of Erotic Risk," in *Studies in the Novel* 22 (1990), 67-81.

Banerjee, A. "D.H. Lawrence as His Taos Contemporaries Saw Him," in *Kobe College Studies* (1998), Dec. 45:2, (132), 1-13.

Bantock, G. H. "D.H. Lawrence and the Nature of Freedom," in *Freedom and Authority in Education*. London: Faber, 1952.

Baron, Helen. "The Surviving Galley Proofs of Lawrence's *Sons and Lovers*, in *Studies in Bibliography* 45 (1992), 231-51.

_____. "Lawrence's *Sons and Lovers* versus Garnett's," in *Essays in Criticism* XLII, 4 (October 1992), 265-78.

_____. "Editing *Sons and Lovers*," in *Journal of the D.H. Lawrence Society* (1994-95), 8-20.

_____. "Disseminated Consciousness," in *Essays in Criticism* (1998, Oct.), 48:4, 357-78.

Bartlett, N. "The Failure of DHL," in *Australian Quarterly* 19 (December 1947), 87-102.

_____. "Aldous Huxley and DHL," in *Australian Quarterly* 36 (1964), 76-84.

Bates, H.E. "Lawrence and the Writers of Today," in his *The Modern Short Story: A Critical Survey*. London and New York: Nelson, 1941, 194-213.

Beer, John and Malcolm Elwin. "Ford's Impression of the Lawrences," in *Times Literary Supplement*, (5 May 1972), 520.

Beirne, Raymond M. "Lawrence's Night Letter on Censorship and Obscenity," in *The D.H. Lawrence Review*. 7, (1974), 321-22.

Bell, Michael. "DHL and Thomas Mann: Unbewusste Brüderschaft," in *Etudes Lawrenciennes* 9 (1993), 185-97/

Bennett, David. "Burghers, Burglars, and Masturbators: The Sovereign Spender in the Age of Consumerism," in *New Literary History: A Journal of Theory and Interpretation* (1999) Spring, 30:2, 269-94.

_____. "Heroic Vitalists of the Twentieth Century," in his *A Century of Hero-Worship* 1944, 205-53.

Bentley, Eric R. "DHL, John Thomas and Dionysos," in *New Mexico Quarterly Review* 12 (1941), 133-43.

Bien, Peter. "The Critical Philosophy of D.H. Lawrence," in *The D.H. Lawrence Review* 17:2, (Summer 1984), 127-134.

Björkman, Edwin. "Introduction," in *The Widowing of Mrs. Holroyd* by D.H. Lawrence. London: Duckworth, 1914, vii-x.

Black, Michael. "A Kind of Bristling in the Darkness: Memory and Metaphor in Lawrence," in *Critical Review* (Melbourne) 32 (1992), 29-44.

_____. "'Theorizing Myself Out'—Lawrence after *Sons and Lovers*: 'The Burns Novel' and 'Esla Culverwell,'" in *Cambridge Quarterly,* (1997), 26:3, 242-62.

_____. "D.H. Lawrence: Spontaneity and Revision as Aesthetic," in *Cambridge Quarterly* (1999), 28:2, 150-66.

Blackmur, R. P. "D.H. Lawrence and Expressive Form," in *The Double Agent*. New York: Arrow Editions, 1935.

Blanchard, Lydia. "Love and Power: A Reconsideration of Sexual Politics in DHL," in *Modern Fiction Studies* 21 (1975), 431-43.

_____. "*Women in Love*: Mourning Becomes Narcissism," in *Mosaic* 15 (1982), 105-18.

_____. "The Savage Pilgrimage and Katherine Mansfield: A Study in Literary Influence, Anxiety, and Subversion," in *Modern Language Quarterly* 47 (1986), 48-65.

Booth, Howard J. "'Give Me Differences': Lawrence, Psychoanalysis, and Race," in *The D.H. Lawrence Review* (1997-98), 27:2-3, 171-96.

Boulton, James T. "D.H. Lawrence: Letter Writer," in *Renaissance and Modern Studies*, 29 (1985), 86-100.

Brennan, Joseph. "Male Power in the Work of DHL," in *Paunch* 63-64 (1990), 199-207.

Bryden, Ronald. "Strindberg in the Midlands," in *Observer*. London, (19 March 1967), 25.

Buermyer, L.L. "Lawrence as Psychoanalyst," in *New York Evening Post Literary Review* 16 (July 1921), 6.

Burwell, Rose Marie. "A Catalogue of D.H. Lawrence's Reading from Early Childhood", *The D.H. Lawrence Review*, ed. James C. Cowan, 111, No.1, Spring 1970.

_____. "Schopenhauer, Hardy and Lawrence: Toward a New Understanding of *Sons and Lovers*," in *Western Humanities Review* 28 (Spring 1974), 105-17.

Butler, Gerald J. "Sexual Experience in DHL's *The Rainbow*," in *Recovering Literature* 2 (1973), 1-92.

_____. (ed.)"This is Carbon: A Defense of D.H. Lawrence's *The Rainbow* Against His Admirers," in *Recovering Literature: A Journal of Contextualist Criticism* (1999), 25, xxii, 151.

Carswell, Catherine. "D.H. Lawrence in his Letters," in *Nineteenth Century*. CXII (November 1932), 631-40.

Carter, Angela. "Lorenzo as 'Closet Queen,'" in her *Nothing Sacred: Selected Writings*, London: Virago Press, 1982, 207-14. (Originally published as "The Naked Lawrence" in *New Society* 31 [13 February 1975], 398-99.)

_____. "DHL, Scholarship Boy," in *New Society* 60 (3 June 1982), 391-2.

Carter, John. "*The Rainbow* Prosecution," in *Times Literary Supplement* (27 February 1969), 216.

Chambers, Jessie ("E.T."). "The Literary Formation of DHL," in *European Quarterly* 1 (May 1934), 36-45. (Also in Chambers [1935]: 91-123.)

Chesterton, G.K. "The End of the Moderns," in *London Mercury* 27 (January 1933), 228-33.

Church, Richard. "Three Established Poets," in *Spectator* (3 August 1929), 164-65.

Clarke, Ian. "Lawrence and the Drama of His European Contemporaries," in *Etudes Lawrenciennes* 9 (1993), 173-86.

Clements, Richard. "The Genius of DHL," in *Central Literary Magazine* (July 1938), 272-78.

Cohen, Marvin, R. "The Prophet and the Critic: A Study in Classic Lawrentian Literature," in *Texas Studies in Literature and Language* 22 (1980), 1-21.

Cooper, Frederic T. "The Theory of Heroes and Some Recent Novels," in *Bookman* 33 (April 1911), 193-196.

Cowan, James C. "The Function of Allusions and Symbols in DHL's *The Man Who Died*," in *American Imago* 17 (Summer 1960), 241-53.

_____. "D.H. Lawrence's The Princess as Ironic Romance," *Studies in Short Fiction*. Newberry, SC, 4, (1967), 245-251.

_____. "Lawrence's Romantic Values: Studies in Classic American Literature," in *Ball State University Forum* 8 (Winter 1967), 30-35.

_____. "DHL's Quarrel with Christianity," *University of Tulsa Department of English Monographs* no. 7: *Literature and Theology* (1969), 32-43.

_____. "Lawrence, Freud and Masturbation," in *Mosaic*, (March, 1995) 28:1, 69-98.

Cox, Gary D. "DHL and F.M. Dostoevsky: Mirror Images of Murderous Aggression," in *Modern Fiction Studies* 29 (1983), 175-82.

Craig, David. "Fiction and the Rising Industrial Classes," in *Essays in Criticism* 17 (January 1967), 64-74.

Cushman, Keith. "Lawrence, Compton Mackenzie, and the 'Semi-Literary Cats' of Capri.," in *Etudes Lawrenciennes* 9 (1993), 139-53.

_____. "Lawrence's Dust-Jackets: A Selection with Commentary," in *The D.H. Lawrence Review* (1999). 28:1-2, 29-52.

Danby, J.F. "DHL," in *Cambridge Journal* 4 (February 1951), 273-89.

Daniel, John. "DHL—His Reputation Today," in *London Review* 6 (Winter 1969/70), 25-33.

Davies, Cecil. "D.H. Lawrence: *The Merry-Go-Round*: A Challenge to the Theatre," in *The D.H. Lawrence Review*. 16:2, (Summer, 1983), 133-163.

Delany, Paul. "Lawrence and E.M. Forster: Two Rainbows," in *The D.H. Lawrence Review* 8 (Spring 1975), 54-62.

_____. "Lawrence and Forster: First Skirmish with Bloomsbury," in *The D.H. Lawrence Review* 11 (Spring 1978), 63-72.

Diez-Medrano, C. "Fictions of Rape: The Teller and the Tale in D.H. Lawrence's 'None of That,'" in *Forum for Modern Language Studies*, (1996, Oct.) 32:4, 303-13.

Dillon, M.C. "Love in *Women in Love*: A Phenomenological Analysis," in *Philosophy and Literature* 2 (Fall 1978), 190-208.

Doherty, Gerald. "The Salvator Mundi Touch: Messianic Typology in DHL's *Women in Love*," in *Ariel* 13, no.3 (1982), 53-71.

_____. "The Nirvana Dimension: DHL's Quarrel with Buddhism," in *The D.H. Lawrence Review* 15 (1982), 51-67.

_____. "The Third Encounter: Paradigms of Courtship in DHL's Shorter Fiction," in *The D.H. Lawrence Review* 17 (1984), 135-51.

_____. "The Darkest Source: DHL, Tantric Yoga, and *Women in Love*," in *Essays in Literature* 11 (1984), 211-22.

_____. "The Throes of Aphrodite: The Sexual Dimension in DHL's *The Plumed Serpent*," in *Studies in the Humanities* 12 (December 1985), 67-78.

_____. "White Mythologies: DHL and the Deconstructive Turn," in *Criticism* 29 (Fall 1987), 477-96.

_____. "The Dialectic of Space in D.H. Lawrence's *Sons and Lovers*," in *Modern Fiction Studies*, (Summer 1993), 39:2, 327-743.

_____. "Death and Rhetoric of Representation in D.H. Lawrence's *Women in Love*," in *Mosaic*, (March 1994), 27:1, 55-72.

_____. Metaphor and Mental Disturbance: the Case of *Lady Chatterley's Lover*," in *Style* (Spring 1996), 30:1, 113-29.

_____. "The Art of Appropriation: The Rhetoric of Sexuality in D.H. Lawrence," in *Style* (Summer 1996), 30:2, 289-308.

Draper, R.P. "DH: on Mother-Love," in *Essays in Criticism* 8 (July 1958), 285-89.

_____. "Great Writers 4:DHL," in *Time and Tide* 44 (24-30 January 1963), 23-24.

_____. "A Short Guide to D.H. Lawrence Studies," in *Critical Survey* ii. No. 4, (Summer 1966).

_____. "The Defeat of Feminism:  D.H. Lawrence's *The Fox* and 'The Woman Who Rode Away,'" in *Studies in Short Fiction* 3, (1966), 186-198.

Eagleton, Sandra. "One Feminist's Approach to Teaching DHL," in *The D.H. Lawrence Review* 19 (Fall 1987), 325-30.

Eggert, Paul. "Identification of Lawrence's Futurist Readings," in *Notes and Queries* 29, (1982), 342-44.

_____. "D.H. Lawrence and His Audience: The Case of *Mr Noon*," in *Southern Review: Literary and Interdisciplinary Essays*, 18 (3), (November 1985), 298-307.

_____. "DHL and Literary Collaboration," in *Etudes Lawrenciennes* 3 (May 1988), 153-62.

_____. "Discourse versus Authorship: The Baedeker Travel Guide and D.H. Lawrence's *Twilight in Italy*," in *Texts and Textuality: Textual Instability, Theory, and Interpretation* (ed. Philip Cohen), New York: Garland, 1997, 207-34.

_____. "C.S. Pierce, D.H. Lawrence, and Representation: Artistic Form and Polarities," in *D.H. Lawrence Review* (1999), 28:1-2, 97-113.

Eliot, T.S. "London Letter," in *Dial* 73 (September 1922), 329-31.

_____. "The Contemporary Novel" (English Text of "Le roman anglais contemporain," in *La Nouvelle Revue Française* 28) (1 May 1927), 669-75.

Ellis, David. "Lawrence in His Letters," in *Etudes Lawrenciennes* (May 1988, 41-49.

_____. "Lawrence, Wordsworth and 'Anthropomorphic Lust,'" in *Cambridge Quarterly* 23, no.3 (1994), 230-42.

_____. "D.H. Lawrence and the Female Body," in *Essays in Criticism: A Quarterly Journal of Literary Criticism*. Oxford, 46:2, (April 1996), 136-52.

_____. "Explaining the Abnormal: D.H. Lawrence and Tuberculosis," in *Writing the Lives of Writers* (eds. Gould-Warwick, Staley-Thomas F), Houndmills: Macmillan, 1998, 204-11.

_____. "Lawrence and Forster in 1915," in *Cambridge Quarterly*, (1998), 27:1, 1-14.

Ellmann, Richard. "Lawrence and His Demon," in *New Mexico Quarterly* 22 (Winter 1952), 385-93.

Empson, William. "Swinburne and DHL," in *Times Literary Supplement* (20 February 1969), 185.

Engelberg, Edward. "Escape from the Circles of Experience: D.H. Lawrence's *The Rainbow* as a Modern *Bildungsroman*," in PMLA, LXXCIII (March, 1963), 103-13.

_____. "The Displaced Cathedral in Flaubert, James, Lawrence, and Kafka," in *Arcadia* (Berlin) 21 no.3 (1986), 245-62.

Farr, Judith. "DHL's Mother as Sleeping Beauty: The 'Still Queen' of His Poems and Fictions," in *Modern Fiction Studies* 36 (Summer 1990), 195-200.

Fenton, James. "Men, Women & Beasts," in *New York Review of Books* (1998, Oct. 22), 45:16, 51, 54-58.

Fiedler, Leslie A. "The Literati of the Four-Letter Word," in *Playboy* 8 (June 1961), 85, 125,28.

Finney, Brian H. "A Newly Discovered Text of D.H. Lawrence's 'The Lovely Lady,'" in *Yale University Library Gazette* 49 (1974), 245-52.

Fisher, William J. "Peace and Passivity: The Poetry of D.H. Lawrence," in *South Atlantic Quarterly*. (9 July 1956), 337-48.

Fjagesund, Peter. "DHL, Knut Hamsun and Pan," in *English Studies* 72, no.5 (October 1991), 421-25.

Flay, M. "Lawrence and Dostoevsky in 1915," in *English Studies* 69 (June 1988), 254-66.

Fletcher, John Gould. "Mr Lawrence's *New Poems*," in *Freeman* 1 (21 July 1920), 451-52.

Ford, George H. "Jessie Chambers' Last Tape on D.H. Lawrence," in *Mosaic: A Journal for the Interdisciplinary Study of Literature*, 6:3, (1973), 1-12.

Forster, E.M. "DHL," in *Listener* 3 (30 April 1930), 753-54.

Foster, D.W. "Lawrence, Sex and Religion," in *Theology* 64 (January 1961), 8-13.

Freeman, Mary. "DHL in Valhalla," in *New Mexico Quarterly* 10 (November 1942), 211-24.

_____. "Lawrence and Fascism," in *D.H. Lawrence: A Basic Study of His Ideas*. Gainesville, Fla.: University of Florida Press, 1955.

Galbraith, Mary. "Feeling Moments in the Work of DHL," in *Paunch* 63-64 (December 1990), 15-38.

Garlington, Jack. "Lawrence—With Misgivings," in *South Atlantic Quarterly* 59 (Summer 1960), 404-8.

Garnett, David. Review of Huxley's *Letters* in *The Saturday Review of Literature* (October 1932).

Garnett, Edward. "Art and the Moralists: Mr. DHL's Work," in *Dial* 61 (16 November 1916), 377-81. (Reprinted in his *Friday Nights: First Series*. London: Cape, 1929, 117-28.)

_____. "Introduction," to *A Collier's Friday Night* by D.H. Lawrence, 1st edition. London: Martin Secker, 1934. v-vii.

_____. "DHL: His Posthumous Papers," in *London Mercury* 35 (December 1936), 152-60.

Ghiselin, B. "DHL and a New World," in *Western Review* 9 (Spring 1947), 150-59.

Gibbon, Perceval. "A Novel of Quality," in *Bookman* 44 (August 1913), 213.

Gifford, Henry. "Anna, Lawrence and the Law," in *Critical Quarterly* 1 (Autumn 1959), 203-6.

Gilbert, Sandra M. "Feminism and DHL: Some Notes toward a Vindication of His Rites," in *Anais* 9 (1991), 92-100.

_____. "D.H. Lawrence's Mexican Hat Dance: Rereading *The Plumed Serpent*," in *Rereading Texts/Rethinking Critical Presuppositions: Essays in Honour of H.M. Daleski* (eds. Rimmon, Kenan, Shlomith, Toker-Leona, Barzilai-Shuli), Frankfurt: Peter Lang, 1997, 291-304.

Gilchrist, Susan Y. "DHL and E.M. Forster: A Failed Friendship," in *Etudes Lawrenciennes* 9 (1993), 127-38.

Glicksberg, Charles I. "DHL and Science," in *Scientific Monthly* 73 (August 1951), 99-104.

Good, Jan. "Toward a Resolution of Gender Identity Confusion: The Relationship of Henry and March in *The Fox*," in *The D.H. Lawrence Review* 18 (1985-86), 217-27.

Gordon, David J. "DHL's Dual Myth of Origin," in *Sewanee Review* 89 (1981a), 83-94.

_____. "Sex and Language in DHL," in *Twentieth Century Literature* 27 (1981b), 362-75.

Gordon, Rosemary. "Look! He Has Come Through!: DHL, Women and Individuation," in *Journal of Analytical Psychology* 23 (1978), 258-74.

Green, Eleanor H. "Blueprints for Utopia: The Political Ideas of Nietzsche and DHL," in *Renaissance and Modern Studies* 18 (1974), 141-61.

_____. "Schopenhauer and DHL on Sex and Love," in *DHL Review* 8 (Fall 1975a), 329-45.

_____. "The *Will zur Macht* and DHL," in *Massachusetts Studies in English* 10 (Winter 1975b), 25-30.

_____. "Nietzsche, Helen Corke, and DHL," in *American Notes and Queries* 15 (1976), 56-59.

_____. "Lawrence, Schopenhauer, and the Dual Nature of the Universe," in *South Atlantic Bulletin* 62 (November 1977), 84-92.

Greenfield, Barbara. "In Support of Psychoanalyzing Literary Characters," in *Journal of the American Academy of Psychoanalysis* 12 (1984), 127-38.

Greer, Germaine. "Sex, Lies and Old Pork Pies," in *Independent on Sunday* (London) (3 June 1990), 9-10.

Gurko, Leo. "D.H. Lawrence's Greatest Collection of Short Stories—What Holds It Together," in *Modern Fiction Studies* 18, (1972), 173-82.

Gutierrez, Donald. "A New Heaven and an Old Earth: DHL's *Apocalypse*, Apocalyptic and the Book of Revelation," in *Review of Existential Psychology and Psychiatry* 15, no.1 (1977), 61-85.

_____. "The Ancient Imagination of DHL," in *Twentieth Century Literature* 27 (1981), 178-96.

_____. "Vitalism in DHL's Theory of Fiction," in *Essays in Arts and Sciences* 16 (May 1987), 65-71.

Hamalian, Leo. "DHL and Black Writers," in *Journal of Modern Literature* 16 (Spring 1990), 579-96.

_____. "England Our England: D.H. Lawrence and George Orwell," in *South Dakota Review*, (1992, Summer), 30:2, 114-27.

Harris, Janice H. "DHL and Kate Millett," in *Massachusetts Review* 15 (1974), 522-29.

_____. "Sexual Antagonism in DHL's Early Leadership Fiction," in *Modern Language Studies* 7 (Spring 1977), 43-52.

Hayman, David. "Attitudinal Dynamics in Narrative: Flaubert, Lawrence, Joyce," in *Journal of Modern Literature*, (Fall, 1995), 19:2, 201-14.

Heath, Jane. "Helen Corke and DHL: Sexual Identity and Literary Relations," in *Feminist Studies* 11 (Summer 1985), 317-42.

Heppenstall, Rayner, "Outsiders and Others," in *Twentieth Century* (November 1955), 453-59.

Herrick, Jeffrey. "The Vision of *Look! We Have Come Through!*," in *The D.H. Lawrence Review* 14:3 (Fall 1981), 217-237.

Hervey, Grant Madison. "The Genius of Mr. DHL." in *Nation and Athenaeum* 39 (21 August 1926), 581-2.

Hinz, Evelyn J. "DHL's Clothes Metaphor," in *The D.H. Lawrence Review* 1 (Summer 1968), 87-113.

_____. "The Beginning and the End:  D H Lawrence's *Psychoanalysis* and *Fantasia*," in *Dalhousie Review*, 52, (1972a), 251-65.

_____. "*Sons and Lovers:* The Archetypal Dimensions of Lawrence's Oedipal Tragedy," in *D.H. Laurence  Review* 5 (Spring 1972b), 26-53. 4 (1970), 319-33.

_____. "*Ancient Art and Ritual* and *The Rainbow*," in *Dalhousie Review* 58 (1979), 617-37.

_____ and John J. Teunissen. "'They Thought of *Sons and Lovers*': DHL and Thomas Wolfe," in *Southern Quarterly* 29, No.3 (Spring 1991), 77-89.

Hirai, Masako. "Mother-Son: The Hahakoi Novels of Tanizaki and Lawrence," in *Kobe College Studies* 662 (1998 Mar.) 44:3 (130, 13-23.

Hoerner, Dennis. "Connie Chatterley: A Case of Spontaneous Therapy," in *Energy and Character: Journal of Bioenergetic Research* 12 (1981), 48-55.

_____. "Ursula, Anton, and the 'Sons of God': Armor and Core in *The Rainbow's* Third Generation," in *Paunch* 63-64 (December 1990), 173-98..

Hoffman, Frederick J. "Lawrence's 'Quarrel' with Freud," in *Freudianism and the Literary Mind*. Baton Rouge, La.: Louisiana State University Press, 1945.

_____. From "From Surrealism to 'The Apocalypse': A Development in Twentieth Century Irrationalism," in *English Literary History*. XV, (June 1948), 147-65.

Holmes, Colin. "A Study of D.H. Lawrence's Social Origins," in *Literature and History: A New Journal for the Humanities* 6, (1980), 82-93.

Honig, Edwin. "The Ideal in Symbolic Fictions," in *New Mexico Quarterly* 23 (1953), 153-68.

Hough, Graham. "DHL and the Novel," in *Adelphi* 30, no.4 (1954), 365-82.

Humma John B. "DHL as Friedrich Nietzsche," in *Philological Quarterly* 53 (1974a), 110-20.

_____. "Melville's *Billy Budd* and Lawrence's 'The Prussian Officer': Old Adams and New," in *Essays in Literature* 1 (1974b), 83-88.

_____. "Pan and 'The Rocking-Horse Winner,'" in *Essays in Literature* (Illinois) 5 (1978), 53-60.

_____. "The Imagery of *The Plumed Serpent*: The Going-Under of Organicism," in *The D.H. Lawrence Review* (Fall 1982), 197-218.

_____. "Lawrence in Another Light: *Women in Love* and Existentialism," in *Studies in the Novel* 24, no.4 (Winter 1992), 392-409.

Hunt, Violet. "A First Novel of Power," (review of *The White Peacock)* in *Daily Chronicle* (10 February 1911), 6.

Huxley, Aldous. "The Censor," in *Vanity Fair*. November 1929, 88-89.Reprinted as "To the Puritan all Things are Impure," in *Music at Night and Other Essays* by Aldous Huxley, London, Chatto & Windus, 1931, (1949), 173-83. Reprinted: as "ditto" in *On Art and Artists,* by Aldous Huxley, ed. with Intro. by Morris Philipson. New York: Harper Brothers, 1960, 69-75.

_____. "Introduction" to *The Letters of D.H. Lawrence*. New York: The Viking Press, Inc., 1932.

_____. "DHL," in his *The Olive Tree and Other Essays*. London: Chatto and Windus, 1936, 199-238.

Ingersoll, Earl G. "The Failure of Bloodbrotherhood in Melville's *Moby-Dick* and Lawrence's *Women in Love*," in *Midwest Quarterly* 30 (1989), 458-77.

_____. "Virginia Woolf and DHL: Exploring the Dark," in *English Studies* 71 (1990), 125-32.

_____. "Staging the Gaze in D.H. Lawrence's *Women in Love*," in *Studies-in-the Novel* 26:3, (Fall, 1994), 268-80.

_____. "Gender and Language in *Sons and Lovers*," in *Midwest Quarterly: A Journal of Contemporary Thought,* 37:4, (Summer, 1996), 434-47

James, Henry. "The Younger Generation," in *Times Literary Supplement* (19 March 1914), 1-2.

Janik, Del Ivan. "Towards 'Thingness': Cézanne's Painting and Lawrence's Poetry," in *Twentieth Century Literature* 19 (1973), 119-27.

_____. "D.H. Lawrence's 'Future Religion': The Unity of Last Poems," *Texas Studies in Literature and Language: A Journal of the Humanities* 16, (1975), 739-54.

Jones, David A. "The Third Unrealized Wonder—The Reality of Relation in DHL and Martin Buber," in *Religion and Life* 44 (Summer 1975), 178-87.

Jones, Lawrence. "Imagery and the 'Idiosyncratic Mode of Regard': Eliot, Hardy, and Lawrence," in *Ariel* 12 (1981), 29-49.

Jordan, Sidney. "DHL's Concept of the Unconscious and Existential Thinking," in *Review of Existential Psychology and Psychiatry* 5 (1965), 34-43.

Kalnins, Mara. "'Terra Incognita': Lawrence's Travel Writings," in *Renaissance and Modern Studies* 29, (1985), 66-77.

Kaplan, Cora. "Radical Feminism and Literature: Rethinking Millett's *Sexual Politics*," in *Red Letters* 9 (1979), 4-16.

Kazin, Alfred. "Sons, Lovers and Mothers," in *Partisan Review* 29 (Spring 1962), 373-85.

Kellogg, David. "Reading Foucault Reading Lawrence: Body, Voice, and Sexuality in *Lady Chatterley's Lover*," in *The D.H. Lawrence Review* (1999), 28:3, 31-54.

Kermode, Frank. "Spenser and the Allegorists," in *Proceedings of the British Academy* 48 (1962), 261-79.

_____. "DHL and the Apocalyptic Types," in *Critical Quarterly* 10 (Spring-Summer 1968), 14-33.

Kim, Sung Ryol. "The Vampire Lust in D.H. Lawrence," in *Studies in the Novel*, (1993, Winter), 25:4, 436-48.

Kinkead-Weekes, Mark. "DHL and the Dance," in *Dance Research* 10 (Spring 1992), 59-77.

_____. "The Genesis of Lawrence's Psychology Books: An Overview," in *The D.H. Lawrence Review* (1997-98), 27:2-3. 153-70.

_____. "An Affair into Art: A Question of Boundaries," in *Rereading Texts/Rethinking Critical Presuppositions: Essays in Honour of H.M. Daleski*, (eds. Rimmon-Kenan-Shlomith, Toker-Leona, Barzilai Shuli), Frankfurt: Peter Lang 1997, 275-90.

Kirkham, Michael. "DHL and Social Consciousness," in *Mosaic* 12 (1978), 79-92.

Kitchin, Laurence. "Colliers," in *Listener and BBC Television Review* LXXV (28 April 1966), 618-19.

Klein, Robert C. "I, Thou and You in Three Lawrencian Relationsips," in *Paunch* no. 31 (April 1968), 52-70.

Knoepflmacher, U.C. "The Rival Ladies: Mrs. Ward's 'Lady Connie' and Lawrence's *Lady Chatterley's Lover*," in *Victorian Studies*, IV (December, 1960), 141-58.

Kuttner, Alfred. Review of *Sons and Lovers*, in *New Republic* (10 April 1915,) ii, 255-57; reprinted as "*Sons and Lovers*: A Freudian Appreciation," *Psychoanalytic Review*, 3, (July 1916), 295-317.

Lainoff, Seymour. "*The Rainbow*: The Shaping of Modern Man," in *Modern Fiction Studies*. 1 (May 1955), 23-27.

Lavrin, Janko. "Sex and Eros (On Rozanov, Weininger, and DHL)," in *European Quarterly* 1 (1934), 88-96.

Leavis, F.R. "DHL Placed," in *Scrutiny* 16 (March 1949), 44-47.

_____. "Mr Eliot and Lawrence," in *Scrutiny* 18 (1951), 66-72.

_____. "Lawrence and Class," in *Sewanee Review* 62 (Fall 1954), 535-62.

_____. "Anna Karenina," in *Cambridge Quarterly* 1 (Winter 1965-66), 5-27.

_____. "Son and Lover," in *Cambridge Quarterly* 5 (1969), 323-61.

_____."The Late Nineteenth Century Novel and the Change towards the Sexual—Gissing, Hardy and Lawrence," in *English Studies* 66, (1985), 36-47.

Liou, L. "The Problematic of a Politics of Sexual Liberation: D.H. Lawrence's *The Rainbow* and *Women in Love*," in *Studies in Language and Literature* 106 (1996, Aug.) 7, 57-87.

Littlewood, J.C.F. "Lawrence, Last of the English," in *Theoria* 7 (1955), 79-92.

Lodge, David. "Metaphor and Metonymy in Modern Fiction," in *Critical Quartery* 17 (Spring 1975), 75-93 (86-88).

_____. "DHL," in his *The Modes of Modern Writing: Metaphor, Metonymy and the Typology of Modern Literature*. London: Edward Arnold, 1977, 160-76.

_____. "Lawrence, Dostoevsky, Bakhtin: DHL and Dialogic Fiction," in *Renaissance and Modern Studies* 29 (1985), 16-32.

Lowell, Amy. "A New English Poet," in *New York Times Book Review* (20 April 1919), 205, 210-11, 215, 217.

_____. "A Voice in Our Wilderness: D.H. Lawrence's Unheeded 'Message to Blind Reactionaries and Fussy, Discontented Agitators,'" in *New York Times Book Review* (22 August 1920), 7. (Repeated as "A Voice Cries in Our Wilderness" in *Poetry and Poets: Essays by Amy Lowell*. Boston and New York: Houghton Mifflin, 1930, 175-86).

Macy, John. From "The American Spirit" in *Nation*. New York, CXVII, (10 October 1923), 398-99.

Magalaner, Marvin. 'DHL Today," in *Commonweal* 70 (12 June 1959), 275-76.

Markert, Lawrence W. "Symbolic Geography: DHL and Lawrence Durrell," in *Deus Loci: Lawrence Durrell Newsletter* 5 (1981), 90-101.

_____. "'The Pure and Sacred Readjustment of Death': Connections between Lawrence Durrell's *Avignon Quintet* and the Writings of DHL," in *Twentieth Century Literature* 33 (Winter 1987), 550-64.

Marks, W.S., III. "The Psychology of the Uncanny in Lawrence's 'The Rocking-Horse Winner,'" in *Modern Fiction Studies* 11 (Winter 1965-66), 381-92.

_____. "The Psychology in DHL's 'The Blind Man,'" in *Literature and Psychology* 17 (Winter 1967), 177-92.

Masson, Margaret J. "DHL's Congregational Inheritance," in *The D.H. Lawrence Review* 22 (Spring 1990), 53-68.

Mather, R. "Patrick White and Lawrence: A Contrast," in *Critical Review*, no.13 (1970), 34-50.

McCurdy, Harold G. "Literature and Personality: Anbalysis of the Novels of DHL," in *Character and Personality* 8 (March, June 1940), 181-203, 311-22.

McVea, Deborah. "A Lost Paragraph in the Cambridge Edition of D.H. Lawrence's Letters," in *Notes and Queries* (1998, June), 45 (243):2, 233.

Mendelson, Edward. "How Lawrence Corrected Wells: How Orwell Refuted Lawrence," in *High and Low Moderns: Literature and Culture 1889-1939* (eds. M. DiBattista & L. McDiarmid), New York: Oxford University Press, 1996, 166-75.

Meyers, Jeffrey. "DHL and Katherine Mansfield," in *London Magazine* new series, 18 (May 1978a), 32-54.

_____. "Memories of D.H. Lawrence: A Genre of the Thirties," in *The D.H. Lawrence Review* 14, no.1 (1981).

Miller, Henry. "Shadowy Monomania," in *New Road* (1945), 113-45.

Miller, Milton. "Definition by Comparison: Chaucer, Lawrence, Joyce," in *Essays in Criticism* 3 (October 1953), 369-81.

Moe, Christian. "Playwright Lawrence Takes the Stage in London," in *D.H. Lawrence Review* 2 (1969), 93-97.

Moore, Harry T. "Lawrence from All Sides," in *Kenyon Review* 25 (Summer 1963), 555-58.

_____. "Some New Volumes of Lawrence's Letters," in *The D.H. Lawrence Review* 4, (1971), 61-73.

_____. "The Great Unread," in *Saturday Review of Literature*, 20: 2 (March 1940), 8.

_____. "Introduction: D.H. Lawrence and the 'Censor Morons'," in *Sex, Literature and Censorship* by D.H. Lawrence. New York: Twayne, 1953, 9-32; London: Heinemann, 1955, 1-38.

Mortimer, Raymond. "New Novels," *Nation and Athenaeum*. London, XLIII, (9 June 1928), 332.

Muir, Edwin. Review of *St. Mawr* in *Nation and Athenaeum*, (30 May 1925), 270-71.

_____. "Contemporary Writers II: Mr. DHL," in *Nation and Athenaeum* 37 (4 July 1925), 425-27.

Murry, John Middleton. "The Nostalgia of Mr. DHL," in *Nation and Athenaeum* 29 (13 August 1921), 713-14.

_____. "On the Significance of DHL," in his *Adam and Eve: An Essay toward a New and Better Society*. London: Andrew Dakers, 1944, 88-101.

_____. "Dr Leavis on D.H. Lawrence," in *Times Literary Supplement* London, (28 October 1955), 638.

_____. "The Living Dead I: DHL," in *London Magazine* 3 (May 1956), 57-63.

Needham, John. "Eavis and the Post-Saussureans," in *English* 24 (1984), 235-50.

_____. "In Search of My Hero," in *PN Review* (1997), Jan-Feb, 23:3 (113), 57-64.

Neilson, Brett. "D.H. Lawrence's 'Dark Page': Narrative Primitivism in *Women in Love* and *The Plumed Serpent*," in *Twentieth Century Literature* (1997 Fall), 43:3, 310-25.

Newton, Frances J. "Venice, Pope, T.S. Eliot and DHL," in *Notes and Queries* 5 (March 1958), 119-20.

Norton, David. "Lawrence, Wells and Bennett: Influence and Tradition," in *Aumla* 54 (November 1980), 171-90.

Oates, Joyce Carol. "Lawrence's Gotterdammerung: The Tragic Vision of *Women in Love*," in *Critical Inquiry*, 4 (1978), 449-78.

_____. "'At Least I Have Made a Woman of Her': Images of Women in Twentieth Century Literature," in *Georgia Review* 37 (1983), 7-30.

Orage, A.R. "Twilight in Mr. DHL," in his *Selected Essays and Critical Writings*: *Part One: The Art of Reading*. (ed. Herbert Read and Denis Saurat), London: Stanley Nott, 1935, 65-67.

Orr, Christopher. "Lawrence after the Deluge: The Political Ambiguity of *Aaron's Rod*," in *West Virginia Association of College English Teachers Bulletin* 1 (Fall 1974), 1-14.

Orwell, George, [pseud. of Eric Blair]. "The Prussian Officer and Other Stories," *Tribune*. London, (16 November 1945).

Otte, George, "The Loss of History in the Modern Novel: The Case of *The Rainbow*," in *Pacific Coast Philology*, 1, 16 (June 1981), 67-76.

Paccaud-Huguet, Josiane. "Narrative as a Symbolic Act: The Historicity of Lawrence's Modernity," in *Etudes Lawrenciennes* 9 (1993), 75-94.

Padhi, Bibhu. "DHL and Europe," in *Contemporary Review* 257 (1990), 83-87.

Panichas, George A. "D.H. Lawrence's Biblical Play *David*," in *Modern Drama* 6, (1963), 164-176.

_____. "DHL's Concept of the Risen Lord," in *Christian Scholar* 47 (Spring 1964), 56-65.

_____. "DHL and the Ancient Greeks," in *English Miscellany* 16 (1965), 195-214.

Parkes, H.B. "DHL and Irving Babbitt," in *New Adelphi* 9 (March 1935), 328-31.

Parry, Albert. "DHL through a Marxist Mirror," in *Western Review* 19 (Winter 1955), 85-100.

Pearson, S. Vere. "Psychology of the Consumptive (With Special Reference to DHL)," in *Journal of State Medicine* (August 1932), 477-85.

Pinto, Vivian de Sola. "DHL, Letter-Writer and Craftsman in Verse: Some Hitherto Unpublished Material," in *Renaissance and Modern Studies* 1 (1957), 5-34.

_____. "The Burning Bush: DHL as Religious Poet." In *Mansions of the Spirit: Essays in Literature and Religion*. Edited by George A. Panichas. New York: Hawthorne, 1967, 213-35.

Pollack, Paulina S. "Anti-Semitism in the Works of DHL: Search for and Rejection of the Faith," in *Literature and Psychology* 32 (1986), 19-29.

Porter, Katherine Anne. Review of *The Plumed Serpent* in *New York Herald Tribune Books* (7 March 1926), 1-2.

Pound, Ezra. "Review of Love Poems and Others," in *Poetry*, (11 July 1913), 149-151.

Powell, Lawrence Clark. "D.H. Lawrence and His Critics. A Chronological Excursion in Bio-bibliography," in *Colophon*, n.g.s.1, (1940).

Price, A. Whigham. "DHL and Congregationalism," in *Congregational Quarterly* 34 (July and October 1956), 242-52; 322-30.

Pugh, Bridget. "Lawrence and Industrial Symbolism," in *Renaissance and Modern Studies* 29 (1985), 33-49.

_____. "DHL: Some Russian Parallels," in *Etudes Lawrenciennes* 9 (1993), 81-91.

Quennell, Peter. "DHL and Aldous Huxley," in *The English Novelists*. (ed. D. Verschoyle.) London: Chatto and Windus, 1936, 247-57.

Read, Herbert. "An Irregular Genius: The Significance of DHL," in *World Review* new series 17 (July 1950), 50-56. (Partly a review of Aldington's biography [1950].)

Renner, Stanley. "Sexuality and the Unconscious: Psychosexual Drama and Conflict in *The Fox*," in *The D.H. Lawrence Review* 21 (1989), 245-73.

Remsbury, John. "'Real Thinking': Lawrence and Cézanne," in *Cambridge Quarterly* 2 (Spring 1967), 117-47.

Richardson, Barbara. "Philip Larkin's Early Influences," in *Northwest Review* 30, no.1 (1992), 133-40.

Rieff, Philip. "Introduction" to *Psychoanalysis and the Unconscious* and *Fantasia of the Unconscious*, by D.H. Lawrence. New York: The Viking Press, 1960a, vii-xxiii.

_____. "Two Honest Men: Freud and Lawrence," in *Listener* 62 (5 May 1960b), 794-96.

Roberts, Warren. "London 1908: Lawrence and Pound," in *Helix* 13-14 (1983), 45-49.

Roberts, William H. "DHL: Study of a Free Spirit in Literature," in *Millgate Monthly* (May 1928).

Rosenbaum, S.P. "Keynes, Lawrence and Cambridge Revisited," in *Cambridge Quarterly* 11 (1982), 252-64.

Ross, C.L. "The Revision of the Second Generation in *The Rainbow*," in *Review of English Studies* 27 (1976), 277-95.

_____. "DHL's Use of Greek Tragedy: Euripedes and Ritual," in *D.H. Laurence Review* 10 (Spring 1977), 1-19.

Rossman, Charles. "'You Are the Call and I Am the Answer': DHL and Women," in *D.H. Laurence Review* 8 (Fall 1975), 255-328.

Ruderman, Judith G. "*The Fox* and the 'Devouring Mother,'" in *The D.H. Lawrence Review* 10 (Fall, 1977), 251-69.

_____. "Rekindling the 'Father-Spark': Lawrence's Ideal of Leadership in *The Lost Girl* and *The Plumed Serpent*," in *The D.H. Lawrence Review*, 13/3, (Fall, 1980), 239-59.

_____. "DHL and the 'Jewish Problem': Reflections on a Self-Confessed 'Hebrophobe,'" in *The D.H. Lawrence Review* 23 (1991), 99-109.

Rudrum, Alan. "Stage Sons, Stage Lovers," in *Listener and BBC Television Review*. LXXV, (10 February, 1966), 214-15.

_____. "Philosophical Implications in Lawrence's *Women in Love*," in *Dalhousie Review* 51 (Summer 1971), 240-50.

Ruthven, K.K. "The Savage God: Conrad and Lawrence," in *Critical Quarterly* (1968), 39-54.

Sackville West, Edward. "A Modern Isaiah," in *New Statesman*. XXVII, (10 July 1926), 60-61.

Sagar, Keith. "Open Shelf and Open Poem:The Stages of D.H. Lawrence's Poetic Quest," in *The D.H. Lawrence Review* 24:1, (Spring, 1992), 43-56.

_____. "DHL and Robert Louis Stevenson," in *The D.H. Lawrence Review* 24 (Fall 1992), 161-65.

Salmon, H.L. "Lawrence and a 'Sense of the Whole,'" in *New Adelphi* 2 (June 1931), 241-44.

Sarvan, Charles, and Sarvan, Liebetraut. "DHL and Doris Lessing's *The Grass is Singing*," in *Modern Fiction Studies* 24 (1978), 533-37.

Scanlon, Joan. "Bad Language vs. Bad Prose/Lady Chatterley and The Well," in *Critical Quarterly* (Autumn, 1996), 38:3, 3-13.

Scherr, Barry J. "Sex, Selfhood, Literature and Politics: The Left Wing Attack on D.H. Lawrence," in *Recovering Literature: A Journal of Contextualist Criticism* (1997), 24.

Schneider, Daniel J. "The Symbolism of the Soul: DHL and Some Others," in *The D.H. Lawrence Review* 7 (Summer 1974), 107-26.

_____. "Psychology and Art in Lawrence *Kangaroo*," in *The D.H. Lawrence Review* 14 (1981), 156-71.

_____. "DHL and *Thus Spake Zarathustra*," in *South Carolina Review* 15, no.2 (1983a), 96-108.

_____."Schopenhauer and the Development of DHL's Psychology," in *South Atlantic Review* 48 (1983b), 1-19.

_____. "'Strange Wisdom': Leo Frobenius and DHL," in *D.H. Lawrence Review* 16 (1983c) 183-93.

_____. "DHL and the Early Greek Philosophers," in *D.H. Lawrence Review* 17 (Summer 1984), 97-109.

_____. "Alternatives to Logocentrism in DHL," in *South Atlantic Review* 51, no.2 (May 1986), 35-47.

_____. "DHL and Houston Chamberlain: Once Again," in *D.H. Lawrence Review* 19 (Summer 1987), 157-71.

Schorer, Mark G. "Technique as Discovery," in *Hudson Review* 1, (Spring, 1948), 67-87.

_____. "Fiction with a Great Burden," in *Kenyon Review* 14 (Winter 1952), 162-68.

Schulz, Volker. "D.H. Lawrence's Early Masterpiece of Short Fiction: 'Odour of Chrysanthemums,'" in *Studies in Short Fiction*, 28:3, (Summer 1991), 363-70.

Schwartz, Murray M. "DHL and Psychoanalysis: An Introduction," in *The D.H. Lawrence Review* 10 (Fall 1977), 215-22.

Scott, James F. "DHL's *Germania*:Ethnic Psychology and Cultural Crisis in the Shorter Fiction," in *The D.H. Lawrence Review* 10 (1977), 142-64.

_____. "Thimble into *Ladybird*: Nietzsche, Frobenius, and Bachofen in the Later Works of DHL," in *Arcadia* 13 (1978), 161-76.

_____. "'Continental': The Germanic Dimension of *Women in Love*," in *Literature in Wissenschaft und Unterricht* (Kiel) 12 (1979), 117-34.

Semeiks, Joanna G. "Sex, Lawrence, and Videotape," in *Journal of Popular Culture* 25 no.4 (Spring 1992), 143-52.

Shaw, Marion. "Lawrence and Feminism," in *Critical Quarterly*, 25, 3 (Autumn 1983), 23.

Siegel, Carol. "Virginia Woolf's and Katherine Mansfield's Responses to DHL's Fiction," in *D.H. Laurence Review* 21 (1989), 291-311.

Sklenicka, Carol. "Lawrence's Vision of the Child: Reimagining Character and Consciousness," in *The D.H. Lawrence Review* 18: 2-3, (Summer-Fall 1986), 151-168.

Spender, Stephen. "Books and the War: IX. DHL Reconsidered," in *Penguin New Writing* 10 (1941), 120-33.

_____. "Writers and Politics," in *Partisan Review* 34 (Summer 1967), 359-81.

_____. "The Erotic Art of DHL," in *Vanity Fair* (January 1986), 88-93.

Spilka, Mark. "Was D.H. Lawrence a Symbolist?" in *Accent*, XV (Winter, 1955), 49-60.

_____. "Lawrence's Quarrel with Tenderness," in *Critical Quarterly* Manchester, England, 9, (1968), 363-377.

_____. "Lawrence's Vitalistic Comedies," in *English Language Notes* (December 1997.) 35:2, 74-79.

Squire, J.C. (Pseud Solomon Eagle). [On the suppression of *The Rainbow*.] *New Statesman* 6 (20 November 1915), 161.

Squires, Michael, "Lawrence's *The White Peacock*: A Mutation of the Pastoral," in *Texas Studies in Literature and Language* 12 (March 1972), 263-83.

_____. "Recurrence as a Narrative Technique in *The Rainbow*," in *Modern Fiction Studies* 21 (Summer 1975), 230-36.

_____. "D.H. Lawrence's Narrators, Sources of Knowledge, and the Problem of Coherence," in *Criticism: A Quarterly for Literature and the Arts*, (Summer 1995), 37:3, 469-91.

Stanford, Raney. "Thomas Hardy and Lawrence's *The White Peacock*," in *Modern Fiction Studies: D.H. Lawrence* V (Spring 1959), 19-28.

Stavrou, Constaine W. "DHL's 'Psychology' of Sex," in *Literature and Psychology* 6 (1956), 90-95.

Stein, Marian L. "Affirmation and Negations: Lawrence's 'Whitman' and Whitman's 'Open Road,'" in *Walt Whitman Review*, 18 (1972), 63-67.

Steven, Laurence, "From Thimble to Ladybird: D.H. Lawrence's Widening Vision," in *D.H. Lawrence Review* 18, 2:3 (Summer-Fall 1986), 239-253.

Stewart, Jack F. "Expressionism in *The Rainbow*,: in *Novel* 13 (1980a), 296-315.

_____. "Lawrence and Gauguin," in *Twentieth Century Literature* 26 (1980b), 385-401.

_____. "Primitivism in *Women in Love*," in *The D.H. Lawrence Review* 13, (1980c), 45-62.

_____. "Lawrence and Van Gogh," in *D.H. Laurence Review* 16 (Spring 1983), 1-24.

_____. "Primordial Affinities: Lawrence, Van Gogh and the Miners," in *Mosaic* 24 (Winter 1991), 92-113.

_____. "Dialectics of Knowing in *Women in Love*," in *Twentieth Century Literature* 37 (Spring 1991), 59-75.

_____. "Metaphor and Metonymy, Color and Space, in Lawrence's *Sea and Sardinia* ," in *Twentieth Century Literature*, (Summer 1995), 41:2, 208-23.

_____. "The Myth of the Fall in *Women in Love*," in *Philological Quarterly*, (Fall 1995), 74:4, 443-63.

_____. "Gender and Language in *Sons and Lovers*," in *Midwest Quarterly* (Summer 1996), 37:4, 434-47.

_____. "Lawrence's Peasant Portraits in *Twilight in Italy*," in *Studies in the Humanities*, (1998), June-Dec, 25:1-2, 24-37.

Storch, Margaret. "The Lacerated Male: Ambivalent Images of Women in *The White Peacock*," in *The D.H. Lawrence Review* 21:2, (Summer 1989), 117-36.

Tedlock, E.W., Jr. "DHL's Annotations of Ouspensky's *Tertium Organum*," in *Texas Studies in Literature and Language* 2 (Summer 1960), 206-18.

Thompson, Alan. R. "DHL: Apostle of the Dark God," in *Bookman* 73 (July 1931), 492-99.

Tietjens, Eunice. "Review of *Amores* by DHL," in *Poetry* 9 (9 February 1917), 264-66.

Tindall, William York. "Introduction" to *The Plumed Serpent*. New York: Alfred A. Knopf, Inc., (1951).

Trilling, Diana. "Lawrence: Creator and Dissenter," in *Saturday Review of Literature* 29 (7 December 1946), 17-18. 82-84.

_____. "DHL and the Movements of Modern Culture," in *DHL: Novelist, Poet, Prophet*, Edited by Stephen Spender. London: Weidenfeld and Nicolson, (1973), 1-7.

Trilling, Lionel. "DHL: A Neglected Aspect," in *Symposium* 1 (July 1930), 361-70.

Trotter, David. "Modernism and Empire: Reading *The Waste Land*," in *Critical Quarterly* 28 (Spring-Summer 1986), 143-53.

_____. "Edwardian Sex Novels," in *Critical Quarterly* 31, (1989), 92-106.

Turner, John. "David Eder: Between Freud and Jung," in *D.H. Lawrence Review* 1997-98, 27: 2-3, 289-309.

Twitchell, James. "Lawrence's Lamias: Predatory Women in *The Rainbow* and *Women in Love* ," in *Studies in the Novel*. 11, (1979), 23-42.

Ulmer, Gregory L. "DHL, Wilhelm Worringer, and the Aesthetics of Modernism," in *The D.H. Lawrence Review* 10 (Summer 1977a), 165-81.

_____. "Rousseau and DHL: 'Philosophes' of the 'Gelded' Age," in *Canadian Review of Comparative Literature* 4 (1977b), 68-80.

Van Doren, Mark. "Review of *Pansies* by DHL," in *New York Herald Tribune Review of Books* (15 December 1929), 15.

Van Ghent, Dorothy. "On Sons and Lovers," in *The English Novel: Form and Function.* New York: Holt, Rinehart, and Winston, Inc., (1953).

VanHoosier-Carey, Kimberley. "Struggling with the Master: The Position of Kate and the Reader in Lawrence's 'Quetzalcoatl' and *The Plumed Serpent*," in *The D.H. Lawrence Review*. 25, (1993-94), 104-18.

Vickery, John B. "Myth and Ritual in the Shorter Fiction of D.H. Lawrence," in *Modern Fiction Studies* V, (Spring 1959), 65-82.

_____. "*The Plumed Serpent* and the Eternal Paradox," in *Criticism* 5 (Spring 1963), 119-34.

_____. "*Golden Bough*: Impact and Archetype," in *Virginia Quarterly Review* 39 (Winter 1963), 37-57.

_____. "*The Plumed Serpent* and the Reviving God," in *Journal of Modern Literature* 2 (November 1972), 505-32.

_____. "DHL's Poetry: Myth and Matter," in *D.H. Laurence Review* 7 (Spring 1974), 1-18.

Vitoux, Pierre. "Aldous Huxley and DHL: An Attempt at Intellectual Sympathy," in *Modern Language Review* 69 (July 1974), 501-22.

Wagenknecht, E.G. "DHL: Pilgrim of the Rainbow," in his *Cavalcade of the English Novel*. New York: Henry Holt, 1943, 494-504.

Watson, E.L.Grant. "On Hell and Mr. DHL," in *English Review* 38 (March 1924), 386-92.

Watson, G. "D.H. Lawrence (in *Women in Love*) on the Desire for Difference and 'the Fascism in Us All,'" in *Cambridge Quarterly*, (1997), 26:2, 140-54.

Way, B. "Sez and Language: Obscene Words in DHL and Henry Miller," in *New Left Review*, no.27 (September-October 1964), 164-70.

Weatherby, H.L. "Old -Fashioned Gods: Eliot on Lawrence and Hardy," in *Sewanee Review* 75 (Spring 1967), 301-16.

Weiss, Daniel. "Oedipus in Nottinghamshire," in *Literature and Psychology* 7 (August 1957), 33-42.

West, Rebecca. "Notes on Novels," in *New Statesman* XVII, (9 July 1921), 388-90.

_____. "A Letter from Abroad: DHL as Painter," in *Bookman* 70 (September 1929), 89-91.

Wexler, Joyce. "D.H. Lawrence Through a Postmodernist Lens," in *The D.H. Lawrence Review* (1997-98), 27:1, 47-64.

_____. "Realism and Modernists' Bad Reputation," in *Studies in the Novel*, (1999), Spring, 31:1, 60-73.

Widmer, Kingsley. "DHL and the Art of Nihilism," in *Kenyon Review* 20 (Fall 1958), 604-16.

_____. "The Primitivistic Aesthetic: DHL," in *Journal of Aesthetics and Art Criticism* 17 (March 1959a), 344-53.

_____. "The Sacred Sun in Modern Literatuire," in *Humanist* (Antioch) 19 (1959b), 368-72.

_____. "Lawrence and the Fall of Modern Woman," in *Modern Fiction Studies* 5 (1959), 44-56.

_____. "The Pertinence of Modern Pastoral: The Three Versions of *Lady Chatterley's Lover*," in *Studies in the Novel* 5, (1973), 298-313.

_____. "Lawrence as Abnormal Novelist," in *The D.H. Lawrence Review* 8 (Summer 1975), 220-32.

_____. "Psychiatry and Piety on Lawrence," in *Studies in the Novel* 9 (Summer 1977), 195-200.

Wilcher, Robert. "D.H. Lawrence (1885-1930)," in *British Playwrights, 1860-1956: A Research and Production Sourcebook* (eds. W. Demastes & K. Kelly), Westport, Conn.: Greenwood, 1996, 251-67.

Wildi, Max. "The Birth of Expressionism in the Works of D.H. Lawrence," in *English Studies* XIX (December 1937), 241-59.

Williams, Linda R. "The Trial of D.H. Lawrence," in *Critical Survey*, (1992), 4:2, 154-61.

Williams, Raymond. "Tolstoy, Lawrence and Tragedy," in *Kenyon Review* 25 (Autumn 1963), 633-50. 9

Williams-Ellis, A. "Mr D.H. Lawrence's Work," in *Spectator* London, CXXVII, (1 October 1921), 434.

Wilson, Colin. "Existential Criticism," in *Chicago Review* 13 (Summer 1959), 152-81.

Winn, Harbour. "Parallel Inward Journeys: *A Passage to India* and *St. Mawr*," *English Language Notes* 31:2, (December 1993), 62-66.

Woodbridge, Homer, E. "Plays of Today and Yesterday," in *Dial* 58 (16 January 1915), 46-50.

Woodcock, George. "Mexico and the English Novelist," in *Western Review* 21 (Autumn 1956), 21-32. (Lawrence, Huxley, Greene.)

Woolf, Virginia. "Notes on DHL," in her *The Moment and Other Essays*. London: Hogarth Press, 1947, 93-98.

Worthen, John. "D.H. Lawrence: Problems with Multiple Texts," in *The Theory and Practices of Text-Editing: Essays in Honour of James T. Boulton*. Ed. Ian Small and Marcus Walsh. Cambridge: Cambridge University Press, 1991, 14-34.

_____. "D.H. Lawrence and the 'Expensive Edition Business,'" in *Modernist Writers and the Marketplace*, (eds. I. Willison, W. Gould and W. Chernaik), Houndmills: Macmillan; New York: St. Martin's, 1996, 105-23.

_____. "The Biographer and Perspective," in *Writing the Lives of Writers* (eds. Gould-Warwick, Staley-Thomas), Houndmills: Macmillan, 1998, 191-203.

_____. "Towards a New Version of D.H. Lawrence's 'The Daughter-in-Law': Scholarly Edition or Play Text?" in *Yearbook of English Studies* (1999), 29, 231-46.

_____. "The First "Women in Love,'" in *The D.H. Lawrence Review* (1999), 28:1-2, 5-27.

Wright, Louise E. "Disputed Dregs: D.H. Lawrence and the Publication of Maurice Magnus' Memoirs of the Foreign Legion," in *The Journal of the D.H. Lawrence Society*, (1996), 57-73.

Yoxall, Henry. "Books and Pictures," in *Schoolmaster* 76 (25 December 1909), 1242.

Zoll, Allan R. "Vitalism and the Metaphysics of Love: DHL and Schopenhauer," in *The D.H. Lawrence Review* 11 (Spring 1978), 1-20.

Zytaruk, George J. "The Phallic Vision: DHL and V.V. Rozanov," in *Comparative Literature Studies* 4 (1967), 283-97.

_____. "DHL's Reading of Russian Literature," in *The D.H. Lawrence Review* 2 (Summer 1969), 120-37.

_____. "Lawrence and Rozanov: Clarifying the Phallic Vision," in *Etudes Lawrenciennes* 9 (1993), 93-103.

NB: A list of journals, and special editions of journals, specific to D.H. Lawrence studies can be found in: Poplawski, Paul. *D.H. Lawrence: A Reference Handbook*. Westport, Connecticut: Greenwood Press, 1996. [p.660]

# Index

## About the Editor

JAN PILDITCH is Senior Lecturer in English at the University of Waikato. Her previous books include *The Critical Response to Katherine Mansfield* (Greenwood, 1995).